Foundations of Social Psychology

WITHDRAWN
UTSA LIBRARIES

Foundations of
SOCIAL PSYCHOLOGY

EDWARD E. JONES
Duke University

HAROLD B. GERARD
University of California, Riverside

JOHN WILEY & SONS, INC.   New York · London · Sydney

Copyright © 1967 by John Wiley & Sons, Inc.

All Rights Reserved. This book or any part thereof must not be reproduced in any form without the written permission of the publisher.

Library of Congress Catalog Card Number: 67–21053
Printed in the United States of America

10 9 8 7 6

ISBN 0 471 44906 7

/ *Preface*

The present book has evolved through a long and complex history. The project was initiated some eight years ago when the first author decided to stop complaining about existing texts and nervously began work on an alternative. Tentative drafts of several chapters were prepared in a burst of initial enthusiasm, but other matters began to assert their priority and the project languished for several years. The present collaborative team was formed late in 1961; its purpose was to freshen the material already written and to revive the flagging enthusiasm of the first author. The team was cemented into a highly cohesive dyad by our opportunity to work together during 1963 and 1964 at the Center for Advanced Study in the Behavioral Sciences. We are deeply indebted to the Center and its staff for providing us with the ideal setting in which to work. There the scope of the project became enlarged, our aspirations raised; we became enthusiastic again about the potential significance of what we were doing. The subsequent months have been devoted to hammering out the details of intellectual resolutions achieved at the Center. Because our collaboration has been so intense and sustained it is no longer possible to identify the source within the team of most of the new ideas presented on the pages to follow. Order of authorship represents longevity of involvement in the project; it does not in any way reflect priority of intellectual contribution.

Our aim has been to write a systematic presentation of social psychology that emphasizes the experimental approach. The fact that we have tried to carry basic ideas from chapter to chapter and that we have been more fatally drawn to experimental than to correlational data means that the final product is less comprehensive than many existing texts. Inevitably, we have made some compromises between comprehensiveness and systematic development. We have not refused to talk about an area of potential theoretical relevance just because the data are weak. Nor, as far as we are aware, have we failed to cover areas possessing substantial data solely because they could not be housed in our systematic framework. We shall be content with the description of our book as more systematic and less comprehensive than existing texts, as long as it is clear that we have tried to maintain a balance between the extremes of selectivity and eclectic data sampling.

Even a cursory review of the pages to follow will confirm our intellectual indebtedness to a handful of fellow psychologists, many of them personal friends and mentors, and all of whom we greatly respect. Our decision to highlight the experimental approach made it a foregone conclusion that we would emphasize the broad strategic contributions of Kurt Lewin and the numerous provocative studies of Leon Festinger. In our opinion Festinger is more than any other person responsible for moving the experimental study of social processes to the center stage of social psychology. His insistence on the role of middle-range theories in the design of experiments, his own ingenious and seminal studies, and the impact of his many excellent students on the field, all testify to his stature as a pre-eminent contributor to our discipline. One of us was a student of Festinger, one of us was not; we are both very much in his debt.

In attempting to provide a framework for relating cognition, decision-making, and action, we found Jerome Bruner's sensible and lucid prose of great value. Fritz Heider's preoccupations have become ours in the discussion of person perception and the attribution process. John Thibaut must be accused of encouraging the first author to begin. He has been a persistent source of support for the project and has read and reacted to most of the chapters. Beyond this, it will be clear that we have made extensive use of the model presented by Thibaut and Harold Kelley for describing patterns of social interaction and the structure of interpersonal relationships.

The list of those true friends and colleagues who have read all or portions of the manuscript at various stages is a long one, so long that in acknowledging our debt we may inadvertently omit a few whose comments and advice were much appreciated. Jack Brehm read an early draft of the entire manuscript and made a number of valuable comments. Lloyd Stires deserves a special note of thanks for his painstaking critiques of several chapters. Many others have read and commented. They include Elliot Aronson, Richard Atkinson, Edward S. Conolley, Lee Cronbach, Keith Davis, Linda B. Fleischer, Jonathan Freedman, Edward S. Jones, Daniel Katz, Martin Lakin, Darwyn E. Linder, Gardner Lindzey, Norman Miller, Judson Mills, Paul C. Rosenblatt, Kelly Shaver, Jerome E. Singer, Joseph A. Thomas, David Tiedemann, Sydney Verba, Michael A. Wallach, Carl Weick, and Roland A. Wilhelmy.

To an unusual extent we have enjoyed the facilities of our respective universities, including the provision of such niceties as paper, postage, and duplicating machinery. We have been especially fortunate in the high level of secretarial help that these universities and the Center have made available to us. Our personal thanks for secretarial contributions beyond the line of duty go to Irene Bickenbach, Judy Edquist, Carol Hausman, Amby Peach, Julie Raventos, Carole Shaver, and Sally Stockman.

Finally, we should like to thank the following publishers for permission to reproduce figures or quotations: The Academic Press; Addison-Wesley; The American Psychological Association, for its various journals; Appleton-Century-Crofts (Meredith); Carnegie Press; Duke University Press; Harper and Row; Holt, Rinehart and Winston; Massachusetts Institute of Technology Press; W. W. Norton; Princeton University Press; Random House; Stanford University Press; Tavistock Publications Ltd.; The University of Chicago Press; and John Wiley. In each case, acknowledgment to the original source is given with the material reproduced.

Edward E. Jones
Harold B. Gerard

Durham, North Carolina
Riverside, California
February, 1967

Contents

1	The Field of Social Psychology	1
2	Research Methods in Social Psychology	36
3	Effect Dependence and Processes of Child Socialization	76
4	Information Dependence and Cognitive Socialization	120
5	The Products of Socialization	157
6	Action, Choice, and Dissonance	186
7	The Impact of Value and Attitude on Perceiving and Remembering	227
8	Perceiving and Evaluating Persons	256
9	Social Comparison Processes	309
10	Consensus and Communication in Groups	331
11	The Conformity Conflict	387
12	Attitude Change	431
13	Dyadic Interaction: A Conceptual Framework	505
14	Power and Influence in Dyadic Interaction: Experimental Findings	537
15	The Impact of Group Membership on Individual Behavior	591
16	Psychological Bases of Group Structure	642
	References	682
	Glossary	707
	Index	721

Foundations of Social Psychology

CHAPTER ONE

The Field of Social Psychology

Social psychology is a subdiscipline of psychology that especially involves *the scientific study of the behavior of individuals as a function of social stimuli*. This definition seems to say something important and to say it with pedantic precision. Yet we might immediately raise a string of questions about it. When, precisely, does a study become "scientific"? Scientific method, as we shall see in Chapter Two, encompasses a broad range of strategies, all intended to protect the scientist from his own fallibility as an observer and interpreter of events. Do we mean to be restrictive in using the word "behavior"? Social psychology is very much interested in thinking, feeling, and desiring; the restriction in the definition merely refers to the fact that these internal states can be inferred only from some form of overt behavior.

Finally, we might raise the most difficult question of all, "What is a social stimulus?" Roughly speaking, a stimulus is some change in the environment that actually or potentially affects the behavior of an organism. Social stimuli are obviously stimuli that come from other people. Or is this really obvious? Are social psychologists still interested when an individual does something, in the absence of people, that was learned in their presence? It would certainly seem silly to draw a line between presence and absence and to say there is no interest when the individual is affected only by the *implicit* presence of people. Even in isolation an individual's behavior may be largely determined by considerations that have their origin in the social environment. Consider several different hypothetical instances.

A small boy, alone in the family kitchen, looks at the cookie jar and, though he wants a cookie desperately, does not take one. We might say that he has learned the bad consequences of this kind of behavior or has "internalized" certain guilt mechanisms relating to violation of family rules. Either way, it seems likely that early in the establishment of moral behavior the child in some way invokes or imagines the presence of the mother and behaves accordingly. He is responding to implicit social stimuli, though we could make this inference more readily if we had observed the history of his interactions with his mother and could relate the nature of these interactions to increasing abstinence in the presence of cookies and other tempting objects.

People sometimes respond to physical stimuli in the environment as if they were social or directly produced by other people. They may violently slam the door on which they have just bumped their head, kick the tire of a stalled automobile, or kiss the ground after a frightening airplane flight. The citizen who not only believes there are flying saucers, but also believes they are manned by observers from Russia, is probably misreading the physical signs of swamp gas, clouds, or meteors as having a social origin. Whether he is correct or not, his behavior would be a proper matter for social psychological study.

Conversely, people sometimes respond to socially produced stimuli as if those stimuli were independent of all human elements. At least some of the information and enlightenment we receive from verbal material is accepted at face value, without regard to the characteristics of the social source. Social psychologists are unlikely to be directly interested in reactions to encyclopedia articles, pronouncements by experts, and other materials assumed to be informative and without ulterior motivation. The same is not true, of course, for reactions to political speeches, moral pronouncements of the church pastor, or other materials commonly evaluated in terms of their source. In principle, at least, we may determine the social relevance of verbal materials by answering the question, "Would the reaction have differed if we had varied the characteristics of the author?"

Historical Perspective

The roots of social psychology lie deep in antiquity, reaching back to man's earliest intellectual probes into his relations to society. Gordon Allport (1954) has contended that most of the major problems of concern to contemporary social psychologists were recognized as problems by social philosophers long before psychological questions were joined to scientific methodology. Certainly there are timeless riches in the insights of Aristotle, Machiavelli, Hobbes, or the Mills. But it is one thing to have problems posed and areas highlighted, and another to be able to support insights with valid observations of behavior. Social psychology has a more recent history than its flavoring ideas. Auguries of and reflections on this more recent development may be found in textbooks that have attempted to give structure to the field. The first two textbooks that contained the term social psychology in their titles were, quite by coincidence, both published in 1908.

One of these books was by the psychologist William McDougall, the other was by the sociologist E. A. Ross. It is hard to imagine two more distinctly different offerings bearing the same essential title. McDougall wrote from the conviction that progress in the social sciences awaited a relevant, systematic psychology that would reveal "the innate tendencies of thought and action that constitute the native basis of the mind" (McDougall, 1908, p. 16). His great and controversial contribution was to frame a theory of human instincts, which he saw as broad, purposive tendencies emerging from the evolutionary process. In his view it was important to understand man's basic instinctual nature before it was possible to deal with the "moralisation" or "socialization" of the individual by society—a process he saw as the fundamental problem of social psychology.

Ross, on the other hand, began his textbook with the statement that "Social psychology . . . studies the psychic planes and currents that come into existence among men in consequence of their association" (Ross, 1908, p. 1). He was particularly concerned with the contagion of emotions in crowd behavior, the sweep of fads or fashions, and other instances of the transmission of social influence from person to person. And yet each author, in his own way, was ultimately concerned with the impact of society on the development and behavior of individual men.

In the decades since 1908 more than fifty textbooks having a central concern with social psychology have been published. Early in this period it was characteristic for a text to root its explanations in individual human nature (*à la* McDougall) or in the forces created by social institutions (*à la* Ross). A common meeting ground began to emerge in F. H. Allport's *Social Psychology* (1924). Here was a sensible, articulate text that derived social behavior and the various predispositions to social life from the elaboration of various innate reflexes by conditioning. Allport essentially extended the principles of associative learning to account for a wide range of social phenomena: emotional expression and control, language development, sympathy and imitation, suggestion, social facilitation of performance, crowd behavior, and, finally, societal institutions. The publication of this book had an important influence on the development of social psychology as a subdiscipline or specialization of psychology. Allport sought to construct a framework for discussing social behavior that avoided reference to mysterious social forces on the one hand or to elaborate instinctive dispositions on the other.

During the twenties the literature of social psychology was largely devoted to discussions about concepts and clashes between points of view. The pros and cons of the instinct doctrine were extensively aired, along with many discussions of the proper way to conceive of groups, and the appropriate level of abstraction for analyzing group properties. Occasional empirical studies did appear in the journals, but these were largely descriptive accounts of such matters as the range of attitudes on a topic and were rarely useful for explanation. During the thirties there was a steady increase in scholarly papers that contained data on problems of both practical and theoretical importance. Can animals be taught to cooperate? Are groups more effective in solving problems than individuals working in isolation? How does the prestige of a speaker or writer affect the listener's response to a persuasive speech? What kinds of people tend to be suggestible? How prevalent are stereotypes about different national and ethnic groups? What happens to information as it is fed into channels of rumor? How can we best characterize the patterns of liking and affection in face-to-face groups? What are the attributes that distinguish between people who become leaders and those who remain followers? What is the distribution of attitudes in different samples of persons and how are these attitudes related to each other? These and other questions prompted many empirical investigations before World War II. Some of these questions would now be phrased in different terms, but the interest in such problems and the methods of solving them has undoubtedly done much to shape the present image of social psychology.

In the midthirties the émigré psychologist Kurt Lewin began to concern himself with theory and research on social psychological problems. His contributions had a far-ranging impact on the methodology of subsequent research in social psychology. Indeed, he may with some justice be considered the father of experimental social psychology, or at least of a major contemporary tradition of (what we shall call in the next chapter) hypothetico-deductive experimentation. A critical feature of Lewin's contribution was his emphasis on the importance of theoretical analysis before conducting research on a problem. The research should be designed to clarify explanatory mechanisms underlying the surface manifestations of observed behavior. Although the particular concepts Lewin suggested did not have widespread or lasting influence, his advocacy of the importance of theory and of conceptual analysis was extremely important. Also import020t historically was an experiment conducted by Lewin and two of his doctoral students on the effect of different leadership atmospheres in children's groups. Lewin, Lippitt, and White (1939) arranged to have the same adults play different leadership roles in directing matched groups of children, attempting to establish particular "climates" of democracy, autocracy, or complete laissez faire. The reactions of the children were systematically observed and detailed notes were taken on the resulting patterns of social interaction—who talked to whom, how much time was spent in aggressive behavior, in horseplay, and so forth. Their experimental designs had many deficiencies, but the autocracy-democracy studies had a liberating impact on subsequent researchers. The attempt to create in a controlled laboratory situation something as nebulous as a democratic social climate required optimism, ingenuity, and dash. The general success of these studies stimulated others to think about experimental stagecraft and the controlled manipulation of complex situational variables. Lewin and his students went on to conduct a variety of additional experiments before his death in 1947.

By the end of World War II the way was paved for an outpouring of experimental research involving the manipulation of experimental subjects' temporary social environment and an examination of the effects of this manipulation on attitudes, behavior, and various emotional states. Questions of behavioral causation could now be examined with closer scrutiny than was possible through questionnaires and interviews. The outlines of an empirical, and especially an experimental, social psychology have clearly emerged. It is our hope to deal with the portions of the outline that are already filled in, and to capture the flavor of the filling process and the most promising strategies for finding out what we need to know next.

In approaching this task, we shall begin with a variety of cases that raise critical questions or illustrate important principles of social psychology. We do this with a number of purposes in mind. For one thing, having been half-hearted and cynical in the provision of a formal, schematic definition of the field, we attempt with greater enthusiasm to define our domain by pointing. We have chosen the cases so that they will present a fair idea of the range and variety of topics with which social psychologists should be, and for the most part have been, concerned. A second purpose of this survey is to give some indication of the similarities between "real life" and experimental settings, as well as the features that distinguish them. In the process the reader can perhaps begin to see how it is possible to gain more precise understanding of cause-and-effect relationships through experimentation than through observation of natural events—even in cases where these observations are made by shrewd and talented observers. The examples begin with relatively anecdotal accounts of social phenomena and move toward cases of increasing rigor and control. Finally, we hope by the spread of examples to provide fodder for the discussions to come. The cases presented raise problems that are dealt with in subsequent chapters of the book. The reader is forewarned, however, that each case differs in many respects from those that precede and follow it; our purpose here is more to arouse and interest the reader than to give him systematic information. Such information, we trust, will come out of the subsequent chapters.

ILLUSTRATIVE CASES OF SOCIAL PSYCHOLOGICAL PROCESSES

Case One. Wild Boy of Aveyron

In 1799 a child of 11 or 12 was found by a group of sportsmen in a wooded region of the French county Aveyron. The child was completely naked and strenuously resisted being taken from the perch in the tree to which he had scurried to elude his captors. To the distress of those like

Rousseau, who tended to idealize the "noble savage," the Wild Boy of Aveyron was a pitiful sight to behold:

> A disgustingly dirty child affected with spasmodic movements and often convulsions who swayed back and forth ceaselessly like certain animals in a menagerie, who bit and scratched those who opposed him, who showed no sort of affection for those who attended him; and who was in short, indifferent to everything and attentive to nothing (Itard, 1962, p. 4).

Pinel, the famous physician for the insane, observed the child and reported him to be mute, insensitive to sounds, incapable of attention, "destitute of memory," without aptitude for imitation, and "insensible to every kind of moral influence." The Wild Boy of Aveyron, Pinel concluded, was an incurable idiot.

A young physician, Jean-Marc-Gaspard Itard, did not share this pessimistic judgment. He undertook to provide special educational experiences for the child, who was given the name Victor, in order to civilize him. Itard needed all the patience and ingenuity that he had in abundance to make the slightest impact on the child. At first Victor showed no response to pistol shots fired next to his ear, snuff in his nose, or extremes of heat or cold. He was discovered several times in the kitchen, picking potatoes out of boiling water and showing no sign of discomfort. He was sometimes observed squatting, half-naked, on the cold winter ground for hours without any evidence of distress. By carefully arranging graded sensory experiences for Victor, Itard was able to develop in him a fairly acute discrimination between temperatures and a preference for warmth, which enabled Itard to teach him to dress himself and spend the night without wetting his bed. Although Victor never lost his fascination for the outdoors (indeed, during the early phases of his training he often ran away into the woods and fields), he did adapt himself with considerable success to the routines of civilized living. However, he never learned to walk properly, and persisted in a crouching shuffle with the aid of his hands to propel him along the ground.

Perhaps Itard's greatest achievement was to teach Victor to do a limited amount of reading. Although he was forced to conclude that Victor was close to being mute, and so insensitive to sounds that he might as well have been deaf, Itard found it possible by slow and painful stages to build in a vocabulary of written words. As a result, Itard could point to the word for book, or cup, or hat and Victor would search for the object symbolized by the word. It is clear that in other respects Victor manifested flashes of intelligence and ingenuity that belied the label of idiocy, though it would be difficult to argue that the boy was not mentally defective (whether through genetic defect or as a consequence of social privation) even at the end of Itard's five years of training.

As for Victor's social and emotional development, there were marked changes over the five-year period. When taken from the Aveyron woods, he would slide from apparent melancholy to immoderate laughter without any event intervening to bring about the change in mood. However, as a result of Itard's painstaking care and training, Victor became capable of shedding tears in sadness and of laughing and squealing with delight when the occasion inspired it. His response to other people also changed radically. From complete indifference to human contact, Victor developed considerable warmth and affection for Itard and the physician's housekeeper. He would embrace and caress them at greeting and leave-taking. But Itard remained for a long time disappointed in the extent of this development, as he felt that Victor's sociability and affection were based on selfish and greedy motives:

> I noticed that after several hours and even after some days, although Victor returned to his guardian with demonstrations of affection, these expressions of delight were proportionate not so much to the length of his absence as to the real advantages which he found on his return and to the privations which he had experienced during their separation (Itard, 1962, p. 89).

Eventually, Itard became convinced that there was, after all, a spontaneous and "civilized" quality to the affection Victor expressed toward his guardian and Itard himself. As one example of this final development, Itard described the boy's reaction to the death of the guardian's husband as reflecting "a sad emotion, belonging exclusively to the sphere of civilized man" (p. 91).

Itard summarized his successes as dramatic in some spheres but disappointing in others. Whereas he had set out primarily to show that Victor could be turned by intensive educational efforts into a responsive and roughly normal child, he encountered severe difficulties and the results were essentially ambiguous. Was Victor mentally defective and *therefore* abandoned as a small child, or were his capacities dulled and stunted through disuse and through the complete lack of human contact? Some have argued that a truly defective child could not have survived the privations of scratching for an existence in the woods. Others have argued that Victor's resistance to instruction marks him as constitutionally (natively) defective. There is obviously no way to resolve this controversy, though we know today that even children who are natively defective are educable to varying degrees.

The case of Victor dramatically suggests the importance of early social experiences in shaping individual personality. The child showed the severe effects of isolation from human contact. We may infer that the period of isolation extended over critical stages of the socialization process. The fact that Itard made so little headway with his conscientious and ingenious efforts to "humanize" Victor indicates that early experiences may be relatively irreversible.

More specifically, Itard's relative failure points up the probable importance of early social interaction in establishing the basis for later interpersonal relations. It did not take long for Victor to recognize the instrumental value other persons can serve—people can reduce pain and bring comfort. It was more difficult for him to develop what Itard calls "civilized" affection. Victor was, after all, deprived of the vast range of complex and subtle social experiences that the normal child routinely encounters. It is tempting to speculate about the effects of this deprivation on Victor's concept of himself as well as his concept of "other person." It has often been suggested that we learn about ourselves from the reactions of others. Obviously Victor was handicapped in this regard.

The fact that severe and irreversible deficit seems to be the result of social deprivation in childhood raises a number of interesting questions that will receive some attention in Chapters Three and Four. From the point of view of scientific method, Itard's report must be treated as a lengthy anecdote from a perceptive medical observer. The account is a compelling one and the descriptions of Victor's behavior are concrete and apparently objective. Nevertheless, if we accept the validity of this report we do so because, by his manner of discourse, Dr. Itard convinces us of his integrity and seems not to stretch the facts to fit an argument. We remain, however, at Itard's mercy: the observations are not systematic or in any way supported by the reports of a second or a third observer. They obviously are colored by the special relationship between Victor and Itard, and it is impossible to estimate the role played by the young doctor's own hopes and doubts in shaping his final account of Victor's progress. In spite of these opportunities for bias and distortion, Itard's report remains a model of one man's honest efforts to conduct a noble and demanding educational experiment.

Case Two. Morale Problems in an Army Training Group

Toward the end of World War II the Army brought together on the campus of a large Midwestern university an aggregation of approximately 100 soldiers. Each of these soldiers had been recently inducted into the Army, each had been through an infantry basic training course, and each had volunteered for a year of specialized training in Japanese language and culture. Each had qualified for the specialized training program by the multiple criteria of at least one year of college, high general aptitude scores, and a demonstrated proficiency at absorbing the vocabulary and grammar of a new language (as measured by a special language aptitude test). The course was to last a year, and most of the trainees arrived in a mood of frank relief that they had been at least temporarily spared the dangers of infantry battle and with a definite interest in the prospect of learning a new and potentially very useful language.

The basic living conditions of the group could hardly have been improved upon. Straight from out-of-doors winter bivouacs in Alabama, or Georgia, or North Carolina, the soldiers found themselves sharing rooms in a relatively new and attractive men's dormitory. The food was excellent and plentiful. Before long it became possible for the married men to invite their wives to town and live with them in nearby apartments. Both single and married soldiers found that, in contrast to the strictly monitored campus Navy unit in another wing of the dormitory, they could leave the campus at any time after classes were over for the day and no military passes were necessary. Only on rare occasions was a curfew enforced, and then there was sufficient advance publicity so that all could be present at bed check.

At first there was considerable challenge involved in the training program. With few exceptions the trainees progressed rapidly in learning Japanese. Many tried to use the language in casual conversations with each other, often with humorous effects, and a few, through outside reading and study, went much faster than the pace of the established curriculum. Throughout the year there was never a dramatic change in the conditions of learning or living, though many of the trainees soon knew almost as much as their teachers—most of whom were American-born Japanese from nearby communities. Notwithstanding the relatively stable and comfortable circumstances, there was an increasing frequency of negative—even delinquent—actions toward both Army and university authorities, and a growth of tension between trainees and their officers. This was in spite of the fact that the officers performed largely benign custodial functions, interfering relatively little with the after-hours freedom of the trainees, and there was an active group of cadet leaders drawn from the ranks of the soldiers themselves.

The increased tension paralleled a steady decline in the morale of the trainee group. This was reflected in both the obstreperous actions of individual soldiers and a shift in what we shall later call group norms * or standards, so that anti-authoritarian actions were not only condoned but actually encouraged by reactions of the group. Before the year was over the following incidents had occurred:

1. A civilian geography instructor asked to see a book that one of the trainees was reading in class. He glanced at the book title, saw it was a

---

* A glossary of technical terms, and of common terms used with restricted meaning in this book, appears at the end of the book.

novel, and threw it casually and with some irritation in the direction of the trainee. The trainee immediately leaped to his feet and threw the book back at the instructor with considerable force. Before being drafted into the Army the trainee had been a graduate student in philosophy at a major university.

2. Sometimes as many as 20 trainees would get up and file casually out of class once the roll had been taken by the sergeant who had brought them there.

3. Trainees were always marched to the first class in the morning, falling into formation after breakfast. It was common practice for some of them to peel off when the formation reached the main thoroughfare and to embark by trolley for a day at the golf course or in the downtown area.

4. The major, who was the executive officer of the entire training program, had the air removed from his automobile tires on several occasions.

5. One trainee, who had finished all but his final thesis for the doctorate in chemistry at an Ivy League school, freely appropriated books from the small library run by the Army in the dormitory and sent them home for storage. This was done without any clear signs that he was in moral conflict over this book stealing.

6. The cadet company commander was severely beaten late one night in a carefully planned attack by two of his fellow trainees. Both attackers, who were eventually found guilty of the attack in a court-martial trial, were married college graduates; one had two children and was an established businessman in a Midwestern community.

7. The war with Japan finally ended while the soldiers were still in training. Two nights after V-J Day several trainees managed to raise a Japanese flag on the campus flag pole in such a way that it could not be lowered. This apparently innocent college prank angered university officials exceedingly, and the municipal fire department spent the better part of a day maneuvering their ladders until they successfully disengaged the flag.

8. The flag incident raised considerable comment around the university and in local press. It was variously blamed on fraternity pledges, disgruntled veterans, and visitors from a rival campus. The actual culprits soon published one early-morning edition of an anonymous newspaper in which the flag incident was exploited as symbolic of the unbearable grievances of the soldiers in the specialized training unit. The newspaper made clear that the flag-raising was undertaken by trainees of the Army unit in order to call attention to the restrictions placed on them. A long list of complaints was aired in the paper, and most of these were laid at the feet of the "incompetent" officers and noncommissioned officers who were in charge of the daily routines, though not the actual classroom work. Copies of this protest paper were sent to the commanding general of the division in which

the unit was located, the colonel in charge of the unit, such columnists as Walter Winchell (no doubt in hopes of starting a crusade), and President Truman.

9. Toward the end of the training year the pace of learning had slowed considerably. Few trainees ever studied outside of the classroom. Several asked to be transferred to any other available unit. At one point almost the entire unit signed a petition asking for immediate transfer overseas. A small number turned in blank examination papers, hoping thereby to be removed from the program.

Some of this obvious deterioration in morale seemed to be a function of the lack of stimulating teaching and the absence of first-rate Japanese language instructors. Some of it undoubtedly was attributable to the news that members of preceding training groups had been sent to Europe rather than Japan, or else to infantry units where they would not be asked to make use of their special training.

The members of this training unit eventually ended up in Japan, where they functioned as clerk-typists, librarians, teachers, military policemen, radio announcers, orderlies, and so on. Only a few made any direct use of their training in Japanese language and culture. Initially many of them experienced a need to complain to others about the year they had spent studying Japanese in the States. This need was soon suppressed when the complaints were met with bitter incredulity from auditors who had fought in the Pacific Islands. The ex-trainees soon realized how irrational their many complaints had been.

The preceding account is reconstructed from the Army experiences of one of the present authors. More than two decades have intervened since the occurrence of the episodes described, so the reconstruction is undoubtedly more selective and fallible than most case studies of ongoing groups in the social science literature. The basic point of interest in this anecdote is that the training group seems to have created an atmosphere of its own, a set of standards or comparison levels that permitted each person to see his lot as mean and shabby. This occurred in spite of the fact that the soldiers were objectively better off than the vast majority of draftees who participated in World War II.

Undoubtedly many factors contributed to the severe decline in morale. There was insufficient intellectual challenge; there were no clear avenues to promotion and no concrete incentives for good performance. Certainly a critical factor, however, was the fact that the soldiers in this group felt deprived *relative to* the civilians in the surrounding community with whom they were prone to compare themselves. In Chapter Three we shall discuss the importance of reference groups. Also in Chapter Thirteen, we shall introduce the concept of comparison level. Both of these notions stress subjective determinants of personal satisfaction. They have been introduced by social scientists to explain certain paradoxes of dissatisfaction in the midst of apparent plenty. We can only assume that had the soldiers compared themselves with those at the fronts of war they would have been more satisfied with their lot. The more salient comparison, apparently, was with civilians at the university who served to remind them of their former freedom.

Case Three. The Invasion from Mars

On a Sunday evening in 1938 Orson Welles' Mercury Theater presented a radio dramatization of H. G. Wells' *War of the Worlds,* freely adapted by Howard Koch. The hour abruptly began with the rich intonations of Orson Welles:

We know now that in the early years of the twentieth century this world was being watched closely by intelligences greater than man's and yet as mortal as his own. We know now that as human beings busied themselves about their various concerns they were scrutinized and studied, perhaps almost as narrowly as a man with a microscope might scrutinize the transient creatures that swarm and multiply in a drop of water. . . . Yet across the immense ethereal gulf, minds that are to our minds as ours are to the beasts in the jungle . . . regarded this earth with envious eyes and slowly and surely drew their plans against us. In the thirty-ninth year of the twentieth century came the great disillusionment. It was near the end of October. Business was better. The war scare was over. More men were back at work. Sales were picking up. On this particular evening, October 30, the Crossley service estimated that thirty-two million people were listening in on radios.

As Welles faded out, the voice of an announcer could be heard in the middle of a weather report. At the end of this brief report, the audience was treated to the music of "Ramon Raquello and his orchestra" coming from the "Meridian Room in the Hotel Park Plaza in downtown New York." After a brief interlude of Spanish music, a second announcer broke in with the following message:

Ladies and gentlemen, we interrupt our program of dance music to bring you a special bulletin from the Intercontinental Radio News. At twenty minutes before eight, central time, Professor Farrell of the Mount Jennings Observatory, Chicago, Illinois, reports observing several explosions of incandescent gas, occurring at regular intervals on the planet Mars. . . . Professor Pierson of the observatory at Princeton confirms Farrell's observation and describes the phenomenon as "like a jet of blue flame shot from a gun." We now return you to the music of Ramon Raquello. . . .

Since something exciting seemed to be happening, the station began to devote more and more of its time to the curious Martian explosions. Professor Pierson was interviewed in his Princeton laboratory by Carl Phillips, described as "our commentator." Pierson was restrained and skeptical. When a report came in that a "seismograph registered shock of almost earthquake intensity occurring within a radius of 20 miles of Princeton," the professor stated that "this is probably a meteorite of unusual size and its arrival at this particular time is merely a coincidence." Further announcements pinpointed the location of the disturbance.

After another musical interlude, Carl Phillips was heard reporting from a farmyard at Grover's Mill, New Jersey, with the breathless announcement that "Professor Pierson and myself made the eleven miles from Princeton in ten minutes." Surrounding the farmyard was a crowd that had gathered to observe a huge cylindrical object that had fallen in a field. Suddenly the top opened and a wriggling monster emerged, "large as a bear and glistening like wet leather." Within a matter of seconds flames engulfed the spectators and it was obvious by the eerie silence that Phillips had been destroyed along with the rest. The studio announcer eventually broke the silence to state, ". . . due to circumstances beyond our control, we are unable to continue the broadcast from Grover's Mill. Evidently there's some difficulty with our field transmission. . . ." The program developed rapidly from this point, and the time relations involved in the unfolding story became increasingly incredible. Armies were decimated, fields and cities were covered with black poisonous gas, and Martian machines began to land in scattered groups all over the countryside. The last announcer before the station break described the apparent end of human life in New York City: ". . . Now the smoke's spreading faster. It's reached Time Square. People trying to run away from it, but it's no use. They're falling like flies. Now the smoke's crossing Sixth Avenue . . . Fifth Avenue . . . 100 yards away . . . it's 50 feet . . ." [silence].

After a station break of 20 seconds, during which it was clearly stated that a dramatization of *War of the Worlds* was in progress, the play changed its tone quite radically and the listener was exposed to Professor Pierson (who had somehow miraculously survived) reading his notes on subsequent events. The notes made clear that considerable time had passed, the Martians had all succumbed to disease bacteria "against which their systems were unprepared," children were again playing on the streets, and so on.

Reactions to the radio dramatization were remarkable. According to Hadley Cantril, who interviewed 135 listeners shortly after the program and carefully examined the results of a survey of 460 listeners conducted by the Columbia Broadcasting System,

Long before the broadcast had ended, people all over the United States were praying, crying, fleeing frantically to escape death from the Martians. Some ran to rescue loved ones. Others telephoned farewells or warnings, hurried to inform neighbors, sought information from newspapers or radio stations, summoned ambulances and police cars. At least six million people heard the broadcast. At least a million of them were frightened or disturbed (Cantril, 1940, p. 47).

From Cantril's interview we excerpt the following samples:

". . . My mother went out and looked for Mars . . . Brother Joe, as usual, got more excited than he could show. . . . Aunt Grace . . . began to pray with Uncle Henry. Lily got sick to her stomach."

. . . .

". . . people started to rush out of the apartment house all undressed. We got into the car and listened some more. Suddenly, the announcer was gassed, the station went dead so we tried another station but nothing would come on. Then we went to a gas station and filled up our tank in preparation for just riding as far as we could . . ."

. . . .

". . . I turned the radio off and ran out into the hall. The woman next door was out there crying too. Then a man ran up the stairs and when he saw us he laughed at us and said . . . that it was only a joke. We didn't believe him and told him to pray, but he finally convinced us. He said he had called the police, and they told him it was a play."

. . . .

"I thought the best thing to do was go away, so I took $3.25 out of my savings and bought a ticket. After I had gone 60 miles I heard it was a play. Now I don't have any money left for the shoes I was saving up for." (Material from Cantril, 1940, pp. 48–54.)

From his interview material Cantril was able to classify most of the listeners in four broad categories: (1) those who checked the internal evidence of the broadcast and realized the program was fictitious; (2) those who checked the broadcast against other information and learned that it was a play; (3) those who tried to check the program against other information but who, for various reasons, continued to believe that the broadcast was an authentic news report; (4) those who made no attempt to check the broadcast or the event. Respondents in the third category were especially interesting. Their main problem was that they checked the program against standards that were themselves ambiguous and that could be interpreted flexibly.

"I looked out of the window and everything looked the same as usual so I thought it hadn't reached our section yet."

. . . .

"I called my mother to find out what to do and there was no answer . . . My only thought was that the flames had overcome my parents."

. . . . .

"We looked out of the window and Wyoming Avenue was black with cars. People were rushing away, I figured."

. . . .

"No cars came down my street. 'Traffic is jammed on account of the roads being destroyed,' I thought."

. . . .

"We tuned into another station and heard some church music. I was sure a lot of people were worshiping God while waiting for their death." (Material from Cantril, 1940, pp. 92–95.)

Our principal interest in this case is that it exemplifies the range of responses people can make to uncertainty. The natural response to ambiguity is to seek clarifying information. It seems apparent from Cantril's carefully collected data that some of the listeners were more interested in finding additional information that would *justify their fears* than in finding information that would reduce uncertainty. In several of the above examples there almost seems to be a wish to believe the worst. What purpose could such a wish serve? What factors are there in the common backgrounds of the listeners that led such a large proportion of them to rely on essentially invalid information to check on the program?

At many points in the chapters to come we shall be concerned with the role that other persons can and do play in the reduction of uncertainty. Especially in Chapters Ten and Eleven we shall see that persons commonly observe the actions of others in an effort to determine the reality that confronts them, to decide how they should feel about that reality, and to evaluate their own abilities to act. The panic resulting from the Orson Welles broadcast seems to reflect a distortion of a basic tendency to compare ourselves with others and to use the information they provide as an aid to decision-making. The word distortion seems justified because panic could have so easily been avoided by such means as checking other stations, examining the radio schedule in the newspaper, calling the police, or even carefully monitoring the program itself. Many of the more affected listeners made the mistake of bypassing nonsocial sources of information to place a too-ready reliance on the reactions of others—others faced with the same uncertainties. The program was, of course, carefully designed to be as realistic as possible. It exploited the reliance people place on radio, normally the first medium (in the thirties) to announce cataclysmic events. Within the framework of the dialogue itself, the program also exploited the credence we normally place in scientific testimony. The distinguished Professor Pierson himself changed his attitude from one of bemused skepticism to one of involved concern that the observed creatures were from an obviously superior civilization. If a skeptical scientist changes his mind, why should the normal listener hold back? The role of communicator credibility in attitude change will be discussed at length in Chapter Twelve.

From the point of view of method the Cantril study can be described as a field survey, but one that was obviously handicapped by pressures of time and the lack of financial resources. Because his interest was primarily that of explaining why those who panicked did so, Cantril interviewed over 100 persons known to have been upset by the broadcast, as determined "by the personal inquiry and initiative of the interviewers" (Cantril, 1940, xi). The interviews were also limited to the New Jersey area. Thus they cannot be described as random in any way, and the study suffers because it lacks sufficient numbers of control cases who were not affected by the broadcast. Nevertheless Cantril has managed to preserve for us the dramatic quality of a celebrated social panic and to capture the rich variety of individual reactions combining to make up the panic.

Case Four. Beliefs, Attitudes, and Behavior

One of the most important social and moral issues of our times is that of civil rights or integration. Historically and at the present time, much of the theory and research of social psychologists is bound up with the study of attitudes: their structure, their relations with one another, and their relations with behavior. In the following case we present excerpts from Robert Penn Warren's small volume, *Segregation* (1956), to illustrate the complexities of attitudes, beliefs, and behavior when a vital social issue is involved. The book itself consists of conversations between the author and a variety of Southerners, both colored and white.

. . . I am in the library of a plantation house, in Mississippi, and the planter is talking to me, leaning his length back at ease, speaking deliberately from his high-nosed, commanding face, the very figure of a Wade Hampton or Kirby Smith, only the gray uniform and cavalry boots not here, saying: "No, I don't hate Negroes. I never had a minute's trouble with one in my life, and never intend to. I don't believe in getting lathered up, and I don't intend to get lathered up. I simply don't discuss the question with anybody. But I'll tell you what I feel. I came out of the university with a lot of ideals and humanitarianism, and I stayed by it as long as I could. But I tell you now what has come out of thirty years of experience and careful consideration. I have a deep contempt for the Negro race as it exists here. It is not so much a matter of ability as of character. Character."

He repeats the word. He is a man of character, it never could be denied. Of character and force. He is also a man of fine intelligence and good education. He reads Roman history. He collects books on the American West. He is widely traveled. He is unusually successful as a planter and businessman. He is a man of human warmth and generosity, and eminent justice. I overhear his wife, at this moment, talking to a Negro from the place, asking him if she can save some more money for him, to add to the hundred dollars she holds, trying to persuade him.

The husband goes on: "It's not so much the hands on my place, as the lawyers and doctors and teachers and insurance men and undertakers—oh, yes, I've had dealings all around, or my hands have. The character just breaks down. It is not dependable. They pay lip service to the white man's ideals of conduct. They say, yes, I believe in honesty and truth and morality. But it is just lip service. Most of the time. I don't intend to get lathered up. This is just my private opinion. I believe in segregation, but I can always protect myself and my family. I dine at my club and my land is my own, and when I travel, the places I frequent have few if any Negroes. Not that I'd ever walk out of a restaurant, for I'm no professional Southerner. And I'd never give a nickel to the Citizens Council or anything like that. Nor have any of my friends, that I know of. That's townpeople stuff, anyway."

Later on, he says: "For years, I thought I loved Negroes. And I loved their humor and other qualities. My father—he was a firster around here, first man to put glass windows in for them, first to give them a written monthly statement, first to do a lot to help them toward financial independence—well, my father used to look at me and say how it would be. He said, son, they will knock it out of you. Well, they did. I learned the grimness and the sadness."

And later, as we ride down the long row of the houses of the hands, he points to shreds of screening at windows, or here and there a broken screen door. "One of my last experiments," he says, dourly. "Three months, and they poked it out of the kitchen window so they could throw slops on the bare ground. They broke down the front door so they could spit tobacco juice on the porch floor."

We ride on. We pass a nicely painted house, with a fenced dooryard, with flower beds, and flower boxes on the porch, and good, bright-painted porch furniture. I ask who lives there. "One of the hands," he says, "but he's got some energy and character. Look at his house. And he loves flowers. Has only three children, but when there's work he gets it done fast, and then finds some more to do. Makes $4,500 to $5,000 a year." Some old pride, or something from the lost days of idealism, comes back into his tone.

I ask what the other people on the place think of the tenant with the nice house.

"They think he's just lucky." And he mimics, a little bitterly, without any humor: "Boss, looks lak Jefferson's chillen, they jes picks faster'n mine. Caint he'p it, Boss."

I ask what Jefferson's color is.

"A real black man, a real Negro all right. But he's got character."

. . . . .

What's coming? I ask the handsome, aristocratic, big grey-haired man, sitting in his rich office, high over the city, an ornament of the vestry, of boards of directors, of club committees, a man of exquisite simplicity and charm, and a member of a segregation group. "We shall exhaust all the legal possibilities," he says. I ask if he thinks his side will win. The legal fight, that is. He rolls a cigarette fastidiously between strong, white, waxy forefinger and thumb. "No," he says. "But it is just something you have to do."

. . . .

What's coming? I ask the taxi driver in Memphis. And he says: "Lots of dead niggers round here, that's what's coming. Look at Detroit, lots of dead niggers been in the Detroit River, but it won't be a patch on the Ole Mississippi. But hell, it won't stop nothing. Fifty years from now everybody will be gray anyway, Jews and Germans and French and Chinese and niggers, and who'll give a durn?"

. . . .

And the old man in north Tennessee, a burly, full-blooded, red-faced, raucous old man, says: "Hell, son, it's easy to solve. Just blend 'em. Fifteen years and they'll all be blended in. And by God, I'm doing my part!"

. . . .

I sit for an afternoon with an old friend, a big, weather-faced, squarish man, a farmer, an intelligent man, a man of good education, of travel and experience, and I ask him questions. I ask if he thinks we can afford, in the present world picture, to alienate Asia by segregation here at home. He hates the question. "I hate to think about it," he says. "It's too deep for me," he says, and moves heavily in his chair. We talk about Christianity—he is a church-going man—and he says: "Oh, I know what the Bible says, and Christianity, but I just can't think about it. My mind just shuts up."

My old friend is an honest man. He will face his own discomfort.

Another man, with a small business in a poor county, "back in the shelf country," he calls it, a short, strong-looking, ovoidal kind of man with his belt cutting into his belly when he leans back in his office chair. He is telling what he has been through. "I wouldn't tell you a lie," he says. "I'm Southern through and through, and I guess I got every prejudice a man can have, and I certainly never would have got mixed up in this business if it hadn't been for the Court decision. I wouldn't be out in front. I was just trying to do my duty. Trying to save some money for the county. I never expected any trouble. And we might not have had any if it hadn't been for outsiders, one kind and another.

"But what nobody understands is how a man can get cut up inside. You try to live like a Christian with your fellow man, and suddenly you find out it is all mixed up. You put in twenty-five years trying to build up a nice little business and raise up a family and it looks like it will all be ruined. You get word somebody will dynamite your house and you in it. You go to lawyers and they say they sympathize, but nobody'll take your case. But the worst is, things just go round and round in your head. Then they won't come a-tall, and you lay there in the night. You might say, it's the psychology of it you can't stand. Getting all split up. Then, all of a sudden, somebody stops you on the street and calls you something, a so-and-so nigger-lover. And you know, I got so mad not a thing mattered any more. I just felt like I was all put back together again."

Case Five. Brainwashing

The American people became dramatically aware of the problem of "brainwashing"—that is, ideological conversion or thought control—toward the end of the Korean War. At that time it became clear that a number of our soldiers and their officers had signed confessions that substantiated such Communist charges as germ warfare, and that at least some of them had been sufficiently convinced of the merits of the Communist cause to refuse repatriation in the United States. The plight of the American soldier in a North Korean prison camp was severe and unpleasant to say the least, but many Westerners in China before and after the Korean War have been subjected to even more intensive indoctrination as prisoners. The experience of many of these persons is described by Lifton (1961) in his fascinating book on *Thought Reform and the Psychology of Totalism.* The descriptions are largely based on interviews Lifton managed to have with ex-prisoners soon after they had been discharged from Chinese prisons and allowed to proceed to Hong Kong.

Although there was no such thing as a typical course of thought reform or indoctrination effort, certain common practices were relied upon to shake the prisoner's convictions and bring him to recognize his "guilt" as an imperialist-capitalist and to accept some of the underlying premises of the Communist ideology. Lifton's accounts reflect a persistent, all-encompassing attempt to assault the prisoner's identity. In the early days of imprisonment prisoners were typically interrogated outside of their cells for long hours and then returned to cells where their fellow prisoners (usually in a more advanced stage of training) badgered and belittled them. When a prisoner was told to confess (without being given much specification as to what he was supposed to confess), he typically resisted. This early resistance was countered by placing the prisoner in chains, making him stand or sit in extremely uncomfortable positions, and under no circumstances allowing him to sleep. The combination of extreme physical discomfort and the degrading experiences of harassment and constant interrogation were invariably sufficient to bring the prisoner to seek a way out of his excruciating dilemma. There followed characteristically a period of making either wild and irresponsible confessions—so absurd as to implicate no one—or confessions that were half-truths and little more than trivial concessions to the charges.

This kind of indiscriminate or grudging confession brought no respite. Furthermore, in most cases the prisoner could not remain unaffected by the unanimous condemnation of captors and fellow prisoners alike. Under such circumstances an individual becomes so permeated by an atmosphere of guilt, as Lifton puts it, that criminal accusations made by others become merged with subjective feelings of sinfulness. Feelings of resentment gradually gave way to the prisoner's feeling that the punishment was deserved and that more was to be expected. This burgeoning guilt was soon coupled with feelings of self-betrayal as the individual was led little by little to renounce the people and organizations that had been the mainstay of his previous life.

At this point the assaults combined with guilt and self-recrimination to produce "the basic fear of annihilation"—the final focus of the prison pressures. This fear was accompanied by considerable confusion and sometimes by hallucinations; the individual reached a state of utter despair and the future seemed hopeless. But then there would be a sudden twist in the direction of leniency. As the prisoner was hovering at the breaking point, the pressures would ease just enough to allow him to feel that there was some hope for adapting to his outer world. A long process might follow when the prisoner, now eager to shape himself in the image of the expectations of those in his environment, would attempt to create a confession that truly encompassed his changed feelings about himself. Each prisoner developed a "creative participation" in the confession process at this point.

His inner fantasies must always make contact with the demands from without. To be sure, these fantasies are painstakingly and selectively molded by officials and cellmates. But they are never entirely divorced from the man who produced them. This means that a good deal of the energy involved in the confession comes from the prisoner himself. His compulsion to confess dedicates him to the task of continuously carving out and refilling his own inner world—under the active supervision and broad moral guidance of his captors (Lifton, 1961, p. 75).

The ultimate results of this process, which for the typical prisoner lasted several years, were variable. Lifton describes three classes of reaction: those who ended up quite confused, shaken by the experience, but puzzled about their new identity; those who became apparent converts; and those who apparently resisted the brunt of the brainwashing experience. Even in this latter group, however, there was considerable repression of underlying feelings and more profound changes in personality than the prisoners would admit.

Although the Western prisoner was usually isolated from supportive social contact of any sort, and cast in with Oriental cellmates who were to varying degrees removed from him culturally and ideologically, Lifton came across one instance where an all-European group was for some reason placed in the same cell, along with eight Chinese prisoners. The group was allowed to maintain itself, with some changes in personnel, for two and one-half years. Eventually the group included a German physician with ardent Nazi sympathies, a highly trained French Jesuit philosopher, a Dutch priest of lowly origin, a successful North German merchant, an adventurous South German businessman, and a French Jesuit science teacher.

The group went through three phases, each marked by the emergence of a different person in the primary role of leadership. During the first phase, the Nazi physician exerted strong influence in the direction of resistance, and Communist pressures were not overwhelming. During the second phase there were much more intensive "reform" activities. This was partly because of the increase of outside pressure and partly because Father Benet, the Jesuit philosopher, had joined the group in the official position of "study leader" because he was fluent in Chinese and was considered a "progressive." He was a brilliant and a complicated person who vigorously urged the group to stop at nothing to convince the officials of the extent of the members' personal reform and conversion. Although the group was not wholeheartedly behind this change in reaction to imprisonment, it gradually moved in a "progressive" direction. The group lost a good deal of its cohesion and inner strength as increasing confusion developed over the difference between the strategy of calculated overt compliance and a more fundamental capitulation to indoctrination pressures.

The final phase was a subtle combination of resistance and adaptation, and it was ushered in by the appearance of still a third leader, the Dutch priest, who was the last of the six to join the group. Father Vechten was a remarkably steady, courageous man who managed to pull the group together and win the clear respect of the other members. Especially with the help of the Nazi physician, Father Vechten was able to develop a definite group policy that involved superficial compliance and enthusiasm for the reform process, coupled with private resistance and conveying of signs to each other that the game was being played.

Vechten, for example, might criticize another Westerner harshly, but at the same time he would try to get across to him some indication that he was merely going through the necessary motions. This could not usually be done overtly, but semantic tricks were exploited by the Westerners to create a communication system which their Chinese cell mates could not penetrate. They sometimes spoke in French or German; when this was prohibited, they interjected single words or concepts from European languages. They also developed special pronunciations to which they ascribed their own connotations . . . "Horse language" became a euphemism for German, and when Vechten would advise some of the others not to use the "horse language," they would know that he meant it "as a friend and not really from the side of the [Chinese] government" (p. 169).

Largely because of their success in following this plan, the individuals in this unique group managed to stave off the ultimate fear of annihilation and preserve much of their identity intact. At the time of release the group members seemed to be better prepared than the average single prisoner to adapt to the change in ideological climate that Hong Kong represented.

Lifton sums up the achievements of the group with the following interpretation of the results of Father Vechten's efforts:

These six men had succeeded in creating a small world of partial independence within the larger threatening universe of the Communist prison. Their independence was never anything like complete, and at times it seemed about to disappear altogether; but its survival created vital alternatives in an otherwise saturated environment. The intellectual alternative—the standing critique of Communist theory—was impressive enough; but even more important was the emotional alternative—the construction through trust and cooperative resistance of a psychological "home" and "family" where each member could find support and spiritual replenishment, and thereby avoid complete dependence on the offerings of reform (pp. 177–178).

Case Six. The Failure of Important Prophecies

In the mid 1950's a suburban housewife (given the pseudonym Mrs. Marian Keech) began to receive messages in "automatic writing" from beings who said they were from outer space and who instructed her to warn the people of the earth of a coming cataclysm, a flood that would inundate the continent from the Arctic Circle to the Gulf of Mexico on December 21. Mrs. Keech told a number of her friends and acquaintances about these messages and before long had attracted a small following of believers. Among them was Dr. Armstrong (again, a pseudonym), a physician living in a college town in a nearby state. Dr. Armstrong spread the word among a group of students who regularly met at his house to discuss spiritual problems and cosmology. He and his wife also visited frequently with Mrs. Keech as the two groups discussed the lessons from outer space and began to prepare themselves for salvation when the flood came.

Initial publicity about Mrs. Keech's messages attracted the attention of a group of social psychologists at the University of Minnesota. They were particularly intrigued with the chance to study what happens to a group that has committed itself to an important (indeed drastic!) prophecy when that prophecy is clearly disconfirmed by events. Elaborate plans were made to "infiltrate" both the Keech and the Armstrong groups with participant observers; the psychologists themselves and those in their employ presented themselves as interested potential members and were eventually accepted into one or the other group. Our information about the group's activities and the responses of the members to the failure of their drastic prophecy comes from the observations of these participant observers (as reported in Festinger, Riecken, and Schachter, 1956).

During the autumn months that preceded the predicted cataclysm, various members of each group made irrevocable commitments to their belief that the world as they knew it was coming to an end. Some gave up their jobs, others gave away their possessions, and nearly all made public declarations of their convictions. In spite of the initial publicity about the messages to Mrs. Keech, it was observed that the groups became increasingly secretive and tended more and more to shun any publicity. As December 21 approached, the believers received some unwanted publicity when Dr. Armstrong was dismissed from his hospital post, an action widely covered in the nation's newspapers. Alerted by this event to the impending cataclysm, representatives of the nation's major wire services converged on the Keech home for a full story. They were turned away. In addition to the reporters, the believers were besieged with potential converts who appeared in person or called on the phone. No attempt was made to convert or proselytize them and they were paid only the most sporadic attention.

By late evening of December 20, the believers began making final preparation for their salvation. Earlier that day Mrs. Keech had received a message instructing the group to be ready to receive a midnight visitor who would escort them to a parked flying saucer that would whisk them away to safety, presumably in outer space. As the moment approached, the two groups, which had merged for the occasion, sat in silence.

The clock chimed twelve, each stroke painfully clear in the expectant hush. The believers sat motionless. . . . Midnight had passed and nothing had happened. The cataclysm itself was less than seven hours away. But . . . there was no talking, no sound. People sat stock still, their faces seemingly frozen and expressionless (pp. 162–163).

Gradually, despair and confusion descended upon the group. The messages were read and reread to see if some clue had been missed. At one point, Mrs. Keech broke down and cried bitterly. At 4:45 A.M., however, she received another message that said the cataclysm had been called off; the little group, sitting all night long, had spread so much light that God had saved the world from destruction.

Mrs. Keech also received a message urging her to publicize the explanation. There followed a period of several days during which the members took turns contacting newspapers, radio stations, and national magazines to spread the explanation of the failure of the flood. Where only hours earlier they had shunned public disclosure, they now became avid seekers of publicity. Active attempts were made to proselytize those who dropped by, again as opposed to the earlier casual attitude toward such visitors.

In contrast to this radical change in the direction of proselytizing activity was the behavior of the students in Dr. Armstrong's group who had not come to Mrs. Keech's home on the fateful night. Although equally committed to their belief in the cataclysm, these students lacked the support of a believing group at the crucial moment. Instead of being activated to proselytize for their beliefs in the messages, the disconfirmation destroyed these beliefs, and there was a corresponding attempt to conceal their earlier membership in Dr. Armstrong's group.

On July 4, 1960, a group of 135 men, women, and children began a 42-day stay in underground fallout shelters in a Southwestern desert community, reacting to a prophecy of widespread nuclear disaster (Hardyk and Braden, 1962). All of these people were members of the same evangelical church. Many had come from congregations in the Midwest, having given up their jobs, sold their homes and many of their belongings, and made the more-than-thousand mile move southwestward. Others were from the local area, but they too made serious sacrifices in contributing labor and funds toward underground shelter construction. The move from the Midwest and the subsequent descent underground were responses to a series of prophecies, the last of which was apparently transmitted through the group leader on the day that they all entered the shelters: "The Egyptians are coming; get ye to the safe places."

Of the original 135 who entered the shelters on July 4, 103 "faithful" remained in the shelters for the full 42 days, at which time they received the word to come out.

At about 9 A.M. they held a joyous reunion in the church, led by their pastor, in which they were asked, "Did you have a victory?" In unison came the reply, "Yes, praise the Lord!!!" [The leader said] their faith had not been shaken, "the Lord has brought the people closer to Him, there is not division, there's a fellowship here and we are the holiness people." Many other church members gave testimony as to how their stay in the shelters had both strengthened their Christian fellowship and increased their belief (p. 138).

The members kept their beliefs intact in part through a reinterpretation of the purpose of their stay. They discovered by looking back over the messages that it had never really been stated that the attack was imminent. God was simply using them to warn a world that was asleep and was, besides, testing their faith.

On the other hand, unlike Mrs. Keech's group in the preceding case, there was little or no evidence of proselytizing activity or any obvious seeking of publicity following the return above ground. The group members were relatively indifferent to the attempts of civil defense officials to contact them and turned away curious tourists who asked to see their shelters.

There are perhaps no problems more central to social psychology than those involved in the relations among a person's various attitudes and between his attitudes and his behavior. We shall deal more formally and systematically with the defining properties of attitudes in Chapter Five; but for the moment let us consider an attitude as an inferred predisposition to behave in an evaluative way toward certain classes of objects or events. Other things equal, we should be able to predict behavior in important social contexts from a knowledge of underlying attitudes. But behavior often reflects the resolution of competing attitudes or of attitudes colliding with external pressures. People conduct most of their affairs within a social structure that defines their relative power to act upon their basic beliefs and values. The white Southerner's desire to segregate himself from the Negro in education, housing, and employment, has obviously been curbed by court decisions and federal legislation. The Western prisoner's desire to act in ways consistent with his fundamental beliefs was even more strongly inhibited by the coercive control of his Communist captors. In less dramatic ways each of us is periodically forced to act in ways that do not fully reflect our underlying beliefs and values.

The social processes of desegregation and brainwashing dramatize the condition of coerced action. What are the effects of such coercion on one's underlying private attitudes? If one is coerced to behave in a manner that runs counter to these private attitudes, does he hold to them all the more tenaciously? Or does there tend to occur a kind of subtle erosion process so that ultimately one's beliefs shift in the direction of one's actions? As we shall see in chapters to come, there are no simple answers to these questions. It depends on the source of the coercing power, its magnitude, the responsibility the individual feels for his own actions, and a variety of other factors. In both the brainwashing case and the segregation case there is evidence of the discomfort that accompanies discrepancies among attitudes and between attitudes and action. We note that the educated Southerner is torn between conflicting pressures and values. He is "cut up inside" as he tries to resolve the inconsistencies within his system of beliefs. We shall discover in the chapters to come that, although people can find various ways to handle discrepant beliefs, the presence of inconsistency is an agent of unrest and the resolution of this condition often involves attitude change.

The pro-segregation Southerner, the Western prisoner of the Chinese, and the member of Mrs. Keech's doomsday cult each confronts cognitive discrepancies and moves in various ways to resolve them. In everyday language we might say that self-justification is a theme that ties the three cases together. The Southerner must justify his discriminatory behavior with beliefs about the Negro's mental and moral inferiority. Insofar as he can be led to accept "the inevitable," for example, the fact that his children *will* go to school with Negroes, he confronts new problems of belief justification. The resolution of these new problems will very likely involve a beneficial change in the Southerner's negative attitude toward Negroes.

The Western prisoner becomes more vulnerable to major ideological changes when he publicly acknowledges minor crimes or indiscretions. At least in the case of some prisoners, such minor confessions produce changes in belief that make further self-deprecation a natural next step. Perhaps this is why Lifton emphasizes the increase in feelings of guilt and worthlessness.

Among members of the doomsday cult, there is another kind of discrepancy between belief and action. Belief led to action and the action was by and large irrevocable; many of the members resigned their jobs, some gave away their money, and all developed a great stake in the occurrence of the cataclysm. But then events did not bear out the belief, thus creating the problem of how to maintain the consistency between belief and action when an irrevocable act can only be justified by a discredited belief. The apparent solution is for the cult member to justify his behavior by seeking social support for the belief. If he can get enough people to agree with him, perhaps he is right in spite of the evidence to the contrary.

Why was this same course of action not followed in the case of the larger religious group that descended into a fallout shelter? There were, of course, many differences in the conditions under which the two groups functioned. Perhaps the fallout shelter group had so much social support from within their membership that they did not need any from new recruits. Perhaps the fact that Mrs. Keech's group was ridiculed and vilified by outsiders (while the shelter group actually had the support of civil defense organizations) was an important precondition for proselytizing. In any event, the absence of proselytizing in the second case emphasizes how dangerous and difficult it is to generalize from one complex natural event to another. The hypothesis that drew the investigators to Mrs. Keech's group was a plausible one. It was supported by the data they collected. But the increase in proselytizing may have arisen out of some circumstances quite special to the group.

Although the preceding three cases share certain themes, they differ radically in the methods of inquiry they exemplify. The material on reactions to desegregation pressures was intended more as a contribution to literature than to social science. Quotations from informal interviews were selected by the author and skillfully ordered to convey as clearly as possible his conception of the present mood of the South. The selections are provocative and their sources are brought vividly to life by the author's descriptions. The representativeness of the selections, of course, is entirely indeterminate. Lifton's account of thought control procedures is based, as we have indicated, on psychiatric interviews with returning prisoners. He used his psychiatric training to take advantage of the unique and tragic stories of a small collection of prisoners. Warren gives the impression throughout his book of letting the participants speak for themselves; Lifton presses rapidly toward such concepts as "basic fear of annihilation" and "creative participation" in an attempt to explain the dynamics of prison conversions.

The case presented by Festinger et al. may be aptly described as a natural field experiment using participant observation techniques. The authors and their students anticipated an "experimental" event, namely the occurrence of an unequivocal belief disconfirmation, and maneuvered themselves into a position to observe reactions to this event. Observations before the disconfirmation were of course important to provide a base line against which to measure the amount of subsequent proselytizing activity.

Case Seven. Bargaining and Threat

Many kinds of relations between people involve bargains of one sort or another. The word bargaining is generally used when two persons or parties have conflicting interests but each feels that an agreement might be reached in which they would be better off than without such an agreement. Some common examples of bargaining relations are: the buyer and seller relationship when the price is not fixed; union-management negotiations; and such international negotiations as those on disarmament, tariffs, or rights-of-way.

In an effort to bring certain features of the bargaining process into the laboratory, Deutsch and Krauss (1960) conducted an experiment using as subjects female employees of the New Jersey Bell Telephone Company. Pairs of subjects came to the laboratory and were introduced to a game in which each subject was to imagine herself in charge of a trucking company carrying merchandise over a road to a destination. One player was assigned the name Acme, the other the name Bolt. Both players were to start from separate points and to go to separate destinations. At one point, however, their paths merged into a one-lane road. On this section of the trip, the trucks, moving in opposite directions, could not pass each other. If both trucks met on this section of road, there was an impasse that could only be resolved if one or the other player (or both) backed up. Each player also had an alternate route that did not cross the other player's path but was considerably longer than the path containing the common one-lane road. Each player was shown the road map pictured in Figure 1.1. It was made clear to each that neither had an initial advantage over the other. Actual movement of the trucks was to be simulated by the operation of an electrical apparatus. By pushing various designated buttons, each could move her truck forward or backward along either the short or the alternative path. The players were located in separate booths so that each could not see the other. They were given no moment-to-moment information concerning each other's whereabouts; however, each was informed by a signal light when the trucks met head on at any point on the one-lane road. At other times, each could only make an educated guess as to the other's whereabouts.

The object of the game was for each player to move her truck to its destination in the shortest possible time. Obviously, both could not do this on the same trial without creating an impasse, in which case one or both parties would have to reverse their trucks in order for either truck to reach its destination. For each trip completed a player was to be given $0.60 minus her operating expenses. No money actually changed hands; the subjects

28 FOUNDATIONS OF SOCIAL PSYCHOLOGY

were paid in poker chips that had an assigned imaginary value. These expenses were calculated at the rate of one cent per second, so that if more than 60 seconds were required to reach the destination on a particular trial, the player would lose money. The game was so constructed that the alternate route took at least 70 seconds to traverse. It was emphasized to the subjects that they were not to concern themselves with whether they earned

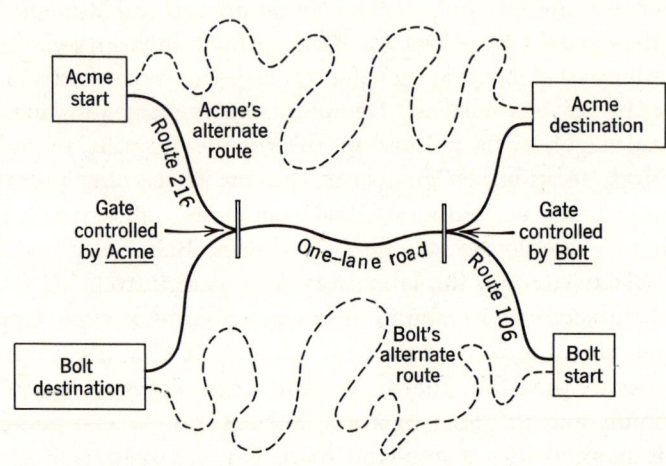

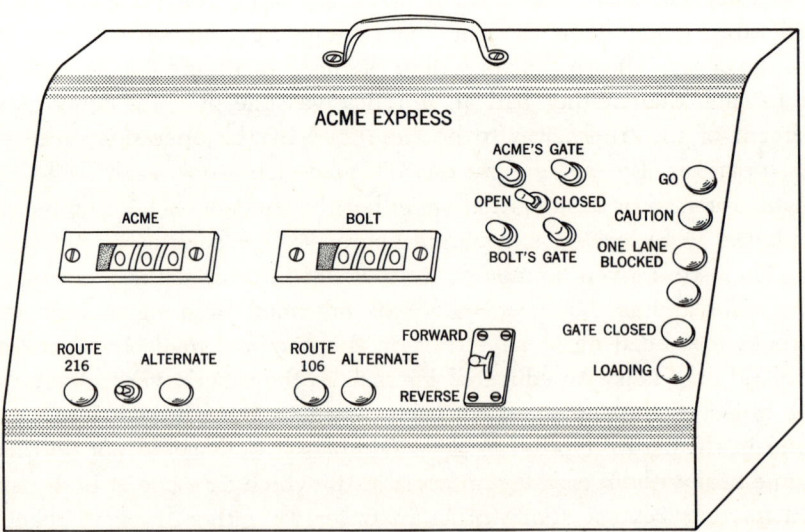

Figure 1.1. The Deutsch and Krauss (1960) trucking game. Top: the road map; bottom: the display panel to indicate moves.

more or less than the other player—they were simply to earn as much money as possible for themselves. The orientation was thus individualistic rather than competitive.

Each pair of players played the game for 20 trials, after having been given $4.00 in imaginary money (poker chips) to represent their working capital. There were three experimental conditions in the experiment. For some subjects the game was further complicated by the possibility that a player could make it futile for the other to travel the one-lane stretch by closing a gate at her end of the stretch. A player who had such a gate under her control could thus prevent the other player from ever reaching her destination by the short route. The fact that she had such a gate was, in effect, a potential threat to the other player. In the *bilateral threat* condition, each player had control of a gate at her end of the one-lane stretch, and thus each could prevent the other from moving beyond that stretch toward her destination. In the *unilateral threat* condition only Acme could control a gate. In the *no-threat* condition neither player had a gate.

The results of the experiment can be measured in terms of the joint payoff to each pair within each condition on each trial. The payoff figures showed that subjects in the bilateral threat condition consistently earned less than subjects in either of the other two conditions. Whereas many pairs in the no-threat condition developed a pattern of alternation (with one subject using the short path on one trial, the alternative path on the next) such a pattern rarely developed in the bilateral threat condition.

Perhaps the most interesting results emerge in comparing the bilateral and unilateral threat conditions. In the unilateral threat condition, Acme's payoff tended to be higher than Bolt's, suggesting that if threat-potential exists within a bargaining relationship it is better to possess it oneself than to have the other party possess it. *But,* Bolt actually did better in the unilateral than in the bilateral threat condition—she was better off not having a gate if Acme had one.

The investigators feel that the very fact that both players have a gate creates the presumption that it will be used, thus arousing antagonism, making it important to "save face," and strengthening whatever competitive motivation exists in the situation. They tentatively suggest that, if the results of their experiment were to be examined for their implications in analyzing international negotiations, ". . . it is dangerous for bargainers to have weapons, and . . . possibly even more dangerous for a bargainer to have the capacity to retaliate in kind than not to have this capacity when the other bargainer has a weapon" (p. 189).

The experimental situation devised by Deutsch and Krauss is an ingenious example of a study designed to simulate conditions in the larger world. To some extent every experiment involves features of simulation; the experimental conditions must have *some* relation to situations outside the laboratory. As we shall see in the next chapter, however, the trucking game experiment has a number of special features that qualify it as a *simulation experiment.*

Such experiments attempt to reproduce some of the complexity of important natural events; they provoke attention to what *might* be the critical variables operating in the real life setting. However, the risk of generalizing from negotiations in a simulated trucking game to international bargaining is a dangerous one. Deutsch and Krauss are cautious and correctly tentative in their discussion of the implications of their results. As we shall see in Chapter Fourteen, the outcome of such simulation games can be radically altered by slight changes in procedure. For example, a study by Gallo (1966) makes it clear that when incentives in the trucking game are real and substantial, there is a high level of cooperation and the threat gates are seldom used. Such a finding, of course, has implications for the international bargaining situation that differ markedly from those of the original Deutsch and Krauss study.

Case Eight. Initiation Severity and Liking for the Group

Aronson and Mills (1959) conducted an experiment to test the proposition that persons who undergo a severe initiation in order to become members in a particular group end up liking the activities of the group and its members better than those who undergo a moderate initiation or none at all. Such an experimental test requires that the investigators expose subjects to the same actual group experience while varying the conditions of becoming a member. Such conditions were impossible to arrange without deceiving the subjects about the reasons for participation; temporary deception is often required in experiments when it is essential to combine control and rigor with conditions that are realistic to the subject. (The problem of experimental deception of subjects—its ethical and methodological implications—will be discussed at some length in the next chapter.) Sixty-three college women served as experimental subjects. Each was assigned to one of three experimental conditions: a severe initiation condition, a mild initiation condition, and a control condition of no initiation. Let us follow a typical subject in the severe initiation condition and then compare her experience as a subject with those who were (randomly, of course) assigned to the two other conditions.

The severe-initiation subject was one of a number of persons who volunteered to participate in a series of group discussions on the psychology of sex. When she arrived at the experimental room to meet with her group she was informed that she was joining a group that had been together for several weeks. She was then given an elaborate explanation of why it was necessary to undergo a "screening test" before joining the group. In this explanation it was pointed out that because the group would be discussing sex it was important to insure that the participants would not be too embarrassed to contribute openly to the discussion. Therefore an embarrassment test had been devised, which consisted of reading aloud some sexually oriented materials. The subject was told that she did not have to take this test, but that she could not join the group unless she did. All but one subject in the severe initiation condition agreed to take the embarrassment test, which actually consisted of reading 12 obscene words plus two vivid descriptions of sexual activity from contemporary novels. In the mild initiation condition the subject went through every step confronting the severe initiation subject except that the screening test was benign and merely involved reading five words like "prostitute," "virgin," and "petting." In every case after submitting to the test the subject was told that she had performed satisfactorily and could join the group. In the control condition there was no mention of a screening test and subjects were led to assume that they would join the group as a matter of course.

The next experimental problem was to expose the subject to the group, so that she could evaluate its attractiveness, without letting her participate in the discussion herself. Her participation would introduce uncontrolled variations into the experiment and it would be difficult to interpret the results. Therefore the subject was presented with two further deceptions: she was told that in order to decrease further any tendencies for embarrassment to get in the way of the discussion, the psychologist had hit upon the scheme of having the group members communicate through an intercom system using headphones and a microphone rather than carry on a face-to-face discussion; second, she was told that the members were discussing the book *Sexual Behavior in Animals,* assigned for discussion at the present meeting, but that as the subject had not read the assignment it was better if she merely listened to the discussion before joining the group herself at the next session. These elaborate preconditions made it possible for the investigators to play the same tape-recorded discussions to each of the 63 subjects, regardless of the experimental condition to which she had been assigned. This was of crucial importance because the interest of the investigator was to vary the conditions of entry into the group while keeping the subjects' experience with the group's activities and members constant.

At this point in the experiment all subjects were exposed to the same tape-recorded discussion, a discussion featuring the comments of three female undergraduates like themselves. The discussion itself was exceedingly dull.

The participants spoke haltingly on secondary sex behavior in the lower animals, "inadvertently" contradicted themselves and one another, mumbled several non sequiturs, started sentences that they never finished, hemmed, hawed, and in general conducted one of the most worthless and uninteresting discussions imaginable (p. 179).

At the conclusion of the recording the psychologist explained that it was customary for each member, at the close of a meeting, to fill out a questionnaire expressing her reactions to the discussion. In consequence, the subject was asked to rate both the discussion she had just heard and the group members on a number of evaluative dimensions (dull-interesting, intelligent-unintelligent, etc.). The results were as shown in Table 1.1:

Table 1.1. Ratings, by Condition, of Discussion and Members [a]

Object of Rating	Condition		
	Severe Initiation	Mild Initiation	Control
Discussion by group	97.6	81.8	80.2
Group members	97.7	89.3	89.9

[a] Adapted from Aronson & Mills (1959). The higher the score, the more favorable the evaluation.

It is clear from these results that those subjects who underwent a severe initiation found the same discussion and the same group members more interesting than did either those subjects who were subjected to mild initiation or those who were not "initiated" at all. Subjects in the latter two conditions did not differ from each other in these ratings.

After the questionnaires were completed, the psychologist explained the conditions of deception to each subject and enlisted her cooperation in not revealing the deception to others. Only one subject expressed suspicions about the procedure; her data were not included in the final results.

Schopler and Bateson (1962) repeated part of this experiment with slight variations in procedure and found similar differences between their severe initiation and their control condition. They found further that if the experimenter disparaged the discussion ("other groups who've discussed this chapter have produced rather feeble discussions") in the severe initiation condition, the subjects rated the discussion content no more interesting than did the control subjects.

A detailed analysis of the Aronson and Mills (1959) experiment is woven into the next chapter. Here we need only comment that the experiment is quite typical, in many respects, of contemporary research in social psychology. A hypothesis derived from theory is tested in a well-controlled laboratory setting. The results are primarily of interest because of their theoretical relevance and not because we can generalize readily to other initiation situations.

SUMMARY

In the present chapter we have tried to introduce social psychology by exemplifying a few of the major problems that characterize the field. In their attempt to study the behavior of individuals as a function of social stimulus variables, social psychologists have been challenged by: reports of uncivilized, feral children; episodes of low morale in the face of objectively comfortable conditions; attitudinal inconsistencies and their resolution; the dramatic phenomena of "thought control" made possible by removing the normal social support for an individual's beliefs; the reactions of a group of believers when the critical feature of their beliefs is clearly disconfirmed; the spiral of self-defeating competitiveness that can characterize interpersonal bargaining; and the tendency of members to like a group better if they have suffered a severe initiation. Each of the cases presented dramatizes the effects people can have on each other and invites theorizing about the processes that mediate these effects.

The examples have been roughly ordered to move from the level of anecdote and descriptive reconstruction to the controlled laboratory experiment. An abiding issue in evaluating the social sciences is whether we truly gain in clarity of insight when we turn from the perceptive but uncontrolled observation to the rigorously designed experiment. In the next chapter we intend to champion the ideal of controlled experimentation and to point out the difficulties of drawing precise conclusions from descriptive accounts of social episodes.

Another issue is whether the social psychologist tells us something we did not already know, and whether the instances of his doing so are frequent enough to justify his existence. As a partial answer to this charge, we offer the following example:

During World War II the Army established a Research Branch of the War Department's Information and Education Division. This branch, which was in existence for about five years, undertook about 300 studies dealing with various phases of the life of American soldiers. These studies included over 600,000 interviews, and, altogether, they give an interesting picture of the state of the soldier's attitudes, his morale, and the perceived sources of his frustration. These materials were intensively analyzed by Samuel A. Stouffer and a large group of collaborators. The results of this analysis were published in a four-volume report entitled *The American Soldier* (1949).

These volumes appeared with considerable fanfare and they were reviewed in a number of major newspapers and commercial magazines. Many of the reviewers were quite sarcastic and raised questions about the investment of time and energy in attitude surveys that came up with such obvious conclusions as the fact that many American soldiers were unhappy in World War II. Partly to answer such criticisms, the distinguished sociologist Paul Lazarsfeld included the following remarks in an *Expository Review of the American Soldier* (1949):

. . . it is hard to find a form of human behavior that has not already been observed somewhere. Consequently, if a study reports a prevailing regularity, many readers respond to it by thinking, "Of course that is the way things are." Thus, from time to time, the argument is advanced that surveys only put into complicated form observations which are already obvious to everyone. . . . The reader may be helped in recognizing this attitude if he looks over a few statements which are typical of many survey findings and carefully observes his own reaction. A short list of these with brief interpretive comments will be given here in order to bring into sharper focus probable reactions of many readers.

1. Better-educated men show more psycho-neurotic symptoms than those with less education. (The mental instability of the intellectual as compared to the more impassive psychology of the man-in-the-street has often been commented on.) . . .

2. Men from rural backgrounds usually are in better spirits during their army life than soldiers from city backgrounds. (After all, they are more accustomed to hardships.) . . .

3. Southern soldiers were better able to stand the climate in the hot South Sea Islands than Northern soldiers. (Of course, Southerners are more accustomed to hot weather.) . . .

4. White privates were more eager to become non-coms than Negroes. (The lack of ambition among Negroes is almost proverbial.)

5. Southern Negroes preferred Southern to Northern white officers. (Isn't it well known that Southern whites have a more fatherly attitude toward their "darkies"?) . . .

6. As long as the fighting continued, men were more eager to be returned to the States than they were after the German surrender. (You cannot blame people for not wanting to be killed.) . . .

We have in these examples a sample list of the simplest types of interrelationships which provide the "bricks" from which our empirical social science is being built. But why, since they are so obvious, is so much money and energy given to establish such findings? Would it not be wiser to take them for granted and proceed directly to a more sophisticated type of analysis? This might be so except for one interesting point about the list. *Every one of these statements is the direct opposite of what actually was found.* Poorly educated soldiers were more neurotic than those with high educations; Southerners showed no greater ability than Northerners to adjust to a tropical climate; Negroes were more eager for promotion than whites; and so on. . . .

If we had mentioned the actual results of the investigations first, the reader would have labeled these "obvious" also. Obviously something is wrong with the entire argument of "obviousness." It should really be turned on its head. Since every kind of human reaction is conceivable, it is of great importance to know which reactions actually occur most frequently and under what conditions; only then will the more advanced social science develop (pp. 379–380).

CHAPTER TWO

Research Methods in Social Psychology

The reader now has some idea about the sorts of problem that interest a social psychologist. In this chapter we want to examine how he goes about formulating and attempting to answer questions that bear on these areas of interest. This chapter is by no means a comprehensive treatment of scientific methodology. We direct the reader who is interested in a broader systematic view to any of several standard treatises (e.g., Cohen and Nagel, 1934; Braithwaite, 1953; and Kaplan, 1964).

We do wish, however, to identify some of the primary goals of any scientific inquiry, including the study of social psychology. We should like to clarify the advantages of experimentation and controlled research without implying that other approaches are necessarily fruitless or irrelevant. As part of this clarification we shall devote considerable space to the laboratory experiment in social psychology and attempt to suggest certain criteria for assessing the meaning of experimental results. We hope the reader will then be in a better position to appreciate the significance and the limitations of the research reports that form a substantial part of the chapters to come. We shall begin with some rather general considerations as a context for our later treatment of those problems of methodology that confront, especially, the social psychologist.

The words "science" and "scientific" are apt to have overly specialized meanings in everyday speech. To many of us these words call up an image of dedicated, remote, dispassionate men surrounded by test tubes or elaborate electronic equipment. To some skeptics from the humanities any reference to a scientific study of human behavior seems a contradiction in terms. How can the essence of human personality be distilled in a psychological beaker? To the natural science skeptic, the social sciences are only "scientific" by analogy, by the use of a few measures and modes of thought superficially similar to those used in physics and chemistry. He may concede that both social and natural sciences share an interest in clear thinking and reliable inference from evidence, but the natural science skeptic also often believes that great differences in measurement possibilities separate the physical and social sciences and emphasize the basic dissimilarity of the two fields.

It is true that many of the claims for scientific status made by students of behavior have the ring of pretense and self-consciousness. Many psychologists wonder whether an adequate psychology will ever emerge from emulation of the physical sciences. Nevertheless, it is important to see the sense in which social psychology is disciplined by the same logic and the same respect for evidence that has characterized the development of physical science.

Any abstract discussion of science must consider two aspects of the term. First, there are the goals toward which scientific thinking and procedures are usually directed. Second, there are the methods that scientists typically employ to achieve these goals. Let us deal with each of these in turn.

THE GOALS OF SCIENCE

The fact that we are talking about science in general makes it somewhat easier to discuss scientific goals than if we were to attempt to answer the question, "What are social psychologists trying to find out?" At the abstract level, three such goals are often bracketed together: prediction, understanding, and control. It is helpful to think of these three possibilities as representing different degrees of scientific achievement. To be able to predict the occurrence of any event is an important step forward in the acquisition of knowledge about that and related events. But prediction may be seen as a first step, one that lays the groundwork for but does not necessarily contain ultimate understanding. Man could make highly accurate predictions of gravitational and astronomical regularities before the contributions of Newton were known, simply on the basis of careful observation and the assumption that what has always happened in the past will continue to happen. No doubt men also observed that various herbs had poisonous or therapeutic effects long before they were able to understand the precise chemical basis for these effects. In our daily interpersonal relations we make successful predictions of human behavior time and time again. We may make the implicit prediction that what we are about to say will not offend the listener or cause him to dislike us. We may predict that if we ask guests to dinner at 7:30, they will not begin to show up until 8:00.

Such predictions are scientific only in a very limited sense, but the observation of regularities, of recurrent event patterns and sequences, lies at the heart of all scientific endeavor. An empirical science that is not built on prediction and predictability is quite inconceivable. Sometimes, in science, statements are made assigning causes for an event that has already occurred and that was not anticipated. Such after-the-fact statements may serve as the basis for future predictions, and unless they implicitly do so they are scientifically uninformative. In fact, a theory or an argument is valuable to the extent that it incorporates predictive statements linking observable events.

But what of the relationship between prediction and understanding? In the usual sense of the word it is obviously possible to think of "understanding" some sequence of events without having predicted it or without using understanding for future predictions. In the stricter scientific sense understanding ultimately rests on prediction because science attempts to establish the validity of explanations and successful prediction serves to validate the understanding that gave rise to the prediction. Intuitive understanding certainly plays a role in the development of scientific formulations, but the kind of understanding that does not lead at some point to predictive statements is not relevant to the scientific process.

Prediction rests on understanding just as understanding implies the ability to predict. A given prediction may, however, represent a very low level of understanding—as in the prediction implicit in the avoidance of certain forms of mushrooms. We never know what level of understanding we have reached until we progress to the next level. The pygmy who kills elephants with poison spears is hardly aware of what he does not know about the ingredients of this poison. A particular scientific theory may be considered valid and useful, and indeed may be, until another comes along to supplant or supersede it. The point is that prediction is vital to understanding (in the scientific sense) but the degree of understanding that predictability brings depends on the fullness and precision of a given predictive account. It also depends on the relationship between a particular prediction and a more general class of predictions. Thus our understanding grows as we move from:

(a) *knowledge that a spear is more likely to produce elephant fatality when dipped in a particular vegetable mash than when no poison is applied* . . .

to

(b) *knowledge that some of the ingredients of this mash are vital to the effect and others are not* . . .

to

(c) *knowledge that the poisoning ingredients have a particular chemical structure* . . .

to

(d) *knowledge that this chemical structure is a member of a class of similar chemical structures having poisonous effects.*

Each step involves prediction, explicit or implied, and yet the order of understanding changes and approaches the goal of scientific generality as we move from (a) to (d). The knowledge represented by statement (a) is an empirical generalization, whereas statement (d) represents a conceptual law, especially when the latter details the precise nature of the interaction between such chemical compounds and animal tissues.

And now, what of control, or the possibility that scientists can take an active role in changing relevant features of the environment to produce predicted effects? Is our understanding further enhanced when we can manipulate the antecedent events in a cause-effect relationship? Perhaps it is better to say that our understanding is more precisely verified and can be more firmly rooted when our predictions are tested under controlled circumstances, when we as scientists have produced or arranged for the occurrence of the antecedent event. Two major points are involved here. First of all, the ability to control—to provide for the presence or absence of critical antecedent conditions—implies that experiments can reproduce a particular cause-effect sequence. This is more than simply a convenience that makes it easier to demonstrate a point or communicate understanding. The operations involved in reproducing the antecedent (causal) event may be precisely specified and made identical from time to time. On the other hand, events that occur naturally, without human intervention, are much less apt to recur in the same form or in the same context. This means that it is more difficult to discern the causal agent when control is not possible, and that the assignment of causal status to one event rather than another is more subject to error. Particularly in psychology, prediction is always a matter of probability. In psychology we rarely gain the kind of control over all variables so that a given antecedent event always leads to another. The probability status of a prediction can be much more easily established through control of the conditions of test and retest.

A second and closely related dividend of control is the opportunity for the systematic variation of antecedent conditions that may always be correlated with other conditions in the natural environment. This is a rather difficult point to understand and one that needs emphasis. If our observations are at the mercy of naturally occurring events in the environment, it is almost always the case that these events are imbedded in complexes of other events. The same antecedent events may tend to be coupled so that we cannot with confidence attribute the observed effect to one rather than the other. The assignment of causal influence to the proper variable may only be accomplished if we can observe what happens when one variable is present and the other is absent.

Correlation versus Experimental Control

The advantages of control over prediction are essentially the advantages of experimental versus correlational research. In experimental research it is useful to distinguish between the independent variable (or variables) and the dependent variable(s). The independent variable is the antecedent stimulus, the potential causal factor. The dependent variable is the consequent response, the effect that is caused by independent stimulus variations. An experiment may be defined as a study in which there is control over the independent variable—the investigator manipulates the state of that variable, its level, or perhaps merely its presence versus absence. For this reason we often speak of experimental "manipulations" to designate the investigator's active role in establishing at least two systematically different conditions whose characteristics are controlled. Manipulation, control, and comparison are, then, the distinctive earmarks of experimentation.

The correlational study, on the other hand, examines the covariation of two or more variables. If the presence or intensity of one variable tends to match or correspond to the presence or intensity of another variable, we say that there is a correlation between them. However, the fact that there is a correlation may allow us to make statements about prediction, but not about causation. We may predict that when X is present, Y will tend to be present also, but we cannot conclude that X causes Y or vice versa. In the correlational approach it is difficult, if not meaningless, to distinguish between the independent and the dependent variable, because all that we can say is that they do or do not vary together. We observe, say, that high productivity in industrial groups tends to go along with democratic supervisory practices. Although we might be tempted to conclude that democratic supervision is good for morale and therefore leads to high productivity, the observed correlation may simply reflect the fact that those groups that were naturally productive made relaxed supervision possible. Or it may be that democratic supervisors are also the most well-informed regarding production techniques and the most efficient way of organizing productive efforts. In order to reach a more complete understanding of the relationship between democratic supervision and productivity, we should have to get better control over these variables.

As another example, the experiment on suffering and liking by Aronson and Mills (1959), described in the first chapter, varied the severity of initiation experimentally by having the subject read either a list of embarrassing words or a list of words that should not prove embarrassing. Subjects in these two treatments were then compared as to how much they liked the recording of a subsequent dull discussion. These investigators might have studied the relationship between suffering and liking by examining a variety of instances in the "real world" outside the laboratory— by looking at fraternity initiations or other cases in which it may be possible to obtain some measure of the relationship between the degree of suffering experienced by a person and the eventual attractiveness of the goal for which he has suffered. If there were a correlation between the severity of fraternity initiations at a particular college and the attractiveness of the fraternity to the members, this could be true for a great variety of reasons. It might simply be, for example, that people are willing to suffer more in order to become members of fraternities that they initially consider to be very attractive on other grounds.

The preceding discussion clearly implies that, because the experiment features control over theoretically relevant variables, it tells us more about causation than does the correlational study. This is certainly true when other considerations are comparable, but there are many occasions in which causal inferences may reasonably be drawn from observed correlations. For ethical reasons it is impossible to study the socialization of children by drastically manipulating their family environments. It is possible, however, to observe the naturally existing differences in family environment and to study the differences in child personality change associated with them.

It should also be noted that logic or a well-developed theory may enable us to draw causal inferences from correlational data with little risk of being misled. For example, suppose we obtain a correlation between group size and the directiveness of the leader—the larger the group the more directive the leader is. Under the circumstances, we are *not* likely to conclude that the group has become large because the leadership was directive. The ambiguity here does not center around the direction of causation; such a finding would be theoretically ambiguous because it is not clear *how* group size leads to directive leadership. In order to understand the factors that mediate the observed correlation, it would be necessary to manipulate and control various other factors that normally vary along with group size. We shall return to this point below.

To summarize, the goal of science is to understand causal relations among events or variables. Scientific understanding must be more than intuitive or retrospective, however; it must lead to testable predictions. Successful prediction validates understanding, but the level and precision of understanding depends on the degree to which we can control and manipulate the antecedent events in a cause-effect sequence. Such control and manipulation are the primary virtues of the experimental method, virtues that distinguish experimentation from correlational studies.

THE METHODS OF SCIENCE

Science seeks to understand the factors responsible for stable relationships between events, whether the events occur in a magnetic field, in a test tube, in astronomical space, in a rat's T-maze, or in a group reaching consensus about a decision to act. The methods employed to achieve this understanding naturally vary in detail, but it is possible to speak meaningfully of *the scientific method* at an abstract level. As a method of achieving understanding, science involves (a) observing relationships between events, (b) testing the generality of the relationships observed, and (c) proposing rational explanations for their occurrence. It is this latter characteristic that inextricably links scientific procedure with scientific theory. If we merely record the fact that event B follows event A with a high degree of probability we have established an empirical generalization, but the fact has only limited value as a scientific statement. If we are able to generalize about two classes of events of which B and A are members we move closer to scientific meaning. If we can postulate some underlying mechanism or process that accounts for the relationship observed and logically implies other observable consequences, we have converted a reliable observation into a scientific statement. If other consequences, which are logically implied by the conceptual statement invented to explain a given empirical relationship, can be observed to occur, this strengthens the conviction that the conceptual statement is useful and worth an effort to relate it to other statements in a more general theory.

In the chapters to come we shall make a persistent effort to relate research data to relevant theoretical concepts. Many different theories have played a role in the development of social psychology and these theories are by no means mutually exclusive. One theory may be particularly useful in highlighting the relationships of a particular area, but another theory may be more useful in other domains. Sometimes two or more theories will make conflicting predictions in a particular domain, and it is then that relevant research becomes especially important and interesting.

The power of a theory is apparent when it successfully predicts relationships in a variety of empirical contexts. An excellent example may be the diverse relationships that can be considered instances of *cognitive dissonance reduction*. Starting from informal observations that people strive to avoid inconsistencies in their beliefs, Leon Festinger (1957) formulated a very general theory of "cognitive dissonance." He proposed that dissonance—that is, inconsistency among related beliefs—produces motivation to do whatever is easiest in order to regain cognitive consistency or consonance among beliefs. Beliefs associated with action or representing a clear choice or commitment tend to be more resistant to change than other beliefs.

In our first chapter we presented two illustrative studies that were based on predictions from cognitive dissonance theory, though they were introduced without particular reference to this fact. On the surface these studies appear to have very little in common. One study predicted that there would be increased proselytizing by a group of believers in doomsday after the failure of their doomsday prophecy. Another study predicted that severe initiations would cause more liking for the group joined than would mild initiations. In both cases the predictions were confirmed, but the point of interest here is the fact that here are two very different relationships that are forecast by the same theory:

(1) Disconfirmation of a prophecy leads to proselytizing.
(2) Severe initiation leads to liking.

In each case the relationship may be explained in terms of the need to reduce cognitive dissonance.

It is probably true that these particular relationships would not have been investigated by social psychologists if they had not been suggested by dissonance theory. It is also probably true that intuition and past experience played an important role in pointing the investigators toward these particular relationships as illustrations of dissonance reduction. Thus it is important to see that theory construction is not merely an irrelevant game of fantasy played by scientists in their spare time. Scientific understanding involves a continuous movement from observed data to more general concepts and back again to other data. Mere observation without theory would at best result in a Sears-Roebuck catalogue of information classified in some arbitrary (e.g., alphabetical) manner. Conversely, theory without observation can have little more than the esthetic significance of internally consistent statements. Clearly, then, theory construction is not something that runs parallel to the research process. The two must intersect at many points to produce the cumulative insight that is the goal of science.

Theory construction is that aspect of scientific procedure that attempts to bridge the gap between observable events. Theories point to causes and to mediating links. Scientific method involves a continuous journey from the general to the particular so that the nature of the concepts is modified by the demands of the data, and the data in turn are forecast by the demands of the theory. But what is the relation between the goal of scientific understanding and the general method we have just described? To appreciate this relationship requires a consideration of scientific method as an aid to persuasive communication about empirical findings.

Science and the Recruitment of Consensus

We have argued that science attempts to achieve understanding of physical and psychological events through an emphasis on prediction and control. But are there not other routes to understanding? What are the special advantages of a scientific approach over casual observation? The rules and procedures that characterize science at its best are basically designed for one purpose: to maximize the chances that a given explanation of reality will be accepted by those attending to the explanation. The methods of science provide an effective way to recruit consensus, to disarm the skeptic, and to reduce the likelihood that alternative explanations could be true. To this end, science attempts to achieve intersubjectivity—a base of explanation that has reference to events transcending the explainer's own subjective experience. When a scientist communicates the results of an experiment to his colleagues he says in effect: "Here is what I have done and why I did it. I found thus and so, and I think it means such and such for these reasons. There is nothing I have done that you cannot also do to reproduce the same effect. In fact, I have described each procedural step so that anyone may do the same study in the same manner." The methods of science are so designed that no statement about reality need to be taken on faith, and that statements endorsed simply by personal assurances cannot compete for acceptance with statements anchored in reproducible observations.

Viewed in this way, science loses much of its majestic apartness as a method of achieving understanding. Science is merely one among many such methods, and it differs from more intuitive and informal appeals to evidence only in degree. Suppose we were to hear a report of a dispute between two acquaintances: "And then suddenly Joe asked Sam why he didn't work harder on the job. This infuriated Sam, since he felt he was the hardest worker in the group and so he hasn't spoken to Joe since." This is more than a simple descriptive observation because of the causal implications of the words "since" and "so" and the reference to Sam's subjective feelings about his own performance. There may be compelling, special reasons why we would accept the cause and effect statements at face value, such as the fact that infuriation is a common response to such a provocative question, the fact that Joe and Sam have a history of not getting along, or the fact that the reporter of the scene is known to be a reliable and impartial observer. It is often true that special circumstances combine to lend credence to an account of motives or to cause-and-effect statements in interpersonal relations. The methods of science merely protect us from the need for such special circumstances. Our agreement with an analysis of a behavioral event need not be affected by the persuasive powers of the reporter, our judgment of his honesty and reliability, or our knowledge of "what most people would do in a similar situation." Scientific discourse should be, and at best is, impersonal, with understanding not ultimately dependent on the special sensitivities of communicator and listener.

Scientific discourse is essentially anchored in two kinds of shared agreement: agreement about what happened and agreement about a rational framework or logical structure within which event relationships may be understood and related to each other. The latter kind of agreement involves complex considerations in both the natural and the social sciences, and progress is made in any scientific field to the extent that an old consensus is challenged by a new finding that does not fit existing theory. The former kind of agreement—agreement about "what happened"—raises special problems for the social psychologist. The physical scientist operates in a realm in which measurement can usually be reduced to "centimeters, grams, or seconds." His variables may be reliably calculated, usually with the use of precise instruments. The social psychologist is not interested in the size, the weight, or the velocity of stimulus events. He is interested in their meaning—their significance for those attending to them. His stimulus and response variables tend to be complex social communications, which are by their nature difficult to quantify or measure precisely.

Yet both the natural and the social sciences make observations that depend on consensus. It may be easier to agree about the number of centimeters in a mercury column than about the number of hostile remarks in a group discussion, but the differences are largely in degree. Physical indicators are often capable of more precise and reliable discriminations than are human observers, and their consistency usually renders the issue of consensus academic. Human observers can operate along many qualitative dimensions of judgment that cannot be indexed by mechanical gadgets, but agreement between observers assumes a greater practical importance because of the human potentialities for unreliability. Nevertheless, reliability in the analysis of complex behavior *can* be achieved by human observers and when this occurs it makes no serious methodological difference whether the data of an experiment are transformed and coded by machine or by a human judge. In the attempt to secure acceptance of findings, which usually involves the agreement of an appropriate group of colleagues, it is not essential to cast data in terms of physical stimulus dimensions. Other methods of recruiting consensus are equally compatible with the spirit and discipline of science and with the specific criterion that the findings refer to something beyond the private, subjective experiences of the investigator.

THE S-[O]-R PARADIGM

In his penetrating analyses of the structure of scientific revolutions, Kuhn (1962) emphasized the great importance of *paradigms* that guide research and thinking about a particular subject matter. A paradigm is essentially a model for asking research questions. Paradigms are partly a matter of broad theoretical outlook or perspective, partly a matter of preferred methods of obtaining evidence, and partly a matter of the standard by which such evidence is to be evaluated. In the developmental history of a particular discipline, a certain paradigm may characterize the outlook of one or more generations of scientists. Eventually, certain anomalous findings may force a shift to a new paradigm, bringing about radical changes in perspective, new suggestions about where to look for evidence, and new standards of evaluation. The change from Aristotelian to Galilean physics represents a very broad paradigm shift. The shift from Newtonian mechanics to Einsteinian relativity provides a more recent example. The point is that these shifts are more than changes in theories appropriate to account for a particular set of phenomena. They are shifts that revolutionize our entire scientific stance and radically change the way in which investigators view their subject matter.

Within the field of psychology, we can also point to such broad paradigms as behaviorism, introspectionism, and psychoanalytic psychology. To a greater extent than has been true in the physical sciences, different paradigms may flourish side by side in the social sciences, giving rise to lively theoretical controversies in some cases and a feeling of "live and let live" in others.

Social psychology has naturally been much affected by the currents generated from controversies in the parent discipline of psychology. There is, to be sure, ample theoretical dispute among contemporary social psychologists concerning many theoretical issues. At a broader level of methodology and overview, however, we believe that social psychology has been in recent years predominantly shaped by a particular kind of experimental approach. We shall try to characterize this approach under the heading of *the S-[O]-R paradigm*, which is exemplified by much of the research discussed in the chapters to follow.

Unfortunately, the S-[O]-R paradigm is not easily described. It involves the making of theoretical inferences about some aspect of "O," the organism. These inferences are tested by experimentation in which social stimulus (S) variables are manipulated and relevant responses (R) observed and measured. In this way a picture of the person as an unobserved construct, intervening between observable stimuli and observable responses, emerges.

Just as the physicist would not be concerned with the nature of matter had he not observed some of its properties, the psychologist would not be concerned with the nature of the person had he not observed human behavior. In both cases the properties have to be understood and this can only be done by inquiring as to the nature of the basic structure underlying these properties.

The experimental physicist makes inferences about the nature of matter by first doing something to a piece of matter and observing an effect. He develops a conceptual view about the structure of his matter from the relationship between what he has done and the observed effect. The psychologist operates in much the same way. He invents hypotheses as to what is taking place inside the person, which might account for the person's response to a particular stimulus. As outlined above, the general paradigm is one in which the stimulus (S) does something to the person (O, for organism) and produces some effect (R, for response). In this paradigm, the particular qualities of the S and the R are of secondary interest; the experimenter chooses to focus on certain stimuli and responses because he thinks they will further his understanding of persons. The research process consists of choosing certain stimuli and observing certain responses that will reveal the nature of O, the unobserved intervening construct.

A serious problem that many psychology students have is a desire to know what the person is *really* like inside; a difficult task for the teacher is to convince the student that this is a pot-of-gold attitude and that the pot is not really there. Psychologists deal in fictions. They create some kind of a model of what they *assume* the person is really like. These models compete and replace one another as one proves to be more adequate than the other.

The atom is, after all, a fiction, but one that is convenient to assume, since if we did not assume its existence the properties of matter would be difficult to understand. The recent overthrow of the parity principle in the atom occurred because this fiction, or assumption, could not explain certain data. Matter has not changed, but the atom, our fictional representation of it, has. It is convenient for you to assume that the page of this book exists or that your roommate exists. Otherwise, you might be hard pressed to explain certain experiences you have had or are having. Whereas constructions in the everyday world take a casual course in their making, science has formalized this process of inventing and testing fictions and has established certain rules for determining whether or not a particular fiction is tenable.

The Stimulus

Students of basic sensory and conditioning processes tend to identify and measure the stimulus in quantitative physical terms. The dimensions of a sound stimulus, for example, would be frequency, intensity, and duration.

A social psychologist is less concerned with the physical characteristics of the stimulus than with its potential meaning. The stimulus for the person—and for the white rat for that matter—will be determined by his history and his current values. The same external events may be interpreted differently by different people depending on their individual histories of interacting with similar events in the past. The pragmatic maxim of Charles Peirce, that meaning inheres in the relevance or the use of the object to the person, is one that lends itself to the problem of defining the stimulus. Two individuals may respond to the same external event in terms of different uses and will therefore attribute different meanings to it. One of the most challenging tasks facing the experimental social psychologist is to control the situation in a manner that will most nearly insure that the subjects in an experiment attribute the same meaning to the external events.

Discovering the Meaning of the Stimulus

Intuition. In an experiment the psychologist can identify the stimulus in various ways. He can, as a preliminary approximation, use his intuition. The typical subject in psychological experiments is the college sophomore. Because the experimenter was once a college sophomore he may rely on his conception of the world of the sophomore in attempting to create some stimulus situation that would appeal in a specific way to the subject. Aronson and Mills attempted to create a stimulus situation that would produce embarrassment and they relied on their own knowledge of the world of the college coed to produce one. When the subjects differ in background from the experimenter, or are removed a great distance in age from him, he runs a clear risk in attempting to intuit what a given stimulus situation would mean to the subjects. Thus, if his subject sample consisted of a number of reform-school inmates, he might commit a very grave error if he assumed that they would be embarrassed by reading a particular list of words. Subjects from different cultures or from different generations may present a difficult challenge to the experimenter's intuitive ability.

In using his intuition the experimenter is using himself as an instrument to identify the stimulus. He puts himself in the subject's place and imagines what the events going on in the laboratory would mean to him. When he has an intimate knowledge of the subject's world this is a fruitful technique and one that is relied on heavily by many researchers. When, however, the subject's world is different from that of the experimenter, the intuitive approach is risky. Intuition is an indispensable aid to the researcher, but he should design his research in such a way as to provide proper checks on its validity. Changes are often made, after pretesting an experiment, when it becomes clear that subjects do not interpret the stimulus situation as the experimenter expected them to.

Verbal Reports. The experimenter can ask the subject what a particular event or set of events means to him. For example, he might ask his subject if reading a particular list of words was embarrassing. The risks are obvious. For one thing, the experimenter and his subject must be clear as to what kind of experience the word "embarrassing" refers to. Even if we assume that there is agreement as to the meaning of the term, how heavily can we rely on the subject's answer? If the subject says "Yes, the experience was embarrassing," we are confronted with at least two possibilities. The experience may indeed have been embarrassing for the subject, or he may be dissembling in order to create a particular impression or please the experimenter. If he believes the experimenter was attempting to create embarrassment he may be tempted to say that he was embarrassed merely in order not to disappoint the experimenter. Another possibility is that the subject may never have considered whether the experience was embarrassing but now that the issue of embarrassment is brought to his attention he may convince himself that it was indeed embarrassing.

If the subject answers "No, it was not embarrassing," we are again left with at least two possibilities. The experience may not have been embarrassing or the subject may have been embarrassed but not want to admit it. Considerations of this sort mitigate against relying entirely on the subject's verbal report as to the nature of the stimulus situation.

Other Evidence. Most researchers use verbal reports as supplementary evidence concerning the meaning of the situation to the subjects but they are cautious about taking such information at face value. Verbal reports are thus examined along with other evidence provided during the experiment. For example, in studying the effects of aggression directed at a subject by someone else, the experimenter may look for signs that the aggression is perceived as intended by noting the subject's facial gestures or monitoring various physiological indicators of stress. A major source of evidence is always the fact that the subjects respond as predicted. If this is the case, then it is usually fair to assume that they have perceived the situation as intended. It is primarily when predictions fail that any evidence about the subjects' perceptions of the stimulus conditions becomes especially crucial. The experimenter must try to determine whether his theoretical inference is wrong or whether he merely has failed to create the appropriate conditions for testing that inference.

The methods used to identify the meaning of a stimulus situation to a subject depend upon the stimulus in question. As we shall see, the psychologist has many techniques available to him, each providing some circumstantial evidence that the stimulus has had such-and-such an impact. Since it is important to establish that the subjects have interpreted the stimulus in the manner intended, these techniques are often referred to as *checking (or validating) the manipulation.*

Homogeneity of the Subject Sample

Subjects should not be heterogeneous with respect to background characteristics affecting the interpretation of experimental stimuli. Different backgrounds predispose subjects to attach different meanings to the same stimuli. A statement made by the experimenter to the subject, praising him for some performance, may be variously interpreted as extremely kind, routine and perfunctory, or patronizing. If the psychologist is interested in the effects of praise on subsequent performance, variations in interpretation of his statement will undoubtedly produce differences in the subject's subsequent behavior. This kind of "error" is inevitable in experiments, but must be kept to a minimum.

In the Aronson and Mills experiment, reading a list of obscene words probably did not produce embarrassment in all of the Stanford coeds who served as subjects. Some may have reacted with aggression toward the experimenter, some with amusement, some with curiosity as to the meaning of the various four letter words in the list, and still others may have been sexually aroused. The subject's behavior would have varied depending on the meaning attributed to the situation.

In the initiation experiment there was a good deal of overlap between the mild and severe suffering treatments in the degree to which the subjects liked the recording of the sex discussion club that followed their initiation. Although, on the average, subjects in the severe initiation treatment liked the discussion better than subjects in the mild one, some severe-initiation subjects liked the group less than some subjects in the mild treatment. These cases may represent deviant interpretations of the stimulus events provided by the experimenters. For example, some subjects in the severe treatment may have developed a great deal of hostility toward the experimenter and this hostility may have colored the evaluation of any aspect of the experiment including the group discussion. Also, as we shall see presently, psychological states other than suffering may have produced the same attitude toward the group. Unless we carefully control the meaning of the situation to the subject we may easily be misled.

Ideally, we would like two homogeneous treatments. In one, *all* subjects undergo equally severe suffering in order to acquire some desired goal; in the other, *all* subjects undergo no suffering or a minimum of suffering to attain the same goal.

In a recent experiment by Gerard and Mathewson (1966) an attempt was made to approximate this ideal more closely. Instead of having the subject read either a list of obscene words or a list of neutral words, the subject was given either very strong shocks or very mild shocks as part of the initiation for entering the sex discussion club; the shocks were part of a supposed "objectivity test" for all prospective members. At the end of the experiment the subject was asked to rate the pleasantness of the shocks. There was no overlap in the degree of pleasantness attributed to the shocks. In the severe treatment practically every subject rated the shocks as extremely unpleasant, whereas in the mild treatment subjects found them only slightly unpleasant. These ratings thus serve as a check on the experimental manipulations. Perhaps because of the clear differences in suffering created by the variation in shock severity, the suffering-liking hypothesis received much stronger confirmation than in the Aronson and Mills study. It is not always possible to find stimulus conditions that lead to interpretations that are so well equated within conditions. Even the response to physical punishment may be quite heterogeneous. Nevertheless similarity of interpretation within and distinctiveness between conditions is the experimental ideal.

Adequate manipulation of the stimulus conditions involves some knowledge about the values and perspectives of the particular subject population. One population may require the manipulation of conditions that, on the surface, appear entirely different from the manipulation used for another population, yet the two apparently different manipulations may have been designed to produce equivalent stimulus meaning. A statement effectively used to praise an eight-year-old would probably be very different from a statement designed to praise an adult. Differences in social status may have to be established in very different ways when repeating at an Ivy League college a study originally carried out at a Southern state university. In attempting to create equivalent stimulus conditions for two different sets of subjects, the experimenter is less intent on following a given set of procedures slavishly than on producing psychologically equivalent stimulus conditions.

Kurt Lewin (1947a) referred to the apparent surface characteristics of both stimuli and responses as *phenotypes* and to the underlying structures they represent as *genotypes*. The same phenotypical procedure, reading a list of obscene words, may evoke in different subjects such different genotypes as embarrassment, curiosity, or sexual arousal. Also, phenotypically different external stimulus conditions, like the application of electric shock in one experiment and having to read obscene words in another, may produce genotypically similar conditions of suffering.

Random Assignment of Subjects. Since there may be differences between subjects in their interpretation of stimulus events in the experiment, subjects should be assigned randomly to the various experimental conditions. What this means, in effect, is that no subject should have a better chance to end up receiving one experimental treatment than another. If assignment to treatment conditions is not random, then there is a good chance that any differences between conditions may be attributable in part to the fact that different kinds of persons are involved in each condition.

Let us consider two examples of the introduction of bias in subject assignment. Experimental subjects often have "volunteered" in order to fulfill a course requirement of experimental participation. An experimenter who makes the mistake of running some conditions early in the semester and other conditions late in the semester may find that he is dealing more in the latter case with people who are less interested in psychology, are more resentful about research participation, more sophisticated about research because they have read further in the textbook, and so on. By running his experiment in this way, the investigator has permitted personality differences to be confounded with experimental treatment differences.

A more subtle problem may arise when subjects in some conditions are given an option or choice to stay in the experiment, while subjects in other conditions are not. If this kind of choice to participate is a variable in the experiment, it may happen that some subjects refuse to continue in the free-choice condition. Because subjects assigned to the no-choice condition have no chance to leave the experiment, subjects partially select themselves for assignment to an experimental treatment. Because the subjects who choose to continue may differ in systematic ways from subjects who choose to leave, there is an obvious factor of bias or nonrandom experimental assignment in such a case.

Evoking, Measuring, and Interpreting the Response

The psychologist makes inferences about the nature of the person from the person's *response* to stimulus conditions. Therefore some measurement of the response must be taken. In order for his response tendencies to be identified, the subject must be given alternative response possibilities. Thus in the initiation experiment the subject had to be given an opportunity to indicate various degrees of liking of the sex discussion club. In investigating the effects of initial success on subsequent performance, we must allow for a range of performance on the subsequent task. Precision of measurement obviously requires sensitivity to relevant response variations.

It is even more obvious that the experimenter must not "load" his questions to obtain the predicted response. He cannot legitimately ask the subjects in the severe initiation treatment, "You liked the group discussion, didn't you?" and load the question the other way in the mild treatment. The *same* opportunity for a number of possible responses in all treatments must be allowed; in each treatment, the predicted response must be pitted against unpredicted ones the subject is equally capable of making. In many experiments this condition is fulfilled by simply administering the same questionnaire in all treatments. In other studies, in which the crucial responses are uncovered through interviewing, it is important to standardize interview procedures. A useful precaution is to arrange the experiment so that the final interviewer does not know which condition his subject has just been through. This makes it impossible for him to bias the interview unwittingly.

Recording a Response Without Distorting It

The hypothesis in the initiation experiment involved studying the effect of degree of suffering on the person's liking of that for which he suffered. A test of this hypothesis requires a measure of the subject's attitude toward the overheard sex discussion. Both the Aronson-Mills and the Gerard-Mathewson experiments used a very simple and straightforward measure. The subjects were asked, on a questionnaire, how pleasant they found the discussion. Such a procedure has certain pitfalls; one is that the very act of measuring a response may distort the subject's real attitudes. The subject may have developed a positive or negative disposition toward the discussion but when asked to evaluate it may suddenly have become sensitized to the reasons why she should or should not be favorably disposed toward the discussion and her unguarded first reaction may have given way to a more "rational," intellectualized response. Or she may have become alerted to consider the experimenter's expectations and ended up shading her responses in the direction of these expectations. The Schopler and Bateson (1962) study, briefly described in Chapter One, exemplifies this; their subjects were influenced by the experimenter's (seemingly casual) remark about the sex group discussion.

Ideally, we would like to eliminate the effects of the measurement process itself on the subject's response. This is a special problem in social psychology because it is difficult to experiment on subjects without their being aware of being subjects, and difficult to get at their reactions to an experiment without asking them pointed questions about it. Schachter (1951) recruited subjects by asking for volunteers to join clubs allegedly established to pursue attractive activities. Once a club assembled for its first meeting, each member's attitudes about other members could be measured by looking at the results of an election to various leadership positions in the club. This experiment will be discussed in greater detail in Chapter Ten. It is a rather rare instance of measurement obtained under controlled experimental conditions but not contaminated by those conditions.

Most investigators have to invent special reasons to give to their subjects in order to justify introducing a questionnaire at some point in the experiment, and these special reasons may themselves color the response obtained. For example, attraction and hostility are often measured in the context of a "first impression" study. Subjects are told that the experiment concerns how people form impressions and are provided with a questionnaire asking them to rate various attributes of a fellow subject. These attributes can be later combined into indices of attraction and hostility, but the subjects may have tried especially hard not to let their emotions influence their ratings because they felt first impressions should be as tentative and as objective as possible.

There are many examples wherein the simple fact of being under observation by a research team affected the behavior displayed to the observers. A frequently cited case of this kind of observer contamination is a study that took place in the Hawthorne plant of the Western Electric Company (Roethlisberger and Dickson, 1939) in which the researchers varied a number of factors they suspected might influence productivity in a work group, such as the amount of lighting, or the number and length of coffee breaks. When they increased illumination in the plant, production went up; when they decreased illumination, production again went up; whatever they did in varying rest pauses also sent production up. It seemed that the mere interest of the researchers in the group's work situation had a salutary effect on morale, leading to repeated rises in production. A parallel situation exists in quantum mechanics, where the beam of light required to observe a subatomic particle influences, however slightly, the path of that particle.

Noncomparability of Responses

When a verbal questionnaire item is used as a response measure, the psychologist has to confront inevitable differences between subjects in the way they interpret the item. This is equally true of spontaneously elicited verbal statements and of rating scales marked by appropriate verbal labels. Although two subjects who both check the scale point "I liked the group discussion very much" will be treated identically in the analysis of the data, the subjects might have in mind quite different levels of liking. One subject might favor superlatives in his speech and, to him, liking something "very much" is to imply that it is only "fair-to-middling." Another subject may be very sparing in his use of superlatives and for him to say that he liked something "very much" implies that it was absolutely "out of this world."

Here, as in the case of other kinds of noncomparability between subjects, the psychologist puts his faith in the random assignment of subjects to conditions, and the fact that quite a few subjects are usually assigned to each condition. The variability between subjects that exists in the population will therefore tend to occur equally in all of the treatments and will appear in the analysis as "error." Any treatment effects would have to be strong enough to "rise above" this "error variance." Where treatment effects are weak, as in the case of many psychological experiments, this type of error will often mask the effects of the experimental variables. The existence of a certain amount of noncomparability between subjects requires that the experimental manipulations be as powerful as possible and that the response measures minimize noncomparability of reactions. Thus, the scale points should be as unambiguous as possible, and techniques of observation should be carefully standardized.

Measurement in the physical sciences is generally much more precise than in psychology. Nevertheless, the method of inference from measurements to variables is no different. The inherent imprecision of many psychological measures increases the importance of repeated observations (replications) and of the use of many subjects in any given experiment. Although the physicist studying the ferromagnetic properties of a particular kind of crystal need only use a relatively small sample of the crystal, the psychologist studying the suffering-liking relationship will need to use a much larger sample of human beings drawn from a population with a fairly homogeneous background. The larger the sample in each treatment the greater will be the confidence he can place in a *given* difference in response between treatments. This relationship derives from certain statistical considerations. The physicist, in selecting his "subjects," can insure that he has a relatively homogeneous sample of crystal wafers. He will often take very great pains in slicing these wafers himself. A social psychologist, on the other hand, must usually take the experimental materials available to him in nature; he normally cannot have a subject sample made to order. Even in a relatively homogeneous sample, such as college sophomores at a particular university, there are very wide differences in temperament and cultural background. The social psychologist must contend with these idiosyncrasies. He must minimize their importance by gaining as much control as possible over relevant stimulus conditions and by measuring those individual difference variables he expects to be important. If individual differences are measured, they may be studied in their own right or comparisons may be restricted to subjects of a certain type.

The Experimenter as Part of the Situation

The physical sciences contain parallels for many of the measurement problems arising in psychology. There is one crucial difference that creates special problems in psychology that do not exist in the physical sciences; the psychologist, especially the social psychologist, can all too easily influence the phenomena of social behavior he is studying without being aware that he is doing so. Human subjects, especially intelligent college students, are often extremely sensitive to subtle cues in an experimenter's behavior. Rosenthal (1963) has presented impressive data showing that experimenters with different private hypotheses about the study they are conducting somehow elicit data from their subjects that are biased in the direction of confirming these private hypotheses. Perhaps the experimenter provides subtle rewards of approval when the subject gives a "correct" response or seems to be moving toward the desired response. Perhaps the subject, correctly or incorrectly, guesses the experimental hypothesis being tested. This could cause him either to make an effort to confirm the hypothesis or perhaps to bend over backward not to be influenced by his secret knowledge.

Whether or not subjects guess the experimental hypothesis, they may pick up certain signs from the experimenter that some ways of responding are more mature, or adaptive, or socially acceptable than others. Most subjects are concerned about the prospect of being evaluated by a psychologist and, as Rosenberg (1965) has argued, they readily develop "evaluation apprehension" in the experimental situation. This apprehension may lead them to be very guarded in response to the experimenter's requests for information and to be very self-conscious in their reactions to the experimental setting.

The subject may also behave in ways that draw the experimenter away from his proper role of treating each subject in precisely the same way. The experimenter may be favorably impressed by one subject and irritated by another. The former may be an extremely attractive coed and the latter may have had considerable difficulty in understanding the experimental instructions. The experimenter may then behave in different ways toward these two subjects, inadvertently creating two different social situations.

Since psychological experiments inevitably involve some kind of social relationship between a subject and an experimenter, it is probably not possible ever to rule out completely the various contaminating factors suggested above. However, there are many effective precautions that, if uniformly taken, can drastically reduce the potential of experimenter bias. At the very least, an experiment should be designed so that the human failings of the experimenter only contribute to the error factor in the experiment and not bias the direction of the results. In other words, steps can be taken to insure that the experimenter does not give off *different cues* in the different treatment conditions. An effective way to accomplish this is for the experimenter to keep himself in the dark about the experimental condition to which a particular subject has been assigned unless and until it is absolutely essential to know. Just as in medical research where a placebo (control) may be administered by a physician who does not know whether it is a placebo or an experimental drug, so in a psychology experiment it is sometimes possible for an experimenter to conceal from himself a subject's condition. Perhaps the basic instructions can be printed and distributed to subjects in a random or disguised way. Perhaps one experimenter can give the instructions and another experimenter, unaware of the condition created by the first, can administer the final interview or questionnaire. In some cases the basic instructions are the same for all conditions, but diverge at some critical point late in the experiment. It is possible for the experimenter to pull from his pocket a slip of paper on which a particular experimental condition has been written. Since he has placed several slips of paper in his pocket, each bearing a different condition label, the choice to put a particular subject into a particular treatment condition remains in the dark until the very last minute.

In many experiments it is quite feasible to put the entire set of instructions on tape, telling the subject quite truthfully that this is for purposes of greater experimental control. The use of tape recordings is especially appropriate in cases where the subjects have been taken to separate booths to await instructions and where these instructions are quite elaborate. Biasing effects present serious problems, but their significance can be very much reduced by the methods we have briefly described and by other more complex procedural safeguards.

Inferences about the Organism

Within the framework of the S-[O]-R paradigm, (a) the stimulus is manipulated and becomes the independent variable, (b) the response is recorded and becomes the dependent variable, (c) inferences are made about various features of the organism that could account for the observed relationship between the S and the R. The properties inferred or attributed to the organism are typically fictitious constructs. They are unobserved and will forever remain so; and there is no necessary implication that a given construct corresponds to an underlying physical structure within O, the organism.

The constructs with which a psychologist works may or may not be a part of an elaborate theory of human functioning. The Freudian scholar who uses the construct "ego" probably sees this construct as embedded in an elaborate framework of additional terms like "id," "superego," "cathexis," and so on. The psychologist exploring the determinants of aggression may use a more limited number of constructs (frustration, aggression, inhibition, displacement) and employ them within a rather skeletonized theory. Legitimate and important research may be stimulated by the barest and most tentative hypothesis. Some research even begins merely with the question, "I wonder what would happen if . . . ," though usually the researcher has at least some hunch about the most likely outcome.

The O term may take an almost infinite variety of forms for different research scholars, and the form it takes for a given investigator has a great deal to do with the kind of research he does and the particular problems he tackles. In the chapters to come we will run across psychologists who are strongly impressed with the importance of incentives and reinforcements. The research with which they are associated will reflect this conviction, and incentive variations will readily find their way into their experimental designs. We will encounter others who are more impressed with a person's informational needs and his abhorrence of uncertainty and ambiguity. Again, we will see this interest reflected in certain experimental designs rather than others.

This is not the place to examine the role of psychological theory in any detail. The main point we would like to make is that research addressed to the R effects of variations in S inevitably must involve some implicit theorizing about O. Every psychological hypothesis makes assumptions about the characteristics of persons, whether these assumptions are actually spelled out by the researcher or not. Quite typically, the particular problem chosen for study, and the particular sources of variation examined, will reflect the investigator's assumptions about O. These assumptions may or may not be explicit; they may or may not be embedded in an elaborate theoretical structure. Nevertheless they exist and they are extremely important determinants of research decisions.

"REAL LIFE" AND THE LABORATORY

Because the psychologist, in setting up his experiment, is attempting to gain as much control as possible over the stimuli confronting his subjects, he may be forced to choose a relatively artificial setting for the experiment, one that may not resemble too closely those real-life settings to which he ultimately wishes to generalize. The natural environment is very complex; many stimuli impinge on the person simultaneously and many response possibilities remain open to him. Because it is impossible for a psychologist to make any firm inference about which stimuli give rise to which responses in such everyday situations, he may prefer to restrict the stimulus input and limit response possibilities by simplifying the relevant environment. Inevitably, this involves the subject in reactions to rather novel and seemingly artificial conditions.

If, for example, a psychologist is interested in studying something about the person's response to finding that his opinion on some issue is discrepant from someone else's opinion, he may limit the stimulus input to a discrepancy of opinion. In order to do this, he may devise a laboratory situation in which the subject does not confront the other person face-to-face. A face-to-face confrontation would provide the subject with additional information about the appearance and status of the other that is extraneous to the mere fact that their opinions are discrepant. These other influences would tend to obscure the effects of the discrepancy variable by introducing error in the form of individual differences in reaction to the communicator's appearance. Depending on what he is looking for, the psychologist provides the subject with a limited number of alternative responses to the discrepancy. This response control may add further to the apparent artificiality of the situation.

The artificiality of the laboratory creates certain problems. It is important to maintain naiveté and spontaneous behavior on the part of the subject. As the artificiality of the situation increases it becomes more and more difficult to get the subject to respond with this naive spontaneity. Often the experimental manipulations within the laboratory tend to become very weak. This is due to the fact that the subject, although he may be mildly curious about what the experimenter is up to, is not involved personally with the situation. Part of the art of setting up an experiment involves engaging important motives or values in the subject—getting him personally involved within the rarified conditions of the experiment. Confronting the subject with an opinion discrepancy under laboratory conditions is unlikely to approximate the involvement he would normally show in a heated political discussion. The trick is to import into the setting some issue about which involvement can be maintained in the face of rarification.

Some form of personal involvement is important to insure that the subject will be himself in some important sense, and not merely play the role of a docile subject anxious to give a helpful, or a reasonable, or a safe response. Fortunately for the psychologist, it is possible to secure substantial involvement even in laboratory settings where there are many elements of artificiality. The fact that a subject has never experienced the particular laboratory setting and its requirements before does not mean that his behavior in that setting makes no difference to him. He may well recognize that fundamental values are being challenged by some feature of the experiment, or that his maturity or his masculinity or his rationality are being put to the test. Thus, though the experimental setting may be artificial in the sense that it differs from any everyday counterpart, it may be a very *real* situation to the subject who wonders, for example, whether he should trust his own eyesight or go along with the majority opinion of a group of fellow subjects. As we shall see in Chapter Ten, this "conformity conflict" can be extremely involving—even upsetting—to subjects, in spite of the fact that they know they are in a laboratory and "it's only an experiment."

Donald Campbell (1957) has made a useful distinction between *internal* and *external validity*. A particular manipulation is considered to have internal validity if it makes a specific difference in the response of subjects within the experimental setting. External validity refers to the ease with which these differences may be generalized to representative life situations. This distinction is similar to that implied above: there is a reality internal to the experiment that may have important emotional implications for the subject; there is also, of course, the reality of life in the natural world before and after the experiment. The experiment may involve few or many elements of a real-life situation. If it involves many such elements, the experiment will probably engage more of the subject's basic motives or values, and the variables will have more internal validity. However, an experiment with questionable external validity may still be powerful in securing the subject's involvement and may feature variables that make a difference in his behavior. This may be a useful experiment from a theoretical point of view.

To put it still another way, in the terms preferred by Aronson and Carlsmith (in press), there is experimental realism (akin to internal validity) and mundane realism (external validity). Each experiment usually involves some form of compromise between these two kinds of realism. Different experimenters prefer to emphasize one more than the other and vice versa. An experiment that is high in mundane realism will tend to be more involving for subjects but will also tend to be complex and thus raise problems about isolating the stimulus factors responsible for the effects observed. An experiment that is very high in experimental realism but low in mundane realism may contribute significantly to the development of a particular theory. The problem here, however, is the difficulty of generalizing from the experimental effects observed to those expected in other situations, especially those of real life. An experiment low in both forms of realism is obviously a poor experiment. Many paper-and-pencil experiments, which merely confront the subject with hypothetical problem situations, run the risk of failing to establish either mundane or experimental realism.

Ethical Issues in Social Psychological Research

By now it should be fairly clear that one of the most difficult and challenging problems confronting the social psychologist is how to secure the personal involvement of his subjects while maintaining careful control over their stimulus environment. This is the problem of creating experimental realism, of getting the subject to behave spontaneously and not to reflect self-consciously on his role in the experiment. In order to accomplish this, it has become a common practice of investigators to deceive subjects with an appropriate cover story. The immediate purpose of the cover story is to give the subject a plausible reason for engaging in the necessary experimental activities. The cover story provides a convenient justification for many procedures that would otherwise appear very artificial and even nonsensical. The ultimate purpose of the cover story is to maximize control and involvement, the two primary ingredients of experimental realism.

A moment's reflection makes clear that meaningful experimentation on responses over which subjects can exercise voluntary control cannot be done if the investigator tells the subject the theoretical hypothesis beforehand. This is such an obvious restriction that subjects do not expect to be told about the experimental hypothesis until after they have provided their data. But the social psychologist often goes beyond the withholding of information to the deliberate fabrication of an experimental cover story. The use of cover stories, often very elaborate ones, is blatant misrepresentation. The experimenter exploits the normal trust of his subjects to deceive them deliberately about the purpose of the study. How may this behavior be justified ethically? What steps may be taken to reduce if not eliminate the impropriety of experimental misrepresentation?

The answer to the first of these questions is very dependent on the importance the psychologist attaches to the behavioral data provided by experimental subjects. Obviously, if he does not believe that psychology makes progress through the accumulation of research findings, he is not likely to believe that the practice of experimental deception is justifiable. Many critics take a more flexible position and weigh the potential results—their likely theoretical and practical significance—against the ethical difficulties created by deception. This involves judging each study on its own merits. Such critics, and we number ourselves among them, tend to view the ethics of human experimentation as very complex. Human welfare is generally advanced by research findings that deepen our understanding of social influences on individual behavior. The extent of this advance must be balanced against the unpleasant necessity to deceive subjects in order to study many social psychological questions in a controlled way. We can offer no glib or easy solutions to the problem. The issues are similar to those involved in the controversy over vivisection. To the ardent antivivisectionist no amount of progress in finding ways to relieve human suffering can justify the sacrifice of animals in biomedical research. Generally speaking, psychologists have a harder time than medical researchers justifying the practical significance of their research to the layman. On the other hand, deceiving a human subject is a more benign and reversible action than sacrificing the life of a stray dog or cat.

If we accept the inevitability of the cover story in certain areas of psychological research, then it is important to face the second question posed above: what may be done to eliminate the negative consequences for the individual subject of experimental misrepresentation? The American Psychological Association has published a code of ethics that establishes certain general guidelines to be followed in human research. This code stresses (a) the importance of weighing the significance of the research problem against any conceivable harmful effects on the subjects; (b) the importance of informing each subject fully about any serious aftereffects which might result from his participation in the research, allowing him complete freedom to volunteer or withdraw; (c) protection of the subject's anonymity in any publication of research results; and (d) the importance of living up to any promises that were made to the subject in return for his cooperation as a subject. Psychologists who violate the spirit of this code are subject to censure and possibly expulsion from the organization.

Perhaps the most important general principle, implicit in several items of the APA code, is that subjects should be treated with respect and their welfare should be carefully protected. Concretely, subjects should be fully informed about the extent of any fabrication and the purposes behind it before leaving the experimental setting. To this end, every experiment should end in a debriefing period during which the experimenter describes what the experiment was all about and, if necessary, allays any guilt or anxiety or self-doubt that the experimental procedures might have generated in the subject. Proper debriefing is a critical step in the experimental process, and it is a step that requires considerable skill and careful training.

The experimenter not only must fulfill his ethical obligations in a debriefing period; the debriefing process is an important step in maintaining secrecy about the experimental arrangements until the study has been completed. Once the subject has been properly informed of the purposes of the experiment, he is asked to agree not to reveal anything about the deceptions involved to prospective subjects. If the subject feels he has been fairly treated, he will almost invariably live up to his agreement not to talk about the experiment. Subjects who have just participated in a deception experiment are often extremely interested in the results of the study and eager to make the experiment a fair test of the investigator's hypothesis. Not only has the subject invested his own time and energy in the project; he is likely to be curious about how others react to the same experimental situation. When research is done in a college setting, especially when introductory psychology students are used as volunteer subjects, it is customary to communicate a summary of the experimental results to the subjects as soon as these results have been analyzed and interpreted. Thus the student not only learns what an experiment is like at first hand; he is able to see how his responses contributed to a set of experimental results having some bearing on our understanding of human nature.

The problems associated with deception in research are just a few of the many ethical issues involved in the entire research process, but these problems are involved to a special extent in social psychological experimentation. The psychologist must remember that he is in a position to create considerable mischief by thoughtless or ill-considered research planning. Fortunately, much of his training is directed toward making him aware of his own power and responsibilities.

STRUCTURAL FEATURES OF THE SOCIAL PSYCHOLOGY EXPERIMENT

Table 2.1 presents in schematic outline a flow chart of the typical experiment from beginning to end. In the top row of the diagram we

Table 2.1. Flow chart of a social psychological experiment.

Operations	(1) Sampling	(2) Instructions	(3) Characteristics of other persons	(4) Task	(5) Process	(6) Outcome	(7) Validating questionnaire	(8) Debriefing
Variables	Intelligence, personality factors, popularity, age, sex, etc.	Interpretive set, motivation, etc.	Status, role, attractiveness, aggressive qualities, etc.	Judge, compare, rate, solve problem, etc.	Content and volume of communication, eye movements, GSR tracings, etc.	Change in attitude, quantity and quality of production, amount learned, etc.	Check constants or independent variables	

Columns (1)–(4): Constant conditions or independent variables (Stimulus conditions)

Columns (5)–(6): Dependent variables (Responses)

have indicated what the experimenter does in the way of operations (that is, procedures) in order to realize the state of affairs depicted in the bottom row. Going from left to right the first four items refer to what he does in order to set up the experimental conditions he requires. This includes manipulating independent variables as well as creating the conditions that will minimize error by reducing unnecessary variation and by stripping away much of the complexity that might confound and obscure the effects of the independent variables.

Sampling

The first column refers to sampling. We have already discussed the importance of maintaining relative homogeneity of the subject sample in order to reduce variations in interpreting and responding to the stimulus conditions. Under certain circumstances, however, we might select our subject sample so that within each condition the subjects are *stratified* in terms of a particular personality dimension. At a minimum this involves measuring subjects on an appropriate personality attribute before the experiment and assigning some high and some low scorers to each condition. Frequently subjects are more finely subdivided into highs, middles, and lows. The inclusion of relevant individual difference variables by this kind of stratification and assignment of subjects may provide important information about the experimental situation and how it was perceived by the subjects. Such information is especially useful when it is not possible to achieve a high degree of control through experimental manipulations, or when a sample of subjects from very diverse backgrounds is the only one available.

An example of subject stratification may be found in Chapter Eleven where an experiment by Mouton, Blake, and Olmstead (1956) is discussed. These investigators were interested in whether subjects, communicating through an intercom system, would tend to conform more to each other if they announced their own judgments after stating their names than if their judgments were given anonymously. The experiment was so designed that half of the subjects in each condition had previously scored toward the ascendant end of an ascendance-submission scale and the other half had scored toward the submissive end. It turned out that only the submissive subjects conformed more when announcing their names than when reporting anonymously. The ascendant subjects were not affected by the experimental variable of anonymity. If the subjects had not been stratified in terms of ascendance-submission scores in this experiment, the results would have been less informative about the determinants of conformity.

In other experiments, when the main object is to compare the productivity or morale of several small groups, it may be very important to control the composition of each group by the careful assignment of subjects. Lewin, Lippitt, and White (1939), in their classic study of children's groups, were careful to insure that each group contained children comparable in intelligence, teacher-rated obedience, leadership, quarrelsomeness, and so forth. This is not to say that each child was the same as each other child on these characteristics, but rather that the distributions of each characteristic were similar from group to group. This was an important procedural step, for it allowed the investigators to concentrate on the main variable of interest: the leadership style of a role-playing adult—who was pre-instructed to act in an authoritarian, democratic, or laissez-faire manner—and the effects of this variable on the productivity and social behavior of the children. Thus careful control over the sampling and assignment of subjects may be used either to manipulate a variable of theoretical relevance or to attempt to hold constant those individual difference factors that can only contribute to errors in interpretation.

Instructions

Instructions may serve many crucial purposes in an experiment: they may be used to induce experimental variables, to control possible confounding factors, and to provide a cover story that diverts the subject's attention from the true purposes of the experiment. In short, instructions control or manipulate "interpretive set"; they help to define the entire situation for the subject and to control his attention to relevant stimuli.

Instructions are viewed here in the broadest sense, and include any information conveyed about the nature and purpose of the experiment. Instructions typically begin at the point of subject recruitment; here the stage is partially set by any descriptive information given about the time, place, sponsorship, or nature of the experiment. The major portion of instructions is usually given at the outset of the experiment itself, though all information conveyed up to the point that the response measure is taken may of course affect that response. For this reason great care should be taken in planning and staging the experiment so that everything that transpires forms a coherent context for the subject's response.

Experimental psychologists have relied on instructional variables for generations. One of the most common variations has been to instruct some subjects that a test is a highly reliable and valid measure of intellectual ability while instructing others that the test is untried or known to be unreliable. This variation has often been used to induce differences in motivation or involvement or the importance of doing well. In its simplest form, the variation has been used in so many experiments that it may no longer be effective with many subjects.

Characteristics of Other Persons

A social psychology experiment obviously involves other people besides the subject. At a minimum there is the experimenter, but there are typically other people present or the presence of others is imagined or anticipated. Many experiments involve a deception that others are in adjacent rooms or booths and that communication will take place via intercom system. In all of these cases, the other person or persons have certain characteristics as persons that influence in unknown ways the subject's reactions to the situation. For this reason it is obviously important to hold constant the characteristics of others involved in the experiment (by having the same person carefully play the same role in the same way) or to make sure that variations in these characteristics are random across conditions and cannot bias the results). Of course there are studies in which the personal characteristics of others are a major independent variable. When this is the case systematic differences in the characteristics presented must be maintained throughout the experiment. For example, Zimbardo, Weisenberg, Firestone, and Levy (1965) wanted to vary the attractiveness of a communicator as a major treatment condition. For some subjects the communicator presented himself as a rather obnoxious and unfair person by berating his experimental assistant. For other subjects, the communicator was very reasonable and decent.

A second example of varying the characteristics of others in the experiment may be found in an experiment by Thibaut and Riecken (1955b). In their experiment subjects attempted to influence both a higher status and a lower status person to comply with a request. Status was varied by telling the subject different things about the accomplishments and academic seniority of the two other persons. This study also exemplifies the attempt to rule out personal characteristics themselves as a variable. Two different experimental accomplices played the role of the targets of influence, and they alternated playing the roles of high and low status persons. This was done to strengthen the argument that differences in subjects' reactions to the two other persons would be mainly a function of the intended variation in status rather than some chance variation in the others' personal attributes.

The Task

In general, a social psychology experiment consists of instructing subjects to perform some meaningful task in some relation to other persons. The task itself frequently provides a vehicle whereby the dependent variable or response measure is obtained. Often certain features of the task are important ingredients of the cover story—in and of themselves unimportant, but necessary to maintain the deceptive picture of the experimental purpose. If the true experimental purpose were to manipulate success and failure experiences, for example, the experimenter would have to design a task on which subjects could plausibly succeed or fail. There may be no true correct answers, and thus the experimenter may randomly assign subjects to success or failure conditions by announcing a false score or by giving false norms. Aronson and Carlsmith (1962) involved subjects in a task of judging which of two photos was of a schizophrenic patient. Actually, the photos were taken from a class album of Harvard students and the task merely provided a plausible vehicle for manipulating the success and failure experiences of the different subjects involved in the judgment task.

The task *may*, of course, be organically related to the true purposes of the experimenter. Thus what the subject is told is a "social sensitivity test" may provide the crucial dependent variable ratings in a first impression study. As in a study by Jones and deCharms (1957) such a test may be included among a variety of other performance tests given in a group setting and actually pick up differences in social perception that are a function of instructional and "other person" variations that have been previously introduced.

Information about Process and Outcome

The major dependent variable in an experiment is obtained in the *outcome* operation as indicated in the sixth column of Table 2.1. Depending on his particular purpose in conducting the experiment, the investigator will want some measure of such outcome variables as whether or not the subject changes his attitude, whether or not he likes or dislikes the other person in the experiment, whether his performance on a task increases or decreases, how much material is learned or remembered, the accuracy of the subject's perceptions, the amount of stress reflected in his galvanic skin response, or his decision to wait by himself while anticipating electric shock or to wait with others in the same boat.

While the outcome variable is usually the measure of response that is most centrally involved in the experimental prediction, the reasoning behind the prediction usually assumes that certain social or psychological *processes* must have occurred in order for the outcomes to take the predicted form. There are many kinds of experiments in which these processes remain hidden and defy scrutiny or measurement. There is no way to record the subtle mental processes involved in learning or perception, for example, or to capture the detailed reasoning that precedes an overt decision. In many group experiments, however, especially when subjects are engaged in free face-to-face communication with each other, it is possible to gain separate information about process and outcome. Thus we have included the fifth column in our table. To cite an obvious example, the experimenter may be primarily interested in whether groups of subjects who have known each other previously perform as well on complex group tasks as groups of strangers. The amount or quality of performance may serve readily as his outcome measure. However, his experiment should also include some attempt to monitor the social interactions that take place in the group prior to actual solution. If the groups of acquaintances proved to be more productive than the groups of strangers, it would be very important to know why this was so. The experimenter might have theorized that acquaintances would more quickly than strangers organize themselves for tackling the task, allocate responsibilities among the members, decide who should be the leader, and so forth. This theoretical reasoning could easily be checked by conducting systematic behavioral observations of each group in action, recording who speaks to whom, noting the content of conversational remarks, and recording instances of leadership and followership behavior. Such information about process can obviously enrich the meaning of the research and clarify the precise mechanisms responsible for the outcomes observed.

The Validating Questionnaire

We have already spoken of the importance of attempting to validate the various experimental manipulations, and of some of the difficulties involved in doing so. Ordinarily, it is quite useful to learn as much as possible from each subject about his perceptions of the experiment, what he thought it was all about, and how he conceived of his task. For this reason experiments often end with a short questionnaire that probes the subject's recollections about instructions and his attitudes about various features of the experiment. By looking at responses to such a questionnaire the investigator may discover that some or all of his manipulations were unsuccessful. This may lead him to redesign a more effective experiment.

Alternatively, the investigator may discover that a few subjects completely misunderstood an important experimental feature, or that they were suspicious of the cover story. In such cases he may decide to discard those subjects on whom the manipulations did not "take." This is a debatable strategy, but one that can be defended if very few subjects are to be discarded before data analysis, and if these cases come equally from the different experimental conditions.

Debriefing

The postexperimental validating questionnaire often leads naturally into a debriefing discussion in which the experimenter reveals the complete purpose of the experiment and probes further concerning the subject's suspicions and perceptions.

Illustrative Overview: the Aronson and Mills Study

By way of summarizing the above discussion let us describe the now-familiar suffering-liking study in terms of the chart. The attempt in that study was to create two different levels of suffering for something that subsequently turned out to be undesirable, and then to detect differences between subjects at the two levels in rated desirability of the goal. By outline the study may be broken down into the following procedural steps:

1. Sampling. A homogeneous group of college coeds, a third of whom were randomly assigned to a condition where they were to take an embarrassing test, a third of whom were to take a less embarrassing test, and a third of whom took no test at all.

2. Instructions. An elaborate cover story was provided. The experiment was described as an investigation of the "dynamics of the group discussion process." It was explained that sex had been chosen as the topic for the groups to discuss so that volunteers for the discussion groups could be obtained without much difficulty. In order to reduce embarrassment, members of the group would communicate from separate rooms over an intercom system. To insure further that embarrassment would not be a problem, the two initiation groups were asked to take an "embarrassment test" involving the reading of very obscene material in the *severe* condition, and of sex-related but not obscene material in the *mild* condition. Subjects in the *control* condition were simply admitted to membership in the sex discussion group.

3. Characteristics of Other Persons. This was a standardized, non-manipulated variable. All subjects confronted the same experimenter who behaved in a standardized way. All subjects listened to the identical tape recording, allegedly representing an ongoing discussion of the sex discussion group. The discussion was dull and banal; the participants spoke dryly and haltingly.

4. The Task. This included the procedure of listening via earphones to the discussion, and making subsequent ratings of the participants. This was presented as a normal procedure; the experimenter explained that after each meeting the group members routinely filled out questionnaires expressing their reactions to the discussion. This fit plausibly with the experimenter's alleged interest in the dynamics of discussion groups.

5. Process. There is no mention of any attention to process in this experiment. The experimenters may have noted signs of flushing and embarrassment in their subjects when the latter read the material in the severe initiation condition. They may also have noted signs of boredom or interest on the part of the subject as she listened to the group discussion.

If so, they did not report their observations, and they would have been quite unreliable and anecdotal in any event.

6. Outcome. The subjects' ratings of the discussion and the participants served as the outcome variables. On both measures subjects in the severe initiation condition showed greater liking than did subjects in the other two conditions, who in turn did not differ from each other.

7. Validating Questionnaire. None was administered in this experiment. Though results on the outcome measures are clearly in favor of the theoretical hypothesis, there remain many questions about the validity and meaning of the manipulations, some of which we have discussed in the body of this chapter. An appropriately designed questionnaire or interview might have provided useful systematic information.

8. Debriefing. At the close of the experiment, the experimenter engaged each subject in a conversation to determine whether or not she was suspicious of the procedure. Only one subject was suspicious and her results were discarded. The purpose of the experiment was then fully disclosed to all subjects.

TYPES OF EXPERIMENTS

Many types of experiments can be performed in science, and each type serves a different function. Kaplan (1964) presents a useful classification of experiments that we shall freely adapt to our purposes.

Methodological Experiments

A technology for research is crucial to any science and a great deal of effort is devoted to developing and improving the methods for manipulating variables and related techniques for measuring responses. The necessary conditions within which to study a particular relationship must be set up and measurements taken to determine the form of the relationship. A critical aspect of the social psychological experiment is to devise stimulus conditions that reflect a relevant conceptual distinction and at the same time are effective in modifying the subject's reactions. Many investigators put considerable time and effort into pretesting (sometimes called pilot study) to discover desired stimulus conditions. This pretesting is a form of experiment that usually involves a great deal of tinkering and post-experimental discussion with subjects before the experimenter can approximate the conditions he wants.

This pretest tinkering must be held in check by a theoretical conception of the independent variable or variables. It is usually possible to keep changing stimulus conditions until they produce the responses the experimenter originally desired or predicted. However, the experimenter may in the process unwittingly introduce stimuli that are not part of the theoretical considerations being addressed by the research. In other words he may demonstrate his skill as a social engineer without really providing a stern test of a theoretical hypothesis.

On the response side, some measures are needed, even if they are such simple operations as counting aggressive responses, to measure as precisely as possible the relevant effects of the stimulus conditions. Much social psychological research is concerned with changes in attitude, opinion, or judgment. Often, by conducting a series of studies along the same line, the investigator sharpens and refines his attitudinal measures so that they are more reliable indicators of the independent variable. A convenient procedure for refining an attitude scale is to conduct an experiment, observe which items in the scale are affected by the independent variable, retain these items for a second (cross-validating) experiment, refine the scale further, conduct a third experiment, and so on. In this way, by conducting series of related methodological experiments, the investigator can develop a more precise measure of attitude or disposition, reflecting the effects of precisely known stimulus conditions.

In recent years research on attitude scaling methods has been abundant, but the results of this research have been used only sparingly in social psychological studies dealing with substantive (theoretical) issues. Unfortunately, the mathematically elegant scales that have been developed are seldom precisely relevant to a particular experiment and are often cumbersome to apply. The subject may worry about whether or not he is responding properly to the procedure or he may become annoyed at the experimenter for putting him through a tedious sequence of judgments.

For the most part, those doing substantive research have paid relatively little attention to refining response measures. Their feeling has been that if the stimulus conditions are powerful enough any rough-and-ready response measure should be sufficient to detect effects, if any. Perhaps, as research problems become more and more refined, more attention will be paid to improving response measures through methodological research.

Hypothetico-Deductive Experiments

The hypothetico-deductive experiment is the type people generally think of when they think of an experiment. Its purpose is to establish a law by testing some particular hypothesis. An empirical finding results from the particular stimulus and response combinations of a given experiment. The unique feature of the hypothetico-deductive experiment is the attempt to embed this finding in a broader theoretical context—to treat it as the reflection of an underlying conceptual law. A single experiment cannot, of course, establish a law. The S-[O]-R paradigm requires that phenotypically different variables be used in different experimental settings to test the same underlying genotypical relationship. The purpose is to shake this genotypical relationship loose from a particular procedure used to test it.

A term that was in vogue some years ago was the "crucial experiment." This is a type of hypothetico-deductive experiment that is supposed to establish, once and for all, the tenability of a particular interpretation of an empirical generalization. However, the facts of controlled experiments, as well as those from casual experience, can be interpreted in a variety of ways. It is always possible by making certain assumptions about what is going on inside the subject, to come up with novel interpretations of an experimental result.

When the data from an experiment support one interpretation and not several others, this gives the experimenter confidence in the tenability of that interpretation, that it makes good sense; but not that it is the only possible interpretation. For example, the experiment by Gerard and Mathewson (1966) compared the suffering-leading-to-liking interpretation of the data from the Aronson and Mills (1959) experiment with several equally plausible interpretations of the data such as curiosity-leading-to-liking or sexual arousal-leading-to-liking. The results of the Gerard-Mathewson experiment also supported the suffering-leading-to-liking hypothesis but did not imply that the suffering-liking hypothesis is established once and for all and for all time. They help, however, to strengthen the case that the original hypothesis used in interpreting the original data is indeed tenable and that the theory from which the hypothesis was initially derived (dissonance theory) provides a useful set of assumptions about processes occurring within the person.

Exploratory Experiments

There is a kind of basic human curiosity expressed by the attitude, "I wonder what will happen if I do *this*." In learning about their world, children appear to be conducting this kind of experiment much of the time. Usually they have some vague notions as to what might happen and are attempting to test them.

In psychology there is a rather lamentable tendency to follow slavishly the pattern of the hypothetico-deductive experiment. At its best this is a powerful approach to scientific advance. However, there is nothing sinful about approaching an interesting phenomenon without explicit ideas as to what might account for it, but merely with a healthy curiosity about it. It helps, however, to have enough of a theory to ask meaningful questions. Galileo might never have performed the experiments from the Leaning Tower of Pisa and Michelson and Morley might not have failed in their attempt to establish the ether theory if it were not for a hypothetico-deductive bent of mind. But a great deal of research in such fields as chemistry and medicine would not have been done without a "let's try this and see what happens" approach.

In psychology there has been a recent renewal of interest in the nature of the hypnotic trance and a great deal is being learned about hypnosis by taking a frankly exploratory tack in carefully designed experiments. When we do not have a tentative explanation for a phenomenon, it is difficult to know what to control and what to vary in an experiment; but people working in an area often have good, implicit hunches without being able to articulate them into a theoretical framework. The work in hypnosis, carried out solely on the basis of this kind of hunch, is leading in several fruitful directions that may eventually play a crucial role in the future of social psychology. A trance can be relatively easily induced and the conditions under which the trance is induced can be carefully controlled. The experimenter, therefore, is in a position to vary first one thing, then another, and then another to see how they affect aspects of the trance state.

There is also a great deal of exploratory work going on now in the study of dreams. In spite of the weakness of theories to account for dreams and hypnosis, there is a good chance that current exploratory experimentation in both of these areas will lead to important findings.

Simulation Experiments

A simulation experiment attempts to create a replica of conditions existing in the real world. Such experiments often work from a model that hopefully contains the essential variables underlying complex natural phenomena. The trucking-game study by Deutsch and Krauss (1960), described in Chapter One, exemplifies a simulation experiment in social psychology. These investigators worked from a model of conflict and negotiation in which such factors as communication and threat potential are prominently featured. Ultimately, Deutsch and Krauss would like to generalize to the setting of international negotiations over disarmament. It is obviously difficult if not impossible to study international relations under controlled conditions; the strategy of the simulation experiment commends itself in this case.

The primary difficulty with simulation experiments is that the investigator may introduce some, but never all, of the complexity and motivational significance of real events. Therefore, the investigator must come to terms somehow with the differences between the simulated and the real situation. As Kaplan (1964) points out, the simulator must translate results from the simulation model to the real world, a feat that involves considerable danger of misapplication. Many experiments using bargaining games of one sort or another have been found to produce misleading results because of the imaginary or small stakes involved (cf. Kelley, 1966; and Chapter Fourteen). Just as a ship or bridge model "will not meet full-scale requirements if we overlook the fact that surfaces increase with the square of the linear dimensions while volumes and masses increase with the cube" (Kaplan, 1964, p. 151), so simulation experiments on negotiation and conflict resolution may misapply their results to negotiations for vital stakes.

Simulation is involved in much applied research; the use of a wind tunnel in applied aerodynamics provides a good example. Many aptitude testing and assessment research programs involve the measurement of reactions to imaginary and contrived situations believed to be representative of real-life situations to which the investigator wishes to generalize. In industry, management may try out a change in production methods or in supervisory practices on a small scale before proceeding on a factory or industry-wide basis. Such trial runs are obviously useful when the costs of large-scale changes are high.

Illustrative Experiments

Finally, we should mention the type of experiment that is done primarily for demonstration purposes, to check on common sense, or to provide material for educational use. There are many experimental studies described in the present book, for example, that are included more for their illustrative value than because they make a theoretically critical point.

Sometimes it is quite difficult to distinguish between hypothetico-deductive and illustrative experiments. One person's theoretical hypothesis may be another person's self-evident truism. Then, too, many experiments start out as hypothetico-deductive, forecasting some subtle or complex result, and end up as illustrative: the subtleties do not occur and all that remains are effects that would have been predicted by almost anyone.

Perhaps the most intriguing kind of illustrative experiment is that designed to dramatize a metaphor or an analogy. An experiment is described in Chapter Thirteen in which two pigeons were taught to play against each other in a game of ping-pong. To some this experimental feat might be looked at as an intriguing analogy of the origins of human competition. Such an experiment proves nothing and adds nothing really new to the knowledge available in the learning literature. However, it may well have the value of stimulating thought—either the experimenter's or the public's—about the basic nature of social interaction.

SUMMARY

We have attempted to characterize in an elementary way the methods of social psychological research. After distinguishing between the experimental and correlational approach to problems, we have singled out the social psychology experiment for detailed analysis. The experiment was presented in the framework of the S (stimulus)–O (organism)–R (response) paradigm. The purpose of research is either to establish some empirical generalization, relating a particular S with a particular R, an approach that is typical of applied research, or to establish some conceptual characterization of processes going on within the O, this being typical of the basic research approach. In discussing the S-[O]-R paradigm, we outlined some of the problems and difficulties of establishing appropriate stimulus conditions and of taking response measures. The experimenter must be able to engage the subject's motives or values so that the stimulus conditions have a measurable impact on him and we must allow him some latitude of response. The social psychologist with a basic research orientation attempts to construct a meaningful, if artificial, environment in his laboratory so that he can observe the average subject's responses and make inferences about the structure of *the* person. He does this by attempting to neutralize individual differences both by using statistical averaging techniques and by constructing situations that are sufficiently clear in their meaning to reduce the effects of idiosyncratic response tendencies. *The* person is a construction derived from the response of particular subjects with given identities and histories. Problems associated with measuring the response without distorting it and scaling problems arising out of the noncomparability that exists among subjects were also discussed.

Our schematic diagram of the flow of events within an experiment showed how operations and concepts are linked in an experiment and how multiple interpretations can arise because of poor coordination between operations and variables. Finally, we discussed the various kinds of experiments that may be devised to serve the different purposes of research.

CHAPTER THREE

Effect Dependence and Processes of Child Socialization

The topic of child socialization is of intrinsic interest to anyone who was himself a child, is currently a parent, or expects someday to be involved directly in bringing about changes in the behavior of others. How have our experiences blended with our native endowments to produce the kinds of person we now are? Have we developed in such a way that certain things about us are now very difficult to change? And in the background is another question: What steps may be taken to insure that our own children can avoid becoming stultified conformists without becoming antisocial deviates?

"Socialization" refers to the adoption and internalization by individuals of values, beliefs, and ways of perceiving the world that are shared by a group. When internalization is effective the individual ends up wanting to behave as others want and expect him to behave as a responsible group member. Strictly speaking, socialization occurs whenever an individual must adjust to the standards of a new group; thus the Army recruit, the fraternity pledge, the new arrival at the home for the aged are all subjected to the pressures of socialization into a group whose standards of conduct are relevant for their behavior. However, most references to socialization in the psychological literature allude primarily to social factors in child development. The specific focus on the social growth of the child is not incompatible with the more general definition of socialization, since the child is learning how to become an accepted member of a group. This chapter concerns itself largely with child socialization, in keeping with the general bias of psychological literature, though we recognize that a complete discussion of the topic should certainly consider other cases of group affiliation and membership occurring in the postchildhood period. The chapter is highly selective in other respects too, since it concentrates primarily on basic processes of interpersonal influence expressed in the parent-child relationship. We do not attempt to survey all that is known about child development.

Few things are more fascinating than the process of internalization that characterizes the impact of group norms on individual characteristics. We can readily understand why an individual publicly obeys social laws and defers to those individuals and groups that have more power than he. But the fascination stems from the fact that most of society's codes and values become part of the very fabric of an individual's personality during the process of socialization. The well-socialized person is rarely tempted to indulge in behavior that flouts cultural traditions; he is not torn with conscious conflict over controlling his impulses. The more completely the individual has been socialized, the less conflict he has when confronted by alternative ways of behaving that are not sanctioned by the culture; in fact, the less he may even be aware of such behavioral alternatives. Through the socialization process we unwittingly lose much behavioral freedom as the number of possible action alternatives is restricted by our experiences with group values. Out of the near-infinite variety of ways in which a human being can conceivably behave, only a few alternatives are actually considered in a given situation by the well-socialized adult. However, as we shall see in Chapter Four, this loss in freedom may be compensated for by the fact that more energy is left to make decisions in areas not covered by clear-cut cultural norms.

The processes of socialization are, unfortunately, as difficult to study as they are fascinating to consider. Most of their dramatic effects are the culmination of long and complicated learning histories. It is unreasonable to suppose that precisely the same kinds of effects could be produced in the brief interactions that characterize laboratory research. Interviews and questionnaires carry their own liabilities. The primary drawback of such approaches is the difficulty of evaluating the remarks of anyone who is asked to reflect on his past history. Such remarks are, to unknown degrees, affected by deliberate as well as unwitting distortions in the recall and reporting process.

There is no single, precisely appropriate methodology for the study of socialization. A coherent account of the major features of the process must rely on some combination of experimental results, interviews, cross-cultural evidence, systematic observation of the behavior of children, intuition, and anecdote. We are not particularly concerned here with a critical evaluation of the data-gathering procedures responsible for current information, but rather with some of the major ideas and theoretical currents that have given some order to research findings in the area, and give promise of generating important research in the future. We are also, understandably, interested in presenting an account of socialization that will set the stage for our later discussions of social influence and behavior modification. In the following account, therefore, we introduce the reader to a number of the central distinctions of the present book, distinctions we shall place on a firmer and more formal theoretical basis in the chapters to come.

For many years we will be exposed to competing accounts of the highlights and the critical variables in the socialization process. For this reason, the present chapter is cast in the spirit of rather playful speculation. We begin with a descriptive account of the socialization process that emphasizes the special features of the child's condition and the social relationships between the child and various socialization agents. In the remainder of the chapter we take a more systematic look at some of the mechanisms underlying the major changes that grow out of the child's dependence on others for rewards and relief from pain. In Chapter Four we consider more specifically the cognitive development of the child and spell out the consequences of his needs for the information others provide. In Chapter Five we shall present a limited set of concepts intended to label the major products of socialization. These constitute (for our purposes) the ingredients of individual personality.

A DESCRIPTIVE ACCOUNT OF SOCIALIZATION

The Dependency Condition

Without the provision of precisely delivered food substances of special kinds, protection from outside dangers, and shelter from wide variations in climatic conditions, the human infant could not survive. From the very first, human beings are enmeshed in social relationships that are required for their very existence. Because the outcomes of the child are so apt to be mediated by actions of the adult—because the child is so *effect-dependent* on the adult—the socialization demands of adults can be successfully applied. The child's dependence on the socializing agent provides essential leverage for the molding of those characteristics that the agent considers important.

The main socializing agents in earlier years are, of course, the child's parents. Through their almost complete control over the stimuli that reinforce the child, the parents have an impressive potential for selecting particular responses of which the child is capable and for increasing the likelihood of occurrence of these responses. Thus they may "condition" the child to expect food at certain regular intervals and to adopt customary patterns of sleeping at night. Or they may apply their considerable power to control rewards and punishments in order to insure that certain responses are forthcoming. This may be done by formulating and enforcing such rules as: You must wash your hands before coming to the table (or you will get no food); you must clean your room before going out to play; you cannot have your allowance until your chores are done; and so on. The parent's power to provide or withhold reinforcements, and generally to set the stage for learning, is an extremely important factor in the socialization of the child.

But the dependency involved in a child's relationship to his parents is not simply a question of who controls rewards and punishments. The child is also very dependent on others for information about the environment, its meaning, and his possibilities for action in it. Naturally he learns much about his surroundings through his own manipulative exploration and via his own senses, but much of the information that is most important to him is mediated by the communications and teachings of others. Because of the child's need for clarification and structure, we speak of his *information dependence*. The distinction between effect and information dependence will turn out to be very useful for analyzing social influence processes in whatever context they arise.

The existence of information dependence implies, of course, that the agents of socialization have a pervasive control over the development of the child's cognitive structure. By selectively presenting certain explanations for events rather than others, the agents can influence the child's conception of reality and his interpretation of his experiences. The fact that parents have the opportunity to "get there first"—often "with the most"—undoubtedly helps to explain the pervasiveness of their influence on the development of assumptions and beliefs about reality. Thus different conceptions of authority and of living and dying are likely to be communicated to the child by parents of varying degrees of religious faith; and attitudes about people of other faiths and colors are notoriously affected by the expressed beliefs and more subtle innuendos of adults. As the child comes in contact with more and more varied sources of information, he customarily learns to discriminate among them in terms of their credibility and their relevance to him. He may even come to reject certain basic attitudes of his parents. Nevertheless, parents and other agents of socialization clearly play a strategic role in providing answers to children's questions by holding a virtual monopoly over the channels of communication to which the child is exposed in the early years. The monopoly is in some respects similar to that at least partially attained by totalitarian governments, which attempt to control the major channels of mass information and education. Whether we are dealing with the national or the family context, the broad human motive to understand and to reduce uncertainties about the nature of reality makes us receptive to those who can offer explanations. These explanations are likely to be accepted to the degree that competing explanations are not available.

Even though the child is later reinforced for different responses from those his parents may have rewarded, and even though, as he grows older, the information environment is more and more mediated by others, his condition of prolonged dependency is of enormous importance. By the time the child is old enough to survive and prosper without parental ministrations and protection other factors have taken over to insure his acquiescence to the demands of the culture. These factors include values, beliefs, and other dispositions that make up the emerging personality of the child.

Socialization Pressures Outside the Family Circle

As the infant becomes a child, and the child then grows slowly into adolescence and adulthood, the socialization process is increasingly affected by the actions of persons outside the family. Teachers, ministers, camp counselors, and Scout leaders play an expanding role in supporting, redefining, and sometimes counteracting parental influence. The child is also increasingly affected by his peers—their ideas about what is fun to do, what is right and what is wrong, who is good and who is bad.

Many social scientists have pointed out that each of us participates in his broader national or regional culture through his memberships in a complex mixture of small groups and associations. Some of these groups are formally constituted whereas others are quite informal and may involve a rapid turnover of members. Not only is there a kind of miniature socialization of each individual into each of his groups, but these experiences combine to form part of socialization into the broader culture. The culture is thus *mediated* by various memberships, with the family being merely one—if the most crucial—of the many groups involved in the socialization process. Although general perspective or frames of reference are initially products of intensive parent-child interactions, many specific attitudes are hammered into shape on the anvil of competing loyalties to various groups.

Since many groups in our society are known to favor certain practices over others, in order to predict the attitudes, beliefs, and values of a particular person we can make an educated guess from listing those groups to which he belongs. This is true both because groups have varying degrees of power over their members to bring about compliance with majority opinion, and also because individuals have some control over selecting which groups they wish to join. If we were to learn that Mr. X, about whom we know nothing else, is a member of the American Legion, we could make a much better than random guess about his attitudes toward admitting Red China into the United Nations. Finding that Mr. Y is a member of the American Civil Liberties Union, we can scarcely err in predicting his feelings about state prohibitions of the sale of birth-control devices.

The problem of predicting attitudes from group membership is complicated, however, by several considerations. First, all the groups and associations to which we belong are not equally important—or equally influential in the formation of attitudes. It may be helpful to think of each individual as centered in a particular social network that is unique for him. This network may be represented as a series of concentric circles representing membership groups. Those circles close to the individual represent groups like the family circle, which control and influence a large segment of attitudinal development. Circles at a greater distance from the individual represent more remote associations such as home town, region, or political party. We often take such differences for granted, and indeed it is newsworthy when a person reports his mother to the FBI because of her pro-Communist sympathies, or when a Southern politician comes out for the inviolacy of the Supreme Court, or when a city council member votes for increased local taxation to support a "down-state" project.

Second, knowledge of an individual's membership in a group, even if we know something about the relevance of the group to his concerns, is not sufficient for accurate predictions of attitudes. The effects of group membership on a person's attitudes are dependent on his position in the group, his reasons for belonging, and the strength of his desire to remain a member. In addition, the attitudes of group members may be quite heterogeneous, and effective prediction may require some further knowledge of the particular subgroup to which the individual belongs.

Third, individuals are often much affected by groups in which they are not members, or by individuals with whom they have no direct contact. A person who cannot afford a country-club membership or secure an invitation to join may nevertheless be extremely affected by the attitudes of members that he meets, and try to pattern his clothes, style of entertainment, and even his political beliefs after his image of the typical club member.

Largely for these reasons, the concept of *reference group* has gained wide currency among social scientists. A reference group is one in terms of which the individual views or evaluates himself, one whose standards are used as a comparison point for the individual's behavior. The more important the reference group is and the more salient it is in a particular situation, the more the individual's actions will be affected by its standards, or "norms."

Hyman first used the concept of reference group in 1942 in a study of subjective social status. This was largely an exploratory study of the criteria most important to people in judging their own relative social standing. Newcomb (1943) found the reference-group concept useful in tracing the changes in student attitudes that accompanied socialization into the liberal college community of Bennington. Although the female students attending the college came largely from conservative, middle-class homes, the norms of the faculty and the more advanced students were not at all conservative and there was active concern with political issues at the time. Through a combination of interview and questionnaire data, Newcomb was able to show that the more liberal a girl was, the more popular and prestigious she tended to be. This could mean either that (a) the liberal girls were rewarded with affection for conformity to the norms of the majority, (b) girls who had more conservative attitudes and resisted conformity were difficult to like for other reasons (they were distant, shy, more maladjusted), or (c) the popular girls became more liberal because they had a better chance to interact with juniors and seniors and to learn their sentiments. While the causes and effects are difficult to disentangle in Newcomb's data, his detailed analysis of attitude change in a field setting has served as a source of many hypotheses in subsequent research.

In the analysis of reference-group phenomena two further distinctions prove useful. One is the distinction between positive and negative reference groups. A person may avoid the adoption of attitudes that characterize the members of groups from which he wishes to dissociate himself. This phenomenon is no more clearly demonstrated than in the rush of many American politicians to be against everything that Communists favor.

A second distinction concerns two quite separate functions reference groups may serve. Kelley (in Swanson, Newcomb and Hartley, 1952) has proposed a distinction between the *comparison* and *normative* functions of reference groups. The former is served when a group provides a standard of reference against which the person may compare his own judgments, attitudes, or performance. During World War II, for example, it was found that noncombat soldiers overseas had relatively high morale because they apparently compared their lot with that of soldiers in combat (Merton and Kitt, 1950). In contrast, soldiers who were assigned to American colleges for special training in such fields as languages or engineering often showed notoriously low morale, since they compared themselves with civilian college students who were subject to far fewer restrictions (the reader will recall the description of an Army special-training program in Chapter One). The comparison function may also involve the reference of a person's own position or status solely to the other members of his particular membership group. Thus it was found, during World War II, that the average military policeman was more satisfied with his promotional opportunities than was the average enlisted man in the Army Air Corps, even though the objective opportunities for promotion in the latter organization were vastly greater.

When only the comparison function is involved, any evaluation of the person by members of the reference group is largely irrelevant. The overseas noncombatant has high morale not because good spirits are expected by, and reinforced by, the combat soldier; the fate of the combat soldier merely serves as a comparison against which to evaluate his own "relative deprivation." When the second, normative, function is added the reference group both sets and reinforces standards. "A group functions as a normative reference group for a person to the extent that its evaluations of him are based upon the degree of his conformity to certain standards of behavior or attitude and to the extent that the delivery of rewards or punishments is conditional upon these evaluations" (Kelley, in Swanson, Newcomb and Hartley, pp. 412–413). Probably the upper-class girls at Bennington served as a normative reference group for most of the freshmen in Newcomb's study, since it may be presumed that rewards of popularity were contingent on acceptance of the group's norms.

It is important to realize that the distinction between the comparison and the normative functions of a reference group is directly comparable to the distinction between effect dependence and information dependence proposed earlier in this chapter. To the extent that a person's reference groups serve a normative function for him, he is dependent on the members of these groups for esteem-building rewards and approbation. To the extent that the comparison function is served, the individual makes use of the information provided by the opinions, values, or other actions of group members. We see, then, that the two forms of social leverage possessed by parents are again present as the child begins to relate to the various groups that characterize the social environment beyond the home.

EFFECT DEPENDENCE AND THE INTERNALIZATION OF VALUES

Every theory of motivation makes the assumption that there are certain states of affairs that persons find more desirable than others. Most theories assume further that persons will act in such a way as to achieve these desirable states and to avoid undesirable ones. Those who wish to theorize about behavior must develop constructs to refer to the factors believed to determine or affect the organism's responses. These constructs, as we saw in Chapter Two, are convenient fictions used by the theorist to account for the behavioral data he wants to explain. The labels he uses will reflect the particular flavor of his assumptions and emphasize those aspects of behavior-environment relations he views as most important. Thus, when we say that persons attempt to "achieve desirable states" we are saying something relevant to a whole range of motivational constructs, constructs that are part of our inheritance from the literature of psychology: reinforcement, drive, incentive, need, aspiration, value.

The proper choice of constructs is an important part of the business of science, and no one can deny the utility of a complex and differentiated terminology in talking about the nuances of motivational phenomena. However, we shall risk the dangers of oversimplification by consistently using the word *value* to refer to much of the broad range of phenomena usually classified as motivational. This concept, value, essentially captures the desirability or undesirability of a state of affairs, which in any given concrete case may be an object, an idea, an event, a person, or any experience that is relevant to an individual's ability to survive and prosper. For the moment we shall not attempt to differentiate between subclasses of values but shall introduce appropriate refinements as the discussion proceeds.

In the present chapter we want to understand how acquired values maintain themselves when the conditions that produced them are no longer present. It is not difficult to see why parents are in a position to manage or control their young children and insure that they behave in a culturally desirable manner. Parents have abundant resources for rewarding and punishing the child, which they are in a position to exploit in shaping the child's behavior. But how do previously neutral events develop into incentives that arouse and channel behavior? How do restrictions imposed from without become inhibitions governing from within? How do self-control and self-regulation supplant a mere responsiveness to external rewards and punishments?

Each of these developments results in the individual applying internal standards to evaluate his own behavior. He monitors himself, as it were, and applies some equivalent of the rewards and punishments that were formerly a part of the reactions of others. The development of these standards and the values that support them is obviously a function of various processes of learning. But we are especially concerned in the following discussion with the maintenance of values once they have been acquired—with their tough resistance to change. As the word internalization implies, the individual reaches a point at which his values become relatively insensitive to the gusty winds of social pressure. A central preoccupation in this chapter is to find an answer to the why of this insensitivity.

Acquiring and Keeping Specific Values

Neutral objects and events acquire value when they are paired with already-valued objects and events. This brief statement expresses one of the most important empirical generalizations in the field of psychology. Its range of application is wide, for it is the very essence of learning that a conditioned stimulus (CS) acquires the capacity to elicit behaviors formerly associated with another stimulus—the unconditioned stimulus (UCS). Thus the CS has taken on value for the responding organism. The value may be positive if the stimulus has been associated with a desired state of affairs, or negative if associated with a state of affairs the individual wishes to avoid. In either case, the CS is evaluated in a different way after being paired with the UCS than before.

Conditioned stimuli may acquire value for the organism either in the framework of instrumental learning or classical conditioning. The Wolfe (1936) study is often cited as an example of instrumental learning; in it chimpanzees worked for poker chips that had previously been useful in obtaining primary food rewards. But the salivation of a dog at a bell (CS) after it has been paired a number of times with meat powder (UCS) or the blinking of a sophomore at a tone that has been paired with an air puff, are conditioned responses that are not instrumental in obtaining the meat or avoiding the air puff. These pairings are instances of classical conditioning because sheer contiguity in time seems enough to "transfer" the meaning of the UCS to the CS.

The distinction between classical and instrumental conditioning is less relevant here than that between establishing a value and exploiting it in the learning process. It seems appropriate to say that a value has been established, if only temporarily, when an organism consistently approaches or avoids an object toward which it was previously indifferent. The establishment of new values involves building on or making use of old values. The use of old values may often involve waiting for the organism to become deficient in the valued commodity. A rat that is completely surfeited with food cannot be taught to press a bar when a light goes on in order to release a pellet from a food magazine.

Switching now to the context of child socialization, it is clear that parents are continually occupied in using certain values that have already been established in the child in order (a) to control his behavior and (b) to expand the number of positive and negative values to which he will respond. As we have said, the parent is in an excellent position to control the child's behavior because he controls many of the resources that the child quickly learns to value: food, warmth, comfort, and so on. But it is certainly in the parents' interest to move out of the stage in which the child has to be monitored continually in order for rewards and punishments to be appropriate into a stage where the child may be trusted to do the right thing without surveillance. Entering this second stage is certainly facilitated by increasing the significance or value of environmental objects or events and thus expanding the number of stimuli the child will attempt to approach or avoid.

The process of *value expansion* which occurs during learning is usually conceptualized in terms of secondary reinforcement. The learning literature (Kimble, 1961) contains abundant evidence that neutral stimuli associated with such primary reinforcing stimuli as food acquire reinforcing properties of their own. Thus the secondary reinforcer (a bell, a light, a click, a maze pathway with distinctive cues) acquires the properties of an incentive; its presentation leads the animal to strive for it. These incentive properties may be inferred from the greater resistance to extinction shown when the primary reinforcer is removed but a secondary reinforcer remains. For example, animals trained to run a maze to obtain food in a distinctive goal box will extinguish more rapidly upon the removal of food if the distinctive cues identifying the goal box are also changed (Saltzman, 1949).

Extending the notion of secondary reinforcement to child socialization, it seems that an increasing attachment of reinforcing properties to previously neutral stimuli should play an important role in maintaining responses desired by the parent. By providing cues previously associated with primary reinforcements the adult may escape the burdens associated with constant surveillance and with the direct administration of primary rewards. In other words, the more stimuli the child comes to value positively or negatively the more vulnerable he becomes to manipulation by anyone having access to those stimuli. Among other things, the mother who dispenses primary reinforcements may herself acquire the properties of a secondary reinforcer, so that her very presence or absence can become "effects" on which the child is dependent.

As important as secondary reinforcement undoubtedly is in the socialization process, a further step is necessary to account for the internalization and persistence of values. Although secondary reinforcers do contribute to a slowing down of the process whereby learned responses become extinguished in the absence of primary reinforcers, there is general agreement among students of learning that the contribution of secondary reinforcement is only temporary. Unless the connection between primary and secondary reinforcers is periodically reinstated, the learned response does extinguish. It is necessary to find some additional mechanism(s) to account for the persistence of values once they are acquired.

Value Internalization and Resistance to Extinction

To say that values become internalized in the socialization process is to imply that they no longer are dependent on their linkage with those primary biological drives on which they were initially based. That is, conditions that originally linked the acquired value to a more basic one may no longer exist, but the acquired value itself persists. Soldiers may sacrifice their lives for values originally learned in the interests of surviving and prospering. Thus it is one thing to understand why behavior persists in the presence of external reinforcements, or reminders thereof, but quite another to understand behavior that persists in their absence.

Many theorists of personality have concerned themselves centrally with the problems of persisting motives. One of the most influential accounts of motive persistence has been that of Sigmund Freud, who was convinced of the decisive importance of early experience in the formation of lasting patterns of motivation. One of Freud's main assumptions was that society, through its adult agents of socialization, exerted a repressive influence on the normal expression of primitive sexual and aggressive urges. In normal development, he held, the content and target of expression are modified in line with society's demands, but the primitive urges themselves remain in the unconscious, later to affect adult behavior in complex and subtle ways. Freud also felt that there are several distinct stages of psychosexual development during which the child is faced with problems peculiar to that stage. He described these stages as first oral, then anal, then genital sexuality, and viewed each as a way-station toward mature heterosexuality. Since problems at a particular stage are not always easily mastered or resolved, he maintained, there are often fixations at an immature level. If the fixation is at the oral level, portions of the general reservoir of sexual energy (the libido) continue to motivate oral strivings or substitutes for them. The resulting motivational symptoms may take the form of extreme dependency manifestations, compulsive overeating or merely pipe smoking and pencil biting. By the use of this elaborate explanatory apparatus Freud attempted to explain why irrational, maladaptive behaviors could persist in adulthood when there were no obvious reinforcing stimuli to sustain them. His answer was that they are fed by motivational sources of which the individual is unaware and over which he has little or no voluntary control.

G. W. Allport (1937) introduced the term *functional autonomy* in an effort to explain, for example, why a sailor who originally signed on for money remains a sailor because of his love of the sea. Allport introduced the concept of functional autonomy as part of a criticism of the early behaviorists' dogma that secondary motives must be sustained by the primary motives they ultimately satisfy. The problem with his alternative—that motives once acquired can become autonomous—is that a description of *how* motives can function was offered as an explanation of *why* they function as they do.

McClelland (1951) has presented a lengthy discussion of the various reasons why certain learned response tendencies persist in spite of changing circumstances. Focusing primarily on the motive to achieve, he sought to explain why a person keeps trying in the face of failure and why some people value achievement for its own sake. Along with many other personality theorists, he sought to find those conditions in childhood that might be favorable to the development of such persistent behavior tendencies. One of the most interesting aspects of this search was his appeal to the known facts of learning for an explanation of persistence. He noted, as others had before him in the more restricted context of learning experiments, that the frequency and regularity of reward has certain paradoxical effects in building up associations. Acquisition of an association occurs most rapidly when reward or reinforcement is systematically and consistently applied. Associations formed under such conditions of consistency are, however, quite easily extinguished. Many people have suggested that the explanation of this paradox lies in the ease with which the learner may distinguish between conditions of acquisition and of extinction. If reinforcement is infrequently or capriciously applied, the association so reinforced may be slowly and laboriously acquired; once acquired, however, it tends to persist when there has been a change in conditions of reinforcement. Why? Because a change cannot be easily perceived.

Avoidance learning provides a clear example of this principle. Consider the following paradigm: a rat in compartment *A* is exposed to a light followed by an electric shock. Initially the shock prompts him to jump into compartment *B* as an escape measure. Before long, however, the light becomes a signal for the onset of shock, and the rat avoids the shock altogether by jumping at the light. Such a learned reaction is known to be extremely stable and resistant to extinction because by avoiding the shock the rat presumably loses any chance to find out whether it continues to occur following the signal. Thus it is impossible, once the rat has performed the avoidance response, for it to discriminate between the condition of acquisition and that of extinction.

Many theorists like Brown (1953) and Dollard and Miller (1950) have played up the role of anxiety in explaining the persistence of acquired values. McClelland argues, however, that it is not the anxiety per se that is important, but the effect of avoidance in depriving the organism of information. Under conditions of partial reinforcement when rewards are only periodically or randomly administered for correct performance, anxiety is not necessarily involved. Yet associations acquired under partial reinforcement are notoriously resistant to extinction. The reason again is that partial reinforcement makes it more difficult to distinguish between conditions of acquisition and extinction.

The relevance of this line of reasoning in the present context stems from the fact that many of the most crucial and permanent associations the child makes are learned in a very complex social-emotional setting, in which reinforcements are indeed capriciously administered. Even when the parent is convinced of his own consistency as a reinforcing agent, the child's capacity to generalize and apply the same label to events adults view as similar may not be up to the task of detecting this consistency.

Lawrence and Festinger (1962) seriously question the preceding explanation. There is little or no dispute about the data: animals or people who learn a particular response under conditions of unpredictable reinforcement tend to persist longer in making that response when the reinforcement is entirely removed. But Lawrence and Festinger do not accept the traditional explanation that this occurs because of the subject's inability to discriminate between the conditions of learning and the conditions of extinction. They argue that there are several conditions of learning besides partial reinforcement that also produce resistance to extinction. If there is a delay between response and reinforcement the subject will learn more slowly but also extinguish more slowly after the reinforcement is entirely removed than if there has been little or no delay. Also, the more effort the subject is required to exert in order to obtain a reward the more slowly he will learn, but again, the more resistant the learned response will be to extinction. These various findings, well established in the learning literature, are not equally susceptible to the "difficulty of discrimination" or confusion explanation.

Taking their lead primarily from the findings on the positive relationship between effort and resistance to extinction, Lawrence and Festinger put forth an alternative explanation that derives from the latter's theory of cognitive dissonance (1957). This theory was reviewed briefly in Chapter Two and will be more fully discussed in later chapters, especially in Chapter

Six. Here, as a special derivation, we present the hypothesis of *effort justification*. Briefly stated, this hypothesis proposes that higher organisms—from the rat on up—will develop a special preference for certain features of the surrounding environment to the extent that effort is expended near these features that is not sufficiently justified by the provision of established rewards or reinforcements. The Aronson and Mills (1959) severity-of-initiation study is one apparent test of this hypothesis. People, as Festinger (1961) has remarked, learn to love that for which they have suffered. In other words, if a person (or animal) expends effort that is not readily justified by the amount of reinforcement received, he tends to create reinforcements out of the stimuli available in the immediately surrounding environment and previously neutral aspects of that environment take on value. This value increase occurs as part of the cognitive work in which the animal or person engages to justify the effort expended.

Lawrence and Festinger (1962) conducted a series of experiments to test several implications of the hypothesis of effort justification. The most telling indictment of the discrimination hypothesis, which states that the organism cannot tell the difference between learning and extinction trials, comes from the results of a large experiment on maze learning involving 146 white rats. By varying both the percentage of total trials that were rewarded and the actual number of unrewarded trials the experimenters directly pitted the discrimination hypothesis against the effort-justification hypothesis. According to the former, resistance to extinction should vary as a function of the ease of distinguishing between the learning phase of the experiment and the extinction phase. This should be a function, in turn, of the percentage of rewarded trials during the learning phase. The greater the percentage of rewarded trials, the easier should be the discrimination task when rewards are no longer forthcoming. According to the effort-justification hypothesis, on the other hand, the percentage of reward should make little difference; resistance should increase as a function of the number and not the percentage of unrewarded trials.

The results of the experiment were dramatic. As long as the same number of trials were unrewarded in learning, the animals showed the same resistance to extinction regardless of the percentage of rewarded trials. But when percentage was held constant, on the other hand, resistance to extinction was more pronounced as the absolute number of trials increased. In short, it appears to be the effort expended in learning, not the confusion about whether or not rewards are still being dispensed, that accounts for the persistence of an unrewarded response. The animals who had been poorly rewarded presumably developed an extra preference for certain features of the situation (the runways, the goal box, and so on) in order to justify the effort expended. Thus removal of the reward in the extinction phase had a smaller effect on their tendency to continue responding since they were attracted to the goal box by those stimuli that had taken on value through the effort justification process.

In other rat experiments Lawrence and Festinger (1962) obtained still further support for the effort-justification hypothesis. In the most direct test of this hypothesis they showed that animals running up a 50° incline to get food took more trials to extinguish than animals running up a 25° incline. Another experiment showed that response effort combined with the effects of partial reinforcement so that extinction of the tendency to run was slowest when there were many unrewarded trials and effort on each was great (because of the 50° steepness of the maze alley).

The Lawrence and Festinger results leave many questions unanswered and offer only a tantalizing glimpse into the role of effort in the acquisition of persistent values. One major question concerns the relationship between resistance to extinction in rats and the internalization of stable dispositions in human children. A second concerns the seemingly opposite theoretical relationship between the effects of effort and the effects of secondary reinforcement. The more consistently a stimulus is paired with an established reward the greater is the tendency for that stimulus to take on the properties of secondary reinforcement. Once these secondary reinforcing properties have developed, we would expect resistance to extinction to be greater. But we have also been arguing that resistance is one result of *inconsistent* reward. We shall take up each of these questions in the process of discussing an experiment by Aronson (1961) that investigated the role of effort by human subjects in the development of extra preference for that with which effort has been associated. This experiment was conceived within the same theoretical framework as the Lawrence and Festinger studies.

Aronson gave female college students the task of fishing for small flashlight cases containing varying amounts of money. Each case was colored either red or green. For any given subject, cases of one color consistently contained money, cases of the other color did not. The subjects could not actually see the color of the case until they had "caught" it. There were two conditions under which the subjects fished. In the *easy* condition, subjects obtained the cases simply by attracting a protruding metal ring with a horseshoe magnet. In the *effortful* condition, they were forced to work with a hook tied to a piece of string and in this condition it took subjects considerably longer to "catch" a container. All subjects were asked to indicate their relative preference for the two colors both before and after the experiment. (They were led to believe this was part of a separate experiment). Change in color preference was the major dependent variable of the study.

If it is true that, in order to justify expended effort, individuals develop special preferences for aspects of the performance situation, we might expect the subjects in the experiment to prefer the nonrewarded color in the effortful condition. However, there are well-known effects of secondary reinforcement that run counter to the effort-justification hypothesis. Previously neutral stimuli associated with rewards, such as the color of a case containing money, are known to develop secondary reinforcement properties and should therefore become more attractive as an outgrowth of the association. Because the level of secondary reinforcement could not be specified in advance, Aronson was forced to make a more complex prediction of relative change: "Since any effects due to secondary reinforcement should remain constant regardless of effort, stimuli associated with lack of reward should become more attractive (relative to stimuli associated with reward) as effort increases" (p. 376).

The results confirmed his hypothesis. The rewarded color was preferred by subjects in the easy condition; there was no preference for either the rewarded or the nonrewarded color in the effort condition. The implication is that secondary reinforcement effects and those associated with effort justification cancelled each other out in the latter case. In the easy condition, on the other hand, the effects of secondary reinforcement were demonstrated.

Where does this rather lengthy discussion of partial reinforcement and value acquisition leave us? Undoubtedly we do learn to value previously neutral objects and conditions associated with rewarding experiences. A large part of the socialization process can presumably be accounted for through the development of more remote and symbolic reinforcers that may stand as incentives in sustaining culturally acceptable behavior. At the same time, however, we have noted that the maintenance of secondary reinforcing systems depends on periodic confirmations that these systems do link up eventually with primary reinforcers. When the environmental context of subsequent performance is similar in structure to the learning environment, the secondary-reinforcement hypothesis is a powerful predictive principle.

However, although secondary reinforcement is an important aspect of the acquisition of values, other things are clearly involved in the internalization process. Internalization results in stable personality dispositions that function *without* the necessary support of primary or secondary reinforcers. We have sought for clues to explain how such dispositions may resist being extinguished when the reinforcements that led to their acquisition are no longer being applied. One promising hint is the hypothesis of effort justification. To the extent that this hypothesis is operative in socialization, we may expect the most durable preferences for distinctive environmental incentives to be those that emerge from situations in which there have been just barely enough primary incentives to bring about learning and in which the effort has been sufficient to require value acquisition as a method of justifying performance. There are presumably many learning situations in childhood that feature the kinds of capricious reward, mixtures of reward and frustration, and so on, specified by the effort-justification hypothesis. We need to learn much more about the specific contributions such situations make to the acquisition of durable values—values that are relatively unresponsive to changing times and conditions.

Inhibition and Impulse Control

Socialization builds in the values that are sanctioned by a culture; the individual learns to desire those things that are consistent with his role in society and therefore support the maintenance of cultural values. In addition, however, socialization involves the control and diversion of those behavior tendencies that potentially threaten group maintenance and solidarity. Unrestrained aggression, promiscuous sexuality, cheating, deceit, or thievery cannot be tolerated in any functioning group. As Whiting and Child (1953) have pointed out, much of the learning of culturally sanctioned behavior comes about through positive learning based on reward. But

. . . conformity to the cultural roles requires more than just a positive habit of following the approved way: it requires also the development of negative habits which will produce avoidance of the disapproved ways of reducing the drive. This is perhaps most uniformly true of the sexual and aggressive drives (pp. 222–223).

Universally, there is general cultural indulgence of impulsive behavior in the early years of infancy. The child is protected from himself and from outside dangers, but there is initially little concern over his aggressive tendencies, his expressions of sensuality, or his urinary and bowel incontinence. Sooner or later, depending on cultural and individual family traditions, indulgence gives way to active attempts by the social agent to control the more primitive urges and the more excessive reactions to stress. From this point on, certain responses are punished in the belief that the probability of their occurrence will decline in favor of more refined behavioral expressions.

Punishment, in the typical case, involves the pairing of a painful (unconditioned) stimulus with some external cue that serves as a conditioned stimulus. As a result of this pairing, the formerly neutral cue (a parental frown, footsteps in the hall) acquires the capacity to elicit responses previously given only to the painful stimulus. That is, the organism learns to avoid the painful stimulus—to avoid making the response that produces it. In short, he develops a *conditioned avoidance response*. The inhibition of punished responses comes about as the organism responds with something like anxiety to the cues provided by his own incipient muscle movements. The striking thing about conditioned avoidance responses is that they are notoriously resistant to extinction. As we have commented earlier, it seems reasonable that a response that reduces anxiety and prevents the occurrence of punishment will at the same time prevent the organism from realizing any change in the occasion for punishment. Thus there is no reason why the response will not persist, unless the organism becomes unduly fatigued or careless and omits the avoidance response, thereby finding that the pain UCS is no longer forthcoming.

It is generally assumed that punishment has rather local and specific effects on the responses that precede it. Instead of learning that aggressive responses to frustration are generally taboo, the child learns to suppress his aggression in situations resembling those in which he has been punished for aggressive behavior, but not in other situations. According to Miller's (1944) theory of conflict and displacement, punishment results in gradients of inhibition along two dimensions. First, there is a gradient that generalizes along the lines of form or type of response. Thus the effects of punishing an overt temper tantrum may extend to inhibit unkind remarks, to some extent, and more indirect sarcasm and innuendo to an even smaller degree. It is thus conceivable that consistent punishment of direct aggression will result in a shift toward more indirect aggression in the face of frustration. This, of course, would be in line with the socialization objective of inhibiting especially disruptive responses in favor of those less threatening to group solidarity.

The other dimension along which punishment produces an inhibition gradient is similarity of the stimulus. The more similar a situation is to one in which punishment originally occurred, and the more similar the punishing agent is to the original one, the greater the inhibition of aggression. Following this line of reasoning, although overt aggression may be inhibited in situation X, the effects of inhibition may not extend to more indirect forms of aggression or to aggression occurring in other situations.

It should be realized, however, that the instigation to aggressiveness also declines as the target becomes less similar to the original instigator. We may therefore speak of a gradient of excitation or instigation as well as a gradient of inhibition. If we were to assume that these gradients are identical in shape, then we would have to predict that aggression would never occur: as aggression becomes more permissible with the decline of similarity, the tendency to aggress declines in camparable fashion. Another kind of assumption is usually made. On theoretical grounds, and with some support from animal experimentation, Miller (1944) proposes that the gradient of inhibition is *steeper* than the gradient of excitation. Thus at some point along the dimension of similarity, the tendency to aggress is greater than the inhibiting tendency and aggression then occurs.

The vicissitudes of aggression, and other antisocial behaviors that are subject to punishment and inhibition by the agents of socialization, may be understood to some extent in terms of the concept of *displacement*. An aggressive response originally instigated by one target may be expressed toward another. This would be a displaced response if aggression toward the first target were severely inhibited and the second target were in some way similar—not similar enough to evoke the same inhibitions, and not so dissimilar as to be a totally irrelevant target. More technically, a displaced response is one that occurs when it does and where it does because it is the strongest and most direct response that may occur when the gradually declining gradient of excitation is above the more sharply declining gradient of inhibition. Figure 3.1 is a schematic depiction of the intersecting gradients of response elicitation and inhibition. By the used of such a diagram it is possible to understand how a child, aroused to aggression by his parent, may end up attacking his little brother.

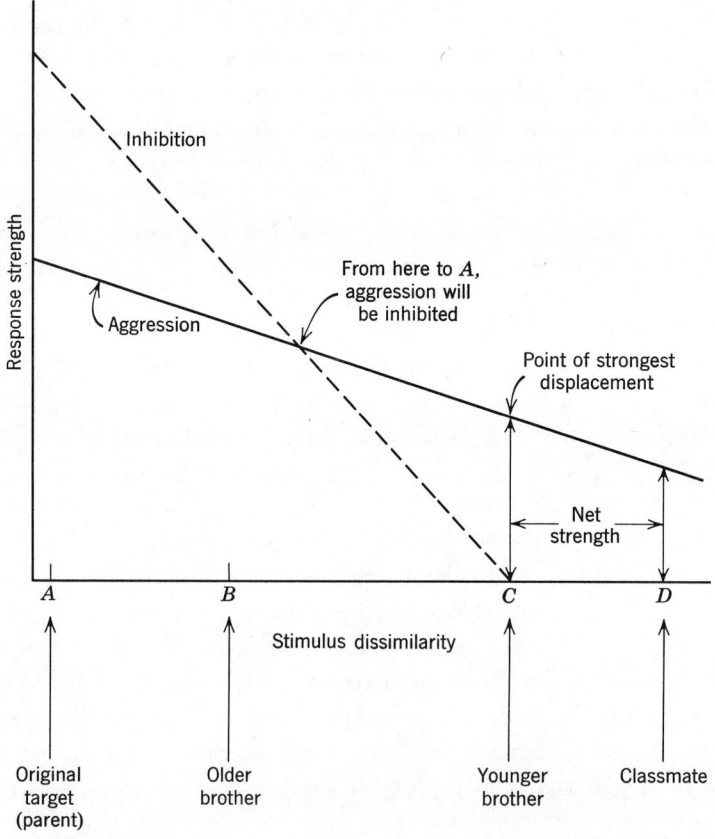

Figure 3.1. *Displacement produced by greater steepness of inhibition than elicitation gradients. Example: a child is angered by his father (adapted from Miller, 1944).*

The main implication of this line of reasoning for our present purposes is that punishment may change the target and form of undesired responses, but children (and people in general) may still be aggressive or dishonest in situations where punishment can be evaded. On the basis of displacement theory, then, we can explain how antisocial responses are suppressed in the presence of agents of inhibition and punishment. However, on this basis alone, we cannot readily explain how the child internalizes society's prohibitions so that they are converted into the dictates of his own conscience.

For the development of conscience to occur the child must learn, in effect, to evaluate his behavior and apply rewards and punishments to himself. Through some process of learning there must be a shift from being under the control of external reinforcements to the incorporation of culturally approved standards for evaluating his own behavior. Such a shift is certainly facilitated by the child's increasing ability to anticipate the consequences of his own action.

Delay of Gratification

It may be assumed that, before the pressures of socialization have begun to take their toll, the child obtains gratification from the direct expression of sexual and aggressive impulses, as well as from those playful expressions of creativity which result in crayoned walls, scissored curtains, and paint-daubed rugs. One of the main tasks of the socialization agent is to devise appropriate rewards and punishments to counteract the gratifications inherent in such "antisocial" actions. Furthermore, these rewarding and punishing sanctions must become anticipatory or the child will never learn to inhibit undesirable responses. This requires that the child develop some capacity to delay acting for immediate rewards in order to avoid subsequent punishments or to obtain subsequent rewards of greater value than the ones foregone. This development of a time perspective seems to be a critical factor in the growth of conscience, since without some appreciation for the long range (delayed) consequences of action, the child would remain a victim of momentary urges to impulsive behavior.

Freud saw that the developing child must move from the immediate demands of the "pleasure principle" to a more mature obedience to the "reality principle." This transition, he argued, is brought about by the emergence of an integrative ego that mediates between the demands of the id (impulse life) and the super-ego (the representative of social reality brought about through incorporation of parental standards). This colorful theory essentially restated the problem in terms of inexorable psychic growth, but it did not carefully analyze how impulse and reality become coordinated.

Mowrer and Ullman (1945) attempted to reformulate the problem of impulse control in terms of the organism's capacity for "integrative learning." They noted that students of learning had long observed a *gradient of reinforcement:* the longer the time interval between response and reinforcement, the less the effects of the reward. If the negative effects of acting or the positive effects of *not* acting were delayed, any immediate reinforcements gained from acting should therefore take precedence in determining behavior. Mowrer and Ullman then posed the question, what factor or factors might serve to bridge the reinforcement delay—to help the organism weigh the delayed and the immediate reinforcements on the same scale? Their tentative answer, based on a delay-of-reinforcement experiment, stressed the importance of symbolic mediation. A rat that is shocked for running immediately to a food trough can be taught to delay only if a signal buzzer sounds throughout the taboo period to "remind" the rat that impulsive running would be shocked. The child, of course, moves rapidly beyond the rat into a phase at which some form of symbolic self-instruction undoubtedly serves the function of the buzzer in the Mowrer and Ullman experiment. In order to understand impulse control, then, it is necessary to discover the variables that facilitate self-instruction, the capacity of symbolic mediation that increases the influence of delayed rewards and punishments over the child's action decisions.

Very little is presently known about such factors, but a recent series of studies by Mischel and his colleagues (Mischel, 1958b; Mischel, 1961a; Mischel, 1961b; Mischel and Metzner, 1962; Mischel and Gilligan, 1964) shows that the problem is amenable to experimentation. To explore the determinants of sensitivity to delayed gratification, Mischel developed a simple procedure of asking subjects to choose between a small immediate reward (say, a five-cent candy bar) and a larger future reward (a twenty-five-cent candy bar). In a preliminary study (1958) with seven- to nine-year-old Trinidadian children, he found that Negro subjects were more likely than East Indian subjects to take the immediate, smaller reward. According to Mischel, this confirmed anthropological observations by "numerous informants" to the effect that Trinidad Negroes are "impulsive, indulge themselves, settle for next to nothing if they can get it right away, . . . etc." (p. 57). In a later study with somewhat older children (average age 13), Mischel (1961a) found that a sample of juvenile delinquents were more likely than normal elementary school children to choose the immediate, smaller rewards offered. In still another sample from the same culture, Mischel (1961b) showed that "need for achievement," as measured by a projective storytelling technique, was correlated with preference for the larger, delayed reward. This is reasonable if we recognize that an interest in achievement for its own sake requires a willingness to delay gratification, to work long hours without immediate reinforcements from the external world.

On the basis of the evidence presented in these three studies, then,

Mischel's simple measure of the willingness to delay gratification appears to be getting at a phenomenon of obvious importance in the socialization process. But it is one thing to establish reasonable cultural and personality correlates of such choices and another to illuminate the antecedents of an ability to delay gratification. Mischel provides an interesting clue pointing in this direction. A child's ability to turn down an immediate, available reward in favor of a larger but more remote one, seems to depend to an important extent on his confidence that the larger reward will actually be delivered. If the child does not trust the person presenting him with the choice, he will doubtless prefer the bird in the hand to any number of birds in the bush. Mischel reasoned that the development of such trust would be weaker if the child had only been exposed infrequently to occasions in which a male socialization agent promised a reward and, after a delay, followed through on his promise. Children whose fathers are absent from the home, either permanently or for long periods of time, should have a more impoverished sense of trust than children from stable homes in which the father is more regularly present.

In apparent confirmation of this reasoning, Mischel did find in two studies and in two cultures (1958b, 1961a) that children from father-absent homes were more likely to choose the immediate reward than those from father-present homes. This factor may account, at least in part, for the Negro-Indian difference in reward preference, since the Trinidad Negro home is frequently fatherless. There are a number of hidden variables correlated with father-absence that may account for the observed relationship with immediate reward preferences. It is interesting to speculate on the importance of experimenter sex in bringing out differences in trust. Would a child from a father-absent home prefer the immediate reward from a female experimenter? Although we do not as yet know the answer to such questions, the establishment of trust as an outgrowth of stable family structure forms a reasonable hypothesis for future confirmation in different cultural settings.

As we would expect, preference for the larger but delayed reward increases as a function of the child's age (Mischel and Metzner, 1962; Melikian, 1959) and decreases as the delay lengthens. This latter effect, consistent with the gradient-of-reinforcement notion, may result from the reduced expectancy that the reward will actually be forthcoming if the delay is long. However, other factors may contribute to the unpleasantness of waiting to be rewarded. The state of deprivation is itself unpleasant, so it may be a question of weighing the unpleasantness of deprivation against the added pleasure of the larger candy bar.

A recent study by Mischel and Gilligan (1964) is especially interesting in showing the relationship between indulging in culturally prohibited behavior (cheating) and preference for immediate reward. Subjects were

49 sixth-grade Boston school children of rather low socioeconomic status. In a first testing session the subjects were administered a delay-of-gratification test and their need for achievement was assessed by McClelland's (1953) picture-storytelling procedure. The delay test included seventeen choice items in which the subject was to indicate his preference for an immediate reward or a larger delayed reward. They were told, "In one of your choices I will really give you the thing that you pick." Items included choices between a small notebook now or a larger notebook within one week, 15 cents now or 30 cents in three weeks, and a small magnifying glass now or a larger one in one week.

At a second session, the child played a shooting-gallery game in which he had to fire a toy rifle at a moving rocket target. The subjects were told that they would receive marksman badges if they scored beyond a certain number of points. Unknown to the subjects, the score of each was controlled so that he could not obtain the prize through his own honest efforts. Each subject, however, was left by the experimenter to score his own hits and misses. This provided him with an opportunity to cheat in an effort to obtain the badges being offered as prizes. The scores were indicated by lights illuminated after each firing. Since they were rigged, the amount and the latency of cheating could be easily scored.

As predicted, there was a relationship between preference for immediate reward and the tendency to cheat. This experimental result is reminiscent of the observed difference between delinquent and normal subjects reported above. Thus resistance to temptation, or impulse control, seems to require placing the importance of immediate rewards in a broader time perspective. At least, the same subjects who resist the temptation of cheating are able to resist the lure of an immediate but small reward. The results involving need for achievement show that variations in the value of the immediate incentive—obtaining the prize—can influence the extent to which children succumb to temptation. Subjects high in need for achievement showed a greater tendency to cheat in order to get an achievement reward than subjects low in the need for achievement. The marksman award was presumably a more valuable prize for the high-need achievers. Thus, although need achievement may generally relate to a capacity to tolerate delays of gratification, it may also push the individual into impulsive behavior when immediate achievement-related rewards are available. Some confusion remains, however, about the role of this variable, as need for achievement did not relate in the Mischel and Gilligan study to the preference for delayed reward.

The line of research exemplified by the Mischel studies opens the whole question of impulse control to empirical analysis in terms of the relative value of immediate versus delayed rewards. Any situational or personality factors that increase the value of the immediate reward—and here we may include those rewards obtained through impulsive actions—will increase the tendency toward selfish, antisocial behavior. Factors in the situation and in the individual that make delayed consequences salient, or make it easier for the child to bridge the delay, promote impulse control.

The all-important capacity to bridge the delay—sometimes referred to as "time-binding"—probably involves explicit or implicit self-instruction concerning the more remote consequences of the action. The more these consequences remain salient to the individual, the more he will tend to inhibit actions that may get him into subsequent trouble with others. But this seems to be an intermediate step in the internalization process, somewhere between response to immediate rewards and punishments and a genuine acceptance of the values important to social functioning. It is one thing to say that a child develops a sense of protecting himself from future punishments as well as immediate ones, or that his sensitivity to rewards bridges across time to include remote consequences. It is yet another to say that a child really internalizes the values of self-control and social responsibility and makes them his own.

In the area of self-control internalization may take the form of self-punishment that at first occurs after a transgression and later becomes anticipatory and thus preventive. The tendency toward self-punishment may itself be learned under the conditions that favor the acquisition of any instrumental response. (See the Bandura and Walters, 1963, pp. 187ff, discussion of "direct training in transgression reactions.") Thus it is possible that some parents reward the child who makes self-punitive statements after a transgression, or that they at least refrain from punishing such a child under circumstances where he has been led otherwise to expect punishment. Aronfreed (1964) presents evidence that self-criticism develops when the adult has criticized the child's response in close contiguity to anxiety reduction. In other words, if the adult labels the incorrect action at the same time he or she terminates the punishments associated with that action, the child will begin to label his own errors and criticize himself.

The Patterning of Deterrents

The conversion of parental control into self-control may be affected in important ways by the timing, intensity, and consistency of socialization demands. Precisely when should punishments be administered if the goal of internalization is paramount? The theories and data of animal learning tell us that punishment should immediately follow the taboo act for it to have the maximum inhibiting effect. Presumably, with their advanced symbolic capacity, children can bridge longer time spans in associating subsequent punishment with prior forbidden actions. Nevertheless, the immediacy of punishment may facilitate the establishment of internalized controls. Two other similar studies, one by Walters and Demkow (1963) and another by Aronfreed and Reber (1965), show that punishment occurring at the initiation of a transgressing act is more effective in establishing internalized inhibition than punishment immediately following transgression. In both experiments the transgression involved playing with or choosing a highly attractive toy. Internalization was tested by observing the child in a subsequent, nonpunishment situation. It is not clear by what mechanism early punishment exerts its superior effects. It may be important that the child does not receive the gratification that would have accompanied completion of the forbidden act. Therefore, when the transgression response has been nipped in the bud, there is not the same mixture of positive and negative reinforcement that exists when punishment follows the completed transgression.

The intensity of socialization demands is another variable of potential relevance to the internalization process. Earlier in this chapter we noted certain paradoxical effects of insufficient reward: responses leading to partial or in other ways minimal reinforcement tend to resist extinction more than responses that are consistently and adequately reinforced. Resistance to extinction is presumably an important aspect of internalization, and such resistance presumably arises out of the subject's attempt to justify the effort expended in learning by attaching positive value to some aspect of the surrounding situation. Even though the standard reinforcement (food, money) is not forthcoming in the extinction period, then, the response persists as long as it maintains the subject's contact with the newly valued stimuli in the environment (the goal box, the maze alley, the color of the flashlight containing money, and so on).

Is there an analogous process stemming from insufficient punishment that may account for internalized self-control? If an individual does not anticipate any punishment for performing an otherwise gratifying act, he tends to perform that act. If he anticipates severe punishment, he does not perform the act. If, however, the punishment is barely sufficient to prevent the occurrence of the act, the individual is in a difficult position. He has refrained from performing the gratifying act, but such self-control is not clearly justified by the weak punishment it avoids. If he has anticipated severe and certain punishment, of course, it is easy to justify his restraint. When the punishment is mild or uncertain, however, the individual tends to mobilize additional reasons why he has refrained from the prohibited action. He might, for example, exaggerate the severity of the anticipated punishment. He might belittle the importance or the attractiveness of the goal to be attained by the forbidden behavior. Or he might convince himself that the action itself was morally reprehensible. The latter two reactions are clearly instances of internalization in the sense that the manipulation of external incentives has an effect on the subject's evaluation of environmental or behavioral events.

Festinger and Freedman (1964) who espouse this *insufficient-deterrence hypothesis* of internalization, argue that parental justification can serve the same role as rewards and punishments. The more reasons a parent offers for not engaging in a behavior, the more justification the child has for not engaging in the behavior. Presumably, then, under most circumstances, the child will not engage in the forbidden behavior. Festinger and Freedman take the example of cheating:

> The child who has sufficient reasons for not cheating—whether it is in terms of desire to receive a reward, avoid a punishment, or avoid social consequences . . . may not develop a moral value or restriction against cheating. He may not cheat because he is convinced it is a bad idea, but, on the other hand, he may not think that cheating is bad per se. In some sense he will be freer in that he does not blindly follow a moral code, but he is also freer in that under appropriate circumstances he may feel free to cheat in much the same way that a child who refrains only from fear is free when the fear is removed. In other words, the child who is given good reasons for not cheating may not develop as strong a moral code as a child who is given less good reasons and told merely that it is wrong (pp. 234–235).

An experiment by Aronson and Carlsmith (1963) nicely bears out the insufficient-deterrence notion. Three- and four-year-old children were individually brought into a playroom in which five rather attractive toys were placed on a table. After the child played briefly with each of the toys the experimenter obtained from him a preference ordering ranging from the most liked to the least liked toy. The toy that turned out to be second most-preferred was left on the table, while the remainder were spread around the room on the floor. The experimenter then told the child he had to leave for a few minutes but he would be back soon.

What he said at that point varied as a function of the experimental condition to which the child had been assigned. In the no-threat condition the experimenter told the child he could play with any of the toys in the room until the experimenter returned. He took the second-ranked toy with him as he left. In the severe-threat condition, the experimenter told the child he could play with any of the toys *except* the one on the table. Furthermore, he was told:

> I don't want you to play with the ———. If you play with it, I would be very angry. I would have to take all of my toys and go home and never come back again. You can play with all the others while I am gone, but if you played with the ———, I would think you were just a baby. I will be right back.

In the mild-threat condition the child was also forbidden to play with the second-ranked toy (the one on the table) along with the following admonition:

I don't want you to play with the ———. If you played with it, I would be annoyed. But you can play with all the others while I am gone and I will be right back.

The experimenter then observed the subject for 10 minutes through a one-way observation mirror. None of the children actually played with the forbidden toy, though some appeared tempted. When the experimenter returned, each child was asked to provide another preference ranking of the toys. If the hypothesis of insufficient deterrence is correct, we would expect the child to decrease his preference for the second-ranked toy in the mild-threat condition, relative to the other two conditions. It is here that the child should be motivated to develop extra reasons for not engaging in a forbidden behavior—including the "sour-grapes" reason that the toy isn't any good anyway. The results, presented in Table 3.1, offer strong support

Table 3.1. Change in Preference for Forbidden Toy [a]
(Adapted from Aronson and Carlsmith, 1963)

	Preference		
	Increased	Unchanged	Decreased
No-threat	7	4	0
Severe-threat	14	8	0
Mild-threat	4	10	8

[a] Difference between severe-threat and mild-threat conditions, $p < .003$.

for the hypothesis. In both severe and no-threat conditions, there was a noticeable trend toward increasing the preference for the forbidden toy, whereas in the mild-threat condition subjects either did not change or decreased their preference.

The link between devaluation of a toy and the development of an internalized prohibition would be clear if children in the mild-prohibition condition later declined to play with the forbidden toy when given the chance. Freedman (1965b) established this link in a study that also showed the long-term effects of insufficient deterrence. Individual second- to fourth-grade children were told by a male experimenter not to play with a very desirable battery-controlled robot, under either high or low threat for disobeying. They were given a five-minute free period during which the toy was present and available. During this period half of the subjects were left alone with five toys, including the robot, and half were not left alone. The latter subjects were considered a control group because, in view of the adult's continuing presence, playing with the robot was not a realistic temptation. Therefore, the child in the mild-prohibition, adult-present condition did not need to internalize the prohibition or invent reasons for not playing with the robot.

Approximately 40 days later, on the average, these same children were brought to the same experimental room containing the same toys, but everything else was done to make the second session appear unrelated to the first. This time the experimenter was a female. She told the child that she wanted him to copy some drawings; after the child complied she said she wanted to score them and while doing this the child could play with any of the toys that someone had left in the room. The main measure of internalization was whether the child in fact played with other toys and still avoided the robot. The results, omitting those children who played with none of the toys, are presented in Table 3.2. They indicate that internaliza-

Table 3.2. Number in Each Condition Who Played with Robot in Second Session (Adapted from Freedman, 1965b)

	Played	Did Not Play
Control		
Severe-threat	13	7
Mild-threat	14	1
Experimental		
Severe-threat	14	4
Mild-threat [a]	6	12

[a] Differs significantly from all other conditions.

tion of the prohibition was most common in the mild-threat condition where the first experimenter left the room. This is exactly what would be predicted.

Aronson and Carlsmith (1963) found that the toy was devalued in the mild-prohibition condition; Freedman (1965b) found very little evidence of devaluation of the robot. He suggests that self-control developed because the children convinced themselves that playing with the robot was immoral, not because the robot lost its attractiveness. Internalization may take different forms depending on the detailed circumstances surrounding insufficient deterrence, and perhaps the robot was simply too magnificent to permit substantial devaluation.

Mills (1958) provides more direct evidence that insufficient deterrence can produce a change in the moral evaluation of a particular class of behaviors. Sixth-grade students were (a) given a questionnaire to measure attitudes toward cheating, (b) strongly or weakly tempted by arranged circumstances to cheat in a contest, and (c) given the questionnaire on attitudes toward cheating a second time. Cheating could be easily detected by a given subject's pattern of answers, since an erroneous set of answers was provided for self-scoring purposes.

As expected, there were many more cheaters in the high-temptation condition than in the low. Of greater interest is the pattern of attitude change as a function of cheating in combination with the amount of temptation. When the temptation to cheat was high, those who did not cheat became appreciably more severe in their indictment of cheating than when the temptation to cheat was low. In contrast, cheaters showed little change in attitude when temptation was high, but became much more lenient toward cheating when the temptation was low.

Apparently, rewards that entice a person into transgression operate in just the opposite fashion from punishments administered. If the rewards derived from immoral behavior are great, a person has less need to justify his immorality. The cheater in the high temptation condition has sufficient (to him) justification for his immoral behavior. When temptation is low, on the other hand, the cheater's problem of self-justification becomes more severe. It is here that he changes toward condoning cheating. The non-cheaters showed a pattern like that shown by the children in Aronson and Carlsmith's (1963) experiment. When temptation is low (analogous to the severe-threat condition) there is little change in attitude. When temptation is high (analogous to the mild threat condition) there is much change to justify the behavioral reaction.

The socialization process is long and drawn out. There are many occasions in which similar responses are met with varying degrees of disapproval by parents and other agents, and there arises the question of the cumulative effects on self-control of different *patterns* of such disapproval. Festinger and Freedman (1964) extend their argument to cover the strength and consistency of deterrence over a longer time span. They propose, in effect, that deterrence that is always effective and stronger than the impulse will produce little or no internalized moral value. Deterrence that is effective half the time will not produce any generalized moral value either, since the person would be busy some of the time justifying his transgressions and busy the rest of the time justifying his morality. But in the range where deterrence is effective much but not all of the time, the internalization of moral values should be greatest. Deterrence is strong enough to insure that the transgression rarely occurs, but weak enough that the need to justify restraint is still present.

The Festinger and Freedman argument is reminiscent of the earlier discussion of the role of parental inconsistency in child rearing. It would, however, be misleading to suppose that consistency in the administration of rewards and punishments is necessarily bad or ineffective. The point is rather that dispositions acquired under circumstances that are highly dependent on external incentives will more rapidly extinguish when those incentives are removed than will dispositions acquired under more chaotic conditions. The socialized product of the more consistent environment, whose parents punish transgressions severely, reward proper behavior lavishly, or both, may be more inclined to transgress when he is not under surveillance; he may also be much better prepared to adjust to new circumstances and new challenges as he goes through life. His morality will be more flexible and he is more likely to redefine, periodically, the specific meaning of right and wrong behavior.

RESOURCE MEDIATION AND IDENTIFICATION

Certainly one of the most striking consequences of the socialization process is the fact that the child adopts many of the parent's own mannerisms and behavior patterns. The child's response dispositions are not only shaped by the direct application of rewards and punishments; they are shaped in more subtle ways by a process of modeling in which the child inadvertently takes over certain distinctive attributes that have been manifested in the parent's behavior. This modeling process is variously referred to as imitation, response matching, copying, or identification. For convenience, we shall use the last term, *identification,* to refer to *the general process whereby the attributes of another are internalized by the one.* Imitation, the reproduction of specific responses in specific situations to attain specific goals, will be more fully dealt with in the next chapter.

The term identification was made part of the psychological vocabulary by Freud. The Freudian analysis (scattered in many sources, see particularly Freud, 1940; and the excellent review by Bronfenbrenner, 1960) credited much of the momentum of the identification process to factors at work in the resolution of the Oedipus Complex. The male child, in particular, passes through a rather definite sequence of orientation with respect to his parents. The boy at first treats the mother in a rather pure and simple way as a love object. He wishes to incorporate the mother, to possess her, and later to love her in a more sexual way. However, it is more and more borne in upon the child that the mother is primarily the sexual possession of the father. This recognition coincides with growing fears in the boy that he will be castrated if he does not in effect renounce all sexual claims on the mother. Out of this combination of factors, therefore, the son suppresses the rivalrous, antagonistic feelings that have been developing toward his father, and instead identifies with him by taking on his characteristics and his values. In the wake of this identification arises the conscience, which Freud felt was one of the two major components of the superego, the other being the ego ideal. In this way, love for the mother is converted into identification with the father through the medium of a fear of decisive physical injury. Although different in its particulars, his account of the female "Oedipus Complex" follows similar reasoning.

A crucial aspect of superego development is clearly the conversion of a fear of certain objective, painful consequences into feelings of guilt or self-punishment. As Freud put it, "The external restrictions are introjected so that the superego takes the place of the parental function, and thence forward observes, guides and threatens the ego in just the same way as the parents acted to the child before" (1933, pp. 89–90).

Probably the Freudian account should not be accepted too literally, though the preceding paragraphs hardly do justice to the subtlety and power of his reasoning. What is especially interesting in Freud's account of superego development is the emphasis on the child's ambivalence as an impetus behind identification. The boy loves and hates his father, but his developing ego structure will not allow these incompatible feelings to exist side by side. The child resolves his ambivalence, therefore, by repressing the negative component and consolidating the positive feelings through identification. This leads to the paradoxical but important possibility that the more intense the unconscious feelings of hostility toward the father (or mother) the more rigid and emphatic the identification with him (or her).

For Freud the concept of identification referred to several related human tendencies, and the term was variously used in different contexts. Freud distinguished identification arising out of loss or withdrawal of the love object from identification with persons who are actively punitive or potentially so. Bronfenbrenner (1960) has suggested the label *anaclitic* (from the Greek "leaning on") to refer to the former kind of identification. The latter notion was captured by Anna Freud's (1946) explicit reference to "identification with the aggressor." In her account she cited a number of instances in which children grimaced and took on the aggressive demeanor of those who were aggressing against them. By identifying with those who may attack us, we quell our anxieties and in a magical way take on the power of the aggressive agent.

Mowrer (1950) has promoted Lair's (1949) distinction between "developmental" and "defensive" identification, which is similar to that between anaclitic and aggressive identification. Whereas Freud was quite aware that through identification the child acquires responses and attitudes other than those primitive injunctions contained in the superego, he did not really give full or systematic treatment to the entire range of identification possibilities. Mowrer's distinction emphasizes the difference between imitative behaviors based on love and gratification on the one hand, and behaviors adopted in response to fear on the other hand. Developmental identification, he feels, arises out of the problem-solving and reinforcement experiences normal to childhood. Because she has been frequently associated with gratification and the reduction of tension, the mother acquires secondary reinforcing properties for the child. The child sooner or later begins to reproduce aspects of the mother's behavior because they are intrinsically satisfying. This reproduction maintains the presence of the satisfying parent when the parent is, in fact, unavailable. Defensive identification is more closely related to the Freudian account of the response to ambivalence arising in the Oedipus situation. As the child grows older, he is confronted increasingly with parental demands and restrictions, and generally with the exercise of the potentially threatening power of the parents. The child is motivated to identify with the parents, partly to reduce the threat inherent in his own relative powerlessness and partly to produce the kinds of behavior that will gain him acceptance and protection.

Mowrer suggests that both kinds of identification occur in response to frustration:

> But the different nature of the frustration in the two instances is noteworthy. In the one case it arises from a sense of helplessness and loneliness: the parents or parent-person is *absent* and the infant wishes he were *present*. In the other case, the frustration arises rather from interference and punishment: the parent or parent-person is *present* and the infant wishes he were *absent* but the latter wish brings the average child into intolerable conflict: while he hates the parent or his disciplinary action he also loves the parent and experiences acute anxiety at the prospect of his really being separated, physically or emotionally, from him (or her) (1950, p. 592).

Since the distinction between the two kinds of identification has appeared in the discussions of many writers, we shall examine the evidence relating to each class or type of identification.

Anaclitic Identification

If it is true that the child's identification with the parent is strengthened by actual or threatened withdrawal of love, then certain testable consequences should follow. If the child never or always experiences love, there is no basis for anaclitic identification. The child who is never loved or nurtured has no need to recreate in fantasy the presence of the parent. The child who is never deprived of the parent's love or even his presence has no need to identify either. If we assume that deprivation, frustration, and parental absence are inevitable conditions of family life, then we are left with the suggestive proposition that the greater the parental nurturance (up to some point that is rarely reached) the greater is the tendency to identify. This proposition is similar to Sears' (1957) argument that high and early nurturance results in a strong dependency drive that, when frustrated, gives rise to "fantasy role playing," or identification.

Several students of the socialization process have proposed that the strength of identification is a function of the type of punishment to which the child is primarily exposed. Type of punishment may, in turn, be highly correlated with degree of nurturance. Whiting and Child (1953), for example, distinguish between love-oriented and nonlove-oriented disciplinary techniques. Included under the former heading are: denial of love, threatened denial of love, and threatened ostracism. Each of these techniques exploits the fear that parents will withdraw their love or isolate the child if he displeases them. In contrast are those techniques of discipline that attempt to control by a more physical means. The parents do not exploit the child's need for their affection, but constrain and control him by shaming or applying physical punishment. Love-oriented punishment clearly involves the manipulation of nurturance and therefore we would expect to find a relationship between the parent's tendency to use love-oriented techniques of discipline and the child's tendency to identify.

Incidental Identification

The evidence supporting the general proposition relating identification and nurturance is not overwhelming, but it is to some extent supportive. One problem, of course, is to develop reasonable indices of identification. The most straightforward measures derive from observations of the similarity between various behaviors of a model and actions of the potential identifier. An experimental study by Bandura and Huston (1961) exemplifies this straightforward approach and provides strong evidence for the importance of nurturance as a precondition for imitation—and, by inference, identification.

In one condition of the Bandura and Huston experiment nursery school children interacted with a highly nurturant and responsive adult accomplice. The adult escorted a child to a room that was full of toys, invited him to play with the toys, sat on the floor with him, and entered into his play in a warm and attentive manner. In the other condition the adult was aloof and avoided interacting with the child. After leading the child into the toy-filled room, she busied herself with paper work at a desk in the far corner of the room. These experimental social interactions between adult and child took place in two 15-minute sessions separated by an interval of approximately five days. Following the establishment of these preconditions the experimenter took each child and adult into another room at the end of the second session.

In this room the experimenter gave instructions concerning a diverting task that would occupy the child's attention while permitting opportunities for his "incidental imitation" of certain of the adult's actions. The task was a discrimination exercise, so planned that the adult was to choose which of two boxes contained a small multicolored sticker with a picture of animals or flowers. After the adult made his choice, the child was also given an opportunity to choose. He could, therefore, look in the same box as the adult or into the other box. Whereas the proportion of imitative versus nonimitative choices was of some interest to the experimenters, they were primarily concerned with the subtler imitation of the manner in which the choice was made. In order to be able to distinguish between the child's imitative responses and those that were coincidentally similar to the model's behavior, the adult model behaved in an explicit and somewhat unusual way:

... on each discrimination trial, the model exhibited certain verbal, motor, and aggressive behaviors which were totally irrelevant to the performance of the task to which the subject's attention was directed. At the starting point, for example, the model remarked, "Here I go," and then marched slowly toward the box containing the stickers repeating, "March, march, march." On the lid of each box was a small rubber doll which the model knocked off aggressively when she reached the designated box. She then paused briefly, remarked, "Open the box," removed one sticker and pasted it on a pastoral scene that hung on the wall immediately behind the boxes. The model terminated the trial by replacing the doll on the lid of the container (Bandura and Huston, 1961, p. 313).

Children who attempted the discrimination task after observing the nurturant model showed more incidental imitation of the marching and associated verbal responses than did those subjects who performed after the nonnurturant model. There was also more imitation of aggression in the former group, but the differences here were not significant. Furthermore, those subjects rated as highly dependent, based on extensive observations of their behavior in the nursery-school setting, showed more incidental imitation than did low-dependent subjects, thus lending support to Sears' (1957) hypothesis relating identification to dependency drive. There were no differences between the two experimental groups in performance on the discrimination learning task, where imitation was rewarded. Presumably, solving the discrimination problem was a more general function of the children's eagerness to make the correct (imitative) response and thus earn the reward.

The Bandura and Huston (1961) study shows that interaction with a nurturant model does affect subsequent imitative behavior, but its support for the broader proposition of anaclitic identification is at best only suggestive. For one thing, there is some question whether "incidental" imitation can be equated with the more fundamental process of identification. Are the effects of two relatively brief interaction episodes comparable to the effects of more sustained and more complex relationships? In addition, the theoretical notion underlying the concept of anaclitic identification would be more precisely confirmed if a further condition were provided that involved the provision of nurturance by a model followed by its abrupt withdrawal.

Such a condition should lead to more incidental imitation than the present nurturance condition. In spite of these reservations the experiment is indeed suggestive and points up the acute sensitivity that children have to the reactions of nurturant adults in their environment. The behavior of adult actors in the immediate environment is readily picked up by the child, especially when he has experienced gratifying relations with the adult in the past.

Identification and Guilt

While incidental imitation may serve as one fairly direct laboratory index of the tendency to identify, another more indirect index is evidence of the capacity to be guilty. Many students of the socialization process have reasoned that refraining from immoral behavior when not under surveillance, or willingness to accept responsibility for one's own errors, reflect the capacity to feel guilty. Since guilt implies internalization of the prohibitions originally imposed by others, it is generally assumed that the capacity to feel guilty increases when identification with such moral arbiters as a parent increases. Thus it follows that the extent to which a person's feelings are characterized by guilt should correlate with the extent to which love-oriented or psychological, versus physical, techniques of punishment were emphasized in his child training history.

In 1933 MacKinnon (in Murray, 1938) placed individual college-graduate subjects in a problem-solving situation where a booklet containing the answers was available. However, the subjects were permitted to look at some of the answers and prohibited from looking at others. A concealed observer noted that about one-half of the subjects in fact violated the prohibition by examining the answers they were not to see. Other evidence about the subjects revealed that the nonviolators were prone to much stronger guilt feelings in daily living than the violators. In later interviews with some of the subjects, all of whom were male, MacKinnon found that 74 percent of the violators showed more preference and fondness for their mothers than for their fathers, whereas only 36 percent of the nonviolators did. The fathers, in other words, were more favored and respected by the nonviolators than the violators. In addition, the nonviolators reported having received a greater proportion of psychological versus physical discipline from their fathers than did the violators. There was little difference as far as punishment from the mothers was concerned. These data are quite consistent with the hypothesis that the nonviolators, who were more prone to guilt feelings, were also punished in a more love-oriented way by the father and were presumably more closely identified with him.

Whiting and Child (1953) tried to explore the hypothesis that love-oriented discipline is related to guilt by examining cross-cultural indices of the former and correlating these with ratings of a person's "responsibility" for his illness. Some cultures tend to view sickness as a sign of weakness or the result of some act of negligence or immorality on the part of the sick person; other cultures attribute the cause of illness to some external agency such as malevolent spirits or hostile neighbors. Whiting and Child felt that patient "responsibility" for illness was one possible index of the extent to which guilt feelings were characteristic in the culture. They did find a relationship between patient responsibility and the prevalence of love-oriented punishment, as predicted, but the relationship was of borderline statistical significance. Two dissertations under Whiting's direction produced additional results supporting the hypothesis:

Hollenberg (1953), for individual differences within a Pueblo Indian group and Faigin (1953), for individual differences within a rural white community, strikingly confirmed the relationship between generalization of guilt feelings and relative predominance of love-oriented techniques of punishment (Child, 1954, p. 684).

Further confirmation of the identification-guilt hypothesis came from a survey by Glueck and Glueck (1950) who report a highly significant difference between parents of delinquents and nondelinquents in the use of physical punishment, the former being more likely to discipline their children in physical ways. Levin (1952) also found a negative relation between physical punishment and identification within our own society, thus adding further support to the general hypothesis that the capacity for guilt is the end product of a chain leading from love-oriented punishment through consequent strong identifications with the same-sex parent.

Some evidence supporting the hypothesis that the capacity for guilt does not develop when the conditions of socialization are less than ideal for identification has been presented by Bandura and Walters (1959) in *Adolescent Aggression*. Their study involved lengthy interviews with 52 adolescent boys and their parents. Half of these boys had histories of aggressive antisocial behavior; this group was matched to the rest of the boys on all related factors except for the history of antisocial behavior. By rating the interview responses on a number of dimensions, the investigators sought to provide evidence to account for the differential development of antisocial aggressiveness.

Bandura and Walters present ample evidence from interview data in support of their main hypothesis that the antisocial boys have a history of greater parental rejection than the control boys, and *also*, that there is more evidence of punishment for dependency strivings among the former. The antisocial boys tend to come from homes in which the parents are more cold and distant, and in which the boys clearly feel more rejected than those in the control group. Though dependency behavior was to some extent encouraged by the mother in both samples, the fathers of boys in the antisocial group tended to ignore or punish dependent overtures and were less inclined to share activities with their sons than were fathers of boys in the control group. Thus in the absence of nurturance, especially given the additional fact that dependency is punished by the same-sex parent, the boys presumably failed to develop the appropriate internal controls over their aggression. Without such controls there is nothing to prevent a boy from being aggressive as soon as he is out from under the external controls applied to prevent aggression in the home.

Considerable further research is certainly needed to analyze variations in developmental identification and to explore their consequences. It seems fair to conclude, however, that the child who comes from a family in which the provision and withdrawal of love is an issue is more apt to "recreate the presence of the parent in fantasy" than children from homes in which nurturance is low or the manipulation of love is not an issue. Out of such identification emerges the capacity to develop guilty feelings into internalized controls over socially unacceptable behavior.

Defensive Identification

The notion of identification in response to the threat of attack, or identification with the aggressor, is an intriguing one because of its paradoxical features. It seems quite reasonable to imitate those whom we like and try to emulate them; it seems less reasonable to speak of modeling ourselves after someone who threatens us. And yet there are strong suggestions that "defensive identification" not only plays a role in child-parent relations but may at times characterize adult responses to extreme stress. In his observations of reactions to imprisonment in a Nazi concentration camp Bettleheim (1943) noted several instances in which prisoners, after extreme physical and moral abuse, begin to take on the attributes and mannerisms of their jailors. There are strong hints that at least some Americans became "collaborators" through this same mechanism of identification with the aggressor in Korean prisoner-of-war camps (Schein, 1958; Kelman, 1961).

Bandura and Walters (1963) express considerable skepticism concerning this phenomenon. A strict interpretation of identification with the aggressor would be that the child's imitative aggression reflects a rather magical, fantasied self-protection. Bandura and Walters point out that the imitation by a child of adult aggression can stem from other than "magically defensive" sources. The child's aggression may be an instrumental reaction to parental aggression—he expresses to them the anger they have expressed to him as a way of fighting back. It is always difficult, furthermore, to prove that the identifier is not being reinforced by others for taking over the aggressor's attributes. This may have been the case, for example, in the concentration camp observed by Bettleheim. The prisoners' imitation of Gestapo behavior may have stemmed in part from a desire to escape group punishments that often followed the transgression of individuals. In this case, then, what might appear to be identification with the aggressor may actually be seen as an instrumental response designed to keep others from actions that invite reprisal.

There is no question that aggressive behavior manifested by an adult is readily imitated by children. Several studies by Bandura and his colleagues (Bandura and Huston, 1961; Bandura, Ross, and Ross, 1961; Bandura, Ross, and Ross, 1963a) make this abundantly clear. The last of these studies shows how children readily attend to and retain in memory rather elaborate and subtle features of experimentally staged adult aggressive behavior. This will be true regardless of whether that behavior is in turn punished. However, the child will not *perform* the learned aggressive actions if the model has been punished for his aggression. Aggressive imitation, then, seems subject to many of the same variables that control the imitation of other responses. The distinctive thing about aggression, perhaps, is that the child will readily identify with the incidental details of the behavior manifested by an aggressive model. It is as if the model releases a tendency to be aggressive that is very near expression anyway, and this tendency is then shaped in detail by observed actions of the model.

Although evidence for an explicit interpretation of identification with the aggressor is sparse, two closely related theories incorporate some of the defensive features of aggressive identification, as well as some of the features of anaclitic identification, and interesting empirical data bearing on their validity. One theory (Mussen and Distler, 1959; Maccoby, 1959) emphasizes the social power of the model, and the other (Whiting, 1959, 1960) emphasizes the child's envy of the model's status. Because the theories are very similar, we shall describe only Whiting's theory, including Maccoby's relevant comments where appropriate.

Whiting contends that identification occurs because of the child's dependence on the socialization agent for the resources he controls. The socialization agent may give these resources (food, solace, praise), withhold them (restrict freedom, withdraw love), or deprive the child of them (spank, criticize, remove privileges). *Which* of these courses of action the adult will follow in a given situation is of vital significance to the child. Thus it is important that he learn to predict the behavior of the "resource mediator." This *cognizance,* as Whiting calls it, is a precondition of the identification process. The child must "know" the role of the parent before he can identify with it. Maccoby also stresses the primary importance of the child's learning to predict behavior sequences of the adult. We learn to anticipate the actions of others in order to coordinate our actions with theirs. The degree of such cognizance will presumably be a function of the amount of interaction required between the two persons involved.

Cognizance is an important precondition for identification to take place, but so is the wish to perform the other's role. This wish, the motive to emulate the resource mediator, derives from the child's envy of the mediator's status. Status in this case refers to the degree to which the model has control over resources, relative to the child's control. The completely indulged child will not identify because his ready access to resources implies that he himself has control over them.

He will, on the contrary, envy the status of those resource mediators who withhold resources from him, deprive him of resources that were formerly his, and consume or enjoy those resources in his presence. This process may be termed *envy of resource mediator*. If the resource mediator withholds a resource from a child and gives it to a third person, this third person will occupy the envied status. Special instances of such a state of affairs are sibling and Oedipal rivalry. We predict that as soon as a child comes to envy a status he will attempt to play the role associated with such a status (Whiting, 1960, p. 118).

Even if status envy and cognizance are both present, the chances are that the child will not be able to play the role immediately and with appropriate skill. His size and immaturity and the various cultural rules that restrict a child from performing adult roles insure that he will not immediately turn into an accomplished mimic who performs all the components of an adult role. But the more a child envies the status of another, the more he will covertly practice the role played by that other. He indulges in a fantasy in which he sees himself as the envied person controlling and consuming the valued resources of which he has been deprived.

Why might this be so, and what function does such fantasy serve? Maccoby suggests:

Presumably, because there will be numerous occasions upon which the arousal of a need in ego will provide the occasion for him to think about an action of alter's. Suppose the child is hungry; if he lives in a household where he is allowed to go to the refrigerator and get the ingredients for a sandwich, he will not engage in any covert role practice. If he is not allowed to do this, but must ask his mother, then, when he becomes hungry, he will think about asking his mother for a sandwich and will imagine a number of things she might say in response, "It's too soon before dinner," or, "If you finish cleaning your room, you may have it." He may decide not to ask her for the sandwich after all, but meanwhile he will have practiced some of her characteristic responses, and added an increment to the habit strength of these responses in his own repertoire. If most things that an individual wants are not under his control but under the control of others, then presumably much of the vicarious trial-and-error that he engages in must involve his trying out various approaches to getting the help or avoiding the censure of others, and imagining the probable responses to these approaches. . . . our position says that a child should covertly rehearse both the rewarding and the punishing actions characteristic of his parents, for both are highly relevant to him in guiding his plans about future actions (Maccoby, 1959, pp. 245–246).

The latent practice described by both Maccoby and Whiting prepares the child for the assumption of adult roles when he approaches adult status. Thus patterns of identification with the parent that are learned in early childhood may assert themselves many years later. On the other hand, the child may adopt roles that are reciprocal or complementary to adult roles, while covertly practicing the latter.

The status-envy hypothesis points to defensive identification in that taking over the attributes of the envied person forestalls deprivation of resources and may increase the likelihood of potential resources being made available. In other words, the child who emulates a powerful parent in fantasy becomes better prepared to cope with that parent and to avoid the dire circumstances of punishment and deprivation.

The evidence for the status-envy hypothesis is either anecdotal or indirect. Whiting himself (1959) examined cross-cultural data to test the hypothesis that identification between father and child would be strongest in those cultures where the father was a regular member of the household. He reasoned that the child would identify with the father to the extent that he saw him as a rival for the love and attention of the mother. This perception of rivalry would be greatest in the monogamous nuclear family (like the family in our own culture), next greatest in the monogamous extended family (where all primary relatives live together), less in polygynous families where the father rotates his domicile from wife to wife, and least in the polygynous family where the father lives by himself or with groups of other men. As his index of identification Whiting again chose the responsibility assumed by the patient in the culture for any illnesses incurred, implying a capacity for the development of personal guilt. Whiting's hypothesis was confirmed: patient sense of responsibility was greatest in the monogamous nuclear family, least in the polygynous mother-child family, and the two other classes of families fell between.

In other investigations it has generally been found that in homes where the father is absent for long periods of time (because of war or business demands), the son develops characteristics that are under normal circumstances more common in girls. Thus Bach (1946) found that the father-fantasies of boys whose fathers were away during wartime were more similar to those of girls than were the fantasies of father-present boys. Sears, Pintler, and Sears (1946) found that father-absent nursery-school boys were less frequently aggressive in a doll-play situation than father-present boys. By testing and interviewing the children of Norwegian sailors, Lynn and Sawrey (1959) established that father-absent boys (compared to father-present boys in a control group) were more immature, tended to be more dependent on the mother, and were more insecure in their interactions with peers. Finally, Whiting (unpublished) found that Harvard students whose fathers had been absent and in the service during the first critical years of their life were more apt than father-present students to be higher in verbal than in quantitative aptitude test scores. The average girl is higher in verbal than in quantitative aptitude; the average boy is higher in quantitative than in verbal skills. Thus it appears that male students who did not have fathers in the early years of development acquired a stronger identification with some subtle aspects of the maternal intellect.

Although the absence of the father for a significant period of time obviously has important consequences for the development of male children, it is not clear that these consequences relate to the status-envy hypothesis. It may be true that the child identifies with the father who is present because presence implies rivalry, but it is certainly possible that his mere availability is significant and that rivalry has little to do with it. This is especially plausible since many tendencies of the male child to imitate characteristics of the father are presumably reinforced by the mother and by others in the society. What is needed is some way of holding exposure to the father constant while varying the extent to which he arouses feelings of rivalry in the child.

Bandura, Ross, and Ross (1963b) attempted to do something like this in an experimental situation. They exposed nursery school children to two adult models in one of two conditions:

(1) *Adult Consumer Condition.* While the child watched helplessly, one adult offered the other adult toys from his large and attractive store.

(2) *Child Consumer Condition.* The child was offered the attractive toys to play with while the other adult looked on.

This initial phase of the experiment was followed by a discrimination learning task similar to that described above in the Bandura and Huston study. The adults performed each trial first, and then the child had an opportunity when it came his turn to imitate various special moves and verbalizations of either of the adults. The experiment showed that the adult who dispensed the toys was imitated to a greater extent than the other adult, regardless of whether the other adult was the consumer of rewards or the ignored person in the child consumer condition.

Bandura, Ross, and Ross (1963b) contend that these results fail to support the status-envy hypothesis, since the child identifies with the dispenser of rewards rather than the recipient. However, the status-envy hypothesis is ambiguous on this point. It is not clear from Whiting's statements whether the child should identify with the rival or with the dispenser. The child should, after all, envy both statuses, because both involve control over resources he lacks. We believe that the experiment is not a crucial test of the status-envy hypothesis for a number of reasons, but the study does point up the ambiguity of Whiting's formulation.

The results shed additional light on the nurturance hypothesis discussed earlier. Because the child identifies with the resource dispenser, whether he receives the resources or not, it seems clear that nurturance and the power to nurture are two different things. The Bandura, Ross, and Ross (1963b) study suggests that it is the *power to nurture* that elicits identification, and not the experience of having been nurtured by the particular model.

It is clear that we have only begun to understand the factors involved in the identification process. Investigation is hampered by the fact that identification refers to the incorporation of personal qualities that are not necessarily reflected in behavior. Also, identification is alleged to be a rather drastic and permanent coming-to-terms with significant figures in the family group, figures with whom there are long and continuous interactions. Thus experiments that study the variables that condition imitation in laboratory situations may or may not be directly relevant to our understanding of the identification process. Cross-cultural studies, with their indirect indices of identification and other subtle processes, have their own limitations as arbiters of theoretical preference. Nevertheless, research in the socialization area has become increasingly sensitized to important theoretical issues, and we may be cautiously optimistic that the expanding volume of both experimental and field researches being conducted will reduce some of our uncertainties about the mysteries of identification.

SUMMARY

The socialization process refers to the internalization of those values, beliefs, and ways of viewing the world that are prevalent in a society or group. In the present chapter we have restricted ourselves largely to the topic of child socialization, and we have been especially concerned with the internalization of cultural values. A consequential feature of human existence is the relatively long period during which the young of the species are dependent on others for surviving and prospering. In fact, this entire book emphasizes that dependence on others continues throughout the human lifetime. It is instructive to distinguish between dependence on others for their role in the direct mediation of outcomes (*effect dependence*) and dependence on others for information about the nature of reality and the adequacy of our abilities for dealing with reality (*information dependence*). Our emphasis here has been on effect dependence as a condition for the internalization of values. In the next chapter we focus the spotlight on information dependence and cognitive development.

It is not difficult to account for the acquisition of values by referring to the standard phenomena of classical and instrumental conditioning. Either form of learning involves the attachment of value to a previously neutral stimulus condition. Without question, the average parent plays an active role in establishing the conditions for learning and value acquisition. As the child grows to endow more and more objects and events with positive or negative value (or, to put it another way, as more stimuli acquire secondary reinforcing properties) he becomes more susceptible to control by others. The increase in this susceptibility clearly opens him to the shaping influence of adults, teachers, and friends, all of whom represent and transmit the values of the culture. But the account of internalization is far from complete when we recapitulate the standard processes of learning or value acquisition. One of the intriguing mysteries of child socialization is that, once acquired, values often show an unusual persistence.

It is widely believed that the basic components of an individual's personality are formed in the early years of family life, and that the person is never again as susceptible to social influence as he was as a young child. This resistance to change, or to "extinction," may reflect the fact that response dispositions learned under rather chaotic, aperiodically reinforcing conditions do not readily disappear when conditions change. A logical reason for this may be that the individual cannot distinguish between the conditions of learning (where reinforcement is present at least some of the time) and the conditions of extinction (where reinforcement is absent). Lawrence and Festinger have contended that this explanation is inadequate. They have suggested that individuals may persist in making unrewarded responses if the tendency to respond is initially acquired under conditions involving a fair amount of effort. This effort-justification hypothesis may account for the development of special preferences for certain features of the learning situation, which is a form of internalization.

Not only must the socialized individual learn to channel his preferences toward certain culturally appropriate activities and goals; he must also inhibit responses that might disrupt or threaten the group. Once again internalization is involved: the individual must move from a condition of responsiveness to external rewards and punishments to a condition of internal control over his impulses. One aspect of this development undoubtedly involves the capacity to symbolize future rewards and punishments so that they will be taken into account when the individual is tempted to transgress to achieve immediate gratification. A number of studies were presented in which preference for small immediate rewards over larger delayed rewards was shown to be related to delinquency, cheating, and certain family conditions conducive to the development of a lack of trust in the promises of others. But, again, the secret of internalizing controls may lie in the patterning and timing of rewards and punishments. Internalization may result when the child is given enough reasons not to do something immoral, but when the reasons are flimsy enough that he must develop additional reasons himself. Severe threats will keep a child from engaging in forbidden behavior, but mild threats may be more effective in setting the stage for internalized abstinence.

Many of the most dramatic aspects of child socialization are in some way tied to identification: the parent presents many mannerisms and behavior patterns that are adopted by the child. Certainly included in this presentation are the adult's values, which the child assimilates at more or less full strength. Whether more or less seems to depend on the extent to which love and nurturance are present in the home; the greater the nurturance, the stronger the identification with the nurturant parent. Theoretically, identification also depends on the extent to which the giving of love is contingent on good behavior, and there is some evidence that the capacity to feel guilty (taken as an index of identification) is greater in homes characterized by love-oriented discipline than in nonlove-oriented homes. In addition to identification arising from the need for love and the desire to maintain the fantasied presence of the loving parent (*anaclitic identification*) we have also discussed *defensive identification*—the tendency to identify with the aggressor. There is some anecdotal evidence in support of the notion that we identify with others to absorb magically some of their power, but there are few if any straightforward tests of the defensive identification hypothesis. One version of this hypothesis, Whiting's proposal that people identify with those whose status they envy, has received indirect support from correlational and anthropological studies but much additional research is needed to rule out plausible alternative interpretations.

CHAPTER FOUR

Information Dependence and Cognitive Socialization

Organisms inherently react to stimuli in the environment. As we move up the phylogenetic scale from more primitive organisms to man, specialization of bodily structure and functions increases. The broadest division of bodily functions, as any psychology student knows, is the division between receptor and effector functions—between functions concerned with stimulus input and those concerned with response output. As to receptor functions, the human organism has highly refined structures that are specifically adapted to receive different kinds of energy. Certain sensory organs convert light into sensations of brightness and color, others turn sound energy into sensations of loudness and pitch, still others control sensations of touch, taste, and pain.

The social psychologist is not likely to be particularly interested in the sensory processes as such, but it is well to keep in mind that all experience of environmental events originates at the specially adapted sensory end organs. A truism that must be mentioned is that events that do *not* provide appropriate energy to be transformed at the various organs of sensory input cannot form a part of the organism's experience. Events that provide such energy are the raw materials for stimuli. Such stimuli may trigger reflex responses, as in knee jerk, eyeblink, and the startle pattern. Or they may give rise to thoughts or cognitions; they may be represented in the cortex of the brain and enter into associative relations with remembered stimulus events, give rise to interpretations, and so on. To put it loosely, the human organism has innate capacities to take in information and either respond directly to it, record and store it, or transform it.

To say that organisms have the capacity to register and make various uses of information is to take but a small step toward understanding the origins of man's information dependence. At various places in this book we shall emphasize the intimate interrelations between information and action. Here we shall be very brief. People, and probably all of the higher animals, gear their information-seeking activities to the possibilities for acting in their environment. Action proceeds from some form of decision among alternatives. These decisions are often implicit, and it would be hard to prove that they always exist as a preface to action. But this is an instance when we assume the existence of implicit decisions because interesting research consequences follow from the assumption. In order to make a decision among alternative courses of action, the actor naturally uses whatever information he has about the consequences of the various alternatives, their costs to him, his ability to carry out the action, and so on. We might say that the actor not only has the capacity to receive information but also *needs* all the relevant information he can get.

There is growing evidence that all higher vertebrates have unlearned, or early and easily learned, tendencies toward active information-seeking (White, 1959). In different organisms this information-seeking takes different forms. Higher animals show striking development, undoubtedly augmented by learning, of varied information-seeking activities. As the next step in the search for the origins of information dependence let us review briefly the nature of the more primitive information-seeking activities in animals and man.

Exploration, Curiosity, and Investigation

Berlyne (1960) provides an excellent summary of the evidence on the apparently universal tendencies of higher animals to explore their environments. He includes under the heading of *exploratory behavior* those responses that afford access to environmental information not previously available. It is assumed that this increased access to information is not a chance by-product of behaviors that are instrumental in reducing the common drives of hunger, thirst, pain avoidance, and so on. Exploratory behavior is a kind of residual category for those responses that cannot be easily accounted for in terms of conventional drive-reducing rewards and that have the additional property of providing greater contact with environmental stimulation.

Berlyne divides exploratory behavior into three major classes: orienting responses, locomotor exploration, and investigatory responses.

Orienting Responses include the "investigatory reflex," a term used by Pavlov (1927) to refer to the highly adaptive tendency in animals and men to orient the appropriate sense organs to the slightest change in surroundings. The basic feature of orienting responses is an increase of attention and acuity stemming from such bodily adjustments as repositioning the sense organs (turning the head in the direction of a sound), changing the sensory organ's state of receptivity (dilation of pupils), increased muscular tonus, expansion of blood vessels in the head, indications of arousal in electrically measured brain activity, and so on. In short, the orienting responses involve a complex set of reactions designed to prepare the organism for efficient reception and attentive processing of information.

Locomotor Exploration involves movement in space when such movement seems to be governed only by the novelty, complexity, or intensity of available stimulation. Thus rats cross an electric grid and absorb a painful shock in order to explore an intricate maze containing miscellaneous objects, preferring irregular or complexly patterned objects to those of more balanced structure.

Investigatory Responses involve active manipulation of an object in the course of inspecting it. These responses expose certain facets of the object to more intense scrutiny. It is not difficult to train an animal to produce stimulus cues that inform him of the correct response. Kelleher (1958) trained chimpanzees to press a telegraph key, which was followed by the appearance of either a red light, signaling that food could be obtained by pressing a second key, or a blue light, signaling that pressing the second key would be fruitless. The building in of information-seeking behavior by reinforcement, so that it has a specific instrumental value in the situation, is referred to by Berlyne as *extrinsic investigation. Intrinsic investigatory responses*—those having no apparent problem-solving function—provide greater intrigue and mystery for the psychologist. Even such lowly animals as mice and rats appear to learn in order to receive a change in stimulation, even if it is only a rise in illumination. Monkeys and apes, as would be expected, engage in a greater variety of manipulative responses to novel objects in their environment.

Investigatory behavior in human infants and children is too common to require special documentation. Its primitive origins may lie, as Piaget (1936) suggests, in "circular reactions" marked by a response (squeezing a toy duck), a reaction from the environment (a squeaky "quack"), and then a repetition of the response that produced the environmental change. At five to seven months the child will pull away a piece of cloth that blocks his view. At eight to ten months he will look for objects that are out of sight in places where they are usually found. The relatively ritualistic quality of the early circular reaction gives way at about eleven months to more systematic experimentation with the novel properties of objects. It seems as if the child is trying to produce as many different effects as he can by holding, pinching, twirling, or dropping objects. At least, the presence of surprising stimuli produced by his actions seems to keep him intrigued and motivated to explore further.

White (1959) feels that there is a whole range of activities, such as exploration, grasping, and manipulative experimentation, that have a common biological significance: they are all part of a process whereby the child or animal learns to interact effectively with his environment. But he does not engage in these activities *in order to* prepare for the future;

they are motivated in their own right. White proposes the term "effectance motivation" because the child or animal seems motivated to discover the effects of his responses on the environment. "Putting it picturesquely," White says, ". . . the effectance urge represents what the neuromuscular system wants to do when it is otherwise unoccupied [with urgent demands from other motive sources] or is gently stimulated by the environment" (1959, p. 321). In other words, in periods between goal-seeking activities aroused by thirst, hunger, or sex, the child or animal engages in recurring transactions with his environment, transactions that are perpetuated by novelty or uncertainty. "Interest wanes when action begins to have less effect; effectance motivation subsides when a situation has been explored to the point that it no longer presents new possibilities" (p. 322).

Psychological experimentation in this area is difficult and the results are often inconclusive. As the child grows older it becomes increasingly hard to distinguish between his extrinsic information-seeking—the search for clues indicating the existence or location of reinforcements—and more intrinsic curiosity. The importance of intrinsic curiosity as a motivating condition is illustrated in an experiment by Mittman and Terrell (1964). In this experiment first- and second-grade children were given the task of pointing to one of three blocks as "correct." The blocks differed from one another either in form or size. If the child picked the correct block (e.g., a cube among different forms) he was allowed to draw a line between two dots in a connect-the-dots puzzle.

By pretesting it was established that no child of this age could tell the content of the finished drawing before connecting at least 30 dots. Presumably the subjects were motivated to continue selecting the correct block by a persisting interest in what the drawing might be. The experimenter varied the extent of the subjects' curiosity by telling them at different points what the complete drawing actually represented. Subjects in the low-curiosity condition were told at the beginning that the dots, when connected, would make an elephant. Subjects in the moderate-curiosity group were given the same information after eight dots had been connected, and subjects in the high-curiosity group were told only after 29 dots. The results showed that avoidance of errors was greatest in the high-curiosity group, next in the moderate-, and least in the low-curiosity group. The study appears to demonstrate that children can be motivated to improve their performance on one task by letting them slake their intrinsic curiosity about an otherwise unrelated stimulus pattern.

There seems to be little question that animals, children, and presumably adults, too, can be motivated by curiosity alone under certain general conditions. Although we are far from being able to spell out the nature of these conditions, Berlyne (1960) makes a constructive proposal about the variables responsible for epistemic behavior. Epistemic behavior is the term he chooses to cover all behavior that augments knowledge. Exploratory behavior may or may not result in the acquisition of knowledge; epistemic behavior is proposed as a further refinement of more primitive tendencies toward exploration.

Implicit in Berlyne's theory of epistemic behavior is the assumption that human exploration and investigation become more selective as the child grows older, and information-seeking becomes more closely linked to decision and action. We do not seek out information, according to Berlyne, unless we are suffering from some conceptual conflict. Conceptual conflict is not easily defined, but the term refers to a condition of the person in which two or more symbolic response tendencies are incompatible. We may have reasons to believe and other reasons to disbelieve the same statements. We may have reason to believe X as well as Y, but X and Y are mutually exclusive and both cannot be true. Or we may perceive an object or animal that possesses features of two different classes—the same stimulus can be ambiguously described by either of two concepts. In each of these cases of conceptual conflict, epistemic behavior or information-seeking should result. The goal is clarification or resolution of the conflict.

Uncertainty and Information-Seeking

Berlyne's theory of conceptual conflict may be recast in the statement that uncertainty leads to information-seeking behavior. But if we consider for the moment the meaning of "information," such a statement is close to being circular. This is not the place to discuss the technical details of Shannon and Weaver's (1949) information theory, but a brief and oversimplified picture of their definition of information may be helpful.

Let us begin by defining an event as any change in physical energy that modifies the state of the environment. Event, then, is a neutral term for any occurrence that may provide stimulation for a person. When an event occurs it may or may not be informative to a particular individual. The degree to which it is informative depends on the amount of uncertainty the event reduces. Before the event occurs the person can entertain the possibility of several things happening. Perhaps the basic assumption of information theory is that the greater the number of things that *might* happen, the more informative a particular event is. To take a simple example, a student's answer on a four-option multiple choice exam is generally more informative than his answer on a true-false test. It conveys more information when a reliable observer tells us that it is a sunny day in Boston than when he tells us that the sun is shining in Tucson, because Boston weather can take more forms than Tucson weather. News about Boston's sunshine is more informative because there is more uncertainty in the first place.

Uncertainty is a function of the sheer number of things that can happen.

It is also a function of the equiprobability of the alternatives. If we restrict ourselves to a concern with whether or not the sun will shine, there is still more uncertainty in the Boston situation. Even though we have reduced the question to sun—no sun in both cities, the probability of sunshine is much greater in Tucson than in Boston. Boston presents more uncertainty because the chances of sun there are more nearly equal to the chances of no sun than in Tucson.

These two components—the number of alternatives and their equiprobability—define the meaning of uncertainty. In the terms of information theory there can be no information without prior uncertainty. Our concern is to take the next step and argue that the condition of uncertainty gives rise to, or motivates, the search for information that reduces this uncertainty. This search often leads in the direction of consulting with or observing others. Thus it is easy to see why uncertainty-reduction is a topic of interest to social psychologists.

Not only is information-seeking selectively increased by the presence of uncertainty, but also some uncertainties are more important than others. The important uncertainties are those, presumably, that precede or are associated with decisions to act. We may be uncertain about the climate of the Siberian steppes or the topography of the moon's dark side, but our need for such information may not be as urgent as for information about road conditions ahead when we are on an automobile trip. As the necessity to take action increases, uncertainties regarding the best course become more and more intolerable and the motive to seek information may be expected to increase.

The strength of the motive to seek information varies with still another factor. This is the subjective probability that reliable information is available. Most of us probably agree that it would be *important* to know whether there is a life after death, because such knowledge would vastly affect our actions here and now. In spite of the significance of this information, most of us do not expend much time or energy in looking for signs of an afterlife. Why? Because, probably, we have learned not to expect reliable information about such matters. Although a few of us believe in mediumism and the possibilities of communicating with the dead, most of us treat reports of such "information-seeking" ventures with considerable skepticism.

The foregoing account provides a three-factor theory of motivation to seek information (cf. Berlyne, 1965). The tendency to seek information on a particular topic will increase with: (a) degree of uncertainty, defined in terms of the number of options available and their equipotentiality; (b) importance, defined in terms of the relevance of the information for action decisions; and (c) subjective probability of success, or the likelihood that a reliable source of information is available to shed light on the topic.

Reduction of Uncertainties by Socialization Agents

It is probably reasonable to take the position that effect dependence precedes and lays the groundwork for information dependence in the growing child. As pointed out in the preceding chapter, the human infant is born into his environment in a remarkable state of helplessness. His world is incalculably more uncertain than the totally nurturant womb from which he has departed, but for many months after birth the child is hardly in any position to provide for his own wants. He is unable through his own efforts and abilities to secure the basic effects of food and comfort. He does, of course, begin to manipulate his social environment through his crying and through expressions of pleasure. The success of such social maneuvering is a crucial phase in the development into, and later partially out of, effect dependence.

As the child grows and becomes more capable of coordinated action on his own behalf his need for information plays an increasingly large role. There seems little question, as we have already pointed out, that the child is born with rudimentary exploratory tendencies that become more and more focused and directed with maturation and learning. These tendencies are the prototype of later epistemic responses designed to reduce uncertainty. It seems reasonable to argue, however, that it is not appropriate to apply the term "uncertainty" until the child reaches the stage where he has hypotheses about the environment and can conceive of alternative events and alternative courses of action. Such hypotheses or predictions do not, in all likelihood, undergo rapid development until the child begins to have sustained and deliberate interactions with events that lead to reward and events that lead to pain and punishment. In short, the child develops cognitions about the environment initially out of a need to anticipate effects or outcomes. As coordinated actions become possible for him, basic categories of things or regions to be approached become distinguished from those to be avoided.

We propose that the need for information grows rapidly and becomes quickly generalized when maturation reaches the point when directed action is possible, when the child implicitly accepts his role in the decision process preceding action, and when the possibility of conceptual conflict exists. Presumably the kind of extrinsic curiosity associated with the need to act appropriately combines with more primitive, intrinsic exploratory tendencies to produce the marked curiosity and constant questioning of adults that may be so easily observed in the two-year-old. In short, information-seeking grows out of a specific concern with approaching positive and avoiding negative events, but it is never entirely restricted to information having high immediate utility. A more intrinsic interest in the nature of reality characterizes the child's orientation to available information and paves the way for his dependence on the information others can provide.

The child is receptive to information from many sources, both social and nonsocial. At least initially, there is information in the fact that his crib rail is hard and his Teddy bear soft. Similarly, the older child interacts directly with his physical environment to become informed about the texture and weight of objects, their typical location, whether they are ever too hot to touch, and whether they sink in the tub. But one fact that highlights man's uniqueness in the animal kingdom is the high proportion of information that is mediated by others.

There are probably many reasons for this heavy traffic in socially mediated information. One obvious factor is the greatly superior communicative skills of the human being. Because of the development of language, human beings are capable of richly textured and precise communications about the states of the world. Another factor is the cooperative adaptability of the human communicator to the capacities of the audience. Cherry (1957) has commented that Mother Nature does not vary her signs to assist the child in interpreting her message. Perhaps less obvious is the role of events that are remote in time and place but that encroach on the child's growing conception of reality. For the lower animal reality is a matter of events occurring here and now. For the human being reality extends back into human history, across the oceans to other cultures, and outward to the kingdom of a god or gods. The amount of such extended information potentially available to the human child is enormous, and a distinctive thing about it is that it can be mediated *only* by other persons, whether directly or indirectly through the pages of a book or the channels of a television set. The child is dependent on others for information about the more remote corners of his reality simply because he is not in a position to experience history, to visit with the spirits of the dead, or to see the roundness of the earth with his own eyes.

Because of his lack of ready access to nonsocial sources of information, the child is peculiarly vulnerable to those social sources appearing and reappearing in the immediate environment. Parents and older siblings find themselves in a position of great power, the power that comes with having answers (right or wrong) to resolve the child's uncertainties. In the early years of socialization, this power is almost monopolistic. Alternative answers or explanations are absent, and the child's earliest contacts with the broader universe are filtered through all the biases and distortions in his parents' conception of reality.

An individual parent's control over information is never entirely monopolistic, however, since the child also gets information from other sources, both social and nonsocial. He soon confronts discrepancies between his own experiences and social communications about reality. He notes that his parents do not always agree. His parents define the world somewhat differently from an older sibling, or a visiting uncle, or, before too long, a schoolteacher. As a consequence the child becomes concerned to know who is correct and grows to realize that not all sources of information are equally accurate or reliable. The uncertainty-reducing function of communications from others thus becomes complicated by a new uncertainty concerning the expertness or trustworthiness of the source.

Modes of Information Transmission

To this point we have used the word communication in a rather conventional sense to refer to a socialization agent describing some feature of reality in verbal terms. It must be emphasized, however, that much information is conveyed through actions other than verbal communication. The child's notion of the world derives both from what his parents say and from the results of their actions as he observes them. During the formative years the child not only processes relevant information conveyed by parental speech and action; he also develops techniques and principles for processing other social information. He learns how to learn from others.

Any action of another person may reduce an individual's uncertainty. The test is whether a question is (explicitly or implicitly) answered, a problem solved, or a conflict reduced. The following modes of information transmission may be identified along a rough continuum of explicitness: decriptive instruction, advice and consultation, social comparison, observational learning, and empathic cognizance.

Descriptive Instruction involves the provision of verbal or symbolic content to clarify some aspect of reality. Such communications are extremely common in conversations between parents and their children. Frequently the information is given in answer to a question such as: "Why is the sun brighter than the moon?" "Where do babies come from?" or "Is there really a tooth fairy?" But often information is given because of the parents' interest in instructing the child about "life" and "the way things are." It hardly needs to be said that most parents feel an obligation to inform their children about aspects of life that extend beyond the child's immediate experience. Parents also play an active role in developing the structural forms of language and providing a framework for the interpretation of subsequent events.

Advice and Consultation differs from descriptive instruction in several respects. The former is concerned with events, relations among events, and the general problem of interpreting reality. The latter centers on the behavior of the child in relation to the restrictions and opportunities of the environment. The child may ask for help in deciding between alternative courses of action. He may ask for an appraisal of his abilities to perform some task, or try to find out from others whether he would like some goal once he had achieved it. Or the parent may provide such advice without being explicitly asked. Advice and consultation thus goes beyond descriptive statement to consider questions of "ought," of values and morality, and the linking of means to ends.

Social Comparison involves a subtler use of information provided in the course of interactions that may be primarily concerned with other matters. In Chapter Three, where the comparison function of reference groups was briefly discussed, it was argued that individuals defined their standing and developed judgments and attitudes with reference to appropriate comparison groups. We shall return to the problems associated with social comparison and cover them in greater detail in Chapter Nine. At this point let us merely note that social comparisons involve several subprocesses all directed to using other persons in defining our beliefs or in assessing our abilities.

Observational Learning covers a variety of processes and outcomes. The concept of imitation in psychology has been influenced by the formulation and research of Miller and Dollard (1941). Eager to place the phenomena of imitation within the framework of reinforcement learning theory, these investigators conducted a number of experiments demonstrating matched-dependent learning, in which a rat or a child learns to make the correct response by paying attention to the rewarded response of another rat or child. In one experiment, 12 fourth-grade children were separately exposed to an apparatus from which they could obtain a gumdrop either by depressing or rotating a lever—two quite incompatible responses. Before making his response, each subject was exposed to a leader who either rotated or depressed the bar, after which the leader received candy. This sequence of leader-response, subject-response was repeated several times, with the leader following a complex schedule of rotations and depressions. The leader was rewarded every time, and the subject every time he made the same response as the leader. The subject quickly learned to imitate the leader, but *not* a second leader who was never rewarded with candy. In short, the subjects responded to the behavior of another person as one of several potential cues in the situation. Since the cue was regularly associated with reward or its absence, learning to imitate (or not) was rapid.

Bandura and Walters (1963) argue, however, that Miller and Dollard focused on only one form of imitation, and a rather trivial form at that. They suggest that the cases described by Miller and Dollard are only accidentally social, and merely involve simple discrimination learning or the attachment of old, previously learned responses to new conditioned stimuli. Bandura and Walters present many examples of imitation that do not fit the matched-dependent framework, examples in which highly novel responses of the model are copied by the subject in the absence of any apparent reward. In one study, briefly referred to in the last chapter, Bandura (1965) was able to show that imitation of novel aggressive responses was easily acquired through observation alone, even though the *performance* of these responses depended on whether or not the model was punished for being aggressive. Children observed a film in which the model engaged in four novel aggressive responses accompanied by distinctive speech. In one condition the aggressive model was severely punished; in a second the model was rewarded with approval and food; in the third condition, no consequences were forthcoming. When later given a chance to manifest the novel aggressive behavior, the subjects reproduced fewer imitative responses in the model-punished condition than in either of the two other conditions, and slightly more in the model-rewarded than in the no-consequence condition. This is roughly in line with Miller and Dollard's notion of matched-dependent behavior in that the subjects learn to imitate the rewarded response. *But,* when later told that they would receive an attractive reward if they could reproduce the model's behavior in detail, the children were capable in all conditions of faithfully doing so.

Much additional research is needed to explore the conditions under which imitation occurs in the absence of specific reinforcements to the imitator. There may be something special about aggression that makes faithful imitative behavior easy to elicit. But probably many actions of others are generally salient to the child and are perceived, remembered, and put to use in appropriate circumstances. Children undoubtedly do not engage in indiscriminate imitation of others, but Bandura's research shows that they are extremely sensitive to others' behavior and, if given appropriate incentives, are capable of reproducing the elaborate response combinations they have observed someone else perform.

It is extremely important in the transmission of culturally desired behavior for children to be so clearly capable of observational learning. Anthropologists' accounts of socialization are rich with reports on the role of observational learning or imitation. In Cantelense (Guatemala) society for example, young girls are provided with a water jar, a broom, and a grinding stone, miniature versions of those used by their mothers. Through constant observation, and in the absence of any direct teaching, the child acquires an appropriate repertory of responses (Nash, 1958). In many other cultures, including our own, children do what they see adults *do* more readily than they do what adults *tell* them to do. The role of pictures, instruction manuals, and other symbolic material obviously facilitates learning in more advanced cultures. Without such symbolic aids to imitation, ". . . members of technologically advanced societies would be forced to engage in exceedingly tedious and often haphazard trial-and-error experimentation" (Bandura and Walters, 1963, p. 49).

Empathic Cognizance refers to the child's ability to anticipate the behavior of significant persons in the environment. In Chapter Three we briefly described Whiting's status-envy theory, which states that cognizance is a precondition of identification, for which the motive force is provided by the child's envy of a model who controls desired resources. Whiting assumes that children pick up recurrent patterns of parental behavior and store them for later use. It may be that cognizance develops out of a primitive capacity for empathy, that is, for intuiting the emotional reactions of others by a kind of immediate inference from their situation or behavior.

Maccoby (1959) argues vigorously that in addition to instrumental learning, in which certain responses are strengthened by reward and others are suppressed by punishment, there is a concurrent process in which a child practices covertly the characteristic actions of other people with whom he interacts. She suggests that in the absence of the parent the child may imagine what the parent might do in a particular situation. This imagery is sufficient to stimulate rehearsal of the most likely parental reaction, whether or not the child overtly performs this reaction. The functional significance of such learning is apparent. Because the child engages in frequent and intricate interactions with the parent, it is obviously helpful for him to have in mind the repertoire of potential parental responses and to be able to anticipate parental actions. A more specific hypothesis is that such observational learning, facilitated by covert practice, occurs as a direct function of the frequency and intimacy of interaction: "The more frequently we interact with another person (and the more our own actions are interdependent with his) the more we must learn to anticipate what he will do if the interaction is to be harmonious; and in anticipating him, we learn the content of his behavior" (p. 244). Along with Whiting, Maccoby believes that these covertly practiced reactions become overt when a child later enters the same position or performs the same role as the parent.

COGNITIVE AND PERCEPTUAL PROCESSES

Cognitive Dispositions and Information Processing

It is difficult to talk long or meaningfully about information and uncertainty without talking about knowledge and understanding. As psychologists we are only interested in information if we can say something about how it affects those who are exposed to it. In order to refer generally to these phenomena of knowledge and understanding we shall speak of cognitions and of cognitive processes. *Cognitive process* is a general term referring to the kinds of mental activity involved in knowing or understanding. These processes do not require outside stimulation; we can reason deductively or daydream in a dark and silent room. Our interest, however, lies in those cognitive processes that are triggered by external events. These are the processes commonly labeled perceptual. The term *perception* covers those cognitive processes that refer to events occurring and objects present in the immediate environment.

Let us begin with a question: what happens to stimulus input once it crosses the threshold of sensory receptors? The brain physiologist has one answer to this question, but we are more interested in a psychological description of how the stimulus input becomes transformed into a cognition—a bit of knowledge or understanding. How is a particular event received and interpreted by the individual? How does present experience join with residues of past experience to produce a meaningful perception?

Until recently "perception psychologists" thought of acts of perceiving in terms closely geared to the basic data of sensory experience. The person perceives colors, sizes, and physical shapes, and we may record his sensitivity to variations in such primary stimulus attributes by asking him rather simple psychophysical questions: "Which line is longer?" "How far must I turn this dial until the colors are matched?" "Can you estimate the number of inches this light moves?"

Because of the persistent pulling and tugging of personality and social psychologists since World War II, the concept of perception has been broadened by most users to include identification of objects. Certainly our own definition of perception emphasizes our interest in the meaning as well as the underlying sensory qualities of stimulus events.

The physical energy impinging on the receptor must contribute to the perceived meaning of an event, but it is obvious that there is no one-to-one relationship between variations in the physical stimulus and in perceived meaning. Words having almost identical physical characteristics may mean entirely different things to a perceiver. Furthermore, the same word may mean very different things in different contexts of other words. The obverse is also true: different physical stimulus values may be represented in the same way. An apple is judged approximately as red both when it is in shadows and when it is under direct sunlight. It is also true that the same physical stimulus may be represented in different ways at different times. Reversible figures, in which first one aspect and then another is perceived, serve to exemplify this class of events.

Two of the most significant accomplishments of perceptual processes are: (a) the screening out of much potential information in the building of a percept; and (b) the addition of predicted information to go beyond that given by the environment itself. Each of these accomplishments will be discussed with reference to a way of looking at perception and cognition put forth by Bruner (1957a, 1957b).

Bruner's analysis emphasizes particularly the cognitive "category" and conditions that affect its "accessibility" to stimulus input. He emphasizes the similarity between perceptual activity and problem-solving in general. Perception always involves a decision process, a placement of incoming information into a network of meaningful categories developed largely from prior learning. The cognitive category is essentially a set of rules for classifying objects as equivalent. The category "plum," for example, specifies particular ranges along several dimensions that are useful for identifying a particular kind of fruit. Color, size, and roundness would probably constitute plum cues for most people. Although each category may be said to have its "typical instances" for each attribute (an average and therefore expected color, shape, size, etc.), a number of values along the dimensions of roundness, size, and bluishness might be accepted as confirming the judgment. Some of these attributes would likely be more criterial than others —would contribute more to the act of placing the object in the plum category. Thus shape and size would be more criterial than color, for most people, since plums have been known to come in a variety of hues.

We should expect to find that people differ significantly in the categories they form and in the particular attributes thought of as typical, or important, or criterial. The anti-Semite's category "Jew" may contain such criterial attributes as stinginess, loudness, clannishness, and flashiness, which would not be included in the same category of others less bigoted. The paranoid often classes neutral events as referring to himself ("they are talking about me"), using cues that others would ignore or use for different purposes. The trained botanist exploits a range of cues that would be ignored by most of the rest of us who are concerned only with whether various plants are edible, aromatic, colorful, or good to throw on a campfire.

In spite of these individual differences it is important that we share enough experiences in growing up (including socially mediated experiences) that there is broad agreement on the more commonly used categories within a particular culture. Without such agreement, amounting to a shared vocabulary of explicit and implicit concepts, meaningful communication is impossible. To say that some of the commonly held categories are *socially mediated* means that communication contributes greatly to the similarity between cognitive structures, as well as being made possible by such similarity. A certain amount of the sharing of object and event categories comes about through similar contacts with the objects in question. All of us have had about the same range of experiences with the sun, for example, or the wetness of water, or the warmth of a fire. Much of the generality of category construction derives, however, from the pulling and tugging of social communication. As people try to understand each other, the pressures to develop common modes of interpreting, perceiving, and labeling have dramatic effects on cognitive structure.

As mentioned, much information is screened out in any given act of perceiving—in deciding, for example, that the object on the table is a plum and not an orange. It can easily be shown why this must be the case. Organisms can only use a tiny fraction of the potential information (the physical signals) reaching the eyes, ears, and epidermis. Even if we could take in more information, there would have to be a selection, out of the total, of that which is relevant for prospective action or for resolving pressing uncertainties. As suggested earlier in the chapter, learning plays an important role in the development of meaningful and adaptive selection habits. The more or less random selection of information that characterizes the infant gives way to an adaptive selectivity of the more reliable and useful cues. This learned selectivity is built into the concept of cognitive category. As we shall shortly see, information that falls within the range of well-established categories is more quickly perceived than information that does not fit nicely into an individual's cognitive structure.

The second significant accomplishment of cognitive processes, as we noted, is the addition of information by the perceiver to that provided by the environment. One kind of addition is implied by our discussion of the categorizing process. Object identification involves the application of a learned structure, a model to be matched more or less precisely with stimulus input. But what is the best way to describe this model and the categories that compose it?

When we categorize an experience we essentially assign it to a meaning class. The conception of meaning is difficult to express with any psychological precision. Bruner proposes that "the meaning of a thing . . . is the placement of an object in a network of hypothetical inference concerning its other observable properties, its effects, and so on" (1957a, p. 126). Such an approximation has interesting implications. We have presented the act of perceptual identification as a decision-making process, but now we see that it is a predictive decision. When our glance reveals a thin rectangular object on the table in front of us, we decide in an immediate, unreflective act of perceptual categorization that it is a book. In making this decision we are really engaged in predicting a series of attributes that are not available to the distance receptors—our eyes, ears, and nose. Our identification predicts pages filled with words arranged in certain combinations that have communicative value. The object also has mass and weight. Its value in keeping the papers it rests on from blowing away is also part of its meaning, and so is the color of the cover, which may or may not blend in an attractive way with the decor of the room. Our percept, book, is like a promissory note: we go from cues to category and back through prediction to other cues, which can only be checked by more detailed inspection.

This going beyond the informative given is a vital aspect of cognition, one that inextricably links the activities of perceiving and inferring. Of course predictions may be in error. We can be tricked by the environment and especially by psychologists who delight in arranging conditions that show the fallibility of human perception. The simple illusions described in introductory courses of psychology serve as examples of this environmental trickery. More complex illusions can be dramatically demonstrated, for example, by rearranging the distance cues in an experimental room. Ames and his associates (Ittleson, 1952) constructed a room giving rise to unsettling illusions of size. A man standing in one of the rear corners appears huge in comparison to another man (actually of equal size) in the other rear corner. The explanation for this apparent difference is that the cues that are usually criterial for distance are in this case subverted by the special construction of trapezoidal walls; whereas the sides of the room appear to recede to an equal distance from us, one is actually much shorter than the other. Therefore, the man in that corner appears much larger because we are tricked into thinking that the men are equidistant from the front of the room.

Such dramatic illusions are not likely to arise in the normal course of everyday living, but we can and do make errors of identification (and therefore of prediction) often enough to realize the extent to which we make a personal contribution to the perceptual process. We dial a phone number, hear a voice, and begin a conversation that may last for embarrassing seconds until we realize things are not going right, and decide that we have dialed a wrong number. Every year we read of unfortunate accidents in which one hunter mistakes another for a deer, or a driver is killed by an oncoming car while attempting to pass on a hill. These are instances in which the individual placed too much weight on an expectancy or a prediction. Usually, as in the first example, the consequences of an identification error are not disastrous. When we go beyond the information given we naturally take chances, but, in the gambler's language, we usually play the percentages. And there is really no alternative to the making of immediate predictive decisions in the give-and-take of everyday life. If we stopped to confirm every perceptual decision we would accomplish very little from dawn to dusk. Fortunately our environment is usually very stable and highly predictable so that most of our errors are minor and fall within the margin of safety adequate for adjustive behavior.

In most cases, furthermore, information does not come to us in a burst that is never repeated. Fortunately for the organism, given his limited capacities for processing information, there is considerable redundancy in the environment. To say that information is redundant is to say, in effect, that not all of it is absolutely necessary for drawing the same conclusion. Different signals, in other words, can point to the same meaning; one or more of these is superfluous under ideal conditions. But conditions are often *not* ideal, and the redundancy contained in an average sentence or a glance at a downtown street often provides an important safety factor in the processing of information. We can miss one part of a message but still retrieve the whole because some of the message could have been reliably predicted from the rest of it. Because of redundancy the parts we see often make up for the parts we miss; thus selectivity is not incompatible with accuracy and we can understand Cherry's comment that because of redundancy "communication is established and maintained in spite of 101 reasons against it" (1957, p. 289).

There are at least occasional messages—signals, stimuli—that are not redundant enough to protect the perceiver against error. One way to study the kinds of errors and distortions that can occur in perception is to reduce redundancy of information in a laboratory and therefore place burdens on the categorizing process. This may be done by providing stimuli too rapidly, at too low a level of illumination, under conditions of noise or distraction, and so on.

Effects of Expectancy on Perception

Category Accessibility

We have seen that information, in the information-theory sense, and uncertainty are closely intertwined. Uncertainty in turn may be viewed as a function of the number of possibilities for interpretation and, ultimately, action. It should follow, then, that any prior information that reduces the number of meanings a stimulus may have should tend to improve perceptual acuity or accuracy and speed of categorization.

In a simple illustrative experiment, connecting two subjects with earphones and using a noisy communications system, Miller, Heise, and Lichten (1951) found that words from a short list (to which both speaker and listener had access) were more accurately heard than words from a longer list—one with more possibilities. A similar kind of demonstration was arranged by D. B. Fry (noted in Cherry, 1957), who made a recording of two men conversing, which artificially so distorted their speech that not a word could be recognized. After the subject listened to the recording, unable to say a single thing about its contents, he was told that the speakers were discussing the subject of buying a new suit. The record was replayed and most listeners were able to follow the entire conversation. In contrast to the first, blind playing, the words seemed to "jump out."

All we need is to assume that past experience creates expectancies that have the same kinds of effects as prior instructions, and we may extend the uncertainty-reduction principle to most perceptual activities. In other words, past experiences in certain kinds of settings lead us to expect certain events with a higher probability than others. Such high-probability expectations presumably operate in the same way as instructions that reduce the number of alternatives an event may signify. It may even be helpful to think of expectancies as self-instruction; the individual tells himself to be on the alert for certain things that have often happened in the past and more or less to ignore the unlikely possibility of rare events.

Such reasoning leads to the prediction that objects and events that have had a high frequency of occurrence will be more rapidly and more accurately perceived than more unusual ones. Two kinds of evidence support such a prediction. First, it has been established that words that have a high frequency of occurrence in the language are perceived and recognized at shorter exposure durations than more unusual words. Howes and Solomon (1951) found that, when word length and word structure were roughly controlled, the ease of recognition of words presented rapidly correlated highly with the general frequency of the word presented, frequency being independently measured by a word count of sizable samples of written English. This finding was confirmed by Postman and Schneider (1951) with the same measure of frequency, and Solomon and Postman (1952) noted the same kind of relationship when differential frequency of contact with words was experimentally established. They presented 100 cards with nonsense words written on them to subjects who were later exposed to some of these words in a tachistoscope (a device for the presentation of stimuli at varying speeds or illuminations). Two nonsense words had occurred 25 times in the 100 presentations, two of them 10 times, and so on, down to words that had only occurred once or had not even been shown. In a subsequent recognition task the words that had been presented with greater frequency were recognized at shorter durations than the less frequently presented words. A related point is made by Miller, Bruner, and Postman (1954), who showed that nonsense syllables were more readily perceived the more they resembled real words in the English language, degree of resemblance being defined in terms of the length of letter sequences in common.

If events that fit readily into established cognitive categories are more easily identified they should also be more easily remembered. One advantage of having cognitive categories should be to make it easier to store relevant information for later use. Many if not most of our cognitive categories are heavily influenced by language in their formation and structure. Numerous investigators have noted that the development of language not only facilitates communication but also is of indispensible value in *storing* experience.

Solid support for the notion that language serves a storage function is provided by a study of Brown and Lenneberg (1954). It has been estimated that color is divisible into 7,500,000 discriminable differences, and yet there are fewer than 4000 color names and only about eight that commonly occur. From this it may be inferred that we tend to map colors into a set of broad equivalence classes in a way that represents considerable informational loss. What is the effect of this categorial mapping on the storage of colors in a memory situation?

Brown and Lenneberg first established a number of indices reflecting the codability of 24 chips of highly saturated color chosen to cover the color space evenly. ("Codability" is Brown and Lenneberg's term for category accessibility.) Certain color chips were more easily named (low reaction time), elicited shorter names ("red" rather than "reddish-green"), and resulted in names about which there was high agreement. Choosing the degree of agreement between judges as the best index of the accessibility of a cognitive category to any individual, Brown and Lenneberg set out to study the relationships between category accessibility (as defined by one sample of subjects) and color recognition (as determined by another). Their basic procedure was to expose one or four color chips and then, after varying intervals of time, to show the complete board of 24 chips and ask the subject to identify the chip(s) initially shown.

The results showed that the greater the codability of the colors originally exposed, the greater was the tendency toward accurate recognition. This was especially the case when four chips rather than one were involved, and the memory task was therefore more difficult. We may infer that language serves an important function in the storage of information about the environment, and that the more precise and unambiguous the cognitive label the more it facilitates the memory and recognition process. This confirms a common-sense expectation that language coding increases the accessibility of a cognitive category to appropriate stimulus input.

A second kind of evidence for the role of past experience comes from experiments in which stimuli with different histories are not singly presented; rather, expectancies are established on the basis of preceding or accompanying stimuli. That is, all perceptions are not only affected by prior repetition of events, they may also reflect expected contingencies or relationships. Thus, given A, B is much more likely to be perceived than C, D, or E. Most college students have learned the highly probable contingency between, say, redness and the six of hearts. When students with this history are then shown a black six of diamonds or a red four of clubs in a tachistoscope, as was done by Bruner and Postman (1949), much longer exposures are required for correct recognition than when normal playing cards are shown. It is interesting that recognition becomes easier the greater is the proportion of incongruous cards in a series of presentations. Apparently the individual can learn quickly to anticipate incongruity if he is tipped off to the nature of the trick being played by the experimenter or the environment.

Assimilation to the Typical Instance

The evidence cited indicates that expectancies about which events are most likely to occur definitely affect the perceiver's preparedness and his efficiency in recognizing and categorizing predicted stimuli. This is true whether expectations are established by instructions, by experimental manipulation of exposure frequencies, or by experience prior to the experiment. Now we may ask whether the kinds of expectancy generated by the development of cognitive categories affect the quality of the perception itself. It seems obvious that recognition should be enhanced when an individual is expecting an event that in fact occurs; but is there a tendency for perceptual distortion when the event that occurs is low in probability?

Is it reasonable to propose, for example, that perception of objects in a particular class tends to be distorted toward the most typical object in that class? From what we have already said about the process of categorizing events, the stimuli are typically identified and placed in particular categories on the basis of learned information about certain salient attributes. The remaining attributes are then predicted, or filled in, in line with the categorizing decision. A rather direct attack on this problem appears in an experiment by Bruner, Busiek, and Minturn (1952). These investigators were interested in seeing whether the distortions of memory that were demonstrated by Carmichael, Hogan, and Walter (1932) also showed up in perception—at least under less than ideal conditions. Simple, line-drawn figures were presented in brief flashes on a projection screen. Some subjects were told before each figure was shown that the drawing was of a particular object ("I am going to show you a figure resembling a pine tree"). Other subjects were given no specific instructions. Still others were instructed that the drawing resembled, say, "either a pine tree or a trowel." In every case the subjects were asked to reproduce the figure. The result was a clear tendency to assimilate the figure to the typical instance suggested by the category label mentioned in the instructions.

Bruner, Postman, and Rodrigues (1951) showed how this same kind of assimilation tends to operate in the perception of color. When subjects were asked to adjust a color wheel to match an ambiguously colored object presented as a tomato, the match had much more red in it than if the object were shaped like and presented as a lemon but objectively colored in the same ambiguous hue.

The point being made here is not too dissimilar from the well-known phenomenon of assimilation in the area of judgment. Sherif and Hovland (1961) reviewed the research concerned with judging the placement of stimulus items on such scaling dimensions as loudness, heaviness, or—in the case of attitude or value statements—favorability. The research in this area is voluminous and cannot easily be summarized. One relevant conclusion, however, is that the individual will be affected in his judgment, for example, of the heaviness of weights, by the manner in which they are presented to him. If, in judging a series of weights, the individual is exposed to one weight much more frequently than to others, that weight will come to serve as an "internal anchor." This means that the other weights will be judged with reference to the one most frequently presented. Furthermore, when the weight being judged is similar to the internal anchor it will be judged as closer to it in heaviness than it actually is. It does not seem too farfetched, in such cases, to note the similarity between the concept of internal anchor in the sphere of judgment and the concept of typical instance in perceptual categorization.

"Contrast effects" are also observed in the judgment of various items in respect to a standard or anchor. If the discrepancy between the anchor item and the presented item is large, the judgment will exaggerate the discrepancy. Here we may be dealing with stimuli falling at or near the boundaries of a cognitive category. The attributes of items belonging to the category are assimilated to the attributes of the typical instance; attributes of items falling outside the category are seen as different, special, or incomparable.

The probable effects of categorization in judgment were shown by Hunt (1941) in a study in which subjects were asked to judge the intelligence of children from their photographs.

Keeping in mind the least intelligent child he had ever seen [—a standard instruction prior to judgment—] would raise [the subject's] judgments of most of the pictures, until he suddenly noticed that one of the children in some way resembled the unintelligent child he had in mind. Then this child would be judged as much less intelligent than previously. Or this [subject] might notice that one child looked exactly opposite in some respect to the ["least intelligent child"] he had in mind. As a result, the child would be given a relatively greater advantage in intelligence than the other children (p. 401).

The process of assimilation is also fundamental to the formation of stereotypes in judgment and perception. The stereotype is a categorical judgment that is relatively oversimplified and resistant to change. Assimilation to the typical instance should be especially marked when the object being judged is highly complex and there is uncertainty concerning many of its attributes. Most stereotypes are formed to come to terms with such complex objects. In regard to the Negro stereotype, for example, Secord, Bevan, and Katz (1956) showed pictures of Negroes and whites to Southern high-school students. The photographs in both sets had been carefully chosen to fall at various points along a dimension of physical "Negroidness," a complex of characteristics including darkness of complexion, coarseness of hair, thickness of lips, and flatness of nose. Subjects were asked to judge the photographed persons on various dimensions related to the prevailing Negro stereotype: superstitious, lazy, dishonest, immoral, and so on. As predicted, the authors found that the assignment of these stereotyped attributes was a function of whether a person in a photograph was Negro or white and not of the *degree* of physical Negroidness of the pictures. The Negro stereotype for this group of subjects apparently consisted of a cluster of predominantly negative attributes. Once the category threshold was crossed by the physical stimulus characteristics of the photographs, all the attributes of a stereotype were inferred at full strength.

Implications for the Prior-Entry Effect

Cherry (1957) argues that any act of perception, the taking in of information from the environment, has two kinds of results: (1) information selects out a response or a specific interpretation of content ("That is a plum"); and (2) modifies the framework of assumptions and beliefs into which subsequent experiences must fit ("Plums can grow bigger than I thought"). In the area of communication, the

> ... hearing of [an] utterance represents a selective action upon your ensemble of hypotheses—strengthening some, weakening others. From that instant on, you are no longer the same person; the experience has changed your "state of preparedness" for other signs (Cherry, 1957, p. 248).

Similarly, if we show a subject a simple square, and he recognizes it as such,

> ... his mental state has undergone a change; his subsequent responses have partly been determined by this event. For example, he may recognize the second card more quickly, or he may respond by saying: "It's like the one before." ... The ... event alters the subject's nervous system in some way, setting him into a different state of preparation for receipt of subsequent stimuli (p. 257).

This position is consistent with our own treatment of cognitive processes. Having emphasized the role of expectancies or pre-established categories in the perception of events, we concur with Cherry that the category both is shaped by the event and shapes it, through such processes as assimilation to the typical instance. But there is an added factor of priority that Cherry's comments do not explicitly contain. We propose that information received early in the growth of a cognitive category is more influential than later information in shaping that category and is less shaped *by* it.

Cognitive categories—expectancies, hypotheses, sets to perceive—never reach the stage of finished construction. The nature of the category can always be modified by experience. However, there are presumably variations in the degree of openness to change during the history of a particular category's development. We may imagine an early formative period in which the defining criteria or central attributes of the category are easily changed by incoming instances that depart from uncertain and tentative expectations. As the individual accumulates more and more instances of the category, the expectancy it represents becomes more ingrained and resistant to change. It is primarily in such well-established categories that we expect atypical information to be distorted and made more congenial, more similar to the average value of the category. The person's cognitive categories also become increasingly integrated—bound together by mutual implication—so that it becomes more difficult to redefine the boundaries of one category without having also to alter related conceptions.

One consequence of this reasoning is that parents and other socialization agents who reach the child early have a disproportionate influence on his cognitive development. As indicated in Chapter Three, the parents "get there first with the most," often establishing nearly monopolistic control over the information reaching the child. Now we are in a better position to appreciate the long-range results of this monopolistic control. The crucial thing is that the parents' control is greatest precisely during the critical early stages of category formation. Owing to their advantage of prior entry with their explanations, definitions, and behavior to be imitated, parents play a special role in shaping the child's view of the world. Other things equal, it is much easier to develop a belief or expectancy where none previously existed than to change one that is already in operation as a consequence of past experience.

A final factor contributing to the importance of prior entry is that much of the information passed on by the parents is definitional and involves assumptions not readily tested or refuted. Thus many basic religious and moral beliefs have a distinctive persistence that later experience does not affect. Undoubtedly many subtle assumptions about language usage creep into the child's own thinking and represent a distinctive and highly stable heritage from interactions with his parents. In short, the fact that much of early learning is not easily refuted by subsequent experiences adds further strength to the prior-entry effect.

LANGUAGE AND COGNITION

The Notion of Developmental Stages

Thus far we have emphasized the *constraining* consequences of past experience. The very notion of the category suggests that the child learns to ignore certain distinctions as irrelevant and to trust his predictions about the characteristics of objects. Even in the discussion of going beyond the information given, we stressed that the person adds predicted attributes in keeping with probabilities derived from past experience.

We have no wish to take back this argument that past experience constrains perception and judgment into certain channels. The argument illuminates many known facts about perception and the persistence of beliefs. But in fairness to other facts about cognitive development, we must acknowledge the rather paradoxical point that the child becomes more intellectually liberated in some respects as he becomes more constrained. Not only do larger ranges of events become categorized with increasing maturity and cumulative experience, but the categories themselves also become more sophisticated and less tied to the superficial similarities of objects. The older child becomes liberated from the immediate demands of external stimulation and multiplies new and more penetrating ways of dealing with events. He moves from the level of identifying particular objects because they look or perform alike to a level of understanding relationships between categories, including some knowledge of rules for transforming certain categories into others. The ninth grader who learns that $(x + y)^2$ is the same thing as $x^2 + 2xy + y^2$ exemplifies this kind of cognitive growth.

Many developmental psychologists have attempted to characterize in some detail the growth of intellectual functioning. Most of them agree that cognitive development proceeds through rather discrete stages. The specific age at which a particular capacity comes into functioning is by no means set, but there are stages in the sense that certain capacities must develop before others and there is thus an ordered unfolding of abilities.

The notion that there are stages has been heavily influenced by the observations and theoretical speculations of Jean Piaget (an excellent summary and analysis of his contributions is Flavell, 1963). In the course of Piaget's writings he has distinguished three major stages through which the child's intelligence passes: sensorimotor operations, concrete operations, and formal operations. The stage of *sensorimotor operations* typically covers the first 18 months of life. During this period the infant develops his coordination of hand and eye movements. He reaches for objects, grasps, and sucks. A subtler feature of this stage is the development of an object concept—the notion that objects exist even when they are not in the field of vision, that they can be looked for, and that an object retains its identity even when it is approached on different sides or viewed under different illuminations. Active experimentation with objects and their properties follows.

The stage of *concrete operations* extends from about 18 months until 11 or 12 years. This long period is extremely critical for the development of language and the ability to represent, symbolize, and put together various combinations of cognitions. The first part of this stage is "preconceptual"; although the child comes to realize that certain objects, pictures, and images can represent other objects, his capacities for grouping and abstraction are quite primitive until approximately age four or five, when he enters a period of "intuitive thought." Here much of the child's thinking involves covert speech. That is, things he earlier had said aloud, he now says to himself. His ability to classify objects in terms of attributes improves, but he is still unable to consider simultaneously the combined effects of several attribute dimensions. For example, until the age of seven or so the child makes serious errors in judging the volume, height, weight, or mass of physical objects. Of two beakers holding the same amount of water, the narrower beaker—and therefore the one with the higher column of water—is almost invariably judged to hold more than the wider beaker. If the child is shown a ball of clay that is then rolled into a long sausage, he concludes that there is more clay in the sausage than there was in the ball, even though the shape of the piece is changed before his eyes. Both errors occur because the child is only able to take account of one dimension (such as length or height) at a time.

In the final stage of *formal operations* the full use of symbolic manipulation is apparent. The early adolescent can put together premises and deduce conclusions. He can keep in mind many different variables or properties of a problem and appreciate how these may enter into combinations. The stage gets its name from the fact that the adolescent can follow the form of an argument while disregarding its content. He may be led by inexorable logic to a conclusion he would like not to believe on other grounds.

Bruner (1964) is convinced that such developmental changes in cognitive functioning cannot be viewed independently of developments in the use of language. Language is the single capacity that most obviously separates man from other creatures. The special feature of language, as opposed to more primitive signaling systems that *may* be found in lower animals, is that

. . . fewer than 100 sounds which are individually meaningless are compounded, not in all possible ways, to produce some hundreds of thousands of meaningful morphemes, which have meanings that are arbitrarily assigned, and these morphemes are combined by rule to yield an infinite set of sentences, having meanings that can be derived. All of the systems of communication called languages have these design features (Brown, 1965, p. 248).

Language thus makes possible a richness of communcation that is crucial for creating and maintaining human culture.

In addition to its critical social role language both shares and contributes to the principles of cognitive functioning already mentioned. On the one hand, language makes possible the storage and retrieval of past experience. We have already cited data (cf. Brown and Lenneberg, 1954) showing that a stimulus that can easily be tagged with a verbal label is more easily stored—and retrieved (remembered)—than one not so easily tagged. In a similar vein we have shown that verbal labels are constraining—they can bias the form of memory and perception by increasing the salience of categories and their typical instances (Bruner, Busiek, and Minturn, 1952). But language is also a dramatic liberating force that frees the human being from his attachments to external events and allows him to combine, to relate, and to invent.

The contribution of language learning to cognitive development is especially obvious in the area of categorization or classification. As Brown (1965) points out, concepts may be learned in any of three ways: (1) from direct commerce with the physical world, without social mediation; (2)

with social mediation that is nonlinguistic; (3) by linguistic social mediation. Most students of cognition would agree that the great bulk of our concepts derive from experiences of the third kind. Initially, language supplies a vocabulary of nouns and verbs to serve as labels for the child's categories. This in itself is a contribution of enormous importance. But the great potentialities of language become apparent when we introduce the notions of subordination and level of abstraction. The rules of combining words, of using words to qualify each other, are enormously important in this respect. The fact that we can refer to the red psychology book and the blue philosophy book has impressive consequences. We recognize their common attributes in spite of their differences. Both are members of the category, book; yet they fall into different categories of color and content.

In Vygotsky's (1962) account of different kinds of categorizing behavior he traces the movement from arbitrary grouping, through a stage when objects are seen as similar if they are associated in some way, to the sophisticated use of superordination. In the latter stage the child is able to view sets of objects or concepts as subordinate members of more inclusive and more abstract categories. If possible, he will apply a universal rule of inclusion for all objects in a given set. A fly and a tree will be seen as "both living," whales and mice as "both mammals"; again, classification becomes more sophisticated as the child grows able to detach himself from the immediate perceptual attribute. As Bruner (1964) puts the argument:

. . . hierarchical classification is surely one of the most evident properties of the structure of language—hierarchical grouping that goes beyond mere perceptual inclusion . . . as language becomes . . . more guiding as a set of rules for organizing events, there is a shift from the associative principles that operate in . . . perceptual organization to increasingly abstract rules for grouping events . . . (p. 11).

Not only does language influence category formation; the child's familiarity with the rules of syntax makes him generally more alert to the ways of putting information into larger structures that are logically related to other structures and that may be transformed, like algebraic symbols, according to certain implicit rules. Above all, language contributes to the crucial change from being stuck with what is immediately perceived to being free to sort, combine, and play with information.

So long as perceptual representation dominates, it is difficult to develop higher-order techniques for processing information by consecutive inferential steps that take one beyond what can be pointed at. Once language becomes a medium for the translation of experience, there is a progressive release from immediacy . . . language . . . has the new and powerful features of remoteness and arbitrariness: it permits productive combinatorial operations in the absence of what is represented (Bruner, 1964, p. 14).

Social Factors in the Learning of Language

Having paused to consider certain broad descriptive features of cognitive and linguistic development, we turn again to our primary task: the role of other persons in bringing about these developmental changes. In the area of language acquisition it is especially clear that simple reinforcement learning cannot account adequately for the dramatic changes that occur in the child's capacity with words. The notion that words are learned in specific response-reward contingencies and extinguished when rewards are no longer forthcoming seems to be misleading or at least incomplete. Much of what the child learns is not specifically taught or, in any obvious way, reinforced by a teacher. The child is constantly exposed to language-speaking models and through this exposure develops a remarkable capacity to discriminate different meaningful sounds, a vocabulary that expands so rapidly that the increase is difficult to chart, and a powerful intuitive sense about appropriate language structures and forms. By the time the child officially studies grammar in school he has already learned the basic elements of grammatical structure, although he has not learned the proper names for them. Of course, he still makes mistakes in constructing sentences, but the mistakes are reasonable and can usually be understood in terms of recurring errors of the model *or* incorrect generalizations of rules.

We are far from understanding all the processes that contribute to language acquisition, but it is safe to say that language develops as it does and at the speed it does because of the active participation of other persons and because of their vital interest in the child's progress. The parent is more than a generator of rewards for correct performance and more than merely a model to emulate. Language acquisition occurs in the framework of complex social interactions in which the model's responses to the child's utterances constitute active imitation. The child, in fact, does not begin his speech by imitating the sounds of others. He babbles, at first in seemingly random fashion. Out of this babbling he may accidentally produce sounds that approximate words. Adult models in the vicinity often seize upon such occasions to repeat the approximation for the child. This reverse imitation may be critical in the early stages of language formation. We have already noted Piaget's remarks on the circular reaction in which the model's verbal response provides the crucial reaction of the environment, which in turn perpetuates the child's initial verbalization. He repeats his accidental syllable because it led to an interesting environmental change.

A case study by Brown and Bellugi (1964) provides a fascinating account of imitation and reverse imitation in the period between 18 and 30 months. These investigators visited each of two children in their homes every second week for an extensive period. They tape-recorded everything said by and to the child. One child, "Adam," was 27 months old when the observations and recordings began. The other, "Eve," was only 18 months. The recordings were transcribed and carefully examined for hunches and clues about the crucial changes in grammar or syntax occurring over the period studied.

The first thing that was made abundantly clear by the transcript is that adults tend to speak to a child in short, grammatically perfect sentences. Knowingly or not, both Adam's and Eve's mothers provided precisely correct models to be imitated. Quite probably the children would have made slower progress in the acquisition of syntax if they were merely allowed to listen to adults speaking to each other. Adult-to-adult speech is often overly complex and ungrammatical, and is studded with self-interruptions, irrelevant interjections, and pronouns with obscure antecedents.

To the extent that the adult provides a meticulous syntactical standard for the child, there is a clear instance of active adult participation in the language acquisition process. The teaching may not be systematic, but there is an apparent concern with presenting the proper model in a form simple enough for the child to assimilate. The importance of providing a correct model is clearly indicated by Braine's (1963) experimental results. In one of his experiments, Braine found that, when children are attempting to learn an artificial language, the mere articulation by the child of an incorrect grammatical sequence—even though he immediately learns that the sequence is incorrect—significantly retards learning. The making of an incorrect response interrupts the delicate acquisition of feeling that a certain way of saying something "sounds right" or seems familiar and therefore correct. The reader may understand this point better if he considers the following example:

... if a foreigner asks whether DIFFERENT THAN or DIFFERENT FROM is correct in English, or whether a sentence like THE CHILD SEEMS SLEEPING is any less correct than THE BOOK SEEMS INTERESTING, one is usually more confident of the answer if one responds at once than if one repeats each alternative twenty times before responding. The very act of repeating the ungrammatical (or less grammatical) sequence a number of times seems to make it momentarily "sound right," and thus removes the usual basis for the judgment (Braine, 1963, p. 335).

The importance of this consideration is highlighted by the fact that the child is exposed almost exclusively to correct instances of linguistic structure. This is not to say that parents are always correct in grammatical usage, even when speaking to their children, but they are more likely to be incorrect through ignorance than inadvertence, and the child readily learns the errors systematically featured in their speech.

The second finding of Brown and Bellugi (1964) is not the least bit surprising. Adam and Eve tended to imitate their mothers. But there was a special feature involved in the imitative responses that is of considerable interest. Their imitations were often quite abbreviated and represented a reduction of the model's utterance:

Utterance	Imitation
1. tank car	1. tank car
2. Wait a minute.	2. Wait a minute.
3. daddy's briefcase	3. daddy briefcase
4. Fraser will be unhappy.	4. Fraser unhappy
5. He's going out.	5. He go out.
6. That's an old-time train.	6. old-time train
7. It's not the same dog as Pepper.	7. dog Pepper
8. No, you can't write on Mr. Cromer's shoe.	8. write Cromer shoe

The child's selection of what to imitate is obviously not random. For the most part the child repeats nouns, verbs, and adjectives. In the foregoing examples the forms omitted include verb endings, auxiliary verbs, articles, and prepositions. The words retained are actually the ones most crucial for conveying semantic content. For this reason linguists call them *contentives*. The ones omitted serve more of a grammatical than a semantic function. The term for them is *functors*. It is as if the child were taking the parents' remarks and trying to make telegrams out of them. At this early age there are, for some reason, constraints on the number of syllables a child can readily string together in an utterance. Words are expensive and they must be used in a way that will convey the most meaning.

As we turn to the reverse side of the imitation process, we notice that the parent adds to the child's utterances precisely the same kinds of words that the child omits in *his* imitations. If the child is guilty of reductive imitation, the adult compensates by expansive imitation. Note the following examples taken from the records of Adam, Eve, and their mothers:

Child	Mother
baby highchair	Baby is in the highchair.
mommy eggnog	Mommy had her eggnog.
Eve lunch	Eve is having lunch.
mommy sandwich	Mommy'll have a sandwich.
sat wall	He sat on the wall.
throw Daddy	Throw it to Daddy.
pick glove	Pick the glove up.

Is the mother doing more than simply helping to teach grammar by this active imitative expansion? Brown and Bellugi (1964) are inclined to think so:

The expansion encodes aspects of reality that are not coded by the child's telegraphic utterance. Functors have meaning, but it is meaning that accrues to them in context rather than in isolation. The meanings that are added by functors seem to be nothing less than the basic terms in which we construe reality: the time of an action, whether it is ongoing or completed, whether it is presently relevant or not; the concept of possession, and such relational concepts as are coded by *in, on, up, down,* and the like; the difference between a particular instance of a class ("Has anybody seen *the* paper?") and any instance of a class ("Has anybody seen *a* paper?"); the difference between extended substances given shape and size by an "accidental" container (*sand, water, syrup,* etc.) and countable "things" having a characteristic fixed shape and size (*a cup, a man, a tree,* etc.). It seems to us that a mother, in expanding speech, may be teaching more than grammar; she may be teaching something like a world view (pp. 147–148).

Searching for the Structure of the Language

The distinction between syntax and semantic content is basic to linguistic analysis. The child not only must learn the meaning of individual words, he must also learn how to put these words together into meaningful combinations—sentences, phrases, paragraphs. He must learn besides how to attach appropriate endings, prefixes, and suffixes. Although we know little about the acquisition of either semantics or syntax, it is probably easier to imagine how words acquire their meaningful content than it is to formulate the process whereby rules of combination, transformation, and sequence are learned. Bruner (1964) proposes that the child passes through three stages in developing modes of representing things. There is first an enactive mode of representation; then representation becomes iconic; and, finally, the stage of symbolic representation predominates.

In the *enactive* mode thought and action are closely linked. Objects are represented as motor responses and they are "thought of" in terms of what can be done with them. A distinctive characteristic of children's definitions is the reference to action: a ball—"You throw it"; flowers are—"to smell"; a hole is—"to dig."

The next development is into the predominant use of an *iconic* mode, in which perceptual imagery takes over the representational task. Children in this stage can recognize and reproduce but cannot create new forms based on rules. With the development of such imagery, the child is able to acquire a large vocabulary of names for things that can be defined by pointing or by simple description.

By exploiting the child's enactive and iconic tendencies, the parent or other socialization agent can get the acquisition of language under way. Since an object may be defined in many ways and at many levels of abstraction, the adult picks out the level most appropriate for the child's stage of development. To use Brown's (1965) example, a ten-cent piece can be called a coin, money, a 1932 Roosevelt, or a dime. To most of us, the word *dime* seems like its true name. To the young child, however, the parent is likely to refer to the coin as "money" in a context where the only thing the child learns about such objects is that one does not put them in one's mouth or drop them down the register. When a child is old enough to be sent to the store, however, the name of a dime for him must be *dime*. It would be a rare and insensitive parent who tried to tell a three-year-old child that a dime was currency in a broad system of monetary exchange that others would recognize as having a standard value. Such a "deeper" understanding of the word dime needs more than enactive and iconic tools to work with.

As the child passes into the third stage, *symbolic* representation, it becomes possible to conceive of things and relationships that cannot be pointed at or visualized. The symbolic mode is dominated by the kinds of combinations made possible through the productive uses of grammar. Toward the end of the child's second year the profound change inherent in the learning of grammar begins to occur. Single word utterances give way to word combinations. The combinations begin to take forms that gradually but inexorably approximate the accepted patterns of grammatical construction—the syntactical rules passed on from generation to generation within the culture.

One of the remarkable things about the acquisition of syntax is that the child must learn that certain structural forms recur with radically different content. If the content is always changing, if the range of content is so great to begin with, how is the structure of the language learned? How does the child appreciate that all verbs have something in common, that adjectives in spite of their great variety typically precede the nouns they qualify unless in predicate form, and so on? A recent series of experiments by Braine (1963) sheds some light on one facet of the problem: learning the proper sequence of words.

In the first experiment 10-year-old children were asked to play a word game that actually consisted of a series of problems in which the child was to decide which of two nonsense words should go first in a two-word "sentence." They were told to pretend that this was like learning a new language. In this way the children were taught by trial and error that certain nonsense words (KIV and JUF) always went first and others (BEW and MUB) always went second. After learning this, the children were given a generalization test. They were asked to complete sentences that started or finished with nonsense syllables they had not seen before by choosing between words whose proper positions they had already learned. For example, the new syllable FOJ would be presented as the first word, to be followed by either KIV or BEW. In this, BEW would be correct because it should always appear as a second or last word. The children's tendency to generalize correctly proved remarkable. Although two particular words had never been in combination before, the child had learned to expect them in a particular position.

A second experiment involved a more complicated task. Although the procedure was similar to that in the first experiment, phrases of variable length, consisting of one or two nonsense words, were used as substitutes for the single words in the previous experiment. Of the three words going first in a sentence, two (JUF and FOJ) were always preceded by a new nonsense word, GED. One of the two always following words (BEW) was itself always followed by a new syllable (POW). The result was that each of the following was a correct sentence: GED FOJ MUB, KIV YAG, and GED JUF BEW POW. Despite the variable sentence length and the fact that phrases rather than single words had to be treated as units, the subjects were able to generalize in completing new sentences, following the rules previously learned by trial and error.

A third experiment showed that subjects of the same age were able to generalize their learning both of the order of phrases and of the order of words within phrases in the construction of new sentences, and to do so simultaneously. Ten-year-olds, and presumably younger children as well, are capable of learning more than one kind of regularity at the same time. In the final experiment, Braine was able to induce generalization of proper order in four-year-old subjects. Pictures rather than words were used because the children were too young to read, and other adaptations were made to accommodate their age and level of experience. Even such young children were able to attend to order and generalize properly in related contexts.

We might ask what kind of learning this is. Does the child learn a rule or a principle of order that he thereafter explicitly applies? Braine is convinced on the basis of his subjects' comments that generalization is induced by a kind of perceptual learning, not by explicit rule application. The subject does not know why he answers as he does; it just seems right to him. The word or phrase belongs, seems familiar, in one position but not in the other.

This line of experimentation is only a beginning step, demonstrating that children of various ages have the capacity to learn the grammatical order of words through a process of "contextual generalization." In other words, the subject who learns to place a verbal segment of whatever length in a certain position in one context later tends to place the segment in the same position in other contexts. However, the actual steps in learning a first language remain obscure.

Almost nothing is known about the sequence in which various structures of English develop, but we do know that at a very early age children play with, and seemingly practice on, word combinations. It is also obvious that when a child begins to produce phrases that contain syntactical structure, this represents more than simple imitation. The child has probably never heard anyone say "I digged a hole," or "Look at the sheeps" and yet he may be heard making these kinds of errors. As Brown (1965) suggests, these are "mistakes which externalize the child's search for the regularities of English syntax" (p. 299). Perhaps the important thing to stress is that the search is an active and intelligent one, in which the child works his speech closer and closer to correct usage. In some dimly understood way, the child absorbs the latent structure of the language. He ends with a sense of what sounds right and what does not, and this feeling of familiarity or appropriateness applies to the forms as well as to the content of the language.

Language as a Determinant of Thought

Are languages merely arbitrary codes for dealing with the same inventory of objects, actions, and events? Or does a given kind of linguistic structure actually determine perceptual discrimination and condition the forms that thinking takes? To use Brown's comparison metaphor, is language a "cloak following the contours of thought" or a "mold into which infant minds are poured"?

One of the most persistent advocates of the "mold" position is Benjamin Lee Whorf. It is his contention that the language of any culture embodies the world view of the people concerned. The formulation of thought is not simply the matter of finding the most suitable linguistic expression for the thoughts. Rather, the structure of the language determines the possible directions of thinking the individual can take and contributes to his basic assumptions about the world. Much of the evidence for this deterministic position comes from the comparative analysis of languages of different cultures—particularly those with different developmental histories.

Anthropologists like Whorf himself and Sapir before him have been impressed with differences between languages that go beyond interchangeable naming responses or the use of different words for describing the same range of objects. These differences take a variety of forms. Not only are there differences in the boundary lines of discrimination between classes (in Hopi all things that fly are called by one name, except birds, which have a separate name; the Eskimos have seven names for different types and conditions of snow); there are also apparent differences in the expressions of relationship in a language and in the interpretive twists assigned to different events. Thus Whorf (1956) notes that most English words are divided into two classes, nouns and verbs, which roughly refer to substance and processes or actions, respectively. The Hopi language, on the other hand, classifies all events in terms of duration. Events of brief duration are always verbs, more protracted events are always nouns. The Nootka language of Vancouver Island has only one class of words for all events, regardless of type or duration. The English language makes frequent allusions to space in reference to time (long or short), whereas in the Hopi language, time has a vocabulary all its own. The question is whether these differences in grammatical structure and verbal usage are accompanied by basically different conceptions of events. An even more controversial question is whether such event conceptions are the effects and linguistic structure is the cause.

It should be no surprise that such questions are difficult to resolve by appeal to controlled experimental data. There is ample evidence that different languages develop different categories and that differentiation in these categories is widest in those areas of greatest concern in the culture involved. It is tempting to assume a strong relationship between perceptual discriminations and the linguistic categories available to report the discriminations. But it is important to consider the task requirements of the discriminator. An experiment by Brown and Horowitz (Maccoby, Newcomb, and Hartley, 1958, pp. 11–12) highlights this problem.

These investigators selected eight colored chips, with barely discernible color variations, from the reddish-violet region of the spectrum and showed them in the proper order to 15 Navajo-speaking and 15 English-speaking subjects. This was repeated for a series of trials and the subjects were asked to group chips as the experimenter had grouped them by his pronunciation of the syllable before each chip was shown. The placing of each chip on each trial was accompanied by a carefully vocalized syllable "identifying" the class into which the chip was to be placed. In all cases, four chips (adjacent in color) were labeled *ma* and four chips, *mo*. However, two *ma* and two *mo* chips were spoken of with the vowels drawn out and the others with the short form of the vowel. In spoken English no meaning is attached to such variations, but in Navajo a shift from a long to short *o* has as much significance as a shift from *o* to an *i* in English. Therefore, it was predicted that the Navajo-speaking subjects would tend to classify the chips into four groups whereas the English-speaking subjects would prefer a simple dichotomous grouping into *ma* and *mo* chips. The results clearly supported the hypothesis. *But,* it is important to note that many of the English-speaking subjects had noticed the variations in vowel length and simply decided they were unimportant. We are dealing here, then, with a decision about meaningful category boundaries, not with linguistically determined differences in auditory acuity.

The study by Brown and Horowitz involved classifications of linguistic differences themselves. Carroll and Casagrande (Maccoby et al., 1958) went beyond this kind of demonstration to show that differences in categorizing nonlinguistic objects may also be related to, and presumably caused by, differences in language structure. Because Navajos use different verbs in association with objects of different shapes and flexibilities, it was predicted and demonstrated that Navajo-speaking Indians were more likely than English-speaking Indians to match objects that were similar in shape but different in color. This result was especially borne out if the shape similarities required the same verbs in Navajo.

On the basis of this experiment it can be argued that language structure affects the perception and classification of objects in the environment. This is more than a truism since neither the stimulus nor the response is linguistic. At the very least, it appears that habits of discrimination developed in the learning of a language are generalized to affect nonverbal behavior in the realm of categorizing.

The broader problem of cause and effect is far from being solved, however, and perhaps it never will be. As Brown has commented, "I don't know of any attempts as yet to show that an independently defined linguistic pattern has either historical or biographical priority over the thought pattern it is supposed to determine" (Brown, 1958, p. 262). It seems plausible to assume that variations in language form and usage share the same status as other aspects of development and change. Linguistic elements are either borrowed or evolve in response to the necessary demands of a physical, economic, social, and religious environment. Without being entirely swept along by the thesis that language ". . . is the shaper of ideas, the program and guide for the individual's activities" (Whorf, 1956, p. 212), we may rest with the conclusion that language is an extremely important factor in perceptual grouping, memory, and the more complex processes of thinking and association. At least some ideas are undoubtedly "shaped" by language, and this is important enough to justify further research into the conditions that affect this process.

SUMMARY AND CONCLUSIONS

Perhaps the major theme of this chapter has been that the socialization of a child is markedly affected by his openness to and hunger for information. Since much of the information that appeases this hunger is passed on by other persons, cognitive development is an appropriate subject for social psychological analysis and speculation.

In tracing man's need for information back to its roots in childhood and infancy we have not been able to draw any firm conclusions. A strong case can be made for the position that we enter the world with a built-in responsiveness to stimuli, out of which develops an active interest in what exists in the environment and a selective attentiveness to changes in stimulation. Berlyne feels that this interest and attentiveness are generated by conceptual conflict—we seek out information when something is happening that does not fit our preconceptions. White focuses on the same kinds of data, but postulates a special "effectance motivation" to account for man's investigative curiosity when other needs are generally quiescent. Neither of these related theoretical conceptions is incompatible with the other, and we may keep both in mind as plausible formulations.

But what are the various ways in which information, to which the child is so naturally receptive, is transmitted by the agents of socialization? Without pretending to develop an exhaustive list of the modes by which information is transmitted to the child, we have identified descriptive instruction, advice and consultation, social comparison, observational learning, and empathic cognizance. The agent may thus serve at different times as instructor, informant, imitation model, or focus for comparison. The process of transmission is exceedingly complex and variable, but its consequences are roughly predictable. The child acquires an outlook that reflects the information to which he has been exposed, though in the course of development the reliability and credibility of the information source are increasingly scrutinized.

The second half of the chapter has dealt largely with perceptual and linguistic dispositions. The impact of information on the child must be assessed in terms of the internal structures developed to select, store, and transform it. These cognitive structures are shaped and changed by information, but they in turn govern the form in which information is processed. We have viewed perception as a problem-solving, decision-making process. The concept of *cognitive category* was introduced to reflect this point of view. The identification of an object or event as more than a confusion of colors, noises, and smells requires a decision to categorize it in terms of combinations of attributes that have been observed in prior experience to identify objects with similar functions. The categorization process involves both the screening out of irrelevant information and the addition of predicted characteristics. The perceiver constantly goes beyond the information given in deciding what a stimulus pattern represents.

Categories are accessible to varying degrees. The more accessible the category is, the less information needed for a decision of identification. When an individual is expecting something like X, he rapidly goes beyond the given information when any component of X appears. Category accessibility also affects the evaluation of attributes, often leading to distortions toward the typical instance. It is easy to move from the role of expectancy in perception and categorization to the effect of prior entry in the socialization process. If new experiences tend to be interpreted in terms of old categories, then the information that created those categories is obviously crucial. Since the parents "get there first with the most," they play an inordinate role in the development of cognitive structure. This is one of the most subtle and important aspects of their influence on the child.

The connections between cognition and language are intricate and defy experimental analysis. It is easier to cite the effects of language on behavior and cognition than to state where language comes from and how it develops. Through the recent work of Brown, Braine, and others, however, we can glimpse some of the points at which the child makes linguistic progress in contact with his social environment. The image we have tried to project is that of an active, experimenting, searching, child in frequent contact with a seemingly omniscient, adaptable, and generally concerned adult. Especially in the little that we do know about language learning we can see that cognitive development is an interactive process: the child and his environment produce changes in each other. Out of these changes are generated the structures that house and give meaning to experience. In the next chapter we comment further on the products of socialization and present a rather simple formulation of the nature of human personality in its social setting.

CHAPTER FIVE

The Products of Socialization

The same object or event may be viewed from several perspectives and often each perspective has its own labeling terminology. In the last chapter the example we gave was the ten-cent piece, but man can serve equally well. Man is a featherless biped, a creature of God, a carrier of the culture, a system that converts stimuli into responses, an advanced primate, and so forth. The biologist, the philosopher, and the psychologist all probe the nature of man, but their perspectives, and hence their vocabularies for dealing with man, differ. Not surprisingly, there have always been pressures in psychology to create general concepts that would have the same meaning in different areas and deal comprehensively with human nature. Especially in theorizing about man it is tempting to want to characterize his many-sided complexity or to construct an exhaustive inventory of his propensities. We propose to resist such temptations. Instead we shall seek to construct a useful *minimal person*—the socialized product of the conditions of effect and information dependence—having only those attributes needed to understand the major phenomena of social psychology.

THE MINIMAL PERSON FOR SOCIAL PSYCHOLOGY

The minimal person for our purposes is a composite of beliefs, values, and attitudes. In our drive to keep things simple we have focused primarily thus far on the concepts of *value* and *cognitive category*. Now we should like to develop these concepts in order to clarify the relations between cognition and motivation—between thought and feeling or desire. We shall introduce the new concepts, *belief* and *attitude,* and argue that attitudes derive from the combining of a belief with a value.

The Belief Concept

It is not a simple matter to distinguish beliefs from cognitive categories because it can be argued that the category *is* a belief relating some label to a characterizing attribute. We may "believe" that lemons are yellow, that Negroes are dark skinned, that the planets are made of green cheese. These attributes help to define what lemons, Negroes, and planets are. The only way that we can really make a distinction between a belief and a category is to propose that some attributes are *defining* and others are *associated*. Yellowness is a defining attribute of lemons; "goes well with fish" is an associated characteristic. It sounds right to say that we can believe lemons go well with fish, but it does not sound right to say that we can believe lemons are yellow or tart. For most people these are presumably defining attributes of the category that, over a certain range, establish whether the object is indeed a lemon in the beholder's mind. Similarly, even the bigot probably distinguishes in his own mind between "Negro blood" and sexual immorality. Negro blood is a defining attribute of the category Negro, sexual immorality is not—though the bigot may deeply believe that most Negroes are sexually immoral. Sexual immorality, in this case, is an associated characteristic. It may be difficult to establish accurate rules to govern the distinction, but it does express a subtle though real difference in the experience of defining an object and believing something about it.

Although such a foundation for the distinction between a category and a belief is a little shaky, we propose that a belief *expresses the relations between two cognitive categories when neither defines the other*. A belief concerns the associated characteristics of the object. Most beliefs may be expressed with greater or lesser precision in the language of the believer, though beliefs do not need to be verbalized or verbalizable. In linguistic terms a belief is, or can be transformed into, an assertion with a subject and a predicate: the righteous will enter the Kingdom of Heaven; yogurt leads to slimness; the Republicans are a divided party. The predicate consists of a connective (relating) verb and an object. The subject and object are both cognitive categories and, in any particular belief, the object is an associated characteristic of the subject. This view is quite consistent with that of Rokeach and Rothman (1965) who define a belief as a unique combination of "two stimuli, each having their separate meanings . . . the unique configuration consists of two components: a *subject* (S), capable of being characterized in many ways, and a *characterization* (C), capable of being applied to many subjects" (p. 129).

The Value Concept

In our usage value refers to a wide range of motivational phenomena. Any singular state or object for which the individual strives, or approaches, extols, embraces, voluntarily consumes, incurs expense to acquire, is a positive value. Anything that the individual avoids, escapes from, deplores, rejects, or attacks is a negative value. Values animate the person; they move him around his environment because they define its attractive and repelling sectors. This is true whether the individual values manure (for his garden) or diamonds (for his true love).

The concept of value expresses a relationship between a person's emotional feelings and particular cognitive categories. Values are thus cognitive in part and affective in part. For a man to say, "War is hell" implies a strong negative value if we assume that hell is the equivalent of "bad." The man is talking about a particular kind of category, war, and is attaching personal affect or feeling to that category.

Most values are conditioned by experience. The more important ones are internalized so that they no longer need reinforcement or justification. But the concept of value is not defined in terms of its linkage to primary drives or the degree to which it is internalized. A value may be a newly formed attitude or a basic and long-standing conviction. We can value or disvalue any member of any cognitive category, whether the category is a food, a person, a group, an idea, an ideology, or the self. Owing to our permissive definition, a value exists whenever an emotion implying liking or disliking attaches to a cognition.

The Attitude Concept: the Syllogistic Conclusion

We propose to treat an *attitude* as the implication of combining a belief with a relevant value. Relevance in this case merely means that the cognitive category, which serves as the associated characteristic in the belief, also serves as the cognitive component (the subject) of the value. The underlying structure of an attitude is best represented as a syllogism.

A syllogism, the basic form of a mediated inference or argument, contains three propositions: the major and minor premises and the conclusion. The term contained in both premises is called the *middle* term; the predicate of the conclusion is the *major* term; and the subject of the conclusion, the *minor* term. The premise that contains the major term is called the major premise, and the premise containing the minor term, the minor premise. Two examples of syllogisms are:

1. *All Negroes are lazy.*
   Lazy people are bad.
   Therefore, all Negroes are bad.

2. *Fluoride is a poison.*
   Poison is bad.
   Therefore, fluoride is bad.

The major premise in each syllogism is the second statement, since its predicate is the predicate of the conclusion; and the first statement is the minor premise, since its subject is the subject of the conclusion.

In each syllogism, the attitude is the conclusion and the two premises generating it represent the structure of the attitude. The major premise of an attitude syllogism is a value statement. The minor premise is a belief connecting one category (the minor term: Negroes or fluoride) with another (the middle term: laziness or poison).

Perhaps it should be said that there are many forms of belief, value, and attitude statements that fit the general paradigm. In many communications one or more of the attitude premises may never be stated, or be stated without the conclusion being formally expressed. Furthermore, there are alternate forms in which the relationship between cognitive categories may be expressed and alternate forms of characterizing the affective component in the value statement. The declaration that "fluoride is a poison, therefore fluoridation must be fought" appears to be nothing more than an attitude generated by a belief. But an implicit value statement links the two; namely, that "poison is bad for the system." We might be more likely to hear this elliptical form of the syllogism in conversation or debate because it is assumed that everyone knows poison (or laziness, in the case of the earlier example) is bad.

Our next step makes the syllogistic approach more complicated but more interesting and useful. To define a belief as an assertion linking two cognitive categories is not to imply that beliefs are simple or that they defy further analysis. A given belief may itself be the conclusion of a syllogism whose premises may be the conclusions of syllogisms, and so on. The syllogisms

1. *All nonwhites are lazy.*   2. *Fluoride is an acid.*
Negroes are nonwhites.   *Acids are poisonous.*
Therefore, Negroes are lazy.   *Fluoride is a poison.*

reflect that syllogisms generate beliefs as well as attitudes. They also show that belief conclusions as well as belief premises may be incorrect.

The value premise in a given syllogism may be the attitudinal conclusion of prior syllogisms. For example:

Councilman Fox favors fluoridation.
Fluoride is bad. (See above.)
Councilman Fox must be fought.

It is apparent that attitudes such as "Negroes are bad" may have complex underlying structures. The premises in the syllogism could be second-, third-, or fourth-order derivatives of other beliefs and values that create a deep "vertical" structure.

We might imagine that the deeper the vertical structure, the more vulnerable the attitude to change since there are more points open to attack. An appropriate metaphor might be the proverbial house of cards. However, it is almost inevitable that the vertical structure is buttressed and reinforced by horizontal support at a number of points. This means that there are different routes to the same conclusion. Thus the belief and value premises

Negroes are dirty.
Dirtiness is bad.

are different from the premises of the previous syllogism, but they generate the same attitude: "Therefore, Negroes are bad." We can easily imagine a wide, horizontal array of syllogisms yielding this general conclusion. Fishbein (1965) has proposed that attitudes are evaluative summaries of a person's various beliefs about an object or concept. Each belief expresses the relation between the concept and some associated characteristic (our belief premise); the associated characteristic is itself positively or negatively valued (our value premise). The summary attitude is the resulting evaluative stance toward the concept taking into account the evaluative direction of component beliefs. The horizontal structure essentially lays out the components summarized by the final attitude statement. Fishbein's analysis, though very close to the present one, ignores the developmental basis of the component beliefs and values and thus says nothing about the attitude's vertical structure.

The complete vertical and horizontal premise structure of a particular attitude can be complex indeed. Figure 5.1 summarizes in schematic outline some of the ingredients that might form the structure of an attitude opposing the admission of Red China to the United Nations. In this example,

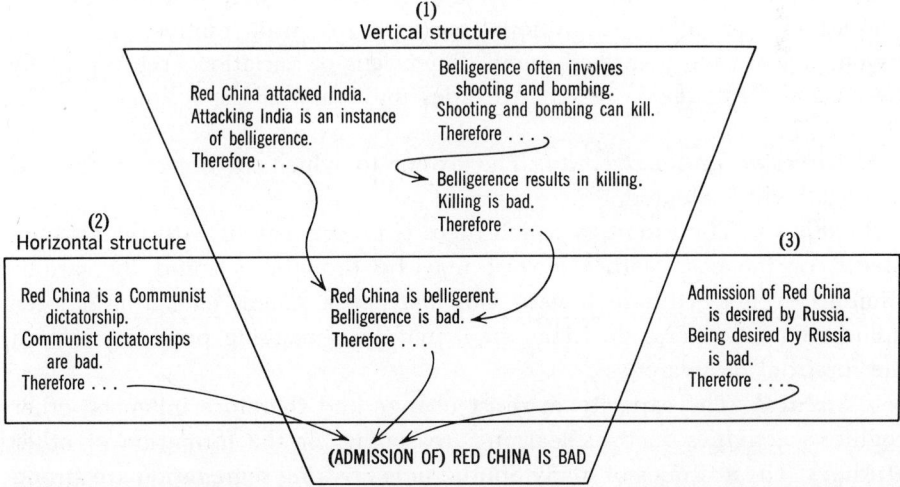

Figure 5.1. Portions of an attitude structure opposing admission of Red China to the United Nations.

a two-step vertical structure is indicated in the central portion of the figure (1). The culminating attitude (*Admission of Red China is bad*) is the conclusion of a belief and value premise, each of which are conclusions of other syllogisms. The same evaluative statement can represent an attitude in one syllogism and a value premise in another. The belief involved in the syllogism generating the value premise is, finally, the conclusion of still a third syllogism (starting with *Belligerence often involves guns and ammunition*). The horizontal structure of the attitude is illustrated by the presence of syllogisms (2) and (3), each having the same conclusion as 1.

RELATED FORMULATIONS AND THE PROBLEM OF COGNITIVE CONSISTENCY

Perhaps no other topic in social psychology has invited as great a volume of discussion and theorizing as the nature of attitudes. As early as 1925, J. B. Watson defined social psychology as the study of attitudes. From G. W. Allport's influential chapter in Murchison's (1935) handbook, through a succession of textbook treatments, the attitude concept has had a thorough examination; it has been defined and redefined, quarrelled over and debated. Some have emphasized its cognitive and affective components (e.g., Krech and Crutchfield, 1948); others have defined attitudes in terms of response consistency (e.g., Campbell, 1950); still others have suggested that the attitude concept should be replaced by more fundamental variables like habit strength and drive (Doob, 1947).

In addition to attempting to define attitude so that it could be distinguished from other dispositional concepts like trait, motive, and habit, psychologists have identified many dimensions of variation (see especially Krech and Crutchfield, 1948). Attitudes may vary in the following ways:

1. Direction and Extremity. The extent to which an object is favored or negatively evaluated.

2. Saliency. The extent to which there is preoccupation with the attitude object, or the ease with which it may be brought to mind by various stimulus events. Attitude toward God may be a salient background force influencing behavioral decisions, or it may be a nagging preoccupation in the forefront of awareness.

3. Strength. The capacity to resist change and therefore influence other cognitive activities such as learning, reasoning, or the formation of other attitudes. The attitudes of many Southerners favoring segregation are strong in this sense, since they often bring about changes in other beliefs. Many such changes may be described as rationalizations. Variations in strength may be viewed primarily as the product of the attitude's horizontal structure: the greater the number of syllogistic paths to the same attitudinal conclusion, the greater the strength of the attitude.

4. Cognitive Differentiation. The degree to which an attitude is cognitively elaborated and to which its belief structure possesses rich detail versus the degree to which the attitude is vague and undifferentiated. This feature seems clearly related to vertical structure, or the extent to which belief and value premises are products of other syllogisms.

5. Action Orientation. The degree to which specific components of action are part of the cognitive pattern supporting the attitude. Though American anti-Semitism is a continuing social problem, anti-Semitic attitudes in this country usually lack the specific and elaborated action components that were part of the attitude pattern in Nazi Germany. Prejudice does not necessarily result in overt discrimination.

6. Verifiability. The extent to which the cognitive (belief) component of an attitude may be subjected to clear test. Most differences in religious belief, for example, rest on fundamental differences in assumptions about God's nature; in the present sense of the word such beliefs are low in verifiability.

Many of these dimensions of variation tend to be highly correlated when we examine and try to describe existing social attitudes. Verifiable attitudes are usually strong; strength and saliency are apt to go together; neutral attitudes are seldom so strong or so salient as extreme ones. Nevertheless, we *can* think of cases where this covariation is broken up, so that the dimensions seem to have some conceptual independence.

Since 1950 there has been an increasing interest in the internal structure of the attitude itself. This interest has derived largely from the marked increase in research on problems of attitude change, but it also reflects active, broader trends in the study of mental organization and internal consistency. We shall review briefly four prominent theoretical models, examine their relation to our own syllogistic formulation of attitude structure, and consider their implications for cognitive consistency. Discussion of a fifth consistency theory, cognitive dissonance, will be deferred until the following chapter.

The Affect-Cognition Model

A view that is closely related to ours, and that is prominent in many recent treatments of the structure of an attitude, considers an attitude to be the resultant of linking certain values (seen as *ends*) with certain cognitions (seen as *means*). Rosenberg (1960) proposes that we consider an attitude toward a particular object as a function of (1) the probability that the object leads to good or bad consequences and (2) the intensity of the emotion expected from these consequences.

This proposal has certain implications for the measurement of attitudes. Focusing on attitudes toward free speech for Communists and Negro housing segregation, Rosenberg (1956) had each of 117 subjects sort 35 cards, each containing a specific goal or value such as: All people having equal rights; People sticking to their own groups; Keeping promises made to others; Having the value of property well protected. Subjects were to place each card in a category from −10 to +10, indicating the direction and intensity of affect attached to the "goal" concerned. After this was accomplished the subjects made separate ratings for each of the two attitudinal issues, appraising the *probability* that granting free speech to Communists or removing Negro segregation would aid or block the attainment of each goal.

By this procedure, Rosenberg was able to compute an "index of affective loading." For each issue the instrumental probability values were multiplied by the desirability value of the goal, the 35 products being summed algebraically. If, for example, a subject saw removal of segregation as having a .7 probability of reducing property values, which in turn had a satisfaction score of −5, the contribution of that goal item to the affective loading would be −.35. Through use of such an affective loading score Rosenberg was able to predict a subject's attitudes toward the free speech and segregation issues as measured by direct questions about the issues.

This view of attitudes comes close to that implied by our syllogistic model. The affect-cognition approach says, in effect, that a person has a particular attitude about an object because the object makes it easier or harder to attain certain values. In other words,

> x *leads to* y (*cognition*)—*with a certain probability.*
> y *is bad* (*affect*)—*to a certain degree of intensity.*
> *Therefore,* x *is bad* (*attitude*)—*to a degree reflecting the product of cognition probability and affect intensity.*

Or, to use some of Rosenberg's own materials, slightly modified:

> *Housing segregation thwarts "having equal rights."*
> *"Having equal rights" is good.*
> *Therefore, housing segregation is bad.*

A proper rendering of Rosenberg's position, and the associated measurement procedures, would require considering a variety of syllogisms all bearing on the same attitudinal conclusion. In our terms, Rosenberg's measuring procedures represent a selected sample of belief and value premises considered relevant to a particular attitude object.

Heider's "Balance Theory"

In 1946, Heider formulated an abstract system for representing cognition-sentiment relations which has since influenced a variety of other theorists. This treatment was further elaborated in his 1958 book. Heider's orientation was that of the naive phenomenologist; that is, one who attempts to see things from the standpoint of his subjects and in terms related to *their* cognitive categories. This orientation led him to consider how persons and objects were seen to be related by the unsophisticated man-in-the-street and to formulate a system of notations and abbreviations to cover the basic features of these relations. A selected sample of these notations (adapted from Heider, 1958) follows:

p = The subject, the person whose cognitions are being considered.
o, q = Other persons.
x, y, z = Objects: impersonal entities, things, situations; all cognitive categories other than persons.
$p\,L\,x$ = p has a positive attitude toward x.
$p\,U\,x$ = x belongs to p in some way.

Heider made a basic distinction between sentiment relations and unit relations. A *unit relation*, represented by the symbol U, is one that connects two objects (cognitive categories) in a relation of belonging. This relation is vaguely specified and may include ownership (Bob owns that house), responsibility for (Jane slapped Jim), relationship to (father and son), and so on. A basic criterion of unit relations is whether the objects are likely to be seen as parts of the same "natural" perceptual configuration from the standpoint of p, the person whose cognitions are being considered. In each of the foregoing instances the same symbolic notation would apply: $p\,U\,x$, where p = Bob, Jane, father; U = belongs to; and x = house, Jim, son.

The unit relation is roughly comparable to our belief premise, though the unit was perhaps meant to include more primitive perceptual groupings than the kind of relations involved in assertions linking two cognitive categories. Obviously unit relations would include definitional statements, and we have tried to rule these out.

Heider's *sentiment relation* is roughly the equivalent of our value premise. Such a relation connects one person to another person or object by the symbols L, for like, or DL for dislike. Thus $p\,L\,o$ means any of the following: p loves o, p is attracted to o, p feels warmly toward o. Intensity is not specified within the notational system either for sentiment or unit relations.

The consistency between sentiment and unit relations and between different sentiment relations was a major interest of Heider's. In his terminology, we may ask whether the cognitions reflected in these relations are *in balance*. When cognitive relations are not in balance, the individual suffers feelings of strain and there are tendencies to change one or more cognitions in the direction of greater balance. A balanced state exists when sentiments toward related cognitions (the members of a "unit") are in the same affective direction. If $p \, L \, o$ and $o \, U \, x$ then $p \, L \, x$ or there will be imbalance. A concrete instance of this is the feeling of strain which a person might suffer if his best friend wears a necktie he considers appalling, or the friend says something with which he violently disagrees. Wearing and saying both exemplify unit relations.

An interesting feature of Heider's formulation is that new relations may be predicted from old ones. Thus if q likes r and p likes q, we may predict that p will like r. If he does not, then this will not be a balanced relationship. Other relationships exemplifying cognitive balance and imbalance include:

Balanced relationships

$p \, L \, o, \; o \, L \, p$
$p \, L \, o, \; o \, L \, p, \; o \, U \, x, \; p \, L \, x$
$p \, L \, o, \; o \, DL \, x, \; p \, DL \, x$
$p \, L \, x, \; x \, U \, y, \; p \, L \, y$

Unbalanced relationships

$p \, L \, o, \; o \, DL \, p$
$p \, L \, o, \; o \, L \, p, \; o \, U \, x, \; p \, DL \, x$
$p \, L \, o, \; o \, DL \, x, \; p \, L \, x$
$p \, L \, x, \; x \, U \, y, \; p \, DL \, y$

Heider's formulation has been the prototype and impetus for other treatments of cognitive consistency, notably those of Newcomb (1953) and of Cartwright and Harary (1956), but he was actually more concerned with the analysis and understanding of interpersonal relations than with elaborating a theory of cognitive structure. We shall review some of the more important implications of his work for the perception of persons in Chapter Eight. Here our main interest is to compare his treatment of cognition-sentiment relations with our own formulation of attitude structure. There are parallels between some of Heider's examples and the belief-value-attitude syllogism. For example, we could construct the following set of premises and their conclusion:

> *Bill owns a new Mustang.*
> *All Mustangs are good.*
> *Therefore, Bill is good.*

This would seem to be the equivalent of: $o \cup x$, $p \perp x$, $p \perp o$. Stated this way the set of relationships does not stray too far from valid syllogistic form, *if* we are allowed to assume that "owns" is an associated characteristic of Bill.

But we may invent other syllogisms that stray further from the canons of logic while remaining "true" in Heider's network of hypotheses about balanced cognitions:

> *Bill owns a new Mustang.*
> *Bill is good.*
> *Therefore, all Mustangs are good.*

This is no more valid logically than to say: x is a y, x is also a z, therefore all y's are z's; or to say gold is a metal, gold is also valuable, therefore all metals are valuable.

In general, Heider's formulation does not distinguish between premises and conclusions and it makes rather strong psychological assumptions relating unit formation (ownership in the example just cited) to valuation. The assumptions help to make Heider's approach interesting, and to extend its flexibility and range of potential application. However, the notion of a belief is poorly represented by Heider's concept of unit formation and we feel that his terminology is more appropriate for suggesting patterns of interpersonal attraction than for expressing the underlying structure of attitudes.

The Psycho-logic Model

Abelson and Rosenberg (1958; Rosenberg and Abelson, 1960) have developed a variation of Heider's balance model that they used successfully to predict the resolution of experimentally induced cognitive conflict. They refer to their model as symbolic *psycho-logic* because, like Heider's formulation, it attempts to deal with the strain toward psychological consistency that characterizes human thinking. In their variation two concepts (cognitions or cognitive categories) must be unrelated, positively related, or negatively related. A positive relation is broadly defined to include: likes, equals, possesses, promotes, affirms—a combination of the L + U of Heider's formulation. Negative relations are also defined inclusively to encompass: opposes, prevents, is incompatible with, and other terms of negation. A major innovation in this model is the provision that the person has positive or negative feelings toward the concepts themselves. Thus rather complex cognitive relations between concepts of different affective values may be readily symbolized. The same relations would take several statements within Heider's symbolic notation. Cognitive relations are seen as balanced in such cases as two positively valued concepts being positively related, a negative and a positive concept negatively related, or two negative concepts positively related.

Rosenberg and Abelson (1960) build an example of an unbalanced relation from the cognitive ingredients: coeds, interference, good grades. If we assume that Yale students like the idea of having coeds around, are fond of good grades, and yet believe that coeds at Yale would interfere with good grades, this would be an unbalanced cognitive relation. Given the psycho-logic of a Yale student in such a state of imbalance, we can predict some change within the cognitive relation. Either the importance of good grades would be devalued, the prospect of having coeds around would pall, or the students would convince themselves that coeds would not interfere with getting good grades.

An important feature of the Rosenberg-Abelson formulation is that imbalance can exist without necessarily creating strains toward consistency. The person has a number of mechanisms for dealing with unbalanced cognitive relations. He may redefine the concepts, insist they are not related, or in subtler ways mentally isolate concepts that are not in balance so that it is not necessary to confront their contradictory implications. This can take the form of never thinking about one concept when thinking about the other.

We have dealt with the simple case in which the subject of the belief is neutral until linked within the syllogism to a value. Abelson and Rosenberg assume that value can attach to both cognitions associated by the belief statement. A syllogism revised to accommodate psycho-logic might look something like:

>   A *is positively related to* B.
>   A *is good.*
>   B *is bad.*
>   *Therefore, . . .*
>   A *isn't as good as I thought.*
>   B *is better than I thought.*

Thus the major adjustment in our formulation required to accommodate the kind of cognitive relation discussed by Abelson and Rosenberg is provision for a more complex value premise and the possibility of at least two different conclusions.

Osgood and Tannenbaum's Congruity Principle

Osgood and Tannenbaum's (1955) introduction of the congruity principle may be viewed as further specification of symbolic psycho-logic when one person makes an assertion in front of another. Their interest in attitude structure developed as an offshoot to a more general interest in the nature and measurement of meaning (Osgood, 1952). For Osgood and Tannenbaum an attitude is essentially the evaluative meaning of a concept, as distinct from other meanings it may have. Two people may have the same attitude toward a concept—attach the same evaluative significance to it—and yet have very different nonevaluative associations to it. An attitude is identified only in terms of its evaluative direction and intensity, not in terms of the beliefs that support it. Two persons can have the same negative attitude toward Negroes and yet one may believe them to be passive and weak, whereas the other may see them as strong and powerful.

Having defined attitude in this general way, Osgood and Tannenbaum turn their attention to communications in which a source makes an evaluative assertion about some object of judgment. Both the source and object fall somewhere on the subject's dimension of evaluative meaning. If both are positively valued, and the source makes a positive assertion about the object, there will be "congruity." Similarly, congruity will exist, for Osgood and Tannenbaum as for Abelson and Rosenberg, if a bad source endorses a bad position, a good source condemns a bad position, or a bad source condemns a good position. Incongruity increases to the extent that the state of affairs departs from these conditions—for example: President Johnson (+) favors Oil Depletion Allowance (−); or *Daily Worker* (−) backs Voting Rights Bill (+). When there is such incongruity Osgood and Tannenbaum predict changes in the evaluation of both source and object. Johnson will be liked a little less, Oil Depletion Allowance will be seen a little more favorably. Which changes the most is a function of which is the most "polarized" to start with. That is, the concept (source or object) that is evaluated more positively or negatively by the subject changes less than the concept that is closer to the indifference point.

The implications of this latter assumption are spelled out in precise mathematical detail by Osgood and Tannenbaum (1955). Such precision is made possible by the assumption that both source and object of judgment can be located on the same seven-point evaluative scale. Thus numerical values can be assigned to the changes predicted in evaluating both the source and the object of judgment. Furthermore, the authors report results that offer good support for the congruity hypothesis.

Since the Osgood and Tannenbaum formulation may be subsumed by the more general model of Abelson and Rosenberg, the former bears the same relation to our syllogism notion. Once again, both formulations deal with a syllogism containing two value premises, one referring to each of the terms related by the belief premise. If these premises lead to the same conclusion there is cognitive balance. If they lead to different conclusions there will be imbalance or incongruity and a tendency toward attitude change. It should be noted that Osgood and Tannenbaum differ from

Abelson and Rosenberg in arguing that both source and assertion will necessarily change, and that they will change in proportion to the relative polarity of each.

ATTITUDINAL CONSISTENCY

In presenting the concept of attitude as the conclusion of one or more belief-value syllogisms, we run the risk of overemphasizing man's rationality. Do different syllogisms ever generate in the person different conclusions about the same attitudinal object? In other words, is the horizontal structure of an attitude always a network of mutually reinforcing premises and conclusions? Without exception, those who theorize about attitude structure would be likely to endorse the same general answer to these questions: there are indeed inconsistencies in the structure of an attitude, but potent forces operate in the direction of consistency. Inconsistency, incongruity, imbalance—these are states the person tries to avoid, although he may not always succeed. There is, then, a general but not unlimited trend toward consistency of cognitive relations.

We may distinguish two different kinds of consistency. First, there is consistency within the structure of a single attitude. Second, there is consistency between attitudes. In order for there to be any issue of consistency between attitudes, the subject of one attitude (the minor term) must be similar in some way to the subject of another attitude. Unrelated attitudes can be neither consistent nor inconsistent with each other.

The Internal Consistency of Attitudes

As Katz and Stotland (1959) argue, "the trend toward consistency exists in its strongest form within the confines of a single attitude; there it seeks to make the components of the attitude congruent with one another" (p. 444). This is because the components of an attitude are all tied to the same object, which must be dealt with in some particular fashion and not in different ways at once. What evidence have we that such a consistency trend operates within the structure of an attitude? The data fall into three categories: prediction of premises from knowledge of a conclusion, distortion of information about premises to fit a desired conclusion, and induction of conclusions by providing appropriate premises.

1. From knowledge of the direction of an attitude, or of behavior from which attitudes may readily be inferred, we should be able to predict that certain premises will be more readily endorsed than others. Anecdotal support for this ability is easy to accumulate but, perhaps because the proposition seems obvious, supporting scientific evidence is fairly sparse.

Feather (1963) found that nonsmokers were more inclined than smokers to accept the premise that smoking led to lung cancer. If we may infer from the habit of smoking a more or less positive attitude toward the practice, this provides evidence for the consistency principle.

Rosenberg's (1956) measurement model itself supports this proposal. As stated earlier, Rosenberg could predict attitudes with a fair degree of success from knowledge of a person's values and his beliefs about things that affected their attainment. By approaching the same data from a different direction, we could successfully predict values and beliefs from a knowledge of attitudes.

One way to test the present proposal is to modify directly and experimentally a person's attitude toward an object of judgment and then observe the repercussions on related beliefs and values. Rosenberg (1960) accomplished this difficult feat by hypnotizing subjects and telling them, for example, "after you awake . . . you will feel strongly opposed to the United States' policy of giving economic aid to foreign nations." No reasons supporting this command were offered, but the subjects showed marked adjustments in the belief and value premises related to the attitude hypnotically changed. This study will be further discussed in Chapter Twelve.

2. From knowledge of attitude or related behavior we should be able to predict that premises leading to conclusions inconsistent with the attitude will be reinterpreted or distorted. Several studies have shown that reasoning processes may be biased in the direction of prevailing attitudes, that wish fulfillment sometimes interferes with logic. Again, we could cite many examples, but the following is typical. Feather (1964) gave his subjects a reasoning test consisting of 40 syllogisms, 24 of which concerned religion. Of the latter, 12 had proreligious conclusions and 12 had antireligious conclusions. In each case six were logically valid, six were invalid. An example of an invalid proreligious syllogism, simplified and paraphrased, follows:

Tolerance toward man creates love and harmony.
Christianity creates love and harmony.
Therefore, Christianity gives rise to tolerance toward mankind.

The subject's task was to indicate whether a given argument was logically sound or logically unsound.

The subject's general favorable feeling toward religion was measured a week later by a questionnaire asking for the degree to which he endorsed the syllogistic conclusions. The major result of the study, for our purposes, was that proreligious subjects overestimated the logical validity of invalid proreligious syllogisms and underestimated the validity of valid antireligious syllogisms. The predicted reverse trend was observed in antireligious subjects, but was less striking.

3. By exposing the person to persuasive communications that enhance the likelihood of a premise being true, we should be able to influence him to adopt appropriate attitudinal conclusions. McGuire's (1960) work comes close to confirming this proposition, although, strictly speaking, belief syllogisms rather than belief-value-attitude syllogisms were involved. McGuire devised a large number of propositions in the familiar form: All A's are B's, all B's are C's, therefore all A's are C's. He then constructed a questionnaire containing three propositions in 16 syllogisms, but dispersed them so that a proposition from one syllogism was mixed in with propositions from other syllogisms. He then asked the subject to indicate his belief in the truth of each of the 48 resulting propositions. About a week later the subjects received persuasive messages arguing for the truth of each of the 16 minor premises, the major premise and the conclusions not being mentioned, and again they indicated their belief in each of the 48 propositions. Another week later they indicated their beliefs for the third time.

The results may be stated in terms of two conclusions: (1) In the immediate after-test of the subject's beliefs there was a significant change toward greater belief in the unmentioned conclusion; belief in the mentioned premise, as expected, changed even more in the direction of the message. (2) In the delayed after-test most of the change in the unmentioned, derived issue was retained, while belief in the directly measured minor premise declined toward its initial state. The latter finding suggests a kind of mental inertia: it takes a while for change to percolate through the belief network to affect derived propositions, and once this happens, it takes time for the effects of persuasion to dissipate.

Since several other studies were *un*able to find any comparable derived effects of a persuasive communication (cf. Hovland and Mandel, 1952), we must accept the McGuire results with some caution. Clearly, more research is needed on this topic—especially research that uses the belief-attitude syllogism format.

It should be mentioned that there are many studies of persuasion and communication in which an attempt is made to change attitudes by changing beliefs. With a few exceptions, however, these studies also mention the desired conclusions along with arguments relating to the premises.

Consistency between Attitudes

Although the internal consistency of a particular attitude presents complex problems of analysis and measurement, the relation between attitudes involves even greater complexities. Merely to begin such a consideration requires some way of detecting relevance, or of deciding when one attitude has implications for the validity of another. The question of consistency across attitudes becomes a question that cannot be answered until certain theoretical assumptions are made and criteria for determining consistency are derived from them.

One way to look at the problem of consistency between attitudes is to adopt a correlational approach. That is, we may start with one attitudinal (pro-con) dimension, locate individuals on it, and inquire into their position on other dimensions which theory or hunch suggest are related. A striking example of this approach is the study of authoritarianism, which may be viewed as the attempt to show that anti-Semitism, for example, is not an isolated attitude, but is embedded in the total structure of personality. In other words, once we know that a person is anti-Semitic, we should be able to predict other things about him. The entire configuration of attitudes has come to be labeled authoritarianism, or the authoritarian syndrome.

An impressive line of research into the nature of this syndrome was launched by Adorno, Frenkel-Brunswik, Levinson, and Sanford (1950). These investigators began their study of the personality dynamics of the prejudiced person with a crude but rather elaborate theoretical network that said something about the correlates of prejudice in other attitudinal realms, the functions that prejudice might serve in the adjustive economy of the individual, and the likely developmental history of the prejudiced person. Exploring first the hypothesis that anti-Semitism was part of a general pattern of prejudice, rather than an isolated attribute, the investigators showed that those who endorsed negative statements about Jews also endorsed similar kinds of statements about Negroes, Filipinos, and other minorities. In addition, the anti-Semite tended to endorse a fairly coherent cluster of authoritarian statements emphasizing deference to superiors, hostility toward inferiors, unwillingness to introspect about his own feelings, and an inclination to project unacceptable impulses. There was weaker evidence, but still significant enough to be interesting, that the now roughly defined authoritarian personality tended to be more conservative in political-economic matters.

By interview and projective tests the investigators then proceeded to explore certain hypotheses about (a) the world view of the authoritarian individual, and (b) his attitudes and reminiscences about early childhood and the family environment. Their findings here gave further support to authoritarian personality theory. For example, high authoritarians report a relatively harsh and more threatening type of home discipline than the low authoritarians. The formers' parents tend to adopt highly conventional goals for their children and to view the child's behavior in terms of their own, rather than their children's needs. Low authoritarians show a greater tendency to be aware of their own unacceptable impulses and feelings, whereas high authoritarians tend both to repress and displace their unacceptable tendencies by attributing them to others. The high authoritarians tend toward idealization of the parent during the interview but occasionally their feelings of resentment break through. In the projective test materials there are more signs of latent hostility toward the parents and other authority figures. The low authoritarians, on the other hand, are characterized more by objective appraisal, and among them aggression in the fantasy material is better controlled and more subtly expressed. In sum, the evidence from various sources—what a subject says about his family and himself, stories he tells to Thematic Appercetion Test cards, his scoring pattern on a battery of attitude scales—combine to form a rather consistent picture of the authoritarian personality syndrome. We can reasonably say that a set of attitudes predicted to be correlated by the theory of authoritarianism are, in fact, quite consistent with one another.

A common feature of all major theories of cognitive balance is the prediction of consistencies across different attitudes. Heider's formulation has several features pertinent to the present discussion. Heider predicted that if two concepts are related in the perceiver's mind—that is, if they "belong together"—there is a tendency to feel the same way about them, to evaluate them similarly. This clearly amounts to a statement about the consistency of attitudes. He did not formally define his notion of relationship, belonging, U, but he illustrated it by a few prominent examples. Because he did not formally provide criteria for determining the degree to which cognitive categories are related, the predictive power of his formulation is low.

Rosenberg and Abelson (1960) are somewhat more explicit about the criteria of relevance between cognitions, but deal only with the dimension of evaluation (*favoring* versus *opposing*). Their formulation and that of Osgood and Tannenbaum (1955) directly grapple with the problem of consistency between attitudes in considering evaluation of both the source and his assertion.

When assertions about different concepts are attributed to the same source, the source can serve as a mediating link between the concepts. Concentrating on the case in which one source was associated with two otherwise unrelated concepts, Tannenbaum (1966) predicted that a change in subjects' evaluation of one concept would alter their evaluation of the source and therefore change their attitude toward the second concept. He confirmed this prediction in an experiment in which the source, a fictitious Professor Samuels, was presented as favoring (or opposing) teaching machines and as favoring (or opposing) Spence Learning Theory. When the subjects later received persuasive information that supported or attacked teaching machines, their attitudes toward Professor Samuels became more or less favorable in line with congruity predictions, and attitudes toward Spence

Learning Theory also varied although nothing further was mentioned about this second topic. For example, if a subject were in the experimental condition where Professor Samuels attacked teaching machines and supported Spence's theory, and where subsequent information supported teaching machines, his attitude toward the Professor and toward Spence's theory tended to become more negative. Thus the attitude change toward the second concept was in a direction opposite to that on the manipulated first concept because of the mediating attitude change toward the source.

We may conclude this section by noting that there is widespread agreement concerning the general tendency for beliefs, values, and attitudes to be organized into broader structures and for this organization to be internally consistent. Beyond this there is general agreement that inconsistencies within and between attitudes tend to generate changes in some or all of the component parts. These changes, predictably, are in the direction of increased consistency. The kind of cognitive inconsistency discussed here is but one instance of the broader notion of conceptual conflict discussed in Chapter Four.

It would be a mistake to exaggerate the prevalence of internal consistency in cognitive organization. Man is not completely rational, nor does he always succeed in bringing his beliefs and values into line with his attitudes. Each of us finds ways to live with inconsistency. These usually involve some form of self-deception, or of segregating inconsistent cognitions. But the more basic point is that there are pressures toward balance—strains toward consistency—that animate our information-seeking activities, our reactions to other persons, and many other features of social life. Much of this book is concerned with the various guises and forms of inconsistency reduction. Our next task is to deal, in broad outline form, with the origins of these consistency pressures in man's relation to the environment and his needs to act adaptively in it.

ENVIRONMENTAL PRESSURES TOWARD PERSONAL INTEGRATION

Our basic position is that consistency across dispositions and the stability of dispositions through time can be dealt with as emerging products of organism-environment relations. This is more fruitful than merely postulating the operation of unifying or integrative forces in personality functioning and treating them as part of the unfolding endowment of each human being. The *capacity* for integration is surely endowed, but the form and extent of integration are determined by the requirements of meaningful action in a complex environment. Let us develop this position and explore the physical and social origins of integration and consistency in the human personality.

Culture Pattern and Cultural Norms

A reasonable first step is to examine the concept of culture and to pursue its implications for our problem. A culture is a system of shared beliefs, values, symbols, and performance styles that characterizes a group. A culture is, in effect, the residue of past efforts of a group to solve its problems of survival and growth. A particular generation within a society confronts a physical and social environment that has been shaped by earlier generations in their attempts to cope with life's problems. The states of the physical environment are infinitely more predictable because of this heritage. Protective clothing, heating and air-conditioning systems, fertilizers that standardize plant growth, flood control techniques, and principles of fireproof construction—these buffers against environmental variations are part of the legacy from past generations.

Of greater relevance to the concerns of this book are those aspects of culture having to do with our being born into a prearranged *social* environment. Cultures tend to differ in both great and trivial respects in the particular systems that evolve for regulating human relationships. Physical inventions are probably more readily transmitted across the boundaries of particular cultural groups than are customs and social conventions. Each identifiable culture is thus to some extent unique and has its own peculiar history.

Cultures increase the predictability of social life. The customs or conventions of a culture reduce the randomness of events and provide a stable framework of expectations within which action can occur. In this sense the culture of a group is a map designating regularities of both the group's physical surroundings and the member's traditional patterns of thinking, believing, and acting. The socialization process involves the teaching and learning of this map—these regularities. Having said this, we must go on to assert that culture is more than a map of a system that exists "out there." A socialized individual not only learns some of the regularities contained in the cultural map; he is himself bound (constrained) in various ways by these regularities and contributes to them.

We have noted that the well-socialized individual is not likely to be too aware of the constraining force of culture. Precisely because he is well socialized, he does not readily perceive alternatives that are not on the map and he is likely to take for granted his culture and its implications for his behavior. Whether or not the individual is aware that he himself is constrained or shaped by cultural forces, there is no question that he is. For the advantages of group membership he knowingly or unwittingly pays the price of conformity to the cultural standards of the group.

A convenient way to conceptualize this cultural penetration of individual life is to reserve the word "culture" to refer to the system of beliefs and practices "out there" and to use the word *norm* to refer to "a pattern of commonly held behavior expectations . . ." (Bates, 1956). For a given individual the impact of culture is mediated by norms, and an important legacy of effective socialization is the ability to intuit or sense the behavioral expectations of others. Involved here is both the building-up of a background of experiences concerning commonly held expectations (which is really another way of talking about learning the social side of the cultural map), and the ability to perceive the motives and beliefs of individuals from the cues their behavior provides.

It is important to realize that our own adherence to cultural norms contributes at least a small increment to their binding character for others. Just as pressures from social norms make it easier to predict the behavior of others, our own conformity to expectations adds to the stability of the cultural system for someone else. When our overt behavior is influenced by cultural norms, we participate in their maintenance and perpetuation. Violation of a norm, on the other hand, threatens its stability and universality and perhaps contributes a small increment to its ultimate modification or dissolution.

Cultural Norms and Social Roles

The cultural map is complicated by the fact that society (the group) comprises different roles for which there exist different normative expectations. Roles are *shared norms concerning the behavior of certain persons in certain settings*. Men confront different social expectations—are constrained by a different set of norms—than women. Adults differ from children, leaders from followers, waiters from customers, in the norms relevant to their roles. The facts of role differentiation introduce complexity but not chaos, however, since the roles of two interacting group members are organized in a social subsystem that is bound together by shared expectations about the behavioral implications of *each* role. A woman expects a man to rise when she enters the room and the man knows that he is expected to rise. Although role differentiation means that cultural norms apply differentially to different persons, there is a sharing of expectations about the norms appropriate for different roles and some understanding of how the roles mesh with one another.

In a less obvious way the concept of role has a wide applicability in all interpersonal relations. Many scientific observers of group formation have noted how the processes of working toward group goals seem to call forth various roles even if none are specified by the formal organization of the group. Thus there may emerge a person who expedites the discussion, a clarifier, a tension reducer, a dispute mediator, and so on, as the group tries to accomplish its objectives. There are also, of course, roles that lead the group astray, such as obstructionist, nitpicker, and self-aggrandizer. No doubt personality differences do in part determine who takes what role, but of greater importance in the present discussion is the fact that one person's actions create expectations concerning his future actions, and once a person makes a few expediting comments it may be extremely difficult for him to leave the expeditor role. This is one of the primary ways in which a miniature cultural system emerges out of partly random and partly personality-based processes of interaction in a group. Roles are assigned, often implicitly and often on the basis of minimum cues, partly because roles increase predictability and stabilize the structure within the broader objectives of the group.

The role concept becomes important, then, in helping us avoid an oversimplified view of the impact of culture on individual behavior. In some respects, cultural norms help make everybody similar. In other respects, culture creates differences out of personal variations that were originally minimal. If a number of relevant group members expect member B to behave like an advisor, or a playmate, or a shortstop—these common expectations or norms define one of B's roles and serve to constrain his behavior in expected directions.

One way to express the character of this constraint is to recognize that the kinds of expectations we are talking about here have both cognitive and evaluative ingredients. A social expectation is typically more than a behavior prediction, since it represents what the expecting person wants to happen and a forecast of what will happen. It is an important feature of cultural and social phenomena that predicted, and therefore "expected," actions become morally correct and good actions. This is the reason why the shared expectations we have defined as norms actually shape or constrain behavior. Because the principles that lie behind manifestations of constraint are both psychologically complex and socially critical, the dynamics of social influence will be discussed in considerable detail in Chapters Nine through Fifteen, and more will be said about the origins and functions of norms in Chapter Sixteen.

Action Under Conditions of Uncertainty

Having tried to make a strong, although brief, case for viewing culture as a systematic determinant of personal consistency, we shall now take back at least part of what has been claimed for culture. Although culture is extremely important in molding group traditions, personality is not just the subjective side of culture, nor is culture merely a term for describing in summary manner the behavior of group members. As Kluckhohn put it, "the concept of culture arises from behavior and returns to behavior but culture is not behavior—it is only one element in human behavior" (1954, pp. 923–924).

For one thing, each of us participates in the broader culture in his own way, differing in sensitivity to and acceptance of cultural norms. Except perhaps in the most homogeneous and isolated societies, the individual's attitudes and behavior are regulated by his membership in different groups and organizations. For example, the college student may have to reconcile the norms of fraternity life with those of his family group, and perhaps of the campus orchestra in which he plays the cello. Role conflicts may develop whenever such important membership groups have different norms.

Quite aside from these points at which the individual is exposed to conflicting cross-currents within the cultural stream, it is also true that cultural norms are for the most part loose and incomplete. Norms tend to reach their sharpest clarity in recurrent situations that nearly everyone confronts, and in which some change in expected behavior is anticipated as an outgrowth of the situation: weddings, leave-takings, graduations, and funerals. But even the most conscientious participant in a culture constantly confronts choices between action alternatives that require something more than a quick reading of the cultural map. There are important regularities in the life situations that face any individual, yet there is always the challenge of situational novelty—unexpected demands, new acquaintances, surprising twists in the flow of events. Even one who is desperate to fulfill norms, to meet the expectations of others, may be unable to determine what these expectations are. The processes underlying the choice of action in such situations are of special interest to psychologists. In the present book we too are primarily concerned with determinants of action in settings that are free of the kind of environmental pressure that completely restricts choice—whether this pressure is cultural, as is the constraint on males to wear pants in our society, or physical, as is the constraint on behavior choice occasioned by a blow on the head from a sledge hammer.

When the individual's course of action is not clearly charted by the cultural map he will choose among available alternatives the path that seems most likely to lead to reward. Of course the individual can rarely be certain of the consequences of a particular action. But still he must act, and in order to do so with any effectiveness he must commit himself in the face of uncertainties. The consequences of action will ordinarily be the same whether the decision to perform the act is difficult and conflicted or easy. The conflict itself, the weighing of pros and cons, may precede but is typically not reflected in overt behavior.

As he stands on the threshold of action the individual cannot both act and not act; and if he decides to act, he cannot act in mutually exclusive ways. Unlike the state of affairs that sometimes obtains in a dream—when dream characters are sometimes in two places at once, when actions can be undone and great distances covered in split seconds—action in reality must come to terms with the limiting properties of the environment. In short, whatever the nature of the conflict, indecision, or playful rumination that precedes action, the action itself is squeezed through the eye of the decisional needle and, for better or worse, its effects inexorably follow.

There are two critical questions that might be raised at this point. (1) Are the consequences that follow from action irrevocable? (2) Is action never equivocal or conflicted? In answer to the first question, at least some actions are irrevocable in a way that thoughts are not. By themselves thoughts have no effect on the environment; they do not alter the existing state of affairs as actions do. It is an unfortunate fact of life for golfers that a bad drive is irrevocable. It cannot be taken back, any more than a chess move can be revoked once the hand has left the piece. Some actions can, for all practical purposes, be undone, but important actions tend to set in motion chains of events that often have a momentum beyond the person's control. Like a missile, once launched they cannot be recalled. Another factor that distinguishes thought from action is that actions are, at least potentially, open to public observation or monitoring. Observed action can be symbolically undone ("I didn't mean it," "I was only kidding"), but the mere fact of being observed marks them as irrevocable in a sense that thoughts never are.

As to the second question, our line of argument has implied that action must be "either-or"—that a person must commit himself unequivocally as a condition for action. We must concede that this is not always so. Not only are conflicted or half-hearted responses sometimes seen, but there are also vigorous compromises, which seems to suggest that people *can* be equivocal in an unequivocal way. Effective compromise becomes possible when there are fine gradations of choice. The majority supports compromise positions on most complex public issues: some—but not too much—money for defense, enough—but not oppressive—federal intervention, movement toward desegregation—but not too rapid or too drastic. If a person wants to paint a garage in a medium green but finds that paint is only sold in dark green or light green, he easily resolves the problem by mixing them.

But many action situations involve discrete, mutually exclusive alternatives and the opportunities for compromise are absent. The boy with a nickel must choose the licorice or the jaw-breaker; he cannot have both or half of each. The voter may feel conflicted and in doubt, but he must filter this conflict through an unequivocal choice in the voting booth. The high-school senior must choose a college out of those that accept him and are within his budget. He cannot combine the good features of each into a new, compromise blend. And the discreteness of behavioral alternatives requires unequivocal action, which in turn sets up pressures that reach back to affect attitudes and cognitions.

We have now arrived at the nub of the argument. It is this reaching-back process that ties attitudinal consistency to the requirements of behavior. As the individual presses toward an *unequivocal behavior orientation*

(UBO), it becomes adaptive to bring his relevant cognitions and values into harmony with each other. The internal dispositions which are the products of socialization serve the important function of preparing the organism for effective, unconflicted action. But for action to be unconflicted, for it to occur at the proper time and with the proper coordination, there must be a minimum of cognitive or evaluative confusion about the considerations involved. When the time comes to act, the great advantage of having a set of coherent internally consistent dispositions is that the individual is not forced to listen to the babble of competing inner voices.

We do not argue that the need to act in an unconflicted way (to assume UBO) always generates a consistent framework of supporting attitudes, but we propose that it is a potent force in the direction of consistency. The individual keeps moving toward the unequivocal decisions that must precede behavior; this in turn promotes consistency or integration at the cognitive level. If we could imagine an organism that never had to act, to do things that affected the environment and his own well-being, we could imagine an organism that could afford the luxury of inconsistent dispositions.

Consistency Over Time

Thus far the examples and the discussion itself have referred to the sources of consistency among attitudes and cognitions at a given point in time. But an equally important feature of human nature is the tendency to act the same when conditions recur, and the tendency for underlying dispositions to show a tough stability. Does the preceding argument, which linked cognitive integration to the requirements of action, apply as well to temporal consistency? Whereas it is obvious that we cannot be in two places at once or approach and avoid the same object simultaneously, we *can* do these things in succession. At the least, time loosens consistency requirements and we can imagine a person making different (vigorous and unconflicted) responses at different times but under comparable circumstances. Although Mr. A cannot vote for a Democratic and a Republican mayoral candidate in the same election, he can surely vote Democratic one time and Republican the next. Unconflicted love before marriage may turn into unambivalent hatred before divorce.

To account for the degree of consistency that *does* exist through time, it is necessary to consider the effects of behavior on the social context in which it occurs. An act that is observed by another has some effect on the other, no matter how small that effect may be. If the effect is positive—if actor A provides observer B with a satisfying outcome—then B will presumably do what he can to increase A's tendency to perform more acts like it. In the language of learning theory, B will reinforce A. Presumably there are a number of things A might do or say that would please B and thus elicit this reinforcement in return: he might voice an opinion shared by B, lend him money, give him advice, and so on. But above and beyond the content of *A*'s particular acts, *B* has an interest in *A*'s predictability per se. Since his own reactions are more easily prepared if his social environment is stable, he will positively reinforce *A* for contributions made to this stability or, more likely, reinforce *A* negatively for evidences of inconsistency in his behavior.

If *A* says on Monday that he deplores capitalism and on Tuesday spends all his savings on stocks, such inconsistent behavior might or might not trouble or raise problems for him. We shall discuss in subsequent chapters some of the mechanisms people have for preventing awareness of inconsistency. However, if *B* had observed both the Monday statement and the Tuesday stock-buying action, he might very well hold up to *A* the inconsistency of his actions and chide him for not practicing his preachments. Since *A* is anxious to avoid such unpleasant outcomes, he will try to anticipate and thus avoid the kinds of inconsistencies likely to produce them. This anticipation involves the individual in attempts to determine the expectations of others and conform to them.

Thus consistency across dispositions grows out of the actor's desire to take a clear stance at a given moment of action, whereas consistency over time develops more in reaction to the social reinforcements provided by others. These reinforcements will be positive when expectancies are confirmed, and negative when they are disconfirmed. In this way the reinforcer does what he can to stabilize *his* social environment. The two consistency arguments merge when we realize that the more stable our environment can be made, the easier it will be to organize our dispositions in preparation for unequivocal action.

The Phenomenal Self

As the individual's dispositions become coordinated to avoid or minimize inconsistency, action in familiar settings can proceed with greater assurance and efficiency. An increasing number of behavior decisions become automated so that larger patterns of action run their course without conscious planning or deliberation. But the entire structure of the interrelated dispositions is potentially available to conscious awareness. Out of the individual's interactions with the environment, in other words, there emerges an overarching cognitive category that contains and relates cognitive subcategories. We may use the concept of *phenomenal self* to refer to each person's awareness of his own beliefs, values, attitudes, the links between them, and their implications for his behavior.

These developments in the social process may appear paradoxical: on the one hand, the development of integrated belief and action clusters makes adaptive behavior more automatic and reduces the role of conscious deliberations; on the other hand, there appears to be an emerging, inclusive cognition of the self that allows greater awareness of the relatedness of acts to each other and to underlying dispositions. The paradox is only apparent, however. The phenomenal self is a potentially available cognition that becomes more differentiated and elaborated as experiences and remembered actions accumulate. Self-consciousness fluctuates markedly, however, as we conduct our daily behavioral business. Potential and actual inconsistency provokes awareness and brings the phenomenal self into focus. This presumably has adaptive significance, as self-consciousness implies a calling to mind of dispositions and a review of their joint implications for behavior. The initial impact of inconsistency, however, may be painful and debilitating, reflecting itself as embarrassment and feelings of awkwardness and inadequacy. Under some circumstances the implications of inconsistency may be so threatening to the person that he represses or dissociates the cognitions involved (cf. Rosenberg and Abelson, 1960).

When the person is confronted with a surprising, unexpected, or novel situation, it is likely that the phenomenal self becomes salient. In some way the person attempts to steer his behavior in directions consistent with his present self-conception. In general, the greater the number of behavior sequences that become automated, the more free energy the individual has to concentrate on novel events. Behavior in novel situations thus calls forth a high degree of self-involvement and the person is apt to be extremely alert to the effects of his actions on the environment—and especially on others.

It might be claimed that the emergence of a phenomenal self is one of the major characteristics distinguishing man from lower animals. The notion of a phenomenal self implies that memories of past actions and outcomes associated with them are available in integrated form to be used to clarify current action possibilities. The actions taken reflect the continuity between the remembered past and the anticipated future. In lower animals, on the other hand, there is no evidence of such conscious reflection over the implications of actions in novel situations, and behavior seems either to involve the arousal of instinctive patterns, the perfunctory application of past learnings, or trial-and-error reactions to immediate events.

As a final comment on the origins of the phenomenal self, the importance of others' reactions should again be stressed. As if to locate and keep track of us in the intricate social web that surrounds them, others endow us with a name, an identity, and a structural endurance. In attempting to come to terms with the expectations that others have of us, we rather naturally take ourselves as a social object and try to see the self as others see it. Thus, in shaping our social environment to make it easier to predict its states, we get caught up in the presentation of a consistent face to others. It becomes easier to predict others who have us as stimuli if we ourselves are predictable and can fulfill their expectations. The emergence of a phenomenal self is both a by-product of and an agency for the maintenance of a consistent public image. The fact that it can be both effect and cause testifies to the circular, bootstrap quality of personal development through social interaction. The phenomenal self enters into the regulation of behavior in critical or novel situations, but it is itself shaped by previous outcomes of behavior.

SUMMARY

In the present chapter we have focused on the products of socialization—the personal dispositions that develop to prepare the individual for adaptive action. Impressed as we are with the psychologist's freedom to select the kinds of dispositions he wishes to emphasize, our candidates have been cognitions, beliefs, values, and attitudes. To put it simply, two cognitions make a belief and a belief plus a value equal an attitude. Thus beliefs express the relationship between concepts or categories and attitudes involve the linking of value or emotion to a concept embedded in a belief. These relations may be conveniently expressed in syllogism form, with the belief serving as the minor premise, the value as the major premise, and the attitude as the conclusion. A given attitude may be the conclusion of several syllogisms, and to the extent that this is so we may speak of the horizontal structure of the attitude. The attitude may also be the outcome of a vertical structure of prior syllogisms whereby the values and beliefs involved are themselves conclusions of prior syllogisms, and so on. The distinction between a value and an attitude is entirely relative, in other words, and makes sense only within the framework of a given syllogism. Today's attitude may be tomorrow's value.

Having presented our own model of attitudes, we have reviewed briefly several related conceptions. These include the affect-cognition model, the theory of cognitive balance, the symbolic psycho-logic model, and the congruity principle. Each of these models stresses either the internal coherence of single attitudes and their components or the consistency among related attitudes held by the person. The evidence supporting these two kinds of consistency was briefly reviewed, with the conclusion that consistency pressures unquestionably exist although there are circumstances in which they are checked by other forces and by various forms of mental compartmentalization.

Next we showed how consistency comes about in response to action in a complex environment. Much of behavior—perhaps more of it than we generally realize—is governed by culture. The culture is mediated by norms or the shared expectations of others, to which the individual becomes responsive through the socialization process. But culture is only a general determinant; it does not determine behavior in detail. In fact, it provides ambiguous or conflicting guidelines in many situations. When the individual cannot determine the proper action course by reading the cultural map he attempts to estimate the course that will be most rewarding and choose that one. There is considerable uncertainty involved in predicting outcomes and the individual tries to reduce this uncertainty by information-seeking and to deny it by moving toward an *unequivocal behavior orientation*. Such an orientation represents a commitment to action in the face of uncertainty. Such a commitment involves the risks of acting inappropriately, but such risks are assumed to be less grave on the average than the risks of hesitant or conflicted action. In the process of preparing for unequivocal action, preparatory attitudes and cognitions are pressed into a coordinated relationship with each other with a resulting increase in consistency.

Consistency through time is heavily conditioned by social reinforcement and the response to approving and critical reactions of others has much to do with the development of the phenomenal self. This is the counterpart in awareness of the person's attitudes, cognitions, motives, and their interrelations. The phenomenal self takes on monitoring and steering functions when the situation is novel or when the individual is in danger of inconsistency.

CHAPTER SIX

Action, Choice, and Dissonance

The higher an organism is on the phylogenetic scale the more complicated must be the models of his behavior because the behavior to be explained is itself more intricate. The more advanced the evolutionary stage, the more stimuli impinge on an organism whose organs are complex and whose response repertory is large. Recent studies of animal behavior by ethologists have led to the development of simple models of so-called innate behavior. Ethologists give the name "innate fixed action pattern" to behavior that is not learned but that occurs in a rigid, mechanical way in response to a specific set of stimulus conditions. Volition appears to be completely absent from this pattern.

An innate fixed action pattern occurs when a particular releaser stimulus is presented. For example, the male stickleback, a species of fish, assumes a threatening posture when sighting another male stickleback approaching his breeding territory; this appears to be an innate fixed action pattern. That the pattern does not always occur for the same individual at different times or for different individuals at the same time is somewhat complicating. Evidently the organism must be in a particular state of readiness for the releaser stimulus to provoke the response. The general model is relatively simple, despite the readiness requirement, and ethologists spend much of their time cataloging innate fixed action patterns and releaser stimuli for particular species.

Up the phylogenetic ladder the proportion of behavior that can be characterized as fixed action patterns decreases and the proportion learned, and hence dependent upon *volition,* increases. Much of the behavior of the higher mammals can be more aptly characterized as a decision rather than an automatic response; an element of choice is involved. The occurrence of an innate fixed action pattern does not depend on prior reinforcing experiences. Given the proper circumstances, individual members of a species exhibit the pattern regardless of whether they have ever performed the response before or have ever seen it performed by another member of their species. Learned behavior, on the other hand, is based on prior experience involving a decision among two or more possible responses. When a response to some set of stimulus conditions pays off by providing a state of affairs preferable to the one that existed before the response, the individual tends, on the occurrence of a similar set of stimulus conditions, to make a similar response. This is a general definition of learning.

The world of the higher mammals is very complex as measured by the large number of potential stimuli that can impinge on the organism through its highly developed sense organs. Rather than having a huge catalog of innate fixed action patterns to deal with this broad range of stimuli, mammals have evolved a large associative cortex that relates incoming stimulation to selected response possibilities.

All learning models acknowledge the elements of volition and choice and most of them contain an account of some change in the state of affairs confronting the organism after his response. This change goes under a variety of names such as satisfaction, reinforcement, drive reduction, and so on. Within our terminology this change is a change in *outcome level*. Outcomes are coordinated with particular values the organism holds. The process of choosing a response is a decision; we mean to use the term decision in this general sense. Decisions are based on cognitive representations of current versus expected outcomes. Although certain actions may reflect implicit, automatic decisions, more important human actions involve the actor's cognitive representation of choice alternatives and his evaluation of their significance for him. An adequate theory of complex human behavior must consider the cognitive precursors and accompaniments of action.

PHASES IN THE SEQUENCE OF PLANNING AND ACTION

Lewin's (1935) conception of the person's "life space" provides one useful model of the cognitive state of affairs preceding action decisions. Lewin held that the person's life space consists of a set of "activities" potentially available to him at any given moment. Certain activities in the life space are perceived to lead to "regions" that are positively valued, others to regions of negative value. Lewin referred to these values as "valences." He believed that at any given moment the person is in some activity region and in possession of needs that require some activity for their satisfaction. Behavior, he contended, involves moving from one activity to another in order to maximize satisfaction or minimize the frustration of a current need. With this framework Lewin analyzed various kinds of motivated behavior.

We conceive, as Lewin did, of certain activities as being *instrumental* and others as being *consummatory*. A white rat presses a bar in order to get a food pellet and a child inserts a dime in a candy machine and pulls a plunger in order to get a candy bar. These instrumental activities lead to the consummatory activities of transacting with the food pellet or the candy bar.

We refer to the transaction experience as providing positive or negative *outcomes*. The sequence begins with cognitive activity during which the person sizes up his environment while determining the alternatives open to him. In this phase of the sequence he is oriented toward acquiring as much information as he can about alternative actions. The alternatives may simply be either acting or not acting; should he buy the candy bar or not? This phase is also characterized by conflict; he weighs the alternatives in terms of how each furthers or frustrates the values he holds; that is, he establishes an attitude toward each alternative. Information-seeking, in the predecision phase, is designed to reduce conflict by illuminating the attitudes involved. If the individual buys the candy he is able to further a value he holds, namely, "candy is good." He then has a positive reason for buying the candy. But buying the candy involves spending a dime he may be reluctant to part with. This generates a reason for not buying the candy. The child has to resolve this conflict between attitudes in order to act.

Any action alternative typically leads to positive and negative values, with expected outcomes associated with these values. At some point the person decides to transact with one object or situation and to forego the other alternatives that may be available. It is at this point that he must begin to come to terms with his act. In order to get the most from the chosen alternative he must maintain what we described in the last chapter as an *unequivocal behavioral orientation* (UBO). The requirement of maintaining this postdecisional orientation typically results in the cognitive work that Festinger (1957) has called dissonance reduction. The rest of this chapter is devoted to examining what is known about the three phases of the action sequence: the predecision phase, the decision itself, and postdecisional accommodation to the act.

Some Considerations of the Predecisional Phase of the Act

There has been a great deal of speculation, mostly fortified by mathematics and some relatively uninformative research, on decision-making. This work has been done by psychologists, economists, and mathematicians. What is known largely consists of two propositions: (1) an individual engages in action that he expects to maximize value attainments; (2) to the extent that action alternatives have similar values it is difficult for the individual to make a decision. Thus, if we ask a person before a decision to evaluate separately each of the alternatives, we can bet on his choosing the alternative he likes best. Further, we can bet that if we confront him with two alternatives that he previously said he liked nearly equally well, it will take him longer to make a decision than if a clear difference exists in his liking for the alternatives. Although these two facts have been clearly demonstrated by controlled experimentation, we know little about the details of the process whereby the person makes up his mind to do or not to do something. Let us speculate about the nature of this process.

The person attempts to do two things in response to a change in information input. As we saw in the previous chapter, he attempts to classify the information into some cognitive category, which in turn is associated through belief premises with other categories. He also attempts to anticipate the relevance of the categorized information to the values he holds. This enables him to establish an attitude of either approach or avoidance toward the topic of information.

Lewin's characterization of the person's life space does not contain the critical feature that is the basis for information dependence, that is, uncertainty. In Lewin's conception activity regions lead to goal regions and goal regions involve transactions with situations having a particular valence. In a few places in his writings he does acknowledge the existence of uncertainty in the person's life space but he does not incorporate it as an essential characteristic of action. This cannot be an accurate characterization because, at any given moment, the person's particular vantage point from which he views action possibilities is characteristically one of incomplete knowledge. Often he has only a vague sense of what will follow particular actions.

The predecision situation may contain various kinds of uncertainty. The person may be uncertain about the appropriate cognitive category to which to assign a particular information change. Are the footsteps coming down the hall those of his boss or of someone else? That object looks like candy, but is it? Uncertainty reduction here involves assigning the object or event to some cognitive category having relevant value.

Another uncertainty in the situation involves whether transacting with the object or event affords the person the outcomes he may anticipate. In other words, is a positive (or negative) attitude justified? If the object is candy will he truly enjoy it?

Other uncertainties have to do with a person's own capacities for engaging in instrumental or consummatory activities. The child may wonder if he has the strength to pull the candy-machine plunger. A sports-car enthusiast may wonder if he has the driving skill to engineer a particular turn. We are never perfectly certain that we will be able to bring about a particular enjoyable state of affairs. Our attitude toward any action alternative is determined in part by our estimates of the likelihood of successful accomplishment.

Cognitive processes during the predecisional phase will be shaped, in ways we little understand, by the nature of competing values at stake and the uncertainties involved. The actor may be quite certain about the consequences of alternative courses of action but may experience predecision conflict because the values achieved by each alternative are evenly balanced.

Here the actor will place an emphasis in his thinking on value review and comparison—"which of these values is really more important to me?" In cases when uncertainty is high, the actor will delay action as long as possible and be extremely hungry for relevant information. The actor may face a choice between an alternative leading to relatively certain but mixed values and a course of action with very uncertain consequences. The resolution of this conflict—whether a bird in the hand *is* worth two in the bush—may depend on various personality factors that influence the tendency to take risks.

Cognitive Dissonance and the Postdecisional Phase

Dissonance theory states that two cognitions held by a person can have one of three relationships: *consonance, dissonance,* or *irrelevance.* Two cognitions are said to be consonant when one follows from the other. Festinger (1957) is not completely clear as to what he means by "follows from." There is some purpose to this vagueness in the theory because there are many bases upon which cognitions may be mutually compatible. They may be compatible because one follows logically from the other. Thus knowledge that I am in New York is consonant with knowledge that I am not in Boston. There are two hidden assumptions in this relationship: a single object cannot be in two distinct places at once and New York and Boston are distinct places. Two cognitions may also be consonant because of certain kinds of experience with the world. Thus, the cognitions that "I dropped a stone in the water" and "the stone sank" are perfectly consonant; the one normally follows from the other in the person's past experience.

Brehm and Cohen (1962), in their expanded version of the theory, point out that cognitions can have different degrees of consonance. Thus an individual's belief that air travel is dangerous may be only mildly dissonant with his cognition that he has arrived safely in an airplane. The two cognitions are relevant, but the second neither confirms nor categorically contradicts the first.

Two cognitions are said to be dissonant when they are either logically inconsistent or incompatible with the person's past experience. Festinger uses the term dissonance to refer both to the relationship between cognitions and to the psychological state this relationship produces. We shall distinguish these by referring to the cognitions as inconsistent or incompatible and to the state of tension produced by their inconsistency or incompatibility as psychological dissonance.

Two cognitions may be inconsistent or incompatible and not produce dissonance if they do not have mutually incompatible behavioral implications. A person may know that a stranger has made two mutually inconsistent statements or may receive two mutually inconsistent weather reports about some remote corner of the world. If he has no intention of interacting with the stranger or of traveling to the distant area dissonance does not arise. The knowledge of these inconsistencies has no consequences for him. Dissonance is produced if and only if two cognitions generate mutually incompatible behavior dispositions, such as approach and avoidance tendencies toward the same object or the desire to be in two distinct places at once.

For Festinger, irrelevant cognitions are those that are neither consonant nor dissonant. We should like to modify this category to concern cognitions that have neither compatible nor incompatible behavioral implications. Thus, knowledge that the sun is shining outside and suddenly remembering that I left my pen in the breast pocket of my suit jacket are likely to be cognitions that have no apparent interactive behavioral implications. If, however, I always write when the sun shines or never write when the sun shines, these cognitions of course interact.

Dissonance Is Drivelike. The basic postulate of Festinger's system is that the tension to which he refers as dissonance is unpleasant and that the person tends to engage in some activity to reduce that tension. He tends to transform dissonant relations into consonant or irrelevant ones.

The Importance and Number of Cognitions. Some further elaboration of the theory is necessary in order to predict the magnitude of dissonance engendered by inconsistent or incompatible cognitions. According to Festinger, dissonance increases as the number and importance of cognitions involved in the relationship increases.

Neither the Festinger book (1957) nor the Brehm and Cohen (1962) book is explicit in defining importance. The definition rests more or less on intuition. Importance can be defined in terms of the value implications of actions based on cognitions, to wit, the *outcome potential* associated with the cognition. Thus the cognitions associated with the automobiles a person might buy loom relatively important as compared with those involved in the choices facing a housewife in a supermarket.

We can see that the importance of a set of cognitions refers to the behavioral implications a person anticipates in acting on the basis of the cognitions. Such anticipations are, in effect, value-relevant beliefs because consequences are predicted that have a positive or negative value for the person. We can expect that as the number of anticipated implications increases the importance of a set of related cognitions also tends to increase. The amount of dissonance or consonance experienced by the person is a function of the *number* of related cognitions having value-relevant behavioral implications.

Decision-Making and Dissonance

The theory of cognitive dissonance is concerned with the situation confronting the person *after* he has made a decision. Knowledge that he has chosen something valuable and rejected something that might have unpleasant consequences produces in the person a psychological state of consonance *because his behavior has been compatible with his values.* Generally, each choice has positive and negative features—that is, both positive and negative behavioral implications. Knowledge that the alternative chosen has negative features and that one or more of those not chosen has positive features produces a state of dissonance. To the extent that he has acquired negative and rejected positive features, the person's behavior and values have been incompatible; there remain tendencies to approach the nonchosen and avoid the chosen alternative. Of course, the greater the net positive balance favoring the chosen alternative, the less will be the person's postdecisional dissonance.

Little empirical work has attempted to study the behavior of the person in making a decision. Festinger (1964) has argued that the predecision situation is characterized by an openness to information regarding possible choices. He suggests that the person takes an objective point of view in order to appraise fully the merits and demerits of the alternatives. He is vigilant and open to information in the predecisional period.

If we could observe the information-seeking behavior of a person as he prepared to make a decision, we would expect him to spend more time acquiring information about an alternative the more he lacked information about it. If equally familiar with the alternatives, he would be likely to spend an equal amount of time seeking information about each. The reason for seeking information would be to evaluate aspects of each alternative insofar as these aspects embody outcomes that might be derived from transactions with them. Given these assumptions about the cognitive work that precedes a decision, it is difficult to maintain, as Festinger apparently does, that the alternatives do not undergo evaluative changes in the predecision period. Given the assumptions, the purpose of seeking information is to assign certain outcome values to the alternatives. Festinger maintains that both the absolute and relative value of the alternatives do not change but that information serves to increase the person's conviction as to the value he had assigned to each alternative at the beginning of the predecision period. This we regard as highly unlikely.

As Festinger points out, it is extremely difficult to study value changes that might occur during the decision process. For one thing, it is difficult to pinpoint exactly when a decision has been made. Typically, the subject in an experiment is asked to inform the experimenter when he has made up his mind between the alternatives before him. When the subject announces his decision, all the experimenter can be sure of is that it was made at some prior time, it being most convenient to assume that it was made immediately prior to the announcement by the subject. The subject, however, may have made the decision several seconds or many seconds earlier and may have spent the interim between his decision and his announcement of it convincing himself that he had made the right choice. Ideally, in order to examine predecisional evaluational changes we would want to measure the attractiveness of the alternatives at the beginning of the decision sequence and then again one or more times before the decision, one of these measurements being taken immediately prior to the decision.

Another problem involved in measuring changes in attractiveness of the alternatives during the decision sequence concerns the influence of the act of measurement itself, which is a general problem in psychological research. Typically, changes in value are measured by asking the subject, in some direct or indirect way, how he values each of the alternatives. When a person is confronted with making such evaluations the situation tends to be disrupted. What assurance do we have that considered evaluations accurately reflect the spontaneous evaluations that would have existed at this point in the decision sequence? When a person begins to consider the value of the alternatives in order to report them verbally to the experimenter he may alter these evaluations for a variety of reasons.

For example, when he becomes reflective he may see implications that he had not previously considered or his evaluations may be affected by how he believes the experimenter expects him to evaluate the alternatives. Although these technical obstacles seem insurmountable there have been attempts at taking measurements indirectly. We shall examine these as we review the research. We shall also discover some of the difficulties in "stopping" the action sequence at a given stage for the purpose of measuring some of its features at that point in time.

Postdecisional Regret

To the extent that one alternative has a clear edge over the others, the decision is easy and postdecisional regret is minimal. The person's choice is consistent with his values and he should be in a state of relative consonance. To the extent that predecisional evaluation cannot establish a clear edge for one of the alternatives, the person is expected to suffer regret on making the decision. The desirable qualities possessed by one or more of the non-chosen alternatives which are not possessed by the chosen one suddenly appear salient to him. He has a "what-have-I-done?" experience. In that respect his choice is inconsistent with his values and he is therefore in a state of cognitive dissonance. If the decision is irrevocable he comes to terms with what he has done by attempting to minimize the regret associated with having given up desirable features of the nonchosen alternatives.

To the extent that the individual maintains an open information-seeking perspective he continues to confront himself with the desirable features that he has given up, and his regret persists. We therefore expect him to be defensive rather than open to any information that tends to favor any of the nonchosen alternatives. He also tends to take an open stance toward information that downgrades any of the nonchosen alternatives. His attitude toward the chosen alternative is the mirror image of this; he tends to be attentive to information that plays up the qualities of the chosen alternative and defensive toward information that highlights any of its negative qualities.

Another postdecisional maneuver the individual might undertake is to increase the importance of value dimensions that favor the chosen alternative and decrease the importance of value dimensions that favor the nonchosen alternative. Let us suppose he chooses a Ford over a Plymouth and Chevrolet and, of the three, the Ford has the highest horsepower. He might increase the relative value he now places on horsepower, perhaps by spelling out for himself the valuable consequences horsepower can bring. Whereas before his decision it was not a significant factor, he suddenly feels that horsepower is much more important than he thought it was. The Plymouth, on the other hand, has a great deal more head room than the Ford but now he feels that head room, which he had previously considered as an important value dimension, is only of minor consequence. He also tends to diminish the importance of values in which the Ford is deficient. Of the three cars the Ford consumes the most gas, a factor he had initially considered to be greatly significant. After the decision he may come to believe that gas mileage is really a trivial matter. At the same time he may tend to exaggerate the importance of factors in which the nonchosen alternatives were deficient.

These are some of the cognitive maneuvers in which the person may engage in order to come to terms with and live with a decision he has made. These maneuvers provide the person with extreme flexibility in the typical decision situation. Distortion is usually easy, especially in decisions involving alternatives with complex attributes. The consequences of this cognitive work is the tendency to upgrade the over-all value of the chosen alternative and downgrade the over-all value of the nonchosen alternatives. This "dissonance effect" derives from the person's attempt to maintain an unequivocal behavioral orientation toward his acts; that is, by reducing his approach tendencies toward the nonchosen alternatives and his tendency to avoid the chosen one, he is able to minimize his regret over his choice.

PRE- AND POSTDECISIONAL INFORMATION-SEEKING

Turning to the evidence bearing on the seeking of information before and after a decision is made, we can make two general predictions. First, there will be openness to information in the predecision phase. This openness will best enable the person to assess the outcome potential of the alternatives. Second, defensiveness derived from the unequivocal behavioral orientation principle will govern such behavior after a decision has been made. The defensiveness will enable the person to follow through and live with his decision.

Information-Seeking in the Predecision Period

There is practically no experimental evidence concerning the relative attention paid by a person to alternatives in the predecision period. An experiment by Gerard (1966) indicates that in the predecision phase there is relatively more attention paid to the alternative that is eventually not chosen. In that experiment the choice was between prints of paintings that the subject had previously evaluated. He was presented with two paintings that were either close or disparate in value for him; the former condition, of course, involving a difficult choice and the latter an easy one. The experimental setup is shown in Figure 6.1. The measurement of changes in attention was accomplished with a small shaving mirror, a light source, and two photocells. The mirror was attached to the back of the subject's head

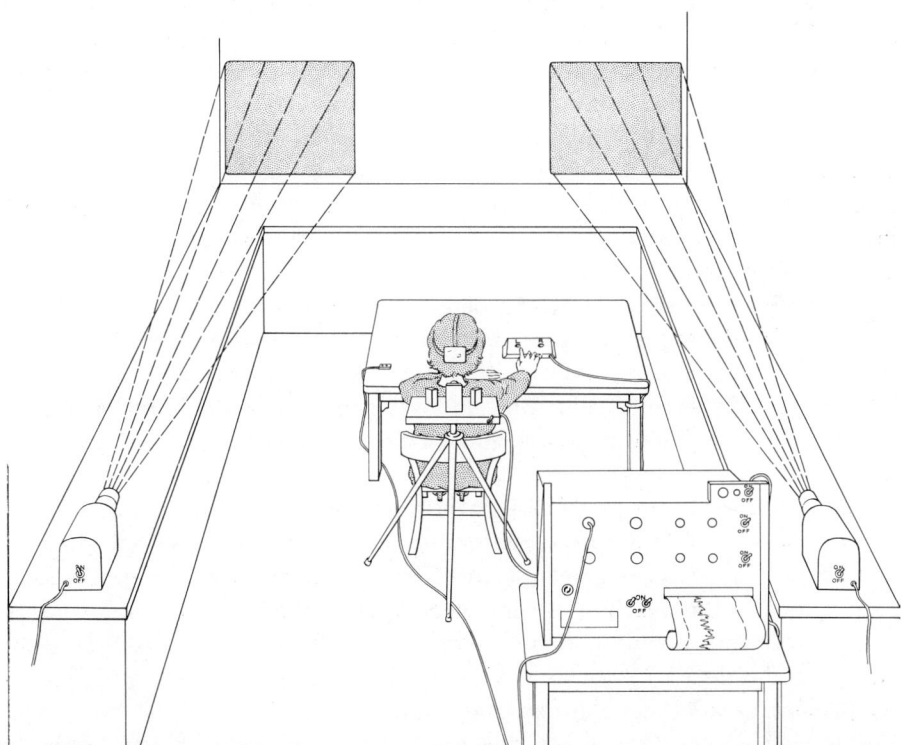

Figure 6.1. Schematic representation of experimental setting in which selective attention may be monitored.

and the two photocells with the light source in between were 12 inches further back. The system was aligned so that when the subject turned to inspect the painting projected on the screen to the right the beam of light reflected from the mirror tripped the left-hand photocell, whereas when he turned to inspect the screen at the left, the right-hand cell was tripped.

Of the 23 subjects in the experiment, 16 spent more time in the predecision period looking at the alternative they eventually did not choose; the ease or difficulty of the choice seemed to have no effect. This suggests that the person attempts, in the predecision period, to come to terms with what it is he is giving up.

It is difficult to conclude very much from this one study but the evidence does appear to indicate that the person is open to information in the predecision period, presumably in order to increase the certainty with which he will eventually make his choice. There is a good deal of evidence about information-seeking in the postdecision period that shows quite a different pattern.

Postdecision Attention to Choice Alternatives

Dissonance is an inherent by-product of a decision, for the person, by his act of choosing, either relinquishes claim to the outcome potential in the nonchosen alternative or must suffer the negative outcomes, if any, associated with the chosen alternative, or both. We would expect this dissonance to be greater the closer in value the nonchosen alternative is to the chosen one. This implies that the greater the conflict engendered immediately prior to the decision by alternatives that are close in value, the greater will be the postdecision dissonance. To the extent that the person cannot revoke his decision, and important behavioral implications follow from it, he tends to maintain an unequivocal behavioral orientation toward his choice. One way of looking at the psychological state of dissonance is that it consists of a compound of ambivalence toward both chosen and nonchosen alternatives. Dissonance reduction involves reducing this ambivalence in a positive direction for the chosen and a negative direction for the unchosen alternative.

The implications for postdecisional information-seeking are clear. In general the person seeks supportive information and tends to avoid information that he suspects will be nonsupportive. His openness during the predecision period is transformed into a biased perspective; he screens and censors information not according to its merit, but according to its usefulness in justifying the decision. Let us see the evidence for this characterization of the person's postdecisional information stance.

It is well known that in election campaigns a voter tends selectively to expose himself to campaign oratory once he has committed himself to a particular candidate. Lazarsfeld, Berelson, and Gaudet (1948) surveyed the voters in Erie County, Ohio, during the 1940 presidential election. They found that those voters who indicated constant voting intentions from May through October showed a marked tendency to be selective in the way in which they allowed themselves to be exposed to the propaganda for Roosevelt and Willkie. Close to 70 percent of the respondents indicated that they tended to listen more to their own candidate than to the candidate of the other party, whereas only slightly more than 30 percent stated that they exposed themselves to propaganda from the other side. Some respondents stated that they exposed themselves equally to both candidates. The investigators assessed the degree of interest of the respondent in the campaign and found that the greater the interest, the greater was the tendency for the voter to program his radio listening in a selective way. If we assume that interest in the campaign is highly correlated with commitment to a candidate, which it probably is, we can take this as evidence supporting a dissonance view of postdecisional information exposure.

Schramm and Carter (1959) report similar evidence in a survey of San Francisco voters immediately after the 1958 California gubernatorial election. Their survey concerned the Knowland telethon that was conducted a day or so before the election. Many more Republicans, who were presumably already committed to Knowland, reported viewing the telethon than did Democrats.

The evidence from these two studies suggests one of the reasons why propaganda campaigns often fail. Campaigns are directed at both uncommitted individuals and those on the other side. For the propaganda to have an effect the target person must choose to expose himself to that propaganda. Since those who are committed to the opposing point of view or candidate are unwilling and unlikely to tune in on discrepant information, the missive fails to hit its mark. Those who are undecided in the campaign are often individuals who are not highly involved and are, therefore, unlikely to expose themselves to the usual campaign oratory.

Clearly, the propagandist's job seems almost impossible. Elections, however, are often decided by a small percentage of the voters, sometimes only a fraction of a percent, as in the 1960 presidential election. Political parties are evidently happy to pour their resources into propaganda that will be listened to primarily by voters who are committed to their candidate with the hopes that some small fraction of the viewing audience will either be uncommitted or members of the opposition.

Evidence on Selective Exposure to and Selective Avoidance of Information

The first study to examine postdecisional information-seeking was conducted by Ehrlich, Guttman, Schonbach, and Mills (1957). This study was not an experiment but was carried out as a door-to-door survey of purchasers of automobiles. The assumption was that the decision to purchase a particular automobile is both a difficult and important one. This kind of a decision is usually difficult because of the number of comparable, competing makes of cars in any price range. Owing to the difficulty and importance of this decision there should be a good deal of postdecisional dissonance and subsequent selective exposure to information about the make of car purchased. Half the sample of respondents consisted of recent car purchasers, whereas the other half consisted of respondents who had bought their cars a year or more before the interview. These two subsamples were compared as a further test of the theory because someone who had purchased a car some time before would have presumably reduced most, if not all, of his postdecisional dissonance. There should, therefore, be selective exposure for recent but not for old purchasers.

Each respondent was asked several questions about the automobile advertisements he had noticed and read since purchasing his car. From these data it was possible to determine how selective the person had been in exposing himself to advertising. Presumably advertisements tout only favorable characteristics of a product; therefore, overexposure to ads for the make of car purchased may be interpreted as consonance-seeking whereas underexposure to ads of other makes of car may be considered as dissonance-avoiding. Ads for three types of cars were considered: those for the car purchased, those for other cars considered at the time of purchase, and those for cars not considered at the time of purchase. The respondents who were recent purchasers of new cars showed a clear tendency to favor reading ads about the make of car they bought, whereas old purchasers showed no such tendency. So far so good. There is a hitch, however; new and old purchasers are equally attentive to ads about cars they considered at the time of purchase but did not buy and also to ads for cars not considered. Thus there is no tendency to avoid potentially dissonant information. These results are not encouraging for the theory.

Another study that attempted to examine postdecision exposure was conducted by Mills, Aronson, and Robinson (1959). This study did not use data on recalled exposure as in the study just described but asked the subject, after he had made a decision between two alternatives, what kind of information he would like to have about each alternative. College students in an introductory psychology course were used as subjects and were told that they could choose the kind of exam they wanted, either an essay or an objective type. The importance of the decision was varied by telling the students that the examination would count either 5 percent or 70 percent toward their grades in the course.

After the subject had made his choice he was told that he could have an article to read about either essay or objective type exams. He was given a list of six different titles describing three articles about objective exams and three about essay exams, and was asked to rank these articles by preference. This was done under two treatments. In the "positive information" treatment the six titles indicated that the articles would give reasons favoring the kind of exam discussed. In the "negative information" treatment, it was clear from the titles that the arguments would be against the kind of exam the article was about. The prediction from the theory is straightforward: that subjects tend to seek out positive information and avoid negative information about their choice. Furthermore, the greater the importance, the more pronounced should this effect be.

The data do not bear out these predictions. There is a definite tendency for the subject to seek out positive information about the exam he chooses but no corresponding tendency to avoid negative information about his choice. He tends to be equally desirous of having negative information about the type of exam he chooses and about the other type. This corroborates the data from the automobile study. The importance factor, whether the exam would count 70 percent or 5 percent of the grade, produced no difference in desire for either positive or negative information. The fact that there was no avoidance of negative information and that importance had no effect on seeking either kind of information is negative evidence for the theory.

A study by Rosen (1961) was, in all essential respects, identical to the study just described except that the student-subjects were at a different university. These results corroborated, in nearly every detail, those of the previous study. There was strong evidence that the subjects sought out evidence that favored their choice but there was no tendency to avoid information that might argue against their choice.

Two studies (Feather, 1962; Brock, 1965) have examined the tendency for smokers and nonsmokers to seek information about the relationship between smoking and lung cancer. We would, of course, expect smokers but not nonsmokers to avoid such information. Once again, in these studies the subject was offered articles to read that, by their titles, supported, did not support, or were irrelevant to the hypothesized relationship between smoking and lung cancer. The evidence from the Feather study indicates that smokers *did not avoid* dissonant information. In Brock's study, subjects actually anticipated being forcibly exposed to the pro or con lung cancer articles. Under these conditions smokers did prefer to read an article entitled, "Smoking does not lead to lung cancer" to one taking the opposite point of view. Perhaps subjects feign having an open mind until put in a situation where they are actually confronted by the information. In addition, smokers may, under certain conditions, seek out discrepant information in order to come to terms with it; if they know there is such information its very existence is dissonant.

No studies have as yet been conducted using ex-smokers. It would be interesting to compare those who recently quit smoking with others who quit smoking a long time ago. People who recently quit presumably still feel the urge to smoke and would therefore be experiencing greater dissonance than those who quit some time ago. We would therefore expect individuals in the former group to be more avid in seeking out consonance-increasing information; namely, reports that add further evidence for the relationship between smoking and lung cancer.

The study by Gerard (1966), in which the subject made a choice between two paintings, measured postdecision exposure. After the choice the paintings remained projected for 60 seconds and the subject's continued inspection of the paintings was recorded. There was a marked alteration in attention. Whereas in the predecision phase 16 out of 23 subjects paid more attention to the alternative they eventually did not choose, in the postdecision phase the situation was reversed; 16 out of 23 paid more attention to the chosen alternative.

Although this study's findings are certainly consistent with dissonance theory, and add interesting information about predecisional exposure to the soon-to-be-rejected alternative, it is not clear that inspection of the chosen object is necessarily dissonance-reducing. Without more precise measures of attention to the positive versus the negative features of the chosen painting, no clear conclusion may be drawn. The automobile advertising survey, the two exam studies, and the smoking-lung cancer studies taken together offer only equivocal support for the theory. It may be that dissonance theory does not clearly apply in the area of selective exposure or that the situations used to test it involve other variables that obscure the role of pressures toward dissonance reduction. One such factor that might account for the equivocal results in the automobile advertising study is the differential interest value of the products involved in the choice. Mills (1965a) proposes that at least two influences are operating on the subject's information-seeking tendencies after choosing between products: the need for decision-supporting evidence and the inherent desirability of the product involved. The greater the desirability of the product the more interested the subject will be in reading advertisements about it. Mills conducted an experiment that attempted to assess the role of dissonance-reduction while controlling for the influence of inherent desirability.

The female university students who participated in Mills' experiment believed they were taking part in a market survey of various kinds of cosmetics. The subjects read descriptions of 10 products such as handcream, deodorant, and hair rinse, and were asked to rank the products according to how much they liked them.

Following the ranking, the subject was given a choice, between the second- and third-ranked products, as to which she wanted as a gift. The subject was then asked how interested she was in reading ads about each of the 10 products. The data revealed that subjects were definitely more interested in reading ads about the products they had ranked high in preference. In an effort to remove the influence of this inherent desirability factor, Mills computed a mathematical function relating the interest value of advertisements for each subject with her rank ordering of the products that were not included in the choice; that is, those products ranked 1, 4, 5, 6, 7, 8, 9, 10. From this function it was possible to compute a predicted interest value of ads about the products ranked second and third—an estimate of how interested the subjects would have been in reading these ads had they not been asked to choose between the products the ads extolled. Any discrepancy between these predicted ratings of interest value for the second- and third-ranked alternatives and how they were actually rated was presumably due to their status as products-to-be-chosen-between. Mills attributed the observed differences to postdecisional dissonance reduction. The discrepancy averaged +1.56 for the chosen product and −1.59 for the rejected product. That is, on the 20-point rating scale used by the subjects, ads about the chosen product were rated more interesting than would have been predicted from the inherent desirability function. Ads about the rejected alternative were *under*rated by approximately the same amount.

Whereas other studies have demonstrated a greater interest in information that would support the chosen alternative, this study demonstrated an actual avoidance of information that might support the rejected alternative. Ever since a study by Brodbeck (1956), investigators have been attempting to devise a refined experimental situation in which the avoidance of dissonant information might be demonstrated. This avoidance is a clear prediction from the theory, and failure to demonstrate avoidance meant either that the theory was wrong or that other forces were operating to counteract and obscure the avoidance tendency. Mills' results suggest that subjects' interest in reading about any attractive object or product may be an important counteracting force. A subject's behavior in *any* experimental situation is determined by a variety of influences, and progress in building a theory requires the ingenuity to identify and control those influences that obscure hypothesized relationships. As Mills (1967) has pointed out in reviewing research in this area, failure to control for the influence of inherent interest in information about attractive alternatives may be responsible for at least some of the conflicting findings in previous studies.

Confidence, Commitment, and Information Usefulness

In a recent study Canon (1964) attempted to control for two other factors that may have been confounded in these earlier studies. If, after a decision, certain apparently negative information is possibly useful in the future, the person may tend to be curious about that information. Thus, even though a subject chooses to take an essay exam he may want to read articles that purport to describe the disadvantages of essay exams in order to prepare himself for possible pitfalls. This tendency would be opposite to that predicted by an unqualified derivation from dissonance theory.

Another factor that might affect the willingness of a person to expose himself to potentially damaging information is the amount of confidence he has in his ability to come to terms with that information. If a person is confident and the discrepant information is seen as potentially useful, we might expect to find a preference for discrepant over consistent information. When confidence is low, on the other hand, we might expect this relationship to be reversed.

Canon's experiment involved an initial procedure of establishing either high or low confidence on the part of the subject in solving certain kinds of problems (labor–management case studies). This was done by having him solve problems and giving him false feedback about how well or poorly he had done on them. The subject was then asked to solve an additional problem and to write a brief essay defending his solution. Half the subjects in each confidence treatment were assigned to a "highly useful" condition by being told that their essays were preparation for a debate in which they would have to rebut opposing arguments. The other half of the subjects were not given this instruction (the control condition). This combination of two factors, confidence and usefulness of information, with two levels of each factor, resulted in a fourfold design. That is, there were four treatment combinations: high confidence–useful, low confidence–useful, high confidence–control, and low confidence–control. Subjects were randomly assigned to each of the four treatment combinations. After the treatments had been established the subject was given an opportunity to rate and rank descriptive titles of five articles: two that, by their titles, favored his decision; two that were opposed; and one that was neutral. The data revealed a definite preference for the negative articles in the "useful" condition, when a debate was anticipated, as compared with the control condition, when the subject received no instructions about an impending debate. The effect of usefulness was accentuated by confidence, the high-confidence subject in the "useful" condition showing a greater preference for discrepant information than his low-confidence counterpart. In the control condition the low-confidence subject showed a greater preference for consonant information than his high-confidence counterpart.

The results of this study and the one by Mills (1965a) show that strict attention must be paid to factors other than the subject's desire to justify his decision, as they may possibly influence his stance toward both supportive and nonsupportive information. One difficulty in the Canon study is that confidence and dissonance are confounded. Presumably, when a person is highly confident of a decision he experiences little dissonance and is therefore much more open to information that might be discrepant with his choice. Canon's study assumed that the amount of dissonance was the same for both confidence treatments, that confidence varied independently of dissonance. On the face of it, we would guess that a person's confidence in making a decision and his postdecision dissonance go together, and it seems highly unlikely that an experiment could be devised in which confidence and dissonance could be varied independently of each other. Freedman (1965a) attempted to replicate Canon's (1964) study, with only partial success. He found no effect of the confidence variation, but subjects again showed a preference for more useful information.

On the strength of the Canon and Freedman studies it appears that usefulness is an important factor in determining postdecisional information exposure. Sears & Freedman (1963), however, found that usefulness was not a critical variable in their study. College students were brought into the laboratory and asked to participate in a "jury study." The subject read a case of a delinquent boy and was asked to decide whether the boy should be convicted or acquitted. In one condition the subject was told that he would merely listen to a discussion and not participate, whereas in a second condition he was told that he would participate in the discussion. This obviously varied information utility, as the subject who was going to be in a discussion would presumably want to prepare himself by exposing himself to arguments supporting the other side, just as in Canon's anticipated debate in his "useful" condition. Commitment was also varied by informing half of the subjects that their opinions regarding conviction or acquittal were final and irrevocable, whereas the other half were told that their opinions would be regarded as merely tentative statements that they could subsequently change. A procedure similar to the earlier studies was used, in which the subjects' preferences for articles that supported or were discrepant with their opinion were determined.

The major findings were that commitment reduced the subject's desire for *both* supportive *and* nonsupportive information and that information utility (participant vs. audience conditions) showed no effect on desire for exposure. Dissonance theory would have predicted that selective exposure to supportive information would occur in the "audience" treatment in which the subject would be seeking to justify his choice, and that there would be exposure to nonsupportive information in the "participant" condition as a way of preparing for the anticipated discussion.

Predecisional Conflict and Postdecisional Information-Seeking

Dissonance theory makes a clear prediction that the greater the dissonance after a decision the greater should be the attempts by the person to accommodate to this decision. This should have clear implications for postdecisional information-seeking; the greater the dissonance the more the person will tend to seek out supportive information and avoid information that is nonsupportive. The greater the conflict in the predecision period, the more uncertain the person should be at the time he makes his decision and therefore the more misgivings he should experience after the decision; that is, the greater his postdecisional dissonance should be. Thus the amount of predecisional conflict will affect the amount of postdecisional dissonance. It follows that everything that we have said about the seeking of supportive and the avoidance of nonsupportive information should be heightened for difficult decisions.

In another study by Mills (1965b) college women were given a choice between two cosmetic products that they had previously ranked along with 18 other products. In one condition the choice was between the second- and third-ranked products and in the other condition the choice was between the second and nineteenth. The former condition would of course represent a more difficult decision and would be expected to arouse greater postdecisional dissonance than the latter condition. Therefore greater information-seeking and avoiding effects should be expected for the difficult as compared with the easy decision. After having made the decision the subject indicated how interested she was in reading ads about each of the 20 products. After correcting for the intrinsic interest value as in the previous study (1965a), the results showed a greater interest in the ad for the chosen product in the difficult choice condition than in the easy choice condition. There was, however, no corresponding greater avoidance of information about the rejected alternative in the difficult decision condition. Here we see the same old problem of demonstrating avoidance as a function of dissonance, but now it occurs even after a correction for intrinsic interest.

Information-Seeking after the Introduction of Discrepant Information

The studies discussed in the previous section attempted to examine information-seeking in response to the dissonance inherent in a decision, since a decision implies giving something up. A number of studies have examined information-seeking that occurs when a person is apprised of discrepant information *after* he has made his decision. Such information tends to produce dissonance and subsequent information-seeking selectivity in order to reduce the dissonance.

An experiment by Festinger (1957) employed an ingenious technique to determine information-seeking and information-avoiding behavior when subjects are confronted with dissonant information after a decision. The experiment was introduced to the subject, a male undergraduate, as a two-person card game and he was asked to decide whether he wanted to be player *A* or player *B*. He was given a "kitty" of $2.50 and he could come away with more or less than that depending on how the game went. He was told that the two sides, *A* and *B*, were not even. The game was biased so that one player was more likely to win than the other, but he was not told whether it was A or B. The following is the description of the game:

There are two players in this game: player A and player B. Before each game, the cards will be shuffled, cut, and seven cards will be dealt out on the table, face up. The values of the seven cards will then be added up. The cards count: ace, 1 point; deuce, 2 points; three, 3 points; and so on up to 10. Tens and picture cards count 10 points each; the maximum total for seven cards would be, of course, 70.

Whenever the total number of points is 48 or less, player A wins. Player A always wins the exact amount of his wager. (You will be asked to state how much you want to bet before each game.) At 49 points nobody wins. Player B wins if the cards add up to 50 or more. His possibilities of winning are as follows: from 50 to 54 points he wins the exact amount of his wager; from 55 to 59 points he wins twice the amount of his wager; from 60 to 64 he wins four times the amount of his wager; and from 65 to 70 he wins eight times the amount of his wager.

The subject was told that there were to be 30 games and for each he could bet from 5 to 25 cents. He was also told that he could switch to the other side once during the 30 trials. If he were A he could switch to B or vice versa. A penalty of one dollar would be exacted if he decided to switch. Since there was a penalty it was important for him to pick the more advantageous side at the outset.

The subject was given as much time as he needed to make his decision and was then asked to keep a trial-by-trial record of his winnings and losses. After 12 trials the experimenter showed the subject a graph purporting to indicate the cumulative probabilities of all possible scores from 10 to 70 and instructed him how to interpret the graph. A different probability graph was used, depending on which side the subject chose; but both graphs, if interpreted properly, implied to the subject that he was on the losing side. The amount of time spent by the subject looking at the graph was recorded by the experimenter. After he set the graph aside the subject was informed that the experiment was over.

By the twelfth trial, there was a wide range of winnings and losses among the 108 subjects used in the experiment. This distribution was equivalent to a manipulation of degrees of consonance and dissonance since winning or losing was determined by chance. If the subject was ahead he probably felt that he had chosen the "correct" side and that continuing to play that side was consonant with his belief. If he was losing, continuing to play on that side was dissonant with his belief; the more he was losing, the greater the dissonance.

The upper curve in Figure 6.2 presents the results of the experiment with the average number of cents won or lost per wager by the subject

Festinger Experiment:

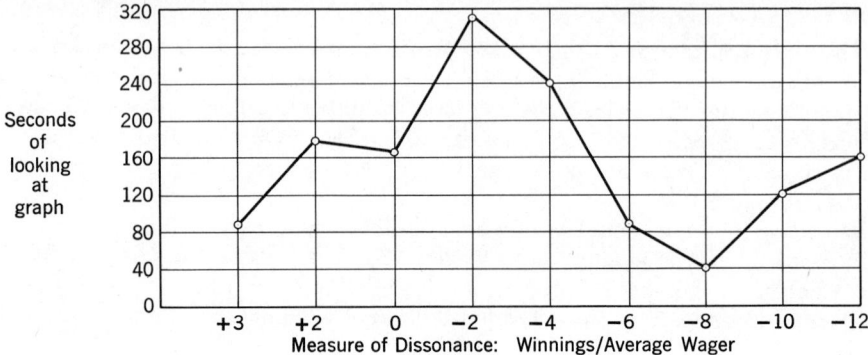

Cohen, Brehm, and Latane Experiment:

Public Condition

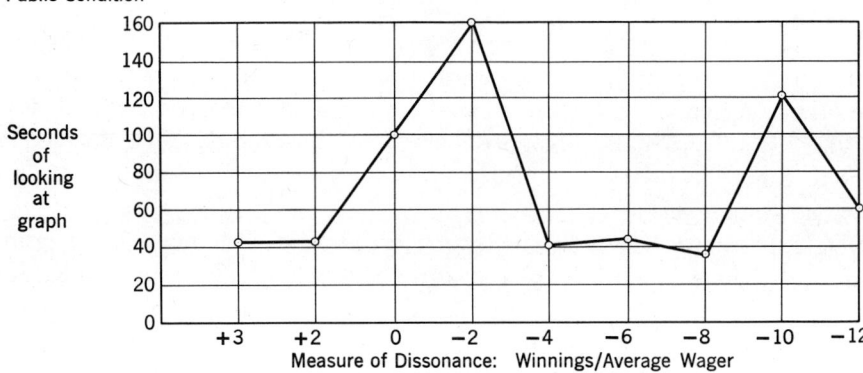

Private Condition

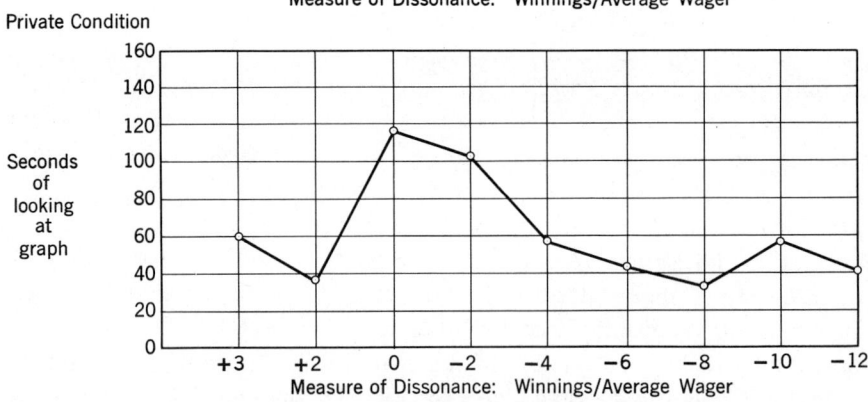

Figure 6.2. Time of exposure to new information for Festinger experiment and Yale replications (public and private conditions). From Cohen, Brehm, and Latané, 1959.

along the abscissa (horizontal axis), and inspection time of the probability graph given to him after the twelfth trial shown along the ordinate (vertical axis). We see inspection time rising to a peak at about minus two cents, then falling to a trough at about minus eight cents, and rising again after that. Where the subject was winning there was little motivation to seek additional supportive information that he had chosen the correct side. Where the subject was losing a small amount these losses were somewhat dissonant with his continuing to play that side. This dissonance produced in him an active tendency to seek supportive information that he was doing the right thing by continuing to play that side.

The large amount of time spent inspecting the probability graph by subjects who were losing moderately presumably reflects this inclination. Those who were losing rather heavily had considerable dissonance and could only expect the graph to tell them that they had chosen the wrong side. The one-dollar penalty was a sufficiently strong commitment to the side they had chosen so that they defensively avoided further evidence that they were on the wrong side. The trough at eight cents presumably indicates this avoidance tendency.

With losses even larger than eight cents per wager the subject suffered even greater dissonance and must have felt certain that he had indeed chosen the wrong side. At this point his dissonance was so great that he may have been willing to undo his commitment and pay the one-dollar penalty in order to change. The increase in inspection time at extreme losses may indicate the reduced defensiveness of these heavy losers prior to reconsidering their decision of which side to play.

This experiment is a complicated one based on assumptions as to what kind of information the subject expected to find in the graph, given his level of winnings. Fortunately, Cohen, Brehm, and Latané (1959) replicated this study. The procedure was exactly the same as that used by Festinger except that the sizes of the "kitty" and the penalty for changing sides were increased to fit a more affluent Ivy League subject population. This was done in order to maintain involvement in the game at the same level as the Big Ten university-student subjects used in the first experiment. Cohen, Brehm, and Latané suspected that the apparently strong commitment to maintaining the same side in Festinger's experiment was due to the presence, in the laboratory, of the experimenter and an observer who recorded the inspection time. This public commitment to the side chosen made in front of these two people may have produced a greater unwillingness to change sides owing to an attempt by the subject to save face.

The replicated experiment was run under two different treatments, a "private" and a "public" one. In the public treatment the subject was told that his performance and the performance of the other subjects in the experiment would be published in the campus newspaper and that his name and the report of his success would appear "probably next Wednesday." This was done to intensify public commitment in order that its effect, if any, would be heightened. By comparing this treatment with one in which commitment was minimized, we would be in a position to estimate the effect of commitment in the first experiment. In the private, minimal-commitment treatment the subject was told that the results of the experiment would be held in strictest confidence.

The two lower curves in Figure 6.2 show the results of the public and private treatments in this experiment. The shape of the curves confirms the original findings and the sharper peak and deeper trough under the public treatment suggest the effect of greater commitment. There was also evidence that the greater his losings, the more the subject expected that the chart would indicate that he had chosen the wrong side. This makes the dissonance interpretation even more compelling since the relationship between losing and expectation of what the chart would indicate is an assumption on which the interpretation of the original experiment was based.

Adams (1961) conducted a field experiment utilizing the opinions of mothers on whether heredity or environment plays a more crucial role in child-rearing. The mothers, whose opinions were ascertained during a personal interview, were exposed to either of two authoritative-sounding communications. One of these took the position that heredity was a more important influence and the other that environment was more important. The experiment was arranged so that half of the subjects heard a communication that agreed with their point of view whereas the other half heard a communication that disagreed with their point of view. The subjects were then asked if they would like to hear a lecture allegedly favoring an environmental view or one favoring a hereditary view. Those subjects who had heard a message that was discrepant from their point of view were much more interested in hearing the subsequent lecture than were those subjects who had heard a message that agreed with their point of view. They were, however, *equally* interested in both topics. They did not favor potentially consonant over potentially dissonant information. They simply seemed to be more interested in finding out more about the general topic. These data, then, do not support dissonance theory but support the idea that a discrepancy piques the person's interest and increases his desire for additional information presumably to resolve the discrepancy.

A study by Brodbeck (1956) does present supporting evidence. Subjects whose confidence in their initial belief had been shaken by a persuasive message that argued against it preferred to seek out others who agreed with their belief to a greater extent than did subjects who heard a message that was consonant with their initial belief. Maccoby, Maccoby, Romney, and Adams (1961) investigated the same problem using female subjects. The issue was the age at which children should be toilet trained. The women were interviewed individually in their homes on three successive occasions. The first interview assessed their initial attitude toward toilet training; the second interview introduced a persuasive message advocating later toilet training than the respondent had advocated on the first interview, with a remeasure of the subject's attitude at that time; and the third interview attempted to assess information-seeking that occurred after the persuasive message, by determining with whom the respondent chose to converse about toilet training in the interval between the second and third interview. The findings were that women who changed their opinion tended to seek out other women who agreed with the new opinion, whereas people who were steadfast in the face of the persuasive message tended to seek out other women who agreed with the old opinion. Presumably a person who has recently changed his opinion is still working through the dissonance occasioned by the change, whereas a steadfast person is less likely to be in a dissonant state. An obvious problem with this experiment, however, is that subjects in effect selected themselves to be changers and nonchangers and the changers may differ from the nonchangers in a variety of ways that may account for the information-seeking difference; for example, the changers may be generally more insecure about any issue.

When Prophecies Fail

When a person committed to a course of action is suddenly confronted by evidence that the course he has chosen is incorrect he may resort to a number of tactics to reduce the dissonance created by the information. He may denigrate the new evidence or its source; he may misperceive or reinterpret the evidence so that it is rendered either irrelevant or consonant with his choice; or he may seek additional evidence to support his initial choice. Other people often serve as sources of supporting evidence, especially if they are committed to the same behavior as the person. After being exposed to the disconfirmation, the person acquires support for his initial decision by convincing other people to engage in the same behavior. This is a form of seeking supportive information by manufacturing it, by convincing other people that they too should commit themselves to the same behavior. Festinger, Riecken, and Schachter (1956) studied a dramatic situation in which such proselytizing behavior was predicted. The nature of the situation has already been described in detail as one of the cases in Chapter One. The investigators assumed that the world would not be destroyed as one doomsday cult had prophesied, and that the members of the cult would be confronted with evidence that was blatantly inconsistent with the belief to which they were heavily committed. The cult members assembled, waiting to be rescued by flying saucers just before the end of the world. When the events the cult members expected failed to occur there was a great deal of consternation and confusion but at some point someone suggested that there might have been a miscalculation in the timing. Most of the members seemed satisfied with this explanation, which was later confirmed in automatic writing that purportedly represented word from the spirits. Before the disconfirmation the group made no attempts to proselytize, whereas after it the members contacted the press and other media in order to provide publicity for their venture, presumably for the ultimate purpose of acquiring proselytes. This evidence supports the derivation from dissonance theory.

The case of another doomsday group was briefly described in Chapter One; these were members of the "Church of the True Word" who descended into fallout shelters to await a nuclear holocaust (Hardyk and Braden, 1962). On the forty-second day the 103 "faithful" who had remained in the shelters emerged to find the world much the same as they had left it. This group was thus in a position like that of the other group that was waiting for the world to come to an end, yet its behavior was quite different. Instead of seeking proselytes it held a "joyous reunion" in the Church and praised the Lord for uniting it even more firmly in Christian fellowship.

It is not at all clear why two such similar disconfirmations, both involving predictions of the end of the world as we know it, should produce such different group reactions. Clearly the reactions of the fallout-shelter group do not confirm dissonance theory, yet the members of this group were presumably as firmly committed to the belief as were the doomsday cult members. There were numerous differences between the circumstances of the two groups, any one of which could have obscured the operation of dissonance-reducing mechanisms in the second case. Perhaps the most likely candidate as a crucial difference was the sheer size of the second doomsday cult. With more than 100 fellow believers, any dissonance associated with disconfirmation might have been easy to handle within the group, without the need for external social support.

Let us briefly summarize the evidence on exposure. Regarding the predecision period the evidence at present is rather thin but does suggest that a person is dispassionately open to information relevant to the impending decision. The major factor in the predecision period is probably the degree of familiarity with the alternatives, although there is no direct evidence bearing on this assumption. Regarding the postdecision phase there is a great deal of evidence, but it appears very confused. There is substantial evidence in a number of the studies that a person seeks out information supporting his choice; but only one study presents evidence that he avoids discrepant, nonsupportive information. Several studies suggest that when discrepant information may be useful in the future a person tends to seek it out. The same information may follow one decision and precede another so that the individual cannot reduce his dissonance by selectively avoiding the information without jeopardizing the wisdom of a future decision.

The Adams study and the one by Sears and Freedman present interesting complementary evidence. Sears and Freedman found that commitment reduced the subject's desire for both supportive and nonsupportive evidence regardless of its potential usefulness. Evidently the subject made up his mind about the evidence for either conviction or acquittal of the delinquent boy and became relatively quiescent in his need for additional information. In the Adams study, in which a discrepancy was introduced after the subject had committed herself to a particular stand, we find heightened interest in any relevant information. The act of commitment in the Sears and Freedman study was presumably preceded by some reduction in uncertainty before the decision was made, whereas in the Adams study the message that provided the discrepant information had the effect of arousing uncertainty and the subsequent need for information that might reduce it. When we deal with social-influence processes later we shall examine a large literature that relates directly to this problem.

An important difference between the studies that support the theory and those that only partially support it is the nature of the measure of information-seeking used. In those studies that support the theory the subject could freely expose himself to information after he made his decision. For those in which the evidence for the theory was ambiguous the subject either was asked to recall what he did or was asked to choose various kinds of supporting and nonsupporting information. The subject's attitude toward this kind of request may be a confounding factor. He may feel that the fair and reasonable thing to do in a case like this is to be unbiased, or at least appear to be so to the experimenter. Further work is required to evaluate the importance of this possible artifact in detecting selective exposure tendencies.

RE-EVALUATION OF THE ALTERNATIVES

The maintenance of an unequivocal behavioral orientation toward his decision requires the person to minimize any regret. Intense regret can interfere with enjoyment of the fruits of a decision and can serve relatively few useful functions. Regret may be minimized through self-justification. We found some support for this attempt to "justify" the decision in the preceding section. The end result of cognitively working through the decision should be a tendency to enhance the value of the chosen alternative and derogate the nonchosen one so that they spread apart in value after the choice. Biased exposure to the alternatives can obviously facilitate re-evaluation, and bias can have more powerful effects when the alternatives are complex, when they have vague behavioral implications, and when there is a large time lag between making the choice and confronting its consequences. The evaluation process is probably very adaptive in the service of behavioral commitments.

The earliest study to examine postdecisional re-evaluation was undertaken by Brehm (1956) whose procedure established a paradigm for many subsequent studies. Basically, the technique is very simple and involves having the subject evaluate a set of a dozen or so objects, having him subsequently choose between two of these as to which of them he would like as a gift, and then asking him to re-evaluate all of the objects after the choice. The same technique was used in some of the information-seeking research already described. Any change in evaluation, up or down, of either choice alternative can be assessed. In his study Brehm used a number of objects such as small appliances and found that after the choice the object chosen as a gift did rise in value for the subject relative to the nonchosen alternative.

The cover story used to present the experiment to college coed subjects was that they would be taking part in a nationwide market research survey in which a number of products were being evaluated. In return for her cooperation the subject was told that she would receive a gift from one of the manufacturers. The experimenter then proceeded to unpack the various objects: an automatic toaster, an automatic coffee maker, a small portable radio, a desk lamp, a silk-screen print, a painting, a stopwatch, an art book, and a sandwich grill. The subject was instructed to take as much time as she wanted to examine the articles and rate each on a rating scale. The experimenter then picked two of the articles and asked which of them the subject wanted as her gift. Half of the subjects were asked to choose between two articles that were close in value for them as indicated in the initial ratings. The other half were given a choice between two articles that were quite disparate in value. The one she chose was wrapped up and given to her.

After a period of time, during which the subject was asked to read research reports written by the manufacturers, she was again asked to rate all nine objects. The reason given for the second rating was that now the subject had really had sufficient time to examine the objects, also had additional research information, and could give a more realistic evaluation.

As stated earlier, a difficult decision, in which alternative objects are close in value, should arouse greater postdecisional dissonance. Hence we should expect more spreading apart of the alternatives in the close- as compared with the disparate-value treatment. In order to facilitate dissonance reduction half of the subjects in each treatment read research reports about the two alternatives involved in the choice, reports containing descriptions of both positive and negative aspects of both objects. The research reports read by the rest of the subjects, in both easy and difficult decision treatments, were about two of the other items that were not involved in the choice. A control condition was run in which the subject did not make a choice but was merely handed one of the articles as a gift. The purpose of this condition was to assess the effects of any change in attractiveness of the chosen article that might occur due to its mere possession.

The results presented in Table 6.1 strongly support the theory. The first two columns of the table indicate change in evaluation of the alterna-

Table 6.1. Reduction of Postdecision Dissonance by Changing the Attractiveness of the Chosen and Nonchosen Alternatives [a]

	Change from first to second rating for:		
	Chosen object	Nonchosen object	Net change
Without research reports			
Low dissonance (disparate value)	+.38	−.24	+.62
High dissonance (close value)	+.26	−.66	+.92
With research reports			
Low dissonance (disparate value)	+.11	−.00	+.11
High dissonance (close value)	+.38	−.41	+.79
Gift (control)	+.00	−	

[a] A positive sign indicates an increase in attractiveness and a negative sign indicates a decrease. Net change is the change for the chosen object minus the change for the nonchosen, which would indicate the net "spreading apart" of the alternatives following the choice; a positive index would be evidence for dissonance reduction (adapted from Brehm, 1956).

tives and the third column presents the net spreading apart. First we see that subjects in the control, "gift" condition, in which there was no choice, showed absolutely no change in evaluation of the object they had received as a gift. In the rest of the table we see tendencies for subjects to increase the value of the chosen and decrease the value of the nonchosen alternative. Over-all, we see more spreading apart when the objects were close in value (high dissonance) than when they were disparate in value (low dissonance). The difference between the close and disparate value conditions was greater when the subject read research reports about the alternatives involved in the choice than when she read reports about two other objects. This is consistent with dissonance theory, too, since in the former condition there is more material to use in working through the dissonance.

The Effect of Overlapping Alternatives

To the extent that available alternatives possess qualitatively different characteristics we would expect greater postdecisional regret. When there is a great deal of overlap in the features of the alternatives, choosing one alternative does not imply giving up the outcomes associated with the others, since these outcomes are to a great extent embodied in either. Theoretically there should be greater spreading apart of the alternatives after a choice insofar as their features are dissimilar.

An experiment by Brehm and Cohen (1959) provides data supporting this derivation. School children were asked to evaluate 16 toys; half were given a choice between toys that were qualitatively similar and the other half chose between toys that were qualitatively dissimilar. A similar choice might have been between two pieces of sporting equipment or two games, whereas a dissimilar choice might have been between a piece of sporting equipment and a game. In both conditions the value of the toy chosen was enhanced relative to the nonchosen toy, with the effect being more pronounced in the dissimilar condition.

Perceived Freedom of Choice

In the original Brehm (1956) study the more equal the alternatives were in value the greater was the apparent postdecisional re-evaluation. This, according to dissonance theory, results from the greater need for justifying a choice the less objective grounds there are for having made it. The subject gives up more when the alternatives are close in value than when they are disparate. Any factor that tends to minimize regret by adding predecisional justification results in less postdecisional dissonance. Thus, if a person were strongly urged or forced to make a choice, postdecisional dissonance would tend to be low because the urging or forcing would have justified making the choice. Also, if the subject were threatened for not making a partcular choice or were promised a large extrinsic reward for making the choice, the choice would be easier than if no punishment were threatened or no extrinsic reward offered.

Evidence supporting this theoretical derivation is found in experiments by Brehm and Cohen (1959) and Cohen (1962). These experiments varied the amount of reward for participating in an unpleasant task, finding that the less the reward the greater was the amount of dissonance reduction as reflected in increased attractiveness of the task. Further research by

Brehm (1962) and Cohen and Brehm (1962) indicates that when a threat is applied to "encourage" a person to make a decision, the less the threat, the greater is the postdecisional dissonance. Thus anything that justifies the decision before it is made tends to reduce the need to justify it afterward. Or, the less the predecision conflict, the less is the postdecision dissonance.

Commitment and Postdecision Dissonance

A point stressed earlier was that a decision had to have some behavioral implications for there to be postdecisional regret. A study by Deutsch, Krauss, and Rosenau (1962) advances strong evidence for the importance of commitment. In their experiment the subjects were engaged in a food-tasting situation under two treatments. In one they were told that their preference reflected upon them personally, whereas in the other their preference had no such implications. Re-evaluation favoring the chosen alternative occurred only in the treatment where the choice had subsequent implications for the subject.

An experiment by Gerard, Blevans, and Malcolm (1964) provides additional evidence for the importance of the consequences implied by the commitment. In this experiment the choices were the paintings used in the Gerard study cited earlier. Here again a comparison between a gift condition, in which the subject chose which of two prints he wanted to receive as a gift, and a preference condition, in which he merely indicated which of two paintings he liked better, revealed significant postdecisional re-evaluation only in the gift condition.

Certainty of Outcome

Two recent experiments, one by Jecker (1964a) and another by Allen (1964), offer convincing evidence for the importance of commitment to a choice as a precondition for re-evaluation. Both experiments used high-school girls as subjects. Each subject was asked to choose between two phonograph records selected from among 15 records she had previously evaluated. In the Jecker experiment the subject was informed before she made her choice that the experimenter had an oversupply of records and that she might very well get both records as a gift rather than just one. Since there were not enough records to give two to every girl participating in the experiment some girls would receive only one. In one treatment the subject was told that 19 out of every 20 girls would receive two records; in a second treatment she was told that only one out of 20 would receive both records. The subject then chose the record of the two that she preferred; she would get this record as a gift in any case. There was uncertainty, however, as to whether she would get the second record as well; in one condition there was a 5 percent chance that she would get it and in the other condition a 95 percent chance.

A postmeasure in which all 15 records were re-evaluated indicated that in neither treatment was there the typical postdecisional spreading apart in value of the alternatives. Another condition in which the subject chose between the two records and was told that she would definitely get one and only one record shows the typical dissonance effect, with the chosen record being enhanced in value and the nonchosen record being derogated. This result is startling since it suggests that unless the nonchosen alternative is definitely and completely excluded after a choice, re-evaluation does not take place. It would have been reasonable to expect that in the condition in which there was only a 5 percent chance of getting a nonchosen record the subject would react as though the alternative was excluded, but this was not the case.

The Allen experiment confirmed Jecker's finding. Four treatments were run, varying the probability of receiving the nonchosen alternative. Systematic re-evaluation occurred only where the subject knew for certain that she would not get the nonchosen record.

Re-Evaluation before or after the Decision?

Earlier we discussed the formidable technical problems involved in determining whether re-evaluation occurs before or after a decision is made. We suggested that re-evaluation tends to occur both before *and* after a decision is made and that the purpose of predecisional cognitive work is to assess the outcome potential of each alternative so that the person can make a wise decision. Postdecisional changes are part of the follow-through, reducing regret and maintaining an unequivocal behavioral orientation. The studies by Jecker and Allen might seem, at least on the surface, to suggest that systematic re-evaluation does not occur before the decision, because in all of the treatments in those experiments a decision was made but re-evaluation occurred only when the nonchosen alternative was definitely given up. This argument is specious, however, since the predecision situation as well as the postdecision situation might be different when the person anticipates giving up something. Furthermore, in all of the studies described thus far the conditions are so arranged that even when the alternatives are close in value one alternative definitely has an initial edge. When the alternatives are exactly equal in value, and any decision is better than none, the person is likely to attach great significance to small differences. In this sense there is probably some motivated spreading of the alternatives even before the decision, or indeed to make the decision possible. Festinger (1964) appears to disagree with this since he favors the hypothesis of complete objectivity in the predecision period. We feel that he overstates the case and that some of the evaluative changes that occur prior to a decision may be systematic—especially in the period immediately preceding the decision.

An experiment by Davidson and Kiesler (1964) attempted to overcome the technical difficulties of getting pre- and postdecisional measurements. Subjects were teenage girls, each of whom was asked to make a decision about hiring a man to become first vice-president in a firm that she owned and controlled. Each was asked to rank, in order of importance, eight personal qualities that make up a good executive. There were two applicants for the job, Mr. Brown and Mr. Jones, and the subject was told that she would receive information about these men in order to make a decision about which one to hire. This information would be provided on 10 printed cards that she would receive in sequence, arranged in order of importance of the information contained, the last two cards containing the most important information of all. Thus the subject was led to believe that it would be virtually impossible to reach a good decision until she had read all of the cards. All subjects, however, received only four of these cards, each containing information indicating that Mr. Jones excelled in one quality in which Mr. Brown was average, whereas Mr. Brown excelled in another quality in which Mr. Jones was average. Taken together the four cards contained eight qualities, four for which Mr. Jones was higher than Mr. Brown and four for which the relationship was reversed. The qualities were the same eight that the subject had ranked initially.

In the postdecision treatment the subject was told after reading the fourth card that although she initially had been asked to wait until reading all 10 cards before deciding, she should decide now on the basis of the information she had read on the first four cards. After her decision the subject reranked the eight qualities. In the other treatment, the *predecision* treatment, the order of these events was reversed; the subject first reranked the eight qualities and then made an early decision. The measure of re-evaluation used in the study was the change in rank of the eight qualities. If the subject chose Mr. Jones an increase in the importance of the qualities in which he was reputed to excel would indicate that his value was enhanced for the subject. Similarly, if she chose Mr. Brown an increase in importance of his qualities would indicate that his value was enhanced. This measure is a good, indirect method for determining evaluational changes.

The results indicate that value enhancement of the chosen applicant occurred in the postdecisional treatment but not in the predecisional treatment. Festinger suggests that the results of this study and of the studies by Jecker and Allen are conclusive proof that re-evaluation does not take place in the predecision period. On the basis of the results of the Davidson and Kiesler experiment, his position is difficult to defend because the subject was told specifically to withhold making a decision until she had read all 10 cards. In the predecision condition the subject was probably doing just that and was not prepared to re-evaluate the two candidates finally until all the evidence was in. In the postdecision condition a "switch" was pulled on the subject by suddenly asking her to stop withholding judgment and make a decision. In the time it took for the subject to make up her mind she could have spread the applicants apart in order to facilitate the decision.

All we can legitimately conclude from the study is that the decision process is followed by re-evaluation. Whether it occurs before or after the decision, or both, is still an open question. We need technology that will enable us continually to track changes in attractiveness of alternatives both before and after a decision without the subject's being aware that we are taking these measurements. Recent work by Hess (1965) suggests that this may at last be possible. He finds that the dilation of a person's pupils correlates with the degree of attraction of a stimulus to which the person is attending. This technique may be the key to the important question of when re-evaluation occurs.

Self-Evaluation and Re-Evaluation of Alternatives

Underlying the discussion in this chapter is the implicit assumption that a person behaves in a manner that increases his welfare. He attempts to move from his present psychological state to some other one in order to increase his outcome level or to prevent his present level from being reduced. This assumption of self-benefit, in turn, derives from a more basic assumption that the person evaluates himself positively. The data presented thus far have, of course, been based on the comparison of what subjects do *on the average* in various treatments within any given experiment; but there are always individual differences in interpreting and responding to experimental variables. Sometimes this variability between subjects can be shown to be a function of measurable personality traits and of recent or remote past experiences.

In all of the experiments investigating postdecisional accommodation through re-evaluation when there was a large dissonance effect in a particular treatment, the implication was that a relatively large number of subjects in the treatment showed the effect. When the data are examined in more detail it is usually found that some subjects in the treatment do not show the effect, and others show a reverse effect; that is, they enhance the value of the nonchosen relative to the chosen alternative.

If a person has a negative self-evaluation that leads to the expectation that he will make poor decisions rather than good ones, we might expect a reverse of the dissonance effect. Evidence for this exists in the study by Gerard, Blevans, and Malcolm (1964), referred to earlier, in which self-confidence was manipulated prior to the decision. The decision involved a choice between two paintings that had previously been evaluated. Perceived self-ability was manipulated by informing the subject, before making his decision, that he had done well, poorly, or about average on an art-judgment test taken a week earlier. The findings are clear-cut. We find the usual dissonance effect, with the alternatives spread apart in value after the choice, only when the subject had a positive evaluation of his ability to make the choice. When the subject's self-evaluation was negative there was a postdecisional *increase* in the value of the nonchosen alternative relative to the chosen one.

Malewski (1962) conducted an experiment in Poland to study the effect of a more generalized measure of self-esteem on the evaluation of objects before and after a decision. Instead of manipulating self-evaluation experimentally, as in the study just described, he used evaluations made of the subject by his schoolmates as the measure of self-esteem. Here he assumed that the child's self-evaluation would be influenced by the evaluations that schoolmates had of him (or her).

Malewski's results are nearly identical to those of Gerard, Blevans, and Malcolm, lending additional weight to the assumption that self-confidence influences the onset of postdecisional regret. Presumably, when self-confidence is high, postdecisional regret is overcome by cognitive work, whereas when self-confidence is low, regret is taken as affirmation of low ability and is not reduced. The results of these studies should help future attempts to account for intersubject variability in postdecisional behavior. Obtaining a prior measure of the subject's self-ability estimate should enable us to predict his postdecisional behavior with even greater precision, though it remains true that most subjects like to believe they make wise decisions and that they choose the most valuable alternative of those offered.

POSTDECISIONAL REGRET

A pesky problem in much of the research on postdecisional re-evaluation is the relatively large number of subjects who make decision reversals. When confronted with the decision alternatives they choose the one they initially ranked lower in value. It becomes difficult to know just what to do with these subjects in subsequent analysis of the data. Did they initially make a mistake in using the rating scales, are the scales unreliable, or did the reversal subjects become confused about the properties of the choice confronting them?

Another possibility is that they knew exactly what they were doing and exactly how to interpret the rating scales but the inversion reflected an important aspect of the choice situation itself. As we have already stated, owing to the limits of present technology it is impossible to know exactly when the subject's decision occurs; all we know is that it takes place sometime before he announces it to the experimenter. It is conceivable that a choice inversion does not represent the initial choice of the subject. He may have made a choice and before announcing it, felt a sudden surge of regret at giving up the nonchosen alternative. He may then have made an impulsive reversal of his initial decision, which he announced publicly. Once having done this he could not reverse himself again without appearing foolishly indecisive.

Perhaps the predecision period is characterized by a sequence of tentative decisions followed by reversals. Dissonance tends to be maximum immediately after a decision is made and before the subject has had time to work through the negative implications of his choice. One implication of this postdecisional regret is that if we were able to track the relative value of the alternatives after a decision the nonchosen alternative would tend first to be enhanced and then depressed in value, relative to the chosen alternative, as the person worked through the dissonance.

If a situation could be devised in which a subject made a decision without definitely committing himself and then were allowed to make the decision again, postdecisional regret could be inferred if the second decision represented a reversal. Festinger and Walster (1964) conducted an experiment in which this was attempted. They used college coeds as subjects and had them first rate photographs of 12 different hair styles—according to how each would feel about having her own hair done in the style portrayed. On the basis of these initial ratings the experimenter picked two styles that the subject had found attractive. In the no-prior-decision condition each subject was then asked to rank the 12 photographs she had previously rated. After this ranking the experimenter explained that the company sponsoring the study was offering each participant a free haircut and set at a nearby salon; however, the subject had to choose between the two hair styles that the experimenter had previously selected. The subject then made her choice.

In the prior-decision condition the same procedures were followed except that the offering of a free styling was made before the ranking task. The experimenter put paper clips on the two photographs that the subject was later to choose between so that the ranking would be made with the subsequent choice clearly in mind. As soon as the ranking was completed the subject chose between the two clipped photographs.

In the prior-decision condition, then, the rank order of the two hair styles was an expression of a decision by the subject. In the no-prior-decision condition the ranking did not imply the same commitment to a choice with behavioral consequences. When the subjects in the latter condition were later confronted with a choice between the two attractive alternatives, it was possible for them to express any regret attendant upon their ranking by choosing the hair style they had initially ranked lower. Twenty-eight percent of the subjects in the no-prior-decision condition chose the initially less attractive (lower-ranked) alternative, whereas in the prior-decision condition 62 percent chose the less attractive alternative. This appears to be strong evidence for postdecisional regret.

An experiment by Walster (1964) attempted to follow, over time, the process of coming to terms with postdecisional regret. In order to track the process experimentally, this investigator felt, it was essential to utilize a decision with important implications for the subject so that the immediate postdecisional dissonance would be extremely high. She was fortunate in getting the cooperation of the Human Resources Resarch Office of the U.S. Army. Army recruits were used as subjects in the experiment and the choice they confronted was to which of two military occupational specialties they wished to be assigned during their two years of service. This setting combined the control that can be exercised in the usual laboratory experiment with the importance of a crucial real-life decision. When the subject came into the laboratory he was asked to rate 10 occupational specialties and was then given a choice between two of them. After his choice the subject rerated all 10 jobs. All this was made to appear very natural and believable. There were four experimental treatments that varied the time interval between choice and second rating: an immediate rerating, a rerating after four minutes, a rerating after 15 minutes, and a rerating after 90 minutes. These time intervals were selected arbitrarily; there was no way of knowing beforehand how long it would take for regret to dissipate if it did in fact occur.

The data shown in Table 6.2 suggest that there was indeed a phase of regret that appears to have occurred during a brief period after the decision was made and was detected up to the four-minute treatment. But should regret not be maximum immediately after the decision? The theory certainly suggests that it should be, but for a decision as important as this one, with so many distant behavioral implications, it may take a few minutes for the regret to build up. We see in the table that by the time 15 minutes had passed considerable dissonance reduction seems to have taken place.

The failure of the spreading apart of the alternatives to be sustained after the 90-minute interval (as shown in the table) is puzzling. It is conceivable that after the dissonance has been worked through the person can again take a dispassionate, nondefensive view toward the alternatives. Initially the alternatives may have been so discrepant in value that it was not necessary to sustain the spread added by dissonance reduction. It would have been interesting to compare the postdecisional pattern, in which the alternatives were approximately five units apart on a 31-point scale, with

Table 6.2.[a] Mean Ratings of Chosen and Rejected Alternatives for Subjects Who Chose the More Attractive [b] Job as a Function of How Long after the Decision the Second Measurement Was Taken

Time of second measurement	Predecision ratings		Change on postdecision		Net spreading apart [c]
	Chosen	Rejected	Chosen	Rejected	
Immediately after	9.80	15.09	.70	.00	.70
4 Minutes after	9.79	15.02	−.37	−.97	−1.34
15 Minutes after	10.04	14.98	1.56	.58	2.14
90 Minutes after	9.91	14.84	.67	−.36	.31

[a] Adapted from Walster (1964). The rating scales had a total of 31 points.
[b] Data from subjects who made a decision reversal (when the subject chose the job that he initially rated as less attractive) are not included in the table. Fifty-one of the total of 244 subjects made reversals.
[c] By "spreading apart" we mean the chosen increased in value relative to the rejected job.

another in which the jobs involved were as close as possible on the rating scale. In this second condition the spreading apart might have been sustained into the 90-minute condition.

Regardless of the problem of the arbitrary choice of time intervals and the problem of the best strategy to be used in selecting initial discrepancy size, the results do suggest that there was postdecisional regret. We must remember that there were different subjects in each of the four treatments, and we are assuming that if it had been possible to take successive measurements on all subjects the same pattern of results would have been generated. Employing successive measurements on the same subjects, although more appropriate for arguments about cognitive changes over time, would certainly have disrupted the subject's cognitive work.

EFFORT JUSTIFICATION AND THE ACTION SEQUENCE

We have found that the closer in value the alternatives are the greater is the dissonance following a choice between them. This was interpreted as having been due to the regret experienced by the person in giving up desirable features of a nonchosen alternative and of acquiring undesirable features of the chosen one. There is another possibility that might also produce this effect: a decision between two close alternatives is more difficult and hence requires greater *effort*. In discussing effort in Chapter Three we presented evidence indicating that to the extent that a person expends effort in attempting to acquire something, the knowledge that it is low in value will be dissonant with the knowledge that he has expended effort to acquire it. Both regret and effort will probably be confounded in a decision, each operating in a manner to create cognitive dissonance and each leading to cognitive justification by the person.

An experiment by Yaryan and Festinger (1961) shows the role of effort. Subjects were asked to prepare to take an examination. In one condition preparation was quite effortful; in another it was not. There was some doubt—initially, the same amount for each treatment—whether the subject would take the examination. When subjects were asked whether they thought they would take the examination, subjects in the high-effort condition considered it much more likely that they would than subjects in the low-effort condition. If the subject knew he was engaging in a great deal of effort in order to take the exam, knowledge that he would not take it would be dissonant. His overestimation of the likelihood that he would take the exam would reduce that dissonance.

Additional evidence supporting the effort-justification hypothesis has been reviewed in Chapter Three. The animal learning research of Lawrence and Festinger (1962), Aronson's (1961) experiment in which subjects fished for containers of different colors, and the Aronson and Mills (1959) severity of initiation study, all provide data that are consistent with the proposition that the attractiveness of a goal object is heightened by the effort put forth to acquire it.

As noted in Chapter Two, any single experiment may be subject to alternative interpretation. The girls in the severe initiation treatment of the Aronson and Mills experiment, for example, may have been attracted to the ensuing discussion and the discussants for a number of reasons having nothing to do with effort justification. Because the severe initiation required the girls to read obscene words and lascivious literary passages they may have found salacious double meanings in the supposedly banal discussion. Or they may have wondered about the meaning of some of the obscene words and assumed that joining the group would enable them to find out what the words meant.

Another difficulty stems from the fact that there was no control in the experiment to determine whether the attraction taken on by the club in the severe initiation treatment was because of some kind of contrast effect. Perhaps any experience that followed the reading of the list would be pleasant in comparison with the embarrassing task of saying obscene words. Unless such a control were provided and the context of the suffering was separated from the context of the club's activities, the data would be consistent with many other theories besides dissonance theory.

The experiment by Gerard and Mathewson (1966) attempted to narrow the number of possible interpretations of the Aronson and Mills experiment by separating the content of the initiation from the purpose of the club and by providing certain additional controls. In all essential respects the format of the experiment was the same as the one by Aronson and Mills. Girls were invited to join a discussion club on "morality on university campuses" and were then subjected to an initiation. When each subject arrived in the laboratory she was told that there had been a lot of trouble in these discussions since formerly just about anyone was allowed to join. The discussions often deteriorated because certain members were not able to maintain objectivity about morals. A new procedure, therefore, had just been instituted in order to screen applicants for the club. The subject was then given an "objectivity test." The test involved measuring her emotional reactions (physiological measurements were simulated) to a series of stimuli: perfume, music, paintings, and electrical shock.

In the severe initiation treatment the shocks were strong, whereas in the mild initiation treatment the shocks were barely above threshold. The subject was asked, as a warm-up and to give her an introduction to the type of discussions she could expect, to listen to a recording of a previous discussion of the club she was a candidate for and was then asked to evaluate the discussion. As in the Aronson and Mills experiment, the discussion was as boring and banal as possible in order to maximize dissonance in the high shock condition. The two initiation treatments were compared with two control treatments in which the procedure was exactly the same except that the subject was not a candidate for one of the discussion clubs but was merely required to evaluate a series of stimuli that included, as the last one, the group discussion. Aronson and Mills had informed all of their subjects that they had passed the screening test. Each subject had thus acquired that for which she had suffered. It was inappropriate in this replication to inform the noninitiate as to how she had done since she did not perceive the situation as a test. In order to take account of the difference between initiate and noninitiate treatments, within the initiate condition half of the subjects were told that they passed the objectivity test, whereas the other half were given no information as to whether they had passed. Thus the not-told initiates were comparable to the noninitiates with respect to performance feedback.

The data for the evaluation of the discussion are presented in Table 6.3. Here we see strong confirmation of the Aronson and Mills experiment. Among the initiates, those who had had a severe initiation liked the discussion better than those who had had a mild initiation, whereas among the noninitiates those who had suffered more severe physical discomfort liked the discussion less. This latter effect is what might be expected from secondary reinforcement; some of the unpleasantness of the shock apparently rubbed off onto the subsequent evaluation of the discussion. This interaction between initiate versus noninitiate on the one hand, and severity of shock on the other hand, is impressive support for dissonance theory. We see

Table 6.3. The Effects of Severity of Shock, Initiation, and Feedback on Evaluation of the Group Discussion [a]

	Initiate				Noninitiate	
	Mild shock		Severe shock		Mild shock	Severe shock
	Told	Not told	Told	Not told		
Participant rating	11.5	26.1	31.1	41.0	19.8	13.2
Discussion rating	11.0	15.6	27.0	28.2	9.1	5.8

[a] The larger the number the more favorable the evaluation. (From Gerard and Mathewson, 1966.)

in the table that the told versus not-told factor does not interact with the severity of the shock. However, there does seem to be a main effect of feedback. Those subjects who were informed that they had passed the test had somewhat lower evaluations of the discussion. This may reflect a desire on the part of the initiates who received no feedback to be in the group. The initiate who knew she had passed was assured of membership and thus before the evaluation her efforts in undergoing shock were at least partially justified.

SUMMARY

In this chapter we have outlined a theory of action in which an act is conceived of as a decision. There are three phases of the act: the predecision phase, the act itself, and the postdecision phase. In the predecision phase the person attempts to evaluate the decision alternatives as to which has the greatest outcome potential for him. This phase, therefore, is characterized by information-seeking for the purpose of evaluation. During this phase of the sequence the person maintains an objective stance toward the information though the information gained may itself bring about systematic evaluative shifts. This is obviously the most efficient way of making evaluational estimates. After some threshold has been established, in which one of the alternatives has a clear edge, the person makes his decision. The size of this threshold is determined by a number of factors including the importance of making some kind of a decision rather than none, the importance of decision consequences, and the relative ambiguity of the alternatives.

The decision itself produces regret, because a decision has inherent in it the giving up of something, namely the potential enjoyment associated with the nonchosen alternatives. The decision also implies some suffering associated with any unpleasant implication of the chosen alternative.

The postdecisional phase is characterized by attempts to come to terms with this regret so the person can maintain an unequivocal behavioral orientation toward the chosen alternative. The extent to which the person tends to work through this regret is proportional to the extent to which he is committed to the alternative he has chosen. Postdecisional behavior is therefore characterized by attempts to seek information that would support the decision as well as the tendency to overvalue the chosen alternative relative to the nonchosen ones.

CHAPTER SEVEN

The Impact of Value and Attitude on Perceiving and Remembering

The distinction between pre- and postdecisional thinking reflects a fundamental division of approaches toward information in the human organism. There is a *basic antinomy* between openness to change and the desire to preserve a pre-existing view or conviction. To understand the nature of this antinomy, let us return to socialization and its products.

The socialization process may be viewed as the set of experiences that establish the strength of the opposing forces of the antinomy. Chapter Five stressed the adaptive significance of consistency in thought. The individual constantly works to simplify his thoughts about the environment and to impose some system on events around him. He is aided in this struggle because it takes place in a framework of tried and tested cultural arrangements and norms. Learning these norms is half the battle; they specify behaviors expected of him by those important to him in society. Further, the individual learns that he is expected to behave in certain ways in certain roles but not in others. The looseness and generality of the cultural map, even in its specification of role behavior, induces the person to learn individualized ways of responding to recurrent situations. This learning also sets the stage for actions in nonrecurrent settings. As the person acts and reviews the results of his actions, he develops a more general cognition of self to regulate behavior in areas not covered by the cultural map or by well-rehearsed individual habits. The more novel or unexpected the situation, the more salient the phenomenal self becomes to the actor, and when there is a break in the consistency of action the self becomes vivid in the form of embarrassment.

Dispositions such as beliefs, values, and attitudes actually develop to help the person anticipate and thus cope with recurrent events. Because these dispositions grow out of the triumphs and embarrassments of the past they are not to be lightly discarded. Reliance on them is part of a fundamental economic or "least-effort" principle: whenever possible, apply past solutions to present problems. The person imposes as much system on the environment as he can get away with in order to free his attention and energy for coping with surprises.

It is an obvious fact of human existence, however, that any system of expectations developed to map events can only estimate the probabilities of the events occurring. The system is at best an oversimplified approximation and is inevitably in error to some degree. Moreover, there is the additional fact that people do not treat their hard-won attitudes, predictive cognitions, or phenomenal selves lightly. These dispositions have a tough, enduring stability, and new events—those not in phase with current dispositions—tend to be responded to in ways appropriate to those older events that resemble them. A rigidity based on commitments to dispositions embraced by the phenomenal self is the price paid for the advantages in time, energy, and security that come from ready-made decisions.

If this were the whole picture human existence would be a dull tragedy of increasing rigidity. Each of us would become victimized by his past and incapable of coping with novelty and change. Although there is an undeniable tendency toward conservatism reflected in the economizing principle of applying past solutions to present problems, there must also be countermeasures that make for openness and flexibility. Cognitive categories, attitudes, and motives change slowly and reluctantly, but they do change ultimately when they are clearly out of tune with changing reality. Insofar as history never repeats and all events are novel, it is self-defeating to cling to certain ways of characterizing and reacting to events. Categorization, as we saw in Chapter Four, inevitably involves distortion and simplification of information.

Yet the thought of a completely flexible organism attempting to map all the nuances of stimulation peculiar to each event imposes even more serious problems. Without change-resistant cognitions and attitudes the environment itself would lose its stability and adaptation would involve little more than a primitive response to immediate events. Thus the antinomy of stability versus openness to change is important, for if either were allowed to dominate behavior for any length of time the consequences for efficiency and effectiveness would be severe.

The notion that human life is pervaded by a basic antinomy of conflicting orientations raises a host of issues that have concerned students of human behavior for centuries. To some extent the antinomy is represented in the controversy over whether motivation must always be extrinsic or whether there are also intrinsic motivational conditions (Koch, 1956). The extrinsic view of motivation is usually associated with concepts of tension reduction or the removal of deficit. This general model (which clearly permeates psychological thinking) seems to emphasize the conservation side of the antinomy. The person strives for quiescence, security, drive reduction, and the economic avoidance of both cognitive and physical effort.

Even among lower animals, however, there is evidence of exploratory activity and behavior seemingly motivated solely by curiosity. In Chapter Four we reviewed the scattered but impressive evidence that children, adults, rats, and chimpanzees (and by inference many other species) are responsive to novelty, seek it out under some circumstances, and find it rewarding. There is, then, abundant evidence both that persons ignore information that does not fit their pre-established categories and that they seek novelty. This evidence is not contradictory if we can establish the general conditions under which the organism is stable, conservative, and self-protecting and the conditions under which flexibility, openness, and self-redefinition have the upper hand.

The previous chapter provides an important clue for any attempt to understand the conditions favoring each side of the antinomy. Without much strain we may coordinate flexibility and openness to the predecisional phase and stability and self-protection to the postdecisional phase. In the predecisional phase the person actively attempts to move, through the proper choices, toward the most gratifying outcomes. He is more or less in control, he is the uncommitted chooser, and as a consequence he hungers for any information that will help him choose adaptively. The less he knows about an alternative, the more he will examine its implications, but his search is not systematically biased by his values or attitudes. After he has made a committing decision information no longer has the same kind of instrumental value for him. He cannot unmake the decision, so information telling him he should have decided otherwise can only arouse subjective strain or displeasure. Thus he will bias his search in the direction of information that is likely to support his decision.

Although the point of decision conveniently divides the two orientations of the antinomy, the important thing is what the decision implies once we identify the decision point. The critical feature of the predecision phase is the prospect that action is possible, and it makes a difference to the actor which course of action is taken. In the postdecision phase action is not possible and the individual is under the fatalistic control of his environment. It is the possibility of action that basically distinguishes pre- and postdecisional situations.

THE ANTINOMY AND EXPERIMENTS ON PERCEPTION

The stage is set for a return to perception. Questions now arise. Does the shift in selectivity when action is not possible also characterize perceptual processes? Do we see things more quickly or in more accentuated form when they support our values than when they run counter to them?

If we can find instances of this perceptual accentuation, can we show that it occurs only in contexts in which action is not possible?

Value Relevance and Veridicality

Before World War II there had been suggestions that the study of perceptual processes could shed some light on the workings of personality, but few took these suggestions seriously as a stimulus for careful research. Social and personality psychologists—especially those influenced by Freud's emphasis on autistic (wishful) thinking, memory distortions in the service of defense mechanisms, and so on—were generally agreed that people to some extent "see" what they want to see in the environment around them, but scholars were not disposed to treat "see" in a literal sense. They usually assumed that the environment was *interpreted* differently, depending on needs and past experiences, but few studies of perception per se took social or personality factors into account. In the late 1940's such psychologists as Bruner, Ericksen, Klein, McClelland, McGinnies, Murphy, and Postman advocated a "new look" at the determinants of perception. A large cluster of experimental studies entered the literature, all concerned with the role of motivational and personality—in short, nonstimulus—determinants of perception. The radical departure of these studies was that they explored the role of personal determinants with laboratory procedures and settings designed for the precise analysis of perceptual identification and the judgment of attributes. Bruner and Postman, especially, wanted to move as far as current experimental methods would allow them from the metaphorical "see" of interpretation to the literal "see" of perception.

The basic argument of the new-look perception psychologist was that perceptions are often erroneous, and that the errors bear some systematic relation to such intrapersonal variables as expectancies, current motive states, stable value patterns, mood, preferred defensive mechanisms, and so on. The strategy was to inject these variables into the traditional settings of perceptual research and to measure the resulting distortion.

The concept of *veridicality* is often used to describe the absence of distortion, but it is important to realize the restrictions on this term. Veridical perceptions are those that correspond to, or agree with, physical description. The perception of two lines as parallel is veridical if, in fact, a ruler shows them to be equidistant at all points. Of course perception is also involved in reading the ruler. Nevertheless, as F. H. Allport (1955) contends, it is possible to distinguish degrees of contact with a physical object and assume that a visual or auditory perception is veridical if increasing contact in manipulation of the object supports or confirms what is perceived. If an object looks like an ink bottle, perception of it is classed as veridical if it also feels like an ink bottle, contains a colored fluid with a distinctive, ink-like odor, and so on. In the realm of sizes, weights, frequencies, and durations, the measurement of veridicality is even more practical because of the reliable instruments available for objective physical description.

Chapter Four emphasized the extent to which what we see is governed by what we expect to see. We can be led to distort reality insofar as unexpected events occur or expectancies are improperly geared to the probabilities of events. But such errors are part of the inevitable price of gaining time for action. That is, we risk the occasional error because we are so often correct, and because a thorough checking of each incident would incapacitate us and drastically interfere with adjustive action.

Although they may occasionally lead us astray, expectancies function largely in the interests of accuracy and realism. But what of the role of desire or value? Do the needs for self-protection and self-enhancement observed in the postdecisional phase of the action sequence play a role in perception? Does the relevance of an event's or an object's value interfere with the ability to achieve a veridical perception of it? Let us examine how the organism might be served by the perceptual distortion of need-satisfying objects. First, if highly valued or need-satisfying objects are actually present in the environment, it is to the perceiver's advantage to locate them as soon as possible and with the least expenditure of effort. It would be functional in perception, then, to perceive selectively valued or needed objects or to recognize them more easily and quickly than other available objects. It seems reasonable to assume that motives and values can help establish expectancies just as past experience does. That is, if certain objects are more comforting or satisfying than others it is to our advantage to be prepared to see them so they are not missed. In Bruner's (1957a) language, our categories for such objects will be highly accessible.

Such accessibility could have disastrous consequences, however. We could be led to misidentify neutral or even negative objects and instead classify them as objects with satisfying properties. We could thus be led to approach rather than to avoid danger and pain. In order for perception to function as an instrument of adjustment there must be some sensitivity to threatening and dissatisfying events, particularly if immediate action is required or is possible. If we are in a position to make a decision whether to approach or to avoid, it behooves us to be vigilant and alert to the occurrence of both congenial and threatening events.

Most experiments conducted in the spirit of the new look have been performed in laboratory situations, where the task of perceiving and recognizing was not presented as a preface to subsequent behavior. The subjects were presumably aware that they were being shown pictures, words, and other symbolic representations of objects that were to be identified or judged but not otherwise coped with. This would seem to be an important consideration in evaluating the predictions and results of these studies. Perhaps we can say that the majority of these experiments have placed the subject in a postdecisional position. When the subject is put in the role of the perceiver, but with no further adjustive action expected of him, he is presumably freed from some of the demands of realism. We would, therefore, expect the positively valued objects to continue to be readily perceived and even invented as possible responses to ambiguous stimuli.

However, by analogy to the person who has already made his decision in a dissonance experiment, negatively valued objects might actually be more difficult to recognize than neutral objects because of the unpleasant associations the former arouse. Since no overt action is anticipated or required the individual will have no desire to punish himself by a special alertness to unpleasant events. The argument may be summarized in the form of two propositions: (1) When perceptual recognition or description is the ultimate performance required in a given situation, the perceiver's categories for valued objects will be highly accessible and those for disvalued objects will be relatively inaccessible. The goal of perception is to perceive so that pleasant and congenial stimuli are dominant over unpleasant ones. (2) When perceptual recognition and description are instrumental to a decision to act, the perceiver's categories for both valued and disvalued objects will be more accessible than categories whose members arouse no tendency to approach or avoid (cf. the similar arguments developed by Solley and Murphy, 1960).

Perhaps the best way to present evidence relevant to these propositions is to discuss first the perception of need-satisfying or positively valued objects in the environment, and second, the perception of painful and threatening stimuli. Studies in the latter category will be further subdivided into those where vigilance would or would not facilitate adjustive action.

Perception of Positive Stimuli

Stimuli may be positive and objects valuable for a number of reasons. The stimulus may be a goal object that reduces some state of tension or deprivation, it may be instrumental to the attainment of the goal object, it may forecast reinforcing events, or it may remind the perceiver of pleasant experiences in the past. These are overlapping possibilities, but they indicate the range of conditions under which stimuli can take on positive value for the individual.

Perhaps the most straightforward approach to the problem of perceiving positive stimuli is to arouse primary motives by depriving the organism of food or water and then observe his perceptions of need-related words or pictures. In fact, this was one of the earliest avenues of investigation. In 1936 Sanford studied the tendency of hungry and satiated subjects to see food-related objects in highly ambiguous, cut-up pictures. Levine, Chein, and Murphy (1942) and McClelland and Atkinson (1948) followed the same general tactic in working with the hunger motive in adults. The results were not exactly clear-cut. Although there seemed to be a tendency for hungry subjects to produce more food responses than satiated subjects when attempting to describe what they saw, this tendency was not pronounced; and even more perplexing, increasing hunger did not lead to uniform increases in the accessibility of food-object categories. The typical finding was that food objects were increasingly perceived up to moderate degrees of hunger and then slacked off.

Both McClelland (1951) and Levine, Chein, and Murphy (1942) have interpreted this decline as a function of increasing realism under high need. Solley and Murphy (1960) argue that it has to do with adaptation to the internal stimuli produced by deprivation. As we grow accustomed to deprivation, in other words, we become better able to cope with it. In any event, the early experiments were difficult to interpret because small numbers of subjects were involved and the stimuli were generally so ambiguous that it seems to stretch things to use the term perception in describing the subject's responses.

More clear-cut findings seemed to emerge from a study by Wispe and Drambarean (1953), which focused on the time taken to recognize food-related words under varying degrees of hunger. There was indeed a relation between recognition time and hours of deprivation, but 10 hours of deprivation produced as much sensitization to food words as 24 hours. To confuse matters further, Taylor (1956) tried to reproduce this effect under almost identical conditions and was unable to do so. About the most we can say is that moderate hunger sensitizes a person to the presence of food symbols (pictures, words) in the immediate environment, though the effects of increased hunger beyond six to ten hours is debatable.

A related approach to the same problem has focused attention on a different response index of perception, the judgment of various attributes that might contribute to the perceived vividness or salience of the stimulus. It is not too farfetched to propose that need-related objects will in some way be accentuated and sharpened by the perceptual process. Gilchrist and Nesberg (1952) were able to show that, as a function of the length of water deprivation, slides depicting thirst-quenching objects were judged brighter than control slides. That is, the thirstier the subject, the greater was his tendency to accentuate the brightness of the experimental slides in a test of short-term perceptual recall. There is little hint in these results of the trend toward realism suggested by Levine and Murphy and McClelland; the accentuation of brightness seems to grow steadily as thirst increases. Differences in procedure are so marked that further research is certainly needed to resolve the differences in results. At least as far as accentuation and thirst are concerned, however, Gilchrist and Nesberg's results are the product of precise and carefully controlled experimentation, and they should be taken seriously.

The attempt to vary need or motive by varying hours of deprivation has a deceptive simplicity but it entails many difficulties. For example, there are clearly learned cycles that overlay physiological hunger. Someone who is six-hours deprived is not necessarily twice as hungry—or even necessarily hungrier—than someone who is three-hours deprived. Also, it is difficult to deprive a subject without focusing his attention on the relationship between being deprived and the purpose of the experiment. Awareness of this relationship may lead to spurious correlations between deprivation and the accessibility of need-relevant stimuli. For this and other reasons, it is interesting to compare the results of experiments on built-in values and interests with those based on the experimental manipulation of primary physiological drives.

One of the most influential studies in this area was conducted by Bruner and Goodman (1947), who showed (a) a tendency for all subjects to accentuate the size of valuable coins more than those of lower value and (b) a tendency for poor children to accentuate the size of all coins more than rich children. This study aroused considerable controversy, and attempts to replicate the findings were a dismaying mixture of success and failure. The problem of measuring the value of objects—especially their value to different people—brought forth a line of studies in which value was established by procedures of experimental reinforcement.

The most direct descendent of the Bruner and Goodman study was the experiment by Lambert, Solomon, and Watson (1949), in which an attempt was made by controlled reinforcement experiences to impart value to previously neutral objects. These investigators studied children's judgments of the size of poker chips after they had had different learning experiences with the chips. An experimental group of 37 subjects found that if they turned a crank 18 times they would receive a poker chip that could in turn be used to obtain a piece of candy. They worked at the crank either once or five times a day for 10 days (the amount of reinforcement per day making no difference in this experiment). The remaining subjects went through precisely the same procedure except that candy was directly produced after 18 cranks of the machine instead of through a chip token. After this 10-day learning period, all subjects judged the size of the poker chips by adjusting a nearly circular diaphragm to a matching size. The experimental subjects who had experienced the value of the poker chips exaggerated the size of the chips much more than did the control subjects. On the eleventh day the subjects were again exposed to the crank but no candy was forthcoming. They were allowed to work on the crank until extinction set in—until they stopped working for an arbitrarily chosen three-minute period—and then all subjects again made a size judgment. The experimental and control subjects did not differ at this point in their judgment of chip size. The difference was reproduced the next day, however, when the subjects were again given candy for eighteen cranks with (experimental) or without (control) the chip.

Even before these studies, Gardner Murphy and his colleagues had investigated the effects of reinforced experience with particular objects on the perception of these objects. Proshansky and Murphy (1942) and Schafer and Murphy (1943) had shown that stimuli that had been recently associated with rewards were more salient and more readily perceived than stimuli associated with failure. Sommer (1957) confirmed this general finding. Using ambiguous figures that could be seen in either of two ways, he found that the previously rewarded alternative was more frequently perceived than a neutral or a punished alternative. (Reward and punishment were determined in all of these experiments by the winning or losing of small sums of money.)

In his experiments Sommer found some evidence for an alternative hypothesis that both positive and negative reinforcements might make the associated stimuli more salient than the mere absence of either. Whereas reward was clearly more potent than punishment in its effects on perceptual recognition, stimuli associated with loss of money were more frequently recognized than neutral stimuli. This indirectly suggests that the old "law of emphasis" may be reflected in perception along with the "law of effect." This conclusion is encouraged by the results of Postman and Brown (1952), who subjected some subjects to failure and others to success on a span-of-attention test. Subsequent to this, all subjects were shown a mixed series of success words (e.g., excellent, winner) and failure words (unable, obstacle) in a tachistoscope. Those subjects who failed perceived failure words at shorter exposures and those who succeeded perceived success words at shorter exposures. It is as if the experience of failure makes words within the broad category of failure words more accessible, whereas the success category becomes more accessible for those who succeed. Understandable as this may be, it does suggest that associations may be aroused and categories made more accessible by factors other than motivation and frequency of past experience. Categories may be made more accessible both by recent experiences (see Postman and Solomon, 1950) and by various mood changes they induce. It could be argued that in the Postman and Brown study the experience of failure served to arouse a mood of pessimism and discouragement with an attendant increase in the accessibility of associated categories.

These studies are representative of many that show some of the effects of motivation and past history on perceptual responses. It is important to avoid the conclusion that perceptions are normally swept along by dominant states of need and become the servants of wish fulfillment. For each study that demonstrates the effect of need on perception there are undoubtedly many, both published and unpublished, that find no reliable effect. Much clearly depends on the ambiguity or difficulty level of the objects in the visual field, the degree of relevance of these objects to the need, and the pliability of the particular responses used to measure perception. But the studies cited do show that the relevance of the object to the need *can* intrude on the perceptual process. The most common effect of this intrusion is to increase the accessibility of the category and to enhance the apparent size, brightness, or general vividness of the stimulus.

But what of threat, danger, and objects that are negatively valued? The two propositions presented suggest the importance of examining the role of perceptual judgment in overt behavior before making predictions in this area.

Perception of Negative Stimuli

If it seems reasonable for people to see desired things more rapidly than neutral things and to accentuate the attributes that make them more vivid, it also seems reasonable for them to have difficulties seeing unpleasant and threatening objects. But this is precisely the area in which there should be evidence of the basic antinomy because the desire for short-term comfort comes in conflict with the need for long-range protection. Thus the perception of negative stimuli should be most disrupted and delayed when no action is possible or necessary.

The history of research efforts on this topic understandably parallels the history of experimental approaches to the perception of positive stimuli. Studies in which the unpleasantness of exposed stimuli is inferred from knowledge of the subject's personality or cultural background give way to those in which unpleasantness is more precisely defined by experimental operations. In 1948 Postman, Bruner, and McGinnies studied the relationship between a person's values and the speed with which he recognized need-related words. Using a standard test that measures the strength of such value areas as religious, political, esthetic, and theoretical beliefs, they found that words in an individual's high-value areas (e.g., for religion: sacred; for theoretical: verify) were more rapidly perceived than words in his low-value areas, and that there was a general decline in speed of recognition from the most to the least valued areas. Also important was the observation that subjects tended to give high-value presolution responses to low-value words. That is, before the words were fully recognized, subjects would give partially informed responses that showed emotional antagonism to or meaningful distortion of the word's actual meaning. Two examples of such distortion are *scornful* for *helpful,* or even *hypocrisy* for *elegant,* the latter a response actually produced by a subject lacking esthetic values. Largely on the basis of these results, along with help from the psychoanalytic theory of repression, the concept of perceptual defense was developed. In an attempt to provide a firmer base for the concept, McGinnies (1949) followed with a demonstration that obscene or taboo words had higher thresholds of recognition than neutral words. The reason was, presumably, that such words were anxiety arousing and therefore painful.

The concept of perceptual defense was quickly welcomed by many psychologists who saw its relevance to the dynamics of personality functioning. The concept was just as quickly attacked by other psychologists, who jumped to explain these experiments on other grounds. McGinnies' taboo-word experiment was particularly challenged because (a) there was good evidence that subjects simply withheld their responses to taboo words until they were certain of them, and (b) the taboo words were probably less frequently encountered than neutral words in the written literature. The experiment by Postman et al. was also criticized on this latter ground. Presumably someone interested in religion, having read more in the area, has more familiarity with religious words; therefore such words should be perceived at more rapid exposure intervals (cf. the discussion of word frequency in Chapter Four).

It has proved possible to hold familiarity with words constant, at least in a general way, by matching experimental and control words on frequency of occurrence in written English. The problem of consciously withholding responses has been by-passed without relinquishing the use of taboo words as stimuli. This has been accomplished by showing the effects of these words in making it more difficult to recognize the words that immediately follow in the series (see McGinnies and Sherman, 1952; and Walters, Banks, and Ryder, 1959). Although these patchwork solutions have yielded some interesting results, there remain serious problems associated with the complex significance of taboo words in diverse experimental contexts. The most meaningful and relevant recent research has come from two different approaches. The first approach has focused on individual differences in the perception of anxiety-provoking words or pictures. This approach often uses projective tests and other clinical techniques to determine which stimuli will tend to be anxiety-provoking for a given individual. A second approach has involved the experimental attachment of negative value to previously neutral stimuli followed by perceptual tests of the now-charged stimuli compared with control stimuli. The following discussion focuses on the latter kind of study.

There is considerable evidence that subjects can be trained to manifest perceptual defense. If shock always follows the exposure of stimuli A, C, and E but never the exposure of B, D, and F, it may be predicted that the A, C, E words will be more difficult to recognize in a subsequent perceptual task even when no threat of shock remains. The results of experiments by Rosen (1954), Dulany (1957), McNamara, Solley, and Long (1958), and

Lowenfeld (1961), essentially support this kind of conclusion. Hochberg and Brooks (1958) were able to show that such effects were not unique to electric shock. In their experiment, figures previously paired with an unpleasant screeching noise were later more difficult to recognize than figures that had not been so paired.

The general conclusion that noxious stimuli impair recognition is supported, however, only when nothing can be done to avoid or escape shock during the training phase. An experiment by Reece (1954) followed the general pattern of (1) a pretraining test of recognition threshold for various nonsense syllables, (2) a training period where certain words were accompanied by shock, and (3) a posttraining test of recognition threshold. If subjects were simply exposed to the syllable-shock couplings during the training phase and could do nothing to reduce or escape the shock, the syllables had to be exposed for a longer time in the posttraining test for recognition to take place. If, during training, the subject could escape the shock by pronouncing the shock-syllable as soon as it appeared, the syllables were later recognized as quickly as in a no-shock control group. In other words, when speed of recognition has proved adaptive in reducing the duration of shock perceptual defense does not seem to occur.

This finding is relevant to situations in which the perceiver has a chance to do something about the threatening stimuli to which he is exposed. As such, the finding indirectly supports the proposal that perceptual defense does not occur when suitable escape or avoidance action is possible. Even more direct support for this proposal comes from Rosen's (1954) study. In this study nonsense syllables were again exposed in a tachistoscope, but shock was actually applied during threshold determination, and not just in a preceding training series. The experimental design involved eight different experimental and control conditions, of which three are most relevant here: (1) a control group that received shock between the presentation of the different nonsense syllables and in a fashion unrelated to the presentation of stimuli or to the recognition of responses given; (2) a "disruption" group that received shock in a random and capricious fashion, but always immediately following a response to a syllable; (3) a "sensitization" group that was shocked for all incorrect responses to each syllable—shock was stopped on the first correct identification of the nonsense syllable as the syllable was presented on successive trials with increasing durations of exposure. Thus all groups were shocked during the recognition task, but only in the third group was recognition instrumental to coping with the painful or noxious event. The results with these groups were clear-cut: subjects for whom shock was avoidable became vigilant and correctly perceived the syllables at shorter durations than control subjects. Those who could not avoid shocks that followed recognition attempts needed longer exposure than the control subjects for accurate recognition to occur.

Undoubtedly, the results of these few studies do not tell the whole story. Hatfield (1959) found that subjects were *quicker* at recognizing nonsense words previously shocked than words without a shock-association history. Although this finding is contrary to previously reported results of experiments using shocked words, there is one feature of Hatfield's procedure that may account for the unexpected evidence for vigilance. During the training phase, when the nonsense words were paired with shock, the pairing was on a partial reinforcement schedule so that the critical words were only shocked 33 percent of the time. Even though subjects were instructed not to report the syllables during the training phase, they may have felt there was a way of avoiding the shock and carried a vigilant orientation into the final recognition test. Mangan (1959) found poorer recognition of previously shocked pictorial stimuli only when the shock had been extremely severe; otherwise the pictures associated with shock were better recognized than the nonshocked stimuli. His findings are similar to those of Pustell (1957), who also paired shock with visual stimuli in a no-escape situation. Pustell found that his male subjects tended to show vigilance, while his female subjects were defensive (i.e., they showed better recognition for nonshocked stimuli). The female subjects in his experiment were probably more upset by the shocks, and what is perhaps more important, the male subjects typically reported that they kept trying to figure out some way of escaping the shock.

Although these studies thus raise questions about the generality of our major propositions on perceptual vigilance and defense, the evidence favoring the propositions is still fairly impressive. However, the conditions of no-escape versus escape must be carefully defined and the noxious stimulus must be quite intense if the propositions are to hold.

The Determinants of Category Accessibility: a Summing Up

It hardly needs to be said again that an individual does not approach situations as a *tabula rasa* on which mirrorlike reflections of the physical and social environment are recorded. The perceiving individual presses toward recognition and identification; he immediately goes beyond the physical description of events to code them into categories of meaning as a first step toward coping with reality.

In this and preceding chapters we have seen that not all categories are equally accessible. Some category boundaries are so easily breached that the slightest clue, the tiniest bit of evidence, qualifies the event for inclusion. Others are so inaccessible that massive and overwhelming confirmation may be needed for perception to be "veridical."

Category accessibility depends on two general sets of factors: expectancies concerning the likelihood of events to be encountered in the environment, and the "search requirements imposed on the organism by his needs and his on-going enterprises" (Bruner, 1957a). Primarily as a function of this latter factor, valued and need-satisfying stimuli tend to be readily perceived and made more salient by the accentuation of such attributes as size and brightness. Stimuli associated with pain or anxiety may be efficiently or inefficiently perceived as a function of the behavioral context in which they occur. Such stimuli are defended against and perception is disrupted when there is no prospect for overt coping behavior. Painful stimuli become salient, however, when action is possible. These conclusions are generally confirmed by the experimental results cited, and they jibe with the position that "perceptual readiness for accessibility serves two functions: *to minimize the surprise value of the environment* by matching category accessibility to the probability of events in the world about one, and *to maximize the attainment of sought-after objects and events*" (Bruner, 1957a, p. 133).

THE LEARNING AND RETENTION OF THEMATIC VERBAL CONTENT

Perceiving prepares the person for action. If we wish to formulate laws concerning the response of organisms to complex social situations it is necessary to consider the manner in which these situations are placed into categories and category systems. It would be rash to say that behavior is determined by perception—this would stretch the meaning of the concept far beyond its usual connotation of representation and classification. But determinants of behavior such as values, habits, and attitudes are aroused only in relation to the perceived environment; events that in no way register on the sensory surface of the organism have no effect on behavior.

Once having registered, however, events can clearly influence subsequent behavior long after their actual occurrence. The line between perceiving and remembering is fine, especially if we treat perception as a categorizing process. Many of the investigations mentioned earlier could properly be classified as studies of immediate memory. A word is flashed at one-twentieth of a second and the subject must organize his impressions of what the word *was*. It is interesting and dramatic that meaningful distortions and disruptions may occur so soon after exposure to the stimulus. What is the fate of these percepts or immediate memories over time? Our special concern is with the retention of meaningful verbal materials that may occur in oral or written communications.

Before examining the empirical findings that bear on this problem, let us consider how individuals cope with various kinds of information in the social environment. To a large extent individuals can control the source, and to some extent the nature, of information to which they expose themselves. Under normal conditions each individual may choose his companions, his reading material, his television and radio programs, and his plays and motion pictures. Of course, no one directly controls the content emanating from these sources, but the voluntary nature of exposure to communications gives each person considerable freedom in constructing his own information environment.

Second, once confronted with a complex communication people may deliberately or unwittingly attend to certain themes rather than others. They decide which themes will be retained, rehearsed for later use, or embellished with reference to other learned materials. Further, the nature of the selection plays an important role in determining what is learned and retained. In fact it is impossible to eliminate or completely control for the subtle differences in attention and selectivity accompanying the differential learning of varied materials. It is usually assumed that even if such factors were held constant learning would be affected by frequency and recency of exposure and the complex relations between what is being presented and what is already known.

It is important to identify these different stages in the process of acquiring and utilizing information. Nevertheless, many psychologists have long been impressed by the common functions served throughout exposure, selection, perception, learning, and retention: namely, the achievement of a congenial picture of the environment, one that is consistent with established attitudes and beliefs. But this tendency to construct a congenial picture is bridled by the demands of reality. Nobody is completely free to fabricate a comforting history of all the things he has read and been told; adjustment and emotional growth clearly require that individuals profit from current experiences and the information they contain. But the latitude for selective memory has been shown again and again to be clearly greater than that for perception. For one thing, perceptions can be more readily checked and subjected to confirmation than memories; the stimulus is either present or so recent that its features remain vivid. In addition, and perhaps deriving from this, the consequences of recall distortion are not likely to be so immediately evident as the consequences of perceptual distortion. It is not too difficult to make grudging and realistic concessions to the existing environment while at the same time glorifying things the "way they used to be." For these and other reasons we can expect social, motivational, and experimental factors to exert a stronger influence on learning, memory, and thinking than on perception. As we shall see, many conclusions reached regarding perceptual research apply to learning and recall to an even greater extent. The following discussion examines representative evidence on this point with special reference to the learning and retention of communications relevant to the learner's attitudes and biases.

If we wish to study the conditions that affect the learning and retention of meaningful material we must establish the general conditions of exposure to the material. It makes little sense to speak of learning or failing to learn if there are doubts that the material was ever initially perceived. Similarly, it makes little sense to speak of retention as a separate process unless we have evidence that the material was at one time learned. Osgood (1953) has contended that few studies of retention have, in fact, controlled for initial level of learning. Our discussion will not attempt to maintain a precise distinction between learning and retention. We shall speak of learning when dealing with the immediately measured effects of repeated exposure, and retention when a period of time intervenes between exposure and measurement.

It should be noted that variations in both learning and retention can reflect a number of factors that are difficult to separate in a particular experiment. Although it is possible to arrange for exposure to the material, it is difficult to control selective attention within the area of exposure. Especially when complex materials are presented, subjects can emphasize or focus on certain elements at the expense of others. This is presumably one reason why some aspects of communications are better learned. In addition, it is impossible to control for the differential rehearsal of various elements during an exposure. We would expect the subject to rehearse more when highly motivated. At least when meaningful materials are involved, performance measures of learning and retention are usually the product of a variety of subprocesses that contribute to the measure.

Past Experience, Expectancy, and Learning

It seems trivial to argue that past experience can affect present learning. Obviously, what we already know well does not have to be relearned in order to be reflected in learning. From this point it is a short step to the argument that material of a generally familiar type will be more easily learned and better retained than unfamiliar materials. The context of associations into which new material fits is alleged to play a crucial role in the ease of learning these materials. This may be demonstrated by comparing the time it takes to learn meaningful versus nonmeaningful paired associates (e.g., skate–rink versus skate–house).

Ebbinghaus, the towering ancestral figure of research on remembering, recognized the kinds of complexity introduced by meaningfulness in the study of learning and retention. By his experimental studies, first reported in 1885, he initiated a line of research on the rote memorization of nonsense syllables that carries through to the present time. His classic curve of forgetting, obtained by using himself as his only subject through countless hours of working with nonsense syllable lists, has stood the test of time as one of the stable functional relations of psychology. The curve simply indicates that forgetting is most rapid at first and then levels off to the point at which retention is almost constant over long periods of time.

For the social psychologist this function is probably less relevant than the more qualitative conclusions of F. C. Bartlett (1932). In his influential book, *Remembering*, Bartlett argued that the laws that summarize the forgetting of rote-learned nonsense materials do not apply in the vast majority of human learning situations when meaningful materials are involved. Bartlett reported several informal experiments in which subjects were asked to reproduce complex and somewhat ambiguous narratives. The results of these experiments offer persuasive evidence that social factors determine the fate of recall. When asked to reproduce a 300-word folk story with a number of unfamiliar notions and obscure connections, his English subjects assimilated the story to their own system of culturally determined cognitive categories, or, as Bartlett called them, *schemata*. This story was both simplified and elaborated to bring the reproduction attempt more in line with expectations. When logical connections were lacking in the original story the subjects provided them. Elements that seemed inconsistent or irrelevant were omitted. The same tendencies toward condensation and rationalization (making the story more sensible from the subjects' standpoint) were even more marked after longer delays.

Bartlett's persuasive accounts of such experiments, and his appeal to cross-cultural data showing differential recall of relevant information, turned many investigators toward an interest in the qualitative aspects of recall phenomena. Of interest here is not how much is recalled per unit time, but what *kinds* of things are retained and what particular form the distortions and errors take. The results of subsequent investigations have left little doubt that the expectancies, categories, and category systems derived from experiences in a particular culture can be powerful determinants of learning and retention of new materials. When the material to be learned is stripped of meaning the laws of rote learning and retention become applicable. The introduction of meaning immediately forces the investigator to consider the particular matrix of expectancies, categories, or schemata that the subject brings with him to the learning–memory task.

The Role of Attitude in Learning and Retention

Under normal circumstances a person may be expected to retain information supporting the attitudes reflected in past actions and to have difficulty remembering those things that imply that his attitudes are inappropriate. This is the self-maintenance side of the antinomy analyzed earlier in this chapter, and most of the studies concerned with the impact of attitudes on retention have assumed the predominance of this side—at least when we hand a subject some verbal arguments and merely ask him to learn them as quickly and as thoroughly as possible.

A survey of the limited research on this point reveals fairly consistent, but not overwhelming, support for the thesis that individuals remember best those things that are consistent with their beliefs. Watson and Hartmann (1939) studied the ability of atheists and theists to recall arguments for and against religion. Each subject tended to recall statements favoring his own position, but the results were not statistically significant. Edwards (1941) divided subjects by means of a simple seven-point scale into groups for and against the New Deal and exposed them to a long verbal passage containing pro and con statements about the New Deal and Communism. Subjects answered a true-false test very much in line with their attitudes, tending to err on those items whose correct answers were opposed to their position.

Whereas Edwards' study is more a study of recognition than learning, Levine and Murphy (1943) investigated the learning and forgetting of two selections, on opposite sides of the Communist issue. They asked five pro-Communist and five anti-Communist students (judged so in terms of their reputation on campus) individually to read and then reproduce the same two passages on five different occasions, each a week apart. This was designated the "learning period." They returned each week for the *next* five weeks and were instructed merely to reproduce as much of each passage as they could remember. This was designated the "forgetting period." At each point in both the learning and forgetting curves, subjects did a better job reproducing the selection favoring their position than the selection opposed to it. That is, at every weekly period throughout the experiment, the pro-Communist subjects were better able to reproduce the pro-Communist than the anti-Communist passages, and the opposite was true for the anti-Communist subjects. However, the evidence for either differential learning or forgetting is slight. Although congenial material is better reproduced at all points in the experiment there is little tendency for the differences between groups to increase as learning or forgetting proceeds. The results of the experiment probably reflect differences in prior learning and expectation as much as the results of attitudinal pressure on the learning of new materials.

A more recent study by Alper and Korchin (1952) attempted to exploit the "war between the sexes" by presenting as a memory test to male and female students a bogus letter from a dean to a professor dealing with problems of coeducation. The letter was generally derogatory toward female students but contained profemale and antimale items as well as promale and antifemale items. Females did retain more antimale items than the males, offering some support for the general hypothesis under investigation. Somewhat stronger support comes from a study by Taft (1954) who presented a passage about a Negro baseball player to 30 Negro and 30 white delinquent boys. The passage contained items both favorable and unfavorable to Negroes, and the Negro children retained more of the pro-Negro items on immediate recall. Interestingly enough, the differential recall of items favorable to Negroes was even more striking in a delayed recall test three days later.

We may conclude from this survey that the ability to reproduce meaningful prose passages from memory can be clearly affected by the relationship between the meaning of the passage and the attitude of the person exposed to it. Quite probably, if we had better and more reliable measures of attitude and better ways of knowing *how* a passage is relevant to a belief, this phenomenon could be more strikingly and consistently demonstrated. Nevertheless, we have been forced by the evidence to restrict our conclusions to "reproduction" and not learning. No one has yet produced firm evidence that the rate of learning new, congenial material is faster than the rate of learning new, uncongenial material. Differences in the ability to reproduce the two kinds of material are usually present after the first exposure and the differences in reproduction are maintained over time. This suggests that differences in speed of learning arise during the first contact with the material and disappear thereafter, or that the differences in reproduction largely reflect the immediate effects of past learning in assimilating new material.

Even if we restrict the general conclusion to the neutral descriptive term, reproduction, it seems hardly likely that the effects of attitudes on the reproduction of thematic content are invariant and not affected by the conditions and context of recall. Attitudes *can* affect the reproduction of relevant materials, but this does not imply that they always do. What are the conditions under which self-maintenance is likely to be superseded by the side of the antinomy that is reflected in vigilance and receptivity to unwanted information?

Let us begin by sharpening this question's implications: under what conditions do we retain themes that are uncongenial or threatening to existing attitudes? There must be some conditions of this sort, for surely we pay some attention to, and are able to retain, arguments with which we disagree. The problem resembles that in the discussion of perception that analyzed the conditions promoting perceptual defense on the one hand and vigilance on the other. We become vigilant to threat when something can be done to escape or avoid the threatening event. Otherwise, perception is likely to be defensively disrupted with delayed or distorted recognition. In line with the urging that perception, learning, and retention are cognitive processes on a continuum, perhaps the distinction between action-impossible and action-possible has some implications in the present context.

A close real-life parallel to the phenomenon of vigilance would be the intelligence agent who is very much against Communism, but who must learn and retain nuances of meaning conveyed by documents, articles in

Pravda, and Kremlin speeches in order to inform his superiors on the most likely course of Soviet diplomacy. A second example might be the case of a political campaigner digging into his opponent's record. In both cases there is motivation to learn, which presumably overrides the normal difficulties of learning and retaining uncongenial evidence. It is interesting to note that the more ominous the news of Russia's intentions and the more his political opponent threatens the election of a candidate, the greater the stake there is in obtaining accurate knowledge of "the enemy."

There seems little question that this factor of the probable usefulness of information, even when it is unpleasant, is an important determinant of selective exposure. We saw in Chapter Six that the dissonance theory prediction of postdecisional selective recall did not hold under certain conditions. When information inconsistent with the alternative chosen was useful for future behavior the actor remained relatively vigilant or unbiased in his exposure preferences. Negative (contradecisional) information was *not* avoided by the subjects in the Mills, Aronson, and Robinson (1959) experiment, presumably because it is important to know the difficulties that are associated with essay (or objective) examinations if the subject has chosen that type of exam and wishes to do well. Usefulness of information was more directly varied by Canon (1964), who led some subjects to expect that they would debate with a person who disagreed with them on a labor-management case, whereas other subjects merely expected to write an essay favoring the position they had chosen. Subjects in the debate, in which information about the other side of the issue was highly useful for preparing the subject's own case, were quite interested in negative, uncongenial information. This finding was strongly confirmed in a close replication by Freedman (1965a).

In turning from selective exposure studies to research in the tradition of learning and retention we find that surprisingly little effort has been directed toward this problem. A study by Jones and Aneshansel (1956) does, however, show the operation of the basic antinomy in the learning-retention sphere. These investigators attempted to establish the conditions under which subjects who disagreed with a set of statements would learn those statements *better* than subjects who agreed with them. Students in a southern university served as experimental subjects; half of the subjects selected were strongly in favor of integration and half of them were strongly opposed. All were given a list of 11 antisegregation statements to read out loud and then attempt to reproduce. This procedure was repeated for five separate trials and a measure of learning was obtained by counting the number of meaningful units within the 11 statements which were reproduced on each trial. For half of the subjects, those in the control group, no further instructions were given. The results for this group showed that on each of the five trials the antisegregation subjects were better able to reproduce the statements than the prosegregation subjects. This finding supports that of Levine and Murphy (1943) and the popular expectation that we retain best those statements congenial to our beliefs.

The remaining subjects, constituting the experimental group, were put through the same learning procedures with the same 11 statements. However, before the statements were presented, these subjects were given the following special instructions:

This is going to be an experiment to see how well you can think up appropriate counterarguments for controversial statements. You will be presented with a number of statements which all argue more or less in favor of segregation. Your task will be to look at each statement in turn, read it aloud, and then give me an appropriate counterargument . . . before getting on with the main part of the experiment, I am first going to show you some antisegregation statements like the ones you may want to use as counterarguments. Your first job is to learn *these* statements as quickly and as completely as you can. Remember, you may want to use some of the statements in the main part of the experiment later on, so it will pay to learn these statements.

As predicted, prosegregation subjects actually learned *more* items than did antisegregation subjects, even though the statements opposed their beliefs. Thus, by a simple change of instructions that made learning the statements instrumental to an important experimental goal, the usual relationship between attitude and learning was reversed. Presumably, the antisegregation subjects viewed the learning task as irrelevant to the performance of the counterargument task since they were well stocked with antisegregation arguments. The prosegregation subjects, on the other hand, could do well only by learning the unfamiliar statements as well as possible.

This experiment shows a counterpart to vigilance in the perception of threatening or negatively toned stimuli. It suggests one kind of restriction on the general hypothesis that persons always learn best those statements that they favor. Although this may usually be true, it is necessary to consider the situation in which learning takes place and the effects of this situation in arousing motives that enhance or impede learning.

Another kind of restriction concerns the importance of separating the general direction of the statement and its plausibility. With sets of pro- and antisegregation statements similar to those used by Jones and Aneshansel, Jones and Kohler (1958) showed that subjects learned plausible statements favoring their over-all position much better than they learned implausible statements. What is even more interesting, subjects learned implausible statements favoring the opposing position much better than they learned plausible statements favoring that position. Presumably both effects reflect an attempt to maintain the image of our own position as more plausible than the image of the opposing position, but it is interesting that people are actually "vigilant" in the retention of extreme and implausible arguments for a position opposed to their own.

Zimmerman and Bauer (1956) have explored the role of still another determinant of recall: the prospect of communicating the material to an audience known to have a particular set of relevant opinions. These investigators reasoned that we frequently confront new information with some image in mind of the audience to which we shall probably communicate it. This image shapes the perception and retention of the information as we anticipate the best way of presenting the material. The American traveling abroad, for example, remembers events largely in terms appropriate to the interests of the folks back home—the most important "prospective audience," let us say, that he carries in his head.

Zimmerman and Bauer set out to test this hypothesis by designing an experiment in which subjects were asked to retain materials to be used in giving a subsequent speech to one of two radically different audiences. Subjects were led to anticipate the task of writing an informal talk about teacher salaries. This brief written statement was to be transmitted either to members of the National Council of Teachers or the American Taxpayer's Economy League. These fictitious organizations were so labeled to suggest radical differences in attitudes toward higher teacher salaries. The experimenter read a series of statements either favoring or opposing higher salaries and (presumably as an aid in subsequently writing the speech) the subjects were asked to recall as many of them as they could. The actual writing of the speech was deferred for a week. Before the speech was written a second recall test was administered.

The results may be looked at in terms of the amount of material correctly recalled at each session. As it turned out, there were no differences attributable to audience or direction of arguments at the first recall session. However, by the second session subjects in the conditions in which the arguments were congruent with the "image" of the audience retained more than subjects in incongruent conditions. Thus recall was good (1) when the speech was to be delivered to the Taxpayer's League and the arguments were *against* raising salaries, and (2) when the Teacher's Council was to be the audience and the arguments *favored* salary raises. Recall was poor when the arguments and audiences were reversed.

These studies suggest some fruitful lines for further research on the conditions that affect the retention of meaningful materials. We may start with the basic presumption that we learn and retain better those materials congenial to our beliefs, but it quickly becomes apparent that such congenial information processing may be affected by many features of the recall situation. It is important, therefore, to specify carefully the context in which meaningful material is to be learned and remembered.

RETENTION AND REPRODUCTION IN NATURAL COMMUNICATION SETTINGS

Two areas of great practical importance that have long concerned psychologists are those of courtroom testimony and rumor. Both topics are primarily of interest because they so often involve distortions of perception, memory, and thought that may have profound social consequences. All of the factors discussed above may be relevant in understanding particular distortions of communication. We shall not dwell again on the variables that influence event cognition itself, but shall use the setting of legal testimony and rumor to exemplify some of the additional factors involved that influence the reporting to others of remembered events.

Attempts to study legal testimony in the courtroom setting in which it naturally occurs are likely to be overwhelmed by complexity. In many trials there are key witnesses whose descriptions of seen or heard events are central to the arguments of either prosecution or defense. If there were some simple test of accuracy and reliability, justice would surely be well served by such testimony. Obviously no such test exists, which means that the jurors and the judge must apply their own standards in assessing the truth value of sworn testimony. Of course, there are certain legal props that help to establish broad standards; for example, the ruling out of hearsay testimony and restrictions placed on the admissibility of the testimony of children. Nevertheless, the outcome of a trial may depend on a complex judgment concerning the reliability of testimony.

Psychological interest in the problem of testimony goes back at least to the turn of the present century and, curiously enough, it has been almost exclusively a European interest. In fact there are several reported instances in which psychological experts have influenced the admissibility of testimonial evidence in European criminal prosecutions. The main conclusion repeatedly established by studies in the area of testimony is that distortions of recall are indeed serious when complex and emotional materials are involved. What are the most likely sources of error in testimony? For one thing, events important to the trial are usually witnessed involuntarily and without any preparatory set. The reader has probably heard of, or even participated in, classroom lessons of testimonial distortion. Students are quietly sitting in the midst of a lecture when suddenly three or four figures, dressed in bizarre garb, dramatically burst on the scene to commit simulated mayhem on the professor and then just as suddenly depart. The amazed students are then asked to recall certain crucial features of the incident and the assailants with results that are usually alarming in their degree of distortion. If the students had been forewarned to expect some dramatic event, undoubtedly they would have done a better job.

A second source of error in testimony is the well-established fact that people remember initial reports of events better than the events themselves. This means that any temporary disrupting factors, such as those of high emotion, present during the first recall of the event may produce errors which will be subsequently perpetuated.

Another important source of bias is the condition under which the event is recalled for public consumption in the courtroom. Particularly under the pressures of cross-examination, recall can hardly be described as free or unbiased. It is well known that leading questions can produce serious errors of testimony or at least place an unwarranted and biased complexion on previously recalled events.

Finally, there is the motivation of the witness to produce a certain effect on his audience. He may have strong convictions of the guilt or innocence of the prisoner that color his testimony and influence his memory. Or he may simply wish to avoid involvement in the case by giving a highly general, nonimplicating report of seen events. On the other hand, he may wish to achieve a moment of personal glory by extending his testimony to increase its importance as a factor in the case.

Many of these same sources of distortion are present in the communication of rumors. Once again, in addition to all the factors that mold the cognitive processes in originally assimilating and retaining information, there are new factors in the communication setting that strongly flavor the report of the rumor. The normal tendency to simplify, rationalize, and make sense out of incoming information is presumably strengthened by the prospect of communicating this information to someone else.

In his studies on remembering Bartlett (1932) used what he called the *method of serial reproduction* to shed some light on this problem. As compared with the *method of repeated reproduction,* wherein the same individual is asked to report his memories of a scene or a passage on several different occasions (perhaps parallel to the situation of testimony), the method of serial reproduction involves the transmission of recalled information through a chain of persons. Bartlett conducted a number of informal experiments in which folk tales, descriptive and argumentative prose materials, and pictorial materials were presented for serial reproduction. As for the general result of these experiments we shall let him speak for himself:

. . . serial reproduction normally brings about startling and radical alterations in the material dealt with. Epithets are changed into opposites; incidents and events are transposed; names and numbers rarely survive intact for more than a few reproductions; opinions and conclusions are reversed—nearly every possible variation seems as if it could take place, even in a relatively short series. At the same time, the subjects may be very well satisfied with their efforts, believing themselves to have passed on all important features with little or no change, and merely, perhaps, to have omitted unessential matters. A subject who takes part in an experiment is, as a rule, more careful than usual, and hence we may reasonably suppose that the changes affected by serial reproduction in the course of the social intercourse of daily life will probably occur yet more easily and be yet more striking than those which have been illustrated in the present tests (p. 175).

In terms of the sheer quantity of material recalled there is no question that the method of serial reproduction is inferior to repeated reproduction. Some of the reasons for this are obvious. Although we have noted that people tend to recall prior remembrances more faithfully than the event remembered, some aspects of the original event may be forgotten for a period of time and yet subsequently recalled. Technically called reminiscence, this phenomenon is typically observed in standard learning experiments when factors (similar to fatigue) that inhibit early recall dissipate more rapidly than the factors promoting recall. Also, subsequent events and associations may make salient forgotten aspects of the initial event, which may then be correctly recalled. In serial reproduction what is lost in one recall effort is obviously lost forever. The final subject in a rumor chain can only be as accurate as the weakest, most forgetful, and most distorting link. For this reason alone we have little cause to attach much credence to any sort of rumor or hearsay.

In addition to this logical factor a host of other sources of distortion lie in the motivational conditions of communication. People like to be the sources of important information. This makes their presence valuable to others and establishes their worth as communicators. Such a consideration should, and undoubtedly does, result in pressures to exaggerate, to overemphasize the dramatic significance of information.

Whether a rumor is passed on at all depends on a host of additional factors. Allport and Postman (1947) have emphasized that rumors are born and circulate when there is a high interest and importance attached to an event and when the actual facts are ambiguous or difficult to ascertain. Their formula, "Rumor = Ambiguity $\times$ Importance," implies that rumors do not thrive when either factor is reduced to zero. This, of course, would apply to the individual agent or communicator of a rumor. If the event is unimportant to *him*, he is less likely to pass it on to others. If he happens to be in a good position to ascertain the facts he is also not likely to pass the rumor on. Just what determines "importance" to an individual is discussed by Allport and Postman with reference to rumors that flourished during World War II. They devote particular attention to rumors that are spread because they relieve, justify, and *explain* emotional tension. Thus a person may relieve his own guilt about not contributing to the war effort by passing on a rumor that Jews are avoiding the armed services. Feelings of panic concerning attack from without may be justified by helping along a rumor that the Pacific Fleet was wiped out at Pearl Harbor. Or a rumor that "they are throwing whole sides of beef in the garbage at Camp X" thrives because it helps to explain the meat shortage. Many of the rumors that arose to support the belief in an invasion from Mars, in the case of the Orson Welles broadcast described in Chapter One, were fear-justifying rather than fear-reducing rumors.

It is difficult to conduct reliable studies of the rumor process. Most of the discussions of rumor in the literature are based on after-the-fact reconstructions. A rumor comes to the attention of someone with research interests and he tries to reconstruct its pathways of diffusion and determine how it got started. Obviously such reconstruction attempts are next to impossible if they involve large numbers of people and extend across many social groupings. Within a well-defined organization it is sometimes possible to reconstruct the history of a rumor by subsequently interviewing everyone in the organization. The main problem with this approach is that people are notoriously poor at remembering from whom they received information and whether or not (and to whom) they passed it on (Back, et al., 1950).

An additional difficulty with the method of reconstruction through interviewing is that it ignores the negative case. We shall not really understand rumor transmission until we know something about the kinds of rumors that die in infancy and therefore do not normally reach the interviewer's attention. Not surprisingly, it has occurred to some social psychologists to plant a false rumor in a well-defined group with elaborate follow-up interviews. Although such studies are difficult to arrange, they do carry the great advantage of allowing the investigator to choose among possible "rumor inputs" the one that best fits his theoretical interest.

Perhaps the most impressive study of this type was that of Schachter and Burdick (1955). Their study was conducted during one typical day at an exclusive girls' preparatory school. The investigators had worked out a careful cooperative arrangement with the teachers to accomplish two objectives that were vital to the study: creating conditions of uncertainty that would promote the spread of a rumor, and planting the rumor. Uncertainty (or "cognitive unclarity") was a major variable of the study: the students in four out of the six classes used were exposed to an event early in the day that was designed to puzzle them and to make them hungry for an explanation. In these classes, the principal entered each classroom within a 10-minute period just at the beginning of school. She interrupted the work, stood in front of the class, pointed a finger at one girl, and announced, "Miss K., would you get your hat, coat, and books, please, and come with me. You will be gone for the rest of the day." The four girls taken from their classes (who actually ended up spending the day with the principal on a tour of the nearby university campus) had been carefully chosen so as to be average in most respects, reasonably popular, and with fair grades. There seems little question that the principal's invitation to "Miss K." aroused cognitive unclarity, since the teachers in the classes visited by the principal were deluged with questions about where Miss K. was being taken.

The rumor itself was planted with two girls from each of four different classes; two of these classes were from the four in which cognitive unclarity was produced. Thus the design consisted of three conditions: (1) cognitive unclarity plus rumor, (2) cognitive unclarity without rumor, and (3) rumor but not cognitive unclarity. There were two classrooms in each of these conditions. The rumor was planted during routine interviews that occurred shortly before the beginning of the school day. Toward the end of each interview, which was mainly about the student's progress, next year's program, and so on, the interviewing teacher said, "By the way, some examinations have been taken from the office. Do you happen to know anything about this?" No such thing had actually taken place, of course, but the rumor was chosen to "fit" with the subsequent episode in which the principal called a classmate from the room.

In order to understand how the rumor might spread it is necessary to know a little about the school routines. Communication was possible between class hours, during morning recess, during gym period, and at the luncheon hour. At 2:00 P.M., a team of 20 interviewers took over the school lunchroom in order to interview all of the girls involved in the study. Each class was interviewed at a time, so that there could not be any communication among the girls about the nature of the interview. As was quickly determined in these interviews, all but one girl in the total of 96 comprising the six crucial classes had heard the rumor by interview time. Since almost all of the girls in the rumor-only condition soon heard about the cognitive-unclarity manipulation, and since almost all of those in the cognitive-unclarity-only condition heard about the missing examinations, it is obvious that we cannot treat the three conditions as distinct. However, the girls in the rumor-only condition should have been less involved in the spread of the rumor. The situation was presumably less important to them because no one in *their* class was removed by the principal and thus implicitly accused of taking examinations.

In line with this recharacterization of the conditions in terms of relative importance, the interview results clearly showed that subjects in the rumor-only condition were less apt to transmit or to receive the rumor. There were approximately twice as many transmissions of the rumor in the cognitive-unclarity conditions as in the rumor-only condition. In addition, some 70 percent of the girls in the cognitive-unclarity conditions reported discussing rumors other than the one that was planted; less than 15 percent of the girls in the rumor-only condition discussed new rumors.

It may be concluded, certainly, that the investigators were more than modestly successful in planting a rumor that quickly "made the rounds."

They were so successful, in fact, that the only measures that revealed differences among conditions were fairly subtle measures of quantity of transmission. A final point of some interest was the fact that there was no indication of distortion in any of the 96 interviews. Though many new and rather bizarre rumors did spring up, "the planted rumor itself came through a day's discussion intact" (p. 370). Schachter and Burdick noted that this was at variance with some of the laboratory studies of rumor conducted by Bartlett (1932) and Allport and Postman (1947), wherein the method of serial reproduction led to considerable distortion. They suggest that there are important corrective tendencies that distinguish the natural field situation from the laboratory setting in which there is a single chain of communicators. In the cognitive-unclarity conditions of the field experiment, at least, there was much recirculation of the rumor. Any girl was likely to hear several versions of the story, so that she could challenge variant versions. It is also probably the case that unreliable communicators are by-passed in the natural setting, or at least that their communicative efforts tend to be more discounted than the efforts of those who have proved themselves reliable informants in the past. Finally, the rumor planted by Schachter and Burdick was a rather simple one, having little of the complexity introduced by Bartlett or by Allport and Postman.

The study of rumor is one of the many fascinating areas in which the principles of social psychological reasoning may be applied. The Schachter and Burdick results emphasize the role of *importance* as a variable, and though *ambiguity* rapidly became a constant (as information about the cognitive-unclarity manipulations was transmitted from class to class), we can surmise that the principal's actions greatly facilitated rumor transmission and helped to account for its rapid spread.

SUMMARY

Fortified with an understanding of certain crucial differences between predecisional and postdecisional cognitive processes, we have examined some of the traditional literature on perception and memory distortion. We began by suggesting that pre- and postdecisional differences reflect a basic antinomy between pressures toward maintaining hard-won dispositions and pressures toward change and responsiveness to novelty. There is fairly impressive evidence in the literature on perception, learning, and memory, that cognitive processes are geared to the construction of a subjective reality that is compatible with beliefs, values, and attitudes. This cognitive construction of events involves varying amounts of distortion or nonveridical representation. But there is also evidence that, under some conditions at least, individuals can be sensitized to threat and show an openness to information that seems likely to question their values.

In the area of perception the issue of distortion versus sensitivity is often framed in terms of perceptual defense versus perceptual vigilance. When events are positive, congenial, or value-promoting, we tend to be alert to their occurrence and to accentuate perceptually many of their stimulus attributes. The adjustive significance of this is that we are better prepared to approach attractive stimuli to the extent that we can readily identify them. In the presence of negative or uncongenial events, on the other hand, we may either defend against perceiving them or be hypervigilant and perceive them faster than neutral events. Whether defense or vigilance occurs depends on which side of the antinomy gains the upper hand. This in turn appears to depend on whether the organism is in a position to take appropriate action. Many perception experiments place the subject in a passive situation, in which he is asked to recognize negative information but has no control over the occurrence of this information. Impaired recognition typically results. When the subject can act to eliminate negative stimuli, on the other hand, he typically shows more rapid recognition and greater perceptual accuracy.

In the closely related areas of learning and retention we can find many parallels to these conclusions drawn from studies in perception. Although there seems to be a general tendency for the learner to remember better those ideas and themes that are consistent with his attitudes, it is not difficult to motivate the learner to retain uncongenial information. The crucial thing, again, is to create the conditions that make this information useful. People will learn well those passages or arguments inimical to their cause, if they must counter these arguments in the context of a subsequent debate.

The chapter concluded with some discussion of the naturalistic settings in which testimony and rumor occur. The principles underlying perception and memory developed in artificial laboratory settings are relevant in considering the exchange of information between persons when events of high value-relevance are being discussed. It should also be clear, however, that such phenomena as those included under the heading of rumor have extremely complex and tangled determinants. It will probably be some time before psychologists can move from reasonable after-the-fact accounts of the operation of these determinants in specific cases to more precise predictive statements.

CHAPTER EIGHT

Perceiving and Evaluating Persons

In the Colette-Ravel ballet, *L'enfant et les Sortileges,* a disobedient child is punished in a most frightening and diabolical manner. Suddenly his world becomes chaotic and unpredictable. The chair on which he sits walks away from him, the clock comes away from the wall and begins to strike ceaselessly, the fire in the grate turns on the child, figures of shepherds and shepherdesses on the curtain descend to sing a song. Later, in the garden, as the child learns from the animals of his former cruelty to them, he shows evidence of his kindness by ministering to their wounds. The child is forgiven; the environment again becomes predictable and the objects perform in keeping with their true nature.

We may glimpse in this fanciful account the harrowing prospect of a chaotic environment, and perhaps sigh gratefully over the stability of our own everyday world. The success of our adjustive behavior hinges to an important extent on our ability to anticipate events, to predict the changes and constancies of environmental objects.

On *a priori* grounds there is no reason why this is any truer for the physical than for the social environment, the environment of persons and their actions. Clearly, if we were completely unable to anticipate and predict the responses of people in general, and of particular persons to a given situation, we would be disadvantaged in preparing our own actions. Most of us would probably contend that the physical environment is more stable and predictable than the social environment. Although there are undoubtedly senses in which this is true, it is important to realize that stability does not inhere in either the physical or social environment; the environment is rendered stable by our learned ability to predict its states. This is true whether we are impressed with the predictability of fellow committee members, who may not be predictable in the eyes of a newcomer, or whether we marvel at the regularity of the seasons, which may appear most irregular to a child.

Long experience with the physical environment makes us aware of its regularities. When the sun sets on Wednesday, we fully expect it to reappear on Thursday; we learn that objects with particular characteristics melt when heated, others harden, and still others explode; an enormously important set of predictions is linked to our experiences with gravity, experiences that help us to predict the velocity of moving objects, possible and impossible ways of building a house, how we should lean while climbing a hill. And, of course, we acquire new knowledge constantly about the physical characteristics of mechanical inventions. We learn that the change in the sound of the automatic washer simply means a new cycle has begun; a persistent knock in the automobile motor forecasts mechanical failure.

In all of these cases our knowledge is based on a consideration of the features of objects *in relation to* environmental events or contexts. A ball, which we would all agree has a "disposition" to roll, will not roll on a completely level surface. Wood is known to burn, but not without contact with fire or extreme heat. It is instructive to extend this line of thought to attempts to predict and understand events in the social environment. Here again, it is obviously important to consider the cues provided by the person-object in relation to the stimulus context in which the object appears. Instead of such observed properties as rolling or burning we are now confronted with the behavior of persons. Instead of intensity of heat and degree of incline we must take into account the constraints on the person—the extent to which his behavior has been provoked or stimulated by the environment. Instead of inferring that an object is combustible or round, we infer that a person is anxious, humane, or devious.

An elementary experimental demonstration of this point may be found in a study by Cline (1956), which dealt with inferences about personal attributes from facial expressions. Cline presented simple outline drawings of three faces, one "glum," another "frowning," and the third "smiling." The faces were not presented in isolation, but rather as pairs to form the experimental stimuli to be judged. The experimenter urged the subjects to consider the situation in which "these people find themselves." The resulting impressions of a particular face in some cases showed drastic changes as a function of the face with which it was paired. To illustrate the types of change that occurred, note the following account for the smiling face:

. . . when paired with the glum face, Smiling is a dominant, vicious, gloating, taunting bully. He is strong enough not only to defeat the other, but to be able to afford a bit of sadism to garnish the victory. Presented with Frowning the change in the significance of Smiling's face is astounding. He is now peaceful and peace-making. He wants to help, be friendly, and be happy. He no longer is deriving pleasure from the misfortune of another, but is instead enjoying an external event of a friendly nature. The purpose and intent of the face has been reversed with the change in the situation (p. 149).

We cite these results to support the conclusion that a person's facial expressions (and, to generalize, his behavior in general) are perceived to reflect underlying characteristics, but always with reference to the total context in which these expressions occur.

AN OVERVIEW OF PERSON PERCEPTION

Person perception subsumes all processes of cognizing or understanding some particular other or forming an impression of him. "Perception" is undoubtedly a misnomer, but its usage is justified by a vigorous if short tradition and there is little danger of being misled by it. It is possible to perceive a person in the strict, literal sense. Persons are physical objects and we can and do "perceive" their bulk, rhythm of movement, texture of skin, and color of hair. But a more metaphorical view of perception concerns us here, a view that conveys the inferring of unseen propensities or dispositions. It is especially these propensities toward which the perceiver gropes in his attempt to comprehend his social environment.

A useful starting point is to examine the implications of the fact that persons are social objects as well as physical objects. Thus persons have a number of characteristics that other physical objects, including the lower organisms, do not share. Because these special characteristics largely define the perceiver's problem of inference and force us to use the term "perception" in its metaphorical sense, we shall review them briefly. In this review we wish to look at the social object from the standpoint of the naive perceiver. We make no claims regarding the true nature of the person as a perceptual object. Because there is no infallible way of deciding what a person "really is," we restrict our interest to characterizing the person as he tends to be seen by others. We shall not attempt to pass judgment on the accuracy of various characterizations.

Perhaps the most important difference between the physical and the social object is that persons, as social objects, are centers of action and intention. We could discuss at great length the philosophical question of whether all behavior is in some ultimate scientific sense determined. But from the perceiver's point of view other persons share a relative autonomy, a freedom of motion and response, and capacities for capriciousness and impulsiveness that do not characterize rocks, flowers, or paramecia. These latter objects seem to be the victims of a fate established by irreversible processes of growth or decay and conditions in the environment.

Another facet of this same point is the extent to which the most relevant attributes of nonsocial objects are revealed by an analysis of their physical structure. The attributes of a rock that are most likely to concern us are its bulk, its weight, its grain and color, and its indestructibility. These properties are readily revealed by examining and measuring the rock's external physical features. On the other hand, it seems likely that the brain surgeon knows little more about his patient's thoughts after, than before, examining portions of the exposed cortex. The important attributes of social objects are not usually revealed by physical states and changes; they are revealed by patterned communications that bear an almost arbitrary relation to the apparent physical structure of their source. Among other things, one implication of this fact is that a social object may be thinking one thing while expressing another. Correlated with this difference in the physical visibility of cues is an additional important distinction. The stimulus patterns basic to person perception are usually more extended over time than those relevant to thing perception (Heider, 1958). This makes sense when we consider how little we learn about a person from a single photograph or an abruptly curtailed sample of speech.

A further difference is that social objects resemble the perceiver in structure and attributes. The fact that the social object is aware of the perceiver and can take attitudes toward him may affect the behavior he presents to the perceiver. Tagiuri (1958, p. xi) has captured this possibility with the remark, "Through his own presence and behavior in the perceptual situation of the other, the perceiver may alter the perceptual characteristics of the person whose state he is trying to judge." The fact of resemblance between perceiver and perceived also has important implications for strategies of inferring the states of others.

A recital of such differences helps to point up the difficulties that we all face in attempting to form an impression of some particular other person. If the other is "capricious," if his attributes are "not usually revealed by physical states and changes," if we as perceivers "alter the characteristics of the person we are trying to judge"—how *do* we reach any conclusions about another person?

Before proceeding further, let us recognize that many of our interactions with others do not require a differentiated perception of unique personal characteristics. We may assign to the other a particular role category that enables us to predict enough of his behavior to get into and out of the interaction successfully. Thus the fact that we live in a socially structured environment is an enormous aid in reducing the need to make complicated judgments about individual persons.

Assuming that our perceiver has some good reason to form an impression of some particular other person, can we make any general remarks about the processes involved? Undoubtedly several distinct processes contribute to the formation of most impressions. In order to appreciate their variety consider the following examples:

1. We are introduced to a man for the first time. Before he tells us anything about himself we "know" that he is *depressed*. And yet we do not know how we know this.

2. We watch a boy working on a puzzle. He is having difficulties but keeps coming back to the same pieces over and over again. Finally the puzzle is solved. We conclude that he is a persistent youngster.

3. We engage in brief conversation with an older man we have never seen before. We feel that he is patronizing us, that behind his pleasant demeanor he feels quite superior and has little respect for us. Later, in thinking about the episode, it suddenly strikes us that the man resembled a pompous, supercilious uncle.

4. We meet a person who has a low forehead and a powerful physique. We are surprised to learn later that he is an exceptional student who has never had any interest in football.

In the first case it is hard to know what process is involved, but psychologists for years have written about "motor mimicry," "empathy," and the like. The notion behind many of these terms is that we unwittingly mimic some component of the other person's reaction. If he is depressed perhaps our own shoulders slump a little or our head imperceptibly sags. Then from our own mimicry we silently and rapidly infer his emotional state though we remain unaware of the basis of the inference. Even in this simple example many other processes might be involved. In addition to empathy, or the state of feeling-with-others, there is the possibility of what Murray (1938) has called *recipathy:* the assignment of characteristics to others to account for our own feelings or behavior. We decide that the other person is depressed because he makes *us* feel depressed; we decide that another is dominant because we find ourselves submitting to him; and so on. There are at least two ways, then, in which we may use our own feelings as instruments to infer the feelings of others: by putting ourself in the other's place and by accounting for our own emotional reaction to the stimuli he provides.

In the second case our impression that the boy completing the puzzle is persistent is based on a generalization that what the person does now he tends always to do. This may be a case of what Secord and Backman (1964) call *temporal extension*—when a characteristic that is momentarily revealed is assumed to be an enduring attribute. Temporal extension also implies a certain amount of situational extension. No two situations are ever alike, so the repeated manifestation of persistence means persistence on a variety of occasions under differing circumstances. Such extensions often occur because, in the absence of further information, they represent a best guess about underlying dispositions.

In the third case another form of generalization is involved—our new acquaintance resembles an uncle, and unwittingly we may attribute some of the uncle's characteristics to him. This may be a case of incorrect categorization, of course. We may have inferred all of the attributes associated with a category that was erroneously applied in the first place.

The final example illustrates both stereotype formation and what is known as metaphorical generalization. Stereotype formation is merely an exaggerated form of category utilization. We may have lazily made a cluster of assumptions about athletes tending to have good physiques, low foreheads, and shaky IQ's. When two of these attributes are present the category is easily entered and the remaining attributes are inferred. Metaphorical generalization is involved to the extent that we associate low brows with low intelligence because (we falsely reason) high brows imply greater brain capacity and therefore greater intelligence. This is similar to the kind of inference involved when a person who has coarse skin or who uses coarse language is considered to be an insensitive (i.e., coarse) person (Secord, Stritch, and Johnson, 1960).

Because we have dealt at some length with categorization as a cognitive activity, and because motor mimicry probably plays a minor role in the understanding of more permanent characteristics, we shall not review these processes extensively. We suspect that metaphorical generalization is ubiquitous in person perception, but there is little systematic evidence to justify further discussion of such inference by analogy. Although we recognize that these other processes feed into the formation of impressions, we feel that the most central process is that involved in moving from behavioral cues to inferences about enduring dispositions. The following discussion emphasizes this process of extension over time and across settings, and epecially examines the conditions under which action is treated as a significant cue or index of an underlying disposition.

FROM ACT TO DISPOSITION

Heider (1958) persuasively argues that a basic goal of the perceiver is to comprehend the structure that underlies and gives rise to events. It is not surprising, therefore, that the person perceiver typically strives to discover the invariances that underlie observable actions. These discoveries are mixed with invention, for the perceiver works with his own set of categories for interpreting action. He has his own theory of personality and the words to go with it. Heider also points out that there are various levels of invariance, and as the perceiver engages in inference he stops at the level that enables him to act effectively. This is a level that is neither too remote from the specific act nor too bound to it. For each perceiver on each occasion there is a form of explanation considered sufficient. For most of us, establishing a *sufficient reason* leads to the attribution of intentions, motives, and traits of character. Through this process of attribution we explain why a person eats, why he gambles, why he drinks. "He eats because he is hungry" seems a sufficient reason for the act of eating. After all, eating is something that a person would do if he were hungry. The person who says "Joe bets heavily because he's an optimist" or "Jack drinks because he's insecure" is also groping for a causal explanation that will be sufficient for his own purposes.

Personal Causality and the Attribution Process

Just as we have distinguished between objects that are only physical and those that are social as well, we may distinguish between impersonal and personal causality. This distinction was clearly drawn many years ago by Fauconnet (1928, pp. 277 ff.) as translated by Heider (1944):

> There exists a causality peculiar to man, different from the causality which connects natural phenomena. Man is, in a certain sense, a first cause, if not of the physical movements which constitute his acts, at least of their moral quality. . . . From this perfect causality originates his responsibility . . . a true antagonism exists between this idea (the idea of human causality) and the scientific idea of causality. First of all, science knows only of secondary causes: every cause, in itself, is also an effect, and causal explanation is a regression which has no feasible end; secondly, the cause is for science a phenomenon like the effect, the laws of causality only describing necessary relations between phenomena. On the other hand, the person conceived as cause is a first cause; the act, said Aristotle, has its beginning in itself; secondly, the two terms are heterogeneous, between them exists, not the relation of phenomenon to phenomenon which a law expresses, but the relation of producer to product, of workman to finished work.

The human perceiver attempts to understand action by finding a sufficient reason, which often involves attributing intentions and values to the actor. But the perceiver ideally attempts to establish for himself that certain conditions obtain before he directly infers value or belief from an act. In Chapter Six we made the fundamental assumption that an act is a choice among alternatives designed to secure maximum outcome at minimum cost. Acts have effects, in other words, and because people act *in order to* achieve these effects there should be direct links of inference between effects and intentions. However, the perceiver observing an act and its effects must first decide whether the actor knew that those particular effects would follow from his act. Consequences of an action that could not have been foreseen by the actor cannot qualify as candidates for what he was trying to achieve. The condition of knowledge is of critical importance within our legal system, in which it is customary to distinguish among levels of responsibility for a crime: (1) intentional (he killed for revenge); (2) incidental (he killed in order to escape); and (3) accidental (he did not know the gun was loaded).

In addition to assumptions or conclusions about knowledge of consequences, the perceiver must also take into account relevant information concerning the *ability* of the actor. An actor cannot achieve his objectives solely by desiring to achieve them—he must have the capacities or skill to move from his present condition of desire to a subsequent condition of attainment and satisfaction. When a person's actions have certain consequences it is important for the perceiver to determine whether the person was capable of producing these consequences in response to his intentions. Especially when an actor *fails* to produce certain effects that might have been anticipated by the perceiver, there may be ambiguity over whether the actor did not want to produce the effects or wanted to but was not able to. Even when effects are achieved the perceiver may have the problem of assessing the relative contribution of luck or chance. When a novice archer hits the bull's eye, we are more likely to attribute this to luck than to skill. There are other occasions when we do not assign intentions to explain effects achieved because we do not consider the actor capable of producing those effects at will. A jury is more likely to believe that a killing is accidental if the defendant, viewed as an average person, lacked the skill (the marksmanship, the strength, etc.) to bring about the crime deliberately.

The perceiver may have certain information about knowledge and ability or he may merely assume that knowledge and ability were probably present or probably absent. Whether the perceiver's conclusion about such matters is correct or incorrect, it obviously affects his perception of the actor's intentions. Knowledge and ability are preconditions for the assignment of intentions. Each plays a similar role in enabling the perceiver to decide whether an effect or consequence of action is accidental.

Sufficient reason may well be provided by the attribution of a simple intention ("he eats because he is hungry"). However, the more important the actor's behavior in the perceiver's scheme of things, the more likely the latter is to treat intentions, once inferred, as cues or indices of more stable dispositions: beliefs, values, and attitudes. To clarify this latter point we return to Heider's persuasive argument that ordinarily the perceiver strives to discover the invariant properties that underly manifest actions, and to do so at the proper level of abstraction.

> The search for relatively enduring aspects of our world . . . may carry us quite far from the immediate facts or they may end hardly a step from them. That is, there exists a hierarchy of cognitive awarenesses which begin with the more stimulus-bound recognition of "facts" and gradually go deeper into the underlying causes of these facts. . . . In the hierarchy of cognitive awareness, each previous layer stands to the succeeding one in the relation of raw material to interpretation (Heider, 1958, p. 80).

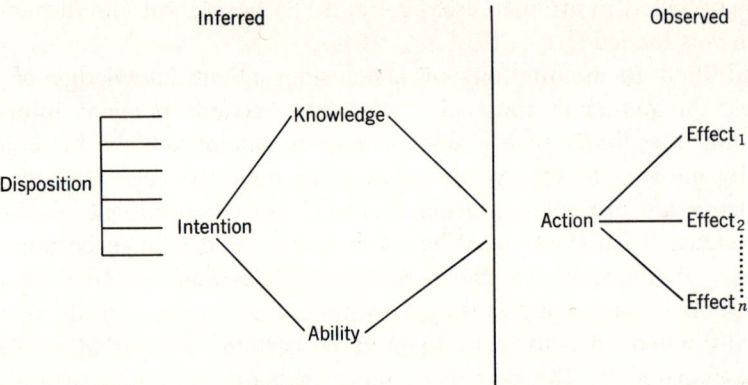

Figure 8.1. The effect-disposition paradigm (from Jones and Davis, 1965).

The foregoing remarks are summarized in Figure 8.1. The perceiver typically starts with the overt action of another and makes certain decisions, concerning ability and knowledge, that pave the way for his coping with the problem of attributing particular intentions. Once attributed, these intentions serve as raw material for further inference about values and other stable characteristics. Reversing the sequence, a person's beliefs, values, and attitudes are revealed through patterns of intentional action and may be inferred by appropriate processing of the data of overt behavior.

The Informational Value of Observed Action

Once the perceiver has made the assumption that at least some of the effects of an action were intended he faces two new problems of inference. He must first make some decision regarding *which* effects were the primary goals of the actor. He must next decide what this tells him about enduring personal dispositions. In both decisions he tries to extract as much information as he can from the behavior observed. The value of this information is much affected by the total setting in which the behavior occurs.

In Chapter Four it was pointed out that "the degree to which an event is informative depends on the amount of uncertainty reduced by the event." How many things could have happened but did not? is one way to put it. There is no reason why the cognitive task of the person perceiver cannot be understood in these same terms. In order to understand the significance of an action he must make some estimate of the number of alternatives open to the person being judged and consider their *a priori* probabilities of occurrence.

Breaking the process down into its essentials, an event is informative if it is one of a large number of equiprobable events. It is uninformative if it was bound to occur—if few other things could have happened and the thing that did happen was highly probable. Thus in the realm of behavior we learn little about a man's personality when he wears shoes to work, when he takes out more life insurance after the birth of his first child, when he deplores violence in the streets. These are actions that have a high degree of *a priori* probability because they are more or less true of everybody. As for inferring dispositions, we are not likely to infer that a man is highly fastidious because he wears shoes or view him as extremely prudent because he insures his life. Usually such highly probable courses of action are constrained by the situation forced on the actor by circumstances.

Just as the person has a backlog of expectancies that he brings to his perception of the physical environment, so has he expectancies about the social world. In any given situation we can imagine the person perceiver attaching probabilities to alternative actions and evaluating the significance of action against this backdrop of inferred probabilities. An action having a low expectancy value because other alternatives are numerous or more likely is informative about enduring dispositions.

Let us illustrate the argument with the results of an experiment by Jones, Davis, and Gergen (1961). The central purpose of the study was to demonstrate that behavior fulfilling clearly defined role requirements is seen as uninformative about the individual's personal characteristics, whereas a considerable amount of information may be extracted from out-of-role behavior. Male undergraduate subjects were exposed to one of four tape-recorded "job interviews" in which the interviewee was either instructed (on the tape) to behave as one who was very interested in qualifying as a prospective submariner or to behave as though he wished to become an astronaut. The subjects were aware that the interviewee was being invited to play a role in a fictitious situation, but they were not told that the entire interview was carefully written as a prearranged script and was recorded by an experimental accomplice serving as the interviewee.

Those subjects who listened to the recording involving the submariner role heard the interviewer describe the ideal submariner as obedient, friendly, cooperative, gregarious—in short, as "other-directed." The remaining subjects listened to a description of the ideal astronaut as one who does not need other people, who has inner resources—in short, an "inner-directed" person. The two interview beginnings were spliced into two different endings, thus creating the four experimental groups. The interviewee either responded with a series of statements indicating extreme other-directedness or he responded with a series of inner-directed statements. On half of the recordings, then, the interviewee-accomplice behaved much in line with the requirements of the occupational role (astronaut–inner condition; submariner–other condition). On the other half the behavior was distinctly out of line with these requirements (astronaut–other condition; submariner–inner condition).

After listening to these tape recordings the subjects were asked to rate the interviewee on a number of trait dimensions ("What do you think he is *really* like as a person?") and indicate their confidence in ratings of each trait. The results were striking and unequivocal. After the two in-role recordings, the interviewee was rated as moderately affiliative, moderately independent, and moderately original. The confidence ratings were extremely low. These findings tended to validate the investigators' assumption that inner-directedness and other-directedness are roughly equiprobable types. In contrast, the astronaut-other was seen as conforming, unoriginal, and affiliative, and confidently rated as such; the submariner-inner was seen as independent, original, and nonaffiliative, again with high confidence. Thus the responses of the interviewee were clearly evaluated in the context of the setting from which they emerged. If other-directedness is called for, an inner-directed response is highly informative. Inner-directedness in the face of a situation that seems to require it, on the other hand, is difficult to interpret. The same kind of contrast applies to other-directedness in the two settings described, providing a replication of the basic hypothesis within the single experiment.

The results may strike the reader as self-evident, but they illustrate a number of more general points in keeping with the argument. In-role behavior is not informative because we can find sufficient reason for it in the stimulus conditions confronting the interviewee. Of course the interviewee must understand those conditions and be responsive to the role definition, but certainly most people would be capable of this. Out-of-role behavior, we may assume, was unexpected in the experimental situation. The subjects had to reduce their uncertainty by locating a sufficient reason somewhere else than in the situation. There are a few scattered reasons why a person would act in an inner-directed manner in response to other-directed role requirements, and vice versa. The interviewee might have been bored or inattentive, he might have felt like pulling the interviewer's leg, or the interview comments might not have been truly representative of extremes of inner- and other-directedness. The most plausible reason for out-of-role behavior, however, is that the interviewee's personality somehow broke through the requirements of the situation. The subjects may have inferred that, try as he might, the interviewee simply could not act in a way that was alien to his nature. Enduring dispositions will out.

The attribution of dispositions by the person perceiver is also a function of the degree of choice the actor is perceived to have in determining his own behavior. Steiner and Field (1960), for example, found that perceivers were much more confident in their judgments about a fellow group member when he could choose his role than when all group roles were experimentally assigned. An accomplice of the experimenter, always presented as a naive subject, took the role of a prosegregationist in a three-person discussion. In some cases this role was assigned to him; in other cases, he *chose* to play this role rather than speak out in favor of integration. In addition to being more confident in attributing prosegregation beliefs to the accomplice in the condition in which he assumed the role, the subjects also tended to like him less in that condition.

A study by Jones and Harris (1967) also indicates the importance of choice and provides interesting data on the combined effects of choice and prior probability. In this study college-student subjects were asked to estimate a stimulus person's attitudes toward Castro from a short speech allegedly written by the stimulus person (hereafter called SP). The SP was presented as a member of the debating team of a neighboring university and the speech was supposedly his attempt to support one side of the debate on Cuba. In two experimental conditions the speech obviously favored Castro; in two others the speech obviously opposed him. Some subjects were told that the SP had been assigned to one or the other side of the question. Other subjects were told that he was given his choice of sides to defend.

After reading the speech the subjects attempted to estimate the SP's true attitudes toward Castro. Table 8.1 presents the results of their estimation attempts. The higher the number, the more pro-Castro the estimate. Several features of the table deserve comment. First of all, it is

Table 8.1. Attribution of Pro-Castro Beliefs

	Choice	No choice
"Pro" speech		
mean	57.7 [a]	41.3
variance	21.0	134.8
"Anti" speech		
mean	22.9	23.7
variance	34.9	50.1

[a] Possible range from 10 (extreme anti) to 70 (extreme pro). The average subject's "own score" was 31.7.

obvious that the speech itself played an extremely important role in the subject's estimate. The SP was obviously judged to be more pro-Castro when he wrote a speech favoring Castro—regardless of the circumstances under which the speech was composed.

Many writers have noted the general tendency of perceivers to attribute more causation to persons as origins than an objective analysis would warrant. Unintended harms and benefits are often ascribed to hostile or benevolent motives; acts classed as bravery are often accidental responses to situational pressures. Heider (1944) discussed the tendency to exaggerate the influence of personal causation with reference to supporting comments by a number of German psychologists and philosophers: Stern, Ichheiser, Nietzsche, and Klages. The present data certainly provide evidence for this bias in the highly significant difference between the two no-choice conditions (41.3 versus 23.7). Logic impels us to conclude that little information is provided by a speech whose direction is dictated by environmental forces. However, the perceivers did not see it this way. Someone who writes a pro-Castro speech is more in favor of Castro than an anti-Castro speech writer, even if neither has any choice in the matter.

Having said this, it is still obvious that the degree of choice is an important factor. The SP who *chooses* to write a pro-Castro speech is seen as more in favor of Castro than the SP who is assigned that task; the SP who chooses the anti-Castro speech is seen as more opposed to Castro than his no-choice control. This is clearly consistent with the argument that the informational value of action is greater when alternative action courses are available.

Another feature of these results merits comment. The choice versus no-choice variable plays a significantly greater role when a pro-Castro than when an anti-Castro speech is written. Why should this be so? Quite probably because of the greater antecedent probability that the speech writer is really against Castro. In other words, in the college population from which both the subjects and the SP were drawn, it is much more likely that a person would be against the Castro regime than for it. (In fact, the subject's responses to an attitude questionnaire showed that this was clearly the case for all but a few of them.)

One final thing may be noted. The ratings of subjects are extremely variable in the no-choice, pro-speech condition. This is what we would expect if there are conflicting or ambiguous cues about the SP's true attitude. Some subjects apparently guessed that he is pro-Castro (because, after all, he did write the speech), others guessed that he is anti-Castro (because, after all, most people are).

To summarize this discussion of the attribution process, some actions are more informative about underlying intentions and dispositions than others. The perceiver identifies intentions by observing the effects of action, once he has decided that the actor knew his behavior would produce these effects and had the ability to produce them. When an effect of action is seen as highly desirable in the culture, the perceiver is likely to assume that the actor intended to achieve it. Such an intention has, we might say, high antecedent probability. Although a perceiver may assign this intention with some confidence, such highly probable behavior is not really informative about the actor's underlying dispositions—little uncertainty is reduced when a middle-class college student writes an anticommunist speech.

Action that produces effects that are not seen as universally desired is more informative about unique dispositions. This is especially true if the action observed represents a choice among several alternatives.

The possibility that an action may lead to several identifiable effects complicates matters. The argument can be extended to choices among multiple-effect-producing action if we introduce the notion of nonoverlapping or noncommon effects. If a chosen and a nonchosen alternative have effects in common, the choice is not informative about intentions to achieve those effects. The reader who wishes to pursue the matter further is referred to Jones and Davis (1965).

THE ORGANIZATION OF IMPRESSIONS

This account of the process whereby a perceiver infers a disposition from an action has been highly simplified, thus far. We have focused on the perceiver who is confronted with the circumscribed actions of a stimulus person, having a certain amount of information about the context in which these actions have occurred. Under certain conditions, using the data of observed action, the perceiver makes rather reliable inferences about underlying dispositions. Now we move on to realize that this may be only the beginning of the impression formation process. Once the perceiver has satisfied himself that the stimulus person has a certain disposition, he naturally makes further inferences about associated dispositions. The tendency to go beyond the information given, in this case to infer one disposition from another, is a remarkable aspect of person perception. Out of a pattern of brief glances, gestures, a few spoken words, and a set of physical appearance cues we develop an impression about a total person. This impression is likely to be organized so that certain characteristics stand out as central and others as subsidiary. Where does this richness of inference come from? How do we come, rightly or wrongly, to make so much out of a downward glance, an ungrammatical expression, or a feeble handshake?

The most obvious answer to such questions is to recognize that each of us is involved in a continuing learning process that results in increasingly sophisticated understanding of the various ways in which human nature patterns itself. Some of this learning is unique to the individual, growing out of his particular experiences with others. Much of it, however, may be broadly defined as "cultural"; embedded in the language itself, it comes to us in the form of synonyms and phrases that include the same recurring combinations of words. Because of the structure of our language, for example, it is easier to say "he is a dominant, aggressive type" than to say "he is dominant and shy." Aggressiveness is suggested or connoted by dominance, whereas shyness is not.

Several students of person perception have suggested that people operate with "implicit theories of personality" in making inferences about others. To the extent that this is true these implicit theories represent an amalgam of personal and cultural experience. In any given case it is extremely difficult to disentangle the unique and the shared associations that compose a personality theory. In the examples to follow we merely attempt to show that certain associative patterns are common to a particular culture and may be studied by the simple strategy of asking subjects to predict certain characteristics from information about other ones.

The Role of "Central" Traits

In 1946 Asch reported a series of studies on organizing tendencies in first-impression formation, which influenced much subsequent research. In these studies Asch employed simple experimental procedures to produce convincing demonstrations of the extent to which certain traits may serve as foci around which others become organized. In one experiment he presented the following list of traits to a group of subjects with instructions that they all referred to the same person: intelligent, skillful, industrious, warm, determined, practical, cautious. The same list was presented to a second group of subjects with the single substitution of the word *cold* for *warm*. Subjects were asked to write a brief sketch of the person and to check the one of a pair of antonyms (for each of 18 antonym pairs) that best characterized the person.

The results showed that subjects can readily take such a list of discrete traits and form a rounded, interpretive impression of the person being described. What is more important, the variation of the words *warm* and *cold* dramatically influenced the selection of particular antonyms. The great majority of those presented with the *warm* list inferred that the stimulus person was also generous (90 percent), happy (90 percent), good-natured (94 percent), humorous (77 percent), and humane (86 percent). In contrast, those presented the *cold* list checked ungenerous (92 percent), unhappy (66 percent), irritable (83 percent), humorless (87 percent), and ruthless (69 percent). It appears, then, that clearly different persons are brought to mind when the traits *warm* and *cold* are exchanged. Nor is this entirely a matter of *warm* leading to positive and *cold* to negative evaluation. Both stimulus persons are described by almost all subjects as persistent, curious, reliable, important, strong, and honest. And yet these traits are all quite positive in a general evaluative sense.

Asch showed through further experimentation along the same lines that: (1) if the words *polite* and *blunt* are substituted for *warm* and *cold,* the differences in impression are very slight; (2) when *warm* is included in the list *obedient, weak, shallow, warm, unambitious, vain,* it loses its comparative importance. What these findings suggest is that certain traits are more central than others in the formation of an impression, and that a trait that is central in one set of traits may be quite peripheral in another. This is not a surprising conclusion, but it suggests that total impressions may be predicted quite well from knowledge of a perceiver's appraisal of the stimulus person along some highly focal dimension.

Asch presented the results of his research to demonstrate his prior conviction that impressions form organic, integrated wholes. Each trait modifies the meaning of every other trait, so that the resulting impression is not merely an additive combination of separate meanings. The *intelligent* of *warm–intelligent* is a kind of creative, spontaneous brightness; the *intelligent* of *cold–intelligent* smacks of craft and calculation. Thus traits are mutually defining and interact in ways that produce meanings not contained in the individual trait.

Luchins (1948) criticized Asch's conclusions as being overgeneralized and maintained, upon examining the data from a similar experiment that he conducted, that many of his subjects had difficulties in integrating the discrete traits. He also criticized Asch's method as artificial and of questionable relevance to impression formation. Contrary to Luchins' criticism, Mensch and Wishner (1947) were able to reproduce Asch's results faithfully and Haire and Grunes (1950) found parallel results in a slightly altered context. The artificiality criticism was at least partly answered by Kelley (1950), who demonstrated similar effects when similar lists of traits, including *warm* and *cold,* were applied to actual people. Students in three sections of a psychology course were told that a guest lecturer would lead the discussion that day, and before he actually arrived biographical notes were distributed among the students describing the guest lecturer as a graduate student considered by people who know him to be "a rather cold (warm) person, industrious, critical, practical, and determined." Half the students in each class received the note containing "warm"; to the other half he was portrayed as "cold." The guest instructor then led the class in a 20-minute discussion. After this he left and the students were requested to fill out a candid impression rating of him. Although two different persons served as guest instructor in different sections, Asch's findings were replicated for both instructors. Whether *warm* or *cold* was in the list made an important difference in the students' rating of the instructor on other traits.

Another result of this experiment was extremely interesting. A record was kept of the number of times individual students initiated interaction with the guest instructor. Students who had received the *warm* notes tended to initiate more interactions than those who had received the *cold* notes. Although this tendency was not quite significant statistically, it is certainly consistent with the basic notion that social behavior is conditioned by social perception—our behavior toward others is very much a function of the way in which these others are categorized. To categorize a person as warm is to expect pleasurable interchanges with him. That is part of the meaning of the word. A cold person is presumably more likely to respond in a crisp, aloof, and not supportive manner. (Kelley found that those subjects more positively disposed toward the instructor initiated more interactions with him. This correlational result *was* statistically significant.)

That our impressions of others are organized around a focus, that component bits of information are not additive, that the characteristics of a person are defined in relation to one another—all these contentions of Asch have been lurking in the wings for years. It has long been known, for example, that when people are asked to rate or judge an individual on a specific characteristic, they are influenced by judgments of other characteristics or by their over-all impression of the stimulus person. This tendency, first mentioned by Wells in 1907, was later christened the *halo effect* by Thorndike (1920). The implication of this concept is that characteristics that may vary independently in actual fact are judged to be highly correlated in ratings.

For years raters were cautioned to adopt procedures that would minimize the halo effect and other sources of bias or error. Only recently have psychologists begun to focus on "halo" as a phenomenon in its own right, one whose determinants need investigation and analysis. The halo effect undoubtedly reflects the fact that perceivers approach the task of judging another person with built-in maps of inference. As already suggested, individuals seem to apply their own implicit personality theories to fill in the gaps created by limited information about a stimulus person. If we could understand how these home-grown theories are applied, we would account for halo phenomena in the process.

Determinants of Centrality

Asch was eager to convince his scientific audience that the meanings of component traits do not merely summate when an impression is formed, but that the impression represents an emergent synthesis of organized meaning. The contention that the whole is greater than the sum of its parts is familiar in psychology, yet often simpler additive models have considerable predictive power. Whereas Asch may have been correct in arguing that traits often combine to form emergent patterns of meaning, we might make more sure-footed scientific headway, given our present limited knowledge and measuring techniques, by assuming that trait meanings are additive. For example, Bruner, Shapiro, and Tagiuri (1958) presented each of 11 different arrangements of four *given traits* to 120 different subjects (total sample size, 1320). The four traits were CONSIDERATE, INDEPENDENT, INTELLIGENT, and INCONSIDERATE. The 11 combinations resulted from taking these traits one, two, and three at a time (without ever employing CONSIDERATE and INCONSIDERATE in the same combination).

Inferences were made from each *given* trait or combination to 59 other *list* traits. Subjects were instructed to indicate, for example, whether "People who are CONSIDERATE and INTELLIGENT . . .

> very often are
> tend to be
> may or may not be
> tend not to be
> seldom are . . ."

aggressive, active, awkward, and so forth, for the 59 list traits. The investigators found that the impression inferred from any of the seven trait combinations could be very reliably predicted from the ratings given (by other subjects, of course) to the four traits in isolation. When the rating assigned to a list trait is the same for two given traits there is no problem of predicting their meaning in combination. When the two or three traits individually yield conflicting inferences the resulting inference from the combined traits may still be predicted by weighting more heavily the component on which there is more widespread agreement. If we are content to predict on which side of the neutral point ("may or may not be") the combined inference will fall, we may do so with 97 percent accuracy.

We should point out that the Bruner et al. study by no means refutes Asch's contention that a trait in combination may have a different meaning than the same trait in isolation. Their procedure was different and the subjects' task was more abstract. However, the study emphasizes that the meaning of traits in isolation is a serviceable predictor of their meaning within a particular combination. This is obviously different from Asch's implied position that the final impression of the whole is unpredictable from knowledge about the constituents. One problem is that it is possible to demonstrate almost any contention of this sort as long as the investigator is free to choose his examples. We might suspect that the words in Asch's stimulus lists were less "additive" than the given traits selected by Bruner et al. Perhaps the latter investigators unwittingly avoided traits that differed in centrality. Wishner (1960) tried to make a refined analysis of the relation between stimulus traits and response lists. In doing so he succeeded in dispelling much of the mystery generated by Asch's contention of emergent meaning. He also succeeded in showing how the centrality of a particular trait in a given context can be predicted on the basis of independent evidence.

Wishner re-examined the particular procedures followed by Asch and could find no stated reason why certain traits were chosen for the stimulus list and others for the response (or check) list. He reasoned that *warm* and *cold* may have been central traits in Asch's experiment because variations along the *warm–cold* dimension happened to correlate highly with checklist ratings, but not with fellow items in the stimulus list. Specifically, the checklist contained such items as *irritable, sociable, unhappy,* and *popular.* The subjects in Asch's experiment rated the person being described very differently on these items depending on whether the stimulus list contained *warm* or *cold.* It was largely on these grounds that Asch argued for the centrality of *warm–cold.* However, on several independent samples of subjects rating different stimulus persons, Wishner found that ratings of *warm* versus *cold* intercorrelated highly with ratings on these other traits. He also went on to show that other seemingly peripheral dimensions such as *blunt–polite* could be made central by modifying the checklist to include traits with which the stimulus dimension is known to be correlated.

The upshot of Wishner's re-analysis of the Asch study is that we are now in a better position to predict which traits will be central in the process of impression organization. By examining the intercorrelations between large numbers of traits, obtained on independent samples, it is possible to make fairly precise predictions about the impression that people will form from a particular set of traits—*provided* that the trait terms in which the impression is to be stated are also specified beforehand. Although Asch himself argued that centrality depended on the other traits in the stimulus list, Wishner pointed up the added complexity that centrality also depends on the traits in the response checklist.

The Search for Basic Factors of Verbal Meaning

Wishner performed an important service in dispelling some of the mystery generated by Asch's discussions of centrality and emergent meaning. His contribution provides certain procedures for predicting the effects on impressions of varying one trait within a combination; it does not, however, illuminate the basic processes involved in impression organization beyond suggesting that these processes are heavily affected by semantic factors. Osgood, Suci, and Tannenbaum (1957) have sought a more general strategy for analyzing the basic dimensions of verbal meaning. Although not primarily addressed to the perception of persons, their work is certainly relevant in the present context. Osgood and his associates have asked whether the meaning of any concept (man, boulder, Catholic, my mother, summer) could not be expressed in terms of a limited set of meaning dimensions or coordinates. By intercorrelating the traits that do and do not apply to (describe) such concepts, Osgood et al. were able to find general clusters of covarying traits that seemed to form basic dimensions of meaning. In their terms, they were able to simplify the description of *semantic space*— if a man or a boulder or a Catholic is rated good (rather than bad) it (he) also tends to be rated fair (rather than unfair), happy (rather than sad), and so on. By sampling a wide variety of concepts and adjectives they were able to show that three independent factors or dimensions accounted for a large proportion of variations in meaning. The first of these factors is *evaluation* (e.g., good–bad), the second is *potency* (strong–weak), and the third is *activity* (active–passive).

Because of the procedures followed in arriving at these factors, they are quite independent of one another. Thus a person or object may be good, weak, passive; bad, strong, passive; and so on. The stability of these factors is suggested by their reappearance in different studies using different concepts, traits, and subjects. In every case, however, the evaluative factor was the most pervasive and accounted for the greatest amount of possible variation in meaning.

In a few experiments dealing with persons and social issues as concepts evaluation again appeared to be the most important and powerful factor involved. That is, if a person is asked to rate Goldwater, then Johnson, then labor unions, then Communism, on a series of identical trait pairs (aligned as opposites) he tends to use all evaluative traits in pretty much the same way. If the concept is positive on one evaluative trait (say, fair–unfair) it will be rated in the same direction on another evaluative trait (say, beautiful–ugly). In such ratings of persons and other social concepts, however, the independence of the other two factors, activity and potency, tends to diminish. Activity and potency seem to covary more with social concepts than do other nouns in the English language; they blend into a broader dimension that Osgood et al. call a *dynamism factor*.

But there is no question about the pervasiveness of the evaluative factor, which will hardly come as a surprise to anyone who has worked with ratings of personality. The evaluative factor is so omnipresent that the permeation of single ratings by a general impression was designated "halo" by Thorndike and others, rather than some more neutral term. It is true in general that if a perceiver attributes one strongly positive trait, the best prediction is that he will attribute other positive characteristics. In everyday speech we seem to recognize this also. We say "He's a nice guy *but* he's kind of stupid," or "She's very talented at making friends *but* I don't trust her." Our impressions are so likely to be packaged in evaluative clusters that inconsistencies along the dimensions of value call for a "but" to alert the audience.

Inconsistencies exist, of course, and, even more important, there are wide variations in the strength of relationships among positive or negative traits as they are assigned to a concept or a stimulus person. Following Osgood, Suci, and Tannenbaum, some of this variation is attributable to activity and potency, but beyond the general case there are clearly nuances of meaning that can be important: activity and evaluation may obviously be correlated when one concept is being rated (*president*) but not another (*flower*). There are strong logical inferences between certain specific traits that are very different in evaluative significance, and equally valued traits can be logically incompatible. The results of Osgood et al. bring home the point that when information about another leads to a trait inference that is distinctly positive or distinctly negative in evaluation that trait serves as a crucial focus for the assignment of other positive or negative qualities. The same is true to an important but lesser extent when activity and potency are concerned.

Organization over Time: Early and Later Impressions

The aforementioned investigations, and indeed most of the studies in the area of person perception, are concerned with *first* impressions. The reasons for this are not difficult to understand. One reason is methodological. If we wish to study the development of impressions over time, this takes more investigative effort than first-impression studies. There are, of course, many natural situations that involve the growth of an acquaintanceship. However, the history of such relationships is so difficult to control that it is hard to make scientific generalizations about the factors that condition the organization of impressions over time. Long-range studies of impression development inevitably involve interaction between the perceiver and the stimulus person so that variations in the resulting impression may be traced as much to the "eliciting behavior" of the perceiver as to the observed behavior of the stimulus person.

Aside from these methodological considerations, it has often been asserted that first impressions are terribly important and worthy of study in their own right. First of all, many significant interpersonal contacts are single and brief; first-impression results may be said to generalize to these common once-only contacts. It may also be plausibly maintained that organizing principles applicable to first-impression formation may be successfully applied to organization at later stages of information acquisition. In addition, there is strong folklore support for the claim that first impressions unduly influence later impressions. To the extent that this is so, the more we know about the organizing foci of first impressions describing a particular person the more we can predict what subsequent impressions of him will probably be like.

This latter claim has been investigated in a number of studies whose conclusions stress the importance of early information in the formation of impressions. One of Asch's (1946) experiments was addressed to this question. The following list of traits was presented to one group of subjects as characterizing a person: *intelligent, industrious, impulsive, critical, stubborn, envious.* A second group of subjects received the same traits presented in reverse order. The resulting impressions of the stimulus person were quite different in the two cases, no doubt because of the deliberate use of lists containing evaluative terms in either a good–bad or a bad–good order. As for the direction of the difference, those who received the list beginning with the good traits (*intelligent,* etc.) were more likely to view the stimulus person as happy, humorous, sociable, and restrained. Thus the subjects in the good–bad group formed more favorable general impressions. On the basis of these and other results Asch concluded that early terms in such a series set up a *direction* that then exerts a continuing effect on later terms, modifying their meaning in subtle ways and thus changing their evaluative intensity.

In another series of experiments Luchins (1957) demonstrated this same kind of "primacy effect" with more descriptive narrative materials as stimuli. He constructed two paragraphs about a boy named Jim, each describing a different sequence of behavior. In one sequence Jim was gregarious, extroverted, sought out the company of others; in the other sequence he was seclusive, shy, introverted. Control subjects were exposed to one or the other paragraph. Experimental subjects read both paragraphs in one of the two possible orders. The results were straightforward; striking primacy effects were obtained in that the impressions of the experimental groups primarily reflected the information to which the subjects were first exposed. In subsequent experiments Luchins was able to destroy the primacy effect by cautioning subjects not to form a snap judgment but to weigh all the evidence. Inserting a series of irrelevant numerical problems between readings of the separate paragraphs was also effective in reducing the importance of the first paragraph. In fact, moderate but statistically significant recency effects were produced under this condition of an interpolated task.

Recent work by Anderson and his colleagues shows the precision and power of primacy effects when evaluative information appears in varying sequences. Using a procedure basically similar to Asch's method of forming an impression of a person from a string of descriptive adjectives, Anderson and Barrios (1961) found strong primacy effects. Subjects were asked to give an evaluative impression rating of a stimulus person described by six adjectives. They were to think of these adjectives as having been given by six different people who knew the stimulus person well. The subjects were much more positive in the evaluation of, for example, a stimulus person described as "smart, artistic, sentimental, cool, awkward, and faultfinding" than a person described in the same terms with their order reversed. Using a very elaborate research design, in which combinations of favorable and unfavorable adjectives were presented in systematically different sequences, Anderson (1965) again found that a primacy effect was in operation, and he attempted to provide a mathematical formula that would predict the amount of primacy to be expected given a particular sequence of favorable and unfavorable adjectives.

Anderson questions whether the Asch interpretation is the best way to account for primacy effects in this kind of situation. Asch argues that the early traits bias the interpretation of later traits so that, given a set starting with positive and ending with negative adjectives, the more favorable shades of meaning would be applied to the later adjectives. The less favorable shades of meaning would be applied to the same adjectives when they appear early in the sequence. Anderson (1965) favors the interpretation that the later adjectives are given a smaller *weight* in the judgment process, not that their meaning undergoes subtle changes. His preference for a "weighted-average" interpretation is based on several additional findings. Anderson and Hubert (1963) found that the primacy effect dissipates if subjects are asked to recall the adjectives before giving their impression response, a result that seems to support the idea that the primacy appearing in the standard version of the task results from decreased attention to and hence lower weights for the later adjectives. Also, Stewart (1965) found that primacy was eliminated when subjects reported their impressions (cumulatively) after each successive adjective of the set.

Several other investigations have dealt with the cognitive integration of contradictory or discrepant information about the stimulus person. Typically they have concluded that (a) such integrations can be achieved even when the information is clearly contradictory; (b) individuals differ in their methods of achieving integration, some merely suppressing one part of the contradiction, others attempting a true integration (see Gollin, 1954, and Pepitone and Hayden, 1955); and (c) the ease of integration depends on initial instructions emphasizing that the traits all apply to the same person. Concerning the last point, for example, Asch (1946) and his student Kastenbaum (1951) showed that the difficulty of integrating conflicting information about a person was much increased if the perceivers were first asked to form two impressions, each based on one internally consistent kind of information, and then told that the parts referred to the same person.

This suggests that the organization of an impression depends not only on the sequence in which information is presented or the extent to which the information is contradictory, but also on whether the perceiver is pressed to make judgmental decisions about the stimulus person after receiving different amounts of total material presented. If the perceiver must commit himself to a decision about the characteristics of a stimulus person, this may affect the use to which subsequent information is put—much in the manner that action decisions alert the individual to information supporting the decision taken (see Chapter Six).

Dailey (1952) studied this problem in a series of well-controlled experiments on premature conclusions in impression formation. He first showed that subjects receiving a certain amount of autobiographical information about a stimulus person could better predict his responses to a personality questionnaire when they made one final rating than when asked to make a preliminary rating after exposure to half of the material. In other words, subjects forced to make premature conclusions seem to be hampered in making full use of subsequent information and end up being less accurate than those who make a final prediction.

We would not expect this conclusion to hold universally. The amount of valid information on which a premature conclusion is based should be an important variable. Indeed it is, as Dailey (1952) demonstrated in a further experiment in which the "importance" of the early information was varied. Here it was shown that only when the early prediction followed rather trivial information did the prediction itself reduce the benefit of subsequent information. Those subjects who received important information first were unaffected in their accuracy by drawing a premature conclusion. A practical implication of these results is that in personality-judgment situations when maximum accuracy is desirable the judge should be asked to express his judgment only after exposure to all available information and not at various points along the way. Also, if possible, the most important information should be presented first.

The importance of initial impressions seems well documented by these studies, but we should be careful not to make our conclusions too sweeping. It is true that primacy effects seem to occur under well-controlled conditions, but this hardly means that information received subsequent to the first impression has no effect. Our impressions of others do seem to fill in and often to shift over time, and we can all cite cases when a first impression was later acknowledged to be almost entirely misleading. But obviously time itself is not a relevant variable; neither is the sheer number of occasions we observe the stimulus person. Common sense tells us that it is the range and variety of our contacts that determine the accuracy and validity of our impressions. We would expect that the more varied and intimate our contacts with others are, the more fully we understand them. Variety of contacts should be important simply because understanding implies the ability to predict, and it is easier to predict behavior in situations resembling those to which we have already seen the stimulus person respond than in situations where much inference and generalization is required.

The role of intimacy raises another interesting set of problems. In the first-impression investigations we have just discussed, the amount of exposure and contact was roughly guaranteed or established by the conditions of the investigation. The perceivers were given the task of perceiving others in the abstract, without any specific relationship between perceiver and stimulus person. It should obviously make a difference if the perceiver is allowed to act on his first impression by responding to the stimulus person and observing his reactions to this response. The perceiver may, and probably often does, test out his first impressions in ways that clearly affect the kind of information subsequently received.

This possibility is well documented by the results of a recent experiment of Davis (1962), who brought two naive and unacquainted college girls together and asked them to discuss arguments to support a position they both endorsed (this being determined by the results of a questionnaire both students had previously taken). Each subject first received authoritative information about the other, authoritative because it came allegedly from an assessment by the other's close friends. In each pair one subject was always told the other was quite dominant, the other was told the first was quite submissive. The members of each pair were actually equal in dominance, according to a standard personality measure of that trait.

The conversations took place in either a cooperative context, in which the experimenter urged the subjects to work as a team to develop the best arguments for use against opposing teams, or a competitive context, in which the task was to see which of the two subjects could develop the most effective arguments for the position they jointly supported. The ensuing discussions were carefully monitored by assistants in the next room observing through a one-way mirror. Reliable indices of dominant behavior (speaking first, talking the most, suggesting rather than reacting) revealed the following: in the cooperative context the subject who believed her partner was dominant was herself quite submissive in her behavior; the other subject in each pair tended to dominate the conversation from beginning to end. In the competitive context, on the other hand, the subject who believed her partner to be dominant tended to be dominant herself; the other subject tended to be submissive.

These different patterns of behavior were predicted before the experiment. The dominance-submission pre-information served in the cooperative context to facilitate role differentiation. It was as if one subject said to herself, "Well, she's probably going to try to take over, so I might as well let her," whereas the other reasoned "It looks as though I'm going to have to step in and assert myself if we want to get anything accomplished." In the competitive context the situation is more complicated, and Davis's predictions were more tentative. He expected the subject facing a dominant opponent to mobilize her own dominance in order to protect herself—to compete effectively. The subject facing a submissive opponent, on the other hand, might be lulled into a sense of false security and put out little effort to lead the discussion. The results support these expectations, by and large, especially for those who scored high in dominance on the previously administered questionnaire.

What were the resulting impressions in the various experimental conditions? As might be expected, subjects in the cooperative conditions felt that the conversation confirmed the pre-information they had received. The final and initial impression ratings on traits related to dominance-submission were almost identical. In the competitive conditions, on the other hand, the subject's impressions changed quite drastically as a function of the conversation. In fact, the opponent's actual behavior was a much stronger determinant of the final impression than the pre-information, which the behavior tended to contradict. One implication of the Davis experiment stands out clearly. When people form an initial impression and are then allowed to engage in meaningful social interaction their subsequent impressions may be a complicated function of many factors *including* their own behavioral response to their initial impression. The cooperative condition was especially interesting in this respect. Because of the structure of the interaction setting, erroneous pre-information led to behavior that merely perpetuated the error. In this case we can reasonably say that the later impression was "determined by" the earlier one. In the competitive context, of course, the intervening behavior served to contradict and upset the earlier impression.

In the freer setting of the everyday environment, when the situation is not carefully defined by an experimenter and the conversation partner is not carefully chosen, a number of new selective factors can operate. Given the normal freedom to choose companions and to choose the topic of conversation with them, it is likely that first impressions can very much influence later impressions by affecting the course of intervening interactions between the perceiver and the stimulus person.

This possibility has been emphasized by the studies and the theorizing of T. M. Newcomb in particular. In 1947 Newcomb proposed what has since come to be known as the *autistic hostility hypothesis* to account for the perpetuation of antagonistic attitudes between persons. The hypothesis is a reasonable one: when persons, for whatever reasons, develop hostility toward each other they tend to restrict or avoid mutual communication, and therefore the hostility cannot be corrected through open communicative contact. Once person A becomes hostile to B, this hostility tends to be perpetuated because A avoids those opportunities for communication most likely to break down the hostile attitude. The perception of B thus becomes autistic because it is not responsive to information that is potentially available, and it cannot be periodically tested against social reality.

The converse of this also seems reasonable, namely, that initial liking or attraction leads to increased social contacts. From this it should follow that persons who initially like each other should get to know each other better than those who initially dislike each other, given the same opportunities for social contact. "Getting to know each other" implies a growth of accuracy in evaluating attitudes and values and in predicting behavior.

Newcomb had a unique opportunity to study these phenomena when he established at the University of Michigan a rooming house for two successive groups of 17 students. In return for one semester's free rent the tenants were to spend four to five hours a week working on psychological questionnaires. The students were carefully selected to be complete strangers to one another and, in fact, all were transfer students. The questionnaires measured attitudes in many spheres: toward issues, events, and persons in the wider environment; toward one another; and toward the self. In addition, at various points during the semester of living together, the students attempted to estimate how others felt about them and what some of the additional attitudes of these others were.

The resulting data were extremely complex and could be analyzed in many ways. Perhaps the most immediately relevant results reported by Newcomb (1961, p. 99) concern the extent to which the students were accurate in estimating others' opinions of each other. Not only did accuracy increase over time, but this was particularly true of students who liked each other. This finding suggests, as hypothesized, that liking someone facilitates communication and in turn facilitates the development of an accurate impression.

To sum up, first and subsequent impressions of others seem to be fairly predictable if we are informed about a few key or focal inferences. The single most important bit of information is whether the perceiver likes or dislikes the stimulus person. Not only is this an important determinant of generalization in "semantic space"; in the natural environment initial evaluation also effects subsequent communication, which in turn may influence the growth of impressions over time. Because the evaluative dimension is of such critical importance in the organization of first impressions, we turn in the next section to consider the determinants of positive or negative feelings about another.

DETERMINANTS OF ATTRACTION AND HOSTILITY BETWEEN PERSONS

It is not difficult to think of personal characteristics that are considered unfavorable by almost everyone in our culture. People generally dislike persons perceived as dishonest, boastful, selfish, complaining, or unreliable. We could make a much more extensive list of negative characteristics without getting into those about which there would be serious disagreements. What are some of the factors that determine whether a trait is valued or disvalued in a particular culture, or within a particular kind of relationship, or by a particular kind of perceiver? More generally, what are the main determinants of attraction and antagonism between persons?

Obviously there are individual differences. Some of us like outspoken extroverts better than others. A smiling, agreeable person might be appreciated by some, and considered intrusive or hypocritical by others. It is also likely to be the case that different characteristics are differently evaluated from one culture to another. Finally, we should expect the context of interaction to affect the linkage between perceived personal attributes and over-all attraction. But we should be able to comprehend individual, cultural, and situational effects in terms of the basic proposition that *persons are valued to the extent that they possess characteristics that facilitate the outcome attainments of the perceiver*. Such a statement is not very helpful in and of itself, but it sets the stage for a more refined analysis of the determinants of attraction. By putting the matter this way we are alerted to those factors that serve to promote or block the perceiver's purposes. The following account attempts to list some of the more obvious factors that have received the attention of social psychologists.

Attraction and Being Liked

A major determinant of attraction to particular other persons is our estimate of their feelings about us. In some contexts, such as that of adolescent dating, this may become of supreme importance, but the intuition or perception that another person likes us is presumably an important inference in a wide variety of social situations. Why is it important that others like us? There seem to be at least two major reasons. First of all, when others like us they generally will do things for us. They can be counted on to facilitate our attainment of desirable objectives in the environment. Thus when others like us we gain some power over them and at least have some leverage to influence their behavior on our behalf. Thibaut and Riecken (1955b) have made the further point that those who are attracted to us will be loyal and tend to act on our behalf even when we are not in a position to check up on them. A second reason is perhaps more basic and yet more nebulous. Each of us is concerned with our worth as a person. There are no clear objective yardsticks of this worth: if the acquisition of material goods and financial success were really valid indicators of this worth much of the fictional literature of our time would lose its point. Instead, our worth is validated largely by the opinions others have of us. The opinions of certain acquaintances may be more important than the opinions of others, but cues that a person is liked by another generally bolster the conception that he has of himself as a worthy, capable, or virtuous person.

It does not necessarily follow that we *like* others who appear to like us even though we need and appreciate their assumed support. Nevertheless, we have begun this section with the proposition that we generally tend to value positively those persons who facilitate our purposes. We include as such a purpose the desire or need to be a worthy person.

The evidence on this point is so strong that we shall merely cite a few representative findings. In a series of investigations Tagiuri has consistently found that his subjects like those whom they perceive as liking them (e.g., Tagiuri, Blake, and Bruner, 1953). From Tagiuri's evidence, however, it is not clear whether we like another person because we perceive he likes us or we assume the other person likes us because we know we like him.

Incidental evidence in studies by Jones, Hester, Farina, and Davis (1959) and Jones, Gergen, and Davis (1962) makes it clear that positive evaluation of the stimulus person follows the receipt of evidence that the stimulus person likes the perceiver. Those who received negative evaluation from the stimulus person were more negative in their subsequent evaluation of the stimulus person than were innocent bystanders exposed to the same derogatory remarks. Our feelings for a given person are determined by how he feels about *us*, above and beyond whether he is inclined to be a generally accepting or critical person.

No one would expect this to be the whole story, of course. We do not respond as positively to favorable evaluations that are undeserved as to those that we feel are to some extent merited. If we evaluate ourselves negatively in certain areas, there is some evidence that we value positively those persons who accurately perceive these weaknesses. Newcomb (1956) has presented data in support of this point. Subjects who accepted unfavorable adjectives in describing themselves, tended to see those they liked as also perceiving these weaknesses or foibles. Along the same line, Deutsch and Solomon (1959) were able to show that subjects who were positively evaluated for a poor performance did not respond as favorably toward their judge as those who were positively evaluated for a good performance, and subjects who were negatively evaluated for a good performance were more unfavorable in their impressions than those negatively evaluated for a poor performance. In both the Newcomb and the Deutsch and Solomon studies, however, subjects also showed a strong tendency to be especially favorable in return for positive evaluation of themselves. Deutsch and Solomon have labeled this the *positivity effect* to distinguish it from our desire for others to see us as we see ourselves. The latter may be called the *balance effect* because it may be derived from Heider's (1958) theory of cognitive balance: taking the self as an object (X), we should like others when their sentiments toward X are the same as our own. In most cases, because we tend to view ourselves favorably, the positivity effect and the balance effect work together to produce strong liking for those who like and appreciate us.

It is not uncommon, of course, for a stimulus person to express his liking for a perceiver and not really mean it. If the perceiver becomes suspicious that he is being flattered or complimented for ulterior reasons he may actually dislike the stimulus person. Dickoff (1961) demonstrated experimentally that subjects highly complimented by a person who had an interest in obtaining a favor were not highly positive in their own subsequent evaluations. "Flattery will get you nowhere"—if you are too obvious about it. It is at least possible that the subjects who performed poorly in Deutsch and Solomon's (1959) experiment were lukewarm toward the anonymous person who presumably evaluated them highly because they suspected some ulterior motivation or at least were incredulous about the discrepant evaluation received.

A factor even more subtle than suspicion of flattery may complicate the relation between liking and being liked. Perhaps because being liked can serve as a sign of our own worth, it is important that the one who likes us is a discerning fellow—one who does not simply like everybody. It may also be that we especially like someone whose early reservations about us we have managed to overcome. Not only would this be proof of that someone's discernment (he obviously does not just like everybody because he did not like us at first) but there may be additional gratification at having achieved a victory over a stubborn opponent—at having really earned the affection of another through an increasing exposure of self. The obverse of this proposition may also be true: we may especially dislike someone who started out liking us but became cool upon further acquaintance.

These related propositions were tested in an experiment by Aronson and Linder (1965). In order to create a situation in which one person might plausibly receive evaluative feedback from another, these investigators arranged an elaborate deception wherein one female subject overheard another female subject, actually an experimental accomplice, making remarks about her to the experimenter. The subject heard these remarks while in an adjacent room, busy at the task of recording the number of plural nouns used by the accomplice in her remarks. This activity was in line with the cover story that presented the experiment to the subject as involving an attempt to increase the use of plural nouns through reinforcement from the experimenter. Between each of seven sets of remarks, the subject entered the accomplice's room and engaged her in conversation for three minutes. The subject believed that she was doing this to see whether the increased use of plural nouns would generalize to some one other than the reinforcer. Actually, of course, this periodic contact was a crucial feature of the experiment because it gave the accomplice a pretext for changing her mind and generally endowed the evaluative remarks with greater personal significance for the subject.

When the accomplice made her evaluative remarks about the subject she supposedly did not know that the subject was listening in the next room.

Thus there was no issue of deliberate flattery or open insult. There were four experimental conditions in the main study. As subjects listened to the accomplice's remarks about them, they learned that she (1) thought highly of them throughout the experiment (steady positive treatment), (2) started out rather negatively disposed but became increasingly favorable (gain treatment), (3) thought highly of them initially but became increasingly cool (loss treatment), or (4) remained cool throughout (steady negative treatment). After the experiment was over each subject was led to the office of a final interviewer who asked her several questions to assess her evaluation of the accomplice. The results, on a scale ranging from "dislike her extremely" (-10) to "like her extremely" ($+10$), are presented in Table 8.2.

Table 8.2. Means and Standard Deviations for Liking of the Confederate (Adapted from Aronson and Linder, 1965)

Condition	Mean [a]	SD
1. Steady positive	+6.42	1.42
2. Gain	+7.67	1.52
3. Loss	+0.87	3.32
4. Steady negative	+2.52	3.16

[a] Condition 2 mean is significantly greater than condition 1 mean ($p < .02$); condition 3 mean is not quite significantly smaller than condition 4 mean ($p < .15$).

From these results it may be seen that the subject likes the accomplice better when the latter begins with negative remarks and grows positive than when she is positive throughout the experiment. The accomplice is liked less in the loss than in the steady negative treatment, but this difference is not statistically significant. These results generally confirm the original predictions made by Aronson and Linder and suggest that there are many subtleties in the relationship between attraction and evidence of being liked. At least under the circumstances of their experiment, it is more important to gain esteem than to have had it all along.

Additional research will be needed to determine the precise mechanisms underlying this relationship, but Aronson and Linder propose that the accomplice in the gain treatment may be better liked because she first upsets the subject, raising her uncertainty level, and then reduces uncertainty. This is consistent with our own view of uncertainty as an unpleasant motive state (see Chapter Four) and is supported by the internal-analysis findings that subjects in the gain treatment who later reported being upset by the initial negative evaluation liked the accomplice more than those not upset. It is also possible, however, that the results reflect the subject's feeling in the gain treatment that she had *earned* the affection of a discerning person.

Attraction and Similarity

One of the cornerstones of Newcomb's position is that we are attracted to those who share our attitudes about things, including ourselves, as the foregoing discussion indicates. In examining similarity as a determinant of attraction, it is important to be precise in attempting to answer the question: similar with respect to what? Typically we associate with people who are roughly similar to us in social status and occupational category. Physicians, college professors, and corporation executives do not, as a rule, seek the company of storekeepers, truck drivers, and stevedores. For some, ethnic and religious factors create boundaries across which associations are rare, lacking in intimacy, or both. Within these sociologically defined "fields of eligibles," what kinds of similarity factors determine selective attraction and association?

There is fairly strong support for the hypothesis that people like others who have similar attitudes, values, and interests. Precker (1952) found that students in a small college tended to associate with other students having similar values. Newcomb (1961) observed that students in his resident housing group were most attracted to persons having similar attitudes toward others in the group and toward a range of other objects. A number of other studies summarized by Lindzey and Borgatta (1954) support the conclusion that mutual friends tend to have similar patterns of interest, value, and attitude.

It is less clear whether other kinds of personal characteristics also conform to the hypothesis that relates similarity and attraction. When we turn to more general characteristics such as traits and needs it is not at all evident that similarity predicts or accompanies interpersonal attraction. In fact, one student of the determinants of mate selection in young married couples has championed the importance of need complementarity as a basis for attraction (Winch, 1958). Though his procedures of data collection and analysis are open to criticism, Winch presents evidence that husbands who score high on a given need variable (e.g., *nurturance*, the need to give aid) tend to marry wives who score low on the same variable or wives who score high on a different but complementary variable (e.g., *succorance*, the need to receive aid). Although Bowerman and Day (1956) were unable to find evidence either for similarity or complementarity in their study of dating couples, Winch's argument is persuasive on common-sense grounds. Whereas it seems reasonable to assume that we like and enjoy others who share our beliefs and values, it also seems reasonable that compatible relationships can be formed when the needs of one person are satisfied by the behavior of the other, and vice versa.

An interesting study by Kerckhoff and Davis (1962) shows that similarity and complementarity may each play important roles at different stages of a relationship. Their subjects were "pinned" or "seriously attached" couples in a coeducational college. The couples were asked about their relationship at the beginning and end of a seven-month interval and classified as "staying the same" or "nearer to being a permanent couple." Subjects within each of these classes were further divided into long-term and short-term couples, the latter having gone together less than 18 months. The study found that similarity was a better predictor of progress toward permanency for the short-term couples, but complementarity was a better predictor for long-term couples. It may be, as they suggest, that "social status variables (class, religion, etc.) operate in the early stages, consensus on values somewhat later, and need complementarity still later" (p. 303).

Newcomb (1956) has acknowledged the argument for complementarity but regards the latter as a special case of similarity. Although an assertive and a receptive partner may be attracted to each other for reasons of their complementarity of needs, this attraction is probably dependent on the similarity of shared attitudes that one partner should be assertive and the other receptive. Such a contention may bring us close to circular reasoning. Perhaps the most reasonable perspective is one that acknowledges that similarities and differences may both be determinants of attraction as a function of several interrelated factors:

1. The stage of the relationship (as argued by Kerckhoff and Davis, 1962).

2. The particular attributes being considered. Whether we are working at the level of interest, attitudes, traits, or needs, some attributes simply require complementary attributes in others for their expression or satisfaction. A dominating person may gain some satisfaction from the knowledge that he is not the only dominator in the world, but he cannot fully express his need to dominate in interacting with other dominant people. Needs are more likely to contain this requirement for complementarity than attitudes, values, or interests. But even in the realm of values, someone with strong political or economic values will be more responsive to and attracted by complementary persons than will someone with strong esthetic values.

3. The degree of similarity involved. If it were possible for two persons ever to have identical values and be interested in precisely the same things, it is questionable whether such a pair would remain strongly attracted to each other. We would expect the relationship to wither on the vine of boredom, there being no point in conversation when the outcome is already inevitable. It is probably fair to surmise that people do not always hold out for carbon copies of themselves when choosing buddies, roommates, or spouses. On the other hand, complete dissimilarity of interest would strain

any relationship regardless of the circumstances. The joint planning of activities and even the maintenance of a direction of conversation would be difficult to achieve.

4. The relevance of similar versus different patterns of interests and needs depends on the nature of the relationship involved. The wealthy Englishman is perhaps more concerned with complementary qualities in his butler than with similarity of interests. When it comes to his companions at the Regency Club, that is a different matter. Extroverts may seek out other extroverts at cocktail parties, but avoid them as roommates. Marriage, of course, involves a wide variety of prospective interactions and calls on different sources of compatibility from those relevant to the relationship between a sailor and his date.

With reference to this last variable, one study by Jones and Daugherty (1959) set out to test the hypothesis that persons with a strong political orientation (interested in manipulating and influencing others) are attracted to similar persons in the abstract, but not when they have to interact with them on a competitive task. All subjects listened to a tape-recorded interview between the experimenter and two persons presented as fellow students. One of these persons expressed strong political values, the other expressed strong esthetic values. One group of subjects was told that this was a tape recording and that they would not meet either of the stimulus persons being interviewed. Another group was told that each person would engage in a subsequent discussion with the stimulus person of his choice. All subjects filled out a rating scale containing a number of positive and negative traits in an attempt to convey their first impression of each stimulus person. The strength of the perceiver's political orientation was made another variable in the experiment. This was measured by a questionnaire designed to tap the person's cynicism about the motives of others and his willingness to manipulate others to attain some personal goal.

When the ratings describing the political stimulus person were examined, those who anticipated competitive interaction with him were more negative in their evaluations if they themselves were strongly political than if they were low in political orientation. There was no relationship of either similarity or complementarity when the stimulus person was presented as a student whose interview had been tape recorded during a previous school year. Thus, when the perceiver anticipated interacting with the person he was asked to describe, certain qualities of that person were apparently made salient. As a result the anticipation of such an interaction increased the role of complementarity as a determinant of attraction. The point is not that the prospect of interaction always increases the importance of complementarity, but we may conclude that the particular requirements of the situation must be considered in order to predict attraction from the needs and values of the perceiver.

Attraction and Being Frustrated or Attacked

We like others who like us because, among other consequences of being liked, this increases the probability that they will help us attain our goals or at least not stand in our way. The obverse is no less true: we are inclined to dislike those who dislike us. People who dislike us may or may not obstruct our purposes and people who obstruct our purposes may or may not dislike us. We would expect, however, that those who obstruct or frustrate our actions are likely to arouse our hostility. This hostility may, and no doubt often does, color our impressions of the agent of frustration so that he is seen in a more negative light than otherwise. Let us consider some of the conditions that determine whether frustration results in a negative impression of the frustration agent.

As background for this consideration it is relevant to summarize a particular theoretical position that has strongly influenced research on responses to frustration. This position is contained in the *frustration-aggression* hypothesis that was first formulated by a group of Yale psychologists (Dollard, Doob, Miller, Mowrer, and Sears) in 1939. Though the main hypothesis and its offshoots are stated in rather "behavioristic" terms the underlying notion owes much to the psychoanalytic views of Freud. The Yale hypothesis, as modified by Miller in 1941, stated that "frustration produces instigations to some form of aggression." We shall loosely define as *frustrating* any condition that directly or indirectly prevents an organism from attaining a desired goal. An *aggressive response* is one that actually or potentially involves injury to some other organism. Such psychological injuries as disagreements, sarcasm, and negative appraisal would be included.

Overt aggression does not always follow frustration, but frustration always produces a tendency to aggress. As frustration persists, those responses that were initially more strongly instigated than aggression (if any) tend to drop out, increasing the probability that aggression will appear.

Though simple in its outlines, the theory of frustration and aggression contains a number of additional propositions that further specify the conditions under which aggression is most likely to occur and the most likely form and direction of expression it takes once the instigation to aggress becomes dominant over other frustration-produced instigations. To consider all of these conditions in turn would take us far afield from our current concern. Our primary interest is in those conditions that affect cognition of the agent of frustration (usually called the instigator) by the frustrated person. In pursuing this interest we shall consider some variables specifically mentioned by frustration-aggression theorists, and some additional ones as well.

Power Differentials and the Inhibition of Aggression

The frustration-aggression hypothesis implies that aggression will be more completely inhibited when the agent of frustration is powerful and capable of retaliation than when he is weak and impotent. Such differences in inhibition are built into social norms: it is certainly more permissible for a father to spank his child than for the child to hit his father. These norms are undoubtedly supported by recurrent personal experiences that lead each of us to realize that aggression against more powerful adversaries does not pay (Berkowitz, 1958).

In the investigation of this problem the differential power of the agent and recipient of frustration has typically been defined in terms of social status and authority. There is ample evidence that aggression is more likely to be expressed toward low-status than high-status instigators. This has been the consistent result of paper-and-pencil investigations in which frustrating situations are verbally presented to the subject and he is asked to give his most likely response. If identical frustrations are perpetrated by parents on one form of the test and siblings on the other, for example, the response of the subject tends to be much less aggressive on the parent items (Graham, Charwat, Honig, and Weltz, 1951; Cohen, 1955).

In a much more realistic experimental situation Thibaut and Riecken (1955a) exposed Air Force Reservists to a frustrating experience in which the frustrater (actually an accomplice of the experimenter) was introduced as a reservist from another unit. He was presented to the subjects as holding a military rank one notch higher or one notch lower than they held. After filling out preliminary rating and impression forms, a subject and the accomplice were assigned to adjacent rooms; the accomplice was to give the subject instructions, by telephone, concerning the placement of military positions on a large map. In doing this the accomplice was pompous, condescending, and self-contradictory. His behavior was carefully designed to instigate the subject to hostility. Although subject and accomplice were linked by telephonic communication, the accomplice did all the talking until a certain point when the subject was finally allowed to communicate his comments and criticisms. A clear result was that more hostility (as rated by independent judges) was addressed to the accomplice when he was low-status than when he was high-status. It seems reasonable to assume that such a finding is representative and that frustrations administered by high-status persons are not likely to elicit open aggression toward the frustrater.

But to speak of overt aggression really gets ahead of the story. We are concerned here with impression formation rather than communicative behavior itself. Considering the way first impressions are usually measured in psychological experiments, we may look upon the impression response as a form of indirect aggression. The subject is typically frustrated and antagonized by a stimulus person, but instead of or in addition to reacting to him the subject records an impression of the stimulus person that he transmits to the experimenter. Presumably, the subject expresses some of his hostility toward the stimulus person by evaluating him negatively, but the determinants of the negative evaluation may not be the same as the determinants of overt aggressive behavior addressed to the stimulus person.

There are several issues involved in considering this question. For one thing, inhibitions against the overt expression of aggression are likely to be stronger than inhibitions against expressing a negative evaluation on a questionnaire to be seen by a neutral person (the experimenter). This would mean that a person's impressions of a high-status frustrater would not necessarily differ from his impressions of a low-status frustrater, even though more aggression was openly expressed toward the low-status frustrater. This is essentially what happened in the Thibaut and Riecken (1955a) experiment, because there was no differential change in private evaluations of the high- versus low-status instigator. On the other hand, the person who is frustrated is likely to make some attempts to bring his feelings into line with his behavior. Except perhaps in cases of extreme power differential, we should expect a moderate relationship between a person's impression and his overt action. However, we have much to learn about the relations between overtly and indirectly expressed hostility.

A further complication involves the notion of *catharsis,* or the possibility that overt expression of aggressive feelings removes or reduces the hostile coloration of the feelings themselves. The authors of the frustration-aggression hypothesis formalized the role of catharsis when they stated: "The occurrence of any act of aggression is assumed to reduce the instigation to aggression" (Dollard et al., 1939, p. 50). Even these authors noted that catharsis would not be effective if the frustration persisted or if the aggressive outburst involved in catharsis led to additional instigation from the target person. If catharsis operates at all the opportunity for openly expressing hostility toward an instigator should actually *reduce* residual negative feelings toward him.

This possibility was investigated by Thibaut and Coules (1952) who exposed undergraduate subjects to a first-impression situation in which they were to exchange notes with another undergraduate. The second undergraduate had been preinstructed to send a particular series of notes about himself climaxed by a strong accusatory and attacking message. At this point half of the naive subjects were allowed to send one more message, half of them were interrupted. All subjects were asked to record their impressions of the other person both before and after the experiment.

The results showed that subjects in the former group communicated mostly aggressive remarks subsequent to the instigation. And, those subjects who were allowed to communicate their negative feelings showed *less* negative change in their impression ratings of the stimulus person. These results are consistent with the catharsis hypothesis, as overt expression of hostility apparently reduced residual hostility. However, the results may simply reflect an increase in hostility of those subjects not allowed further communications, because the interruptions by the experimenter may have represented additional frustration. Thibaut and Coules ran a variation of the initial experiment that pointed up the plausibility of the second explanation, although catharsis was not ruled out.

Pepitone and Reichling (1955) also found evidence consistent with the notion of catharsis—that is, an inverse relationship between overtly aggressive behavior and residual hostility as tapped by a rating scale. The subjects in their experiment met in pairs and were severely insulted by a graduate-student experimenter. The experimenter then departed and the subjects were left alone with a hidden microphone in the room. Their postfrustration conversation was classified in various categories of content including hostility directed toward the experimenter. Half of the subject-pairs had been previously led to believe they were high in mutual compatibility; the other pairs were told they had little in common and probably would not get along too well. The former pairs, designated as "high cohesive," showed a reliable tendency to be more aggressive toward the absent experimenter in their postfrustration conversation than the "low cohesive" pairs. On the other hand, in a subsequent questionnaire, the high cohesive subjects indicated a *more* favorable attitude toward the experimenter than did the low cohesive subjects, suggesting less residual hostility in the former group.

It is tempting to interpret this evidence as demonstrating catharsis, rather than merely being consistent with a catharsis hypothesis. However, this study again exemplifies the difficulties of ruling out alternative explanations for catharsislike phenomena. It is conceivable that subjects who expressed more hostility in their conversations suffered more guilt or anxiety as a consequence. The favorableness of their subsequent ratings may thus reflect the inhibition of residual hostility rather than its absence. This same explanation may be applied to a striking study by Feshbach (1955), which purportedly demonstrated the cathartic effects of aggressive fantasy on subsequent ratings of an insulting experimenter. Subjects who were insulted and then allowed to express their generalized hostility in stories told in response to pictures were later less hostile toward the experimenter than subjects who performed a neutral, nonfantasy task after being insulted. Feshbach provides some evidence that indicates that guilt aroused by the fantasy was not the primary determinant of this difference, but as Berkowitz (1958) noted, the guilt measures have not been validated.

Thus it is difficult to draw clear conclusions about the effects of catharsis in reducing residual hostility. Nevertheless, the fact that a number of studies present evidence consistent with the catharsis hypothesis suggests that opportunities for overt or fantasy aggression should be carefully controlled if we are interested in measuring the effect of frustration on a person's impression of the frustrater.

Another reason for such controls is that catharsis is not the only cause of discrepancies between direct aggression and subsequent expressions of residual hostility. Strictly speaking, catharsis refers to the purely expressive "draining" of something like a reservoir of frustration-produced hostility. Aggressive behavior may also serve an instrumental function in bringing about certain changes in the conditions of frustration. If aggression succeeds in modifying the behavior of the instigator, such as securing an apologetic promise that "it won't happen again," there should be much less residual hostility. This point was demonstrated in an experiment by Thibaut, Coules, and Robinson (described in Thibaut and Riecken, 1955a) in which psychology class sections were lectured by a guest who was patronizing and officious. In all sections the students were asked to write notes evaluating the guest lecturer, but the notes were handled in a different way in each section. In one section the lecturer received the notes, silently read them, and indicated that he would try to take the criticisms into account in the remainder of the lecture (hit-steer treatment); in another, the lecturer also read the notes but indicated that he would not let the suggestions govern his remaining remarks (hit-no-steer treatment); in a third, the notes were delivered to the regular lecturer who collected them "for research purposes" only (no-hit-no-steer treatment). As predicted, students in the first (hit-steer) treatment were less hostile than students in either of the other treatments in subsequent ratings of the guest lecturer. Their criticism was instrumental in modifying the lecturer's behavior and therefore there was less residual hostility.

Returning to the role of differential power in the facilitation or inhibition of hostility, we see that a final set of considerations involves the role of group support as a condition affecting response to frustration. Thus far we have considered an individual subject being frustrated by an agent either higher or lower than himself in social status. Presumably another determinant of the frustrated subject's response is the extent to which his relative power is increased by the feeling that others are on his side. The Pepitone and Reichling (1955) study was primarily concerned with this possibility. It will be recalled that those subjects who were led to believe in their similarity of backgrounds and mutual compatibility made more hostile remarks about their tormenter than subjects who were allegedly low in compatibility. It might be said that members of a united or cohesive pair subjectively feel more power in confronting the insulting graduate-student experimenter than do members of a less cohesive pair. Because the measure of hostility was based on a "private" conversation between the subjects the results can probably be more easily interpreted as reflecting the freedom from conversational restraints implied by Newcomb's autistic hostility hypothesis. That is, the subjects in the high cohesive pairs may have been no angrier than the low cohesive subjects, but simply felt greater freedom to express their irritation because of the intimacy produced by feelings of compatibility.

A more unequivocal interpretation may be placed on some results obtained by Strickland, Jones, and Smith (1960). In this experiment one member of a small group of subjects presented arguments either in favor of or opposed to big-time athletics to a stimulus person in another room. This person (actually a standard tape recording) always responded to these arguments and their originator in a rejecting and insulting manner. The major variable of the experiment was: half of the subjects were led to believe that the group approved of their arguments, the other half that the group disagreed with the arguments chosen although it was in favor of the position represented. The subject was finally asked to record his impression of the stimulus person on a form that would be shown only to the experimenter. The results showed that subjects who believed that the group supported their arguments were much more hostile in evaluating the stimulus person than those who believed that the group disagreed with their arguments. The interesting aspect of this general result is that not only does the feeling of support probably make a person more fearless in expressing his feelings, but the presence or absence of support actually affects the subject's cognitive impression of the stimulus person even though it will be transmitted only to a neutral party.

The Perceived Cause of Frustration

Frustration produces instigations to aggression that are most strongly aroused in relation to the perceived agent of frustration. There is simple logic in the feeling that "He's responsible therefore he's the one I'm mad at." The authors of the frustration-aggression hypothesis largely ignored those factors that determine the perception of responsibility, and yet a consideration of such determinants is crucial in understanding what acts are frustrating in the first place.

If we define frustration as the blocking of goal-directed activity, two persons can be equally frustrated, objectively, but be differentially instigated to hostility. Let us consider some possible reasons for differential instigation. One relevant factor seems to involve the actor's expectation at the moment of frustration. If he has strong expectations of success, of reaching the goal, then anyone who prevents this is likely to arouse more antagonism than one who blocks attainment of an unlikely goal. The role of expectancy has been noted by several writers (e.g., Zander, 1944; Pastore, 1952; Berkowitz, 1962), but the linkage of expectancy and acceptance of frustration presents a problem for the scientist who wishes to avoid circularity of definition. It is easy to say that frustrations that do not instigate hostility must have been more or less expected by the person frustrated.

A closely related fact that may actually be subsumed under expectancy is the *arbitrariness* of the frustration. Presumably, an arbitrary frustration is one that would not normally be expected under the circumstances. The behavior responsible for the frustration may or may not be seen as a legitimate response and one sanctioned by the culture. Thus children are likely to be much less disturbed when punished by a parent than by an adult neighbor. Soldiers are probably less frustrated when "chewed out" by a top sergeant than by an acting squad leader. If we knowingly violate a law we are less likely to be frustrated by the fine than if our violation was unwitting. Both Pastore (1952) and Cohen (1955) demonstrated the importance of arbitrariness as a determinant of hostility by presenting hypothetical situations of each type through a paper-and-pencil test. In both cases arbitrary frustration situations clearly led to more hostility than nonarbitrary situations.

An interesting study by Burnstein and Worchel (1962) examined the issue of arbitrariness against the background of frustration-aggression theory. These authors sought to determine whether the relative absence of aggression following nonarbitrary frustration was a function of lower instigation or greater inhibition. They reasoned that if the latter were the case they should observe a greater displacement of aggression after nonarbitrary than after arbitrary frustration. In their experiment three small groups of subjects were to discuss the case of a delinquent boy and to reach a unanimous conclusion, within a specified period of time, about what should be done with the youth. In each group one of the members was a prerehearsed accomplice of the experimenter. In a control, or *no frustration*, condition the accomplice merely played the role of an average member and did nothing to impede progress toward unanimity of decision. In the *arbitrary frustration* condition, the accomplice kept interrupting his fellow group members with such remarks as "I don't follow you" or "why did you say that?" until failure to reach agreement within the time limit was assured. In the *nonarbitrary frustration* condition, the accomplice also prevented agreement by his questions but he obviously wore a hearing aid and was having difficulty adjusting it. At the close of the experiment, the subjects were asked to evaluate the other members of the group, the experimenter, and themselves.

The results showed that there were no significant differences between the two frustration conditions in evaluation of the accomplice, although both groups liked him much less than in the no frustration condition. On another measure reflecting evaluation of the accomplice, a measure indicating whether the subjects wanted to work with him again, the arbitrary frustrater was more severely rejected than the nonarbitrary one. However, the most intriguing and theoretically relevant findings concern the subjects' evaluations of the experimenter and themselves. Presumably these evaluations should serve as measures of displacement and provide indices of the amount of inhibition of aggression. It turned out that the experimenter was rated as less competent, intelligent, likable, and so forth, in the *non*arbitrary than in the arbitrary condition. Similarly, the subject tended to blame himself and to berate his own contributions more in the former than in the latter condition. Although it is extremely difficult to draw firm conclusions from experiments in this area, Burnstein and Worchel's findings seem to give greater support to the notion of differential inhibition than to that of differential instigation. The more arbitrary the frustration, the more direct the expression of aggression.

The study also makes clear the likely connection between arbitrariness and perceived causality. Factors such as the perceived intent of the frustrater or his responsibility for producing the frustration seem to be basic determinants of the amount of aggression. Many students of frustration and aggression have noted that the subclass of frustrating events most likely to instigate hostility is attack or hostility itself. Frustrations that are a by-product of the legitimate pursuits of other persons may be taken in stride, but frustrations that involve an aggressive attack on the subject especially seem to call forth retaliatory aggression. It is true, of course, that a perceiver may occasionally consider a hostile attack on himself justified or legitimate. Children sometimes prefer a spanking or tongue-lashing to being ignored, and we all are sometimes aware that we have deserved someone's criticism. But when we perceive a deliberate intent to harm us our most natural reaction is hostility and, if the occasion presents itself, overt aggression.

We can, of course, attempt to flee from or avoid the attacker—perhaps spurred more by the emotion of fear than of hostility. However, to the extent that the attacker intends to hurt us as an end in itself, rather than as a by-product of other pursuits, hostility and counterattack are the natural reactions (cf. the discussion in Jones and Davis, 1965).

The perception of intent brings us back to the matter of inferring dispositions on the basis of the alternatives available to the actor. Even though A may be fully aware that B is attacking, belittling, or blaming him, the extent to which this arouses A's hostility depends on his perception of B's freedom in the situation. Consider the following situation in which B might verbally attack A: (1) B has instructions from his superiors to attack anyone who behaves as A has done; (2) B is required by the social codes to which both A and B adhere to punish people like A; (3) B is known to be maladjusted or neurotically ill and is lacking in voluntary control over his hostility. Each of these diverse cases has one thing in common: the instigator, B, does not have full responsibility for or control over his actions. For one reason or another he is a passive victim of situational requirements, compelling unconscious motives, or the absence of appropriate skills. To the extent that A perceives these requirements to be operating we may expect A's reaction to B to be less aggressive than otherwise.

There is some evidence that this is the case. Jones and deCharms (1957) planted an accomplice in problem-solving groups of five or six members. His behavior was standardized as much as possible; specifically, he had been instructed to fail a particular pattern of tasks. Half of the groups were set up so that each individual could win a reward for effective performance regardless of how well or poorly anyone else did (individual fate treatment). In the remaining groups rewards were administered on an all-or-none basis so that everyone had to do well for anyone to get the reward (common fate treatment). The experimental accomplice, by his poor performance, always prevented the group from attaining a reward in the common fate treatment and was the only one who did not obtain the reward in the individual fate treatment. It is hardly surprising that the subjects were more negative in their evaluations of the accomplice when he prevented their attainment of the reward, although his behavior was actually identical in both treatments.

An additional variable makes this experiment especially relevant for the current discussion. Half the subjects in each of the treatments were led to believe that the tasks on which the members were to work were *unrelated* to intelligence but highly related to motivation—the desire to do well. The remaining subjects were told that the tasks were discriminating measures of intellectual ability. As predicted, in the subgroup combining common fate and motivation instructions, the accomplice tended to be more negatively evaluated and to be seen as less dependable than in the other groups. The effect was not a powerful one and there were considerable differences between individual raters. Nevertheless it may be argued that the more negative evaluation of this crucial subgroup occurred because the accomplice was capable of doing better but did not. In other words, a person has more control over how hard he tries on a task than over his intelligence or basic competence to perform well. We may infer that the accomplice in the common fate–motivation treatment is seen as a more direct and responsible cause of the other subjects' frustrations or their failure to obtain the reward.

It is important to note that phenomenal causality is a two-edged sword whose effects are also important when goal attainment is facilitated instead of obstructed. It seems reasonable to predict that a stimulus person who is instrumental in improving our fortunes will be more favorably evaluated when he is perceived to help us as a matter of choice than when he is seen as helping us because he has no alternative. Thibaut and Riecken (1955b) verified this prediction in two related experiments. The basic design called for one naive subject and two experimental confederates. One confederate was initially presented as of higher status than the other; he was either a graduate student or a law student, whereas the low-status confederate was a freshman. The naive subject then attempted to get the other "subjects" to do something for him. In both experiments the confederates eventually complied to this influence attempt.

A subsequent exploration of the subjects' perceptions of the two confederates showed two major findings: (1) The high-status confederate was generally perceived to be more genuinely, spontaneously responsible for complying to influence, whereas the low-status confederate was seen as having little choice in the matter, as being pressured by the relatively superior power of the subject to comply with his request; the investigators speak of the former's behavior as "internally caused" and the latter's as "externally caused." (2) The subject's impressions of the two confederates were obtained before and after the successful influence attempt. Ratings of the high-status confederate either changed more in the positive direction (experiment 1) or less in the negative direction (experiment 2) than ratings of the low-status confederate. This differential favorability or acceptance was predicted; the high-status confederate was seen as complying even though he clearly had the capacity, by virtue of his superior status, not to. Thus we see that the actual locus of perceived causality, whether internal or external to the person, is an important determinant of evaluation in situations of frustration and facilitation.

Cognitive Balance, Attraction, and Evaluation

No discussion of the determinants of attraction would be complete without considering the relations between cognitions that are relevant to the perception of a particular stimulus person. We have emphasized that the arousal of positive or negative feelings about another is determined by the functional significance of that other in facilitating or blocking the perceiver's aims. Changes in evaluation may also reflect certain internal adjustments that are made to bring cognitions about objects and events into balance with one another.

As documented in Chapters Five and Six, the assumption is prevalent in contemporary social psychology that normal individuals try to avoid having incompatible, dissonant, or imbalanced cognitions; when imbalance is introduced there is accompanying strain until a new realignment of beliefs is achieved. The following discussion briefly examines certain consequences of this family of notions.

1. As a first case of cognitive imbalance, consider the coexistence of positive and negative information about a particular stimulus person. It is at least implied in Heider's theory that a certain amount of strain should be generated when a person has conflicting sentiments about the same "unit." But simply to hear about the existence of a person who has positive and negative attributes should not be a powerful producer of strain. Dissonance

theory suggests that the strain from imbalance would lead to cognitive work only *if* there were some anticipation of interaction with a stimulus person about whom both good and bad things are said. The predecision–postdecision framework should be applicable here. If the perceiver is in the position of choosing whether to interact with the stimulus person, both positive and negative characteristics are relevant. Once the individual has decided to interact or not to interact—has committed himself to approach or to avoid—we should find that some resolution of the ambivalence toward the stimulus person has occurred. Especially in the case of a commitment to approach there should be a tendency to suppress or distort negative information and resolve the ambivalence in the positive direction.

Some indirect evidence on this point comes from a study by Cohen (1961), who presented highly contradictory traits to undergraduate subjects in an impression-formation study. In the list, for example, were traits such as extremely generous, ruthless, very kind, overly conceited. Half of the subjects (transmission tuning condition) were told that they were to communicate with others about the stimulus person, the remaining half (reception tuning) were told that others would communicate with them about the stimulus person (cf. Zajonc, 1960). The results showed very clearly that subjects in the transmission tuning condition tended to organize their impressions around either the positive *or* the negative pole; subjects in the reception tuning condition were much more likely to attempt an integration of the disparate information into a single, complex impression. Perhaps it is not too farfetched to argue that the reception tuning condition features more aspects of the predecision phase ("more information to come, don't make up your mind") and the transmission tuning set is more postdecisional in character.

In a more directly relevant study by Darley and Berscheid (1967), college-student subjects were given information about two other persons and were convincingly told that they would interact with one of these persons at a subsequent session. The future partner was designated randomly by the experimenter, who then asked the subject to study available information and to evaluate both stimulus persons on a number of trait dimensions. The results showed that the subjects definitely were more positive in their evaluations of the future interaction partner. The investigators suggest that such positive feeling arises because the subject already sees herself in a "unit relationship" with the partner. Positive evaluation thus reflects cognitive work that results in balance between unit formation and sentiments (see Chapter Five for a discussion of Heider's terminology).

Mirels and Mills (1964) provide data that further refine the hypothesis that negative characteristics will be played down when interaction is anticipated, by further suggesting that the perceiver may compensate for his awareness of negative characteristics in a partner by attributing more positive qualities in other spheres. Female college-student subjects were led to believe that they were going to work with a partner on a problem-solving task and that the top teams would receive a gift certificate. The subjects then received personality questionnaires allegedly filled out by their partners-to-be or by nonpartners. The information conveyed on these questionnaires either suggested that the respondent was rather unpleasant or that she was neutral with respect to pleasantness. After examining the questionnaire assigned to them, the subjects were asked to rate the respondent on a variety of characteristics. Some of these characteristics provided a measure of perceived pleasantness, and some provided a measure of perceived competence (about which no differential information had been given to the subjects). As in the Darley and Berscheid study, the respondent was seen as more pleasant when she was a partner than when she was a nonpartner—*but*, this was only true in the condition in which the respondent's answers revealed her to be quite unpleasant. Mirels and Mills suggest that knowledge about the unpleasantness of a partner is dissonance-producing, and therefore the subjects in this condition tend to minimize the partner's unpleasantness. A second finding, also predicted from dissonance theory, was even more interesting. The unpleasant partner was seen as more "competent" than the neutral partner or the unpleasant nonpartner. Apparently the dissonance associated with the anticipation of working with an unpleasant partner can be relieved if the partner can be seen as competent.

Obviously further research is needed in this area, but each of the foregoing studies could be readily extended to test the proposition that ambivalence toward a stimulus person is resolved in a positive direction when there is commitment to future interaction with that person.

. . . . .

2. A second case of cognitive imbalance is that which may occur between person *A*'s feelings about person *B* and *A*'s perception of *B*'s feelings about him. Clear evidence has been presented that indicates a normal congruence between a person's choice of friends and the guess that they choose him. In the natural, everyday environment it is difficult to find instances of clear imbalance so that the effects of imbalance may be studied. However, it is possible to produce imbalance experimentally as in a study by Harvey, Kelley, and Shapiro (1957). In a classroom setting these investigators asked students to rate themselves on a number of important characteristics. At a second session each subject was asked to rate another person in class, in some cases a person who knew him and in other cases a person who did not know him. The subject was then shown ratings of himself that had presumably just been made by that other person but that in reality were fictitious. These ratings tended to be lower than his previous self-ratings by small or large amounts; that is, they were more negative than the subject's own self appraisal. The subject then rerated himself, rerated the per-

son whose ratings he had just seen, and completed a brief questionnaire concerning his feelings about the ratings and the other person. Finally, he was asked to recall how the other person had rated him. The subjects were thus exposed to impressions of themselves that were to varying degrees more negative than their own ratings. In some cases these impressions were made by a trustworthy source (a person who knew them well) and in other cases by a stranger.

The results may be summarized as follows: (1) There was a slight tendency toward devaluation of the self after receipt of the unfavorable ratings; (2) there was a more marked tendency toward devaluation of the rater, especially when he was a stranger, or an acquaintance who was not liked very much to start with; (3) the recall test showed that distorting the received ratings in a direction more favorable to the self was especially likely when the ratings were by acquaintances and did not depart too far from the self-ratings; (4) the subjects were more inclined to doubt that the ratings were actually made by the alleged sources when the raters were acquaintances and the raters extremely discrepant from self-ratings.

The results are complex but generally plausible. They indicate the variety of ways in which cognitive balance may be at least partially restored when the individual receives information discrepant from his established picture of himself. It is of further interest to note that subjects ether tend to devaluate the source or to distort his rating; they are not inclined to do both. Thus there is some evidence in this particular study that the ways of restoring cognitive balance in this situation may substitute for each other.

· · · · ·

3. A third case of cognitive imbalance concerns the relationship between attitudes toward different persons who in turn are related in some way. Thus if A likes B and knows that B likes C, these cognitions are out of balance with A's *dis*like for C. Imbalance would also exist if A liked both B and C but perceived that they disliked each other (Heider, 1946; see Chapter Five).

One way to study the effects of the tendency toward balance in cognition of social objects is to present subjects with hypothetical relationships exemplifying various conditions of balance and imbalance, asking them to record the degree to which such a relationship would be a pleasant one. In one such study, for example, Jordan (1953) found that subjects reported more unpleasantness (or "cognitive strain") when they imagined themselves in relationships that Heider would classify as imbalanced than in balanced relationships. Thus the hypothetical situation "I dislike person O, I like object X, O likes X" was not generally viewed as a pleasant relationship. Jordan also found that more strain was produced when the imbalance involved liking between persons than between persons and objects (Xs) and that either balanced or imbalanced relationships involving disliking were judged more unpleasant intrinsically than those predominantly involving liking.

Another strategy has been to present hypothetical relationships in which the lines of liking and disliking are only partly filled in. The subject's task is to complete the missing links of interpersonal affect. Morrissette (1958) adopted this experimental strategy in a study involving three- and four-person relationships. Although he was primarily interested in exploring predictions from the more complicated balanced model of Cartwright and Harary (1956), the general results were in line with Heider's general prediction. That is, the subjects filled in and specified the missing relationships in a way that tended to make their cognitions as balanced as possible (as defined by the model).

From Heider's (1946) and Cartwright and Harary's (1956) general considerations and the empirical support the preceding studies offer, it appears that a perceiver's evaluation of a stimulus person about whom he has little evidence may be clearly affected by his cognition of the attitudes of others toward that stimulus person. We like those whom we perceived to be liked by our friends and disliked by our enemies.

But all this is from the vantage point of a particular perceiver. He may achieve balance by distorting the actual direction and status of his friends' and enemies' attitudes. Is there any evidence that the pressures associated with the tendency toward cognitive balance actually operate in determining how people feel about each other? Is there a tendency for affective relations between group members to take a balanced rather than an unbalanced form, or is the balance tendency merely a phenomenon of internal cognitive structure?

A study by Kogan and Tagiuri (1958) has shed some light on this question by studying perceived and actual relationships in ongoing groups. Using as subjects the members of five groups of Navy enlisted men (12 to 22 persons in size), these investigators asked each group member to indicate the three crew members with whom they would like most to spend a 72-hour liberty. In addition, subjects were asked to identify the choices made by each of the other crew members. This was not an inconceivable task, for each crew had been working together for at least two months on board ship.

By cross-tabulating the responses for each group, Kogan and Tagiuri could see whether there was a tendency for three persons chosen by a particular person also to choose one another. When the number of such choices were compared to a chance baseline, the number of mutual choices within such trios departed significantly from chance in three out of the five groups and a similar trend was observed in the remaining two groups. In the four-person units studied, then, it could be predicted with some success that O, Q, and R would like each other simply because they were all liked by P.

On the cognitive or perceptual side the tendency toward balance was even more evident. In each of the subject groups (though in one not quite significantly) the perception of balanced relationships was greater than the actual degree of balance and, of course, much greater than the chance level. Thus, whereas interpersonal relations tend toward balanced states within well-defined groups, the degree of balance *perceived* is actually an accentuation of the degree of mutual choice that obtains.

Studies of this sort provide an interesting avenue into the dynamics of group behavior and we can expect to see many other explorations of cognitive and interpersonal balance in existing groups. The possibility of being able to predict the nature of unobserved from observed relationships is naturally an attractive one to the social scientist, and the possibilities of balance models in making such predictions are being vigorously pursued by many investigators.

• • • • •

4. A fourth case of cognitive imbalance is that in which we behave toward another in some way not in keeping with our feelings toward him. More precisely, the cognition associated with our overt behavior is dissonant or not in balance with the cognition associated with our private feelings about the person. It may be that we strongly dislike a person and yet have to interact with him on some cooperative job, as his neighbor, or as his subordinate. Or it may be that we like the person but feel obligated to criticize and be stern with him for his own good. To the extent that imbalance or dissonance is produced in such settings, we expect a tendency to make our cognitions more balanced. This can be most easily accomplished in the situations described by modifying our feelings to bring them more in line with our overt behavior.

Reasoning such as this led to an experiment by Davis and Jones (1960) in which subjects were requested (no-choice treatment) or coaxed (choice treatment) to deliver a negative, hostile evaluation to another subject who was presumably in the next room. Subjects in the no-choice treatment were merely presented this task as an unavoidable part of the experiment; those in the choice treatment were allowed to choose between a positive or a negative statement but in every case were gently persuaded by the experimenter to read a negative one. It was assumed on the basis of several previous studies that there would be more dissonance created in the choice treatment than in the no-choice treatment, in which it was possible for the subject to see himself as merely the temporary agent of the experimenter.

In this situation the greater the dissonance, the stronger should be the tendency to change a private evaluation in the negative direction to justify behavior. But this would not necessarily be the case if other means of dissonance reduction were available. To check on this possibility, half of the subjects in the choice and in the no-choice treatments were told that they would meet and be able to explain (and take back) their hostile behavior immediately following the experiment (anticipation condition). The remaining subjects were explicitly told that this would not be possible (nonanticipation condition). Because the anticipation of seeing and disabusing the person in the other room provided a clear prospect for dissonance reduction, less negative change in impression was predicted for the anticipation subjects. The results were clear-cut. Only in the combined condition of choice-nonanticipation treatments was there a decided change toward more negative evaluation of the stimulus person. In the other three conditions dissonance either was low to start with (no choice was allowed) or else there was an obvious alternative way of anticipating the reduction of dissonance.

Thus our impressions and evaluations of others may be influenced by our behavior toward them as well as the reverse being true. One of the most obvious ways of justifying our behavior to ourselves is to bring our other feelings and attitudes in line with it. The Davis and Jones study shows that this is particularly likely to happen when the individual feels he has had some choice in deciding on his overt behavior. A person does not feel pressured to justify behavior that someone else has imposed on him or that the situation seems to have required.

A more recent study by Glass (1964) supports the same conclusion, and shows in addition the importance of the subject-perceiver's self-esteem. Glass first induced high or low self-esteem in undergraduate males by providing them with a bogus report of psychological test results. Subjects in the high-esteem treatment were assured of their personal maturity, freedom from conflict, and so on; low-esteem subjects were informed that their poor "pattern of (test) responses" indicated a weak personality and a low degree of personal maturity. Each subject was then introduced to another "subject," was asked to make a first impression judgment of him, and was then induced to administer electric shocks to the other "subject" in the process of training the latter in a learning task. The other subject, an experimental accomplice, was not in fact shocked. As in the Davis and Jones experiment, some subjects were clearly given the choice of going ahead with the shocking procedure or backing out and others were simply instructed to proceed with the training. All subjects actually agreed to the shock procedure and were later asked to record their impressions (for the second time) of the person they had shocked.

Glass assumed that dissonance would be greatest in the high-self-esteem-choice condition. His reasoning was that the more highly a person thinks of himself, the greater the inconsistency in acting to injure an innocent person. Therefore in the high-esteem-choice condition we should expect to find evidence of dissonance reduction. An obvious way to reduce dissonance is to feel less friendly toward the accomplice after shocking him than beforehand. It is easier to justify hurting someone—if your high self-esteem and your role in *choosing* to hurt him make such justification important—when you have convinced yourself that the someone is not very attractive or likable anyway. The predictions were confirmed. There was a significant drop in attractiveness ratings after the shock-training session, but only in the high-self-esteem-choice condition.

SUMMARY AND CONCLUSIONS

The perception and evaluation of persons is a relatively new focus for experimental study in social psychology, but, as the present chapter demonstrates, the quantity of relevant studies is already substantial. And this is as it should be, for the perception of persons underlies and conditions most social psychological phenomena. If we wish to understand behavior in response to social stimuli it is obviously crucial to investigate the determinants of those cognitive processes by which such stimuli are comprehended by the actor.

In this chapter we have tried to select the most critical features of person perception for discussion. Perhaps the most pervasive emphasis of the entire chapter has been on the role of contextual factors in the interpretation of action. The significance of a given act must be viewed against the background of the setting to which it was a response. We have attempted to give the notion of context a more systematic meaning by stressing the importance of perceived choice (how many alternatives did the actor have?) and the perceived normative baseline (which action alternative is most likely to appeal to the average person?). This model was used to clarify the process of inferring stable dispositions from observed actions. Once the perceiver has decided that the actor is capable of performing a given action, and is aware of the consequences it will produce, then the clarity of attribution becomes a function of the number of alternative actions available and their equiprobability. The value of this model was most clearly demonstrated in a study involving the attribution to an essay-writer of a particular set of attitudes about Cuba's Castro. In this study attribution was seen to depend on the amount of choice involved in the (anti- or pro-Castro) behavior observed and whether or not the speech was in line with cultural expectations. In short, the degree of choice was seen to be important in determining the attribution of private attitudes when the observed behavior went against prevalent norms.

After having discussed some of the major factors conditioning inferences about dispositions from observed action, we turned to a discussion of how dispositions are inferred from each other. Clearly, if a perceiver has reason to believe that the stimulus person is "warm" rather than "cold," this affects his hunches about many other related attributes: generosity, friendliness, creativity, sense of humor, and so on. In discussing this problem of how impressions become organized we reached a number of tentative conclusions. It is clear that some assigned traits play a more important or central role than others in providing a focus for the organized impression. The problem of predicting which trait will be central, however, is difficult to resolve. The prediction of centrality depends on a detailed study of the full range of information provided (the "given traits") and the manner in which the resulting impression is measured (the "list traits"). At least one study has shown that considerable headway can be made in predicting how traits will combine in an impression, simply by combining the implications of the individual traits.

A full discussion of impression organization must obviously pay some attention to the problem of order effects and, more broadly speaking, the relations between initial and subsequent impressions. There is a fair amount of evidence supporting the importance of a "primacy effect" in first impressions, especially if the individual is asked to record his impression after receiving an initial communication about the stimulus person. However, the importance of such a primacy effect is probably obscured in natural interactions by the more important role of the perceiver's own behavior. In other words, his first impression causes the perceiver to behave in a certain way toward the stimulus person, which in turn elicits further information that may be compatible or incompatible with what is already known. One study has shown that the compatibility of subsequent information can be predicted from a knowledge of the interaction setting.

Any discussion of centrality in the organization of impressions eventually must acknowledge the crucial importance of evaluation in the person perception process. Whether the perceiver likes or dislikes the stimulus person is the single most important piece of information the psychologist can have if he wants to make detailed predictions about the attributes perceived. For this reason we turned next to a consideration of the major factors which determine social attraction. (1) It is clear that attraction begets attraction, that we like those who appear to feel positively about us. There is some evidence that we like those who perceive us as we perceive ourselves better than we like those who are indiscriminately positive, but this relationship is very much affected by the particular experimental setting. (2) Perceived similarity is also an important determinant of attraction, though here again there are many exceptions and qualifications that must be taken into account. It is necessary to know something about the nature of the characteristics being matched for similarity, the interaction setting, the stage of the relationship, the degree of similarity involved, and so on. (3) An obvious response to attack or frustration at the hands of another is to withdraw affection from that other. We discussed various mitigating and enhancing factors that affect the link between frustration and aggression, including the relative power of the attacker, the degree of choice he is perceived to have had, and the extent to which the attack was a by-product or an end in itself.

Finally, we have examined the implications of balance and dissonance theories for our understanding of attraction and its determinants. Here we found fairly good evidence in support of the following propositions: (1) especially if interaction is anticipated, the person will tend to smooth over conflicting information and ignore or play down the negative attributes of the stimulus person; (2) information will also be distorted to avoid the recognition that a person likes someone who does not like him; (3) balance theory enables us to predict that a person likes those who like the same people he likes; (4) if a person is induced to behave toward another in a way that conflicts with his private feelings about the other, there will be a tendency for him to change his private feelings to accord with his actions.

CHAPTER NINE

Social Comparison Processes

The present chapter is the first of several that deal with the modification of beliefs, attitudes, and verbal behavior as a direct consequence of social influence pressures. The distinction between information and effect dependence, already featured prominently in our treatment of socialization, will serve as a major organizing principle in the chapters to come. It is now fitting, therefore, that we reconsider and refine this distinction with particular emphasis on the use of information from others. How may this information be usefully classified, and how do various types of reference persons function as information sources?

A FURTHER CONSIDERATION OF INFORMATION AND EFFECT DEPENDENCE

The distinction we have made between information and effect dependence is by no means novel; similar distinctions have been proposed by Festinger (1950), Kelley (1952), Deutsch and Gerard (1955), and Thibaut and Strickland (1956). These formulations all recognize the dual nature of the person's dependence on others around him, that is, his dependence upon them for both outcomes and information. In order to appreciate fully the genesis of the present distinction we would like now to review the earlier formulations.

Festinger's Distinction: Group Locomotion and Social Reality

Festinger (1950) postulated that pressures toward uniformity exist in groups and are brought to bear on the individual group member in such a way that he will tend to conform to the opinions and behavior patterns of the other group members. In Chapter Ten we shall consider the way in which these pressures operate. For the moment we are concerned with what Festinger had to say about the sources of these pressures toward uniformity.

Group Locomotion

One basis for pressures toward uniformity derives from the assumption that a group has some goal or set of goals and that the actions of the individual members, separately or in concert, move the group toward or away from the group goal or goals. When it is necessary that the beliefs or behavior of the group members be changed in order for the group to "locomote" toward the goal, pressures toward uniformity will be exerted by members of the majority to bring deviant members into line. Since this frequently involves threats of rejection for obstinacy and implied approval for "going along," pressures based on the need for group locomotion are essentially pressures trading on effect dependence. In addition to the outcomes implicit in rejection and approval there are outcomes associated with successful goal attainment. Often the members of a minority position in a group would rather achieve the goal preferred by the majority than achieve no goal at all. This recognition may be an important factor in generating eventual uniformity within the group.

Social Reality

The other source of pressure is the need on the part of the person to establish the correctness of his beliefs, values, and attitudes. Let us imagine, Festinger says, a continuum along which any given belief or attitude may be said to lie and that this continuum reflects the physical evidential basis for the belief or attitude. At one extreme are beliefs whose evidential basis consists of the hard facts of incontrovertible physical reality. For example, if the person has observed that when a china dinner plate is dashed against a wall it will shatter, he will be confident in his belief that all such dinner plates so treated will suffer the same fate. This kind of evidence is directly given to the senses, and when a belief is so supported the person will be very secure in the belief. In the example given, he will attach a great deal of *subjective validity* to his belief about the fragility of china plates. It would be very difficult for someone to talk him out of that belief.

At the other end of the continuum indisputable facts are not available to support a given belief or attitude. Many of the beliefs we hold—probably the more important ones—lack a firm evidential basis and cannot easily be checked against physical reality. Beliefs about the nature of God, about ethical standards, about what would have happened if a particular event had or had not occurred, are some of the types of beliefs for which a physical check does not exist. We may, for example, hold a very strong belief as to what would have happened in the area of foreign affairs had John F. Kennedy not been assassinated. But there is obviously no way to check the correctness of such a belief; we can only speculate about it.

How does the person establish confidence in beliefs that are not supported by hard fact? There are two general bases for establishing the subjective validity of such beliefs: an autistic base and a social base. The former base, which Festinger does not consider and to which we will only briefly allude, derives from the possible contamination of beliefs by deep-seated and important values. Much of Chapter Seven was devoted to a study of the impact of values on cognitions about the nature of reality. It seems reasonable to propose that a person's confidence in the subjective validity of his beliefs will be strong to the extent that these beliefs justify important personal values. In much of perception this autistic base colors what is perceived.

Festinger's concern is with the social base for beliefs unsupported by hard fact, and not with autistic, intrapersonal supports. To the extent that other people around him share his belief, the person will attach validity to that belief. This holds for values as well. That is, to the extent that a given value is shared by others, the value will seem correct or proper. Festinger goes on to say that,

> Thus where the dependence upon physical reality is low, the dependence upon social reality is correspondingly high. An opinion, a belief, an attitude is "correct," "valid," and "proper" to the extent that it is anchored in a group of people with similar beliefs, opinions, and attitudes (1950, p. 272).

Values would be included since values, by our definition, are for most purposes equivalent to attitudes.

It is important to point out here that there are many beliefs that are based on support from a combination of physical, social, and personal sources. A shred of physical evidence may be twisted in such a way that it supports some personal, autistically based conviction or it may be incorporated in such a manner that it conforms to the dictates of social reality. For example, seeing a Negro lolling on a park bench in the afternoon sunshine when everyone else is at work may be taken as evidence to support an already established belief that Negroes are lazy and unwilling to work. But this particular Negro may work the night shift or be on vacation. Support for many strongly held beliefs is augmented in this way by substantiating the belief with poorly chosen or irrelevant instances of physical evidence. A final ingredient might be a selective sampling of the opinions of friends on the topic of Negro characteristics to establish how shiftless they "really are." Physical and social evidence may both be interpreted so as to give support to beliefs to which the person is strongly committed.

It is, of course, not necessary that all people everywhere agree with the person, but it is important that some relevant "reference group" share his beliefs or values. Once an individual has begun to utilize the beliefs or values of a particular group whose members provide points of reference, pressures are exerted on him to reduce any belief discrepancies. The subjective validity of a belief cannot be very high if the belief is not shared by relevant comparison persons.

In a later paper Festinger (1954) reformulated his theory about social comparison, considering primarily the processes set in motion by information dependence or the need for establishing social reality. He postulated that there is a basic drive in human beings to evaluate their opinions and abilities; he stated once again that when physical reality checks are not available in making these evaluations the person will use others as points of reference.

Our own position is that the self-evaluative drive postulated by Festinger as a given, innate characteristic of the person can better be seen as a derivative of the requirements of action. Because a person usually has various courses of action open to him, and because he wants to maximize his outcomes, he seeks to know the requirements, advantages, and pitfalls of each possibility. It is in this search for knowledge that his opinions are formed through referral to the most reliable sources of information available to him.

This formulation of the social reality base for beliefs and values implies that there will be information dependence on others. Festinger's formulation of the way in which others are utilized as information sources was incomplete, as we shall see, but it provided the foundation on which subsequent, more refined formulations were developed.

Kelley's Normative and Comparison Functions

In a paper written shortly after Festinger's original formulation, Kelley (1952) made explicit a dual function of reference groups. According to Festinger, the response of group members to uniformity pressures was the same regardless of the *source* of these pressures and differed only as a function of their magnitude. Implied in Kelley's distinction, however, was the possibility that the processes of reference-group comparison based on information dependence are different from those based on effect dependence.

In examining the literature on reference groups Kelley found that the concept of reference groups had been used to describe two different kinds of relationships between the individual and some group or class of persons. The first usage referred to situations in which the person wanted either to maintain or to improve his status in a group, and therefore sought the acceptance of group members. By virtue of the rewards and/or punishments that the other group members are able to mete out the person becomes susceptible to their influence and is motivated to avoid disagreement with their expressed beliefs and attitudes. The assumption here is that if he disagrees with them they will either punish him or withhold rewards. If he is attempting to gain acceptance in the group, holding a deviant opinion about matters that are important to the group members may automatically preclude his being accepted. If he is already a member of the group, holding a deviant opinion may have a detrimental effect on his status within the group and may even result in his being dropped from membership.

Kelley gives as an example of this usage of the reference-group concept, Merton and Kitt's (1950) interpretation of a study conducted during World War II by the Research Branch, Information and Education Division of the War Department. Three groups of soldiers were interviewed: a group of men who had not as yet been in combat and who were in units composed entirely of men like themselves; a group who had not as yet been in combat but who had been assigned as replacements in combat units that had been temporarily pulled out of the front lines; and combat veterans themselves in the latter units. Combat veterans typically do not glamorize combat. On the contrary, their attitudes toward combat tend to be very negative and, as a consequence, they usually express very little eagerness to get back into the front lines. The data from the three different populations of soldiers indicated that whereas 45 percent of the recruits in unseasoned units were ready to get into an actual battle zone, only 15 percent of the combat veterans felt ready. The recruits assigned as replacements to seasoned units fell between these two figures, with 28 percent expressing eagerness to get into battle.

Using the 45 percent figure for recruits in unseasoned units as a baseline, Merton and Kitt interpret the intermediate 28 percent figure for the recruits in seasoned units as indicating that

> The replacements, seeking affiliation with the authoritative and prestigeful stratum of veterans, will move from the civilianlike values toward the more tough-minded values of the veterans . . . For replacements, the assumed function of assimilating the values of the veterans is to find more ready acceptance by the higher status group, in a setting where the subordinate group of replacements does not have independent claims to legitimate prestige (p. 76).

Kelley's second usage of the concept of reference group closely resembles Festinger's social reality concept. In this usage the person attempts to evaluate a belief or attitude that may be about some aspect of his external world or about himself. Kelley uses examples taken from Hyman (1942) on the psychology of status. The group functions as a bench mark or standard against which the person makes some judgment. Thus if a person is asked how poor he thinks he is his answer will depend on the comparison group he is using to estimate degree of poverty. A pretty girl who is applying for a job as a model will evaluate her appearance in comparison with other models rather than waitresses in the agency lunchroom. In spite of actually being very pretty, she may think of herself as very ordinary-looking because of the standard of comparison she has chosen.

On the basis of the two ways in which the reference-group concept had been used, Kelley distinguished two functions that reference groups can play in the determination of a person's attitudes. The first of these functions is the setting and enforcing of standards for the person. Because such standards are generally referred to as group norms, Kelley denoted this as the *normative function* of reference groups. A group can exercise this function only when members are in a position to reward or punish the person for adhering to or not adhering to the norms of the group. The group functions as a normative reference for a person "to the extent that its evaluations of him are based upon the degree of his conformity to certain standards of behavior or attitude and to the extent that the delivery of rewards or punishments is conditional upon these evaluations" (Kelley, 1952, p. 413). A point that must be emphasized here is that under this normative pressure propriety or correctness is not defined by the person in terms of any evidential basis for a belief or attitude. He may feel perfectly confident about the correctness of a belief that disagrees with group norms, but if the group members become aware of the discrepancy between their beliefs and his the person's status will be in jeopardy. He will be under pressure to behave, *at least overtly,* in a manner that is "pleasing" to the other group members.

The second function distinguished by Kelley is the informational one in which the person uses the beliefs or attitudes of the group members as a standard of comparison against which to evaluate the correctness of his own beliefs or attitudes. This *comparison function*—and this is the crucial point—considers the act of reference as an end in itself, whereas the normative function involves referral as a means to an end, that is, as a tactic for gaining acceptance. It is also apparent that there are two notions of correctness here; under normative pressure the person behaves in a manner that the group deems correct, whereas when he compares a belief with the beliefs of others he is seeking to establish a feeling of correctness regarding the belief itself.

Deutsch and Gerard's Normative and Informational Social Influence

By now it must have occurred to the reader that the normative and informational functions of a reference group are in many cases inextricably entwined with one another and occur simultaneously within the same group setting. The other members of a group may punish a person for holding a discrepant belief because the fact of his holding that belief may shake their confidence regarding the correctness of their own belief. They may dole out rewards to him in order that he conform to their beliefs and hence remove the threatening discrepancy. Thus if person A is in a position to reward person B for changing his belief to agree with A, and B publicly affirms to A that he has changed his belief, A may then increase the subjective validity with which he holds *his* belief. Here we see both the normative and informational functions operating simultaneously. A's motive was informational and B's motive was to gain acceptance. In reviewing the research literature it became clear to Deutsch and Gerard (1955) that in most experiments on social influence these two processes are confounded; that is, they are both occurring in the same experimental session. After pointing this out they designed an experimental situation, which will be described in detail in Chapter Ten, in which the effects of each process could be separately evaluated. Whereas Kelley derived the normative and informational distinction from an analysis of the nonexperimental literature on reference groups, Deutsch and Gerard derived essentially the same distinction from considering psychological experiments on social influence.

Thibaut and Strickland's Group Set and Task Set

A highly similar distinction was made by Thibaut and Strickland (1956) with the concepts of *group set* and *task set*. These are regarded as two orientations that the person can take in evaluating the beliefs and attitudes that are communicated to him by others.

> The person's set depends on his orientation toward the communicating individuals. In a group set, the person is concerned with achieving or maintaining membership with the individuals whose attitudes are being communicated to him. When the person is threatened with loss of membership, when he is motivated to gain membership, when the group informs him that "integrative" behavior is necessary for group effectiveness or survival, he may be expected to adopt a group set (Thibaut and Strickland, 1956, p. 115).

The last reference to "integrative" behavior harks back to Festinger's "group locomotion." Thibaut and Strickland go on to say that

> ... in a task set, the person is disposed to view the other individuals in the group as "mediators of fact." The person utilizes the other individuals as perceptual or judgmental instruments or surrogates for his own perceptual equipment. In responding to the perceptions and attitudes of others, the person is concerned, not with achieving or maintaining a social relationship, but with achieving or maintaining cognitive clarity about his environment (pp. 115–116).

THE ACTION SEQUENCE AND UTILIZING INFORMATION FROM OTHERS

It is now appropriate to relate the notion of information dependence to the course of decision and action. In Chapter Six the characterization of the "action sequence" was basically similar to Lewin's (1935) portrayal of the person locomoting within his life space. We would now like to examine the action sequence in a little more detail, starting with a brief review of the discussion in Chapter Six.

Lewin depicted the external regions of the life space as consisting of activities and the internal regions as consisting of needs. He used activity in a very general sense to refer to any kind of behavior engaged in by the person. Certain activities are consummatory whereas other activities are instrumental. That is, the person may have to pass through a number of activity regions in order to engage in some positively valued consummatory activity. The term "goal" referred to activity regions with positive consummatory value. Naturally the person attempts to avoid activity regions that have negative value. Behavior, for Lewin, involved action in which the person moves or locomotes through various activity regions in order to end up in one in which activity is intrinsically satisfying. Whether an activity is satisfying depends on the inner state of the person—whether certain needs fulfilled by the activity are salient at the moment.

In order to move from one activity region to another certain abilities are required. Lewin did not make much of the ability aspect of action, but did at one point (1936) discuss the motoric regions of the person that are roughly equivalent to his ability repertory. He did not develop the idea to any extent, nor did he attempt systematically to tie it into his characterization of action. Lewin depicted illustrative action sequences in diagrams. A typical diagram is shown in the upper half of Figure 9.1. The person is represented by an encircled P and is shown in his present activity region, which is the leftmost one in the figure. The desired end-state, temporary as it may be, is depicted in the rightmost region and contains a plus to note its need-satisfying potential as perceived by the person at the time. The large central region could be any activity or set of activities the person perceives that he must engage in to move from where he is to where he wants to be. For example, the diagram might refer to a person who wants to read a particular book but does not as yet have the book in hand. His present activity region could be described as a state of not having the book, the desired activity region, the goal, as a state of reading the book, and the various activities involved in going to the library to sign the book out could be represented as the large intermediate region.

Using a terminology more useful for our present purposes, the person's situation may be diagrammed as in the lower half of Figure 9.1. He is in a present state, S_0, that has associated with it some outcome level, OL_0, that he is currently experiencing; he perceives that some act or set of acts, $R_1, R_2, \ldots$, will lead to some new state, S_1, with an

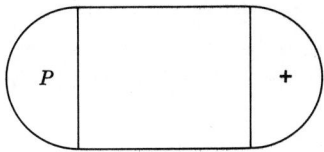

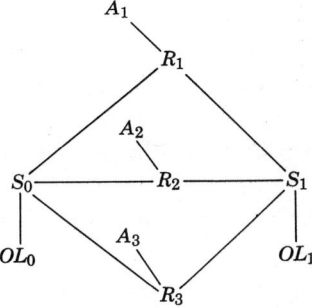

Figure 9.1. Representations of action. The top diagram is typical of those used by Lewin. The bottom diagram is a schematic picture of our "action sequence."

associated outcome level, OL_1. Each R may itself represent a sequence of responses. The outcome level being experienced by the person in S_0 or anticipated in S_1 will be determined by the various *values* fulfilled by being in those states. Certain abilities, $A_1, A_2, \ldots$, are shown as being associated with the acts that are contemplated. Thus the person must know how to use the library in order to get the book he wants; he must be able to walk up the library steps or get there by some other means; he must be able to speak a language the library clerk understands; he must be able to fill out the necessary forms; and so on. Each of the subactivities involved in finally getting the book has associated with it some requisite skill or skills.

The person may realize that alternative courses of action probably lead to the same end state. Thus if he has a secretary he can ask her to charge the book out for him; or he may have some special arrangement with the library so that all he has to do is pick up the telephone and ask that the book be sent over. In any case each alternative course of action requires different skills, different amounts of energy, different risks of incidental embarrassment, or different subjective probabilities of success or failure. The situation is often further complicated by other states the person anticipates finding himself in as a result of pursuing the desired state of having the book. He may anticipate meeting someone he knows on the way to the library and this may be a pleasant, neutral, or unpleasant prospect.

What we have been describing is a schematic model of the action sequence highlighting the more essential features. But what about beliefs and values, the concepts on which much of our earlier discussion was based? They are both an integral part of any act. We have depicted the action sequence as it is perceived by the actor. He has beliefs about the various acts available to him and beliefs about the consequences of these acts—what sorts of desirable or undesirable state they will lead to. He also has beliefs about the amount of ability he possesses to perform these acts. He further has beliefs about the outcomes to be expected from achieving certain states; that is, whether these states will really fulfill the values he holds. The outcome level or anticipated outcome level associated with any state of the world will determine the value the person places on that state.

The major difference between our conception and Lewin's is the important role that knowledge plays in the assessment of a given course of action. It is this knowledge that the person seeks when he is uncertain about one or more aspects of a given action sequence and it is here that he will often rely on other persons as information sources.

TYPES OF REFERENCE PERSONS

What factors determine to whom the person will refer for information? This is a problem that has been only vaguely considered in the literature. For example, Festinger (1950) notes the difficulty of independently defining which groups are and which groups are not appropriate reference groups for a particular individual, and for a particular opinion or attitude. It is often the case that the person refers to others to whom he has referred in the past, but this observation contributes little to theoretical understanding. Perhaps we can make a start toward such a contribution by casting the problem of referral within the context of our action sequence. Conceiving of the problem in these terms, the most important and obvious point is that the individual's choice of a reference person (or group) will be determined by the aspect of the action sequence about which he is unclear, that is, the amount of ability required, how satisfying the new state will be, and so on. He will turn to someone or some group that he believes can serve as suitable referent for the particular kind of unclarity he is experiencing. Let us now consider some of the characteristics of these reference persons and the kinds of referral that are possible.

The Expert

One type of reference person is someone with superior knowledge about some aspect of the action sequence. For example, if there is a question regarding the ability required to move from one state to another, the person may turn to someone who has successfully navigated such a move himself and knows something about the difficulties involved. He may seek out someone noted for his special background or his astuteness in evaluating the abilities of others. In short, he may turn to an expert to remedy the unclarity he perceives. An expert is someone who can inform the person how best to move from his present state (S_0) to the state he wants to enter (S_1). He is able to clarify for the person the likelihood that particular sequences of acts will lead to the desired state. Depending on the action sequence being considered, the expert might be a golf pro, an economist, a marriage counsellor, or just an acquaintance with some special knowledge of the requirements for the action being considered.

The Co-oriented Peer

The decision to act, as we have already indicated, is itself based on an estimate by the person that his present outcome level can be improved, that other available outcome levels might be better than the one currently being experienced. When he relies on others in making *this* estimate he ordinarily refers to someone he believes has an outlook and values that are similar to his own, a *co-oriented peer*. Presumably the co-oriented peer has experienced or will be experiencing similar rewards and frustrations in transaction with the state of the world confronting the person, as well as the state of the world the person might envision for himself. Thus, in "measuring" his present outcome level, or anticipating a future level, such peers will be the most likely candidates for referral. A member of the Ku Klux Klan will evaluate his particular satisfaction or dissatisfaction about the way Negroes in his home town are behaving with other Klan members rather than with a Northern liberal. Furthermore, in attempting to change what may be happening in his home town, he will estimate the desirability of some new state of affairs by referring to what fellow Klansmen think about it. A student, in deciding what college to go to, may refer to an expert—his guidance counsellor or someone who is already practicing the profession to which he aspires. The same student may also attend carefully to comments by co-oriented peers to determine what attributes of a college he should weight most heavily in making his decision. His peers may convince him that prospects for dating and fraternity life are important matters in choosing a college.

Co-oriented peers may help an individual decide what states he likes and whether a particular outcome will be enjoyable. They may, in other words, influence a person's values through direct and indirect communication. Peers may also be used as reference points to determine current level of satisfaction. The amount of deprivation a person may feel at any moment is often influenced by what he perceives to be the outcome status of others like himself. Merton and Kitt (1950) demonstrate this point with data on the degree to which certain groups of enlisted men felt deprived during World War II. For example, they found that married soldiers felt more deprived as a result of being in the Army than did single soldiers, presumably because they compared their outcome levels with those available to other married men, whereas single soldiers compared themselves with other single men. Because nearly all able-bodied single men were in the Army, single soldiers did not feel deprived relative to their co-oriented peer group. Married soldiers, on the other hand, knew a large proportion of their peers had evaded the draft and were enjoying the comforts of civilian life. They therefore felt deprived.

Expertise and co-orientation have certain similarities and certain differences. The similarity between the co-orientee and the expert is that each augments the ability of the referring person to judge some aspect of the situation. The difference is that the expert does so because of a perspective superior to the person's own perspective, whereas the co-orientee's augmentation stems from being able to provide a check on the person's own estimate of situations by virtue of attributed similarity of value perspective.

Having made the theoretical distinction between co-orientation and expertise, we must readily acknowledge that a single individual may at times act in both capacities. He may have the same outcome perspective as the person himself and he may also have a great deal of experience and expertise in attaining these outcomes. Under certain circumstances the parent may assume this dual role toward the child—for example, in teaching him to hunt and fish; under other circumstances the generational difference between parent and child renders the parent "square" and he cannot function as a co-orientee. The parent may not understand why a child is transfixed by rock-and-roll music, and the child, knowing this, would be unlikely to refer to the parent in other matters of musical taste. Hitler's great appeal to the German people rested on his assuming both functions. He was able to personify the "typical" German's outlook and demonstrate expertise in achieving the outcomes associated with that outlook.

To recapitulate, then, the co-oriented peer, by virtue of his similarity of value perspective, functions as the reference person for evaluating the goodness or badness of the person's present state, S_0, or the state or states, S_1, S_2, . . . , to which he may aspire. The expert, on the other hand, functions as a reference person in informing the person as to how he may move from one state of the world to another. He sheds light on the skills likely to be required, the costs of action, possible dangers and side effects, or other matters on which goal attainment may be contingent.

THE PROCESSES OF ACQUIRING AND UTILIZING INFORMATION

In Chapter Four we briefly described several processes whereby information provided by others is acquired: instruction, advice, social comparison, observational learning, and empathic cognizance. Information about the aspects of action may be acquired by one or another of these processes. The person typically seeks instruction from an expert and advice as to the value of trying to reach a new state of the world from a co-oriented peer. He may improve his ability to attain a desired end state from observing the performance of someone with proved ability. The child may, through empathic cognizance, learn to anticipate the moves of others so he will be better able to coordinate his actions with theirs.

Information acquired from others is not necessarily used immediately. A particular ability may be exercised for the first time long after it is acquired. For example, a person may have learned a foreign language in school but may not be called upon to use it until he one day visits some foreign country. He may have acquired some beliefs about Negroes without ever having known a Negro and then years later may be thrust into a situation in which he is forced to interact with one. As we pointed out in Chapter Three, behavior tendencies acquired by the child through empathic cognizance may not finally be invoked until the child has become an adult, though it is assumed that covert practice goes on during the intervening period.

All of these processes of information acquisition prepare the person for action; that is, to evaluate where he is and where he would like to be and how to accomplish the change.

Social Comparison

We now single out one of these processes of information acquisition, the one that has been a major focus of attention in social psychology. Social comparison can in turn be analyzed into two basic and different processes, *comparative appraisal* and *reflected appraisal*. In the former the person determines his *standing* on some attribute, whereas in the latter process he derives an *impression* of his position on some attribute through the behavior of another person toward him. Let us examine the two processes in some detail.

Impression and Reflected Appraisal

The person often receives evaluations from others of his ability to perform a given action, of the correctness of his beliefs or opinions, or the appropriateness of the values he has attributed to situations. He may directly solicit the evaluation by asking for it or he may discover the other person's impression by interpreting the other's behavior toward him. Often such information is conveyed unintentionally and not as part of the manifest content of interaction. We use the term impression to refer to an estimate about our own worth or ability inferred from the words and gestures of another person.

Reflected appraisal contains a peculiar combination of information and effect dependence because typically the person is very likely to be more sensitive to the judgments of someone on whom he is effect dependent. Thus a boss's estimate of his employee's ability, conveyed either through a subtle hint or by direct confrontation, may well affect the employee's self-ability estimate to a greater extent than an estimate given by someone of lesser rank.

The person may arrange the situation to improve his chances of obtaining the information necessary to infer an evaluation of himself. In the example given above a subordinate may want to know how his boss evaluates his work but may dread the immediate consequences of a possible negative evaluation in answer to a direct question. Instead he may contrive a situation in which, by his boss's behavior toward him, he can infer the evaluation. At lunch he may affect a casual air in a comment about some aspect of a new procedure he would like to introduce and estimate his boss's evaluation of him by the response to his comment. Alternatively, he may contrive to have a fellow subordinate, whom he knows to be held in high regard by his boss, join them at lunch. During the conversation our main character may compare the boss's responses to him and to his fellow subordinate to extract clues about the boss's impression of him.

We should emphasize here that the person has a dual orientation in a situation of this kind. He wants to see himself honestly, as others really see him, but he also wants to see himself in the best possible light; most people would like to think that they are worthy. The tension that exists between these two orientations, to receive an honest versus a favorable impression, determines many features of comparison behavior. The person tends to see himself through rose-colored glasses but he nevertheless must come to terms with evaluations that are patently discrepant from the image he has of himself. Experiments by Deutsch and Solomon (1959) and Harvey, Kelley, and Shapiro (1957), described in Chapter Eight, show some of the ways in which these discrepancies are managed.

Some evaluations are sought by the person; others are unsolicited. As we saw in Chapter Three, a child comes to evaluate himself from the way in which his parents respond to him. This sensitivity to the other's responses, from which the person infers his stimulus value to the other, extends beyond the nursery and the immediate family circle into the world at large, where the person continually receives evaluative information in encounters with others. Much of this information is in the form of ability estimates. It is conveyed in encounters ranging from order of choice in a pick-up baseball game, through the number of valentines received, to the results of class elections.

As we pointed out in Chapter Five, embarrassment is often a sequel to a statement made by another in which the person infers an evaluation of himself that is at odds with the evaluation he had assumed the other person had of him. The person is confronted with the choice of changing his self-image (a drastic solution), assigning some special and innocuous interpretation to the evaluation, or deciding that the evaluator is unreliable or in a grouchy mood. Some people make complicated inferences about how they are regarded from some remark to which the other person may have attached little evaluative import; others are remarkably insensitive to all but the most fulsome praise or the most devastating insult.

This process of inferring evaluations about oneself from the behavior of others was referred to by the American sociologist Charles Horton Cooley by the apt phrase "the looking-glass self." Cooley (1902) emphasized the human tendency to imagine how we are perceived by others, and the further tendency to let our self-feeling be determined by this attributed perception. Thus we see ourselves reflected in the mirror that others hold up to us and we are pleased or displeased depending on the appearance of this reflection.

Since Cooley's time the point has often been repeated that the person's self-concept reflects the reactions of others to him. It is additionally assumed by most psychologists and sociologists that the early encounters of the growing child are primary determinants of his basic self-esteem and lay the groundwork for evaluating the significance of later encounters. In recent years an increasing amount of research has attempted to explore the reactions of subjects to the receipt of standard evaluative comments by others (see Chapter Eight, pages 283–287). Even more recently experimentation has begun on the determinants and consequences of various modes of self-presentation. The encounters that give rise to reflected appraisal are complicated, for the individual must evaluate the impression he creates in terms of the representativeness of his own behavior. If he has gone out of his way to elicit a positive appraisal the appraisal may not be very informative concerning how he strikes others over longer time periods or in off-guard moments. Some of the issues involved in the relations between self-presentation and reflected appraisal are discussed in Chapter Fourteen.

Reflected appraisal usually occurs with reference to self-ability estimates, and we are using ability in a very broad sense to refer to the potentialities for action given certain environmental circumstances. Our use of the term ability is broad enough to cover most aspects of personality. Each of us is judged by others in terms of our potentialities for interacting with them. Their behavior toward us will be conditioned by their perceptions of us in relation to their own beliefs and attitudes. The problem facing the individual who wants to make use of reflected appraisal data on himself is that of separating the impression he commonly creates from the impression he creates in an idiosyncratic or biased observer. But each impression a person makes has its own validity in the particular circumstances as long as these circumstances are properly weighted. In each social relationship we are treated as a different person because each other person we interact with has different reasons for interacting with us. We are treated as father, husband, student, friend, employee, employer, date, tennis opponent; and in each of these relationships we take on certain attributes that are peculiar to it; our stimulus value varies from setting to setting.

Comparative Appraisal

A person can also acquire information regarding a particular aspect of himself by comparing himself with other people. Modeling behavior or imitation shade into this kind of information but the intent is different. In imitation a person attempts to master a situation by copying relevant features of someone else's behavior. In the process of comparative appraisal he is trying to estimate where he stands on some attribute *relative* to other people.

Comparative appraisal is similar to reflected appraisal in that the person's evaluation is anchored in the social reality of information provided by others. In reflected appraisal the evaluation is mediated by the behavior of the other toward the person himself, whereas in comparative appraisal the person evaluates an aspect of himself by determining his relative standing without any reference to the other's behavior *toward him*. Thus comparative appraisal has another element in common with imitation, for in both the other person, the referent, need not be aware of his being used as a reference person. Reflected appraisal and direct instruction have in common the fact that some form of confrontation is required.

By far the greatest proportion of laboratory research on the utilization of information from others has been done on comparative appraisal. Most of Chapter Ten will be devoted to a review of that work. As a curtain raiser on its contents, let us briefly consider the types of evaluations that have been used as a focus for research on comparative appraisal. In so doing we will be able to illustrate further the nature of the process.

In principle, comparative appraisal may occur with respect to any attribute that is elicitable as overt behavior. A person's observable behavior can act as a point of reference for someone else. Four general classes of attributes to which observable behavior can be coordinated are beliefs, abilities, attitudes, and emotions. We recall that attitudes are derived values and we use the term emotion here to refer to a strong attitude. All four of these attributes have been the focus of research on comparative appraisal.

Belief

In Chapter Five we defined a belief as a propositional relationship between cognitions. This would include such things as an estimate of the distance from one side of a chasm to the other, an estimate as to the amount of ability required to swim the English Channel, an estimate as to whether a particular presidential candidate will carry the deep South, or an estimate of whether the ancient man-like inhabitants of the Olduvai Gorge in East Africa had a spoken language. Beliefs in themselves are not evaluational but consist of cognitions or combinations of cognitions that may have motivational relevance when considered within a given action context.

Let us suppose that several companions are on a winter camping trip and come upon a frozen stream that blocks their route. The most direct way of crossing the stream would be to walk across its frozen surface but the question is whether it will hold the heaviest member of the party. A belief about the solidity of the surface must be formed as a prerequisite to action. If the belief formed is that the ice is thick enough, the crossing will be attempted without further ado, whereas if the belief turns out to be that the ice will give way, then the party must find another way across.

An easy way to form a correct belief would be for the heaviest member of the party to test it, but this has its risks. Instead the evidence is considered in a discussion, during which the party relies on those of its members who have had experience reading nature's signs relating to the probable thickness of the ice on a stream at this time of the year. Out of the deliberations will come some belief for which there may be more or less consensus, and subsequent action will be predicated upon this belief. Although there are a few scraps of physical evidence, the belief is rooted in the social reality provided by the members of the group. If the belief agreed on is that the ice will hold, the subsequent crossing will be a test of the correctness of the belief. If the decision is that it will not hold, subsequent action will not provide the test and there will always be some room for doubt about the belief.

As we indicated earlier in this chapter, some beliefs are amenable to an ultimate test, as in the foregoing example, but other beliefs are anchored in groups and their correctness cannot possibly be determined. Even when it is possible to put a belief to the test we often, as in the frozen-stream story, decide on an action that leaves the belief unchallenged by potential negative evidence; yet an important action may have been predicated on the belief. A company's hiring policy may be based on a belief, which is strongly anchored in the social reality provided by the boss's membership in certain social groups, that Negroes make inefficient and disloyal employees. This belief may never be put to the test because of the complete unwillingness of the boss to do so. When such beliefs are put to the test they are often proved wrong.

We use the beliefs of others as a frame of reference, a source of social reality, against which to measure the correctness of our own beliefs. Such group-anchored beliefs often take on a legitimate, highly salient reality of their own and, for the same reason that they were originally not amenable to checking against physical evidence, they are often extraordinarily difficult to change.

Abilities

The person may also measure an ability by social comparison. In the case of a belief the behavior provides a point of reference that is usually a statement regarding the object of the belief. In the case of an ability a performance is taken as the comparison point. Again, when there are no clear criteria against which to evaluate performance, the person will compare his performance with that of a relevant reference person or group. Shooting par at golf is a performance that meets a rigorous and meaningful performance criterion. Receiving the Nobel prize is a rigorous criterion in certain fields of science. We can think of such bench marks in many areas of endeavor to which one may aspire. For the person of modest ambition or capacity or for the person who is at an early stage in developing his ability, prominent bench marks like these are unrealistic. Are there other bench marks available to him? Performance standards are often modified to fit a particular age group or the efforts of novices at a particular activity. Frequently, instead of or in addition to these standards, there is a performance peer group against which the person may judge his ability and estimate his progress.

From a fairly extensive literature on the determinants of a person's level of aspiration (LOA), we know that he will generally want to do somewhat better than his immediately preceding performance. His feelings of success or failure will be determined by how far his new performance exceeds or falls short of his past performance. Thus, when possible, the person uses prior performance as a bench mark to evaluate present performance. Other research has demonstrated that the person's LOA, that is, what he deems success or failure, will be modified if he is told what someone else's performance was. The direction in which his LOA shifts will depend on the ability he attributes to the person or group of whose performance he was apprised (Chapman and Volkmann, 1939; Festinger, 1942). Thus, if he finds that his performance is below someone to whom he attributes little ability, his LOA will be raised; he will be spurred on to increase his performance level. If it is above someone to whom he attributes a great deal of ability, he will tend to lower his LOA; he will slacken his efforts. These comparison effects occur both for abilities with a clear, external evaluational criterion, such as running ability, and for those with no clear criterion, such as poetry writing.

It is not at all certain which kinds of ability would be more vulnerable to such social-comparison shifts of LOA. With an ability like running it is easier to establish a frame of reference by providing the person with information about the performance of someone else who has characteristics relevant to running ability, such as age and experience, against which the person may compare himself. Yet his own running performance is also fairly well anchored and provides a strong point of reference for him. It may be difficult for him to improve. With an ability like poetry writing, for which less clear and obvious criteria exist, his own performance provides less of an anchor but the performance of others also provides a less effective frame of reference because the characteristics that make another person a relevant comparison referent are also less clearly discernible. No research has been done to examine the factors that determine whether a particular ability will be more or less vulnerable to self-evaluation shifts in response to knowledge about the performance of others. We know, however, that those abilities that have been studied all show such shifts.

Thus far we have referred to social-comparison effects on self-evaluation when the person engages in a performance like running or throwing darts. Information about the performance of another person will affect the person's self-estimate to the extent that the other is seen as a relevant competitor. There are certain abilities that can only be measured with any accuracy with reference to an opponent. Tennis and wrestling are highly contingent games in this sense, for a player can only measure his ability by the success of his response to a response of his opponent or by the failure of his opponent to respond adequately to him.

Especially in such cases of contingent performance, persons seek out those of equal talent to test their ability. If the opponent were distinctly inferior there would be no challenge and no easy way to measure the discrepancy in ability. The person would only know that he was to some degree better than this opponent, but would be unable to determine his standing with any degree of accuracy; the resolving power of the information is low. The case would be similar for a person facing a vastly superior competitor. If we assume that in general the person wants to combine accuracy of information received with the chance to improve as he goes along, he should seek out a competitor who is slightly better than himself. The person who hates to lose might settle for slightly inferior opponents, thus reducing the chance to improve his performance through competition over time. This operates in much the same way as LOA; the person tries each time to surpass his previous performance. The way to do this when competitive ability is involved is for him to keep selecting competitors who are slightly better than himself. Because his goal is to surpass his previous performance, he can do this by beating an opponent who is rated somewhat better than he is.

Obviously, each of the competitors (assuming that there are two) cannot select someone who is slightly better than he. Because there is usually some indeterminacy in pegging a person as to his standing, most often equals, or near equals, tend to be competing with one another. As one of the players tends to improve more rapidly than the other he begins to lose interest in playing with this opponent and is likely to search for someone better. Research relating to these considerations is more fully discussed in Chapter Ten.

Values and Attitudes

As defined in Chapter Five, an attitude is a tendency to make a motivationally relevant response of either approach or avoidance to some object or class of objects, and is derived from a syllogistic structure containing a belief and a value. Because attitudes are derivative values we shall use the two terms synonymously.

In the case of abilities, we saw that the person's experience of success or failure depended on his performance expectancy. With attitudes the situation is similar. When the person expects to experience a decrease in outcome level in transaction with a particular object his tendency is to avoid it, whereas if he expects an increase in outcome level he tends to approach it. Thus he will not knowingly drink quinine but he may be eager to eat a piece of chocolate. We can say that he has a negative attitude toward quinine and a positive one toward chocolate. The referent for many of the person's attitudes is his previous outcome level, which in turn leads to present expectations.

Attitudes, even toward various food substances, are modifiable by experience. Punishment for eating certain foods adds a negative value to the experience and tends to produce avoidance. Similarly, social approval for eating certain foods adds a positive value and produces approach. We examined these processes in some detail in Chapter Three. There are many instances when a person may be uncertain about the appropriateness of his attitude toward some object or class of objects. If there is a relevant reference group of co-orientees he will compare his attitude standing relative to the group and thereby determine for himself the extent to which his attitude is just or valid. Should he like (or dislike) the attitude object class the way he does?

The group norm essentially defines what is the natural or appropriate position for the person to take. A southern white whose attitude toward Negroes coincides with those of his reference group does not see himself as prejudiced. His attitudes seem completely natural to him; this is the way of the world. The group attitude standard in this case is seen neither as positive nor negative, but someone who deviates from that standard in *either* direction is regarded as having an incorrect positive or incorrect negative attitude. The southern white may at times be confronted with attitude standards of other groups that differ from his own group-anchored attitude. To the extent that the members of these other groups are seen as relevant comparison persons, that is, as co-orientees, he tends to see his own attitude as incorrect and to experience some pressure to change it. If these other groups are seen as irrelevant for comparison purposes he experiences no such feeling of incorrectness.

Emotions

Emotions are the momentary expression of strong attitudes (or values) aroused in transaction with a particular object. We speak of emotional dispositions in much the same way as we speak of attitudes as dispositional tendencies. Thus a person is said to fear the dark, to hate war, and to love children. In each of these instances the emotion defines and is indistinguishable from a strong attitude. The emotional label implies something about conditions that will induce a strong reaction of either approach or avoidance or of pain or pleasure. As with attitudes, a given emotion may be based primarily on an innate disposition, such as a fear response to falling, or the disposition may be learned, such as a fear of ghosts. A particular emotional response may have both learned and unlearned components.

As with attitudes, information as to how others tend to emote under the particular circumstances confronting the person may affect the degree to which he believes his emotional response to the situation is appropriate. If the circumstances that provoked his response are novel he may be uncertain as to how exactly to label the response he is experiencing. Is it fear, anger, or disgust? In that case comparison information from others may serve actually to give the experience a name. At times we may respond viscerally to some situation with a free-floating, unidentifiable emotional response. As we shall see in Chapter Ten, information from others can help to label or measure the intensity of such an experience.

SUMMARY

In this chapter the focus was on the distinction between information and effect dependence and some of the precursors of this distinction were identified. We then tried to lay the theoretical foundation for the three chapters to follow by casting information and effect dependence within the framework of typical action sequences. In the absence of a physical evidential basis for a belief, attitude, or ability estimate, the person may rely on others as a source of information in making that estimate.

We singled out two basic processes through which the person may acquire such information: reflected appraisal and comparative appraisal. In reflected appraisal the person acquires the information by inferring it from a response made toward him by another person in a face-to-face confrontation. This information may be about a belief, value, or ability. The person who is attempting to make the evaluation is usually effect dependent on the evaluator.

In comparative appraisal confrontation is not a necessary condition because the person uses the beliefs, attitudes, or performances of others as bench marks against which to evaluate some aspect of himself.

There are two basic kinds of reference persons: the expert and the co-oriented peer. The expert is relied on in making evaluations of aspects of the action sequence that have to do with how to move from one state of the world to another, whereas the co-oriented peer, by virtue of the fact that he shares the value perspective of the person, is relied on in evaluating the outcome level being experienced or to be expected from a given state of the world.

CHAPTER TEN

Consensus and Communication in Groups

The pervasive fact of cultural uniformity in opinions, attitudes, dress, and all manner of response to social and nonsocial situations has been a source of continued and deep interest to social scientists. The most notable early attempts at understanding this uniformity were made by the French sociologists Gustav LeBon, Gabriel Tarde, and Émile Durkheim, who started a tradition in sociology that began at the end of the last century and continues to the present time.

LeBon (1896) was fascinated by the transforming effect that a mob can have on a person. How is it, LeBon asked himself, that a normally levelheaded person can get caught up in the whirl and passion of mob action and mob violence? He answered this question by proposing that the situation of the individual in the mob is like that of the subject in a hypnotic trance. Impressed with the work of Charcot, a fellow Frenchman, in demonstrating the marked alteration undergone by a subject or a patient under hypnosis, LeBon's explanation was more than an analogy, for he firmly believed that the person in the mob has his rational faculties suspended and is in an extreme state of suggestibility. He is reduced to a primitive state and is swayed not by logic but by emotionally charged words uttered by the leader of the crowd. LeBon attempted to develop a theory about how it is that an individual can, under certain conditions, come under the influence of a crowd and commit acts he is normally not capable of committing. The details of the process whereby the individual succumbs to the group were not worked out beyond the stage of metaphor. How could it have been otherwise, because the nature of the hypnotic trance itself was not clearly understood then and remains to this day a baffling mystery for the most part? Only recently has the supposed extreme state of suggestibility represented by the hypnotic trance been subjected to systematic experimental investigation. Research evidence suggests that the hypnotic trance is not as discontinuous with the waking state as LeBon and others had thought (Hull, 1933; Orne, 1959).

Tarde (1903) was concerned with the broader societal context. He was more a sociologist and less a social psychologist than LeBon. Whereas

LeBon was interested in the dynamics of direct contact between the person, the group, and the group leader or demagogue, Tarde was interested in statistical regularity. He wanted to understand the basis for the uniformity of dress and manners apparent in a particular culture. His attempted explanation embodied three laws of imitation: (1) the inferior classes imitate the superior classes; (2) imitation progresses geometrically, spreading rapidly once started; and (3) the individual imitates things within his own culture before imitating those of an exotic culture. Presumably if we observed the spread of a new fad it would tend to follow the course suggested by Tarde. His explanation is more in the nature of a description of the way innovation spreads than a theory about underlying psychological mechanisms. His "laws," however, represent an important early attempt to describe certain regularities in social influence processes.

Durkheim was the giant of this trio of Frenchmen. His comprehensive theory about cultural uniformity took as its starting point events occurring in the human brain. He referred to these basic neural events as "sensations" and to the ideas in consciousness that emerged through their combination as "individual representations." The collective synthesis of these individual ideas, which emerge when people interact, he called "collective representations." Collective representations, or norms of belief and behavior as we would call them today, develop a constraining or controlling power over the individual. Deviation from the norms of his group, or a complete absence of norms, leaves the individual in an uncertain, vague, and uncomfortable state. In his complex social world the person needs guidelines for his behavior. An extreme form of reaction to their absence is suicide. Based on his theory of collective representations and their relationship to individual psychological security, Durkheim (1897) made predictions as to the rates of suicide in various religious groups. He proposed that the suicide rate would be inversely proportional to the number of group norms that define specific beliefs and behavior patterns for the individual. On the basis of his knowledge about the number of rituals and cultural proscriptions among Protestants, Jews, and Catholics, he predicted that Protestants would show the highest and Catholics the lowest suicide rate. This prediction was clearly confirmed. The study is still, even judged by modern standards, an impressive piece of empirical research. Other investigators have since conducted further studies of suicide and discovered similar relationships.

These findings illustrate in bold relief the inextricable dependence of the person on the norms of his group. The work we shall discuss at the end of this chapter is, in a sense, a corollary to Durkheim's study, for it examines the tendency for a person to seek out the company of others when thrust into an uncertain, normless state. Although Durkheim's theory is principally sociological, implicit in the theory is the assumption of a fundamental need on the part of the person to give form and structure to his complex world, a purpose at least partly served by the development of group norms and standards. This assumption is compatible with major trends in contemporary social psychology, although there is currently more interest in the more refined analysis, through experimentation, of normative development.

SOCIAL INFLUENCE BROUGHT INTO THE LABORATORY

In 1920 F. H. Allport conducted a highly influential experiment in which he compared a person's evaluation of the pleasantness of odors and his estimation of weights when alone and when in the presence of others. In the latter case the subject was unaware of the others' judgments. Allport found, with both odors and weights, that the person was more conservative and gave less extreme judgments when in the presence of others than when making judgments alone. H. T. Moore (1921) took the next step and exposed his subjects to a majority opinion and the opinion of an expert on ethical judgment, language usage, and musical preferences. He found for both sources of opinion a marked effect on individual judgment. In Chapter Eleven we shall deal more extensively with the conformity situation of which Moore's experiment is the prototype.

A generation later Sherif (1935) found that not only is the person making a judgment influenced by other people's judgments, but this modified judgment (the norm, as Sherif called it) tends to persist in the absence of those who were originally instrumental in shaping it. Sherif's experimental work on the development of norms had a strong impact on subsequent research and theory on the nature of social influence.

An even more critical development was probably the fact that with the rise of Nazi Germany and the coming of World War II Kurt Lewin became increasingly interested in group influences on a person's attitudes and decisions. Always intrigued by the challenge of applying theoretical considerations to the solution of important practical problems, he became interested in the possibilities of changing food preferences to accord with available supplies or nutritional needs. Because of the shortage of popular foodstuffs during the war the United States government was interested in developing a program to convince consumers to utilize the less desirable, cheaper cuts of meat. Lewin examined various techniques for changing the deeply ingrained attitudes of housewives toward serving intestinal meats to their families. This investigation, as we shall see, had the effect of raising a number of intriguing research questions.

The Group-Decision Experiments

Lewin suspected that when a decision or a judgment was anchored in a group, that is, had group support, it exerted a special compelling quality over the individual. The experiments (Lewin, 1947b) contrasted the effectiveness of a lecture as against a group discussion followed by a group decision, to get housewives to change certain food-buying practices. In the lecture condition a speaker presented the case for having the audience adopt the behavior in question. In the group discussion condition, a discussion leader made the same points that the lecturer made, encouraged the members of the group to participate in the discussion, and asked them to reach a consensus regarding the discussion topic. Parallel experiments were run on the serving of intestinal meats, the feeding of milk, orange juice, and cod liver oil to babies, and the consumption of whole-wheat bread. The general paradigm for all the studies was much the same. After the experimental influence attempt, the participants went their individual ways. They were interviewed several weeks later to determine if they had in fact been influenced in the advocated or consensual direction. In all of the experiments a greater proportion of women in the group discussion treatment stated that they had since adopted the new behavior. Figure 10.1 shows the results of three of these studies.

Many questions and problems immediately come to mind. For example, the women in the group discussion condition in most of the experiments expected a follow-up interview, whereas the women in the lecture treatment did not. Also, Lewin implicitly assumed that most of the housewives in the lecture treatment had made *individual* decisions to adopt the practice advocated by the lecturer. It is also hard to tell from a description of the studies just what went on in the group discussion. Each discussion must have been in many ways unique, for it was to a great extent formless. In

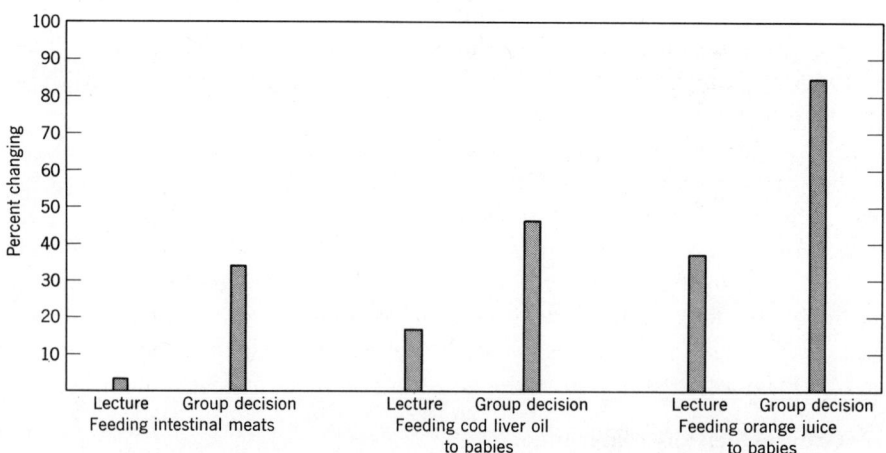

Figure 10.1. The effects of group decision vs. lecture method of changing the behavior of housewives (adapted from Lewin, 1947b).

some of the experiments the qualities of the lecturer and the group discussion leader were not controlled; that is, the person who gave the lecture was not the same person who led the group discussion. We may also legitimately ask to what extent the statement by the housewife in the follow-up interview actually reflected what she was doing in her household.

In spite of these and other shortcomings of the research, Lewin and his students came away from it with a fairly strong conviction that something mysterious, wonderful, and fundamental to human behavior was going on in these group discussions. Lewin believed that a decision reached in a group somehow "unfroze" the individual's prior attitude and carried him along to a new conviction; direct appeals to the isolated individual were far less effective in dislodging the individual from his prior convictions. This is reminiscent of Durkheim's collective representations and the constraining power they have over the individual. Although the effectiveness of such organizations as Alcoholics Anonymous and Synanon (which uses methods similar to those of AA to get drug addicts to "kick" the habit) does not offer systematic evidence of the kind we require to test hypotheses, it does provide strong anecdotal evidence in support of Lewin's ideas.

A study by Bennett (1955) attempted to overcome some of the shortcomings of the earlier experiment in a situation that involved a decision to participate in a psychology experiment. That is, after exposing a group of college students to various inducements to participate in a psychology experiment, the crucial datum observed by Bennett was whether or not the student actually showed up at the time he was scheduled.

The subjects were students in small discussion sections of a large introductory course in psychology at the University of Michigan. Each section was divided into two groups and each group received either a lecture treatment or a group discussion treatment. The groups were carefully matched across all of the experimental conditions in their degree of initial favorableness to participating in psychological experiments. The graduate students who acted as lecturers and discussion leaders were each used in the various experimental treatments in order to control for their own personal characteristics. These graduate students were carefully trained and rehearsed beforehand in order to standardize their behavior—there were actually dress rehearsals with groups that were not going to be used in the experiment. A control treatment was also used in which subjects were exposed neither to the lecture nor to the group discussion.

Four decision conditions were applied across each of the three presentation methods (discussion, lecture, control). In one no decision was required of the subjects. In a second the subjects wrote their decision down anonymously on a slip of paper, which was then collected. In a third condition the leader asked for a show of hands. A "plant" in the class quickly noted down who had volunteered in this "partially anonymous" decision. The fourth condition involved a show of hands and a taking down by the leader of the names of those people who volunteered.

Several days later each of the 488 subjects received a letter asking him to appear at a specified place to give the "Committee for Recruiting Experimental Subjects" his name, phone number, and class schedule so that he could be placed on file with the other volunteers. Whether the subject showed up was the crucial dependent measure.

Contrary to what we might expect from Lewin's earlier work, there was no difference in the proportion of subjects in each of the three methods of presentation (lecture, discussion, control) who showed up to put their names in the volunteer file (the action criterion). About 20 percent showed up in each case. There was also no difference among methods in the percentage of subjects who said they would volunteer when asked for a decision. About 75 percent did so in each. The only effect of method of presentation was a tendency among subjects who volunteered to participate and then did not show up to report their original decision falsely on a postexperimental questionnaire. The greatest amount of falsification occurred in the discussion treatment, next greatest in the lecture treatment, and least among the controls.

Asking for a decision did affect the action criterion. A greater proportion of subjects who were asked to make a decision than those who were not showed up to place their name on file. However, the particular experimental variation of how the decision was made (anonymous, partially anonymous, public) did not seem to have any affect on action. The experiment suggests that the greater the consensus in a favorable direction, as indicated by the show of hands, the more favorable was the subject's subsequent attitude. This, then, may have been the factor that accounted for the results in the original Lewin experiments. The power of a group over an individual may have been a result of his perceptions that other people in his group favored the action advocated by the discussion leader. In Lewin's work the group discussion did end with a show of hands or public statements by the group members, whereas the lecture method did not.

WESTGATE AND WESTGATE WEST

Shortly before his death in 1947 Lewin organized the Research Center for Group Dynamics at the Massachusetts Institute of Technology. The Center had a dual research and training function. Three members of the Center, Leon Festinger, Stanley Schachter, and Kurt Back, decided to get some firsthand systematic knowledge of social influence and chose a circumscribed social setting to observe the effects of particular group memberships and friendship patterns on attitudes. Two married-student-housing developments at M.I.T. were available for study. The material we shall review here is reported in a book entitled *Social Pressures in Informal Groups* (1950).

The two communities, Westgate and Westgate West, were similar to each other. The residents in both communities were M.I.T. students, so they were fairly homogeneous with respect to age, social status, and professional goals. Within each community all of the tenants moved in at about the same time and were allocated to the dwelling units on a random basis. As we shall see, this original random assignment is an important feature of the research setting. The architecture of each community was such that natural groupings tended to develop. In Westgate, which was a garden-type apartment development, the units were arranged around courtyards, whereas Westgate West consisted of 17 two-story buildings, each containing 10 apartments. By and large, people tended to form their closest associations within the community among people living in their court or, in the case of Westgate West, in their own apartment building.

Fortunately for the researchers, a controversial issue developed within both communities at about the time the research got under way. The issue was whether a newly formed tenants' organization served a useful purpose and should be supported. Actually the organization had been in existence for several months, but tenants of Westgate West had only recently been invited to join. They had a uniformly positive attitude toward the tenant organization, but as yet very few residents had become active in it. Each apartment building within Westgate West showed a uniform pattern, with very few tenants expressing a lack of interest in or a negative opinion of the organization. In Westgate, on the other hand, the courts differed markedly from one another in attitudes expressed toward the organization.

The investigators puzzled over why this should be so. The two communities were made up of nearly identical populations and yet were so different in the pattern of attitudes exhibited. An aspect of the situation that they suspected might be the key to understanding the difference was that residents of Westgate had had a considerable amount of experience with the tenants' organization, had discussed it with each other, and in so doing had developed attitudes toward it. In Westgate West the tenants had just been confronted with something new, which seemed, on the face of it, like an excellent idea. The researchers noted, when they collected their attitude data about the tenants' organization, that in Westgate the courts differed from one another with respect to the favorableness of the attitudes of the members, but within each court there was relative homogeneity of attitude. Thus most of the people in one court might be very favorable toward the organization, whereas in another court most of the tenants might be unfavorably disposed toward it. The courts also differed in the amount of uniformity of opinion within the court. In some courts there were relatively few deviates from the general attitude, whereas other courts had many deviates. If, as the researchers suspected, the attitudes developed were formed through social contact among members of the court, the degree of uniformity or homogeneity of attitude within a court should correlate positively with the amount of contact among the court members.

In the initial interview each tenant had been asked to name the three persons within the community with whom he had the most contact. The data provided by the answers to this question were used to derive a measure of the proportion of their social life the residents of a given Westgate court spent within their court. The investigators reasoned that the measure would be a rough index of how much time the residents of a court spent communicating with other members of their own court. They found a significant negative correlation within a court between the number of opinion deviates on the tenants' organization issue and the size of the index for that court. The greater the index, the less was the amount of deviation from the group standard, that is, from the modal attitude of the court members toward the organization.

Table 10.1 presents the two measures for each of the courts. In effect, when the attitude within the court was homogeneous there were few out-

Table 10.1. Cohesiveness of Court and Strength of Group Standard (Westgate) (Adapted from Festinger, Schachter, and Back, 1950)

Court name	Number of residents	Percent deviates	Cohesiveness index
Tolman	13	23	.529
Howe	13	23	.500
Rotch	8	25	.523
Richards	7	29	.433
Main	7	29	.527
Freeman	13	38	.419
Williams	13	46	.447
Miller	13	46	.485
Carson	13	54	.403

Note: The rank order correlation between percent deviates and cohesiveness = −.74.

of-court friendship choices. Unfortunately, there was no analysis reported for either of the two communities comparing each individual's deviation from the group standard and the proportion of his choices made within his court. This would have been a more convincing confirmation of the hypothesis relating deviation to amount of contact. Following the researchers' argument we would predict that a person who made all three choices within the court would probably be a conformer, whereas a person who made no choices within his court would stand a better chance of being a deviate.

There is other evidence in the study to indicate that actual social contact with other people was the key factor in establishing group standards. Those people who were physically isolated from possible chance contact by virtue of the location of their apartments tended to be deviates rather than conformers. These people also tended to give and to receive fewer in-court choices than people who were more centrally located. In Westgate West there was no correlation between the extent of contact among the residents of a building and the degree of homogeneity of attitude in that building. On the basis of this and other evidence the investigators argued that the attitudes toward the tenants' organization within Westgate West were, because the issue was new, largely determined by idiosyncratic individual factors rather than by group pressure exerted through informal social communication.

The investigation did not indicate, nor attempt to examine, why one court would tend to develop negative attitudes and another court to develop positive attitudes. Which way a court went may have been determined by the initial attitude of some relatively dominant person within the court or by an influential clique. The researchers might have been able to examine this problem if they had had a measure of the positivity or negativity of attitude toward the tenants' organization when it first became a topic of conversation and attempted to see whether the more highly chosen members of a court changed less than those who were seldom chosen.

There is the possibility that the positive relationship between homogeneity of attitude and cohesiveness (the measure of the amount of presumed contact within the court) might have been accounted for by a process working in the reverse direction. That is, the degree of initial homogeneity of attitude within the court may have affected the proportion of in-court friendship choices made. The difference in this respect between Westgate and Westgate West suggests that deviation was the effect rather than the cause of low cohesiveness, but these sorts of questions can best be resolved by controlled laboratory experimentation. This was the course taken by Festinger and his students in the work that followed the housing study.

Before examining this work, let us outline the theory that grew out of the housing study and that generated and was modified by subsequent experimentation. The sequence whereby the hunches suggested by a field study subsequently generated systematic thinking and experimental research on social influence is an example of the way in which careful observation within a rich natural environment can provide a useful and sometimes necessary step in exploring certain psychological phenomena.

FESTINGER'S THEORY OF COMMUNICATION AND SOCIAL INFLUENCE

The theory of informal social communication (Festinger, 1950) had a strong likeness to Lewin's (1936) theory about the spread of tension within the need systems of the individual. Lewin's notion was that when a particular need was salient the psychological tension represented by this salience would spread to neighboring regions. This diffusing tendency would, in the end, result in the equilibration of tension across the entire need system. That is, the regions neighboring the region initially in tension would be raised somewhat and the original region somewhat lowered until all neighboring regions had the same level of tension. The amount of tension spread between two regions was assumed to be proportional to the tension difference between them, their closeness to each other, and the permeability of their common boundaries. This kind of a model is familiar in science and variations of it have been used to characterize various physical and biological systems.

Festinger (1950) conceived of individual group members as regions or parts of the group and a difference of opinion between members as a tension differential between the parts. The greater the difference of opinion between any two group members, the greater would be the tendency for opinion equilibration to occur. He introduced the concept of cohesiveness (operating like permeability in the Lewinian model), which is the sum total of the "forces" attracting each member to the group. Group members may differ in opinion on issues that vary in their relevance for the basis that made the members dependent on one another. This concept of relevance is somewhat reminiscent of Lewin's concept of distance between need regions. That is, distance in Lewin's model is a measure of how relevant tension in one need region is to tension in some other region.

The degree of opinion equilibration between two members of a group will be directly proportional to the difference of opinion between them, the cohesiveness of their relationship, and the relevance of the opinion issue to their relationship. There are three manifestations of opinion equilibration: an individual in disagreement with another may (1) attempt to influence the other, that is, to change the other's opinion so that it agrees with his own opinion; (2) change his own opinion to agree with the other's opinion; or (3) redefine the boundary of the group by rejecting the other person. Rejection would naturally result in a smaller group, but one in which opinion differences have been equilibrated. Rejection is likely to occur after influence fails and in the event that the person is unable to change his own opinion. Any basis on which the person can predicate a difference between himself and the other makes it easier to reject him.

Why does this tendency to equilibrate opinion differences exist? As we indicated in Chapter Nine, Festinger postulated two basic underlying causes: the need for "social reality" on the part of the individual member and the requirement that the group reach whatever objective it has. Adhering to Lewinian terminology, he referred to this latter basis as the need for "group locomotion." The concept of a person's standing, relative to others, and the process of comparative appraisal whereby he determines his standing (see Chapter Nine) are the equivalent of Festinger's social-reality principle. It is apparent in Festinger's original theoretical statement and in the research leading to and following from it that his real theoretical and empirical focus was on comparative appraisal. This is not entirely clear in the early work but became explicit in the theory of social comparison (Festinger, 1954).

The cornerstones of the theory are the assumptions made about the content of a belief or attitude (its *relevance* to group purposes) and the nature of the relationships between the individual and the other group members (their *cohesiveness*). Naturally the two factors are interdependent, for the importance of the bond between any two people—that is, their dependence on each other—derives from the satisfactions they mediate for each other. Their attraction for each other has relevance to specific satisfactions; therefore, any disagreement they may have will be felt more strongly the greater its relevance to the basis that binds them together. We may thus expect greater tendencies toward opinion equilibration the more relevant the issue about which there is disagreement.

Certain difficulties arise in interpreting the results of most of the experiments generated by Festinger's theory, because subjects are typically tied to their experimental groups through bonds of both information and effect dependence. Festinger states explicitly that both types of dependence should have exactly the same effects on the influence process. As we shall see, different types of dependence do have different implications for communication and tendencies to reach *and remain in* agreement. As a corollary to the tendency toward blurring the distinction between information and effect dependence, we should also expect to find no distinction in the research between what we have called the co-oriented peer relationship and the expert relationship. In some research this distinction is certainly implicit, but in the early work there was no systematic exploration of the social influence implications of co-orientation as compared with referral to an expert.

Cohesiveness and Attitude Change

The first experiment to follow the Westgate–Westgate West study was conducted by Back (1951). This study focused on the effects of different sources of interpersonal attraction on communication and opinion change.

In this experiment and in the others to follow we shall use the terms attraction and cohesiveness as roughly substitutable although we realize that they are not strictly the same. Cohesiveness refers to a property of the relationship that exists between two people from the perspective of a third person and attraction refers to the relationship from the point of view of one of the individuals. In our terms both are coordinate with *the sum of all of the outcomes mediated by the relationship.*

Festinger's theory predicted that pressures toward uniformity would be a positive function of cohesiveness. To test this prediction Back attempted to create a controlled laboratory situation in which to study the relationship observed in the housing study between the cohesiveness of the group and uniformity of opinion within the group. Each experimental group consisted of two subjects who had not been previously acquainted. In half of the groups the subjects were made to feel, by appropriate instructions, that being in the group with the other person was very desirable (the high-cohesive treatment). In the other half of the groups the two subjects were given instructions that made them feel that being in the group was not especially desirable (the low-cohesive treatment). Before meeting each other, each subject was asked to write a story about a set of three pictures. After the subjects had written their individual stories they were brought together to compare their respective interpretations of the three pictures. The amount of communication during this discussion was recorded by an observer. After the discussion each subject was asked to write, individually, a final version of his story. By comparing this final version with the initial one, written before the discussion, changes in the direction of the partner's interpretation could be estimated. The results of the analysis of the communication data during the discussion itself showed a greater tendency for the partners to attempt to influence each other in the high-, as compared with the low-cohesive treatment, as well as a greater tendency for the subjects in the high-cohesive treatment to change their stories more in the direction of their partner. The results indicated that greater pressures toward uniformity were apparently generated in the high-cohesive groups.

This is only part of the story, however, because overt signs of resistance to influence were also more evident in the high-cohesive treatments. High-cohesive subjects tended to be active and argumentative in discussing their stories, so that the greater amount of ultimate change was in fact preceded by higher temporary resistance. Back attempts to explain this by contending that low-cohesive subjects would be expected to behave in a passive, withdrawn manner featuring polite overt agreement and obstinate private resistance. It may also be noted that each high-cohesive subject has both more power to influence *and* more power to resist influence than each low-cohesive subject. This feature of cohesive groups will be discussed further in Chapter Fourteen.

In the experiment attractiveness was based either on anticipated congeniality, receiving a prize for a good story, or working with someone who was presumably good at writing such stories. Only one basis for either high or low attractiveness was induced in any given experimental group. This was done by appropriate, convincing statements to the two subjects before their discussion began. For inducing anticipated congeniality or expectations about how good the subjects would be at the task, both subjects were led to believe (falsely, of course) that the experimenter had the kind of knowledge about each of them, obtained from previously administered questionnaires, that would enable him to predict with great assurance the course of their relationship.

All three bases of attraction showed essentially similar results, there being no differences among them in over-all generation of and response to influence pressures. However, Back did observe that subjects in the congenial condition tried to transform the discussion into a long and pleasant conversation, those in the prize group were brisk and efficient, and those in the prestige groups were cautious and self-conscious.

Deviation and Rejection

The results of deviation in a group were brought into direct focus in an experiment by Schachter (1951). In the housing study it was found that a person who deviated from the court standard showed low attraction for the people in the court, and they showed low attraction for him. Because the data are correlational, it is impossible to know the direction of causation. That is, did deviation cause low attraction or did low attraction make the individual feel free to deviate from the standard? It may be that both processes were operating.

Schachter chose to examine whether deviation from the group standard would result in rejection and how this would be affected by variations in relevance and cohesiveness. Both relevance and cohesiveness should heighten the attempts of group members to bring the deviate into line. If the deviate remains adamant after initial influence pressure, there should be a tendency for the other group members to redefine the boundaries of the group to exclude him. This tendency to redefine the boundaries should be greater, the greater are the cohesiveness of the group and the relevance of the issues.

The experiment was distinctive in combining laboratory control with realism. Students were recruited not as experimental subjects but ostensibly as volunteer members of clubs that were to be formed. Each club was actually an experimental group and eight clubs were organized around each of four different topics. There were case study, editorial, movie, and radio clubs. The case study and movie clubs made up the high-cohesive groups because all the members had expressed a strong interest in joining such clubs. The editorial and radio clubs were low-cohesive groups because the members had expressed little or no interest in joining these clubs. This club assignment was made possible by the fact that the prospective subject, that is, club member, did not know which kind of a club he would be assigned to before coming to the laboratory. The movie and case study clubs were, as planned, more attractive to the average volunteer—as measured by the desire to continue after the first club meeting. Each group eventually ended up discussing the same topic, a fictitious case history of a juvenile delinquent named "Johnny Rocco."

In the case study and editorial clubs the case history was introduced as relevant to the purpose of the club. In the case study club the relevance was obvious and in the editorial club the case history was to be the basis for a feature article. In the movie and radio clubs a short time was spent either seeing a movie or listening to a tape recording of a broadcast and the case study was introduced as an atypical diversion. Thus the case study was irrelevant to the expressed purpose of each of these latter two types of clubs. These manipulations produced four types of groups: the high-cohesive-relevant groups (the case study clubs), the high-cohesive-irrelevant groups (the movie clubs), the low-cohesive-relevant groups (the editorial clubs), and the low-cohesive-irrelevant groups (the radio clubs).

Each group consisted of five to seven naive subjects and three well-trained, paid participants who posed as naive subjects. Each of the latter was assigned to one of three roles in the club. One of the paid participants adopted the modal position of the rest of the club. Another, the "slider," started out as a deviate and gradually came to agree with the majority of the group members. The third started out and remained a deviate to the end of the discussion. These three roles were systematically varied among the individuals who served as paid participants so that any of their personal attributes could not affect the over-all results. Each of the paid participants contrived to state his opinion about once every five minutes. The subjects and the paid participants initially stated their opinion as to what should be done about Johnny Rocco, on a seven-point scale ranging from very lenient treatment at one end to very harsh treatment at the other end. The case was constructed so as to produce a sympathetic reaction from most people, and the overwhelming majority of the subjects did choose positions at the lenient end of the scale. The slider and deviate, therefore, started out at "opinion 7," which recommended the harshest treatment of all.

During the discussion an observer kept a record of various aspects of the communication process, notably who spoke to whom and whether the speaker supported or attacked the person to whom he spoke. After the meeting an ingenious technique was used to get a measure of rejection. The discussion leader discussed the club's future and suggested that the club organize several committees to expedite its functioning. The committees were to be an executive, steering, and correspondence committee, with their importance described in that order. The subjects were then asked to nominate, on a secret ballot, the members of the club for the various committee assignments. In addition, a so-called sociometric measure was taken. The members were told that it might be necessary to reduce the size of the club and that each, therefore, should list the other members of the club in the order in which he would like to have them remain in the club.

Table 10.2 indicates how the deviate, mode, and slider were ranked on the sociometric questionnaire; the higher the number, the greater the evi-

Table 10.2. Mean Sociometric Rankings of the Paid Participants (From Schachter, 1951)

Condition	Deviate	Mode	Slider
High-cohesive-relevant	6.44	4.65	5.02
Low-cohesive-relevant	5.83	4.70	4.56
High-cohesive-irrelevant	6.51	4.68	4.44
Low-cohesive-irrelevant	5.67	3.83	5.03

dence for rejection. The data clearly indicate that in all four experimental conditions the deviate was rejected to a much greater extent than either the mode or the slider. The table also shows a greater tendency to reject the deviate in the high- as compared with the low-cohesive groups. There does not appear to be any effect of relevance on the rejection of the deviate.

Committee assignment data are presented in Table 10.3 in terms of percentages above or below the frequency of assignment expected on a chance basis. The assignment of the slider and the mode varies closely around chance, whereas the picture for the deviate is very different. In all but the low-cohesive-irrelevant condition the deviate is overnominated for the correspondence committee, and undernominated for the executive committee. The deviate is relegated to a peripheral role in the group, that is, to the correspondence committee, more in the relevant than in the irrelevant treatment.

The sociometric data show an effect of cohesiveness, whereas the committee-assignment data show an effect of relevance. This seems reasonable in view of the fact that the sociometric question probably reflected the subject's response to the personal attributes of the deviate whereas the committee assignment probably reflected his evaluation of the deviate's ability to contribute to the group. For the most part, these data support the initial predictions. Rejection tends to be more intense the higher the cohesiveness of the group and the greater the relevance of the discussion to the purpose of the group.

Table 10.3a. Percentage of Subjects above Chance Assigning "Mode" to Committees

Group	Executive	Steering	Correspondence
High-cohesive-relevant	−4.56	+6.76	−2.22
Low-cohesive-relevant	−9.83	+20.15	−10.44
High-cohesive-irrelevant	−0.08	+6.85	−6.93
Low-cohesive-irrelevant	+3.70	+3.70	−8.07

Table 10.3b. Percentage of Subjects above Chance Assigning "Slider" to Committees

High-cohesive-relevant	+1.76	−5.93	+4.16
Low-cohesive-relevant	+7.32	−7.86	+0.50
High-cohesive-irrelevant	−4.97	+4.38	+0.39
Low-cohesive-irrelevant	+2.69	−3.52	+0.16

Table 10.3c. Percentage of Subjects above Chance Assigning "Deviate" to Committees

High-cohesive-relevant	−14.00	−8.34	+22.31
Low-cohesive-relevant	−17.58	−7.81	+25.26
High-cohesive-irrelevant	−16.41	+4.83	+11.44
Low-cohesive-irrelevant	+10.16	−9.40	−1.30

(All data from Schachter, 1951)

The communication data are not clear-cut. They do, however, show a slight tendency for subjects in the high-cohesive-relevant condition to decrease their communication to the deviate toward the end of the discussion, whereas no such tendency occurs in the other three experimental conditions. This is evidence that there was some attempt to redefine the boundaries of the group in the condition where pressures toward uniformity should, according to the theory, be greatest. The figures on communication to the mode and slider provide control data. Communication to the mode is uniform throughout the discussion, whereas communication to the slider tends to fall off as it becomes apparent that he is adopting the position represented by the group's consensus. Emerson (1954) repeated the experiment using high-school students and manipulated cohesiveness but not relevance. His results were similar to those of Schachter, though there was a stronger tendency for the younger subjects to be less certain of their opinions and more easily influenced by the deviate and the slider. As a consequence there was less rejection and less of a tendency to cease communication with the deviate.

Several further studies specifically examined the pattern of communication to the deviate. Because it is the deviate who creates problems for the other members, bringing him into line is presumably the group's paramount task. Various questions arise. What does the deviate do in response to the influence exerted on him? What are the conditions under which the other members of the group give up attempting to influence him to agree with them? What effects do outside anchorages of opinions have on the course of influence in a group?

Group Heterogeneity and Communication

An experiment by Festinger and Thibaut (1951) investigated the manifestations of pressures toward uniformity under a variety of experimental conditions. The setting involved a group discussion carried on through written messages. The instructions varied the importance of reaching a unanimous decision, as well as the degree to which the group members were allegedly heterogeneous—that is, differed in co-orientation and expertise. The content of the discussion problem was also manipulated to vary the degree to which members presumably had outside anchorages for their opinions. To the extent that unanimity was required, group members would be more intense in their efforts to convert the deviate, the deviate himself would be more prone to conform to the group consensus, and extremely recalcitrant members would be rejected after all efforts to convert them had failed. To the extent that members differed in co-orientation and expertise, we would expect a reduction in conversion attempts especially by members who felt inexpert. When members had strong outside anchorages for their opinions in past experience or in other membership groups they would be expected to have more confidence in these opinions, be more adamant in expressing themselves, and be less likely to change in response to group pressure. When outside anchorages were weak the group presented a medium in which new norms had to be developed for the individual members.

The experiment used approximately 600 undergraduates as subjects in groups varying in size from 6 to 14 members. The subjects in each group were seated facing each other at tables arranged in a circle; each subject was identified by a letter of the alphabet that was boldly displayed in front of him. These letters were used to identify the addressee of the messages written during the discussion. One of two problems was assigned to each of the groups. The problem for half of the groups was a variant of the "Johnny Rocco" case, whereas for the other half it involved football strategy. The Johnny Rocco case was presumed to be an issue on which the subjects were likely to have opinions that were strongly anchored outside the discussion group, whereas the football problem was presumed to be an issue about which a group norm would be easily formed within the discussion. Each subject selected an opinion on a seven-point continuum. For the case study problem, one end of the continuum emphasized a very lenient attitude toward the delinquent whereas the other end emphasized a severe attitude. For the football problem, one end of the continuum recommended a very daring strategy, whereas the other end recommended a very conservative one. Using appropriate instructions, three levels of pressures toward uniformity were induced: high, medium, and low. In the high-pressure treatment the group was strongly encouraged by the experimenter to reach agreement; in the medium-pressure treatment only mild encouragement to reach agreement was given; in the low-pressure condition no mention was made of reaching agreement. Possibilities for group subdivision were created by telling subjects across the three pressure levels that the group was very heterogeneous with respect to the interests *and* abilities of the members. This probably created impressions of a lack of co-orientation and impressions that the group probably contained people who were experts on the topic. A homogeneous condition, also applied across the three pressure levels, emphasized to the group that it was composed of people who were as nearly alike as possible in interests and abilities, which probably led the subjects to believe that no one in the group was an expert and that everyone was co-oriented. There were 60 groups in all, averaging about 10 members each, with 5 groups assigned to each of the 12 treatment combinations.

Each subject had a pad of note paper secretly marked (by the position of the staple) so that the experimenters knew, when they analyzed a message, who had written it. The identification letter of the target person was indicated by the sender at the top of the message but he did not indicate his own letter. When any subject looked around the room he saw a distribution of opinions as indicated by an opinion card in front of each subject. When the subject wrote a message he could choose to write to someone whose opinion was extreme relative to his own or to others who held opinions between his own and this extreme view. If unanimity of opinion were to be achieved, the best strategy for a given subject would be to convert the others in the group who held views that were extreme in relation to his own view. A greater volume of communication directed at others with extreme views relative to the sender would be evidence for a tendency to achieve consensus.

Each message was analyzed in terms of the distribution of opinion at the time it was delivered. If the note were written by someone with "opinion 4," anyone at either "1" or "7" would be considered extreme relative to the subject. If there were no one at either of these opinions, then subjects holding either opinion "2" or "6" would be considered extreme, and so on. If a subject wrote a message to someone holding an opinion between his own opinion and the extreme, the direction of this message was coded as some number of opinions away from the opinion most extreme to the sender's. Thus, if a subject at "4" wrote a message to someone holding opinion "6" (or "2") when there was someone else at "7" (or "1"), this message was coded as being sent 1-away from the extreme. If there were no one at either "7" or "1," then the message was coded as going to the extreme. If, at the time, more than one person bore the same relationship to the sender as the addressee, the message was weighted by dividing it by the number of people in that relationship. Thus, if three people in the group held extreme views relative to the sender, the total number of messages written to all of them was divided by three.

Figure 10.2 presents the direction of communication data separately for those groups discussing the football problem and those discussing the case study problem averaged over the other two experimental variables, location of the addressee and weighting. The obvious conclusion in examining the curves is that pressures toward uniformity were indeed operating. The tendency to communicate is greater, the more extreme the other person's view relative to the sender of a message. The pattern for both discussion problems is the same although there appears to be a greater volume of communication about the football problem. This is apparently a result of the fact that for the case study problem a subject can rely more on perviously established beliefs for his conviction.

It is possible to compute the mean distance from the extreme that messages were sent for each experimental condition. This figure represents the average distance from the extreme for all messages sent in that particular condition. Table 10.4 presents these indices for the first and second 10 minutes of the discussion. A tendency to form subgroups, that is, to exclude individuals holding extreme opinions, would be reflected by a subject writing fewer messages to extreme deviates and more messages to individuals holding less extreme views. The more a subject tends to write to others having

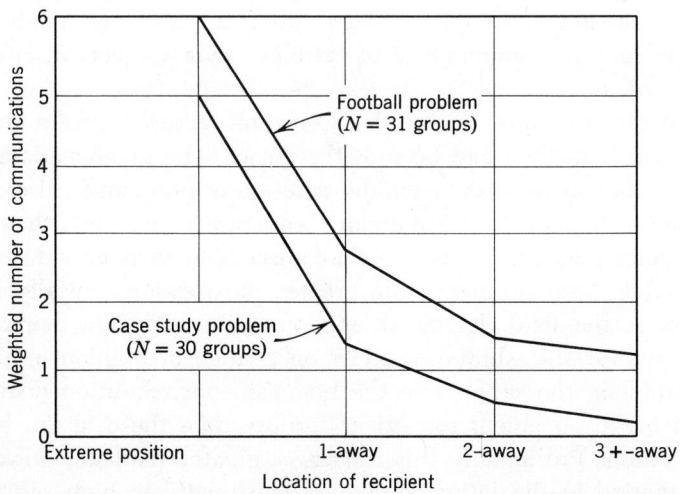

Figure 10.2. Patterns of communication (first 10 minutes) (from Festinger and Thibaut, 1951).

Table 10.4. Mean Communication Distance from Extreme
(From Festinger and Thibaut, 1951)

	Football Problem					
	First 10 Minutes			Second 10 Minutes		
	High	Medium	Low	High	Medium	Low
Hom.	.68	.85	.88	.74	.63	.86
Het.	.83	.83	.86	.75	1.30	.99
	Case Study Problem					
Hom.	.27	.62	.48	.35	.56	.74
Het.	.31	.50	.31	.30	.72	.78

less extreme views, the *larger* will be his "direction of communication" index. Although the pattern in the table is not completely consistent, we see a tendency for the index to increase for the second 10 minutes for subjects in the heterogeneous condition under the medium- and low-pressure treatments, indicating a tendency to cease comparison with the deviates. When pressure is high, however, the index does not increase; that is, subjects continue to strive for unanimity by attempting to influence extreme deviates. In the homogeneous condition, when the individuals see themselves as being all co-oriented and of equal ability, there appears to be no systematic tendency for decreasing communication to people who are extreme relative to the sender. The table shows a strong difference between the two types of discussion problems. Subjects discussing the case study show a greater tendency to communicate to extremes than subjects discussing the football problem.

The changes in opinion during the discussion tended to make the groups more uniform than they had been at the outset. The greater adamance inferred from the previous data for the case study problem is also reflected in the data on change: there is a greater tendency to change in the direction of other group members in the football discussion than in the case study discussion. For both problems, the greater the pressure initially induced, the greater is the final degree of opinion uniformity. The homogeneity-heterogeneity variable shows an effect on change of opinion only for the football problem, the subjects in the homogeneous condition displaying a great deal more movement toward uniformity than those in the heterogeneous condition. Presumably this reflects a greater tendency toward subgroup formation in the latter condition. The relatively high resistance to change for the case study problem apparently made the added effect of homogeneity or heterogeneity negligible.

The data from this experiment bring to light various aspects of the social influence process. Where unanimity of opinion is important to group members, influence is directed at extreme opinions. With relatively low pressures toward uniformity, the possibility for subgroup formation produces a tendency to exclude people with extreme opinions. There is also a readiness to change on the part of group members so as to achieve greater unanimity of opinion.

Minority and Majority Influence Patterns

In a subsequent study Gerard (1953) examined these same processes in a group discussion in which it was possible for the subject to disagree with someone else about two aspects of a problem. All groups discussed the same problem, which concerned opinions toward Federal aid to education. The two aspects of the problem were whether the Federal government should help the individual states in designing curricula and whether Federal financial help should be given to the states. The subjects, who were seated in a circle as in the previous experiment, indicated which issue they felt was the more important to discuss, funds or curriculum, and also indicated to the experimenter, on seven-point continua, their opinion on each of the issues. Only their opinion on the issue they thought was more important was displayed on a card to the other members of the group. One end of each opinion continuum recommended complete Federal domination and the other end recommended complete state autonomy. As in the first experiment, both pressures toward uniformity and the heterogeneity-homogeneity variable were manipulated experimentally. In the high-pressure condition the experimental group was told that it would shortly have a debate with some local experts on the problem. In the low-pressure condition no such debate was anticipated. There were only 4 experimental conditions in this experiment rather than 12 as in the previous ones. These were: high-pressure-homogeneous, high-pressure-heterogeneous, low-pressure-homogeneous, and low-pressure-heterogeneous.

With only minor differences, the findings from this experiment supported those of Festinger and Thibaut (1951). Communication was greater toward those holding extreme opinions and went to less extreme opinions only when subgroup formation was possible, that is, in the heterogeneous condition. Only when pressures toward uniformity were high and the subjects perceived the others as co-oriented peers of equal ability was there any significant movement toward uniformity of opinion.

The division in the group concerning which issue was more important, the curriculum or fund issue, created in all but four groups (where there was an equal split) a majority versus a minority. The majority exerted much more effort in attempting to influence the members of the minority to change their opinions on the issue they had chosen than vice versa. On the other hand, influence was much more intense within the minority than within the majority. Thus the minority members exerted much more internal pressure on each other than on the members of the majority, whereas the majority exerted more pressure on the minority than among themselves.

In both studies it is impossible to determine the source of the pressures toward uniformity. In the first study the subjects may have exerted influence in order to please the experimenter, because in both the high- and medium-pressure conditions he had admonished them to reach a consensus. However, in the low-pressure condition there was some movement toward uniformity and a strong tendency to exert influence on those holding extreme views; therefore, this cannot be the complete answer. In the second experiment the instructions did not even hint at any desire on the part of the experimenter for unanimity even in the high-pressure condition, and yet the subjects attempted to achieve uniformity of opinion.

In the majority-minority experiment there was some indication that many subjects in the heterogeneous condition assumed that the others were more expert than they in discussing Federal aid to education. In the homogeneous groups subjects tended to be dependent for information on all members of the group equally, whereas in the heterogeneous condition subjects may have responded differentially to messages from different people, assuming that some were experts and some were not. This is a clear case of the inconsistency and confusion that runs through the early experiments in this tradition: differences in co-orientation and expertise were confounded with each other because the instructions emphasized, in the heterogeneous condition, that the group comprised individuals who differed in both interest *and* in ability, whereas individuals in the homogeneous treatment were similar in both respects. When differences in interests are involved any difference is grounds for rejecting an opinion. When differences in ability are involved the subject tends to reject the opinions of inferiors and be readily influenced by superiors. The data in these experiments do not separately examine the responses of those subjects who perceived the others as better or as worse than themselves in ability or of those who responded in terms of co-orientation.

Reactions of the Deviate

Festinger, Gerard, Hymovitch, Kelley, and Raven (1952) focused on the reaction of a person to discovering that he is a deviate from group consensus. By creating conditions of differential attraction to the group, their experiment could investigate the nature of information dependence on a group of peers rather than an expert.

This experiment also was conducted as a note-writing discussion. The discussion topic was a labor-management dispute and concerned a prediction as to what the union leaders would do at their next meeting with the representatives from management. A fictitious history of the negotiations up until that point was read by each subject, who indicated his prediction of union response on a seven-point scale ranging from complete adamance (1) to complete capitulation to management (7).

A departure from the procedure in the earlier experiments was made here. The subject did not display his opinion or his identification letter to the others in the group. Instead, he wrote them down on a slip of paper that was collected by the experimenter. Each subject in the group had been assigned the letter D, and each believed that he was the only D in the group. Because the subjects were physically well separated from each other this was easily done by writing the letter D on a slip of paper and placing it on each subject's writing table. The tables themselves were arranged in a large circle. After turning in his opinion statement the subject received a fictitious tally of the opinion distribution in the group. If he was selected (on a random basis) to be a deviate he discovered that he, D, was alone in his opinion with one other subject two opinion positions away and the rest of the group one opinion position beyond that. If he were chosen to be a conformer he found himself as D, in agreement with all but two subjects, one of whom was one opinion away from himself and the rest of the group, and the second two opinion positions beyond that. Typical tallies are shown in Table 10.5.

Table 10.5. Sample of Form Given to a "Conformer" or a "Deviate" [a]
(From Festinger, Gerard, Hymovitch, Kelley, and Raven, 1952)

Opinion	Given to Conformer	Given to Deviate
1		
2		
3		
4	DCBFG	D
5	A	
6		A
7	E	CBFEG

[a] All subjects were D.

Two degrees of cohesiveness were induced with a verbal manipulation similar to the technique used to induce congeniality in Back's experiment. The subjects were told that in assembling the group either a good or a poor match had been made based on information about personal preferences obtained from a form filled out when they were recruited. Assignment of a group to a particular treatment combination was strictly random, as before, and the instructions had no necessary basis in fact. In addition to these instructions there was a warm-up note-writing session for all groups, in which the subjects wrote and received several notes. The notes were intercepted and instead a set of prewritten, false notes was delivered to each subject in the group. In the high-cohesive condition the notes indicated a great deal of interest in the experiment and in the other subjects on the part of the note writers, whereas in the low-cohesive condition only minimal interest was expressed.

Superimposed on this manipulation was another factor. Half of the groups were led to believe that there were experts present, this having been determined, they were told, from the recruiting forms and from telephone contacts with these knowledgeable members to verify whether they were in fact skilled regarding the issues involved in this kind of problem. No one, of course, had received a telephone call, so each subject assumed that he was not an expert but that some of the others were. The other half of the groups were told that everyone in the group was approximately equal in the skills and abilities required to make the kind of judgments involved in the problems they were going to discuss.

An additional variable, the belief that a correct answer was or was not available, was also induced. Half of the groups were told that they would soon find out what actually happened in the labor-management dispute whereas the other half of the groups were told that the Federal government stepped in to arbitrate the dispute, changing conditions so drastically that no correct answer really existed.

These manipulations yielded 16 treatment combinations that, along with the number of subjects in each, are shown in Table 10.6. Data from the

Table 10.6. Distribution of Subjects in Each Experimental Condition (From Festinger et al., 1952)

	Correct Answer		No Correct Answer	
	Experts	No Experts	Experts	No Experts
Conformers				
High-Cohesive	19	22	22	19
Low-Cohesive	22	26	22	20
Deviates				
High-Cohesive	35	35	34	29
Low-Cohesive	34	35	35	34

questionnaire administered when the experiment was over indicated that all of the variables were successfully induced, producing attitudes and perceptions appropriate to the cohesiveness, conformer-deviate, expert, and correct-answer factors.

The false information about the opinions of other group members had to be tailor-made for each subject, exhibiting his identification letter at the opinion he chose and showing the others distributed in the manner shown in Table 10.5 for deviate and conformer, depending on the treatment to which each had been assigned. Thus the subject had not chosen to deviate or conform but found himself in the position *after* stating his opinion. On receiving this false consensus he was asked for his new opinion, and was then instructed to engage in the note-writing session.

Between the first and second opinion statements 23 percent of the deviates changed their opinion, all but one person in the direction of the rest of the group. Only 4 percent of the conformers changed. The communication pattern for the conformers is much the same pattern as exhibited by most subjects in the previous experiments; the greater the opinion difference between themselves and another person, the greater was the tendency to communicate with that person. Deviates, on the other hand, tended to behave like the members of the minority group in the Gerard experiment. They communicated less to those members who were in the agreeing majority three positions away. As in the previous experiments, in computing the amount of communication each message was weighted by the inverse of the number of people holding the same opinion as the addressee of the message.

The communication data suggest that the subject, confronted with a choice between persons to influence, perceived that it would be more difficult to dislodge a member of the entrenched majority than to influence the lone individual who was both closer to him and lacked group support for his opinion. These data also show that deviates who changed their opinions communicated less than either subjects originally assigned to the conformer treatment or deviates who did not change. This suggests that alternative reactions to pressures toward uniformity may substitute for each other—one reaction precludes the need for others. Cohesiveness appears to affect the deviate but not the conformer. In the high-cohesive conditions, both the changing and nonchanging deviates communicated more than they did under the low-cohesive treatment, whereas the conformer communicated an equal amount in both conditions.

When the subject believed that some of the group members were experts there was a decline in the amount of communication both for the conformer and deviate. They presumably believed that it would be difficult to influence an expert.

When a correct answer would be revealed shortly, deviates tended to change a greater number of opinion steps than when no correct answer existed. When there was a correct answer, it was presumably a matter of being right or wrong. Thus when the deviate changed he tended to change all the way toward the other group members who, he assumed, had hit on the correct answer. There was also less communication when there was a correct answer as compared with when there was not. This probably reflects less information dependence on the group for reaching a consensus because the correct answer was shortly to be divulged.

An important experiment by Hochbaum (1954) followed up on the previous one by examining the expertise factor in greater detail. This study used the familiar note-writing format, the discussion centering around a clinical case study of a boy named Horace. The task involved predicting, from the case material, what Horace would do when confronted with a particular critical problem. The subject took his position along a five-point opinion continuum and then received a fictitious, tailor-made opinion distribution of where the others in the group stood. As in the previous experiment, the subject found himself to be either a conformer or deviate. Before reading the case of Horace, all subjects in the group had worked on five short practice cases and, irrespective of their opinions on these practice cases, half of them were privately informed that they had predicted the behavior reactions correctly in all five clinical cases and that the others in their discussion group had not done nearly as well. This constituted the high-ability treatment. In order to induce the perception of low ability, the other half of the subjects were informed that they had done poorly relative to the rest of the group. This ability manipulation, combined with the conformer-deviate induction, yielded a fourfold design of high-ability-conformers, high-ability-deviates, low-ability-conformers, and low-ability-deviates. As in the previous experiment, each subject was asked to restate his opinion and his confidence in it immediately after the conformer-deviate induction and before the note-writing discussion. The same marked-pad note-writing technique, with only the addressee's letter indicated on each note, was used. False notes were delivered at the end of the note-writing session instead of the usual procedure of delivering notes the subjects actually wrote. A third opinion and confidence statement was then required of each subject.

The results are in accord with those of the previous experiment with one qualification. The deviates changed their opinions more than conformers; however, ability had a considerable additional effect on opinion change. High-ability conformers and high-ability deviates changed less than their low-ability counterparts. The data show that 23 percent of the high-ability deviates, 83 percent of the low-ability deviates, 6 percent of the high-ability conformers, and 24 percent of the low-ability conformers changed their opinions. These results clearly show effects of both factors, and that the effect of ability was much greater on the deviates than on the conformers. The note-writing communication data are consistent with this. The deviates attempted to exert less influence than the conformers on the others. However, for both conformer and deviate, the greater their ability the more influence they exerted. Also, the deviate who changed his opinion showed an increase in confidence, whereas the confidence of the deviate who did not change remained the same throughout. Remembering our discussion in Chapter Six, this may reflect the changing deviate's attempt to bolster his decision by cognitive work.

The Hochbaum experiment confronts an issue that was not made fully explicit in the previous research: the relationship between opinion and ability comparison. In Chapter Nine we pointed out that the extent to which one person will be information-dependent on another is a function either of the other person's expertise or of his degree of co-orientation. In referring to another person's estimate of a situation, a person is in effect augmenting his own ability to make such an estimate. An opinion or a belief statement can be regarded as a performance, the quality of which will be judged either by its ability to predict the future accurately or, if no prediction is involved, the degree of expertise attributed to the maker of the statement. The person's confidence in an opinion will be determined by the degree of competence he attributes to the person holding the opinion. This person, of course, may be himself. In several of these experiments the results may be interpreted as an attempt by the person to augment his own competence.

The Anchorage of Opinions in Reference Groups

An experiment by Gerard (1954) focused specifically on the effect of prior group anchorage on vulnerability to social influence. The degree of cohesiveness and unanimity within a reference group were both manipulated experimentally since it was hypothesized that both factors have an important influence on a group member's confidence. We might expect degree of agreement to have a greater effect on confidence the greater the tendency the person has to refer his opinion to those agreeing with him.

Six undergraduate subjects appeared in the laboratory for each initial experimental session. The labor-management case study was used for the discussion topic and in this experiment there was actual face-to-face discussion. The subjects read the case and each privately stated his opinion and his degree of confidence in it. Two groups of three subjects each were then formed and each group carried on its own discussion in a separate laboratory room. The group assignment was based on the opinion statements. There was an attempt to get a range of intragroup consensus across all of the experimental groups. Some of the groups were composed of subjects who were in complete agreement about the labor-management case study, whereas in other groups there was a great deal of disagreement. The separation into the two three-person groups provided a plausible pretext for inducing cohesiveness. The high-cohesive groups were informed that an attempt had been made to compose a discussion group of people who would find one another congenial and that the match in their group was indeed excellent. They were told that the other three subjects who were sent to the other room were leftovers in that their preferences, as stated on the recruiting form, could not be met in the group. For the low-cohesive induction, subjects were told that they were leftovers and that the subjects in the other room were the only ones who could be matched for congeniality. The postexperimental measure of attraction indicated that this manipulation was successful.

In order to heighten their dependence upon the group, subjects were told just before the discussion that there was no correct answer. After a 15-minute discussion each subject was again asked to indicate privately his opinion and his confidence in it. The discussion data are in line with the data from the other experiments. Subjects in the high-cohesive treatment attempted more to influence their compatriots and changed more toward them than did subjects in the low-cohesive treatment.

In order to measure the effect of prior anchorage, each subject was later confronted by a challenge from someone he believed was another subject like himself. This second meeting, held approximately one week later, was introduced as a discussion between representatives of two of the prior groups. The other "subject" was actually an accomplice of the experimenter who was trained to argue effectively from various positions on the issue. In each session he took an opinion two positions away from the subject. A careful observational record was kept of the degree to which the subject exerted, accepted, and rejected influence.

In the test situation, when the subject was defending his view against the accomplice, a medium level of cohesiveness was induced so that a subject from a high-cohesive reference group would be referring back to a more attractive group and a subject from a low-cohesive group to a less attractive group than his present one, made up of himself and the accomplice. It was assumed that both agreement and disagreement would have a greater effect on subjective validity the more attractive the referent. That is, we would expect the effect on confidence of different degrees of agreement to be more pronounced in the high- than in the low-attraction groups. Confidence should be reflected in attempts to influence the accomplice. Table 10.7 presents these data.

The three levels of degree of consensus were based on the average deviation of opinion within the three-person reference group at the end of the first discussion. In the low-attraction treatment the greater the agreement in the reference group the more the subject attempted to influence the accomplice. Under high attraction this linear relationship did not hold. The figure for the high-attraction–strongly-disagree condition suggests that under circumstances when confidence is extremely low, as it should be when a person is in disagreement with others who are attractive, there may be a special interest in recruiting support.

Table 10.7. Average Number of Influence Attempts on the Paid Participant as Affected by the Degree of Attraction to and the Degree of Agreement with Others in the Reference Group
(From Gerard, 1954)

	Degree of Agreement		
	Agree (0.0 to 0.5)	Mildly Disagree (1.0)	Strongly Disagree (1.5 or Greater)
High-attraction	50.7	27.9	36.7
Low-attraction	40.5	34.5	32.9

Table 10.8 presents the percentage of subjects changing their opinion toward the accomplice. The accomplice attacked the subject from a position that would tend to pull the subject away from his reference group. The subject was thus caught between two pressures. The data show that in

Table 10.8. Percentage of Subjects Changing Toward the Paid Participant as Affected by the Degree of Attraction to and the Degree of Agreement with Others in the Reference Group
(From Gerard, 1954)

	Degree of Agreement		
	Agree (0.0 to 0.5)	Mildly Disagree (1.0)	Strongly Disagree (1.5 or Greater)
High-attraction	7	13	25
Low-attraction	20	38	8

general it was easier for the paid participant to pull the subject away from a less attractive group with low consensus than from a group with high consensus that was more attractive than his present one. The low frequency of subjects who changed in the low-attraction–strongly-disagree condition, however, defies ready explanation.

Kelley and Volkart (1952) found much the same evidence in a field experiment. They measured the degree to which a communicator was effective in pulling the subject away from the norms of his reference group, in their case a Boy Scout troop, as a function of how much the subject valued his membership in that group. The communicator was less effective the more the subject valued his membership in the troop. We shall report this study in more detail in Chapter Twelve.

In another study by Kelley (1955), which we shall also consider in more detail in Chapter Twelve, the salience of the subject's reference group, in this case the Catholic Church, was manipulated by verbal instructions before a counternorm communication was delivered. There was evidence that the more salient the reference group, the more resistant to change the subject was to a counternorm communication.

The Bennington Study

Newcomb (1943), in a classic study to which we have already referred, traced the changes in attitudes toward political affairs that occurred among Bennington coeds during their four years of college. The typical Bennington freshman in 1935, the year the study began, came from a wealthy, northeastern, conservative home and expressed typically conservative political attitudes in a questionnaire administered to her on arrival at Bennington. She was soon exposed to the more liberal attitudes of the faculty, and of popular and prestigeful older students who also tended to be very liberal. At the outset, Newcomb found in a cross-sectional survey that the longer the student had been at the school, the more likely she was to have developed nonconservative attitudes. In addition to comparing the freshman class of 1935 with sophomores, juniors, and seniors in 1935, Newcomb traced this entering class through their college career and discovered that year after year their attitudes became more and more nonconservative. It was obviously "in" to be politically liberal. A coed received approval from the faculty and from upper-classmen for expressing liberal views.

The attitudes formed in this way were not a mere passing fancy in the lives of these girls. Some 25 years later, Newcomb (1963) reinterviewed nearly the entire graduating class of 1939. In spite of what might be expected, there was very little reversion to the conservative attitudes held by these women when they had entered Bennington as freshmen three decades earlier. Compared with a comparable sample of American women of the same socioeconomic level, these women were found to be markedly more liberal in their political views. Their husbands also expressed far more liberal views than would be expected from men at this socioeconomic level.

Newcomb attempts to account for this high level of liberalism among the husbands by suggesting that the Bennington graduates sought out marriage partners who would provide a supportive environment for their newly won political beliefs. On returning to their families, they were probably confronted with dissonance-arousing, antiliberal persuasion from family members. Being firmly committed to liberal beliefs anchored in the cohesive Bennington reference group, their reaction may have been to seek out a supportive mate who shared their views. There are, of course, other motivations for choosing a spouse who shares similar views, but the suggestion offered here is one consistent with social comparison theory, the focus of this chapter. It is also possible that this generation of Bennington coeds chose typical members of their socioeconomic group and proceeded to indoctrinate them with the views they had acquired at Bennington. This possibility brings to mind the proselytizing behavior of the doomsday cult described in Chapter One. Without further evidence it is not possible to choose between various interpretations of the findings. Perhaps multiple processes were at work.

COMPARISON OF ABILITIES

In his general theory of social comparison Festinger (1954) attempted to extend his earlier theory of communication and influence to the evaluation of abilities. The revised theory focused exclusively on comparative appraisal, and in its extension to ability comparison relied heavily on the earlier literature dealing with how an individual sets a level of aspiration in performing some task.

As described in Chapter Nine, in the typical level of aspiration experiment the subject performs a serial task, such as throwing darts or ring-toss hoops, and is asked after each trial to predict the score he will make on the next trial. When the subject is given information as to how some comparison group has performed, he tends to use his previous performance and that of the comparison group as points of reference in estimating his own future performance. If we consider an opinion statement a performance, the level-of-aspiration situation is strikingly similar to the situation confronting a subject in the opinion experiments we have just described. If the subject has had a great deal of previous experience with the issue or has other external anchors he is less likely to be influenced by the judgments of others. Similarly, if a subject has had extensive experience with a particular task he relies more heavily on his own past performance to predict his future performance. On the other hand, to the extent that he has no clear-cut basis for holding an opinion or making a performance estimate, he relies on the opinions or performances of others. This is restating the fundamental assumption underlying the process of comparative appraisal.

Whereas the process of opinion comparison manifests itself in social influence mediated by communication, ability comparison appears as competitiveness. Given a range of performances in a group, the individuals involved tend, over time, to become more uniform in performance through competition. As in opinion comparison, both the importance of the performance to the person and its relevance to the particular comparison group affect the degree to which performance comparison takes place. Also, as in opinion comparison, an individual tends to compare himself with others who are close to him in performance rather than with those who are different.

A study by Chapman and Volkmann (1939) clearly demonstrates a group effect on level of aspiration. The subjects, college students in psychology courses, were given a test of "literary acquaintance" that contained 50 multiple-choice items. Before the test they were told the average score made by the members of a particular group. There were three treatments. In one the score was purportedly made by a group of literary critics; in a second treatment the score was made by a group of psychology students; in the third treatment the score was attributed to a group of high-school students. There was also a control condition in which the subjects received no performance information about another group. In all three experimental treatments the fictitious score attributed to the other group was exactly the same. After being given this false information, the subject was asked to predict the score he himself would make on the test.

The experimental treatments showed clear effects on the subject's stated aspiration level; the greater the presumed expertise of the reference group, the lower was the subject's expected score. When the norm was purportedly that of a group of psychology students, the subject's score expectation was similar to that of the control group. When the score was attributed to experts, his score expectation was lower than the control group's, and when the score was attributed to inferiors, that is, high-school students, the subject's score expectation was above that of the control group.

A second experiment by the same authors showed that when the subject had had considerable experience with a particular type of test and could therefore estimate accurately how he would perform on a similar subsequent test, knowledge of the score of some reference group had little or no bearing on the score he predicted for himself. To the extent that the subject has some factual basis for checking his estimate or judgment, he is less likely to rely on social reality.

Festinger (1942) performed an experiment with a similar format. The subjects, who were college students, believed that they scored either above or below one of three reference groups: high-school students, college students, or graduate students. There were clear effects of the prestige of the reference group on the subject's level of aspiration. When told that he had performed above the average score of the reference group, the subject lowered his level of aspiration more, the greater the prestige of the group, whereas if told that he had scored below the average score of the reference group he increased his level of aspiration less, the greater the prestige of the reference group.

An experiment by Dreyer (1954) attempted to arrange conditions in which ability comparison could be studied with the precision that earlier studies had used in investigating opinion comparison. Dreyer assumed that the social comparison of an ability manifests itself as a desire to compete. Using elementary-school children in a card-sorting task, he created three experimental treatments. The subject found himself scoring well above, at, or well below a group performance norm. Over time, the subject who assumed that he was scoring close to the group norm tended to be more involved in the task than the subject scoring well below or well above the norm. This degree of involvement or competitiveness was measured by the subject's desire to continue performing on successive trials of the card-sorting task. There was also evidence indicating that the subject's self-evaluation, as measured by successive level-of-aspiration statements, was stable when he scored near the group norm as compared with subjects who scored above or below it.

It thus appears that when a person's performance is close to that of relevant other persons, he receives more reliable information, which in turn anchors his self-evaluation more firmly. The increased competitiveness for those subjects in Dreyer's study who were close to the norm is also evidence that they were definitely attempting to maintain comparison. They presumably competed with the "typical" member of their group, even though they were performing the task alone.

The possibility exists, of course, that those subjects who scored near the norm were trying to impress the experimenter. Those who scored above the norm had presumably already succeeded in impressing the experimenter, whereas those who scored below the norm consistently gave up trying to create a good impression. This other possible interpretation of the findings presents a serious problem, one that plagues most research of this kind. The relationship between the subject and the experimenter is undoubtedly complex and only recently, as we pointed out in Chapter Two, has it been receiving due attention. This experiment could, of course, be rerun to reduce the probable importance of this factor by removing the experimenter from such close face-to-face contact with the subject.

An individual's level of aspiration is detectable from his experience of success or failure in a particular performance. If the individual feels he has failed he tends to lower both his performance expectation on a subsequent task and his estimate of his own ability, whereas if he experiences success the opposite results. These relationships have been well documented (Lewin, Dembo, Festinger, & Sears, 1944).

Gerard (1961a) examined the effect of performance information about a reference group on the person's experience of success and failure as measured by changes in his self-ability estimate and changes in his level of aspiration. The subjects, college students at New York University, took a test of their spatial visualization ability and each was asked on a questionnaire before receiving his test score to estimate his ability and the score he had made on the test. A few days later the experimenter returned to the classroom and wrote a false score distribution on the blackboard. Each subject was handed a slip of paper with what was presumably (but not actually) his score written on it. The fictitious distribution and the fictitious score given to the subject were such as to make all subjects appear to deviate from the group average. Half of the subjects received scores that placed them in the upper 5 percent of the class, whereas the other half received a score that placed them in the lower 5 percent of the class. These scores bore no relationship to how the subject had actually performed on the test. The subject was then asked to state the score he might have made had the testing conditions been ideal and was also asked to re-estimate his spatial visualization ability. The effects are clear cut and are as we would expect them to be. Those subjects who received high scores increased their estimate of their own ability, whereas subjects who received low scores did the reverse.

An interesting sidelight to the experiment involved the role of publicity. Half of the subjects involved were told that the roster of scores would be posted on the bulletin board so that each person could see how he did in relation to his friends and the rest of the class. Other subjects were told that their scores would be kept in the strictest confidence. This factor was introduced in order to detect what was referred to in Chapter Nine as reflected appraisal. When the subject received his score in private—that is, when it was not going to be divulged to the other members of the class—we would expect only comparative appraisal to be operating. When the score was to be made public we would expect effects of reflected appraisal as well, effects deriving from the subjects' expectations of being evaluated by their classmates.

The subject who received a high score *increased* his self-evaluation *more* in the public than in the private condition. On the other hand, the subject who received a low score *decreased* his self-evaluation *less* in the public than in the private condition. It appears that the high scorer in the public treatment is responding to the anticipated praise for his high score, whereas the low scorer is responding to the anticipated derogation. To have success revealed publicly enhances its effect. Failure, on the other hand, seems to be much easier to accept privately than publicly. The "public-failure" subject resisted lowering his self-ability estimate, presumably in anticipation of having to maintain his position in the group. Subjects who, on a previous personality questionnaire, revealed a high dependence on reflected appraisal information, showed more marked effects on their self-estimates in the public condition than subjects low in their dependence on such information. This last finding adds further support to the assumption that the public condition produces reflected appraisal. Additional evidence in line with these findings may be found in a similar study by Mischel (1958a).

Earlier we stated that tendencies toward ability comparison would manifest themselves in competitiveness. As in opinion comparison, a person tends to compare his ability with that of someone who is relatively close to him in that ability. Thus, if a person's performance in a game reflects an underlying ability, he chooses to compete with someone who is close to him in the ability rather than someone who is distant. We would also expect this tendency to choose an equal rather than a superior or an inferior to be greater the more the measurement of his ability is important to the person.

Hoffman, Festinger, and Lawrence (1954) ran an experiment to examine these relationships. They created a competitive bargaining situation involving trading jigsaw-puzzle pieces in which the subject's success was presumed to measure his intelligence. In one treatment subjects were told that the bargaining test was an extremely good measure of intelligence, whereas in another they were told that the measure was of questionable validity, thus varying the importance of good performance. Three subjects were run at a time. In order for any subject to do well, he had to form a coalition with one of the other two and exchange jigsaw pieces. Otherwise no one could make the rectangle, which was the assigned goal. These coalitions could be made and dissolved at will and the game consisted of each individual attempting to jockey for position by entering into successive coalition agreements about how the spoils (points) would be divided. In each group one of the players was an accomplice posing as a naive subject. In an equal-ability condition the three subjects were told that, by consulting their school records, they were chosen to be of approximately equal intelligence, whereas in another condition they were told that one of the players was superior to the other two. In all of the groups, the accomplice, by immediately assembling a puzzle, achieved an initial advantage over the two naive subjects. It was clear to the two naive subjects that, in the treatment in which one subject was supposed to be superior, it was the accomplice who was, indeed, the one. They could easily discern this from his performance.

From the theory we would predict that there would be less reluctance to form a coalition with the accomplice when he was presumed to be of superior intelligence than when he was presumed to be of equal intelligence. When he was superior there were grounds for rendering him noncomparable; there was no threat implied in helping him gain points since he was clearly superior anyway. In the equal-ability condition the desire to compete with the accomplice should make the subject reluctant to enter into coalition agreements with him. As long as one naive subject forms coalitions only with the other naive subject, it may be possible to reach and overtake the accomplice in the game.

According to the theory, to the extent that the subjects considered the game a good measure of their intelligence, and their performance was therefore important to them, this greater tendency *not* to form coalitions with the accomplice in the equal-ability treatment should be enhanced. Results shown in Tables 10.9 and 10.10 clearly support the predictions.

Table 10.9. Average Percentage of Coalitions Having the Accomplice as a Member (From Hoffman, Festinger, and Lawrence, 1954)

Task Importance	Accomplice's Ability	
	Equal	Superior
High	46	55
Low	52	75

Table 10.10. Average Points Earned per Trial by the Accomplice (From Hoffman, Festinger, and Lawrence, 1954)

Task Importance	Accomplice's Ability	
	Equal	Superior
High	1.43	2.07
Low	1.91	3.45

The accomplice fared more poorly when he was considered equal in ability than when he was considered superior, in terms of both the number of coalitions into which he entered and the number of points he got per coalition. He also fared much worse in the high- as compared with the low-importance treatment; that is, when the test was purported to be a valid measure of intelligence. This latter finding, based on the cross-cutting importance factor, further bolsters the social comparison interpretation because it is exactly what the theory predicts.

The basic assumption underlying social comparison theory is that in the absence of information of some kind as to the quality of his performance (or opinion) the person's self-estimate will be unstable. Evidence for this assumption has been recently reported by Radloff (in Latané, 1966) in an experiment in which the subject had to perform a task involving hand-eye coordination. The subject received false feedback about his performance on one set of trials and then worked on a second set. Radloff's data suggest that when the subject finds that others have performed at about his level his self-estimate on a closely related subsequent task tends to be more stable than when he has been told others have done much better or worse. In addition, the subject's estimates of his own performance tend to be more accurate when he has previously received feedback showing his performance as modal.

These experiments present evidence that comparative appraisal occurs with respect to abilities as well as opinions. In ability comparison the performance of the comparison person is the benchmark. There is usually a clear and obvious connection between performance and the inference made about the other person's ability. The situation for opinion comparison is more complicated. What kind of inference does a person make about someone else when he knows that other person's judgment or opinion on an issue? How much credibility should he attach to the other's judgment or opinion? In order to determine this the person will attempt to make inferences about the expertise and co-orientation of the reference person. As suggested, an opinion statement is a performance that may reflect either or both of these attributes. One implication of this difference between ability and opinion comparison is that, owing to the greater room for inference, it is usually much easier to render another person either comparable or noncomparable when comparing opinions than when comparing abilities.

Attraction and Comparison

In both the 1950 and 1954 versions of the theory, Festinger postulated a relationship between the attractiveness of the reference person and the tendency to use him as a source of comparison information. Interest in this relationship appears in a number of the experiments on opinion comparison and in at least one experiment concerning ability comparison (Festinger, Torrey, and Willerman, 1954). In both versions the relationship is stated by fiat and the dynamic that might underlie the relationship between attraction and comparison is not specified. The data are quite clear. In nearly every experiment that manipulated attractiveness a clear effect was observed between this variable and the strength of the comparison tendency. In terms of the distinctions made in Chapter Nine three possibilities for explaining the relationship suggest themselves.

The first of these is fairly obvious. When the person can be identified with his opinion, as in experiments in which he has an opinion card in front of him, his motivation to conform may be to avoid ridicule. Presumably he would like to maintain his status in the eyes of the other subjects in the experiment; the more attractive they are, the more important it is for him to do this. When the subject is told, in the high-attraction condition, that the group is well matched for congeniality, being in disagreement would violate the expectations of the other subjects and also, incidentally, of the experimenter, whose skill at matching congenial persons would therefore be brought into question. The desire to meet others' expectations is not a manifestation of comparative appraisal, as Festinger would have it, but of reflected appraisal based on effect dependence. In experiments in which a condition that provides the subject with anonymity is compared with a condition in which the subject openly takes a stand, marked differences in conformity behavior favoring the public treatment are found. We submit that the added effect may be a result of normative pressures derived from reflected appraisal in the public treatment. We shall discuss some of this research in Chapter Eleven.

Another process that might account for the attraction-comparison relationship is the attribution of co-orientation to the group. When a subject is a member of a group that has been carefully assembled with congeniality and common interests in mind, he may easily attribute a common perspective to the members of the group and thus regard them as co-oriented peers. Insofar as the aspect of judgment being compared has anything to do with the determination of values or goals, there will be a greater tendency to rely on the judgments of co-oriented others.

Another possibility, addressed experimentally by Berkowitz (1957), is that an individual will attribute expertise to someone he likes. Berkowitz was struck, as are we, by the lack of theoretical underpinning for the attraction-comparison hypothesis. His experiment involved an artillery game in which the subject, who was the "battery commander," received information on target distance from a fictitious "observer." On the questionnaire administered after the game there was a positive correlation between the subject's liking for the observer and his estimation of the observer's accuracy in reporting target information. There was also a greater tendency for the subject who liked the observer to rely more heavily on the target information supplied by the observer. This is evidence, then, for the operation of expertise attribution as a way of accounting for the attraction-comparison relationship.

We would expect each of these processes to operate under different conditions and to have different behavior implications. Obligation would be more likely to operate in a situation when surveillance of the subject by the other members of the group is possible, as in an experiment in which subjects face each other in a spoken or note-writing discussion. Any changes of opinions or performance would be transitory. With surveillance removed, the subject would tend to refer to his initial opinion or performance. Co-orientation attribution would be likely to occur when comparison concerns present or future outcome levels. For example, in discussing a clinical case study, a "love" or "punishment" perspective on what should be done with a delinquent would be more likely to involve reliance on a co-oriented peer than on an expert. On the other hand, a discussion involving Federal aid to education might elicit dependence on an expert. There is obviously a great deal of room for further work on these problems.

COMPARATIVE APPRAISAL AND EMOTIONS

Individuals should be attracted to others they anticipate will provide uncertainty-reducing information and should also be attracted to others who have in fact provided such information. In the experiment by Festinger, Gerard, Hymovitch, Kelley, and Raven (1952), conformers were found to be more attracted to the group, as measured in the postexperimental questionnaire, than were deviates. This is presumably a reaction on the part of the conformers to the uncertainty-reducing value of the information provided by the others in the group. In the majority-minority experiment by Gerard (1953) the subjects were administered a projective test developed by Libo (1953), which was designed to measure the individual's attraction to a group. The data from this projective test revealed a positive correlation between closeness of the subject's opinion to the rest of the members of the group and his attraction to the group. It is at least conceivable that the conforming subject is attracted to fellow group members *because* they have reduced his uncertainty, and not that some subjects conform because they are especially attracted to the group.

Brodbeck (1956) examined the effects of opinion uncertainty on the subject's choice of a discussion partner from among seven other subjects who had opinion cards displayed in front of them. At the beginning of the experimental session each subject had stated on a questionnaire whether he was in favor of wire-tapping and how confident he was of his opinion. He then heard a tape-recorded, persuasive communication that argued either on his side or the other side of the issue. After answering a second opinion questionnaire, subjects were classified into one of three categories: those whose opinion agreed with the opinion advocated in the persuasive communication; those whose opinion disagreed with the message but whose confidence was lowered by it; and those who disagreed and did not lower their confidence. Brodbeck reasoned that, in comparing these three types of subjects, those who disagreed and lowered their confidence would be most uncertain, whereas those who agreed with the message would be least uncertain. Those who disagreed with the message and who did not change their confidence ratings would fall between the other two groups. Each subject was then asked to choose a partner for further discussion. He was free to choose someone who agreed or someone who disagreed with him. The data showed that the greater the assumed uncertainty, in the rank order discussed above, the more likely the subject was to choose someone who agreed with him. It is plausible to assume that in making this choice the subject was motivated by a desire for comparison information in order to reduce uncertainty.

Radloff (1962) shed further light on the problem, using a somewhat different technique with college coed subjects. After determining the subjects' opinions as to who should pay for the cost of higher education, the students themselves or the government, he exposed some and not others to a false consensus. In one treatment the consensus purportedly summarized the opinions of a sample of high-school students, that is, the subjects' inferiors. In another treatment it summarized the opinions of co-oriented peers, other college students; and in another, the opinions of experts in the education field.

Following this each subject indicated the strength of her desire to join a discussion about financing higher education. Those subjects who received no consensus information were most strongly interested in joining the discussion. They were presumably the ones most in need of comparison information. Next in order of intensity of interest were those subjects receiving the consensus of inferiors. Next were those receiving the consensus of co-oriented peers. Those receiving the consensus of experts were least anxious to join the discussion group. The ordering of these treatments is what we would expect in terms of the adequacy of the comparison information available to the subject. Questionnaire data support the assumption that the subject's desire to join the discussion was motivated, at least in part, by the need for comparison information.

Singer and Shockley (1965) tested the uncertainty-attraction hypothesis in an ability-evaluation context. Subjects took an ability test and received their scores; some were given information as to how others had done on the test, the remainder were not. Subjects were then given a choice of waiting alone or with others while the experimenter got ready to administer an additional test. Those subjects who received no norm information showed a stronger desire to affiliate than did those who received such information. Questionnaire evidence indicated that this desire to affiliate on the part of the subjects who received no norms was best interpreted as a result of their desire for comparison information.

Fear, Uncertainty, and Affiliation

A program of research by Schachter has been especially influential in dramatizing the significance of uncertainty and information-seeking as factors leading to affiliation. This work resulted from a convergence of two somewhat different interests. It is clear from his contribution to basic issues of opinion comparison that he was thoroughly immersed in problems relating to comparative appraisal. The other line of interest was stimulated by the work of Hebb and others. (See Heron, 1961, for a review of these studies.) Hebb and his colleagues discovered in a series of experiments that when a person is cut off from a large proportion of the sensory information input that he is normally accustomed to receiving, the situation becomes unbearable after a few hours and strange hallucinatory effects can occur. The subjects in these experiments were asked to lie in a small, unadorned room. Each had translucent caps over his eyes, his ears were plugged, and his hands were covered so that he could not touch anything. In spite of the fact that subjects received a high hourly rate of pay for their services, few were able to bear the deprivation of sensory information much beyond 24 hours. There appeared to be an obvious connection between this work and social comparison, and Schachter wondered whether similar effects would occur with an impoverished social information input. After exploring several situations he decided that the importance of social information input could best be studied by confronting the subject with a novel situation and examining the strength of his desire to be with other people.

Schachter's (1959) experimental paradigm was elegantly simple. The college coeds used as subjects in the experiment were assembled in the laboratory in groups of five to eight members each and were confronted by "Dr. Gregor Zilstein of the Medical School's Department of Neurology and Psychiatry." "Zilstein" wore a white laboratory coat and had a stethoscope dribbling from his pocket. He told the girls that they had been selected for an experiment to study the effects of electric shock. In the high-fear condition the subjects were further told that:

> What we will ask each of you to do is very simple. We would like to give each of you a series of electrical shocks. Now, I feel I must be completely honest with you and tell you exactly what you are in for. The shocks will hurt; they will be painful. As you can guess, if, in research of this sort, we're to learn anything at all that will really help humanity, it is necessary that our shocks be intense. What we will do is put an electrode on your hand, hook you into apparatus such as this [Zilstein points to the electrical-looking gadgetry behind him], give you a series of electrical shocks, and take various measures such as your pulse rate, blood pressure, and so on. Again, I do want to be honest with you and tell you that these shocks will be quite painful but, of course, they will do no permanent damage.

In the low-fear condition Zilstein gave the following instructions:

> I have asked you all to come today in order to serve as subjects in an experiment concerned with the effects of electrical shock. I hasten to add, do not let the word "shock" trouble you; I am sure that you will enjoy the experiment. What we would like each of you to do is very simple. We would like to give each of you a series of very mild electrical shocks. I assure you that what you will feel will not in any way be painful. It will resemble more a tickle or a tingle than anything unpleasant. We will put an electrode on your hand, give you a series of very mild shocks and measure such things as your pulse rate, blood pressure, measures with which I am sure you are all familiar from your visits to your family doctor.

The subjects were then asked to indicate on a questionnaire how they felt about receiving the shocks. Next they were told the main laboratory room would have to be cleared to prepare the equipment for the experiment. During this delay they could have their choice of waiting alone in some of the additional rooms or in a room with some of the other girls. They indicated, on the questionnaire, the waiting situation they preferred and, on a rating scale, how strongly they felt about the situation they had chosen. After this, they were given an opportunity to leave if they desired. This ended the experiment. No shocks were actually administered.

The results were clear. First, the induction of differential fear was successful. Subjects who expected to receive strong shocks indicated that they believed the experience would be much more unpleasant than those who expected mild shocks. Also, about 20 percent of the subjects in the strong-shock treatment refused to continue, whereas none in the mild-shock treatment refused. The waiting-situation question provided the subject with three options: waiting "together," "alone," or "don't care." In the high-fear condition 63 percent of the subjects chose to wait together, compared with only 33 percent in the low-fear treatment.

Obviously, the results of this first experiment can be interpreted in many ways because any number of motives could have been aroused in the high-fear treatment that could account for the higher desire for affiliation in that treatment. To narrow the range of possible motives, Schachter ran a second experiment. This one was designed to determine if the relationship between fear and affiliation had anything to do with characteristics of a suitable waiting partner. Would the highly anxious subject choose to wait with anybody, or was it important that the waiting partner was herself to undergo the same experience? The same procedure was repeated as in the first experiment except that only the high-fear manipulation was used, with two different waiting-option treatments. In one the subject could wait with others in the experiment who were about to receive strong shocks themselves; in the other, if the subject chose "together," she would wait in a room where other girls were waiting to see their professors.

Again the results are clear. The fate of the waiting partners makes a great difference. When the subject could wait with others about to undergo the same shock experience, 60 percent chose to wait together, whereas in the other treatment not a single subject elected to do so. Obviously, the motive or motives involved for wanting to wait together rest heavily on the perception that the waiting partners are about to undergo the same fate as the subject herself, or, as Schachter puts it, "Misery doesn't love just any kind of company, it loves only miserable company" (p. 24).

If we assume that the high-fear treatment created more uncertainty than the low, the former confronting the subject with a novel and strange situation, her desire to be with others can be interpreted as an attempt to get a fix on her own emotional state. This somewhat threatening situation has worked up her feelings, yet she is not quite sure how to interpret them. Is she angry at the experimenter? Or is she worried that she might not measure up to the trial? Or is she afraid that the shocks might be too painful to bear? Her feelings may also seem to her to be quite variable. At one moment she may feel quite fearful and in the next moment her worked-up state may subside somewhat. She may also wonder if what she feels is *appropriate* to the situation. Ought she feel as worked-up as she does about what is going to happen to her?

Another possibility is that both high and low fear produced the same degree of uncertainty in the subject about her worked-up condition but it was more important for her to resolve this uncertainty in the high- than in the low-fear treatment. The data presented so far do not enable us to choose between these possibilities; that is, between the possibility that the high-fear treatment produces more uncertainty or that it produces the same amount of uncertainty but makes self-evaluation more imperative because of the greater magnitude of the consequences.

We would be in relatively good shape if choosing between these two alternatives were the only problem here. Unfortunately, there are many other plausible interpretations of the data. Some of the subjects may have been a little bit incredulous about whether or not "Zilstein" would really be so mean as to shock them. After all, a gentleman does not do that kind of thing to a defenseless young lady. The subject may have wanted to get together with the other girls to discuss this possibility. She may also have entertained the possibility that if they got together she and the others might figure out some way of talking the experimenter out of shocking them. Still another motive that might have been operating for some of the subjects was a desire to be with others for reassurance that things were not as black as they seemed. Any or all of these motives may have been present in different subjects or in some combination in a single subject.

Schachter reasoned that he could narrow the range of possible interpretations if he could demonstrate the fear-affiliation relationship in a treatment in which the waiting situation was restricted so that subjects could not talk about what was going to happen. In a third experiment, then, two factors were varied: the level of fear, as in the first experiment, and the nature of the waiting situation. In one treatment subjects were told that if they chose to wait together they could talk about anything except aspects of the experiment. In a second treatment the subjects were told that if they chose the "together" situation they could sit in the same room but could not talk to one another. By this manipulation Schachter hoped to rule out all interpretations that relied on communication between the subjects. He assumed that the comparison hypothesis did not require such communication but that the subject could pick up the necessary cues that would help her to evaluate herself just by looking at the other people. The experiment thus contained four experimental conditions: high-fear—irrelevant-talk; high-fear—no-talk; low-fear—irrelevant-talk; low-fear—no-talk. The data showed an approximately equal proportion of subjects choosing "together" in all four. This experiment, therefore, did not rule out the vast array of possible explanations. An internal analysis of the data did show a relationship between how afraid the subject said she was on the postexperimental questionnaire and the choice of "together" in *both* types of waiting situations. Such correlational evidence is suggestive but is heir to many inherent weaknesses. For example, those subjects who said they were very afraid may always prefer the company of others to being alone, regardless of the circumstances. We may therefore be dealing with some personality characteristic rather than an experimental effect. Taken together, the data from the three experiments certainly point to the possibility that comparative appraisal motivated at least some of the "together" choices; however, the suggestion must, for the moment, be only tentative.

Rather than pursue the problem further by varying aspects of the waiting situation, Gerard and Rabbie (1961) took a different tack. If the desire for comparison information motivated a "together" choice, providing the subject with clarifying information should tend to reduce the subject's desire to wait with other subjects. This prediction was tested using essentially the same experimental paradigm as in the Schachter experiments. A feature of Schachter's procedure that might have affected results in the third experiment was that the five to eight subjects sat in full view of one another while the fear manipulation was being induced. They could thus look around the room and see the other girls fidgeting, blushing, perspiring, biting their nails, and so on. This is just the kind of information that Schachter expected would motivate a "together" choice in the irrelevant-talk and the no-talk waiting situations. If the subject already had that kind of information, comparative appraisal would be eliminated from the possible motivations to want to be together. Therefore Gerard and Rabbie ran their experiment, using four subjects per session, with each in a separate isolation booth. The subject had no information about how the others were responding to the instructions other than the information the experimenter chose to give them. Each subject had a pair of electrodes attached to his hand which were used to measure changes in his skin resistance. Skin resistance changes are known to reflect the psychological stress a person is experiencing; a decrease in resistance generally accompanies an increase in stress. An electrocardiograph electrode was attached to the subject's forearm, which was then strapped to an arm rest. The subject was informed that the electrode on his hand registered skin resistance and that the arm electrode measured muscle tremor. He was further told that with this information his emotionality could be accurately determined both before and during the administration of the shocks. Actually, the forearm electrode was a dummy but the electrodes on his hand were operative and measured changes in skin resistance.

After high or low fear was induced, using Schachter's original severe- and mild-threat instructions, each experimental group was assigned to one of three information treatments. In one treatment (information–self-and-others) the subject was told:

As you no doubt may guess, even the anticipation of getting a shock may affect you emotionally and hence produce physiological reactions. In front of you there are four meters which have been calibrated to register the emotionality index I referred to earlier. We thought that you would like to see how you yourself and the others are reacting to the prospect of getting shocked. As you can see, each meter goes from zero to a maximum of 100. The first meter to register will show your own index; then the other meters will be connected so that you may see how emotional the others are.

The subject's meter was then switched on and a few minutes later the other three meters were also switched on. Each of the four subjects was in the same situation. Each had four of the "emotionality index" meters lined up in front of him and the third meter from the left, which he assumed was his, was the first to register. In the high-fear treatment—that is, when the subject expected strong shocks—it read 82. When the other meters were turned on they had approximately the same reading. Under low fear, when the subject expected weak shocks, his meter read 32. The other three meters were approximately at the same level. In another treatment (information–self) each subject had one meter in front of him that registered 82 in the high-fear treatment, and 32 in the low-fear treatment. A third treatment (no information) was run in which no emotionality information, either about the subject or about the others, was given. All subjects were then given the same Schachter instructions about waiting together or alone and were asked to make a choice. They were also asked to set a dial to indicate how strongly they felt about the waiting situation they chose.

The critical difference between the information–self-and-others and the information–self treatments was that in the former the subject had comparative information from others that validated his own standing (his own meter reading). There are, as we suggested, a number of possible motives operating that in Schachter's original experiment would cause a subject to choose "together." If one of these motives involves comparative appraisal, the subject's desire to wait together should be *lower* when he already has information about the others' reactions than when he does not have this information. All but 12 of the 100 subjects chose to wait together, but, as may be seen in Table 10.11, the subjects who chose "together"

Table 10.11. Strength of Affiliation for Subjects Choosing "Together"
(From Gerard and Rabbie, 1961)

Level of Fear	No-Information	N	Information–Self	N	Information–Self–and–Others	N
High	66.8	15	70.5	16	55.1	11
Low	54.5	17	64.1	17	47.7	12

showed a weaker desire to be together when they had information about themselves and the others than where they had information only about themselves. This is true both under the high- and low-fear treatments. The somewhat weaker desire for affiliation shown in the no-information as compared with the information–self treatment is puzzling. It may be that subjects who are exposed to their own meter reading become especially curious about their standing in the group. The subject's uncertainty is not reduced if he is assigned a number on a scale and does not have a clear idea what the number really stands for. Radloff (1959) found a similar effect with an opinion comparison. There is also greater affiliation in the high- as compared with the low-fear treatment, presumably because it is more important to obtain comparative information under high fear.

The major assumption made in Chapter Nine was that information-seeking would occur when the person was uncertain. In discussing Schachter's experiments we stated that the greater desire for comparison information in the high- as compared with the low-fear treatments could have been a result either of greater uncertainty or the increased urgency of reducing the uncertainty. The results of the Gerard-Rabbie experiment suggest that both were, in fact, operating. Information about the others did reduce affiliation, but the desire to affiliate was stronger in the high- than in the low-fear treatments under both information levels.

In still another experiment (Gerard, 1963) the uncertainty factor was approached from a different direction. The fact that in the previous experiment information about the others reduced the desire to affiliate suggests that uncertainty is indeed a factor producing affiliation. However, the data for the no-information treatment raise problems for this interpretation. The matter might be pinned down if uncertainty could be varied holding the level of fear constant. Stronger affiliation would occur the greater the uncertainty. We would thus have converged on the comparison theory hypothesis both by varying internal states that are assumed to elicit social comparison behavior and by varying external information that is assumed to reduce that behavior.

The procedure employed was similar to the one used by Gerard and

Rabbie (1961) but an attempt was made to vary the subject's certainty about the intensity of his emotional reaction. Each of the four subjects, who were in isolation booths, had one meter in front of him labeled "emotionality index." Each was hooked up to the skin resistance electrodes and the dummy muscle tremor electrode and was told to watch his meter, which would register momentary changes in his emotionality index. After the "strong shock" instructions used in the previous experiments, the subject in the uncertain treatment saw his meter needle describe wide and erratic excursions with an average reading of 75. In the certain treatment the meter needle was fairly steady, again with an average of 75. This meter-watching uncertainty induction lasted for three minutes, after which the subject was given the alone-together choice and indicated the strength of his desire for the waiting situation he chose. According to comparison theory, we would expect the wavy needle induction to produce greater affiliation than the steady needle induction, if greater uncertainty about the subject's emotional state was indeed induced with the wavy needle. The data bear this out.

Another aspect of the experiment attempted to examine, under the wavy needle treatment, the effect on the strength of affiliation of different kinds of information about the other three subjects. The subject was given information implying that the others were equal, lower, or higher than he in emotionality. According to the theory, the subject tends to compare himself with someone else to the extent that the other person is similar to himself in attributes relevant to the comparison. Assuming, as we have so far, that affiliation reflects the strength of the subject's social comparison tendency, we would predict that affiliation strength should be greater when the others are reported to be similar in emotionality than when they are reported to be either higher or lower than the subject himself. Again, the data bear out this prediction.

In the experiment just discussed the uncertainty felt by the subject concerned his own emotional reaction to the impending threat. As we have already suggested, there are other kinds of uncertainty that may exist in the situation. One of these concerns the nature of the impending experience itself; that is, will it really be painful and if so, how painful? Two recent experiments have examined social comparison under this type of uncertainty.

Rabbie (1964), using Schachter's fear situation, induced differential uncertainty by telling half of his groups that the shocks would be painful for everyone and telling the other half that the shocks are experienced as painful by approximately one in four people. Subjects in the latter, high-ambiguity condition had a greater desire to be with others than subjects under low ambiguity. As in the Gerard-Rabbie experiment the subject was given fictitious emotionality readings on the other three subjects in the group. One of the others was purported to be highly emotional, one moderately emotional, and one low in emotionality. The subject received no information about himself but did indicate how emotional he felt. By and large, subjects tended to seek out their own emotionality level in choosing a waiting partner, although the "moderately emotional other" tended to be overchosen by subjects reporting that they themselves were highly emotional. These data add further support for the theory.

Darley and Aronson (in Latané, 1966) attempted to design an experiment to discriminate between fear reduction and uncertainty reduction as bases for affiliating with others. A subject might choose to wait with others in order to *clarify* his own feelings or in hopes that he could *reduce* the intensity of felt emotion. Darley and Aronson gave high- and low-fear instructions to groups of three coeds per session, following this with false emotionality information to each subject about the level of fear they were experiencing. One girl was reported to be slightly more fearful than the subject, the other girl was considerably less fearful. Thus, in making a choice regarding *which* fellow subject to wait with, the subject would reveal whether her interest in reducing fear (by choosing to wait with the calmer person) was stronger than her interest in comparison per se (by choosing to wait with the person most similar to her). As it turned out, subjects in the high-fear treatment preferred to wait with the person who was slightly more fearful than with the calmer person. This was, however, not true under low fear.

In a third condition subjects were given information about the shock that was explicitly designed to raise their uncertainty about whether the shock would be painful. The instructions referred to the fact that ". . . this is one of the first groups we have run" and concluded with "we just don't have data on the pain caused by electric shock." Interestingly enough, when confronted with the same choice between a slightly more fearful companion and a considerably less fearful one, these subjects tended strongly to prefer the latter or to wait alone. This raises problems, of course, for a strict social comparison interpretation of the affiliation research and suggests that at least two motives are operating when uncertainty is high: the subject wants to discover the appropriate level of fear but also wants to discover that the appropriate level is low.

It is conceivable that the subject under high fear preferred to wait with a slightly more anxious person in order either to reduce her own anxiety by the favorable contrast with the other girl or because she felt motherly toward her and wanted to comfort her. In an attempt to rule out these possibilities, Darley and Aronson ran another treatment (under high-fear instructions) in which one of the girls reported a slightly higher fear level and the other reported exactly the same fear level as the subject. The data effectively rule out the other interpretations, for the subject overwhelmingly preferred to wait with the girl who was exactly as afraid as she. Another possible interpretation, which requires an additional experiment before it can be ruled out, is that the subject may attribute other similarities besides fear level to the girl who shares her fear and therefore may tend to find her more attractive as someone to sit and converse with while waiting for the experimenter to get things ready.

The Results of Emotional Comparison

The evidence from this series of experiments seems to imply strongly that social comparison processes are involved in labeling or measuring emotions, at least under certain circumstances. From the subject's point of view, the experiments described so far were fortunately abortive. After she made her alone–together choice the experiment was over. She experienced neither the waiting situation nor the shocks. What actually happens when a person has an opportunity to compare his emotional reactions with those of others? If comparative appraisal does ensue, we would expect to observe some of the phenomena found in the studies of opinion and ability comparison. For example, we would predict convergence of emotional self-estimates among the members of the comparison group as information is exchanged during the waiting period.

An experiment by Wrightsman (1960) extended the investigation of emotional comparison in this way by studying the effects of actually being with others while awaiting a dire event. Four college-student subjects used in each experimental group were placed in separate rooms; in each room there was a tray containing hypodermic needles and various medicaments. Each was told that the experiment would study the effects of drastic changes in glucose level on mental activity, and that the injection of either a glucose additive or a glucose depressant he was to receive would be quite painful and might produce some bizarre symptoms. The subject was then asked to indicate on a scale how ill-at-ease he was feeling. Again the subjects were told that there would be a waiting period while the room and experimental equipment were made ready. Three waiting-situation treatments were applied, with one-third of the subjects being randomly assigned to each treatment. In the together–talk treatment the four subjects were assembled in a waiting room and told that they could talk about anything at all during the waiting period. In the together–no talk treatment the subjects were assembled in the room but were not permitted to talk during the waiting period. In the alone treatment the subjects remained in their individual rooms during the waiting period. After five minutes of waiting the subjects again stated on the same rating scale how ill-at-ease they felt. As a measure of the degree of convergence in emotionality a ratio was computed of the initial range of emotionality ratings in each four-person group divided by the range after the waiting period.

The alone condition showed no convergence whatsoever, whereas both "together" conditions showed some convergence. When the initial range was either very small or very large there was no convergence in the "together" groups. The groups in which the subjects were initially very close to each other presumably had very little room in which to converge, whereas subjects in groups with an initially wide range presumably saw each other as not comparable. This latter situation produced a condition similar to the heterogeneous condition in the earlier experiments on opinion comparison. Those groups that had neither a wide nor a narrow initial range showed considerable convergence that, we assume, was a result of the comparative appraisal occurring in the "together" situation.

Some Evidence for Reflected Appraisal

In all of the experiments that involved a choice of waiting situation, some subjects actually chose to be alone. In the Gerard and Rabbie (1961) experiment, those subjects who chose to wait alone were among the most emotionally aroused subjects. For these subjects there was a strong positive correlation between their desire to be alone and the amount of emotionality they showed. After the experiment some of the subjects spontaneously expressed a concern about not showing their emotions in public. Males seemed more concerned about this than females. They evidently did not want the others to think that they were sissies. This may be evidence for anticipated reflected appraisal. There appears to be a parallel between these results and those of the Gerard space-relations ability experiment in which the subjects in the private-failure condition lowered their self-evaluation more than subjects in the public-failure condition. Apparently it is easier, at least for some people, to accept failure or a weakness in themselves if it is not to be publicly disclosed. If it is possible to do so, the person prefers to be alone while displaying behavior that may cast him in a bad light and thus open him to possible censure and ridicule. Any such tendency operates in direct opposition to affiliation induced by comparative appraisal.

An experiment by Sarnoff and Zimbardo (1961) provides evidence directly concerning the effects of anticipated reflected comparison on the desire for isolation. The experiment employed the same threat and choice of waiting period paradigm with two different types of threat, one involving electrical shock as in many of the previous experiments, and another involving "oral anxiety." There were two levels of anticipated shock and two levels of induced oral anxiety, yielding a total of four treatments. The two levels of anticipated shock were induced with the same technique used in the previous studies. The two levels of oral anxiety were induced as follows: subjects in the high-oral-anxiety condition anticipated that they would have to suck on a number of objects commonly associated with infantile oral behavior. Each object was to be sucked for two minutes while certain physiological responses were recorded from electrodes attached to the region of the mouth. On a tray in front of each subject were baby bottles, oversized nipples, pacifiers, breast shields, and lollipops. In the low-oral-anxiety treatment the word "suck" was not used and the things the subject was to put in his mouth were innocuous objects like whistles and pipes.

The choice-of-waiting-situation data show that the low-oral treatment did not differ from the low-shock-threat treatment, with nearly all subjects choosing "together" in both. In the high-shock threat treatment, nearly all subjects chose "together," whereas in the high-oral-anxiety treatment fully half of the subjects chose to be alone. These subjects were presumably embarrassed about revealing their emotional reaction to the prospect of sucking the objects they saw. We may conclude that the desire for comparative information may at times be opposed by an unwillingness to face certain implications of public exposure. The behavior produced by these conflicting tendencies for company or isolation will, of course, depend on which is stronger.

Emotional Uncertainty and Suggestibility

To reiterate, when a person is uncertain about some aspect of himself, and having an evaluation of that aspect is important, he will be open to information that may facilitate the evaluation. This information may exist in his immediate environment or he may be forced to seek it out. The information may derive from his physical environment, his prior experience, or from the performances of others. In the case of attitudes and emotions there is both a cognitive and an affective component. This affective component is a tendency to approach the object or situation cognized if there is an anticipation of pleasure, or a tendency to avoid it if there is an anticipation of pain. This affective reaction is presumed to be accompanied by some degree of physiological arousal.

In discussing the action sequence in Chapter Nine, we distinguished the beginning and the end states of the sequence from those acts required to move from one to the other. The beginning and end of the sequence involved estimates of outcomes. A state associated with a relative positive outcome is one that the individual would like to be in, that he will approach, whereas a state having a relative negative outcome is one that the person will avoid if at all possible. Thus present and future end states have a value or an affective tone for the person. An attitude toward a particular object or situation involves the outcome level or affect attached to the state of possible transaction with that object or situation. An emotion is an attitude with a strong affective component.

In estimating present or future outcome levels, as we have said, the person compares his present or possible future state with those of co-oriented peers. In the experiments just reviewed that involve attitudinal or emotional comparison, the relevant comparison persons were clearly co-oriented peers. In Schachter's second experiment, in which the subject could wait either with others about to undergo the same threatening experience or with others waiting to see their professors, the importance of co-orientation was clearly demonstrated. Zimbardo and Formica (1963), in a similar experiment, offers further supporting evidence for this contention. In Gerard's wavy-needle experiment the symmetry in the relative rejection of others who were either higher or lower in emotionality than the subject also suggested that the lack of co-orientation was the deciding factor.

When a person is, or anticipates, transacting with a particular object, he may not necessarily know how to respond emotionally to it. Under these circumstances we would expect him to refer to co-oriented peers if they are available in order to discover the "correct" emotional response. At other times the person may experience a strong reaction to aspects of his environment but not quite be aware of the specific stimuli that produced the reaction. He will be open to information that might possibly supply the cognitive component of the emotional reaction—to endow the reaction with meaning.

The latter possibility is reminiscent of the theory of emotions advanced by William James (1892). James's theory was that an emotional response consisted of an initial affective reaction followed by an awareness of what it was in the environment that produced the reaction. A person suddenly confronted by a lion about to spring would, according to James, initially feel an affective surge of bodily response and would then "interpret" his response as fear upon seeing the lion. The research that we have been reviewing deals with a "slow-motion" version of this, in which the cognitive input is supplied by comparison persons.

Pursuing the Jamesian argument, Schachter and Singer (1962) attempted to separate the affective and cognitive aspects of an emotion. They argued that if an emotion has separable cognitive and physiological components, it might be possible first to arouse a person physiologically and *then* to supply him with different cognitive content and by so doing induce different emotional experiences. The initial state of physiological arousal would be precisely the same; only the cognitive content would differ. Depending on the cognitions supplied, the emotion might be experienced as fear, anger, joy, or whatever. A corollary to James's theory is that if the person were in a state of physiological arousal, with no appropriate cognitions to apply to the state, he would be uncertain as to how to interpret his feelings and would therefore be suggestible to any cognitions that might be immediately supplied by his environment. If, on the other hand, he were physiologically aroused and had an appropriate explanation for this arousal, he would not be uncertain and would then be relatively invulnerable to cognitions that might suggest a different interpretation for his physiological state. A further implication of the theory is that if the person were supplied with the cognitions appropriate to a particular emotion without any accompanying physiological arousal, he would have no genuine emotional experience.

Schachter and Singer (1962) used an ingenious procedure to test these hypotheses. The experiment was introduced to the subject as a study of the effects on vision of a vitamin supplement called suproxin. Actually suproxin was a fictitious label and the subject received either an injection of epinephrine or a placebo of salt water. Epinephrine is a synthetic form of adrenalin that, when in the blood stream, usually causes a dramatic increase in the discharge of the sympathetic nervous system. The resulting state appears to mimic quite well the state of bodily arousal when the individual is emotionally excited. There was one placebo condition, which was introduced as a control, and three epinephrine conditions.

In the "epinephrine-informed" (epi inf) condition, the subject was told that suproxin has certain side effects such as hand tremor, increased heart rate, and possible face flushing. The subjects in this treatment, then, had an appropriate explanation for what was to happen after they received their injection of epinephrine. In the "epinephrine-ignorant" (epi ign) condition, the subject was given no information about any possible side effects. In order to control for the possibility that the subject's preparation for side effects and his possible introspection to discover them might influence his behavior, another condition, "epinephrine-misinformed" (epi mis), was run in which the subject received completely erroneous information as to what side effects he should expect. He was told that his feet would itch, that he would feel numb, and that he might get a slight headache. These subjects, just as those in the epi ign treatment, would be prepared for side effects, though the appropriateness of the preparation differed.

The cognitive input was introduced by a procedure similar to the one used by Wrightsman. Another subject, who was actually an accomplice of the experimenter, was brought into the room and introduced as a subject who had also just been injected with suproxin. Both were to wait together until the suproxin took effect. In one treatment the accomplice behaved euphorically and in another treatment he simulated anger.

In the euphoria treatment the accomplice acted in a bizarre, slap-happy manner, starting off with rather mild antics and ending up in a veritable frenzy. He began by tossing wads of paper into the waste-paper basket, first doing set shots, then elaborate lay-ups. He then engaged in a number of other activities that included flying paper airplanes, building a tower out of manila folders, and finally demonstrating his skill with a hula hoop that just happened to be in a corner of the room.

In the anger treatment both subjects were told to fill out a questionnaire while waiting for the suproxin to take effect. The questionnaire began by asking innocuous questions and became more and more personal. The later questions concerned such things as family income, personal hygiene habits of family members, and how neurotic the various members of the subject's family were. Toward the end there were questions that asked the subject to give ·intimate details about his own sexual life and the sexual life of others in his family. The stooge, while working on the questionnaire and reading the questions aloud, began to simulate annoyance and gradually built up to a high pitch of anger. After reading the last question, he vehemently ripped up the questionnaire and tossed it into the waste-paper basket.

The euphoria treatment was administered to some subjects in the placebo, epi inf, epi ign, and epi mis conditions. There were no epi mis subjects in the anger treatment. Table 10.12 presents the experimental design with

Table 10.12. The Design of the Euphoria-Anger Experiment
(From Schachter and Singer, 1962)

	Accomplice's Behavior			
Euphoria		N	Anger	N
Epinephrine-Informed		27	Epinephrine-Informed	23
Epinephrine-Ignorant		26	Epinephrine-Ignorant	23
Epinephrine-Misinformed		26		
Placebo		26	Placebo	23

the number of subjects assigned to each combination. After the attempt by the accomplice to induce emotion, a questionnaire was administered that included questions designed to measure the subject's happiness or anger and to determine the effects of the injections.

What pattern would we expect the results to take? First of all, we would expect the epi inf subjects to be least susceptible to either emotion-provoking induction because they already had an explanation for their feelings. We would also expect the epi ign and epi mis subjects to report and show a good deal of emotional arousal since neither type of subject has cognitions that can appropriately interpret the physiological arousal he is experiencing. Furthermore, we would expect the placebo condition to show some emotional arousal owing to the fact that the stimulation supplied by the accomplice was sufficiently provoking to arouse the subject physiologically to some extent even without an epinephrine injection. An index was computed from the happiness and anger questions on the postexperimental questionnaire to reflect the subject's degree of euphoria or anger. Also, an activity index was constructed from observational data collected by an observer behind a one-way mirror.

Table 10.13 presents the data for the self-report and activity indexes in the euphoria treatment. The data for the anger treatment show parallel effects, with the direction of emotion of course reversed. We see from the

Table 10.13. Self-Report [a] and Activity Indices [b] in the Euphoria Treatment
(Adapted from Schachter and Singer, 1961)

Condition	Self-Report Index	Activity Index
Epi Inf	0.98	12.72
Epi Ign	1.78	18.28
Epi Mis	1.90	22.56
Placebo	1.61	16.00

[a] The higher the index the greater the happiness.
[b] The higher the index the greater the activity.

table that the hypotheses are generally confirmed. The most striking fact is that the epi inf subjects show an even lower index than those in the placebo treatment. Presumably, they could understand their bodily reactions in terms of the cognitions originally supplied by the experimenter and thus appeared to be relatively immune to the subsequent cognitions supplied by the accomplice's behavior. This, again, is reminiscent of the experiments on opinion and ability comparison. That is, when there is a prior basis for forming a judgment, impression, or level of aspiration, the person is relatively invulnerable to social influence.

SUMMARY

The focus of this chapter has been on certain implications of information dependence on other people. We began the chapter with a brief historical sketch presenting some of the highlights of the developing interest in this general problem area. We traced this development from the French sociologists to Lewin's work on "group decision" that brought us to the brink of the modern era in social psychology. His students and colleagues, and in turn their students, have been responsible for many of the further theoretical developments in the areas of social influence and social comparison.

Experimental studies of social influence have focused on several manifestations of comparative appraisal: a tendency for individuals, in a relatively uncertain situation, to converge on a group norm by (a) influencing those who disagree with them, (b) being vulnerable to influence from others, and (c) rejecting deviates as not relevant comparison persons. The tendency to converge, by any of these means, is heightened by factors that increase the attractiveness of the members to each other, the evidence that members are similar, and the degree to which opinion issues on which there is discrepancy are relevant to the basis for group membership.

Research on ability comparison shows that the subject's level of aspiration and self-ability estimates are also shaped by the performances of others, especially when the person has little in the way of his own prior performance on which to base his self-estimate. We attempted to clarify the relationship between ability and opinion comparison by showing that much of the research on opinion comparison can be interpreted only if we assume that an opinion statement is regarded by the subject as a performance that is taken to reflect the performer's ability. A person is more likely to rely on the opinion of an expert than someone presumed to be inferior to him in ability. In this connection we also examined the different roles played by the expert and the co-oriented peer. As we developed the distinction in the previous chapter, there will be dependence on an expert when some instrumental aspect of the action sequence is involved, whereas there will be dependence upon a co-oriented peer when outcomes are being measured.

Decisions regarding the quality and intensity of emotions are also influenced by the actions of co-oriented peers. When a person is uncertain about his emotional state or some other aspect of himself, he will often seek out comparison persons to reduce his uncertainty. A series of experiments on the conditions of affiliation strongly suggest that this does in fact occur. When comparison persons do come together each is likely to supply cognitions relevant to the other's emotional experience. These cognitions may be transmitted in very subtle ways to exert measurable effects on the content and intensity of felt emotion.

CHAPTER ELEVEN

The Conformity Conflict

In the typical experiment described in Chapter Ten processes of communication and social influence were examined in group settings that featured a complex interplay among the responses of group members. Each subject was therefore confronted with a somewhat different stimulus situation depending on his own particular opinion, ability level, or emotional experience. Although such group experiments have the advantage of simulating the complex events associated with achieving consensus in real life, this very complexity precludes precise analysis of individual behavior. In order to bring into sharper focus the person's reaction to a discrepancy between his own opinions and abilities and others', the nature and direction of this discrepancy must be carefully controlled. Asch (1951, 1956) achieved a high degree of control over this aspect of the situation by arranging a rather dramatic experimental setting that placed subjects in a conflict between trusting their own judgment and accepting the discrepant judgment of peers.

THE ASCH CONFORMITY SITUATION

The Basic Setting

Imagine observing the following situation. Eight undergraduates are sitting facing a blackboard and the experimenter informs them that they are about to participate in an experiment concerned with the accuracy of their visual perception. He rests two oblong white cards, three feet apart, on the blackboard sill. The card on the left has a single black line on it; the card on the right has three black lines, each of a different length, one of them being equal in length to the single line on the left-hand card. A typical set of standard and comparison lines is shown in Figure 11.1.

The experimenter asks the subjects to decide on each trial which of the three comparison lines is equal in length to the single standard line. They are asked to announce their judgments one after the other, beginning with the person on the far left in the front row. On the first trial each subject

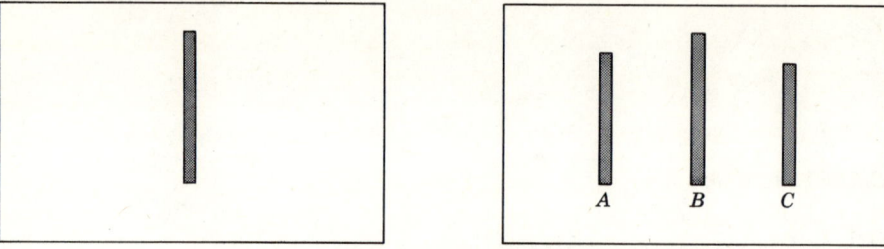

Figure 11.1. A typical line judgment stimulus.

announces his judgment in turn with no apparent difficulty. The comparison lines are clearly different in length and it is obvious which one is equal to the standard. The second trial, with a different set of lines, runs off as smoothly. On the third trial, however, something strange appears to be happening. The first subject announces his judgment. The second subject announces his, concurring with the first. The third subject agrees with the second, and so on. As the judgments are announced with apparent conviction and confidence, the next to the last subject appears to become more and more agitated. He has been squinting, tilting his head, crossing and uncrossing his legs; he is obviously distressed by the proceedings. When his turn comes he hesitates a long time but finally announces his judgment with a quaver in his voice. The final subject then announces his judgment in an affirmative tone indicating no apparent problem. The next to the last subject then raises his hand and inquires of the experimenter as to what exactly they are supposed to be doing. The experimenter answers him, in a matter-of-fact tone, to the effect that they are supposed to state which of the three comparison lines is equal in length to the standard. On the fourth trial the next to the last subject appears to experience the same difficulty and turmoil as he did on the previous trial. During the remaining 14 trials he, and he alone, continues to exhibit periodic, marked disturbance.

In order to find out what is happening here let us look at the situation from this particular subject's point of view by reconstructing in his own words what he was thinking about during the sequence of trials. This reconstruction has been paraphrased from some of the interview protocols reported by Asch (1956). After the experimenter had given the instructions, if we had been able to listen in on the subject's thoughts, this is what we might have heard:

This should be a cinch since I know my eyes are real good. I wonder what it is he's trying to prove. There, he just put up the first pair of cards. That's no sweat, line 2 is the correct one. Let's hear what the first guy says. Sure enough, line 2 it is. Naturally everyone agrees. Now it's my turn. "Line 2." The last guy agrees too. That makes it unanimous. Okay, here comes the second pair of cards. That's cinchy too, it's line 1. That's right, we're all in agreement. Here comes the third pair. It's line 3. This is the easiest . . . What did the first guy say? He couldn't have said line 2. It's much too long. I guess I didn't hear him correctly. The second guy just said line 2. What's going on here? Am I seeing things, or hearing things? The third guy just said line 2. Maybe my head is tilted. No, whichever way I look at it it still looks like line 3. The fourth guy just said 2. Relax, take it easy, there must be some explanation for this. Maybe it's where I'm sitting. But the guy in front of me is seeing it from the same angle and he said 2. The fifth and then the sixth guys both said 2. Is this some kind of optical illusion? Maybe they're seeing something I'm not. What am I going to say, it's my turn? I know I'm right but they'll think I'm some kind of a jerk if I disagree with them. They all can't be wrong—or can they? Maybe they're just playing follow the leader. Yes, that's it. The first guy made a mistake and now they're all just being sheep. But why would they? What do I do? This is completely mad! Well, it's my turn so I'd better tell him what it looks like to me. "Line 3." What a pall just came over the room! They must certainly think I'm some kind of a nut. But what can I do, I have to call them as I see them. This isn't as easy as I thought it would be, although 3 still looks right, or does it? The last guy just went down the line with the others. I sure would have felt better if he had agreed with me. I'd better ask the guy running this what it's all about; maybe I'm doing something wrong . . . Nope, he says I'm doing what I'm supposed to. Let's see what happens with the next set. There they are. There can be no mistake about it—it's line 1. Let's see what the first guy says. He just said line 2. Well, that's what I thought I heard. But that's too short! One of us is nuts! The second guy just said 2. Here we go again. My hand is beginning to tremble. I sure wish I could have a drink of water. They must be right, but how *can* they be since I see it differently. It either is or isn't right. There are no two ways about it! They're beginning to look at me kind of funny. I sure wish I had a ruler and could go up there and measure the lines. Then I'd know for sure who was right and who was wrong. Then I could prove my case. I wonder what they would say then. The third guy just said 2. Gee, I'm going to stand out like a sore thumb again! Maybe I ought to go along with the crowd. What's the difference anyway—it's only an experiment. But how can I if I am supposed to tell him which one *I* think is correct. I'm sure they won't speak to me when this thing is over. I can't remember when I've been so uncomfortable about something as I am about what's going on here. I've always relied on other people, but how can I here? I've always assumed people see things the way I do. Maybe I don't see things clearly and they are actually right. If I say line 1, I may be wrong and then I'll really be out on a limb. But if they're wrong and I agree with them, then we're all wrong together and maybe that's not so bad. It's my turn. What should I do? "Line 2." There I said it. They seem pleased now and I feel a little better about it. Why did I do it though? It still looks like line 1 to me. Next time I think I'll stick by my guns . . .

Actually, there is a perfectly reasonable explanation for what the subject was experiencing. He was really the only naive subject and the others were accomplices of the experimenter. On 12 of the 18 trials the others announced false judgments and were completely unanimous in their choice of comparison lines. The first subject had a little card with the sequence of judgments written on it and the others just followed his lead. Table 11.1 presents the actual lengths of the standard and the three comparison

Table 11.1. Majority Responses to Standard and Comparison Lines on Successive Trials (Adapted from Asch, 1956)

Trial	Length of Standard (in Inches)	Length of Comparison Lines (in Inches)			Majority Choice
1 a	10	8¾	10	8	10
2 a	2	2	1	1½	2
3	3	3¾	4¼	3	3¾
4	5	5	4	6½	4
5 a	4	3	5	4	4
6	3	3¾	4¼	3	4¼
7	8	6¼	8	6¾	6¾
8	5	5	4	6½	6½
9	8	6¼	8	6¾	6¼
10 a	10	8¾	10	8	10
11 a	2	2	1	1½	2
12	3	3¾	4¼	3	3¾
13	5	5	4	6½	4
14 a	4	3	5	4	4
15	3	3¾	4¼	3	4¼
16	8	6¼	8	6¾	6¾
17	5	5	4	6½	6½
18	8	6¼	8	6¾	6¼

a Neutral trials (majority made correct judgment).

lines for each of the 18 trials as well as the bogus group consensus on each.

The Nature of the Conflict

The composite of thoughts attributed to our subject gives some indication of the nature of the conflict confronting him and the forces at work contributing to the conflict. On the surface, the judgment involved may seem inconsequential. In actuality a very critical skill is being tested here. Throughout his life the subject has relied on his ability to make estimates of distance and length and has come through childhood and adolescence relatively unscathed. He can usually grasp things he reaches for and is able to cross the street without being hit by an automobile. In the process he has learned to put a good deal of trust in his ability to make estimates of the kind required in the present experiment. On the other hand, he has also learned to rely on other people as credible sources of such information. In a situation like this he assumes that the others possess approximately the same perceptual capacities as his own and are able and willing to report accurately what they see. How, then, can there be a discrepancy? These considerations make up the informational side of the conflict.

There is also the problem of "standing out like a sore thumb," as the subject put it. The individual is concerned with the kind of impression he is making on the others. He assumes that the others expect him to agree with them. If he reports what he sees, he will disagree with them—which he assumes will displease them. This, in turn, leads to his losing status in their eyes. They will not be favorably disposed toward him, a fact that will lower the degree to which he can rely on them for outcome mediation in the future. Thus both information and effect dependence are involved in the conflict. We should therefore expect, as we get into the literature on the conflict, to see evidence that both comparative and reflected appraisal are operating.

The subject has two alternatives. He can choose the line he sees as correct or he can voice the group choice. Each alternative has both positive and negative consequences for him. If he states the choice he believes to be correct, he is true to himself and is following what he believes to be the experimenter's instructions. On the negative side he runs the risk of actually being wrong and also of incurring disfavor from the others. If he yields to the group choice, the situation is reversed; he is false to himself and is not following instructions, but on the other hand, he does not run the risk of incurring the group's wrath. Furthermore, if he is wrong, at least he is not the only one. Besides, if he assumes he is the victim of some optical illusion, the group's choice may actually be correct. The subject's resolution of the conflict will depend upon such things as the importance he attaches to being true to himself versus avoidance of potential ridicule and loss of status. The weight he assigns to these two prospects depends on many characteristics of the situation and certain of his own idiosyncrasies. Both deep underlying personality dispositions as well as momentary, fleeting influences may be operating simultaneously.

Some Highlights of the Original Experiment

Asch's first experiment was concerned with examining the magnitude of the effects produced by the situation just described. Data on the frequency of "yielding" were gathered from 123 subjects recruited from three different college populations. One sample was drawn from a small private college with high educational standing, another from a large municipal college, and the third from a state teachers' college. As a control group, 37 subjects were run in the absence of group pressure. With one or two exceptions every control subject turned in an errorless performance suggesting that the visual judgment itself was unambiguous. When confronted with a discrepancy between his judgment and the judgments of his peers, only about one subject in four was completely free of error in performance. On the average subjects made between four and five errors out of a possible 12. This proportion of yielding has been confirmed in a number of subsequent studies.

There were wide individual differences among subjects. Some did not yield on a single trial, whereas others yielded on all 12 trials. Although Asch expected that there would be differences in the amount of yielding among the three college samples, the differences that did occur were slight and statistically unreliable. Approximately the same proportion of yielding responses has been found in a number of subsequent studies using samples from different populations of subjects.

Asch did not find an increase in the "majority effect" over time. If a subject yielded he tended to do so early in the series. Those subjects who started out being independent tended to remain so until the very end of the experiment. This seems somewhat paradoxical, as we might expect that with successive disagreements the subject's confidence would decrease to the point at which he might be ready to accept the group's judgment later in the series. We shall have more to say about this finding presently.

THE OPERATION OF COMPARATIVE AND REFLECTED APPRAISAL

In examining the subject's running commentary, it is clear that he has two salient concerns. He is concerned with being correct and also with what the others will think of him if he violates what he assumes to be their expectations. This is clear in the extensive protocols reported by Asch (1956) from which our commentary was paraphrased and also in the protocols collected by Tuddenham and McBride (1959). The available data suggest that processes of both comparative and reflected appraisal are operating.

Identification of the Two Processes

In Chapter Nine we argued that uncertainty about some aspect of the action sequence engaged comparative appraisal, and outcome dependence on other persons engaged reflected appraisal. What details of the situation confronting the subject in the previous experiment tend to elicit either process?

The Factor of Physical Isolation

If the subject were to state his judgments in private he could not be held publicly responsible for them. Under these circumstances the amount of reflected appraisal should be minimal. The subject would presumably be using the others only as he would use measuring instruments or benchmarks, in the sense described in Chapter Nine in our discussion of comparative appraisal. An experiment by Deutsch and Gerard (1955) introduced a procedure in which the subject was physically isolated from the group. By this technique the experimenters hoped to separate the effects of the comparative appraisal component from the combination of effects produced by the face-to-face bogus consensus; that is, from the effects of *both* comparative and reflected appraisal. In order to do this a variation of the original procedure was devised, in which the subject could respond without being identified publicly with his response. The results using this anonymous condition were then compared with results using the original face-to-face procedure developed by Asch.

In the anonymous condition (similar to one independently designed by Crutchfield, 1955) four naive subjects were seated side by side and separated visually from one another by partitions. Each subject had a display panel on his table that consisted of 12 red signal lamps arranged in four rows and three columns. The rows were labeled "1," "2," "3," and "4" to designate the four subjects present and the columns were labeled "*a*," "*b*," and "*c*" to represent the three comparison lines. The experimenter stood at the blackboard and displayed the same standard and comparison line judgments in the same sequence used by Asch.

On his table the subject also had a small box containing three pushbuttons labeled "*a*," "*b*," and "*c*," and was asked on each trial, when his number was called, to press the button corresponding to his choice of comparison line. He was told that the subject numbers, "1," "2," "3," and "4," were assigned at random so that no one could be identified personally with his choice of comparison line. Each person had an envelope containing a card with his subject number written on it. A ruse was resorted to here: each subject had the number "3" written on his card and assumed that the others were "1," "2," and "4." The experimenter further informed all four that the judgments of each of the subjects would appear, as they were made, on each person's display panel. The judgments would appear in the row corresponding to each subject's number. Thus the judgments of subject "1" would appear in the first row of each of the display panels, the judgments of subject "2" would appear in the second row, and so on. In actuality the panels were so wired that each subject's own response appeared only in the third row of his own panel and also on a monitor panel in an adjacent control booth, from which his responses were recorded by an experimental assistant. This assistant also fed in false information to each subject as to what the supposed judgments of subjects "1," "2," and "4" were on each of the 18 judgmental trials.

The sequence on each trial was as follows: the experimenter displayed the two stimulus cards, with the card containing the standard line on the left and the one containing the three comparison lines on the right. He then asked for the judgment of subject "1." After an appropriate pause the experimenter's unseen assistant pressed a button that displayed the preprogrammed fictitious response in the first row on all four panels. The experimenter then asked for the judgment of subject "2" and his assistant pressed the button that displayed what was presumed to be "2's" judgment on all four panels. The experimenter then asked for subject "3's" judgment. All four subjects were subject "3," so they of course responded simultaneously to this request, their individual responses being displayed on their own panels and on the assistant's panel from which they were recorded. Subject "4's" judgment was then asked for and displayed by the assistant on all four panels. As in the original experiment, the bogus majority was in agreement on all 18 trials and gave the set of responses shown in Table 11.1. A total of 36 trials were run, presenting the Asch series of 18 twice.

There was more yielding in the face-to-face than in the anonymous treatment. When confronting the group subjects agreed with the others on an average of 7.08 out of a possible 24 critical trials, whereas when the subjects were visually isolated from the others, and therefore not identifiable by them, they made an average of 5.92 such "errors." This difference is statistically significant but is not so large as might be expected from the prior discussion. Two aspects of the cubicle situation may have worked against producing a truly anonymous psychological situation. For one thing, the subjects saw each other going into the cubicles and expected to see each other on emerging. Immediately after the experiment, a number of subjects in the "anonymous" treatment expressed concern about what the others would think of them and what they would say in a subsequent public confrontation. Some subjects said they wished that they could sneak out after the experiment without being seen but knew that they could not. Clearly, there appears to be a great deal of reflected appraisal operating here. The aspect of the procedure that creates this problem is the fact that the subject's response is displayed not only on his panel, but, he assumes, is also displayed on the panels of the other three subjects. Perhaps he is not entirely convinced that he will not be identified, in one way or another, as the errant responder. If this semipublic feature were somehow eliminated from the procedure, making the condition truly anonymous, the treatment difference might be quite large.

Another procedure of the same genre was used by Argyle (1957) in a social-influence situation involving esthetic judgments. The stimulus was a rather ambiguous modern painting presented for evaluative comments to two subjects, one of whom was an accomplice of the experimenter. The confederate waited for the subject to state his judgment and then challenged him with written messages. In this procedural respect the experiment was similar to some of the work described in Chapter Ten. After a period of note writing each subject was asked for a final judgment. This was done under one of two conditions. In the public condition the subject and the accomplice announced their judgments in full view of each other. In the private treatment each wrote his judgment on a slip of paper. Again, there was more change toward the accomplice in the public treatment.

Identifying One's Self Publicly

Another experiment, by Mouton, Blake, and Olmstead (1956), also manipulated anonymity utilizing a somewhat different bogus consensus procedure. Each of four subjects, seated in separated rooms, was asked to estimate the number of metronome clicks he heard on each of a series of nine trials, with the number of clicks on each trial being either 14, 32, or 49. The clicks were sounded at a rate of three per second. By a ruse similar to the one used in the Deutsch and Gerard experiment, each subject gave his judgment fourth in the sequence. Three voices presented as those of subjects "1," "2," and "3" had been prerecorded and were heard by each of the four naive subjects, who then responded simultaneously. On six of the nine trials the fictitious majority either over- or underestimated the number of clicks. Two treatments were run, with 24 subjects in each. In the public treatment each subject (including of course the members of the fictitious majority) announced his name before making his judgment, whereas in the private treatment no names were announced. Considerably greater yielding occurred in the public treatment. The difference was due primarily to subjects who had scored high in submissiveness on a previously administered test of ascendance and submission. This combined effect of experimental treatment and a highly relevant personality trait lends additional support to the assumption that a public confrontation engages the process of reflected appraisal. If we assume that in the public treatment the effects are a result of both reflected and comparative appraisal, the greater conformity in the public as compared with the private treatment is a result of the additional effects of reflected appraisal.

The Anticipation of Future Interaction

Finally, an experiment by Raven (1959) again used a format similar to the one employed in some of the earlier research. The stimulus material was the now-familiar "Johnny Rocco" case, describing the antisocial behavior of a juvenile delinquent. Between 10 and 14 subjects participated in each experimental group and were asked to state their judgments as to what should be done with Johnny. They generally tended to advocate lenient treatment and were subsequently confronted by a false group consensus (a distribution of judgments written on the blackboard), which indicated that the vast majority of the group was on the harsh side of the seven-point continuum. Each subject was then asked to write a description of the case as he saw it. In the public treatment he was told that each subject's individual description would be passed around so that all the members of the group could read it. In the private treatment the subject was led to believe that his individual description would not be read by anyone. The subjects were then asked for a final statement of opinion about what should be done with Johnny. Again a clear effect of "publicity" emerges. In the public treatment 39 percent of the deviates changed toward the group norm, whereas only 26 percent did so in the private treatment.

Clearly, we can safely say that conformity pressure tends to be greater when the subject can be publicly identified with his judgment. This is presumably due to the effect of adding reflected appraisal to the ever-present effect of comparative appraisal.

The experimental situation developed by Asch is useful primarily because of its simplicity. The issues used to create disagreement in Chapter Ten were complex and it was relatively easy for the subject to make the others noncomparable and thus reject their opinions. Here, however, because of the simple basis of the judgment involved, rejection of the other persons is more difficult and the subject must come to terms with the discrepancy. The subject's initial conviction as well as the convictions purporting to be those of the majority can be fixed by this procedure. Owing to this close control over the discrepancy confrontation, attention can be focused on the impact it creates; extraneous factors that tend to affect the size and strength of the discrepancy are not simultaneously operating.

INFORMATIONAL FEATURES OF THE SITUATION AND COMPARATIVE APPRAISAL

Characteristics of the Stimulus

Ambiguity

When a person has to decide which of several options is correct, his task becomes more difficult the more similar the choices are to one another. We use such terms as "ambiguous" or "equivocal" to characterize stimulus situations that confront the person with this type of difficulty. The greater the ambiguity, the more uncertain the person will be and, therefore, the greater his information dependence. We would expect that when a subject has chosen one alternative and the majority has chosen another, there will be a greater tendency for him to give the majority the benefit of the doubt to the extent that the stimulus material is ambiguous.

In addition to the large original experiment, Asch conducted several subsidiary experiments, one of which was designed to explore the role of stimulus ambiguity. In this experiment a standard line was presented along with a single comparison line, and the size of the discrepancy between the two was varied systematically. The subject's task was to judge whether the comparison line was shorter, longer, or equal in length to the standard. On the neutral trials the standard was presented with a comparison line that was equal to it in length and the accomplices did in fact judge the two as equal. On the critical trials the group judged a shorter comparison line as being longer than the standard or a longer comparison line as being shorter. As we might expect, the proportion of errors made by the subject was greater the smaller the discrepancy between the two lines. That is, the more ambiguous the judgment to be made, the greater was the influence of the group.

An experiment by Kelley and Lamb (1957) provided further evidence of the effects of stimulus ambiguity. They used a novel technique to vary the ambiguity of the stimulus which involved the use of phenylthiourea (PTU), a substance that is tasteless to some individuals but has an extremely bitter taste to others. Tasting apparently behaves as a dominant gene and nontasting as recessive, the ratio of tasters to nontasters being approximately 3:1. Each subject was tested before the experiment to determine whether he was a taster. There were 30 three-man groups, 15 consisting of one taster and two nontasters, and 15 consisting of one nontaster and two tasters. Each subject was first seen individually and asked to lick three gummed labels and then to rate the pleasantness of the taste of the different substances with which each was coated. The first label had no additional coating, the second label was coated with a pineapple flavoring, and the third was coated with a combination of PTU and cherry flavoring. The last label tasted bitter to a taster and sweet to a nontaster. This tasting was repeated in the group setting; the two majority persons, whether tasters or nontasters, announced their pleasantness ratings first.

The minority person in each group observed that the two other people had found the pineapple-flavored label about as pleasant as he did, but disagreed markedly with him in their rating of the PTU-coated label. When the subject's initial private rating was compared with the rating given after hearing the ratings of the other two group members, nontasters of PTU showed a marked shift in the direction of the majority, that is, in the direction of the two tasters in their group. The tasters, on the other hand, showed absolutely no majority effect. During the initial private tasting the subject had also indicated his confidence in the pleasantness judgment he made about the taste of each of the substances. There was a clear difference in certainty between the tasters and nontasters: the tasters were much more certain of their evaluation than the nontasters. This difference in certainty, which we may view as the subjective side of stimulus ambiguity, appears to account for the difference in vulnerability to the majority judgment.

Similarity of the Judgment Alternatives

The matter of ambiguity raises an issue discussed at length in Chapter Ten: the relationship between conformity and judgmental discrepancy. We have implied that conformity to the majority's judgment will be greater the smaller the discrepancy, because it is easier for the individual to accept a judgment that is closer to his own as being correct than a more distant one. Supporting evidence for this hypothesis was found in Asch's experiments using three comparison-line stimuli. There is considerably more conformity when the majority chooses one of the two incorrect lines that is closer in length to the correct one.

Fisher and Lubin (1958) found the same relationship in an experiment where the subject discovered that his estimate of the number of paratroopers in a photograph of a parachute drop differed from a bogus estimate of another subject. Subjects were run in one of six discrepancy treatments. The greater the discrepancy, the smaller was the proportion of the distance "moved" by the subject between his initial estimate and the bogus estimate of the other subject. Up to a moderate discrepancy the subject changed his estimate more, although not proportionally more, the greater was the discrepancy. When the discrepancy exceeded some moderate value, however, even this "absolute" movement declined.

In Chapter Ten we found, in examining the relationship between discrepancy and communication, evidence of rejection when another person's opinion was beyond some value. We appear to be dealing with the same phenomenon here, as measured by the amount of change in judgment. Apparently the subject renders another person as not comparable when the other's estimate is beyond a certain value. The range of values around his own judgment that he considers acceptable—that would conceivably be correct—is finite. This range is greater, of course, the greater the stimulus ambiguity. When someone else's estimate is beyond this range, however, it is rejected as improbable. We shall have more to say about this "latitude of acceptance" in the next chapter.

The Effect of the "Pull" of the Physical Stimulus

In the Deutsch and Gerard (1955) experiment one of the factors in the design varied another type of ambiguity. It may be recalled that subjects responded twice to the same series of 18 sets of Asch's standard and comparison lines. During one series the cards were exposed on each trial while all of the subjects were making their judgments—as in the original procedure used by Asch. During the other series the cards were exposed on each trial for only a few seconds and removed before the first subject announced his judgment. This "memory series" produced many more errors than the series in which the stimuli remained present. The subject was much more vulnerable to the social information because physical information that he could use to check and thereby bolster his initial judgment was missing.

Varying the Number of Choices

Asch obtained some curious results by varying another aspect of the stimulus situation. Seventeen subjects were put through a treatment in which only two comparison lines were presented, the physically correct line and the line chosen by the bogus majority from the two incorrect lines in the original procedure. The only difference between this and the original procedure was that in the original there had been another comparison line on the card that was neither correct nor chosen by the majority. A greater number of errors were made, on the average, in the two-comparison-line variation, but the more interesting fact concerns the way in which these errors were distributed. The distribution in the original experiment was more or less rectangular—there were approximately equal proportions of subjects in each category of error, with the exception of the zero-error category, which contained the greatest number. In the two-comparison-line variation the proportion of subjects in the no-error category was the same as in the first experiment, but the rest of the subjects showed consistent yielding. Evidently, confronted with an either-or choice, the subject tends to resolve the conformity conflict relatively quickly, either remaining steadfast throughout or yielding early and continuing to yield till the end of the experiment.

After these subjects had made their judgments in the two-line series, Asch introduced the original cards containing the three comparison lines and found that the subject's behavior was markedly consistent with his behavior during the two comparison line series. Those who yielded on the first series continued to yield on the second, whereas those who were independent on the first series remained independent on the second. We shall return to a subsequent consideration of these results.

The Effect of Majority Size

When the stimulus situation is ambiguous the subject may assume that "several heads (or pairs of eyes) are better than one." In the absence of information concerning the ability of the others relative to himself he has no reason to conclude that anyone is more likely to be correct than anyone else. Therefore, assuming the situation is sufficiently ambiguous, he is more likely to rely on several independent estimates than just his own. We do not expect ambiguity to lead to much conformity when the subject is pitted against only one other person, as in the Fisher and Lubin experiment, because he is likely to assume that the other person's guess is as good as his own. There is no evidence relating the simultaneous effects of ambiguity and size of majority to conformity, but there is some evidence from an experiment by Asch (1951) on the effects of majority size alone on conformity. An offhand prediction might be that the effect will increase with greater majority size, but is that really the case?

In the usual series of line judgments, the subject was exposed to a discrepant majority of 2, 3, 4, 8, or 16 members. In addition to these five majority sizes, there was a treatment in which the subject confronted disagreement from only one other person. Table 11.2 presents the average

Table 11.2. Errors of Critical Subjects with Unanimous Majorities of Different Size (Adapted from Asch, 1951)

Size of Majority	Control	1	2	3	4	8	16
N	37	10	15	10	10	50	12
Mean number of errors	0.08	0.33	1.53	4.0	4.20	3.84	3.75

number of errors made by subjects in each treatment. The table also includes the data from the original control group of 37 subjects who were not exposed to any discrepant judgments. We see that opposition from one other subject has only a minimal effect, which increases sharply when the subject is opposed by two people and still further when a third person is added to the majority. Beyond three, however, there appears to be no increase. The tendency shown for the effect to decline for a majority size of eight and again for a majority size of 16 is not statistically reliable. As anticipated, when opposing a lone individual the subject attaches no more credibility to the other's judgment than to his own. With a minimum majority of two dissenting members, however, it becomes more difficult to reject the discrepant information. With a third, the majority effect is marked. Still, many subjects remain independent or partially independent, the information from their *own* eyes being more direct and compelling.

A natural question arises here, and the answer to it might disentangle a possible informational influence from the total "majority effect." This question came up earlier. Does the subject perceive that the members of the majority are "following the leader" and, if so, what effect does this have on his tendency to follow along too? The sharp rise in conformity when the majority is increased from two to three, which is really something of a mystery, might be interpretable if we were able to answer this question. Perhaps the subject, when confronting a majority of two, assumes it is likely that the second person is following the first; he just happens to be a sheep. When a third person is seen to go along it may be difficult for the subject to believe that there are two sheep in the group. We could assess the effects of perceiving possible mutual influence among the others by comparing the situation used in these experiments with one in which the subjects were confronted with estimates that the others had made independently of each other. The standard sequential situation, featured in the Asch paradigm, could be either more or less potent than a situation in which everyone's responses are independent—depending on the relative importance of comparative versus reflected appraisal. If comparative appraisal is more important and the subject is primarily concerned with accuracy, then he should be more impressed with judgments that are independently in agreement than with judgments expressed in a sequence. However, if reflected appraisal and the concern with creating an impression are important, the sequential situation may be more potent than the independent one. A subject may assume that because the others have followed the leader he, too, is expected to follow along.

Relative Ability and the Response to Discrepancy

In considering stimulus ambiguity we have already alluded to attributions of ability to self and others as a determinant of the subject's decision to yield or remain independent. In reviewing the research on ambiguity we made the rough assumption that the subject regards himself and the others as equal in ability to judge the stimulus material in question. We suspect, however, that a great deal of the variability in conformity behavior among subjects in these experiments is a result of wide differences in the certainty with which they hold the judgments in question. This certainty derives from how good they believe they are at making the judgments. As we pointed out in Chapter Nine, a person's information dependence on others is determined in part by the degree of expertise he attributes to them relative to himself.

Several attempts have been made to confirm this proposition. The general paradigm for testing it involves a two-stage experiment. In the first stage the subject is either given bogus feedback in a judgment task about his ability to make certain judgments (Mausner, 1954a; Samelson, 1957; Goldberg and Lubin, 1958), or about the ability of the other subject or subjects (Mausner, 1954b), or he is given some special information that will make him an "expert" (Snyder, Mischel, and Lott, 1960). In the second stage he is systematically exposed to a discrepant judgment from the other subject or subjects. The general finding is the same in all of these studies and confirms our prediction: the greater the subject's assumed ability relative to the others, the greater his independence in the face of the discrepancy.

Impact on the Deviate

We may be led to assume from the uniform results of these experiments that the high-ability person has relatively little difficulty in remaining steadfast, that he simply discounts the discrepant information as unreliable. It is rather the low-ability person who is victimized by majority judgment. But is the low-ability subject the only one troubled by a discrepancy? The psychological impact of disagreement on individuals of different ability was explored in two studies, one by Smith (1936) and another by Gerard (1961b). In the first study the independent variable was based on naturally given differences in certainty, whereas in the second study certainty was varied by experimentally inducing differences in ability.

Our interest in ability stems from its role in the action sequence. A person's estimate of his ability affects the confidence with which he holds his beliefs and the certainty with which he makes a decision. In the research discussed thus far the person's confidence in a judgment he has made correlates positively with his estimate of his ability to make that judgment. The Smith experiment examined the effect of confidence per se on the subject's reaction to a discrepant majority. Naturally other factors, such as the ambiguity of the stimulus, may produce differences in confidence, so that in using confidence as an independent variable we may be dealing with factors other than ability. However, in view of the format used by Smith, it is likely that subjects who were confident of their judgments also tended to consider themselves better informed, which is tantamount to a high self-ability estimate.

Even though Smith's experiment was conducted 30 years ago it is similar in many procedural aspects to much current conformity research. Several weeks before the experimental sessions the subjects gave their opinions on 20 statements, indicating agreement or disagreement. Also, on a five-point scale, they recorded the intensity of their convictions on each statement. During the experimental session each subject, tested individually, had his hand attached to electrodes that measured changes in his skin resistance (a decrease in skin resistance is known to accompany an increase in stress). The subject was asked to state his opinion again on the 20 statements, but this time he was informed before stating his opinion how the majority of students like himself felt about each of the statements. For 10 of the items the subject was given a fictitious majority opinion that agreed with his own opinion; for the other 10 items he was confronted with disagreement. In general the subject showed greater reactivity (a greater decrease in skin resistance), the greater was his initial confidence. This was true primarily when the subject found himself in disagreement with the majority; the greater his confidence, the greater was his physiological reaction to disagreement with the majority. This seems paradoxical in terms of our discussion above, but before trying to explain the paradox let us consider the results of the study by Gerard (1961b).

The experiment used the Asch line-judgment task with subjects partitioned from each other and responding via display panels comparable to those used by Deutsch and Gerard (1955). Ability was varied by giving the subject false information about his performance on a prior task. The subject was told that he was better than the others, approximately equal, or poorer in the ability required to make the line judgments—regardless of his actual ability level. By the familiar ruse, each of the four subjects believed that he was "3" and that the others were "1," "2," and "4." Because the purpose of this experiment was to study the impact on an individual when he discovered that his judgments deviated from the group consensus, he had to be prevented from yielding by not knowing about the consensus until he had responded. To this end, all judgments on a given trial were displayed simultaneously. As in the earlier experiments with mechanical feedback, each subject was exposed to a false but unanimous consensus on his display panel so that he found himself a deviate on 12 of the 18 trials; the false consensus was correct on the remaining 6.

The results show a similar effect of ability on reactivity to the one observed by Smith. The greater the subject's ability relative to the others, the greater was the stress he experienced as measured by the change in skin resistance.

How can we interpret these puzzling findings? In both experiments the members of the majority had presumably made their judgments independently. It was therefore not simply a situation in which the rest of the group followed the leader. The subject could not resolve his dilemma that way. The group consensus no doubt assumed high credibility for the subject. When his own ability was high he was confronted with *two* highly credible sources of information that were discrepant with each other, creating a conflict that was difficult to resolve. Which source was he to discount? In the Gerard experiment there was some tendency for the subject in the high-ability condition to level off in his reactivity in the later trials. This presumably was an indication that he had begun to resolve the conflict by assuming that either he or they were correct. To the extent that the subject is able to discredit the majority *or* his own judgment he can escape from the "bind" created by the discrepancy confrontation.

The experiments discussed earlier showed an inverse relationship between conformity and the subject's ability, a fairly obvious prediction. The situation is one of informational dependence in which the subject has data on comparative ability that dictate the relative reliance he should place on himself and the others; the greater his relative self-reliance the less he yields. When, however, the subject's behavior is fixed so that he cannot yield, as in the Smith and Gerard experiments, and a high degree of credibility is attached to the majority judgment, a relationship that is not as obvious was found. Here, the higher the person's ability (or confidence), the greater was his emotional reaction to being in disagreement with the majority.

The Effects of Co-orientation

In Chapter Nine we also pointed out that relative ability is likely to be the important factor determining information dependence when beliefs about aspects of the action sequence itself are concerned. When a person is uncertain about the attitude he should take toward his present condition and toward prospective situations, he tends to compare himself with co-oriented peers. Kelley and Woodruff (1956) investigated some of the effects of co-orientation in an experiment featuring an ingenious false-consensus procedure. Their subjects, students in a teachers' college that was characterized by a very modern and progressive educational philosophy, were asked to listen to a tape recording of a speech espousing a strongly traditional approach to education. The pretext given the subject for listening to the speech was that the experimenter wanted to get his help in evaluating the diction and delivery of the speaker. Seven times during the 10-minute tape recording one of the speaker's major points was followed by applause from the audience that was apparently listening to the speaker. In the "members' applause" (co-oriented peer) treatment, the subject was told that the audience consisted of present and former members of their college, whereas in the "outsiders' applause" (non-co-oriented peer) treatment, the audience was described as composed of outsiders from a neighboring city who were college-trained people interested in community problems related to education. A questionnaire that determined the subject's attitude toward the modern approach in education was administered both before and after he heard the speech. The measure indicated that when the subject confronted apparent approval of a discrepant attitude by his peers there was a greater change toward the point of view advocated in the speech than when the approval of the discrepant position was attributed to outsiders.

When the issue concerns the measurement of present or the estimation of possible future outcome levels, the attitudes expressed by an expert should be irrelevant—the expert functions as a source of information regarding ways in which the person may move from one outcome state to another but he cannot serve in defining whether the outcome level is enjoyable. Similarly, information from a co-oriented peer about how to move from one state to another will be given less weight than such information supplied by an expert. For example, a worker relies more heavily on fellow workers in "measuring" his satisfaction (or lack of it) by comparing himself with them; when concerned with the best way to gain a promotion he might depend more upon information from his work supervisor regarding work procedures and training measures.

The Effect of a Nonunanimous Majority

Asch (1951) conducted several variations of his experiment in which the subject found a "partner" among the others present. In one variation a member of the pre-instructed majority gave the correct judgment on every trial. This procedure drastically reduced the amount of yielding of the naive subject. In another variation, this partner started out giving correct judgments but deserted the subject halfway through the procedure. Here the subject, after being initially independent, returned to the yielding level found in the original experiment. In a third variation, one of the instructed majority joined the subject halfway through the experiment with the effect of markedly increasing the subject's independence. Apparently having one other person in agreement with the subject has a profound effect on his willingness to disagree with seven or eight other people. As Asch pointed out, this cannot be a matter of mere numbers, because when alone against a majority of three the subject tends to yield as much as he does against a majority of 16. It is not clear, however, whether this effect owes more to the partner's role in reducing the subject's uncertainty about the correct answer, or to his role as an ally in case the majority were to react with ridicule. As in most of the findings in the conformity area, a well-established result may reflect a variety of underlying psychological processes.

An experiment by Gerard and Greenbaum (1962) examined some of the details of the situation in which a member of the majority "joins" the subject. In earlier experiments by Gerard and his colleagues, interviews with subjects who had been in conformity conflict experiments revealed a stereotyped pattern of attitudes toward "1," "2," and "4." The subject tended to see "1" as the leader, "2" as a sheep, and "4" as a good-for-nothing culprit, because he had the choice of going along with "1" and "2" or confirming the subject's own judgment by agreeing with him. This pattern of attitudes was extraordinarily uniform among the vast majority of subjects. We would expect the subject's attitude toward "4" to change markedly if "4" joined him at some point during the experiment as in one of Asch's "partner" variations. Another aspect of the situation revealed in the interviews was that the subject tended to become more uncertain of his judgments with each succeeding trial, accounting for the increased stalwartness of the subject when he is joined by a partner. If the subject's uncertainty grows with each trial, and if having a partner reduces uncertainty, then a partner who joined the subject late in the series would serve to reduce greater uncertainty than a partner joining him early in the series. As pointed out in Chapter Nine, uncertainty is an unpleasant drive state and the individual will attempt to reduce it. Any agent that is instrumental in reducing the drive will act as a reinforcer and in the process will take on positive value in its own right. In the situation we are concerned with here it follows that the later the subject is joined by a partner, the more attractive the partner will be for the subject because he is reducing more uncertainty.

The Gerard and Greenbaum procedure of varying the point at which "4" joined the subject was straightforward. The subject, who was always number "3," responded to 18 sets of Asch lines with the bogus judgments of "1" and "2" arranged in the usual manner so that they disagreed with him on 13 of these trials. The bogus judgment of "4" was the factor that was varied experimentally. There were 14 treatments in all. In one treatment "4" agreed with the subject on every trial ("all agree"). In another ("all disagree") "4" was always in agreement with "1" and "2" and therefore in disagreement with the subject on all but the five neutral trials. In addition there were 12 treatments in which "4," after initially disagreeing with the subject, switched over to him (and away from "1" and "2") by choosing the physically correct comparison line. Once having switched in these treatments he agreed with the subject on all subsequent trials. The 12 switch-trial treatments were distinguished by the earliness or lateness of the critical trial on which "4" switched. In earlier research, to be reported presently, it had been discovered that when the subject wrote down his judgment before finding out the judgments of the others, he remained virtually invulnerable to the bogus consensus. This feature was employed in order to prevent the subject from yielding to "1" and "2," a condition that of course had to be met in order to test the hypothesis. The subject was asked after each trial to indicate, by setting a dial on his panel, the degree of confidence he had in his judgment on that trial. Immediately after the last trial the subject indicated, on a questionnaire, the order in which he would prefer the others as friends.

The confidence data show clear effects of "4's" switch: the later his switch, the greater was the increase in the subject's confidence affected by the switch. This suggests that the resistance to influence pressures observed by Asch in the "partner" variations occurred, at least in part, because of an increase in confidence brought about by the partner's support. In the treatment that resembled the basic procedure used in the previous experiments (the "all disagree" condition) all subjects were uniform in the way they ranked the members of the majority. Subject "4" was the least attractive of the three and "2," the sheep, was ranked below

"1," the leader. In the treatment in which "4" was an ally who agreed with the subject from the beginning, he, "4," was ranked first. For those treatments in which a switch occurred, the predicted relationship between the attractiveness of "4," the uncertainty reducer, and the lateness of his switch occurred only for the later switch trials when uncertainty before the switch was high. That is, for these switch-trial treatments, the later the switch, the more attractive was "4" to the subject. The fact that the relationship did not hold throughout the complete range of switch-trial treatments raises problems of interpretation. It may indicate that the effect will not occur below some threshold of uncertainty.

ACCEPTANCE BY THE GROUP AND REFLECTED APPRAISAL

In the experiments described earlier, in which the person was identified personally with his decision to conform or deviate, we found evidence that when he can be held accountable to the group for his decision, reflected appraisal occurs. This is more pronounced the greater the person's effect dependence on others in the group. When A is effect-dependent on B, B's appraisal of A has future outcome consequences for A. A therefore tends to behave in a manner designed to elicit a positive evaluation from B. At the least he avoids displeasing B, for if he incurs B's displeasure he may place his prospective outcomes in jeopardy. If we assume that A attributes to B a preference for agreement rather than disagreement then A should be aware that disagreement with B may lead to potentially negative consequences for himself.

Inducing Effect Dependence Experimentally

Presumably a certain amount of effect dependence inheres in the public situation. The public confrontation itself contains a sequence of immediate or anticipated subtle social exchanges that are difficult to identify. There have been several attempts to study reflected appraisal by superimposing explicit effect dependence over and above that which normally exists in this kind of an experimental situation. An increase in effect dependence would be expected to lead to an increase in conformity.

Supplying a Group Goal

An attempt to strengthen the role of effect dependence was made in the Deutsch and Gerard (1955) experiment. In one condition the four subjects were told that each member of the five groups making the fewest total errors would receive a pair of tickets to a play. By this instruction a group goal was introduced, the desire for which presumably induced mutual effect dependence. This treatment produced a striking increase in the number of group-influenced errors, with many subjects yielding on all or nearly all of the critical trials.

Even in the "group goal" condition some subjects remained uncertain about the proper course of action—especially if they concluded that the group was probably wrong. Such a subject might go along with the group because it would be impossible to win the tickets if he did not. Also, by some improbable chance the group might actually be correct and then it would be possible for them to win. He might reason that one correct judgment would be better than none in trying to get a good score for the group, but on the face of it, this seems unlikely. If the subject were to receive information that certified the accuracy of the bogus consensus, or information that certified his own judgment, his residual uncertainty about the group being correct would be reduced and yielding or independence therefore should be maximum.

This reasoning lay behind an experiment by Jones, Wells, and Torrey (1958). Instead of lines the subjects (in groups of four) matched airplane silhouettes. One of three comparison silhouettes was to be matched to a single standard on each trial. The booth arrangement, with an assistant operating the display in each cubicle, was the same as that used in the Deutsch and Gerard (1955) experiment, except that each subject responded fourth rather than third in the sequence. Two basic treatments were compared, one in which the subjects were merely asked to strive for individual accuracy (the "individual accuracy" treatment), and another in which theater tickets were promised to the five groups making the fewest errors as a group (the "group accuracy" treatment). Within each of these treatments three feedback conditions were compared. In one condition the experimenter openly confirmed the judgment of the majority on both the critical false-consensus trials and the trials in which they gave a correct consensus. This confirmation was arranged by his reading the "correct" answer after the subjects had made their choices on each trial. In another condition the experimenter gave the physically correct answer regardless of the majority consensus. In order to compare the effects of proconsensus and proreality feedback, a control condition was included in which the experimenter provided no feedback, but was merely a bystander as in the previous studies. The subjects in the "individual accuracy" treatment were liberal-arts coeds, whereas the subjects in the "group accuracy" treatment were nursing students. Although the experimenters did not anticipate any effect of the difference in background of the two subject samples, a separate study indicated that nursing students appeared in general to be significantly more resistant to social influence than the liberal-arts coeds.

With this factor taken into account, the data in Table 11.3 are quite clear. In the "individual accuracy" treatment, comparing the two feedback con-

Table 11.3. Mean Number of Yields out of 16 Possible Yields by Accuracy and Feedback Conditions (Adapted from Jones, Wells, and Torrey, 1958)

Feedback	Individual accuracy (Liberal Arts)	Group accuracy (Nursing)
No feedback	7.50	4.58
Proconsensus	9.67	13.90
Proreality	1.96	1.50

ditions with the control, we see that proconsensus feedback only slightly increases yielding to the group, whereas proreality feedback drastically reduces the amount of conformity. In the "group accuracy" treatment we see a marked effect of both proconsensus and proreality feedback: in the proconsensus condition 6 out of 16 subjects yielded on every critical trial. On the average, subjects yielded on all but two critical trials.

This overwhelming group effect presents residual problems of interpretation, however. We cannot assume that the mere presence of an expert in the person of the experimenter automatically causes the subject to suspend his own critical faculties, because this did not occur in the "individual accuracy" treatment, in which fully half of the judgments were nonconforming. One possible explanation is that the effect dependence induced in the "group accuracy" treatment superimposed reflected appraisal on comparative appraisal, an interpretation that is in line with the ideas being developed in this section. Such an interpretation received some support in the Deutsch and Gerard "group goal" condition, in which a number of subjects reported feelings of obligation to the group and a concern with the group's reaction to their performance.

Another possibility is that many subjects in the typical conformity experiment report what they themselves see regardless of what they assume must be correct. Thus the subjects in the conditions in which the total group score was emphasized in both the Deutsch and Gerard and Jones, Wells, and Torrey experiments may have decided that the group was more to be trusted than the evidence of their own senses.

Because both the group and the expert (the experimenter) supported the erroneous choice in the Jones, Wells, and Torrey experiment, it may be argued that the effect was a result of comparative rather than reflected appraisal. Hence, even though the effect is overwhelming and dramatic the underlying process is not clear. As Jones, Wells, and Torrey point out, in order to unravel the problem another treatment is needed in which a theater ticket or some other prize is offered on an individual basis to those subjects getting the greatest number of correct judgments. If the bogus proconsensus support from the experimenter has the same effect as in the "group accuracy" condition, a strong argument will be provided for assuming that the effect of proconsensus support in the "group accuracy" condition was largely informational in significance; that is, that the subjects went along with the group consensus in order to be correct. If, on the other hand, this new "individual prize" treatment produces results similar to the "individual accuracy" treatment the effect of proconsensus feedback in the "group accuracy" treatment may then be safely attributed to the operation of reflected appraisal; effect dependence had presumably been induced when a group prize was offered. Until such an "individual prize" variation is tested we are unable to choose between the two interpretations. Our intuition, however, coupled with the informal evidence of postexperimental comments by the subjects involved, leads us to prefer temporarily the reflected appraisal interpretation.

Inducing Cooperation

Another experiment, by Thibaut and Strickland (1956), varied the importance of reflected appraisal in a less equivocal manner than either the Deutsch and Gerard or the Jones, Wells, and Torrey experiments. In the "group set" condition of their experiment the instructions construed the judgment task as a test of cooperative ability and stressed that each group was competing with other groups *on this dimension*. The subjects in this condition also evaluated each other, before the judgment task, thus making reflected appraisal a salient feature of the situation. The informational or "task set" condition emphasized that the experimenter was primarily interested in the accuracy of individual judgments.

In both conditions six naive subjects, seated in separate cubicles, were given a vague and unfamiliar task of judging the "friendliness" of four separate arrangements of 24 thumbtacks that were to be regarded as representing persons in a group. Friendliness was associated in the instructions with similarity. Each of the four arrangements was in a separate quadrant of a display board, an identical copy of which was in each of the six cubicles. The apparent "friendliness" of the tack arrangements was suggested by variations in the homogeneity of the color and shape of the tacks and by differences in the density of their dispersion. The tacks were so displayed that a particular ordering of the four arrangements would naturally be favored by the subjects.

Ten balloting trials followed, in which each subject's rank ordering of the arrangements was communicated by written ballot to each of the other five subjects. These ballots were intercepted and bogus ballots were substituted that indicated a consensus opposed to the subject's initial ordering. The ballots simulated more and more unanimity with successive trials until complete unanimity was finally reached. In the "group set" treatment, approximately 60 percent of the subjects changed in the direction of the fictitious majority, whereas in the "task set" treatment only 30 percent changed. This certainly is strong evidence for the operation of reflected appraisal.

Half of the groups in this experiment were composed of freshman pledges, each group being recruited from a different fraternity on the campus, and the other groups were composed of strangers. There was significantly more conformity within the pledge groups than within the groups of strangers, which offers further evidence of reflected appraisal because presumably persons who know each other will be more concerned about the impression they are making on each other than will strangers.

Acceptance by the Group and Conformity

Chapter Ten presented, in a number of experiments, a positive relationship between conformity to the group and a person's attraction to it. We interpreted this as a relationship mediated by effect dependence. The individual in an attractive group conforms in order to maintain a favorable position in the eyes of the other group members. This increases the likelihood that the members will subsequently produce good outcomes for him. This potentiality for producing positive outcomes is what makes the others attractive in the first place. It is reasonable to assume that the more attracted a person is to his fellow group members the more concerned he will be with their opinion of him. But if he is confident that he is held in high esteem by the other members, if he perceives his status to be very high and secure, will he still conform to the others against his own initial judgment?

Clearly, there must be a relationship between the person's estimate of his status in the group (his value to the other group members) and his tendency to make overtures to the others by yielding to their judgments. In general, we would expect that the higher his status the less likely he will be to conform. This relationship must be qualified, however, to take account of the ratio of the status increment the person may gain by conforming to the loss he may suffer by deviating. A high-status person may have little incentive to conform in order to increase his status further but may have a high incentive not to deviate for fear of losing status. The higher his status, the greater the number of perquisites he can claim, that is, the greater his claim on the outcome mediation abilities of the other members. He will presumably want to maintain this advantage. The argument suggests a positive relationship between the person's status, the value others place on him, and his attraction to the group, the value he places on his group membership.

Another obvious complication further qualifies the relationship between conformity and status. The person's concern with maintaining his status in a particular group will be influenced by his outcome potentials in groups similar to this one. He may have very high status in a group, yet not value his membership in it because other groups afford him even higher outcomes. The situation for a low-status person will be different but may be equally complex. A person is not necessarily attracted to those who find him attractive. We shall deal with these problems at length in Chapter Thirteen. The only reason we raise these issues here is to anticipate some of the difficulties in interpreting the experiments we shall now review that bear on the relationship between a person's conformity and his feelings of acceptance in the group.

Hollander (1958) puts some of these considerations in an interesting light. He suggests that the person's status in a group be thought of as an accumulation of "idiosyncrasy credit" that accrues to him or is lost by him as he interacts with the other group members. Idiosyncrasy credit is made up of the sum of the positive dispositions of the others toward the person. These credits are bestowed on him as rewards for meeting the expectations of the other group members or taken away if he fails to meet their expectations. The greater his accumulation of credit the higher the person's status is and the more he is accepted by the others. Furthermore—and this is the crucial point—the more credit the person has the freer he is in being able to deviate from the group norms, that is, from the expectancies of the others. When he deviates, however, he loses credit because he has violated expectation. The person's status or credit balance is the algebraic sum of the merits or credits and demerits or debits he has at that moment. Someone who has built up a lot of credit has a great deal of freedom to do as he pleases whereas someone whose balance is thin must be careful in what he does lest he lose the little credit he has. The person is no longer regarded as a functioning member of the group when his balance reaches zero.

Conformity and Induced Feelings of Acceptance

Kelley and Shapiro (1954) assembled groups of five or six Yale freshmen and led them to believe that they would be divided into two subgroups of two or three members each. The subjects were told that great care would be taken in composing subgroups of compatible persons. After an initial period of get-acquainted discussion, the subjects evaluated each other and then were led to positions separated by partitions so that they could not see one another. The evaluations having been collected and tabulated, each subject was given a notice assigning him to a subgroup that in all cases was composed of himself and his two highest choices. (Subjects were separated, so it was not possible for them to detect inconsistencies in the group assignments.)

Two levels of acceptance *by* the subgroup were induced by attaching fictitious ratings to the notice given to the subject, indicating either that he was highly accepted by his fellow subgroup members or that he was not. The attachment of these ratings was made to appear an error by the experimenter, but after some pretended confusion on his part the experiment continued.

Effect dependence was induced by informing each subgroup that it would be competing against a dozen or so similar groups for a $15.00 prize. The task of the subgroups was to judge which of two squares had the greater number of dots. The subjects received a consensus allegedly from the other subgroup members which favored the incorrect choice. It became increasingly apparent, with each successive trial, that the bogus consensus was incorrect. Conformity was measured by the number of times the subject agreed with the consensus.

The results showed no relationship between conformity and perceived acceptance as manipulated by the false ratings of himself that the subject received at the beginning of the experimental session. There was, however, a negative correlation between conformity and the *actual* acceptance of the subject, as determined from ratings that the others had really made of him but were intercepted by the experimenter. The greater his actual acceptance the less he conformed. There is, of course, no way of inferring definite conclusions about what caused what from this kind of after-the-fact correlation. It may be that in the initial introductions those subjects who appeared to be fairly independent characters tended to be highly rated, or that the subject actually sensed the rating made of him by the others and paid more attention to this sensing than to the bogus ratings he received—thus behaving in line with the hypothesized relationship. There is no way, however, of deciding from the data in the experiment what was cause and what was effect.

A previously discussed difficulty arose in attempting to establish experimentally the two levels of acceptance through the bogus personal ratings. A postexperimental measure of the subject's valuation of his membership—his attraction to the group—was lower in the low-acceptance than in the high-acceptance treatment. In Chapter Ten we discussed the empirically well-established relationship between conformity and attraction. It is likely here that attraction, which was inadvertently varied by the experimental manipulation of acceptance, affected conformity in a direction opposed to the predicted relationship between conformity and acceptance. As compared with a subject who is not well accepted, one who is highly accepted should conform less, on the basis of acceptance alone, but should conform more because of his higher, inadvertently induced attraction to the group. Certainly, there are some difficult knots to untangle here!

In a subsequent study Dittes and Kelley (1956) tried to take account of the effect of acceptance on valuation of membership by attempting to induce and maintain a high level of attraction toward the group across four levels of experimentally varied feelings of acceptance. The subjects met in five- or six-man groups and were promised a large cash prize and prestigious recognition for working well together. These inducements were designed to make the group highly attractive for all subjects. The subjects were also told that in order to develop into an efficient group they could, at any point, reject undesirable members by indicating their wish to do this on an evaluation questionnaire that was to be administered periodically. Under the pretext of a warm-up session, the subjects discussed their views about the relative qualities of two delinquent gangs described in simulated court records that each had read. In the group's rating of the two gangs the experimenter forced a consensus by refusing to record any rating until there was complete agreement. At three points during this initial discussion, the subjects were asked to rate each other on a scale of desirability as a group member. After each rating, the experimenter pretended that no one had received a rating low enough to warrant his rejection from the group. At the end of the discussion the experimenter let each member see bogus ratings of himself under the pretext of assuming that everyone wanted to find out how he was rated. Without regard to the actual ratings, some subjects found they were rated very high, some that they were rated average, some that they were rated low, and some that they were rated very low. After this perceived acceptance induction there was a continuation of the problem discussion of the gangs. Now the attempt was made, by introducing new information privately to each subject that would negate the original consensus, to get the subject to deviate from the previous group decision. Final statements of opinion, both public and private, were solicited. After this, another task, the dots problem used in the Kelley and Shapiro experiment, was presented to the group. Conformity was measured by the subject's agreement with a false bogus consensus on a series of 10 trials.

The results of the experiment are complicated, primarily because of the difficulty that appears to plague this kind of investigation; conformity was again confounded by the effect of acceptance on the subject's valuation of his membership in the group. The high- and average-perceived-acceptance treatments did not differ in how much subjects valued their group membership (as measured on a questionnaire). Unfortunately, however, in the low-acceptance treatment valuation was lower than in the high- and average-acceptance treatments and was still lower in the very-low-acceptance treatment. As the data stand, we can give the hypothesis a fair test only by comparing the amount of conformity in the high- and average-acceptance conditions, in which valuation of membership was the same. In comparing these treatments we find, as indicated in Table 11.4, that both for the gang and dot problems there is greater conformity in the average-

Table 11.4. Average Conformity Score for the Four Experimental Conditions of Acceptance [a]
(Adapted from Dittes and Kelley, 1956)

	Experimental Conditions of Acceptance			
	High	Average	Low	Very Low
Gang problem scale position shift	−.92	.57	−.05	.02
First dot problem estimate change	39.0	43.4	33.2	36.4

[a] Positive values indicate change toward conformity from the subject's initial estimate to his estimate after he has been presented with the bogus consensus.

as compared with the high-acceptance treatment. We also see that in the very-low-acceptance treatment the subject tends to conform somewhat more on the dot problem than in the low treatment. This may reflect their greater fear of rejection. Other aspects of the data supported the proposition that for one who values the group but is not entirely secure in it (the average condition), "conformity is unquestioning and extends to private opinions as well as public behavior. On the other hand, persons who are on the brink of unwelcomed rejection [the very low condition] manifest conformity only at the public level, presumably as a means of forestalling such rejection (Dittes and Kelley, 1956).

Conformity and Sociometric Position in a Group

Harvey and Consalvi (1960) examined the relationship between conformity and acceptance in a group in which an explicit hierarchy of acceptance had existed for some time. They assumed, as did Hollander (1958), that the leader-follower dimension in a group carries with it implications of varying degrees of acceptance by the group; the higher up the person is in the hierarchy the more valued he is as a group member. They examined the conformity-acceptance relationship within cliques of delinquent boys in a state training school by studying the relative conforming tendency exhibited by the highest-ranked, the next-highest-ranked, and the lowest-ranked members of 27 cliques in the school. Each clique averaged four or five members. The clique structure was determined by a sociometric questionnaire administered to all the boys before the experiment; by asking the boys whom they preferred as friends, the investigators were able to construct a "map" of the informal social structure of the school that revealed the various cliques that were subsequently studied. In nine cliques the highest-ranked member was the subject, in nine the second-ranked member was the subject, and in the remaining nine the lowest-ranked person was the subject. In each case the person chosen to be the subject was exposed to a discrepant consensus from the other clique members.

A novel and ingenious technique made the use of accomplices unnecessary. The subject and the other clique members were in a completely dark room, unaware of a partition separating the subject from the other group members. In this way a stimulus could be presented to the subject that was different from the stimulus seen by the rest of the group, even though all believed they were seeing the *same* stimulus. Each stimulus consisted of brief simultaneous flashes of light that were either 12 or 48 inches apart. In an initial session the subject and the other group members saw 20 repetitions of the 12-inch-apart stimulus. During a second series the subject and the other group members made 20 private judgments in which the other group members continued to see the light flashes that were 12 inches apart, whereas the subject saw the 48-inch pairs. Following this, these same stimuli were judged for another 20 trials, with each person announcing his judgment aloud, the subject being the last person to respond. Because the other group members continued to announce judgments of about 12 inches, and the subject had privately stabilized his estimate at about 48 inches, conformity in this final, "influence" series was measured by the degree to which the subject reduced his estimate of the distance between the two flashes of light. The average estimates of subjects in the first, second, and lowest positions in the clique during this influence series were 32, 18, and 27 inches, respectively. Thus the second-ranked member was influenced most by the others and the leader least. The lowest-ranked member was influenced less than the second-ranked member, presumably because he had a lower valuation of membership.

Taking into account the possible differences in valuation of membership by the clique members, these results are compatible with those of Dittes and Kelley (1956). In this case, however, acceptance was coordinated to the sociometric status of individuals in actual groups. An obvious problem remains in interpreting these data. If the leader had accepted a great deal of influence it would be an abdication of his status. If leadership and authority are involved, and not simply the person's popularity, he cannot afford to relinquish his decision-making function and still maintain his leadership position. One of the responsibilities of leadership is innovation, the setting of new standards, and trying out new methods of coping with the world external to the group. The leader gets credit for this even though he is breaking away from the usual pattern of doing things. Often leaders are expected not to conform, and to do so would result in a loss of status. This raises a complication for Hollander's (1958) theory.

The procedure of using members of different status levels in existing groups raises another problem in interpreting the results. Acquired status might be associated with high intelligence, high confidence, or both, so some such factor or combination of factors may be contributing, in part, to the effects observed. The usual procedure of assigning subjects at random to the experimental treatment obviates this problem and is to be preferred whenever possible.

Quite probably, the conformity observed in these studies was to some extent motivated by the subject's attempt to make a favorable impression on the others. He wanted to enhance his status by pleasing them. Under certain circumstances such public commitment to a stand that disagrees with the person's own conviction may lead to private opinion change. In Chapter Twelve we shall study the conditions under which public avowal of a belief that is discrepant from the person's actual belief leads to private change. There are undoubtedly many situations in which the person can sustain a difference between his private beliefs and those he professes publicly so that others will accept him.

Private Beliefs, Overt Behavior, and Acceptance

When a person is attempting to convey a favorable impression of himself for purposes of improving his position in a group he often publicly avows a belief that disagrees with his private convictions. This was clear in Asch's protocols and from reports of subjects in subsequent conformity experiments. Assuming that the person highly values his membership in the group, the lower his perceived acceptance the more likely he will be to dissemble if he believes that expressing a view in disagreement with the group norm will injure his status in the group. As we have seen in the Dittes and Kelley (1956) experiment, even when valuation of membership is only moderate, persons who perceive that they are close to being rejected are high public conformers.

A study by Menzel (1957) examined this relationship in a real-life context. A large sample of physicians was interviewed to discover their attitudes toward certain new drugs. These publicly stated attitudes were compared with the physicians' private attitudes by examining the prescriptions they had actually written, as revealed in the records of local drug stores. On the average, there was a tendency for the physicians to express attitudes that were more modern than their privately held beliefs.

Each physician's sociometric position among his colleagues was also determined by asking each of them which of his colleagues he was most likely to call on for advice. The physician's sociometric position was inversely related to the degree to which his publicly expressed attitudes were distortions of his actual private beliefs. That is, the less likely he was to be called on for advice, the more likely he was to express public attitudes favoring the new drugs that belied his actual prescription-writing behavior. Undoubtedly there are other explanations for this relationship, but the data are consistent with the hypothesis that the lower the physician's rank in the community of physicians, the more he strives for status by presenting himself in a favorable light. There is no indication in the study as to the probable status of the interviewer, certainly a critical feature, for we must assume, in order to apply the hypothesis, that the interviewee was attempting to project a positive image of himself to his colleagues. We must then further assume that a desire to improve status in a given group will lead to attempts at impression management beyond the confines of that group, especially about issues that are germane to matters upon which status in the group rests. It follows from these assumptions that the physician being interviewed was trying to impress the interviewer much as he would his colleagues.

The foregoing area of research is very important, but one in which it is extremely difficult to produce clean experimental manipulations. An individual's feeling of acceptance may dispose him to allow himself to come under the sway of the group or may lead him to resist influence and seek the benefits of group membership elsewhere. The perquisites and obligations of leadership are important dimensions of position in a group, dimensions that play into the complex nexus of factors that determine whether an individual will conform to a group consensus.

THE ROLE OF COMMITMENT

Commitment, Conformity, and Independence

Chapter Six laid great emphasis on the factor of commitment in the action sequence. Once a person has committed himself to a course of action, he tends to remain on that course and engages in cognitive work that will sustain his decision. One of the major themes of this book has been to emphasize the distinction between pre- and postdecisional processes.

Earlier in this chapter we examined certain evidence bearing on the role of commitment, which we shall take up now. Asch discovered that when a subject started out being independent—by making correct judgments on the critical trials—he tended to remain independent until the end of the series; that is, a subject made yielding responses early in the series or not at all. There was further evidence on the importance of commitment in the two-comparison-line variation, in which there tended to be either complete independence or complete yielding. This carried over into a second series of judgments in which the subject was confronted with the three-comparison-line cards. Asch suggested that the subject's behavior on the second series was influenced by his rapid resolution of the conflict produced by the two-comparison-line situation. This seems likely, but it is difficult to argue for this interpretation from his data alone. We are not justified in comparing the behavior during the three-comparison line variation of subjects who had been exposed to 18 previous trials (even though these trials were of a somewhat different type) with subjects in the original experiment who had had no previous exposure whatsoever before they made their 18 judgments. It may be that if the subjects in the original experiment had made 18 previous judgments they too would have shown the same marked bimodal reaction pattern. There is a suggestion here, though, that commitment was operating to sustain the behavior.

Initial Self-Commitment and Public Commitment

One feature that was uncontrolled in the original Asch experiment was the extent to which the subject had initially committed himself to his judgment upon seeing the stimulus cards and before hearing the other's judgment. We would expect that a firm initial decision as to what the correct line was would insulate the subject against the discrepant majority. In order to examine the effects of initial commitment, three treatments were compared in the Deutsch and Gerard (1955) experiment. In one treatment the subject wrote his choice on a sheet of paper before finding out how the majority had judged the stimulus. In a second treatment he was asked to write his choice down on a "magic writing pad," a device with which he was undoubtedly familiar from childhood. Anything written on it with a stylus can be erased by lifting the two top sheets. The subject was asked to erase his choice after each trial. His commitment on any given trial was therefore only tentative. In the third treatment there was no written commitment whatsoever. As might be expected, the written commitment produced the greatest independence, the tentative magic-pad commitment somewhat less, and the no-commitment condition the least.

In assessing Asch's discovery that if a subject started out being independent he tended to remain so until the end of the series, we may wonder to what extent the effect is a result of the subject having committed himself publicly to the others. In comparing the face-to-face condition with the anonymous cubicle condition in the Deutsch and Gerard experiment, we find the tendency to remain independent exhibited only in the face-to-face condition. This indicates that public commitment was probably a salient feature of Asch's procedure in producing sustained independence (Gerard, 1963). In the anonymous condition subjects who started out being independent were just as likely to yield later on as to remain independent.

Both the initial self-commitment procedure (in which the subject wrote his choice) and the face-to-face procedure confronted the subject with negative consequences for changing his decision. When the subject initially committed himself to his judgment, conforming would violate his image of himself as one who is true to his conviction (which was staring up at him from his sheet and could not be erased). In the magic-writing-pad condition, constraints against conforming were lowered because, in effect, the evidence of his initial decision was destroyed after each trial. Constraints were even further reduced when there was no initial written commitment whatsoever.

In the face-to-face condition the subject could not erase from the minds of the others the memory of what he personally had done on previous trials. He knew what they presumably also knew about him. Once he had openly conformed or deviated, constraints were imposed against changing because this would have been a public avowal, as well as an avowal to himself, of inconsistency; such constraints are much the same as those imposed when a judgment is written down in the initial commitment treatment.

In a more recent study Allen and Crutchfield (1963) found that when a subject yields to the group on relatively unambiguous judgments he is likely to yield on subsequent judgments that concern more ambiguous stimulus material. We can interpret this finding as having been due to the commitment established on the early series.

Anticipating the Discrepancy as a Way of Resolving the Conformity Conflict

Fisher, Rubenstein, and Freeman (1956) found evidence confirming the effects of initial self-commitment that were observed in the Deutsch and Gerard experiment. In addition, they introduced an experimental variation that carried the analysis of commitment in a different direction. The subject's task in their experiment was to estimate the number of dots on each of a series of 50 slides that were presented as 5 blocks of 10 slides each. There were actually five different slides, each of which was repeated twice within each block. The subject stated his estimate under one of two different commitment treatments. In one treatment, which was similar to the original Asch procedure and the no-commitment condition in the Deutsch and Gerard experiment, the subject heard an estimate by an experimental accomplice posing as a more experienced subject and then stated his own. The accomplice always overestimated the actual number of dots by an amount that was preprogrammed and was independent of the subject's estimates. In the commitment condition the subject first stated his estimate, then heard the accomplice's estimate, and then made a second estimate. This was tested under two different discrepancy conditions. In one of these conditions the accomplice's estimate was based on the same program used in the no-commitment condition—he overestimated by an amount that was fixed and that was independent of the subject's estimate. In the second condition the accomplice's estimate was always based on an amount that was added to the subject's initial estimate.

The subject showed a greater tendency to conform to the accomplice's estimate, especially when the discrepancy was large, in the no-commitment than in the fixed-discrepancy commitment condition. However, the difference was much smaller than we would expect from the results of the Deutsch and Gerard study. This small difference may have resulted from an unexpected effect of the commitment procedure. In the commitment conditions the subject attempted to anticipate the accomplice's estimate. Because this estimate was always higher than the true number of dots, the accomplice's judgments could be roughly predicted. The subject in the commitment condition, after a trial or two, began to make initial estimates that were greater than the true number of dots. Because of his tendency to anticipate the accomplice's judgment, the subject showed relatively little intratrial conformity—if conformity is measured by the difference between his initial and final estimate on each trial. That influence did occur was inferred by comparing the subject's initial estimate on each trial to those given by control subjects who simply estimated the number of dots on each slide. Also, in the second commitment condition, when the discrepancy was always added to the subject's initial estimate, initial estimates from trial to trial climbed markedly to a point at which they were well over three times the actual number of dots on the slides! Here again, the intratrial changes themselves were rather small.

The cumulative social-influence effect observed in this study appears to be an appealing resolution of the conformity conflict in situations when judgments of highly similar materials are being made over and over. In the typical Asch situation, such a resolution is hardly possible because the majority showed no consistent bias, sometimes choosing the larger, sometimes the smaller of the incorrect lines, in addition to being correct on a third of the trials.

Postcommitment Accommodation

In Chapter Six we discussed in detail the evidence indicating that a person will engage in dissonance-reducing cognitive work once a decision has been made. Such dissonance reduction serves the purpose of supporting and confirming the decision. Because the basic decision of the subject in the experiments just considered is whether or not to yield to the false group consensus, we expect to find evidence of cognitive bolstering of the decision reached. Relatively little work has focused on this problem, but the existing evidence suggests that such bolstering does take place.

One way for the subject to justify his decision to conform or deviate is for him to attribute characteristics to himself and others that would be consistent with his decision. From what was said of the effects of ability on the decision to conform or deviate, we might expect postdecisional ability attributions to serve the purpose of further justifying the behavior.

The decision itself, after the process of comparative appraisal, has probably followed from such attributions in the first place. But to the extent that the decision is difficult and irreversible, the person may engage in additional *post hoc* justification to further justify his decision. This cognitive bolstering makes the chosen behavior even more likely the next time such a decision is required. Influence tends, by this process, to be circular and cumulative, making a decision to conform more likely with each successive decision to do so. This also holds for a series of decisions in which a person chooses to deviate from the group.

Postdecisional Ability Evaluations

Some correlational evidence from an experiment by Gerard and Rotter (1961) suggests that cognitive bolstering accompanies a commitment to conform or deviate. The subjects, working in the cubicle situation, were presented with four series of nine line judgments, with the bogus consensus incorrect on six of the nine trials in each series. After each series of judgments the subject answered a questionnaire in which he evaluated his own ability, the ability of the others, and also attempted to guess the evaluations they would make of him. Each of these three evaluations was either positive or negative.

In terms of the discussion of cognitive balance in Chapter Five, we would expect these three evaluations to be made consistent with each other. As stated earlier, balance exists when all three evaluations are positive or when any two are negative and the third is positive. Otherwise the configuration is not balanced. Here the subject's performance is the "object" being judged by himself and the others, with his appraisal of them being the third in this triad of evaluations. Each evaluation can be either positive or negative, so there are eight possible evaluation triads. These are shown in the column headings of Table 11.5 and described in the footnote to the table.

We will assume that the subject anticipates a negative evaluation from the others for deviating from them and a positive evaluation for conforming. Asch's interview protocols as well as the data in Table 11.5 support this assumption. Of the 25 subjects who made no errors or only one error, 19 expected a negative evaluation from the others on the final questionnaire. Of the 24 subjects who made 11 or more errors, 17 expected a positive evaluation from the others. These assumptions as to the others' evaluation of the subject eliminate I $(+++)$, II $(++-)$, V $(-++)$, and VI $(-+-)$ as possible triads for a deviate, because in these triads the second evaluation, which is the anticipated evaluation of the subject by the others, is positive, and III $(+-+)$, IV $(+--)$, VII $(--+)$, and VIII $(---)$ as possible triads for a conformer, because in these the second evaluation is negative. Triads III and VIII are also inconsistent for

Table 11.5. Initial (First Questionnaire) and Final (Last Questionnaire) Distribution of Triad Types by Total Judgment Errors (Adapted from Gerard, 1965)

Total Errors	I(+++)[a]		II(++-)		III(+-+)		IV(+--)		V(-++)		VI(-+-)		VII(--+)		VIII(---)	
	Init.	Fin.	Init.	Fin.	Init.	Fin.	Init.	Fin.	Init.	Fin.	Init.	Fin.	Init.	Fin.	Init.	Fin.
0–1	7	6	[b]		9	4	7	15					2			
2–4	4	7	1		9	5	6	7	1				2	3		
5–10	12	11	1		7	5	2	6					2	2	1	1
11–24	12	17			5	4	1		1	2			4	3	1	1
Total	35	41	2	2	30	18	16	28	2	2			10	8		

[a] The first of the three signs indicates a positive or negative self-evaluation; the second sign indicates the evaluation the subject guessed the others made of him; and the last sign indicates the evaluation the subject made of the others.
[b] An empty cell indicates no cases.

a deviate because the subject would not have deviated had he evaluated the others positively as in III nor would he evaluate both himself and the others negatively as in VIII, because surely someone was correct.

By this process of elimination, triads IV and VII remain as internally consistent given the (probably implicit) decision to deviate. By the same reasoning, triads I and VI are consistent for a conformer. It follows from our argument that triads II, III, V and VIII are incommensurate with both deviating and conforming. Our argument relates the condition of balance regarding these three evaluations to the subject's behavior in the situation, that is, to whether he has conformed or deviated. To the extent that he conforms consistently or deviates consistently he tends to have evaluations that are internally consistent and also consistent with his behavior.

The 96 subjects in the experiment were grouped into four approximately equal categories according to the number of total errors they made over the four series of nine trials each. A maximum of 24 errors was possible because there were six critical trials in each series. The 25 subjects in the "0–1" error category were deviates and should, by our argument, show evaluation triads consistent with deviation, whereas subjects in the "11–24" error category are those who tended to conform; their evaluation triads should therefore be consistent with conformity. Table 11.5 presents the distribution of evaluation triads as indicated by the subject on the initial questionnaire after the first nine trials and again on the final questionnaire after the fourth series. Irrespective of the number of times he yields, there appears to be an overwhelming tendency for the subject to evaluate himself positively; only nine subjects do not. We would therefore expect a deviate to support his behavior with a type IV $(+--)$ triad and a conformer to support his behavior with a type I $(+++)$ triad.

Examining the distribution of initial triads we see that this is the case; there is a greater likelihood for a subject to have a type I triad the more he yields, and for him to have a type IV triad the greater his independence. This comparison can be made by looking up or down the columns for triads I and IV. If we compare the initial to the final distribution we see that these tendencies become more marked over time. Within each error category (the rows) the same subjects are redistributed among the triad types, from the initial to the final evaluations. It is easy to see what has been happening over time by examining how the initial distribution of triads within a given error category redistributes itself on the final questionnaire. A number of subjects change from a type III $(+-+)$ triad, which is not balanced, to either a type I if they tend to conform or to a type IV if they tend to deviate. The other changes are also in the direction of greater balance. Evidently III is a transitional state and if there were additional questionnaires after further judgmental trials, more subjects would probably change out of that state to one that embodies a balanced triad. On examining the column totals, which indicate what has been happening on an over-all basis, we see that there is an increase from 51 to 69 subjects having either a I or a IV triad type.

The theoretical reasoning proposed to account for these data is simple. First, a discrepancy in judgment calls into question the person's estimate of his own ability. Furthermore, because the others have seen his judgment, the subject assumes an evaluation by the others of himself that accords with how he behaved toward them; if he has conformed he assumes that they have evaluated him positively, whereas if he has deviated he assumes that they have evaluated him negatively. He then supports his behavior by bringing his evaluation of them into balance with his self-evaluation and the evaluation he assumes they have of him.

There are some problems here. The initial distribution of triads shows either that the balancing process was well under way after the first nine judgments or that a certain amount of balance existed before the first discrepancy confrontation, which in turn determined whether the subject conformed. It is likely that the process is circular and cumulative, relative ability evaluations leading either to conformity or to deviation, as we saw previously, and the behavior in turn leading to evaluational changes that tend to bolster and thus further justify the behavior. The dramatic example of brainwashing illustrates the process of behavior leading to changed evaluations. The technique involves getting the person to commit himself just once to a behavior that would not ordinarily follow from his beliefs and values. The first commitment typically involves behavior that is of minor importance to the person. But this can be the first step down the road to a completely reorganized set of values resting on subsequent counterattitudinal commitments involving more important matters, each successive commitment requiring additional cognitive accommodation. This accommodation involves not only the specific attitude that is violated by the behavior but related beliefs and values that may have vertical or horizontal connections to it. We described these kinds of connections in Chapter Five.

This internal analysis of the data in Table 11.5 of course raises the possibility that the relationship might be spurious. After all, subjects have selected themselves for the different error categories that we have treated as the independent variable in this analysis. As discussed many times before, this kind of self-selection has many inherent dangers. In order to pin down the relationship we have been studying it is necessary, by experimental control, to assign subjects to the behavioral categories in question. We can then be fairly certain that whatever prior bases exist concerning which subjects may differ these will affect each experimental condition similarly. It is we who decide, rather than the subject himself, the treatment to which he will be assigned.

Controlling Conformity and Deviation in the Study of Postdecisional Accommodation

The previous experiment disclosed an overwhelming tendency for the subject to evaluate himself positively, a tendency that made triad types I $(+++)$ and IV $(+--)$ the balanced configurations for the conformer and the deviate, respectively. If negative evaluations had existed, types VI $(-+-)$ and VII $(--+)$ would also have been possible as balanced configurations. In an experiment by Gerard (1965) an attempt was made to produce both conformity and deviation experimentally, and also to induce both a positive and a negative evaluation. In line with the earlier argument, conformity and deviation will produce anticipated evaluations made by the group members of the subject himself that are respectively positive or negative. Thus the experimental manipulations of self-ability estimate and conformity-deviation act to fix two evaluations in the triad and tendencies toward postdecisional balancing may be estimated by measuring the third component, the subject's evaluation of the others.

Forty-eight subjects were run, three at a time, in the now-familiar cubicle situation, each being informed that he was subject "3." The subject was first exposed to one of two ability treatments in which his task was to select, from a pair of multipointed stars that were briefly flashed on the projection screen, the one having the greater number of points. Figure 11.2 shows a typical stimulus. The subject pressed one button with his left index finger if he chose the left-hand star, or another button with his right index finger if he guessed that the right-hand one had the greater number of points. Only he and the experimenter knew what his responses were during this first series. After each judgment he indicated his confidence, and then a lamp on his display panel lit up if he had made a correct star choice. Half of the subjects were arbitrarily informed, irrespective of whether they were actually correct, that they had chosen the correct star on 14 of the 15 judgments, whereas the other half of the subjects found that they were

Figure 11.2. A typical star judgment stimulus.

correct on only five of the 15. Subjects in the former, high-ability treatment showed a steady increase in confidence over the 15 trials, whereas subjects in the latter, low-ability treatment showed a decrease.

After the ability induction, dummy electrocardiograph (EKG) electrodes were strapped to the subject's forearms and he was led to believe that his first impulse to use either his right or his left index finger could be detected from his forearm muscles. He was instructed to keep his arms motionless and, when it was his turn to judge the stars, his first impulse would be displayed on his lamp panel. During this series, the subject was also told that each person would see the first impulses of the other two subjects. By the familiar ruse, each subject was "3" and believed that the two others were "1" and "2." Each subject's turn, he was informed, would first be signalled by a green light on that subject's panel and his choice tendency, as detected from his forearm muscles, would be the impulse displayed to himself and to the other two subjects.

During this "dummy electrode" series, the subject saw one of two pre-programmed sequences of false first-impulse judgments displayed on his panel. One sequence gave him the impression that his first impulse was to conform to the others regardless of whether they were correct, whereas the other sequence gave him the impression that he chose the correct star, regardless of which star the others chose. The first impulses of "1" and "2" and the subject's own presumed first impulse were displayed in what appeared to him to be a naturally paced sequence. The same 18 star pairs were presented both to subjects in the "deviate" and the "conformer" conditions. On the first three trials, "1," "2," and "3" (the subject himself) all chose the correct star. On trial 4, "1" chose the incorrect star, whereas "2" and "3" chose the correct one. On trial 5 they all chose the correct star again. On trials 6 and 7, "1" and "2" both chose the incorrect star. Up to this point everything was the same for both the conformer and deviate induction. On trial 8 the separation occurred, the conformer finding that his first impulse was to go along with the first impulses of "1" and "2," who both chose the incorrect star, whereas the deviate discovered that his first impulse was to continue to choose the correct star, and thus not to go along with the others. From this point on until the end of the series the conformer found that his first impulse was to go along with "1" and "2" whether they were correct or incorrect; the deviate found that his first impulse always was to choose the correct star.

After this conformer-deviate induction, the subject was given a projective test, the Group Picture Impressions Test devised by Libo (1953). This test has been shown to measure a person's evaluation of others in his present social situation. In taking the test, the subject is shown four stylized pictures in succession that depict an individual in different group situations, and he is asked to write a story about each of the four pictures. The subject's stories are later coded for content indicating approach or avoidance reactions to the others by the main character in each of the pictures, an approach statement being scored plus and an avoidance statement, minus. The subject's score is the algebraic sum of the number of positive and negative statements totaled over all three stories. After taking this GPI test the subject answered a questionnaire that was designed to provide an additional measure of his evaluation of the others and also to check on the experimental variation of ability and conformity-deviation. He estimated how many correct judgments he and the others had made on the first series of 15 star-pairs, and also how many times there was complete agreement during the second series. This last question, the check on the conformity-deviation induction, showed a marked difference between the treatments, the conformers estimating approximately 14 out of 18 trials of complete agreement, and the deviates estimating approximately 8 out of 18, which accurately reflected what happened.

The GPI data, as well as the ability attributions, are shown in Table 11.6. Here it may be seen that the low-ability conformer rated the others'

Table 11.6. Self and Other Evaluations [a] and Group Picture Impressions (GPI Scores) [b] for Conformers and Deviates of High and Low Ability

	Conformer			Deviate		
	Est. of No. of Own Judgments Correct on First Series	Est. of No. of Others' Judgments Correct on First Series	GPI Score	Est. of No. of Own Judgments Correct on First Series	Est. of No. of Others' Judgments Correct on First Series	GPI Score
High ability	14.07_a[c]	12.10_b	5.12_m	13.67_a	10.32_d	1.67_n
Low ability	6.47_c	9.54_d	2.67_n	6.00_c	10.60_d	6.00_m

[a] Both of these evaluations are guesses made by the subject on the postexperimental questionnaire.
[b] The subject's score on this projective test is the algebraic sum of the number of approach and avoidance statements in all three stories.
[c] Figures with the same subscript are not significantly different from one another at the .05 level by a t test. The correct judgments and GPI scores are, of course, not comparable, so that their subscripts are not to be compared. An analysis of variance shows a significant main effect for the ability manipulation on self-estimate of correct judgments and a significant interaction between the two experimental variables on the estimate of the number of correct judgments made by the others. There is also a significant interaction of the GPI scores.

ability as low, whereas his high-ability counterpart rated the others' ability as high. The deviate, on the other hand, rated the others high relative to himself if he were low, and low relative to himself if he were high in ability. Assuming, as we have, that a conformer estimates that the others will evaluate him positively and that the deviate will anticipate a negative evaluation, the data confirm our predictions. The high-ability conformer's evaluations show a type I $(+++)$ triad, and those of the low-ability conformer, a type VI $(-+-)$ triad. The evaluations of the high-ability deviate show a type IV $(+--)$ triad, and those of the low-ability deviate, a type VII $(--+)$ triad.

All four cells show positive GPI scores that indicate a general positive evaluation of the others. When, however, we compare the degree of positive evaluation among the four cells, we find the same trends as in the questionnaire data, which are, therefore, in line with the predicted evaluations. These data, then, place us on firmer ground in drawing the conclusion that evaluation consistency follows a behavioral commitment to conform or deviate. In interpreting the GPI data we have assumed that the subject's general approach or avoidance tendency has as a salient component his evaluation of the others' ability because the situation is such as to make ability a potent consideration. This assumption is supported by the close agreement between the GPI and ability data.

Certain problems remain. The last experiment does not actually pin down *how* cognitive consistency is achieved after a behavioral commitment. The process suggested is that the evaluation the subject makes of the others follows from our having fixed two of the evaluations in the triad. In our proposed sequence the evaluation he guessed the others had made of him was assumed to be fixed by his act of conforming or deviating. It may be, however, that the subject's behavior first fixes his evaluation of the others so that his guess of their evaluation of him may then follow in a consistent way from his evaluations of them and himself. Let us see how that might work. The conformer who finds that his judgments and the judgments of the others are similar may assume that his ability and their abilities are also similar, whereas the deviate might assume a difference in ability because of a difference in judgment. Additional research is needed to determine the immediate effect of a behavioral commitment of this kind; that is, whether it first produces a comparative appraisal of the others relative to what the subject knows about himself, or whether the behavior produces an assumed reflected appraisal of the subject by the others.

SUMMARY

We began this chapter with an examination of the original conformity experiments of Asch in which he discovered that a subject was strongly influenced by the judgments of a group of peers that differed from his own judgments of a simple visual discrimination. The experimental situation provides an ideal setting in which to study certain aspects of the influence process. The judgments are simple and unambiguous; this lends a dramatic impact to the disagreement confronted by the subject.

The first set of experiments examined were concerned with the effect of a subject's being personally identified with his judgment on his decision to conform or deviate from a discrepant consensus. The fact that more conformity occurs when the subject can be held personally accountable to the group than when he is protected by anonymity was interpreted as providing evidence of reflected appraisal in the original experiment. When the subject has anonymity, comparative appraisal alone is engaged; he uses the judgments of others merely as a frame of reference for estimating the correctness of his own judgment.

We then examined separately the literature concerned with the comparative appraisal process and that concerned with reflected appraisal. Comparative appraisal was found to be affected by attributes of the stimulus being judged, such as its ambiguity and the number of alternatives available to the subject. The size, relative ability, and degree of co-orientation of the majority were also shown to affect the resolution of the conformity conflict.

Reflected appraisal was shown to be affected by the degree of interdependence among group members and the degree to which the person feels accepted in the group. Here we were confronted with complex issues, of far-reaching significance, having to do with the relationship between the valuation the person perceives others placing on his membership in the group and the attractiveness of the group for him.

Finally, we inquired into the postdecisional cognitive effects of conforming or deviating. We examined evidence indicating that the person bolsters his decision by cognitive work, adjusting either his self-evaluation or his evaluation of the others, or both, in the process. The results reviewed are consistent with the hypothesis that whether conformity or deviation occurs, the result will be a consistent or balanced attitudinal structure that supports the behavioral commitment.

CHAPTER TWELVE

Attitude Change

Attitudes are formed through experience and, in spite of their relative stability, can be changed through experience. Consider the variety of daily events that are deliberately arranged to affect our opinions and the way we behave. Editorials may direct our attention to some social or political grievance in the hopes of stimulating us to action; advertisements reach out to us through every conceivable medium of communication; speeches are made by those in government to enlist our support for legislative proposals or executive actions; political campaigners appeal to our sense of logic and often our prejudices and passions in an effort to influence our vote; church sermons try to curb our egocentric impulses and indicate the beliefs and actions required of those of faith in a troubled world. In short, our beliefs and actions are the target of many missives that create pressures toward changing our attitudes and inducing behavior in which we would not otherwise engage.

There are also counterforces operating to bolster current attitudes. For attitudes to persist they must survive competing pressures. Clearly many of our attitudes appear to be able to withstand the onslaught. Nevertheless, among all persuaders (which includes each of us in one situation or another) there is the conviction that every belief has its vulnerable spot, that tactic and art can successfully change it if adroitly applied.

The advent of the mass media of the newspaper, radio, and television has given impetus to the study of attitude. Selling a product, electing a political candidate, reducing prejudice, or attempting to get the public to approve the addition of fluorides to drinking water all rest ultimately on the success the communicator has in shaping or changing the attitudes of his audience. These concerns are especially great in a democratic society where the individual citizen has freedom of choice in such matters as how he spends his money and which particular political candidate will best represent his interests. Even a dictatorship ultimately depends for its existence on maintaining some degree of popular support for its policies and methods.

In his role as a scientist the psychologist is vitally concerned with understanding these phenomena. The scientific student of attitude change is interested in the varied settings of persuasive communications because he hopes to extract from them a set of broadly defined variables and to be able to specify how these variables fit into the process of attitude change. To this end, the psychologist seeks to discover why one message succeeds when another fails and to relate such a discovery to the general underlying principles that govern value acquisition, perception, and behavior.

In order to understand why people change their opinions it is essential to inquire into why people have opinions in the first place. What are the major functions that opinions serve, and can knowledge of these functions lead to an understanding of opinion change?

An attitude is a predisposition to approach (positively value) or to avoid (negatively value) a certain class of objects. Opinions are the verbal expressions of such underlying dispositions. Because opinions are thus defined as concrete expressions of attitudes it is probably more appropriate to inquire into the functions of attitudes themselves.

We can, perhaps, gain some idea of the significance of attitudes for normal human functioning by imagining what life would be like in their absence. An attitudeless organism could not easily make decisions between alternative courses of behavior. Instead such an organism would have to perform an intensive calculus of anticipated rewards and punishments in each new situation. We need only think of the enormously increased effort that would be involved in shopping if the housewife, with her grocery list in hand, had no attitudes toward brand names. Or, similarly, we can imagine the dilemma confronting an individual selecting a television program, a movie, or a novel, if he were without the capacity for forming evaluative preferences.

Not only would such an organism be inefficient, but the social consequences of being without attitudes would also be dramatic. Normal human intercourse would certainly be more primitive and reflexive if it were not possible for one actor to generalize about the preferences and predispositions of another. Our anticipations of the actions of others would be limited to highly general knowledge of behavior specific to the species and would provide no guidelines to enable us to anticipate individual differences in behavior.

This brief fantasy about an organism without attitudes points up two major functions of attitudes: (1) Attitudes promote adjustive economy by providing the individual with a ready basis for making decisions. They are dispositions toward objects belonging to certain cognitive categories. (2) Attitudes confer greater stability and social predictability on an individual, making possible the precise and intricate interactions that characterize human beings in contrast to lower organisms. Knowing that individuals tend to respond with consistently positive, neutral, or negative feelings toward particular classes of objects increases the chance that the person can learn about many of the relevant variables that affect another person's behavior. Thus we can derive one set of functions by focusing on the individual person and his adjustive requirements, and another set by examining the conditions necessary for social interaction and group formation.

HISTORICAL BACKGROUND

It is not surprising that the first known set of principles governing the art of persuasion were enunciated in ancient Greece, a relatively large-scale democracy, where reading and writing were regarded as difficult and unnatural. The political system operated through the direct speech of citizens among themselves and to their magistrates. Political agitation succeeded or failed by word of mouth. The art of rhetoric was purportedly first codified in the fifth century B.C. when schools of rhetoric were being established. In the fourth century Aristotle in his *Rhetoric* saw the use of persuasive speech as a technique divorced from the particular content involved.

The use of persuasive speech is to lead to decisions. (When we know a thing, and have decided about it, there is no further use in speaking about it.) This is so even if one is addressing a single person and urging him to do or not do something, as when we scold a man for his conduct and try to change his views. . . . Nor does it matter whether we are arguing against an actual opponent or against a mere proposition . . . we still have to use speech and overthrow the opposing arguments . . . (1941 edition, p. 1408).

Of the modes of persuasion furnished by the spoken word there are three kinds. The first kind depends on the personal character of the speaker; the second on putting the audience into a certain frame of mind; the third on the proof, or apparent proof, provided by the words of the speech itself. Persuasion is achieved by the speaker's personal character when the speech is so spoken as to make us think him credible. We believe good men more fully and more readily than others; this is true generally whatever the question is, and absolutely true where exact certainty is impossible and opinions are divided. . . . Secondly, persuasion may come through the hearers when a speech stirs their emotions. Our judgments, when we are pleased and friendly, are not the same as when we are pained and hostile. . . . Thirdly, persuasion is effected through the speech itself when we have proved a truth or an apparent truth by means of the persuasive arguments suitable to the case in question (pp. 1329–1330).

In these statements Aristotle laid out the general problem of persuasion and attitude change in a form that is still viable. We have only to pick up a modern influential treatment of this field, *Communication and Persuasion* by Hovland, Janis, and Kelley (1953) to see a close reflection of Aristotle's views in the organization of that book. When we separate out the time-bound and culture-bound opinions expressed by Aristotle, we are left with an impressive set of interrelated insights as to the basic nature of the persuasion situation. Such insights provide a starting point in the quest for systematic, substantiated knowledge.

Our approach to attitude will be within the framework of the syllogistic paradigm described in Chapter Five. The reader will recall that the major premise is the value, the minor premise, the belief, and the conclusion is the attitude itself. We can anticipate that strategies for changing attitudes focus on changing either the underlying belief or value premises. Later in this chapter we examine some research in which the attitude is changed directly by having the subject advocate a position he initially disagrees with.

The persuasive communicator is in a real sense a trainer who is attempting to develop or change behavior by altering a disposition that controls it. Let us look at the problem of persuasion within the framework of the learning paradigm.

THE LEARNING PARADIGM

Propositions are generated either deductively, that is, as consequences of other propositions, or are derived inductively from experience. For the fine points underlying the distinction between deduction and induction, the reader is referred to Cohen and Nagel (1934). The process whereby the person derives a proposition from experience is what we usually refer to as learning. The paradigm of so-called classical conditioning (or learning) proposed by Pavlov can be represented as a syllogism. Pavlov trained a dog to salivate to the sound of a bell. He did so by pairing the sound of the bell with the presentation of meat powder to the dog. After a number of successive pairings of the bell and meat powder, the dog was found to salivate to the sound of the bell alone. In this paradigm the bell is called the conditioned stimulus (CS); the meat powder, the unconditioned stimulus (UCS); and the salivation, the response (R). We have three terms and three propositions. The major premise is a built-in relationship for the dog that states a value: meat powder is good. (We have substituted the major term *good* for the response of salivation, as salivation itself is presumably a response to goodness.) The minor premise associates the bell with the meat powder, expressing the fact that the two tend to occur together temporally. This is the belief premise. The new, evaluative response of salivating to the bell ("the bell is good") is the conclusion of the syllogism deriving from the dog having learned the association between the bell and meat powder.

The belief that the bell and the meat powder were associated was derived from a limited number of experienced instances—as may be a person's belief that Negroes are lazy. Like the bell and the meat powder for the dog, Negroes and laziness are associated for that person. The dog's response to meat powder—that it is good—is transferred to the bell; the person's response to laziness—that it is bad—is transferred to Negroes. We are presumably dealing with a primitive mechanism that, in the case of human beings, becomes elaborated by cognitive work.

As pointed out in earlier chapters, many beliefs held by the individual are anchored in groups. A person may have had no direct experience that relates Negroes and laziness, yet may firmly hold the belief that Negroes are lazy if this is a belief of those around him—either those he considers experts or co-oriented peers. Beliefs, of course, can be adopted through the operation of both informational and effect dependence.

The Three Types of Persuasion

The communicator may have one of three tasks: he may wish to create an attitude, change the sign of an existing one, or increase its intensity. When he wishes to create an attitude toward some object or object class he typically relies on a value premise that he knows is held by his audience and attempts to point out why the object or object class furthers that value or detracts from it. He attempts to establish a belief premise or set of premises containing the new object class. Thus someone who is speaking to an audience that knows nothing about the effects of adding fluorides to water attempts, in shaping a new attitude toward the use of fluorides, to associate fluorides with a value already held by the audience: the absence of cavities is good.

A communicator who seeks to change the sign of an attitude from positive to negative or vice versa typically attempts to discredit the belief premise (or premises) supporting the initial attitude—and thus make the value premise irrelevant to the conclusion—or to connect other values with the cognitions related by the belief, attempting to change the sign of the conclusion. Thus, if the audience believed that fluorides were bad because they have an adverse effect on the mind, the communicator would attempt to discredit this belief by citing relevant evidence. He would also try to point out the benefits for dental hygiene to be gained from fluoridation.

If the communicator were addressing an audience that was favorable to his position and his purpose were to get the members to take action, he would attempt to increase the importance of the attitude. This might be accomplished by emphasizing the importance of the value premise, thus increasing its saliency, or by emphasizing the number of important values mediated by the attitude. Thus, if he were talking to a profluoridation audience and his purpose were to get them to canvass their neighborhoods for signatures in support of a fluoridation proposal, he might emphasize the immense hygienic advantages of having good, sound teeth. He might also tie his arguments in with other advantages (values) such as saving on dentist bills, being a progressive person, having attractive children, agreeing with scientific findings, and so on.

As we shall see when we examine the research on persuasion, there has been little attempt to specify which part of the structure underlying the attitude is being attacked by a given message. Instead, the work has proceeded with rather gross and usually implicit assumptions concerning the premises underlying particular attitudes. The current body of available research represents only a beginning in the search for knowledge about the attitude change process.

In this chapter we examine this work from the perspective of the preceding chapters and also in terms of the syllogistic learning paradigm. We take Aristotle's approach by distinguishing those factors characterizing the communicator, the message, and the audience in the attitude change situation. Our concern is primarily with the informational side of the process and we shall therefore frequently cross-reference the findings in Chapters Ten and Eleven.

THE COMMUNICATOR

We should expect to find that those aspects of the communicator that appeared to enhance his effectiveness in the social-influence and conformity situations discussed in Chapters Ten and Eleven also enhance his effectiveness here. Thus, if he is attempting to undermine a particular belief by an appeal to facts, the degree to which he is perceived to be an expert determines how successful he will be. If, on the other hand, he has chosen to attack the value premise underlying an attitude, he will be effective to the extent that he is perceived as a co-oriented peer. When his values do not coincide with those of his audience, the force of his message is reduced. For example, if he is seen as benefiting personally from a change in attitude on the part of the audience, the audience tends to resist the content of the message. The owner of a soap company tends to be less effective in selling a brand of detergent his company manufactures than someone who can assume the role of the typical housewife.

Expertise, "Prestige Suggestion," and the Sleeper Effect

The research has not distinguished systematically between expertise and co-orientation, both of which tend to affect the amount of credibility attributed to the communicator. Instead, studies have often attempted to build up an effect by combining both factors in one experimental treatment.

Thus the credible source is typically represented as someone who has expert knowledge and also shares the values of the audience.

One of the earliest studies dealing specifically with the effects of communicator credibility was conducted by Hovland and Weiss (1951). Each subject received a booklet containing articles on four different topics: the future of movie theaters, the feasibility of atomic submarines, the steel shortage (who is to blame?), and antihistamine drugs (should they be sold without a prescription?). A favorable and an unfavorable article were prepared for each topic. Also, each article was attributed either to a highly credible source or to one that was not very credible. For example, the article discussing the future of movie theaters was attributed either to *Fortune* magazine or to a syndicated woman movie gossip columnist. Various combinations of affirmative and negative articles, each credited to a high- or low-credibility source, were used. Thus each subject received a booklet that contained two affirmative and two negative articles, each on a different one of the four issues, in which one of each type of argument was attributed to a high-credibility source and one of each to a low-credibility source; in this way each subject served in both the high- and low-credibility treatments. The main dependent measure was the amount of change in opinion (in the direction of the attitude advocated by the communicator) on each of the issues. This change was determined by comparing the subject's responses on a questionnaire administered five days before he read the communications with his responses on questionnaires administered immediately after the communication and again four weeks later. In comparing the net change from before to immediately after the communication, the high-credibility source was found to have been considerably more effective. This appears to correlate with a tendency for the subject to attribute greater fairness and reasonableness to the high-credibility source.

Opinions for those issues on which the subject had received a communication attributed to a high-credibility source showed some loss over the four-week period, whereas opinions on issues for which the subject had received a communication attributed to a low-credibility source were slightly *more* influenced by the communication after four weeks than originally. This latter result is referred to by Hovland and Weiss as a "sleeper effect." The net effect was such that there was ostensibly no difference between the "final" opinions of subjects in the high- and low-credibility treatments. Hovland and Weiss found some evidence of a tendency for the subject to dissociate the source from the message after the four-week interval. Thus the message itself was recalled but there was a tendency to forget who had said it.

One possibility that may account for the immediate effect of the communication is that the subject paid greater attention to a high- rather than a low-credibility communicator and thus was more open to the information in the message attributed to the high-credibility source. That interpretation does not hold up, however, as there was no difference between treatments on a measure (included in the postquestionnaire) of the degree to which the subject correctly comprehended the content of the various communications. The immediate postexposure effect of credibility is therefore probably based on the degree to which the subject "accepts" the arguments in the message.

In Chapter Seven we discussed the Gestalt position on how values may influence the nature of the object perceived. Asch (1948) exemplified this view by suggesting that the actual meaning of a statement would be determined by who purportedly said it. Take the statement: "I hold it that a little rebellion, now and then, is a good thing, and as necessary in the political world as storms are in the physical." Asch (1948) argued that the meaning of this statement was different depending on whether it was attributed to Jefferson or Lenin. He interpreted Lorge's (1936) finding, that statements associated with a positive source were accepted and those associated with a negative source rejected, as being mediated by differences in meaning the subjects attached to the statement itself. When the statement in question was attributed to Jefferson (the actual author), the word "rebellion" was interpreted as meaning "agitation," whereas when the statement was attributed to Lenin, "rebellion" was interpreted to mean "revolution."

This process, suggested by Asch, introduces some complexity into our Pavlovian attitude model; an attitude object may take on certain stimulus attributes by virtue of its association with some other attitude object. Thus a value may be attached to a stimulus object and may also modify characteristics of the object itself. It may be that the Hovland and Weiss results are to be accounted for by the latter process. Although apparently equal attention was paid to the communication, irrespective of the credibility of the source, the communication may have taken on a different meaning depending on the source to which it was attributed. If we extend our definition of "meaning" to include the probability that a statement is true, this certainly fits Asch's suggested process. It may be that other aspects of meaning may also have been affected by source attribution.

Are there any real differential consequences of the Aschian versus Pavlovian position? The "sleeper effect" discovered by Hovland and Weiss is a consequence that Asch could not predict. According to Asch, the meaning, and hence the effect of a message, are inextricably tied to the context of who made the statement. The evidence in the Hovland and Weiss experiment suggests that the message and source tend to become *dissociated* over time. Any handicap or benefit that was initially imparted to the message as a function of source credibility had been vitiated after four weeks. These data certainly call for either a revision of Asch's position or a detailed investigation of the nature of the sleeper effect that might reveal a process that is not inconsistent with his position.

It could be argued that asking the subject to read four communications, one right after the other, with each attributed to a different source, might not provide the most ideal circumstances for a subject to remember who said what. The work on memory suggests that this kind of situation would produce a great deal of interference between memory traces. That this is not the case in the Hovland and Weiss experiment is demonstrated by findings in a subsquent experiment by Kelman and Hovland (1953) in which a communication on a single issue was used.

The communication was a tape-recorded speech recommending leniency in the treatment of juvenile delinquents. The speaker on the tape was given one of three introductions. In the high-credibility treatment he was introduced as a juvenile court judge; in the low-credibility treatment he was introduced as someone with a shady past who had recently been picked up for peddling dope; and in the neutral treatment he was introduced as someone chosen at random from the studio audience. Opinion measurements were taken before, immediately after, and three weeks after the communication. The immediate effect of the communication was in line with the findings of the previous experiment. The change toward leniency was greatest for the high-credibility communicator and least for the low-credibility communicator. Half of the subjects in each credibility treatment had the identity of the communicator reinstated after the three-week interval, before they answered the final questionnaire, whereas no mention was made of the identity of the communicator for the other half of the subjects in each of the three treatments. This latter condition was, of course, the same as the one used in the Hovland and Weiss experiment. If we are correct about the tendency of the subject to dissociate source and content over time, there should be a "sleeper effect" only in the nonreinstatement condition. This is in fact what was found; without reinstatement the difference in opinion produced by the high- and low-credibility speakers had again washed out, whereas with reinstatement the difference was approximately the same as the difference observed immediately after the communication. This is shown in Figure 12.1.

Discrepancy and Expertise

In an experiment that ties in with some of the work on the effects of discrepancy discussed in Chapter Ten, Bergin (1962) attempted to reconcile the findings of some studies which indicate that change is greater as the discrepancy between the communicator and target person increases, with findings of other studies showing the reverse trend. In studies by Cohen (1959), Goldberg (1954), and Zimbardo (1960) the amount of change appears to increase with increasing discrepancy. Others have found, how-

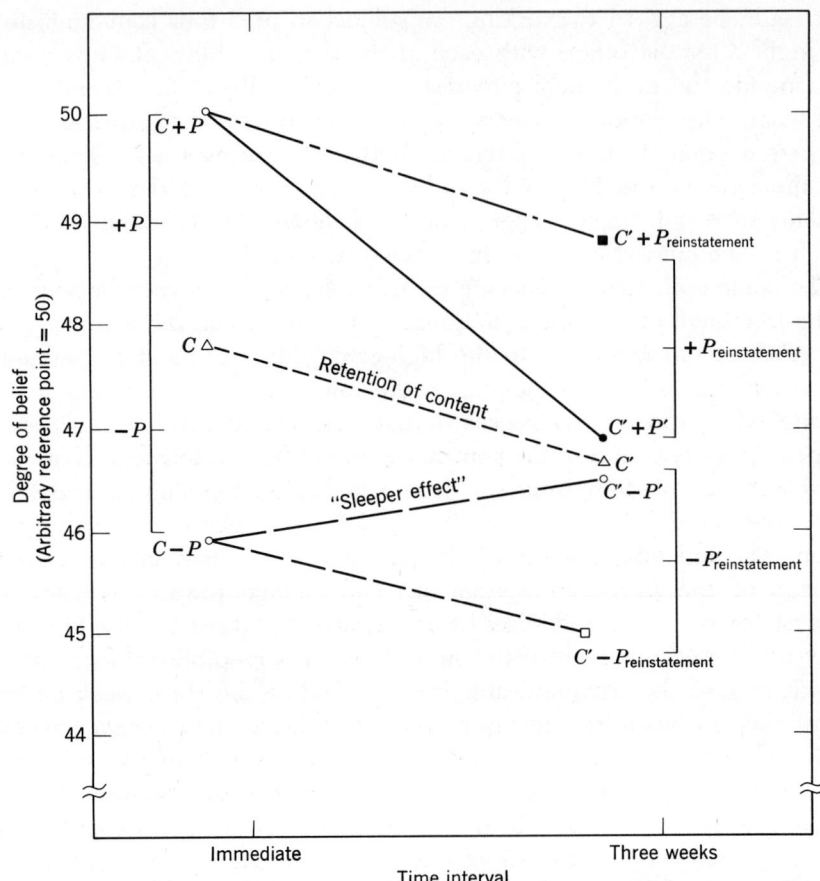

Figure 12.1. Effects of content and prestige factors on degree of belief immediately after the communication, three weeks later without "reinstatement" of the communicator, and three weeks later with "reinstatement" of the communicator (adapted from Kelman and Hovland, 1953). The values for C and C' (effects of content immediately after and three weeks after exposure to the message) are hypothetical and have been selected to be consistent with the data. The value for C + P represents the immediate effect of the content when attributed to a positive prestige communicator and C − P represents the immediate effect of the content when attributed to a negative prestige communicator. The values for C' + P' and C' − P' represent the delayed effects of the content when attributed to a positive prestige and a negative prestige communicator under nonreinstatement conditions. The values for C' + P$_{reinstatement}$ and C' − P$_{reinstatement}$ represent the delayed effects of the content when attributed to a positive and negative prestige source under reinstatement conditions. All of the values are shown relative to C + P, which is given the arbitrary value of 50. The effects or reinstatement are based on the questionnaire attitude data.

ever, that beyond a certain discrepancy the effectiveness of a communicator decreases (Fisher and Lubin, 1958; Hovland, Harvey, and Sherif, 1957). There are at least two possible ways of explaining the inconsistency. Perhaps in the former set of studies the maximum discrepancy was not large enough to show a diminished effect beyond a certain point, or maybe there was something about the communicators in the different studies that made it more or less easy for the subjects to discount or reject them. In Chapter Ten we discussed two modes of coming to terms with a discrepancy that would also be possible in the experimental situation we are discussing here. The subject can reduce the discrepancy by changing his attitude so that he is in greater agreement with the communicator or he can discredit the communicator and thereby reject the opinion he advocates. Bergin attempted to vary the possibility of discrediting the communicator by varying his credibility. The manipulation of credibility was combined with three levels of discrepancy between opinion advocated in the communication and the subject's opinion.

In the high-credibility treatment the college-student subject was led to believe that he was participating in an important personality assessment project being conducted by the university medical school. The room he reported to was purposely arranged to look impressive, with many books, elaborate medical equipment, and even a large portrait of Freud. The experimenter was introduced by the receptionist as the director of the project. The subject was told that the purpose of the study was to compare a person's self-ratings on personality traits with some standard, reliable, objective measures. He filled out a self-rating form that included a rating on masculinity-femininity and then took a battery of tests, which also included one on masculinity-femininity. Several days later he returned and was shown his supposed test scores presented in a very impressive format and it was pointed out to him that there was a discrepancy between his self-estimate of masculinity-femininity and the score (fictitious) he made on the highly reliable test of that trait. This was presented on a 13-point scale on which the discrepancy was either six (high), four (medium), or two (low) points.

In the low-credibility treatment the subject reported to a shabby room, where he filled out the self-ratings. During the second session he interacted with a confederate of the experimenter, who was introduced as a high-school student. The confederate then pretended to rate the subject on the various personality traits. These ratings had been prearranged to place the subject into one of the three discrepancy conditions using the two-, four-, or six-scale-point discrepancy.

In all six treatment combinations (two credibility levels × three discrepancy levels) the final task of the subject was to rerate himself on the traits, a task for which a sufficiently reasonable rationale was given.

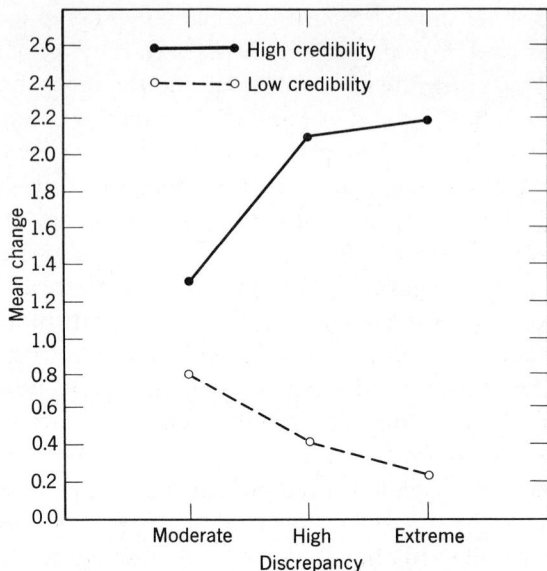

Figure 12.2. Mean change in most-acceptable rating as a function of communicator credibility and communication discrepancy (adapted from Bergin, 1962).

The primary datum was the pre- to posttreatment change in the subject's masculinity-femininity self-rating. The results are most dramatically portrayed in Figure 12.2, where the discrepancy treatments are shown on the abscissa of the graph and the average change for the conditions on the ordinate. The effect is strong and clear. Under high credibility change is greater, the greater the discrepancy, whereas under low credibility the relationship is reversed.

These results not only confirm our prediction but also point out that persuasion effects can occur with respect to self-attitudes as well as with attitudes toward external objects and events. Data from a similar experiment by Aronson, Turner, and Carlsmith (1963) are consistent with these findings.

Co-orientation

A component of the credibility of a message is presumably the degree to which the audience perceives the communicator as co-oriented. We have suggested that a co-oriented peer would be more effective in undermining a value premise than he would in undermining a belief. Unfortunately, there has been no research specifically designed to examine this problem.

Co-orientation raises a strategic question: what is the most effective way for the communicator to inform the members of his audience that he shares their values? Does he tell them directly that he is just like them, or can he use a more subtle method? No research bears directly on this comparison, but a study by Weiss (1957) examined the effectiveness of establishing prior attitude congruence on an issue other than the one involved in the persuasive communication. In that study the issue about which the communicator wished to persuade his audience concerned fluoridation of drinking water. The subject in one treatment was exposed to the communicator's position on academic freedom, which coincided with his own attitude, whereas in another treatment no prior congruence was established. The communicator was more effective on the fluoridation issue when there was prior attitude congruence. This suggests that values on one issue can be used to establish assumed co-orientation for purposes of influencing an audience on another issue. This may be mediated by a value "halo"; the subject may attribute general value congruence between himself and the communicator if he has evidence of congruence on a specific value.

Aronson and Golden (1962) exposed elementary-school children to a communication stressing the importance of studying arithmetic. In one set of conditions the communicator was presented as an M.I.T. engineering graduate and, in addition, he was either Negro or white. In two other conditions the communicator was introduced as a dishwasher who, again, was either Negro or white. When the effectiveness of the communication is analyzed in terms of the questionnaire-measured amount of anti-Negro prejudice of the listener, a strong and clear effect appears. Prejudiced listeners are less influenced by a Negro in both the "engineer" and "dishwasher" treatments than are unprejudiced listeners. Those who scored low in prejudice, on the other hand, were more influenced by the Negro than by the white communicator. The data are not interpretable by assuming that the prejudiced listener attributed less expertise to Negroes, because a postexperimental questionnaire indicated no difference in the degree of intelligence attributed by prejudiced subjects to the Negro and white engineers.

Aronson and Golden interpret the reduced susceptibility of prejudiced subjects to a communication from a Negro in the "engineer" treatment as simply "irrational." We think that the finding is better accounted for by the assumed lack of co-orientation with a Negro on the part of the white, prejudiced, sixth-grade pupils. Prejudice of this sort may lead to the assumption that what is good for the group against which he is prejudiced is *ipso facto* not good for the subject himself because this group possesses an opposite value orientation to his own. This may not be a particularly "rational" approach on the part of the prejudiced person, but it suggests a process whereby the data may be rationally understood.

There is obviously a great deal of room for further research on co-orientation.

Perceived Intent of the Communicator

An aspect of the communication situation that is closely related to co-orientation concerns the intent attributed to the speaker by his audience. If he is out to influence them it is presumably in pursuit of some value that he holds; otherwise why would he make the effort? Unless he can convince his audience that the value he is pursuing is something they should also pursue, the effectiveness of his communication will be blunted. Thus, if someone is hawking toothpaste on television, he has the seller's perspective, whereas his viewer has the perspective of a potential buyer. The viewer takes what he hears with a grain of salt because of the obvious intent of the seller to make money. It follows that a communication overheard accidentally might be more effective than one that the person perceives had been specifically intended for his ears. Television commercials often use techniques that attempt to capitalize on this "overhearing" effect. The two housewives having a casual conversation over the back fence about some new washday product comes to mind as a good example. The setting and their behavior is designed to affect a candid, private situation in order to disarm the viewer into believing that the housewife extolling the virtues of a particular detergent to her neighbor really has nothing to gain from influencing the viewing audience. To make the situation even more compelling, some commercials attempt to remove the slick quality from the appeal by using candid-camera techniques.

There is evidence for this "overhearing" effect in an experiment by Walster and Festinger (1962). College-student subjects were permitted to listen in on a conversation in the next room. In one condition the individual subject was led to believe that the speakers were aware of their being overheard (the "regular" treatment), whereas in a second treatment the subject believed that he was eavesdropping (the "overheard" treatment). The conversation the subject listened in on in both conditions consisted of a discussion of some common misconceptions concerning the causal relationship between smoking and lung cancer. Evidence was cited indicating that the relationship was not nearly so clear-cut as people have been led to believe. A week later the subjects received a questionnaire in their classrooms that was represented as a health survey. Among the many questions on a variety of health issues there were several key questions concerning the student's opinion about the causal relationship between smoking and lung cancer. The subject's responses to these questions indicate that in the "overheard" treatment he became more skeptical about the causal relationship, thus confirming the greater effectiveness of the overheard conversation. The experiment was repeated, using the same technique, with two other issues: "Student husbands should spend a great deal more time at home" and "Junior and senior women should be allowed to live off campus if they desire." The subjects in this second experiment were all women.

For the "smoking–lung cancer" issue, smokers were more influenced by the overheard than by the regular communication whereas for nonsmokers there was no difference in the effectiveness of the two treatments. On the "student husbands" issue, married women were more susceptible to the overheard than to the regular communication, whereas for single women there was no such difference. On the "off-campus-living" issue the effect was reversed, with the single women being more susceptible to the overheard than to the regular communication and with no difference for the married woman. Walster and Festinger attribute the results to a difference in involvement in the issue. When the subject was involved the overheard communication had a greater effect. Why this should be so is mysterious. In all cases the message advocates a position that the involved listener would like to accept (e.g., smokers would want to believe that the evidence for smoking leading to lung cancer might not be convincing). Why, then, should an involved listener be less vulnerable in the "regular" treatment, that is, when the communicator knows that he is being overheard? It is conceivable that we are especially guarded and sensitive to ulterior motivation when we are especially tempted to believe a communicator. This goes little beyond describing the results, however, and hardly explains them.

A recent study by Brock and Becker (1965) contributes further to the mystery. In their "regular" treatment the communicator received a phone call in the subject's presence and tried *not* to be drawn into a conversation with the caller. In spite of the obvious evidence that the communicator-experimenter did not want to discuss the opinion issue in front of the subject, when he finally did so his remarks had little effect compared to an "overheard" condition where the experimenter took the call in an adjacent room (from which his voice was clearly audible). Once again the importance of overhearing was established, and yet the connection between the overhearing manipulation and the concept of the speaker's intent to influence remains obscure. The intriguing problem of determining what accounts for the overhearing effect is well worth pursuing.

In each of the experiments just described there was little basis for the subject to assume that there was an intent to influence him even in the treatment in which the speakers knew they were being overheard. Because the subject in that treatment had no basis for assuming an intent, it is not clear that the experiment actually compared the effectiveness of an intentional versus an overheard communication. If anything, it could be argued that the differences observed in the experiment were not so large as they would have been had the perception of intent been effectively controlled. The experimental situation introduced by Walster and Festinger is an ideal one for separating out and studying the independent effects of expertise and co-orientation. We would not expect credibility based on expertise to have any differential effect in an overheard versus an intentional communication, whereas the effectiveness of these two types of communications should be sensitive to similarities and differences in co-orientation.

THE COMMUNICATION

Clearly, without a communication of some sort there can be no persuasion. The skill of the communicator in phrasing and organizing his message will, in part, determine his effectiveness. Aristotle was deeply concerned with the nature of arguments, their logical coherence, their emotional appeal, and the language used by the speaker to get these various aspects of the message across. His interests here covered the broad range of problems involved in human communication and the nature of language itself. Other rhetoricians since Aristotle have also been concerned with these issues. In their initial efforts to study these problems systematically, social psychologists have focused on some of the more obvious questions that come to mind. For example, when two points of view are in contention, is it better for the communicator to present only his side or should he present and criticize the opposite viewpoint as well? If the communicator has decided to present both sides, should he offer his own or the other side first? Should he draw an explicit conclusion in his message or should he organize it so that the members of the audience take an active part in drawing the conclusion for themselves? Should he state his point of view at the outset or is it more strategic for him to draw his conclusion later in the message? Should he be matter-of-fact in his presentation or should he attempt to trade on or arouse the emotions of his audience? Obviously, the domain of inquiry is larger than these few questions indicate, but the investigation of even this narrow range has led to some extremely interesting and provocative results.

One-Sided versus Two-Sided Communications

A practical question and, as we shall see, one with broad theoretical implications, concerns whether it will advance or hurt a speaker's cause to apprise his audience of the arguments supporting an opposing viewpoint.

As we might expect, the question turns out to be complicated, with an answer that must be hedged and qualified.

The earliest experimentation explicitly directed to this issue was conducted by Carl Hovland and his colleagues during World War II under the auspices of the Information and Education Division of the War Department. The Army had developed an extensive information and education program that involved weekly orientation and information presentations to men in every theater of operations. A special I-and-E officer was in charge of this program in every major unit and installation. A situation was thus provided in which realistic field experiments could be performed and psychologists working in the I-and-E Division capitalized on this opportunity. This initial work laid the foundation for the postwar studies carried out by Hovland and the other members of the Yale Communication and Attitude Change Program.

One of the problems confronting the U.S. Army when the German surrender appeared imminent was the inclination of the average soldier to believe that the war in the East with Japan would end quickly. Such a belief was inimical to the further prosecution of the war. The men would become overconfident and lose their motivation to learn the skills of soldiery. Talks were prepared in an effort to dispel this overconfidence. Hovland and his associates (Hovland, Lumsdaine, and Sheffield, 1949), were able, using I-and-E orientation sessions, to design an experiment that enabled them to explore the effectiveness of two kinds of arguments, one-sided versus two-sided.

It can be argued that when a communicator wishes to advance a particular point of view citing evidence that leads to an opposing viewpoint may raise doubts among members of his audience. On the other hand, it can also be argued that failure to deal with this negative evidence may make the communicator vulnerable to a charge of being unfair, especially if the negative evidence is based on fairly well-known facts. This feeling that the communication was unfair would create resistance to the acceptance of the communicator's conclusion. The strategic question here concerns the relative amount of risk the communicator is taking with each type of argument, whereas the theoretical question pertains to the nature of the processes that underlie this risk-taking.

Each of the argument treatments was presented to 214 men, with an additional 197 serving as a control group that received no communication. Prior attitudes were measured in all three groups approximately one week before the experimental session. The communications in the two experimental groups were radio transcriptions, both arguing that it would take at least two years to end the war with Japan. The "one-sided" presentation lasted 15 minutes and pointed out such things as the logistic problems created by the great distances involved, the remaining large Japanese resources, and the size of the Japanese Army. The "two-sided" communication contained all of the information in the one-sided version, except that four minutes of additional "negative" information was woven into the message when relevant. This negative evidence consisted of pointing out such factors as the superiority of the U.S. Naval forces and the greater concentration of effort we could muster in changing from a two-front to a one-front war. An after-measure of the projected length of the war with Japan was taken in the two experimental groups and also in the control group immediately after the presentation of the message to the experimental groups. In determining the effects of both messages, the net change toward believing that the war would be longer was computed (net change was used because some men changed in one direction whereas others changed in the opposite direction). This was corrected by changes occurring in the control group that were presumably the result of extraneous factors unrelated to the messages.

Compared on an over-all basis, the one-sided and two-sided communications produced substantially the same net change, but interesting differences emerged when initial attitude was taken into account. The results were analyzed separately for men who were initially favorable toward the viewpoint expressed in the communications and for those who were initially unfavorable. As suggested earlier, someone who was initially opposed might consider the one-sided presentation unfair and thus be less vulnerable to it. The data presented in Table 12.1 show that for the unfavorable group

Table 12.1. Net Percentage [a] Changing toward the Commentator (by Increasing their Estimate of the Length of the War) among Men Initially Opposing and Men Initially Favoring the Commentator's Position Who Were Exposed to One of the Two Arguments

	Initially opposed		Initially favorable	
One-sided argument	36%	Net effect, 12% favoring two-sided	52%	Net effect, 29% favoring one-sided
Two-sided argument	48%		23%	

[a] Net percentage change takes account of those men who changed in the opposite direction to the point of view advanced by the commentator by subtracting this percentage from the percentage changing toward the commentator. The percentages are also corrected for any changes occurring in the control group (adapted from Hovland, Lumsdaine, and Sheffield, 1949).

the two-sided argument did have a greater effect than the one-sided argument, whereas the effect in the favorable group was reversed. The greater effectiveness of a one-sided presentation for the favorable group may indicate that the two-sided presentation raised doubts among men with an initially favorable disposition.

We might expect (and Aristotle suggests) that the higher the educational level of the audience the more critical they will be in evaluating the communicator's message. We might therefore expect the more educated members of the audience to be more impressed with the two-sided communication. Indeed, the more educated men were more vulnerable to a two-sided argument, the reverse being true for the less educated men. The results become even more dramatic when the data are broken down by educational level *and* favorableness of initial estimate. Table 12.2, which presents this

Table 12.2 Net Percentage of Men Increasing Their Estimate of the Length of the War for Graduates and Nongraduates Who either Initially Favored or Opposed the Point of View of the Commentator and Who Heard a One-Sided or a Two-Sided Argument (From Hovland, et al., 1949)

	Graduate		Nongraduate	
	Initially opposed	Initially favored	Initially opposed	Initially favored
One-sided argument	30	39	44	64
Two-sided argument	44	54	51	− 3

breakdown into the eight subgroups formed, shows that for the more educated men the two-sided argument was more effective irrespective of initial disposition, whereas the one-sided argument is overwhelmingly more effective for the less educated men with an initially favorable attitude. These results clearly indicate that the effectiveness of the type of argument used in the communication depends on certain characteristics of the audience. In the study reviewed, the initial attitude and educational level of the audience appear to be very crucial.

We can look at the results in the previous experiment from an action-sequence perspective. Those subjects who were initially favorable were convinced of the communicator's point of view and were not confronted with a choice of which attitude to hold. Those who were unfavorable, on the other hand, were presented with a conflict; they had to choose between their initial "side" and the communicator's "side." They had presumably made a decision that they were now being pressed to re-evaluate. In the introduction to this chapter we distinguished the two types of influence situations represented here. When the audience is initially unfavorable the communicator must accomplish two things. He has to unfreeze the initial decision and put his audience in a choice situation. He must then convince the audience that his view is the one it should prefer. It may be that the one-sided presentation is not able to unfreeze the initial commitment to the opposite viewpoint, owing to the subject's defensiveness. In acknowledging the evidence supporting the negative argument the two-sided communication may effectively disarm the subject by making it unnecessary for him to muster counterarguments. By this reasoning, then, the two-sided presentation unfreezes the initial decision and presents the subject with what is essentially a new choice.

An experiment by Lumsdaine and Janis (1953) bears on this interpretation. They used essentially the same procedure as in the previous experiment, except that the issue was one about which the subject population was not heavily involved or well-informed. The experiment was run some months before the Soviet Union exploded its first atomic bomb and the issue was the length of time it would take before the Russians would be producing large numbers of atomic bombs. The communicator was in the position of establishing a belief when, if one already existed, it was only of the vaguest sort. Both the one-sided and two-sided messages were presented as radio transcriptions and both argued that it would be at least five years before the Russians would be producing a large quantity of bombs. Lumsdaine and Janis were primarily interested in comparing the ability of subjects exposed to both treatments to withstand subsequent counterpropaganda. One week after hearing the communication half of the subjects in the one-sided treatment and half in the two-sided treatment were exposed to counterpropaganda in the form of a second message that took the opposing viewpoint. The final questionnaire was administered to all subjects immediately after this second message.

The data presented in Table 12.3 are clear-cut. For those subjects not

Table 12.3. Net Percentage Change toward the Position Advocated by the Communicator for Subjects Who Were Exposed and Those Not Exposed to Counterpropaganda Who Initially Heard either a One-Sided or Two-Sided Argument (From Lumsdaine and Janis, 1953)

	Not exposed to counterpropaganda	Exposed to counterpropaganda
One-sided argument	64%	2%
Two-sided argument	69%	61%

exposed to counterpropaganda in the second session, both types of argument appeared to be equally effective. On the other hand, a marked difference in effectiveness of the counterpropaganda is shown by the ability of subjects who were exposed to the earlier two-sided communication to resist this second message. Thus, even though in this experiment and in the original Army experiment, the two types of argument appear to be equally effective on the average in changing or establishing beliefs, the two-sided argument in this experiment was more effective in sustaining the belief against counterargument. The reasons behind this finding that a two-sided approach increases resistance to change will be discussed later in this chapter when we consider the creation of defenses against propaganda through inoculation.

Surprisingly enough, there has been little additional research comparing the direct persuasive effects of one-sided versus two-sided communications. There are many important problems that must be given attention. In both aforementioned experiments, the negative side in the two-sided message was given much less coverage than the positive side. We might argue that the more attention given to the negative side the less effective the message would be. On the other hand, insufficient attention to the negative side might emphasize the communicator's lack of fairness. Presumably there is some optimal proportion of negative to positive arguments. Another question: Should the communicator present all of the negative arguments or should he confine himself to covering only those familiar to the audience? An experiment by Thistlethwaite and Kamenetsky (1955) suggests that the introduction of novel negative evidence may decrease the effectiveness of the communication. These and other questions await the definitive answers that further research may provide.

The Order of Presenting Arguments

In the two-sided communication used in the foregoing research, negative evidence was woven in at different points in the message. Is this an effective way of dealing with the negative side, or should all of the negative evidence be grouped together? This question has not been specifically addressed in any research, but the relative effectiveness of the order of grouped arguments has been examined. Assuming that the arguments have been grouped into those for the point of view to be advanced and those against it, is it better to present the arguments for the case first or second? The research conducted has rephrased the question in this form: Is there a primacy effect or a recency effect in communication? Does the material presented first interfere with the assimilation of material presented second, or does material presented second retroactively interfere with material presented first? Aristotle argued in favor of a primacy effect. His prescriptions outlined the strategy to be taken when opposing sides were being argued in a political debate or in the courtroom. The side being presented first, he asserted, had an advantage. "For just as our minds refuse a favorable reception to a person against whom they are prejudiced, so they refuse it to a speech when they have been favorably impressed by the speech on the other side" (1941, p. 1447). Aristotle held that this initial advantage could be overcome if the person presenting his argument second begins by carefully refuting his opponent's argument. This prescription, however, takes us beyond the research evidence. Let us backtrack and examine the evidence that exists for primacy or recency. We will ignore the complex questions raised by the role of refutation and deal with a simpler question: When two sets of evidence for opposing viewpoints are presented serially to an audience, which set has the advantage in persuading the audience of its point of view, the first or the second?

Lund's study (1925) confirmed Aristotle's surmise in a seemingly conclusive way. Three groups of subjects were each presented with a different issue. These issues were "Should all men have equal political rights?", "Is the protective tariff a wise policy for the United States?", and "Will monogamous marriage continue to be the only socially accepted relation between the sexes?". A positive and a negative communication was prepared for each of these issues. Within each group the subjects received both the positive and negative communications with the order counterbalanced, half of the subjects in the group receiving the negative communication first, and the other half receiving the positive communication first. Each subject's attitude on the issue was measured three times, once before the experiment, once after the first communication, and again after the second communication. The data showed a shift after the first communication in the direction of the position advocated and another shift in the opposite direction after the second communication. The second shift, however, was not large enough to overcome the shift produced by the first communication. The final result, therefore, gave the advantage to the communication presented first—a primacy effect.

This long-standing conclusion was suddenly clouded by Cromwell's (1950) finding of an unmistakable recency effect. His experiment, which used Federal medical aid as an issue, measured the subject's opinion only twice, once before the experiment and again after he had heard both messages (as in the Lund study, the order of the arguments was counterbalanced, half of the subjects receiving the pro-con order and the other half receiving the con-pro order).

How can the recency effect in the Cromwell experiment be reconciled with the primacy effect found earlier by Lund? Was there a critical difference in the procedure that might reconcile the two findings? Would we expect the only apparent difference between the two studies, an attitude measurement after the first communication, to account for the primacy effect in Lund's study? In pursuing this question let us consider for a moment the conformity research discussed in Chapter Eleven. The typical conformity experiment is essentially a two-sided situation. The subject has to choose between the evidence of his own senses, which he receives first on seeing (or hearing) the stimulus to be judged, and evidence based on the reports of the other subjects, which he receives second. In the Deutsch and

Gerard (1955) experiment, a commitment to the evidence received first (when the subject wrote his choice down) markedly reduced the subject's vulnerability to the evidence received second, that is, to the bogus consensus. Perhaps the same factor of commitment was operating in the Lund experiment. Hovland, Campbell, and Brock (1957), led by this reasoning, confronted the problem in an experiment. Two communications were prepared, one favoring the reduction of the legal voting age to 18 years, the other opposed to lowering the age. Half of the subjects in a "commitment" treatment and half in a "no-commitment" treatment received the pro-con order and the other half received the con-pro order. Subjects in the commitment condition expected their opinion on the issue to be publicized in the school paper, whereas the subjects in the no-commitment treatment did not commit themselves publicly. As in the Deutsch and Gerard experiment, subjects in the commitment condition were much less vulnerable (as measured by change of opinion) to the subsequent counterpropaganda than were subjects in the no-commitment condition. The results of this experiment suggest that when a primacy effect is observed it may be mediated by the subject's commitment to the communication heard (or read) first.

The confusing picture presented by studies of the effects of the order in which both primacy and recency have been observed may be attributed, at least in part, to a certain amount of noncomparability in experimental procedures. For example, the issues usually chosen in these studies were quite familiar to the subject population involved. In most cases, therefore, the subjects had been exposed to prior formal and informal communications, both in the near and distant past. A communication introduced by the experiment, then, was one of a long series on the same issue. With no control over the subject's previous information exposure, anything and everything can happen in the way in which the communications are perceived, attended to, and accepted.

An experiment that goes far in placing this matter in perspective was conducted by Miller and Campbell (1959). They used an issue that was completely unfamiliar to their subjects, a court case based on a transcript of an actual trial involving a suit for damages allegedly incurred by a defective vaporizer. Two communications were prepared, one favoring the plaintiff and the other favoring the defendant. The presentation and measurement procedure were designed to examine different conditions under which a recency effect would be likely to occur. It was assumed, based on what is known about rates of forgetting over time, that the communication presented second would be favored on any measure of recall and presumably in its effect upon the subject's attitude. From the original work of Ebbinghaus (1885), and from subsequent work on forgetting, we know that a person's memory for newly learned material decays rapidly but at a decelerating rate. Thus there is a great deal of forgetting immediately after something new is learned but the relative rate of forgetting decreases over time. On the basis of forgetting curves alone, therefore, only a recency effect would be expected. If there were a time lapse between the presentation of the first message and the second, the recency effect (based on the forgetting curves of each of the two messages) would be more marked, especially if the opinion measurement were taken immediately after the presentation of the second communication. With a time interval both between messages and between the second message and opinion measurement, this recency effect would tend to be reduced because forgetting occurs more rapidly immediately after learning.

In order to examine these predictions Miller and Campbell compared four experimental treatments for the recall of content in the two communications and the measurement of subsequent attitudes in favor of or against the plaintiff. In one treatment the second message was presented immediately after the first, with recall and opinion measurement made immediately after the second message. On the basis of forgetting alone, we should expect a small recency effect here. In a second treatment the two communications were presented one right after the other but the subject's recall and opinion were measured a week later. Here we would expect any recency effect to have just about disappeared, because, relative to the long delay between the second message and the opinion measurement, the two messages occurred close together in time. In a third treatment the second message was presented a week after the first and the subject's recall opinion was measured immediately thereafter. Here, of course, we would expect a strong recency effect because memory of the first message would have had a considerable time to decay. In a fourth treatment there was a delay of one week between the communications and again between the second communication and the recall and opinion measurement. Here we would expect the recency effect to disappear but not so completely as in the second treatment.

In predicting the relative degree to which the four experimental treatments would favor a recency effect, Miller and Campbell assumed that the first message would have an initial advantage, a *prior-entry effect*. This initial advantage would be outweighed to the extent that the relative memory decay for the two messages favored the second message. Thus the second condition, in which both messages were received in succession with a subsequent delay in measurement, would be the one most likely to favor a primacy effect. After such a long measurement delay, both memory traces would be expected to have decayed to nearly the same extent in spite of the fact that the first message started off with an initial advantage. By a similar argument, the third condition would be the most favorable to a recency effect. The first and last condition are indeterminate unless the actual amount of relative advantage to the first message (of prior entry) were known.

In Table 12.4, which presents the attitude data, it is clear that the derivations based on the process of memory decay are borne out. Higher scores

Table 12.4 Mean Attitude Scores
(From Miller and Campbell, 1959)

Condition	Pro-con presentation	Con-pro presentation	Difference	Direction
1(X_1X_2O) [a]	5.94	5.88	0.06	
2(X_1X_2–O)	4.50	6.61	−2.11	Primacy
3(X_1–X_2O)	6.00	4.33	1.67	Recency
4(X_1–X_2–O)	5.47	5.58	−0.11	

[a] The shorthand characterization of the conditions employs a standardized symbolization of experimental treatments (Campbell, 1957), in which X_1 and X_2 represent the experimental stimuli, O represents the process of observation and measurement, and spacing from left to right represents the time dimension.

indicate that the subjects thought the plaintiff was at fault—which would indicate persuasion to the "con" point of view (accepting the defendant's position). In the analysis the relative strengths in persuasive power of the pro and con messages were equated by the usual expedient of having half of the subjects receive the pro message first and half the con message first. The attitude scale was a nine-point scale with opinion "five" as a neutral midpoint. Thus, a score of less than five favored the plaintiff, whereas a score greater than five favored the defendant.

On an over-all basis, it appears that the "con" argument was more persuasive. Because the argument was alternated, however, we can measure the relative advantage to the second message (the recency effect) in each of the four presentation-measurement conditions by subtracting the score in the con-pro column from the score in the pro-con column for that treatment. This difference is shown in the third column, where a strong primacy effect appears for the second condition and a strong recency effect appears for the third condition, confirming the predictions. It is probable that part of the confusion created by conflicting results in previous studies may be accounted for by differences in exposure and measurement times. This possibility becomes all the more plausible when we recall that the issues used in the previous studies had been familiar to the subjects beforehand and were therefore issues about which they had received communications at various times before the experiment. The experiment broke into a naturally occurring sequence of exposures.

One explanation for a primacy effect offered by Hovland, Janis, and

Kelley (1953) was that subjects may not pay attention to the second message after having heard the first. If the material in the second message is not attended to, its effectiveness becomes blunted. In their study Miller and Campbell tested this interpretation by asking the subjects to recall the items of information contained in both messages. The only factor that appeared to affect recall was the time interval between messages and between the second message and the recall measure. Strong recency effects obtained in both conditions three and four. Under none of the conditions was a primary effect observed, a finding that gives no support to the proposition that subjects do not pay attention to the second message after hearing the first. While the recall data show no primacy effects, a measure of the number of statements contained in each message that were checked as acceptable to the subject showed primary effects in the first and second conditions. The investigators conclude that "coming first gives a statement no greater probability of being remembered, but does give it greater probability of being believed" (Miller and Campbell, 1959, p. 8).

In a recent experiment Insko (1964) replicated the Miller and Campbell study using additional timing intervals and found substantially the same evidence for the recency effect as a function of timing of arguments and measures but failed to find any evidence for a primacy effect when both arguments were presented successively followed by a long delay before measurements were taken. Thomas, Webb, and Tweedie (1961) also found no evidence for a primacy effect.

Conclusion Drawing

Aristotle prescribed that the rhetorician not be obvious in the way he draws his conclusion. He says that of all arguments "those are most applauded of which we foresee the conclusions from the beginning, so long as they are not obvious at first sight—for the part of the pleasure we feel is at our own intelligent anticipation; or those which we follow well enough to see the point of them as soon as the last word has been uttered" (1941, p. 1428). He apparently believed that the audience members would be persuaded by a conclusion to the extent that they participated in drawing the conclusion themselves.

Hovland and Mandell (1952) chose to investigate the relative effectiveness of conclusion-drawing by the communicator and by the audience. From Aristotle's reasoning we would expect conclusion drawing by the audience to be more effective. However, unless the conclusion is explicitly known by the audience after exposure to the message, the method of leading the horse to water would be ineffective. Conclusion-drawing by the communicator, therefore, increases the chances that his recommendation will be explicitly known and able to have its effect. We might guess that the intelligence level of the audience (in putting two and two together) would play a role in the effectiveness of the two types of presentation.

Hovland and Mandell prepared two communications supporting a proposal to devalue the American dollar. The messages were identical in every respect except that in one the communicator explicitly drew the conclusion at the end and in the other it was left implicit for the audience to draw. Some simple economic conditions were outlined, conditions under which devaluation of currency was desirable (the major premise). Then specific conditions existing in the United States were described that fit the general conditions (the minor premise). The conclusion that devaluation was desirable could be drawn from the two premises.

The two communications were presented as radio transcriptions. Data from a postquestionnaire indicated that over twice as many subjects changed their opinion in the direction of believing that devaluation was desirable in the explicit conclusion condition than in the implicit condition. Furthermore, there appeared to be no difference in the degree to which subjects with different intelligence levels were affected in the two treatments. Thus the results apparently do not support Aristotle's prescription. There is some evidence, however, from a study by Cooper and Dinerman (1951) showing that an antiprejudice film in which a conclusion was not explicitly drawn was more effective for the more intelligent members of the audience. We obviously cannot generalize about the effectiveness of conclusion-drawing because the type of issue, the complexity of the argument, and characteristics of the audience all play important roles, singly and in combination. When a conclusion is obvious the audience may feel insulted by the communicator if he belabors it by explicitly drawing it. Also, on some issues, some people like to feel that they are making up their own minds; so drawing a conclusion for them might be risky.

BELIEF AND VALUE APPEALS

In his role as information source the communicator may attempt to change the attitude of his audience by introducing beliefs, or by arranging them in some order. That is, he may apprise his audience of new facts or he may organize facts or beliefs already known, in such a way that they support his conclusion. Here he is trading on the information-dependent orientation he may have established between himself and his audience. He may also appeal to the values of his audience by attempting to associate his point of view with potential maximization of outcome for his audience; he is serving (or promising) to mediate outcomes for them. His effectiveness in this role will depend, of course, on how convincingly he presents himself as such a mediator.

Appeals to Beliefs

Staats and Staats (1958) used a classical conditioning situation to manipulate the belief premise of an attitude and then measured the degree to which the middle term transferred to the minor term the value originally associated only with the major term. Two experiments were conducted, one in which the minor term was one of six nationalities: German, Swedish, Italian, French, Dutch, and Greek; and one in which it was one of six boys' names: Harry, Tom, Jim, Ralph, Bill, and Bob. In each experiment one of these minor terms (or CS's) was presented contiguously with a number of middle terms (UCS's) all having a positive value, for example: gift, sacred, happy; and another minor term was presented contiguously with a number of middle terms having a negative value, for example: bitter, ugly, failure. The other four minor terms in each experiment were presented contiguously with neutral middle terms, for example: chair, with, twelve. The procedure involved projecting the six minor terms 18 times in a random order (a total of 108 stimulus presentations). On each presentation the subject, while looking at the minor term, heard the middle term pronounced by the experimenter and then pronounced it again to himself. Thus for one group the word Dutch was always paired on each of its 18 presentations with a different positively toned word (e.g., happy), whereas the word Swedish was always paired with a different negatively toned word (e.g., bitter), with the other four nationalities always being paired with neutral words. For another group the nationalities were reversed, so that Dutch was paired with negatively toned words and Swedish with positively toned words. In the second experiment, Tom and Bill were the names singled out for manipulation.

After the conditioning procedure the subject received a questionnaire in which he was asked to indicate, on a seven-point scale, how positive or negative he felt toward each of the six nationalities (or boys' names). The results clearly indicate that the conditioning procedure was successful in imparting a positive or negative value to the two selected nationalities or names; an *attitude* was induced. In our terms, the procedure involved the use of existing value premises such as "happy is good" or "bitter is bad," to establish a belief by pairing the subject of the value premise (happy or bitter), the middle term, with another stimulus word (a nationality or a boy's name), the minor term, and thereby producing a new attitudinal conclusion.

Staats and Staats used familiar words as the minor term in the experiment and by their classical conditioning procedure added either positive or negative value to the subjects' initial evaluation of the term. Presumably, we could use this procedure to change a positively valued stimulus to a negatively valued one or vice versa, or we could take a term that was completely neutral and impart either a positive or a negative value to it. Staats and Staats make reference to work by Razran (1938, 1940) in which values were conditioned to stimuli that were presented in the presence of unpleasant odors or while the subject was happily munching away on a free lunch. Subtle and powerful effects such as these are probably being induced in us without our awareness during the course of a normal day.

From these inadvertent effects that can be produced by classical conditioning let us turn to a consideration of techniques based on conscious cognitive inference. Carlson (1956) used a procedure designed to change a white audience's attitude toward segregation. The initial step was to measure the subjects' attitude toward allowing Negroes to move into white neighborhoods. The subject was then asked to indicate the importance to him of each of 25 value statements. Four of these values were selected for use as major premises in the attitude change process. These values were: "high international prestige for America is good," "high real estate values are good," "having all people realize their particular potentials is good," "being broadminded is good." The subject then indicated the degree to which he believed that each of the 25 values would be furthered or thwarted by having Negroes move into white neighborhoods. This "perceived instrumentality" measure attempted to get the subject to state a belief that, combined with the value, would lead to a positive or negative attitude toward segregation. The change procedure involved presenting the subject with evidence that desegregation would further rather than thwart attainment of the four values in question. A postexperimental measure of attitude indicated that, in general, the change procedure was effective, although extremely prejudiced subjects showed little or no change.

A similar experiment was run by DiVesta and Merwin (1960) on changing the attitudes of a group of college freshmen toward teaching as a career. The value premise used was the subjects' need for achievement. Presumably most, if not all, subjects in a college sample, especially freshmen who are not yet jaded, would feel that "achievement is good." Three message treatments were tried, one in which it was argued that teaching as a career (the minor term) would facilitate achievement (the middle term), one in which it was argued that teaching as a career would hinder achievement, and another in which irrelevant assertions were made. The changes in belief about the potentiality of teaching as a career for facilitating or hindering achievement corresponded to the direction of the positive and negative messages. The postexperimental questionnaire also indicated corresponding changes in attitude toward teaching as a career.

Appeals to Values

Creating a new value or making an existing value salient is another technique that can be used to tap the underlying structure of an attitude and thereby change it. Here the communicator attempts to exert outcome control over his audience. In conditioning a dog to the sound of a bell, the experimenter first deprives the dog of some valued outcome, such as food (or water), and then presents the dog with repeated pairings of the bell with a small amount of food (or water). It has been found that the rate at which conditioning occurs is related to this deprivation level, that is, to the salience of the value involved. In propaganda appeals it is not enough to argue, for example, that "permitting Negroes to move into white neighborhoods will increase America's prestige internationally," if the audience has little or no interest in the state of America's prestige overseas. The propagandist must either trade on important, already existing values, or he must expend some effort in making existing values salient, or in creating new ones.

It may have already occurred to the reader that value manipulation is itself an attempt to change attitudes; it is changing one attitude to affect another. In attempting to manipulate a value, the communicator must start with another value that he knows already exists and is salient for his audience. Thus, if he is trying to convince his audience that its members should brush their teeth regularly because having sound teeth is important, he must either assume that they have as a salient value "having sound teeth is good," or he must create that value by appealing to other values that he knows are strongly held. He must thus induce a positive attitude toward having sound teeth by appealing to such things as the positive effects of good teeth on appearance or by appealing to the dire health consequences that can result from tooth decay. Unless these attitudes or value premises exist, or can be made to exist, the toothbrush salesman or dental hygiene spokesman will not be successful in inducing a positive attitude toward tooth brushing.

Janis and Feshbach (1953) were among the first to subject value appeals in propaganda to experimental study. They prepared three different illustrated lectures each containing the same basic information about the causes of tooth decay and the same series of recommendations concerning oral hygiene practices. The lectures differed only in the amount of fear-arousing material included. One lecture emphasized the painful consequences of tooth decay, diseased gums and other dangers that often result from improper care of the teeth. A second variant of the lecture was more moderate in its appeal, the dangers being described in milder terms. The third variant contained material that was only minimally fear-arousing. The strong appeal contained such statements as:

. . . if you ever develop an infection of this kind from improper care of your teeth, it will be an extremely serious matter, because these infections are really dangerous. They can spread to your eyes, or your heart, or your joints and cause secondary infections which may lead to diseases such as arthritic paralysis, kidney damage or total blindness (p. 79).

It is clear that the communication was trading on existing salient values regarding good general health in attempting to develop a positive attitude toward having good, sound teeth. The strong fear appeal had a total of 71 references to bad consequences resulting from the improper care of the teeth. The moderate appeal had 49 and the minimal appeal had 18 such references. The slides used to illustrate each of the lectures were chosen to be consistent with the level of fear being induced. In the strong appeal treatment the audience saw realistic photographs of badly decayed teeth and serious mouth infections. The moderate appeal audience was shown milder examples of oral pathology, whereas the audience exposed to the minimal appeal was shown neutral material that posed no threat.

In addition to three experimental groups, one exposed to each of the three fear treatments, a control group received a lecture having nothing to do with oral hygiene. One week before the lecture the subjects answered a general health survey that included questions about oral hygiene. Immediately after the lecture a short questionnaire, bearing on attitudes toward oral hygiene, was administered. One week later a final questionnaire was administered in an attempt to see if there were any lasting effects of the three types of lectures.

The postexperimental questionnaire indicated that the three treatments had their intended effect, subjects in the strong appeal treatment being the most aroused emotionally and subjects in the minimal appeal treatment being the least aroused. Some open-ended questions in the questionnaire administered after the last lecture enabled the subject to give his impressions of various aspects of the lecture. Some of the comments reveal that values were being appealed to:

Leave out the slide that shows the rottenness of the teeth and have more in about how to brush your teeth.

. . . . .

I did not care for the gory illustration of decayed teeth and diseased mouths, but I really think that it did make me feel sure that I did not want this to happen to me.

. . . . .

Some of the pictures went to the extremes but they probably had an effect on most of the people who wouldn't want their teeth to look like that.

. . . . .

I think it is good because it scares people when they see the awful things that can happen (Janis and Feshbach, 1953, p. 83).

The change in oral hygiene attitudes and practices (e.g., amount of tooth brushing) were measured in the questionnaire administered one week after the lecture. The treatment groups showed no real difference in attitude but did reveal differences in reported oral hygiene practices that were exactly opposite to what was predicted. The strong appeal group showed a net change of 8 percent in reported conformity to the recommendation in the communication; the moderate appeal group showed a net change of 22 percent, and the minimal appeal group a net change of 36 percent. The control group showed no net change whatsoever. Furthermore, the minimal appeal condition showed the greatest resistance to a subsequent communication that contained counterpropaganda.

How may we account for this inverse relationship between fear and reported change in oral hygiene practice? It is possible that the induced fear produced certain kinds of interference that blunted the effectiveness of the appeal. Some of the subjects' comments certainly suggest this. It may be that the material used in the strong and moderate appeals was much too threatening and there was not enough remedial information. The authors suggest that "when fear is strongly aroused but is not fully relieved by the reassurances contained in a mass communication, the audience will become motivated to ignore or minimize the importance of the threat" (Janis and Feshbach, 1953, p. 92). It may be that this type of defensive reaction produced a boomerang effect, at least in certain subjects.

The results of the study point up the precarious nature of the effects produced by fear-arousing appeals. An experiment by Goldstein (1959) suggests that when a person is threatened, as in the Janis and Feshbach experiment, there are two things that he can do. He can *cope* with the threat by adopting the belief advocated by the communication and subsequently change his oral hygiene practices; or he can *avoid* anything and everything that might sustain the fear in the present or re-arouse it in the future. If he reacted defensively with avoidance, he would be less likely to show concern with dental hygiene practices subsequent to the threat.

In discussing research on the effects of order, we entertained an "attention hypothesis" to account for a primacy effect: after having heard the first message, the subject may have been less attentive to the second. There was no evidence in support of this hypothesis in that research, but it might explain the inverse relationship between reported change in practices and fear arousal. It is possible that the greater the fear induced, the more disturbed the subject was and therefore the less able he was to pay attention to the communicator's subsequent recommendations regarding preventive practices. Janis and Feshbach tested this hypothesis by asking the subjects in each experimental treatment to recall what the lecturer had said. Recall was equally good in all three treatments, indicating that a differential in attentiveness was *not* produced by the different lectures. Further evidence confirming the lack of such differences comes from a subsequent study by Janis and Milholland (1954).

The basic contention of Janis and his colleagues seems to be that fear appeals are apt to boomerang unless the recommended way to reduce fear is salient and sufficient. If this is true, a positive relationship between magnitude of fear arousal and degree of recommendation acceptance might be observed when the recommendation involves an immediate fear-reducing action. Leventhal and Niles (1964), in attempting to examine the arousal-acceptance relationship for immediate and more remote recommendations, seized upon the opportunity for replicating the Janis and Feshbach study at the New York City Health Exposition. Experimental lectures were held in a small theater in the Coliseum in New York City and were presented as part of an attempt to evaluate certain public-health programs. Two levels of fear arousal ("high" and "medium") were produced with a technicolor sound movie on lung cancer. In the high-fear treatment the entire film was shown, the climax of which was a closeup view of a surgical sequence showing a lung cancer operation in technicolor. In the medium-fear treatment, the film was ended just before the operation began. In a third, low-fear treatment the subject merely read a pamphlet presenting the evidence for the relationship between cigarette smoking and lung cancer, and did not see any portion of the film. After exposure to one of these three treatments the subject was given recommendations to stop smoking and to take a chest X ray in the mobile unit located in the exposition hall. The former recommendation represented a remote and difficult one, whereas the latter could be done immediately with practically no effort.

For the immediate action of taking an X ray there were no differences in the stated intention to take the X ray or in the proportion of subjects in the treatments who actually entered the mobile unit to have one taken. However, smokers in the low-fear condition showed a greater intention to stop smoking than those in either the high- or medium-fear condition, with no difference between the latter two conditions. As we know, smoking is a notoriously difficult habit to give up. In the face of the strong resistance to change of cognitions associated with smoking, the audience might have engaged in cognitive work that would discount the recommendation of the lecturer's message. The greater the fear aroused, the greater the dissonance and hence the greater the tendency to discount the message.

It is interesting to consider the relationship between these studies and the mild versus severe prohibition study described in Chapter Three (Aronson and Carlsmith, 1963). There, it will be recalled, children who were prohibited from playing with a toy ended up judging the toy as less attractive when the threatened consequences were mild than when they were severe.

In the Janis and Feshbach and the Leventhal and Niles studies the differential threat appeals involved forbidden behavior (incorrect tooth brushing and smoking) in which the subject was actively engaged, whereas in the Aronson and Carlsmith experiment the subject committed himself not to engage in the forbidden behavior. As we would predict from dissonance theory, the effect of differential threat on attitude would be exactly reversed as a function of whether the behavior was engaged in or avoided. This is what the results clearly show. When a person commits himself to behavior he should not engage in, the more dire the consequences, the greater the dissonance. When he commits himself to not engaging in an activity, the *less* the threat, the greater the dissonance.

It would be nice if the total picture were as simple as the above discussion suggests; but it is not. Leventhal and Niles performed an internal analysis of their data and found *positive* correlations within both the medium- and high-fear-level treatments between the subject's fear (as stated on the questionnaire) and his desire both to stop smoking and to have an X ray taken. Correlational data in general are difficult to interpret but, however we interpret the relationship here, doubt is cast on the generality of the inverse arousal-acceptance hypothesis. Furthermore, when the low- is compared to the medium- and high-fear treatments, an inverse relationship between arousal and acceptance was found for the remote, long-range recommendation (stopping smoking) but not for the short-range recommendation (having an X ray taken). This was opposite to the prediction derived from the defensive dissonance reaction theory proposed earlier. The waters thus appear to be very muddy.

It is possible that the prospect of having an X ray was more threatening for a smoker than stopping smoking if he saw a chest X ray as a possible prelude to chest surgery. Making this assumption might help to salvage the defensiveness interpretation of the Janis and Feshbach results. In pursuing this line of reasoning Leventhal, Singer, and Jones (1965) induced two levels of fear, using a pamphlet that described what happens to a person who has contracted tetanus. In the high-fear condition the description was embellished with photographs showing a child in a tetanic convulsion, a gaping tracheotomy wound, urinary catheters, tracheotomy drainage, and nasal tubes. These procedures are actually used in severe cases. After the fear induction it was recommended that the college-student subjects have free tetanus shots at the student health service. Questionnaire data and actual follow-ups showed that there was a positive relationship between fear, as induced by the two pamphlets, and the subject's stated intention to get a shot, but there was no relationship between fear and the likelihood of the subject actually showing up for his shot. The data on stated intentions are in line with the defensiveness interpretation of the Janis and Feshbach study if we assume that getting a tetanus shot is an easy recommendation to follow and if followed it will reduce the induced fear. The data are also consistent with a direct drive reduction hypothesis, that fear acts as a drive leading to the acceptance of recommendations that are perceived as reducing that drive; the greater the fear the more readily will the recommendation be accepted. We introduced this section with that hypothesis in mind.

In an attempt to lay the defensiveness hypothesis to rest, Leventhal and Singer (1966) used the original dental hygiene issue in which the recommendation involved a long-term action and which Janis and Feshbach argued may have been inadequate to reduce the fear aroused by the gory arousal procedure. Arguing from this surmise and the results of an earlier study by Cohen (1957), which we shall discuss shortly, Leventhal and Singer reasoned that the positioning of the recommendations should have marked effects on fear reduction and hence on their acceptance. If, for example, the recommendations precede fear arousal they should be less effective in reducing fear than if they follow the arousal. A condition in which arousal statements and recommendations are intermixed, as in the Janis and Feshbach procedure, should show an intermediate level of acceptance of the recommendations.

The Leventhal and Singer experiment was run in the Hall of Health at the New York State Exposition in Syracuse in 1963. The theater used for the study held a maximum of 12 subjects and they were put through the same basic procedure as in Janis and Feshbach's experiment. The data regarding acceptance are clear-cut. Acceptance was greater in the high- than in the low-fear treatment and there was no effect of recommendation positioning on acceptance. Under high fear there was, however, the predicted effect of positioning on affect arousal (as measured on a questionnaire), with the "recommendations first" treatment showing the greatest arousal and the "recommendations last" treatment showing the least. Evidently fear reduction is not a necessary condition for acceptance. These results bring into question the basic assumption of the defensiveness hypothesis, that the recommendations in the Janis and Feshbach study were inadequate to reduce the fear.

It is possible to hedge a bit here and propose that under high fear the recommendations must reduce fear below some minimum before we can get the positive relationship between acceptance and fear reduction. Janis and Feshbach might also argue that because a different setting and subject population were used the low-fear treatment aroused so little fear that the subjects were disinterested. On the face of it these arguments would seem difficult to maintain, but if we wanted to pursue them, a more refined experiment would be in order.

A final experiment by Berkowitz and Cottingham (1960) is worthy of mention. These researchers argued that the relevance of the issue to the audience may be a key factor in determining whether a direct or inverse relationship is found between arousal and acceptance. They suggest that with a highly relevant issue a high-fear appeal would tend to elicit defensiveness and thus be blunted and induce less acceptance than a low-fear appeal, whereas if the issue were not relevant to the audience defensiveness would not be elicited by a high-fear appeal and it would tend to be accepted more than a low-fear appeal.

The communications used by Berkowitz and Cottingham attempted to induce a positive attitude toward using seat belts in automobiles. The low-fear communication was matter-of-fact, whereas the high-fear one included the showing of gruesome slides depicting car accidents. A control group was included that received no communication but merely answered the postmeasure. The same experiment was run with two different experimenters and two different populations of subjects. All subjects in both experiments had answered a premeasure questionnaire a month before the experiment. They were assigned to the different relevance conditions on the basis of how often they drove a car.

In one of the experiments there was an interaction between arousal and acceptance that fits the prediction. Under high relevance (subjects who drove a lot) the relationship was like the one in the Janis and Feshbach study—that is, the high-fear communication induced somewhat less change than the low-fear one—whereas under low relevance the relationship was reversed. In the other experiment subjects were assigned to three rather than two relevance categories. Although the same inverse relationship did not obtain under high relevance, subjects were more receptive to the communication the lower the relevance of the issue for them.

Clearly the relationship between value arousal and acceptance is a complex one that needs much further study. Two factors that probably confound the level of arousal are the interest value of the communication and its credibility. Some of the high-fear appeals that have been used may have been intrinsically more interesting to the particular audience involved. Leventhal and Singer (1965) used the same dental hygiene issue that had been used by Janis and Feshbach and found a positive relationship between arousal and acceptance. This may have resulted from the fact that, as compared with a college audience, a high-school audience found the high-fear communication more interesting and therefore were influenced more by it. Or the college audience may have discredited the high-fear communication because of their greater sophistication regarding factors other than tooth brushing that cause tooth decay.

Another feature of the situation that was not controlled in these studies is the degree to which the subject voluntarily exposed himself to the dissonance-arousing information. In this respect the Janis and Feshbach study differed from a number of those by Leventhal and his colleagues. In the former study the subjects were members of a captive audience in a classroom situation, whereas in the latter studies the subjects just happened to wander into the exhibit. In Chapter Six we found that degree of commitment makes a considerable difference in the amount of dissonance produced by a decision. Perhaps subjects who voluntarily expose themselves to a health lecture are more committed to accepting the recommendation offered.

It may turn out that whether a direct or inverse relationship, or neither, prevails is dependent on some as yet unspecified features of the issue, recommendations, setting, or subject population or some combination of these. The problem here is theoretically interesting, practically important, and tractable to further experimental attack.

Order Effects and Value Appeals

When appealing to a value is it more effective to present the value appeal first, followed by the new belief, or vice versa? The same problems are involved in asking whether it is better to have the dog experience the contiguity between the bell and the meat powder and then deprive him of food, or vice versa? In learning studies it is assumed that the value (drive) must be present in order for learning to take place. We would expect the same effect to be observed in propaganda appeals. Leventhal and Singer (1966) found a greater reduction in drive (fear) in a message when the recommendation followed rather than preceded the value appeal (fear induction) but they did not find an accompanying difference in acceptance of the recommendation. A study by Cohen (1957) compared the two procedures and found the predicted effect. A highly realistic fear appeal followed by information that would reduce the fear was contrasted with a condition in which the information preceded the fear arousal. The subjects in the experiment were college students and the appeal aroused their anxiety about grades by raising the possibility of a general toughening of grading standards. The information that was designed to reduce the subject's anxiety argued that the method of grading on a curve was the most preferred and equitable method. The two treatments differed only in the order of their messages; anxiety was aroused either before or after the change in grading was recommended. A postmeasure indicated that the fear-arousal–information order was far more effective in establishing a favorable attitude toward grading on a curve than the presentation in which that order was reversed. As Leventhal and Singer (1966) point out, it is impossible to know in the Cohen study if recommendations following arousal increase acceptance or recommendations preceding arousal decrease acceptance. A control condition offering recommendations, but without any reference to more extreme, anxiety-provoking alternatives, should have been run in order to choose between these interpretations.

The Direct Manipulation of Values

In an experiment by Rosenberg (1960) each of 11 deeply hypnotized subjects was given posthypnotic suggestions with regard to two attitude issues on which he had been previously tested. Examples of these are:

> When you awake you will be very much in favor of Negroes moving into white neighborhoods. The mere idea of Negroes moving into white neighborhoods will give you a happy, exhilarated feeling. . . . Also, when you awake you will be very opposed to the city-manager plan. The mere idea of the city-manager plan will give you a feeling of loathing and disgust (Rosenberg, 1960, p. 43).

The subjects were told that they would have no memory of the suggestion when they awoke from the hypnotic trance. The same value and "perceived instrumentality" questionnaires that had been used earlier by Carlson (1956) and Rosenberg (1956) were administered to the hypnotized subjects and to a control group of nonhypnotized subjects both before and after the trance session. On these two questionnaires each subject rated 31 values as to their importance for him and also evaluated the extent to which each value was furthered or hindered by having Negroes move into white neighborhoods. In the comparison of the pre- and post-questionnaires the hypnotized subjects showed a greater change than the nonhypnotized control subjects in the structure underlying their attitude toward the issues. The experimental subjects had adjusted their beliefs concerning the perceived instrumentality of furthering or hindering their values to bring them more into accord with the hypnotically induced change in attitude.

Our review of the research in this area has shown that the manipulation of beliefs and values can lead to attitude change and vice versa. Evidently there is a strong tendency for the person to maintain internally consistent attitude structures. Change can be induced only by disrupting this consistency so that it is below the level usually tolerated by the person.

THE AUDIENCE

Obviously, the effectiveness of any message is determined by how successfully it is tailored for its intended audience. A communication intended to induce new tooth brushing habits in an audience of eight-year-olds would not have the same impact on an adult audience. Factors such as the pre-exposure attitude of the members of the audience, their degree of familiarity with opposing points of view, their education and background, and their degree of commitment to their initial positions all affect the degree to which they will be susceptible to a given message. We would also expect the degree of attention paid to the message and the degree to which the audience actively engages in supporting or refuting its arguments to determine partly its impact.

Audience Attitude as It Affects Response to the Message

What effect does the initial attitude of a member of the audience have on his understanding of the message? Misconstruction of the meaning of a message is common in oratory, political exhortation, and everyday conversation. If the listener has not been able to avoid exposure to a discrepant message he can use a variety of mechanisms, one of them being misinterpretation, for coming to terms with the dissonance introduced by the information.

In a series of interview studies of the effectiveness of antiprejudice propaganda, Cooper and Jahoda (1947) reported some dramatic instances of evasion by misinterpretation. A number of these instances occurred in the course of several studies of the effectiveness of cartoons in getting across an antiprejudice message. The main character in the cartoons is depicted as a bigot and is made, as a result of his bigotry, to appear ridiculous. The supposition underlying this kind of message was that a prejudiced person reading the cartoon would be struck by the ridiculous antics of "Mr. Biggot" and would make an effort not to identify with him, in the process reducing his own prejudice. For example, one of these cartoons showed Mr. Biggot lying in a hospital bed, with a doctor in attendance, saying that for his blood transfusion he wanted only "sixth-generation American blood." A respondent, whose interview was quoted by Cooper and Jahoda, at first saw the humor in the cartoon but then engaged in tactics that would differentiate himself from Mr. Biggot. He claimed that he himself was eighth-generation and that Mr. Biggot's blood might not be particularly good blood. As the interview progressed the respondent showed more and more disdain for Mr. Biggot, treating him as a lower-class individual. These machinations served to sidetrack the prejudice issue that was the intended message of the cartoon.

Another form of distortion discovered by Cooper and Jahoda is illustrated by the reaction of some prejudiced respondents to a set of cartoons attempting to expose the absurdity of generalizations about various groups. The concluding message was "live and let live." These respondents often followed the whole story, accepting the message, but finally added that "it's the Jews that don't let you live; they put themselves outside the golden rule."

In another study cited by Cooper and Jahoda a radio dramatization told a story of a Jewish couple who were saved from the Nazis through the efforts of the local villagers. The story was followed by an appeal made by Kate Smith for tolerance toward Jews. Prejudiced respondents tended to negate the message by seeing the story simply as thrilling wartime adventure, thus robbing it of its intended message.

These accounts illustrate the flexibility and adaptability of human interpretive processes. Obviously, an understanding of the techniques that the person can use to blunt the intent of a message is necessary if we are to have an adequate picture of the over-all attitude change process. The first principle of rhetoric, enunciated by the ancients and still valid, is the importance of getting across the message so that it may have its effect. Intrapersonal processes that screen messages so as to change their meaning stand between the rhetorician and his goal of successfully influencing his audience.

In Chapter Seven we discussed the role of values in sensitizing the person to certain stimuli in his environment and in facilitating or inhibiting the perception and retention of attitude-relevant information. At that time we noted the repeatedly observed finding that subjects show better retention for verbal material that supports their attitudes. We also saw that there are boundaries on this relationship and that persons can, under appropriate instructions, be induced to be vigilant in perceiving and remembering information dissonant with their attitudes.

While the studies dealing with the learning and retention of verbal material involved comparing subjects who scored pro versus con on an attitude scale, it is also possible to establish different expectations by laboratory instructions and to study the effects of these expectations on the interpretation of subsequent events. A study by Janis, Lumsdaine, and Gladstone (1951) investigated the reaction of an audience to a news event after having had a briefing that was relevant to the event. The briefing was found to have had a marked effect on how the event was interpreted. In June, 1949, before the Soviet Union was known to have an atomic bomb, opinion measures were taken on members of an audience one week before and again one week after exposure to an "optimistic" communication that maintained that the Soviet Union would not be able to produce a stockpile of atomic bombs for a long time to come. Three months later President Truman announced that the Soviet Union had exploded its first bomb. The researchers capitalized on this unanticipated event by taking a third opinion measure on the likelihood of the Soviet Union being able to stockpile atomic bombs. The experimental group that had been exposed to the "optimistic" message showed far greater resistance by changing less in the pessimistic direction than a control group that had not been exposed to the earlier message. Thus the significance of the event was apparently conditioned by the prior exposure of the subject to certain other relevant information. The information in this prior exposure created a particular context in which the event could be interpreted.

Assimilation and Contrast within a Given Frame of Reference

A more detailed analysis of contextual effects was conducted by Hovland, Harvey, and Sherif (1957). Their experiment investigated how a person's initial position on a controversial issue affects his reaction to a message supporting a point of view discrepant from his own. An understanding of these reactions may help us reconcile instances of messages that boomerang. Whereas the majority of subjects in attitude change experiments alter their opinions in the direction of the position advocated by the message, there are usually some who move in the opposite direction; that is, for whom the message boomerangs. What determines whether the person will change toward or away from the position advocated in the message? The authors suggest that the extremity of the subject's initial position on the issue might be a crucial determinant. This surmise rests on a body of evidence concerning basic perceptual processes of assimilation and contrast.

Psychophysical research has demonstrated that when a person is comparing some fixed point on a stimulus continuum, such as a particular weight, with a second, variable stimulus he tends to introduce a discontinuity into the comparison. Comparison weights that are close to the standard (the fixed point) tend to be judged as more similar in weight to the standard than they actually are, whereas stimuli that differ from the standard tend to be judged as more different than they actually are. In other words, if a comparison stimulus falls within some region on either side of the standard it is *assimilated* to the standard, whereas if it falls outside that region it is *contrasted* with the standard. The standard is often called the anchor stimulus.

In translating these findings into the study of attitudes, Hovland, Harvey, and Sherif have termed the region of assimilation the person's "latitude of acceptance," and the region of contrast his "latitude of rejection." Thus, if a person has a particular attitude on an issue, statements that reflect an attitude similar to his own will be acceptable and judged closer to his own attitude than they actually are, whereas statements that fall into the person's latitude of rejection will be perceived as being more different from his own attitude and will tend to be rejected. These authors argue, with some support from prior experimental findings, that the width of the person's latitude of acceptance is an inverse function of the importance of the issue for him. Thus, holding discrepancy constant, the greater the importance of the issue, the more likely the subject will be to find unacceptable a statement that reflects a discrepant attitude. Other studies have shown that the more extreme the person's attitude, the greater is his commitment to the stand he has taken and the greater the importance of the issue for him. Middle-of-the-roaders tend generally to be less involved and less committed to their position. From this we would expect that those at either extreme on an attitude continuum would have a narrower latitude of acceptance than those in the middle.

In Chapters Ten and Eleven the issues in the studies discussed were for the most part rather bland and deliberately chosen so that the subjects would *not* be highly involved in maintaining their attitudinal position and thus be resistant to change. The experimental strategy of studying attitude change requires that issues be used that permit the effects of different persuasion treatments to show. Hovland, Harvey, and Sherif (1957) were primarily interested in studying the phenomena of judgmental assimilation and contrast under conditions of relatively high involvement. They thus chose a topic in which their subjects were keenly interested and about which there was considerable controversy.

Their subjects were residents of a then "dry" state, in which prohibition was a lively issue. Some of the subjects were members of the Women's Christian Temperance Union. The technique the researchers used consisted of taking premeasures of the subject's attitude toward drinking and then exposing him to one of three different communications, a "wet" message that advocated unlimited sales and drinking of liquor, a "dry" message that advocated complete prohibition, and a moderately "wet" message that advocated drinking with fairly strict controls. The subject was presented with the following nine statements that represented prevailing stands toward drinking:

(A) Since alcohol is the curse of mankind, the sale and use of alcohol, including light beer, should be completely abolished.

(B) Since alcohol is the main cause of corruption in public life, lawlessness, and immoral acts, its sale and use should be prohibited.

(C) Since it is hard to stop at a reasonable moderation point in the use of alcohol, it is safer to discourage its use.

(D) Alcohol should not be sold or used except as a remedy for snake bites, cramps, colds, fainting, and other aches and pains.

(E) The arguments in favor and against the use of alcohol are nearly equal.

(F) The sale of alcohol should be so regulated that it is available in limited quantities for special occasions.

(G) The sale and use of alcohol should be permitted with proper state controls so that the revenue from taxation may be used for the betterment of schools, highways, and other state institutions.

(H) Since prohibition is a major cause of corruption in public life, lawlessness, immoral acts, and juvenile delinquency, the sale and use of alcohol should be legalized.

(I) It has become evident that man cannot get along without alcohol; therefore, there should be no restriction whatsoever on its sale and use (p. 246).

These statements are not strictly continuous because several side issues are brought into a number of them, but they are roughly arranged from "dry" to "wet."

In the first session the subject was asked to underline the statement that came closest to his own point of view on the issue and to indicate which other statements he did not really object to. He was then asked to cross out the statement he found most objectionable and to indicate other objectionable statements. This procedure yielded the subject's attitude position and both his latitudes of acceptance and rejection.

At a second session some weeks later the subjects were exposed to a 15-minute communication. Some subjects heard a "wet" message, some a "dry" message, and others a "moderate" message. Following this, the subjects again indicated their most and least preferred of the original nine statements as well as their latitudes of acceptance and rejection. In addition, the subjects in the "moderate" communication treatment also checked, on a rating scale ranging from extremely "dry" to extremely "wet," the position they thought most nearly represented the stand taken by the communication they heard. It is the data from the moderate message treatment that are of interest in examining the phenomenon of displacement by assimilation or contrast. The data show both assimilation and contrast effects but the contrast emerges much more strongly. "Dry" subjects considered the moderate message to be wetter and "wet" subjects considered it drier than it indeed was. Subjects near the center of the continuum, that is, who were moderate themselves, were more accurate in judging the stand taken by the message and also showed some tendency to displace the position of the message toward their own position.

Table 12.5 presents the data on the size of the latitudes of acceptance and rejection for subjects holding extreme attitudes and for those holding moderate attitudes. As expected, when compared with a subject who is moderate, an extreme subject has both a narrower latitude of acceptance and a wider latitude of rejection. This difference, it was assumed, is mediated by greater involvement with and commitment to the issue among persons holding extreme views.

Earlier in this chapter we examined evidence indicating that the interpretation a member of an audience makes of a message is, in part, determined by characteristics he attributes to the communicator of the message. The foregoing data indicate that interpretation of the message

Table 12.5. Acceptability of Statements in Relation to Extremity of Subjects' Position on Issue (From Hovland, Harvey, and Sherif, 1957)

S's positions	N	Mean number of items acceptable	Mean number of items not checked	Mean number of items rejected
1. Extreme (A, B, G, H, I) [a]	193	2.81	1.48	4.71
2. Intermediate (C, D, E, F)	37	3.05	2.24	3.70

[a] The letters refer to the various attitude statements.

may also be affected by characteristics the person himself possesses, specifically his initial stand on the issue in question. Clearly, if a message is to have its intended effect, the communicator must take steps to control or counteract these types of interpretive process.

Forewarning and Distracting the Audience

As pointed out by Hovland (1959), one of the features that distinguishes field studies from laboratory experiments on the effects of propaganda appeals is the lack of forewarning given to the subject in the laboratory that he will be exposed to a persuasive communication. In the "real world" the person usually exposes himself voluntarily to propaganda. This difference, Hovland suggests, might account for the greater relative effectiveness of propaganda attempts studied in the laboratory where the subject is captive. Other factors might also account for this discrepancy between the data collected in these two settings, such as the difference in commitment the person usually has in real-life issues as compared with his commitment on those issues that are tailor-made for a particular laboratory experiment. Nevertheless, the forewarning hypothesis suggested by Hovland deserves attention, not necessarily as a basis for explaining differences in findings between laboratory and field studies but as an interesting hypothesis in its own right.

Some evidence for the hypothesis is provided by Ewing (1942) who, in a forewarning, led half of his subjects to expect that a subsequent persuasive communication would oppose their point of view and led the other half to believe that it would agree with their point of view. The subjects in each treatment were exposed to the same communication. Those who expected disagreement were more resistant to it than those who expected agreement. It is difficult to know from this study whether the difference is a result of the subjects in the "disagree" treatment being more resistant or those in the "agree" treatment being more compliant.

The latter may have changed merely to conform to what the experimenter believed their opinion to be.

A subsequent study by Allyn and Festinger (1961) provides further evidence for the hypothesis that forewarning creates resistance. In the experiment a prepared speech was delivered to high-school students in support of increasing the driver-eligibility age in California from 16 to 21. This issue was chosen because it was one on which high-school students' opinions were extreme and homogeneous. In instruction booklets passed out before the talk, half of the subjects were asked to pay attention to the message, which would be about the menace of teenage drivers. They were further informed that they would be asked for their opinions about teenage driving at the conclusion of the talk. This was the "opinion orientation" treatment. The instruction booklets for the other half of the subjects did not describe the nature of the talk, only that it was to be about driving. These subjects were told that the researchers were interested in finding out how members of an audience formed impressions of the personality of a speaker and that they would be asked later, in a questionnaire, to give their impressions of the speaker's personality. This was the "personality orientation" treatment. Thus in the opinion orientation treatment the members of the audience were forewarned that the intent of the speaker was to persuade them that the minimum age for drivers should be raised, whereas the members of the audience in the personality orientation condition knew only that the speaker was going to discuss driving but they had no prior notion as to what, if any, point of view the speaker would advocate. In his talk the speaker stressed the average teenager's lack of a mature sense of responsibility and strongly advocated raising the minimum age for drivers.

Because the speaker's message advocated a position that was antithetical to the views held by the members of the audience, dissonance was presumably aroused by the message. Allyn and Festinger investigated two modes of reducing this dissonance. One avenue open to the subject would be to reduce the discrepancy between his own opinion and that espoused by the speaker. Since the position of the speaker was unequivocal, this would manifest itself as a change in the subject's opinion toward greater control over teenage driving. Another possibility for reducing the dissonance would be for the subject to discredit and reject the speaker and thus reduce the force of the opposed opinion. Allyn and Festinger argue that when the subject has been forewarned of the speaker's intent "he will approach the situation with hesitancy, suspicion, and perhaps some hostility" (p. 36). This type of orientation is more likely to lead to rejection of the speaker than the other orientation, in which the subject has not been forewarned and concentrates on forming an impression of the speaker's personality. In this latter condition, owing to the lack of preparedness, we would expect the message to produce a greater amount of opinion change.

Table 12.6 indicates the effect of the message on both opinion change

Table 12.6. Opinion Change and Rejection of Communicator for the Two Experimental Conditions (From Allyn and Festinger, 1961)

	Experimental condition	
	Opinion orientation ($N = 41$)	Personality orientation ($N = 46$)
Average change of opinion	+.49	+.63
Percentage changing appreciably [a]	20%	43%
Percentage saying communication was very or somewhat biased	80%	61%

[a] An appreciable change is defined as a change of two or more points in the direction of the communication.

and rejection of the speaker. The opinion-change measure was based on a comparison of each subject's opinion about teenage driving on both the pre- and postexposure questionnaires. The rejection measure was based on a question in the postexposure questionnaire. The data show that forewarning can fortify the individual by producing a skeptical attitude toward the speaker.

People probably expose themselves selectively and with a particular orientation to different kinds of propaganda. If they anticipate that a bit of propaganda will support their own convictions they will assume an open and receptive orientation toward it. If, however, the speaker is known to hold views that are antithetical to the person's own views, he will either avoid the message or, if he does choose to listen to it, he will be prepared to take what he hears with a grain of salt.

There are some difficulties inherent in the experiment. The major problem concerns the manipulation of forewarning. Subjects in the opinion orientation condition were forewarned, whereas in the personality orientation the subject was not only not forewarned but he was also distracted from attending to the content of the message. A comparison between the two treatments, therefore, is not strictly justified.

As we pointed out in Chapter Two, in order to evaluate the effect of a given factor on some behavior we must compare treatments that differ only in the level (or presence versus absence) of that particular factor with everything else held constant. Because these conditions were not met by the experimental manipulation Festinger and Maccoby (1964) designed another experiment to examine the effects of distraction alone, with forewarning held constant. Their hunch was that the results of the Allyn and Festinger (1961) experiment were the effect of distraction rather than forewarning. In the opinion orientation condition the subject could pay strict attention to the arguments of the speaker and could, *ad libidum*, conjure up counterarguments in order to refute the arguments presented by the speaker. In the personality orientation condition the subject could not readily do this as he had another task to perform, to evaluate the personality of the speaker. He would thus at best have only part of the time available in which to focus on the content and conjure up refutations. If we make these assumptions about the relative availability to the subject of time to engage actively in silent argumentation with the speaker, it follows that a more passive listener (with respect to the speaker's arguments) was created in the personality orientation condition.

In the Festinger and Maccoby (1964) experiment a sound film was prepared that argued against college fraternities. In one version of the film a young college professor, who introduced himself as having been a member of a fraternity while in college, presented a strong case as to why fraternities should be abolished. The distraction version had exactly the same sound track but instead of seeing the young professor while he spoke, the audience saw excerpts from a film, *The Day of the Painter*, which is a rather amusing silent film depicting the creative efforts of a modern abstract painter. Because the visual content of the presentation had absolutely nothing to do with the case against fraternities, the subject would be distracted; this distraction would presumably disarm him and make him a more passive target. The experiment was conducted at three different universities, using both fraternity and nonfraternity men. An after-only design was used, with an opinion measure and a measure of the subject's attitude toward the speaker administered in a postexperimental questionnaire.

The data from two of the colleges, at which there are strong fraternity systems, offer support for the hypothesis that the distraction version of the communication was more effective than the ordinary version of the film. In the third college, where fraternities are apparently on their way out, no difference was produced by the two treatments. In one of the schools both fraternity and nonfraternity men were exposed to each version of the film. If we assume that distraction disarms the listener and prevents him from counterarguing we should find a difference between the two presentations only for fraternity men; nonfraternity men would presumably not be initially opposed to the speaker's point of view and should not, even when given the opportunity, conjure up counterarguments. There was still an opportunity, however, for the speaker to influence the nonfraternity men because the views he expressed were even more extreme than the views of most nonfraternity men. The data show that the distraction version was indeed no more effective than the ordinary version for the nonfraternity men, whereas it was more effective for fraternity men.

There is a strong suggestion here that, when listening to a speaker with a point of view that is antithetical to his own, the listener engages in some sort of silent dialogue in his efforts to come to terms with the discrepancy between his own and the speaker's point of view.

Freedman and Sears (1965) replicated the Allyn and Festinger experiment, endeavoring to come to terms with the difficulties involved in interpreting its data. Their procedure counterbalanced distraction with forewarning so that both the opinion and personality orientation treatments were tried with and without forewarning, yielding four combinations. Exactly the same procedure, with the same kind of introductory booklets, was used as in the original Allyn and Festinger study. All combinations were tested simultaneously in a high-school auditorium with the booklets for the various combinations randomly distributed to the members of the audience. Thus some booklets contained the warning–personality orientation instructions, other booklets contained the no-warning–personality orientation instructions, and so on. Again a postmeasure of attitude toward teenage driving was compared with a premeasure. The data in Table 12.7

Table 12.7. Mean Attitude Change for the Various Conditions of Warning and Orientation (From Freedman and Sears, 1965)

	No-Warning	Warning
Content orientation (no distraction)	1.54	0.75
Personality orientation (distraction)	1.83	1.31

show effects of both variables, although a statistical evaluation of the differences indicates that the effects were not overly strong. Both forewarning and distraction can apparently operate in altering the vulnerability of the audience. Freedman and Sears sifted the evidence in their experiment in an effort to examine three mechanisms that might be differentially affected or engaged by either forewarning or distraction: rejection of the speaker, failure to pay attention, or active conjuring up of counterarguments. They found no evidence for either of the first two but some evidence that active counterargument was occurring. This evidence dovetails nicely with the Festinger and Maccoby (1964) results.

Additional evidence for this active process of counterarguing comes from an experiment by McGuire and Papageorgis (1962) in which some subjects were sensitized to counterarguments beforehand and others were not. The propaganda missive, a short paragraph, attacked certain basic health truisms that are generally accepted as foregone conclusions (e.g., "everyone should get a chest X ray each year in order to detect any tuberculosis"). A distraction manipulation similar to the one used by Allyn and Festinger (1961) was employed to vary the subject's orientation toward the message. In one treatment the subject was distracted by being asked to pay attention to the expository style of the message rather than to content, whereas in another treatment the subject was told, in effect, that the message was designed to influence his opinion. As in the other studies the message proved more effective in the distraction condition. This study also adds evidence supporting the contention that the mechanism mediating the increased resistance of the nondistracted subject, the forewarned subject, or both, is the active conjuring up of counterarguments. McGuire and Papageorgis compared the effectiveness of each of their two types of orientation on subjects who had been previously apprised of counterarguments and on subjects who had received no such training. They found a marked difference in the effects of distraction for those who had received prior training, whereas distraction appeared to have no effect on subjects who were unprepared with counterarguments. This finding is all the more telling when we realize that the issues used in the other studies were controversial ones. The sensitization procedure used by McGuire and Papageorgis served to transform what had been cold, self-evident truisms into controversial issues.

While the results of this set of studies are generally consistent, a number of questions and loose ends should stimulate further research in this area. An obvious question concerns how far we can go in distracting the audience. At one extreme it is possible, of course, to introduce sufficient distraction to obliterate the message completely. Until this extreme is reached it may be that distraction is effective because it makes more demands on the subject, involving him more in the total situation, and thus increasing his susceptibility to all of its aspects. This would seem a possibility worth looking into. There is some indirect supporting evidence. Zajonc and Dorfman (1964) review the literature on what is called sensory interaction, in which a subject is simultaneously exposed to two or more different kinds of stimuli. They cite a good deal of evidence to indicate that, under certain circumstances, stimulus input in one sensory modality heightens rather than detracts from sensitivity in another modality. For example, a subject's sensitivity to sound tends to be heightened when he is shown, during the presentation of the auditory stimulus, a visual stimulus to which he had previously been conditioned by electrical shocks (Dorfman, 1961). Here the light can be considered as a distraction, as was *The Day of the Painter*.

There seems to be another viable interpretation of the Festinger and Maccoby results. It may be that the film *The Day of the Painter* is so pleasant and amusing that anything associated with it takes on positive value. An obvious test of this interpretation would be to present the sound track with visual material that was equally distracting but less pleasant. These are some of the questions that may be pursued in future research on this most intriguing and important problem.

Inoculation against Counterarguments

In a series of ingenious, interrelated experiments McGuire and his students have studied various forms of inoculation against arguments that attack certain basic attitudes the person holds. The earlier research in Hovland's program at Yale provided the background for these investigations. Recall that in the one-sided versus two-sided communication studies, the two-sided presentation imparted sustaining power to the belief in question. Both types of presentation produced approximately the same initial amount of attitude change but the two-sided treatment seemed to freeze the new attitude, as evidenced by much less backsliding. Could it be that the two-sided treatment inoculated the subject against subsequent exposure to arguments from his peers and from media sources that might cause him to revert to his original belief? Perhaps he was provided with ammunition in the form of arguments that he could use in countering attempts to persuade him to revert to his original belief. We saw evidence of inoculation in the experiment by Janis, Lumsdaine, and Gladstone (1951) in which subjects who were previously indoctrinated to expect otherwise resisted changing their beliefs about the Soviet Union's atomic bomb potentiality after a Russian atomic bomb explosion had been announced by President Truman. McGuire brought these crude and loosely articulated findings into sharp focus.

McGuire argues that just as it is possible to stimulate the body's defenses against germs by the inoculation of small doses of the germ in a weakened form, it may be possible to stimulate a person's attitudinal defenses by inoculating him with a weak form of the counterattitudinal arguments he is likely to encounter. This inoculation should be strong enough to stimulate his defenses but not to overcome them. The person's defenses against a disease might also be built up by supportive therapy, that is, by sufficient bed rest and an adequate diet. This kind of support, however, is likely to prove less effective in the long run than immunization by inoculation of a weakened form of the disease. Similarly, it should be possible to build up the person's resistance to arguments that oppose a belief he holds by providing him with arguments that support his belief. Arguing from the disease analogy, however, this technique should be less effective than providing him with small doses of arguments he would have to counter in order to maintain his belief intact. A refutational defense should therefore be more effective than a supportive defense.

Beliefs that tend to exist in a "germ-free" ideological environment were chosen as the attitude target in McGuire's investigations. This choice is analogous to transplanting an Eskimo into the dense hustle-bustle of midtown New York or Tokyo, where there are germ concentrations of high density against which the Eskimo has no defenses. Cultural truisms, according to McGuire, are beliefs that meet the germ-free requirement. Such beliefs are so widely shared that the person has never heard them attacked and would have every reason to doubt that they could be attacked. Examples of the truisms used in McGuire's research are: "It's a good idea to brush your teeth after every meal if at all possible"; "Mental illness is not contagious"; "The effects of penicillin have been, almost without exception, of great benefit to mankind"; "Everyone should get a yearly chest X ray to detect any signs of TB at an early stage." These are beliefs for which a person can muster relatively little support in the way of arguments when confronted by a massive attack; he has never felt any need to seek support for these truisms and therefore has had little practice in doing so. McGuire has shown, as we shall see, that in the face of a direct attack these beliefs do prove to be quite vulnerable. An inoculation technique providing him with counterarguments should enable the person to defend any of them.

The basic condition that makes the person defenseless is his assumption of the belief's unassailability, so it would seem that the first step in an inoculation procedure would be to undermine the assumption by making it appear that the truism is indeed vulnerable. The inoculation should therefore, as a first requirement, be mildly threatening in order to motivate the person to think up the necessary arguments.

The format for all of the experiments was essentially the same. There was a defense-building session followed by an attack. McGuire then determined the relative amount of resistance conferred by various types of defense inoculations by taking opinion measures after the attack.

In the first experiment (McGuire and Papageorgis, 1961) supportive and refutational defenses were compared. A supportive defense, according to the theory, should not be so effective as a refutational one in building up the person's defenses. In the supportive defense treatment the subject read the truism, followed by four supporting arguments and a paragraph that spelled the arguments out. In the refutational defense the truism was followed by four arguments against the truism and then a paragraph that refuted them. Each subject received a refutational defense for one truism and a supportive defense for another truism. Two days later he received two messages, each attacking one of these truisms, and a third message that attacked a truism for which no prior defense had been provided. After the attacking session opinion measures were taken on these three truisms. The subject's opinion on a fourth truism, which had neither been defended nor attacked, was also measured. Of course the truisms were rotated so that each one appeared an equal number of times in each of the four treatments. The data clearly support the theory by showing the superiority of the refutational over the supportive defense. Table 12.8 indicates the over-all effectiveness of the four treatments.

Table 12.8. Mean Belief Levels [a] in the Truism after Attack with Different Prior Defenses
(From McGuire and Papageorgis, 1961)

Refutational Defense plus Attack	Supportive Defense plus Attack	Attack only	Neither Defense nor Attack
10.33	7.39	6.64	12.62

[a] 15.00 indicates complete adherence to the truism; 1.00 indicates complete disagreement.

An interesting sidelight to the experiment concerns the direct strengthening effect of the two types of defense. In a measure administered immediately after the defense-building session, the supportive defense showed a superiority over the refutational defense. This apparent strengthening was only a "paper tiger" effect because, as indicated in the table, this direct strengthening after the supportive defense did not sustain the truism against attack as the refutational defense did. In this respect the supportive defense provided only minimal resistance to attack. This finding illustrates in a dramatic way the danger of equating a person's apparent depth of conviction or extremity of opinion with the strength of this opinion in resisting counterarguments. However, we must bear in mind that the McGuire and Papageorgis experiment used cultural truisms. To the extent that a belief is not a truism, depth of conviction may be correlated with resistance to change.

In the first experiment the refutational defense used the same arguments later used in the attack. We could argue that the superiority of the refutational over the supportive defense stemmed from the surprise value of the attack when the belief had a supportive defense, because the subject had no prior exposure to the arguments. Also, the refutational defense did prepare the subject by providing him with counterarguments for the very arguments contained in the attack. McGuire's theory would have it that the superiority of the refutational defense was primarily a result of its capacity to stimulate the person to consider and refute various counterarguments and not simply a matter of differences in exposure to specific attacks and refutations. A more direct test of the theory would be to confront the person with novel counterarguments when the truism is subsequently attacked. This was accomplished in an experiment by Papageorgis and McGuire (1961).

The procedure, which was essentially the same as that used in the first experiment, compared the effectiveness of the refutational defense when the attack involved the arguments used in the defense-building session (the "refutational-same" treatment) with the effectiveness of earlier refutation when attacked with novel arguments ("refutational-different"). The evidence confirms the theory in that the refutational defense not only produced resistance to the same counterarguments but also generalized this resistance to the novel counterarguments. On the 15-point scale used in the previous study, where 15 represented maximum belief in the truism, truisms with no defenses yielded a score of 5.73 as compared with 13.23 for truisms that were neither defended nor attacked. The refutational-same treatment yielded a belief score of 9.25, whereas the refutational-different treatment yielded a score of 8.70, a difference that favors only slightly the treatment in which the attacking arguments were the same as those the subject learned during the defense-building session.

McGuire's theory assumes that the ineffectiveness of the supportive defense rests on the lack of stimulation of a defensive stance. If the subject were mildly threatened before receiving the supportive arguments, he would presumably be more receptive to those arguments and they would therefore confer resistance. In a third experiment (McGuire, 1961a) a refutational-different defense was followed by a supportive defense. The theory was again confirmed, as the resistance effect of the combination of defenses was greater than the sum of the effects of each type of defense administered separately.

In another study, Anderson (1962) produced the reverse effect of forewarning by reassuring the subject that all of his peers in the experimental group were unanimous in their belief about the truisms. This treatment was compared with one in which the subject received no such reassurance. The reassurance condition *weakened* resistance as compared with the no-reassurance condition. The reassurance may have served to induce even greater complacency in the subject about the cultural truisms and thus to make him a sitting duck for the subsequent counterarguments. This finding is in direct contradiction to the results of the Gerard (1954) experiment described in Chapter Ten. In that experiment the subject's resistance to direct attack on his belief was found to be positively correlated with the degree of unanimity in his reference group. Here again, as in the case of the direct strengthening of supportive defenses, the effects of support for truisms may be quite different from support for controversial beliefs. Anderson's results point up our lack of knowledge. We obviously have to know more about the boundary conditions that determine the relationship between vulnerability and reference-group consensus.

In several of his studies McGuire compared active versus passive inoculation treatments. In the active treatment the subject was asked to write an essay either supporting the truism or refuting arguments that might be made against it. In the passive inoculation treatment the subject was merely asked to read prepared material that was either of a supportive or refutational nature. Because the subject had previously paid little attention to the grounds for believing in the truism, active inoculation would tend to be threatening; he would suddenly be confronted with the task of arguing in favor of a truism and unable to muster arguments because he had never given the matter much thought. A passive refutational defense, on the other hand, would serve both to threaten the subject mildly and to reassure him by providing the necessary counterarguments. The active participation condition should, therefore, create less resistance to attack than the passive condition, because a threat alone, without reassurance, should make the subject more vulnerable than a treatment in which reassurance follows the threat (cf. Cohen, 1957). This prediction was borne out in the study by McGuire and Papageorgis (1961) where passive and active defense treatments were applied. In still another experiment (McGuire, 1961b) a combination of both types of defense was found to be superior to either one alone.

Arguing from the assumptions of the theory, McGuire reasoned that a refutational defense would generate more persistent resistance over time than a supportive defense. The argument here assumes that a refutational defense is threatening and hence will induce vigilance in the person concerning arguments that might bolster his belief. He will therefore be sensitized to any available supportive information in his environment. We should then expect that over time the resistance-creating effect of a refutational defense will increase as the subject musters up more and more supportive information. The supportive defense, on the other hand, because it does not threaten the subject, does not induce vigilance. Instead its resistance-creating potential tends to diminish over time as the subject forgets more and more of the supportive information; there is really no incentive for him to remember it. This prediction was tested (McGuire, 1962) by comparing the resistance to attack of the refutational and supportive defense immediately after, two days after, and seven days after inoculation. As predicted, the supportive defense shows a decay with time in its resistance-creating potential, whereas the refutational defense shows an increase after two days and then a decrease by the seventh day. This decrease presumably reflects forgetting after the subject has acquired all available supporting information following the threat. The rise and fall parallels the disease analogy. Following inoculation, immunization gradually builds up to a maximum as antibodies are formed and then gradually decays, making periodic booster shots necessary.

This review of McGuire's work has touched on the highlights without going into many of the subtle nuances derivable from his inoculation theory. The experimental results examined will probably be qualified by future research into important boundary conditions, such as the degree to which the belief involved is controversial. Nevertheless, the collection of studies by McGuire is unusually coherent, considering the complexity of the theoretical issues involved.

ACTIVE AUDIENCE PARTICIPATION

In McGuire's work a passive defense was found to be superior to an active one in creating resistance to persuasion. McGuire was dealing with cultural truisms about which little specific supportive information was available to the subject in his prior, nonlaboratory environment. In the active defense treatment he had little information to rely on, whereas in the passive defense treatment such supportive information was provided by the experimenter. This difference between the two treatments is presumably the basis for the superiority of the passive defense in creating resistance to counterarguments. What would be the effect of an active participation defense on a controversial issue when the subject is able to muster up the necessary support for his attitude? A series of studies, following that by Janis and King (1954), has examined in detail the effects of the various factors involved in participation. The research served initially to provide support for the theory of cognitive dissonance and gradually became a battleground for competing theoretical explanations.

Role-Playing

A procedure extensively used in both training and psychotherapy requires that a person play the role of someone else. In management training, used in some industrial concerns, the trainee may be asked to play the role of his boss or his subordinate. This role-playing experience presumably gives the trainee some idea of what it is like to be the person whose role he is taking. He is able to develop an approximate version of the way in which the other person perceives his world and in so doing comes to develop some understanding of what is producing the other person's attitudes and behavior. In Chapter Three, we indicated that taking the role of the other appeared to be a natural tendency in an interaction situation. This was a view espoused by the sociologist George Herbert Mead (1934). In Mead's terms, however, the person's perspective in the situation is still very much his own; the person assumes that the other person is responding as he would himself respond to his own gestures and speech. The role-playing situation, on the other hand, is one in which the person is forced to take the perspective of the other person. Used under carefully supervised conditions role-playing appears to be a very effective technique for opening the eyes of a person to the life situation of another person, and dramatic changes in attitude toward the other person and his role have been claimed for it.

Role-playing has been used as a trouble-shooting technique in situations where people are in conflict owing to opposing, and apparently irreconcilable, points of view. As a technique that attempts to get the person to see things from the perspective of the other person it appears to possess all of the earmarks of an attitude change procedure. But in the work reviewed earlier in this chapter we saw the person confronted by arguments supporting an attitude different from his own that were being advanced by someone else—the communicator. In role-playing the tables are turned. The person is being asked, in effect, to assume the role of communicator and is therefore put in the position of having to advance arguments that are discrepant from his own attitude. Being thus forced to look at the situation from the other point of view exposes him, at least to some extent, to the arguments, beliefs, and values, that serve to generate the opposing attitude.

In the everyday life situations in which role-playing has been used there have been no systematic studies attempting to explore the factors that determine the effectiveness of the technique. The claims are based on anecdotal evidence. This is understandable because therapy and training situations are inherently complex and it would be difficult to ferret out the individual factors responsible for the success of the techniques.

Janis and King began their exploration of role-playing in a situation of drastically reduced complexity. The question they raised was a simple one: Is it the fact of verbalizing statements concerning the other person's point of view or is it simply a matter of being exposed to his point of view that produces the change in attitudes claimed for role-playing? In effect, Janis and King were asking whether role-playing was really any more effective than the typical attitude change procedure of exposing the person to arguments that support an opposing viewpoint.

Three subjects were used in each experimental session. On a preexperimental questionnaire each subject had his attitude measured on each of three controversial issues. At the beginning of the experimental session each subject received an outline of a talk on only one of the three issues. The outline embodied a completely one-sided, extreme point of view. Each subject, using the outline provided, spoke extemporaneously on the issue he was assigned and was asked by the experimenter to speak as though he really favored the point of view he was advocating. While each subject talked the other two listened. Thus each was passively exposed to arguments on two issues and was actively exposed to arguments that he himself verbalized on a third issue. When the amounts of change toward the viewpoint advocated in each of the three talks are compared, there is a clear difference favoring the active, role-playing talk. The subject changed more toward the point of view advocated in his own talk than toward the point of view advocated in the talks given by his fellow subjects. Unfortunately, ambiguity in the procedure weakens the conclusion that we would like to draw here, that role-playing is indeed more effective than passive exposure. When the subject spoke on an issue he not only was exposed to the arguments presented to him in the outline but, in the course of his talk to the experimenter and the other two subjects, he may have also come up with additional, novel arguments. If he did not mention all of the arguments in the outline he would have been the only subject of the three who had been exposed to all of the arguments, those in the outline and the novel ones he invented. Furthermore, to the extent that the arguments presented by the other two subjects were weak or did not mention arguments contained in the outline, the subject was exposed to weaker arguments on their issues than on his own issue. This possible difference in exposure to arguments would also account for the superiority of the active over the passive exposure conditions. It is impossible to choose between this and the role-playing interpretation.

The design of the second experiment (King and Janis, 1956) was based on the assumption that the results of the first did indeed show that role-playing was more effective than passive exposure in producing attitude change. The investigators singled out two aspects of role-playing as possible factors that might account for its assumed efficacy as a technique: the self-produced improvisation of the subject that may have resulted in self-convincing, and the satisfaction he may have experienced with his own efforts at public speaking; that is, the "saying is believing" effect may result from the subject's having convinced himself by his own arguments or from the pleasure associated with giving the talk that may then rub off onto the point of view advocated in the talk. King and Janis saw these as the two most likely determinants of the attitude change found in the first experiment.

The second experiment had essentially the same format as the first except that only one issue was used. There were three experimental treatments, with each subject being exposed to only one treatment. In the passive-control treatment the subject merely read the discrepant communication silently to himself. In a second treatment the subject read the script aloud. In the third treatment the subject was required to give an improvised talk after reading the message silently to himself. The authors argued that a comparison of the effects produced by reading the message aloud and improvisation after silent reading counterposed the two factors that were singled out for this inquiry, namely, improvisation and satisfaction. They argued that subjects should be more satisfied with their performance when reading a message aloud than when having to ad-lib a speech. We might, however, question this assumption. On a postquestionnaire measure 98 percent of the subjects in the improvisation treatment showed some change toward the point of view advocated by the message, as compared with 54 percent in the reading-aloud treatment. In the passive-control treatment, where the message was read silently, 65 percent showed some change. The difference between the latter two treatments was relatively small but it is in the direction opposite to what a "satisfaction theory" would predict. The improvisation condition is clearly higher in the amount of change produced than either of the other two conditions. Here again we have something of the same design problem as in the previous experiment because in the improvisation condition the subject not only read the material read by the subjects in the other two treatments but was also exposed to his own improvisations, which may have contained both variations of the arguments in the written message as well as novel arguments he himself invented on the spot. This weakness in design limits the conclusions we are able to draw about the effects of improvisation.

Studies by Zimbardo (1965) and Greenbaum (1966) highlight this weakness in Janis and King's interpretation of the efficacy of improvisation. They both found that when subjects are carefully observed in conditions designed to produce spontaneity, they engage in very little actual improvisation. Furthermore, when there was improvisation, the amount of attitude change bore no relationship to its quality. In addition, Zimbardo found no treatment difference in attitude change between improvisation and active reading. McGuire (1962), too, points to the possibility that the superiority of a passive over an active defense may have resulted from the fact that most of his subjects were inept at improvising an active defense. This additional evidence makes more tenable the interpretation that the superiority of the improvisors in the Janis and King studies may have resulted from the confounding of double versus single exposure to the arguments.

Role-Playing and the Action Sequence

In the role-playing situation the person is asked to take a stand or assume a point of view that is discrepant from the stand that would follow from the attitude he actually holds. When asked to play the role the person is confronted by a choice: should he or should he not play the role he is being asked to play? If he agrees to go along with the trainer, the therapist, or the experimenter we must assume that the incentives or outcomes associated with taking the discrepant stand outweigh the incentives associated with refusing to do so. In an experiment he may go along for a number of reasons, among which may be not wanting to hurt the experimenter's feelings, not wanting to appear a poor sport, interest in advancing science, or any number of other reasons. There may be one or some combination of reasons that would justify his choice of cooperating with the experimenter. The fact remains, though, that there is one very good reason why he should not cooperate: his actual attitude is supported by certain of his beliefs and values. This is assumed; otherwise he would not have the attitude in the first place. The values he holds that support his private attitude presumably have certain associated outcomes. There are, therefore, two sets of outcomes associated with the decision to advocate a discrepant attitude or not, one set supporting one alternative and the other set supporting the other.

This analysis suggests that the role-playing decision, like any other decision, involves all of the elements of the action sequence. Let us therefore examine the implications of casting role-playing into an action-sequence analysis.

The Effects of Rewards and Incentives for Role-Playing

Because the ratio of predecisional, anticipated outcomes affects the amount of postdecisional dissonance we expect the amount of attitude change to be related to the strength of the incentives offered to the subject for advocating the discrepant stand. What should be the nature of this relationship? Role-playing is the chosen alternative here, so the over-all outcome balance must have favored role-playing as against turning the experimenter down by refusing to advocate the discrepant stand. In Chapter Six we hypothesized that the closer the alternatives were in value, the greater would be the postdecisional dissonance and therefore the greater the tendency for the subject to engage in cognitive work in order to support the decision. In the situation under consideration here, the subject has a set of cognitions (beliefs and values) that supports his actual attitude. Let us regard these cognitions as relatively fixed. In the predecision situation, what, then, will affect his postdecisional level of dissonance? An aspect of the predecision situation that can vary is the set of outcomes associated with advocating the discrepant stand; the greater the incentive for doing so, the easier the decision and the *less* the postdecisional dissonance. This is so because the greater the incentive for taking the discrepant stand, the further apart the alternatives will be in the postdecision situation, resulting in less dissonance and therefore less need to justify the decision.

As we saw in Chapter Six, the person may reduce dissonance in a number of ways. Generally speaking, he can either enhance the value of the chosen alternative or denigrate the value of the nonchosen one. For example, he might come to believe that the experimenter is a nice guy, that he has some important reasons for having asked the subject to assume the role he has, that there is some important scientific hypothesis at stake. If the subject has been promised money for participating he might come to feel that he really needs the money very badly. Another method for justifying his behavior would be to find merit in the position he is advocating. He might come to realize that this discrepant attitude really furthers important values he holds. Because holding his initial attitude is inimical to the opinion he is advocating, he may at the same time attempt to downgrade his initial attitude by questioning its connection with beliefs and values he holds. There are a number of ways in which the person may reorganize his beliefs and values so that they realign themselves to support the position being advocated. Another possibility, of course, is for him to change the beliefs and values themselves. The research in this area has not advanced far enough in attempting to understand the nature of this accommodation process. The evidence we do have points to the fact that some sort of accommodation indeed takes place; variations in incentives do result in attitude change.

The first systematic attempt to study the relationship between attitude change and incentives for taking a discrepant stand was made by Kelman (1953). The subjects in Kelman's experiment were 12-year-olds and the attitude issue had to do with two kinds of comic books: jungle comics like *Tarzan* and fantastic hero comics like *Superman*. On an initial attitude measure it was found that most of the children in the sample liked fantastic hero comics better than jungle comics. The intent of the experiment was to change their attitude so that they would tend to increase their liking for jungle comics. The experiment was conducted in the subjects' classrooms and the experimenter gave a short talk in which he extolled the virtues of jungle comics and played down the virtues of fantastic hero comics. In one treatment the class was asked to compete for theater tickets to the movie *Huckleberry Finn* by writing essays in favor of jungle comics. In a second treatment *everyone* who wrote in favor of jungle comics would receive a pair of theater tickets. In the second treatment it was made clear to the subjects that the experimenter expected everyone to cooperate. This latter treatment, Kelman suggests, represents one in which the subject was offered a high incentive (a sure reward and a great deal of pressure from the experimenter) for advocating a point of view that was different from his private attitude, whereas in the first treatment the subject's incentive was small because, owing to the competition, it was unlikely that he would receive the tickets and there was little pressure from the experimenter.

In terms of a dissonance analysis, we would expect more attitude change toward the position advocated in the low- as compared with the high-incentive treatment. For those subjects who did write in favor of jungle comics, the results support this expectation. There are, however, three difficulties in the design that affect confidence in the conclusion. The condition called low-incentive may indeed have been a high-incentive condition because competition itself may have been a strong incentive to write in favor of jungle comics. Another difficulty, which is not unrelated to the first, is a problem of subject self-selection because a greater proportion of subjects in the high-incentive treatment wrote in favor of jungle comics than in the other treatment. There is no way of knowing, of course, what kind of confounding this difference produced. One possibility is that the smaller percentage of subjects taking the discrepant stand in the low-incentive condition were actually those children who liked to compete and were therefore operating under a high incentive. When there is a self-selection problem anything can happen, and there really is no good way of knowing just what did happen.

Another source of difficulty with the experiment concerns the results from a control group. This group was more or less free to write either in favor of jungle or fantastic hero comics. When left to their own devices, over 40 percent of the subjects chose to write in favor of jungle comics. This may reflect the persuasiveness of the initial pitch by the experimenter in favor of jungle comics. If this message was indeed effective then many of the subjects in the two experimental treatments who wrote in favor of jungle comics were actually not taking a stand that was discrepant from their own new private attitude but were writing in favor of what they believed to be a better type of comic book.

A more careful study of incentives in role-playing was conducted some years later by Festinger and Carlsmith (1959). In that study subjects were induced to perform a monotonous, boring task and were subsequently asked to lie to the next subject who was waiting to participate by telling him how much fun the task had been. The next subject was actually an accomplice of the experimenter. The ruse used by the experimenter was to tell the subject that the experiment involved a study of the effect of "set" on how boring or interesting a person finds a task and the next subject was to approach the task with the set that the task would be interesting. He was also informed that the one who usually told this lie could not make it that day. The subject was asked not only to lie to the next subject but also to be on call if he was needed to misinform additional subjects. Two incentive treatments were compared. In one treatment the subject was told that he would receive 20 dollars for helping out, whereas in the other treatment he was offered only one dollar for doing so. The prediction was that the subject would end up liking the task more in the one-dollar than in the 20-dollar treatment because in the former a low incentive for lying would produce greater dissonance from the lesser justification for doing so. The subject could have invented a number of justifications (e.g., that the experimenter was a "nice guy"), and he may have resorted to them, but one clear justification for his behavior was for the subject actually to change his attitude toward the task so that it would support the discrepant statement he had made. After the subject made his spiel to the accomplice, his attitude toward the task was measured and it was found that in the low-incentive condition he did, in fact, end up liking the task more than his counterpart in the high-incentive condition.

In a further extension of this study, Cohen (in Brehm and Cohen, 1962) used four rather than two incentive levels. Yale students were asked to write an essay against their private views on a current campus issue. There had been some recent student riots opposing actions of the local town police on the campus and the vast majority of the students were, as a result, antagonistic toward the police side of the issue. The subject was asked to write an essay supporting the police action. They were offered either 50 cents, one dollar, five dollars, or 10 dollars to write this essay. The guise under which the essay was solicited had to do with the importance for the research team investigating the issue of getting arguments on *both* sides. Because they had a number of arguments on one side of the issue (the side the subject privately favored), they said, they were asking the subject to present arguments favoring the other side. Table 12.9 pre-

Table 12.9. Mean Attitude [a] Toward Police for the Different Incentive Conditions (From Brehm and Cohen, 1962)

$10.00 Condition	2.32
$ 5.00 Condition	3.08
$ 1.00 Condition	3.47
$ 0.50 Condition	4.54
Control Condition [b]	2.70

[a] The higher the mean, the more positive the attitude toward the police.
[b] The control group received no incentive and wrote no essay. They merely responded to the attitude questionnaire.

sents the data showing the average degree of favorableness toward the police. The inverse linear relationship of attitude with incentive shown in the table offers strong support for the dissonance interpretation of the role-playing choice.

Some recent research has questioned the dissonance interpretation of the inverse relationship between reward and attitude change under forced compliance. Janis and Gilmore (1965), in criticizing Festinger and Carlsmith, suggest that a subject offered 20 dollars for telling a little lie would become suspicious and take a generally negative attitude toward the experiment, which would in turn make him change less in the direction of the opinion he was asked to advocate. We must remember, though, that the payment in the Festinger and Carlsmith experiment was offered not only for lying to the next subject but also for being on call for possible lying to future subjects. Twenty dollars may not have seemed such an overpayment for all this. Besides, it is difficult to maintain that the difference in the predicted direction between the one-dollar and the 50-cent conditions in the Cohen experiment can be accounted for by greater suspicion having been aroused in the one-dollar condition. Just on the face of it, this seems highly unlikely. Nevertheless, Janis and Gilmore tested the "suspicion" interpretation by asking all subjects to write an essay, for one dollar or 20 dollars, in favor of the proposition that a year of physics and math should be a college requirement at Yale. Note here that the subject in the 20-dollar treatment was given the money merely for writing an essay *and nothing else*. This might indeed arouse suspicion. Furthermore, Janis and Gilmore made the tacit assumption that in writing the essay *all* subjects would be taking a counterattitudinal stand, without presenting evidence that this was in fact the case. Some subjects may have believed that physics and math should be required. In the light of these difficulties, it is not surprising that the results failed to confirm the findings of the earlier studies; there was no difference between the treatments in posttest favorableness to the opinion they advocated.

In another experiment Rosenberg (1965) suggests that the typical subject is probably concerned with the experimenter's evaluation of him and that if he were to write an essay for a lot of money it would appear that he could be bought by a bribe. This "evaluation apprehension," according to Rosenberg, would induce resistance in the subject to a change in his opinion because he was paid for writing an essay against it; the larger the reward, the greater the resistance. The hidden premise here is that the subject assumes that the experimenter is bribing him not only to write the essay but also to change his attitude. In testing this hypothesis Rosenberg used Cohen's procedure with college-student subjects at Ohio State University. The university administration had just turned down an invitation to the football team to play in the Rose Bowl and student opinion was strongly polarized against the administration. The subjects were asked to write a pro-administration essay for fifty cents, one dollar, or five dollars. Whereas in the Cohen study the request to write the essay was made by the same experimenter who took the final attitude measurement, in Rosenberg's experiment the request was made by one experimenter and the postessay attitude measure taken by another. In addition, as far as the subject could tell, the second experimenter did not know that he had been offered a bribe, this being a critical condition for eliminating evaluation apprehension. This was accomplished by convincing the subject that he was participating in two unrelated experiments. He came to the first experimenter's office only to find him temporarily occupied. The first experimenter then recalled that someone, a graduate student elsewhere in the building, had asked him for help in recruiting subjects for another experiment and encouraged the subject to participate in this other experiment until he, the first experimenter, was free. After going to the second experimenter and writing the counterattitudinal essay for differing amounts of money, the subject returned to the first experimenter's office and filled out a questionnaire containing items on a wide variety of issues—including opinions toward the administration stand on the Rose Bowl.

Turning to the results, we find that the relationship between attitude and amount of reward was direct rather than inverse as in Cohen's study; that is, the greater the reward, the more favorable the subject was to the administration. This is strong evidence for a reinforcement rather than a dissonance effect. Unfortunately, Rosenberg did not run a set of parallel conditions in which the request and attitude measurement were made by the same person. If his reasoning were correct, the results predicted by dissonance theory should obtain when evaluation apprehension is not ruled out. A puzzling fact here is that in the Festinger and Carlsmith (1959) study the measure was taken by a person other than the one making the request and there *was* an inverse relationship between favorableness of attitude and reward. Nevertheless, assuming that Rosenberg's experimental situation was similar to Cohen's in all respects except for the fact that a second experimenter took the attitude measure, the results seem to embarrass dissonance theory.

There are actually a number of other differences between the Cohen (in Brehm and Cohen, 1962) and Rosenberg (1965) experiments. A subtle but basic one is that Cohen offered the subject the money before he committed himself to write the essay and before he agreed to participate at all; in Rosenberg's experiment, the subject essentially committed himself to participating in a second, vaguely described experiment before learning how much money was involved. In the latter case the monetary reward may have acted as postdecisional reinforcement rather than as a determinant of dissonance. It is the *decision* to comply for an insufficient reward that produces the dissonance. Once the subject has committed himself to participate, any additional inducement, even a small one, would tend to sweeten the flavor of the task rather than induce a need for justification.

Two recently completed and as yet unpublished studies emphatically illustrate this point. Jones and Cooper conducted an experiment in which students were asked to write an essay in favor of a ban on "disloyal" speakers at their university. Quite understandably, they were initially very much against such a ban. Subjects were paid either $0.50 or $2.50 for writing the essay, and were either allowed to decide to write the essay, knowing the amount of money, or were told to write the essay and informed of the amount of money they would receive just at the moment they were to begin. The money was, then, either offered as part of the framework of the decision (free decision condition) or after the essay-writing task was assigned (prior commitment condition). The results (in Table 12.10)

Table 12.10. Mean Attitude toward Speaker Ban, by Condition

Incentive	Prior Commitment	Free Decision
$0.50	1.66 [a] $n = 10$	2.96 $n = 10$
$2.50	2.34 $n = 10$	1.64 $n = 10$
Control [b]		1.60 $n = 10$

[a] The higher the number, the closer the attitude to the position advocated in the essay.
[b] Subjects in this condition were simply asked to fill out the attitude measure and were not asked to write an essay.

support the prediction in showing a significant dissonance effect only in the free decision condition; in the prior commitment condition there is a contrasting reinforcement effect—the more the subject is paid to write the essay, the more he subsequently agrees with the position endorsed.

In a second unpublished experiment, Linder and Cooper attempted to replicate Rosenberg's experiment by following his procedures as closely as possible, including the separation into two allegedly unrelated experiments. The issue was that of *in loco parentis,* and the college-student subjects were asked to write an essay in favor of more stringent paternalistic supervision by the college administration. Linder and Cooper obtained essentially the same results as Rosenberg did when they followed his procedures to the letter: the more the money offered, the more the change in attitude toward the position espoused. However, in a second set of conditions a reversal of this reinforcement effect was predicted and obtained. Believing that Rosenberg's procedures pre-committed the subject before he learned how much money was involved, Linder and Cooper had the first experimenter add a comment that the subject should not feel obligated to participate in the other study but was merely to listen to what would be required and feel free to decide. The results of this study are presented in Table 12.11. They show that the dissonance effect—the greater the attitude change the smaller the incentive—appears only when the subject still feels free to choose *not* to write the essay when he hears about the amount of money involved. When the subject is in any way pre-committed

Table 12.11. Mean Attitude toward *In Loco Parentis* by Condition

Incentive	Choice Emphasized	Choice De-emphasized
$0.50	3.64 [a] $n = 10$	2.70 $n = 10$
$2.50	2.72 $n = 10$	3.46 $n = 10$
Control [b]		2.56 $n = 10$

[a] The higher the number the closer the attitude to the position advocated in the essay.
[b] Subjects in this condition were simply asked to fill out the attitude measure and were not asked to write an essay.

by the actions of the first experimenter, the money acts as a bonus and a reinforcement effect is observed.

The results of this last study raise serious doubts about the adequacy of Rosenberg's "evaluation apprehension" explanation as a way of accounting for alleged dissonance effects. Even when the essay-writing task is performed for one experimenter and the attitude is measured by another, dissonance effects can be obtained—provided that the first experimenter does not commit the subject before the latter is exposed to the nature of the task and correct information about the incentives available.

One of the many differences between the Cohen and Rosenberg procedures and the one used by Festinger and Carlsmith is that in the former the subject was asked to write an essentially anonymous essay, whereas in the latter he was asked to advocate an opinion publicly and openly in the act of convincing someone else. This public avowal would be more likely to induce dissonance than the mere writing of an essay. This may account for the lack of a dissonance effect in the Janis and Gilmore study. Following this reasoning, Carlsmith, Collins, and Helmreich (1966), using the basic Festinger and Carlsmith format, asked some subjects to role-play to convince a prospective subject that a dull task was interesting, whereas other subjects were asked to write statements that the same task was interesting. These statements might or might not be used by the experimenter in his future work. Each of these treatments was run under a fifty-cent, a one-and-a-half dollar, and a five-dollar treatment. The data in the role-playing treatment showed an inverse relationship between subsequent favorableness of attitude toward the task and size of reward (dissonance effect) whereas the relationship was direct in the essay treatment (reinforcement effect). The researchers expected to find an inverse relationship in both treatments, but a more marked one under role-playing. Why there was a positive relationship between reward and attitude change in the essay treatment is puzzling and neither we nor the authors have a ready explanation for it. It is also difficult to understand why Cohen found a dissonance effect with essay writing and Carlsmith, Collins, and Helmreich did not, though there may be more dissonance inherent in taking a stand in favor of the local police than in helping the experimenter prepare arguments about the pleasantness of a task for his future use.

This series of studies presents a confused picture and all the parts cannot be readily fitted together. One thing is clear, however: whether different reward levels are directly or inversely related to attitude change, or neither, is sensitive to the many subtleties of the procedures used. These subtleties will have to be dissected experimentally and cast within a theoretical framework large enough to house dissonance theory, concepts of secondary reinforcement, and perhaps several other theoretical positions.

The problems here are worth a great deal of further research effort and are being pursued in laboratories throughout the world. One important reason for not relinquishing the problem is that it deals with a fundamental aspect of everyday life. In the normal course of a day the typical person commits himself to acts for which he does not have unequivocal attitudinal support and thereafter presumably engages in adding further justification for his acts. The experimental paradigm used in these studies should therefore not be considered a unique situation concocted merely for laboratory purposes, but is rather one that captures the essence of much of our day-to-day behavior.

Other Forms of Prior Justification

The implication of a dissonance analysis of role-playing is that the technique will be effective to the extent that the justification for engaging in discrepant behavior is minimal. Ideally, the person should be gently coaxed and cajoled up to the point at which he is just willing to go through with taking the discrepant stand. He should be eased over the choice line with barely sufficient justification. A shotgun approach of heaping as many incentives as possible on top of one another as an inducement should be the least effective method for bringing about attitude change through role-playing.

A number of studies have manipulated incentives other than money. Using a format similar to the essay-writing study above, Cohen, Brehm, and Fleming (1958) employed two levels of justification for having subjects write essays that argued against their own private attitudes. In a high-justification treatment many incentives were heaped one on top of the other. The subject was told how much the experimenter appreciated the help he was getting from the subject, how important it was to stand back and view the other side of an issue, how helpful and willing other students had also been, and how important the results of such a study could be to social scientists. In a low-justification condition the subject was simply asked to write the essay and was assured that he did not have to comply unless he really wanted to. Everything was done to bring pressure down to a minimum, short of the point at which the subject would refuse to write the essay. The data indicate that there was less change under high than under low justification.

A similar experiment by Rabbie, Brehm, and Cohen (1959), essentially a replication of the Brehm, Cohen, and Fleming study, demonstrated fairly conclusively the negative relationship under these conditions between attitude change and justification.

Varying the Attractiveness of the Communicator

An experiment by Zimbardo, Weisenberg, Firestone, and Levy (1965), modeled after an earlier one by Smith (1961), investigated the attractiveness of the communicator as a variable affecting attitudes toward discrepant behavior induced by him. The subjects were persuaded to eat grasshoppers by an experimenter who assumed one of two attitudes. In one treatment he was completely affable, casual, and relaxed, whereas in the other treatment he was cool, stiff, and forbidding. After the subjects had eaten or refused to eat the grasshoppers, they answered a questionnaire in which they indicated how much they liked grasshoppers as a food. As we would expect from dissonance theory, the subjects who chose to eat the grasshoppers were *less* favorable toward eating grasshoppers in the "nice guy" condition than in the condition when the experimenter was forbidding. Presumably when the experimenter was nice there was extrinsic justification for eating the grasshoppers so no additional justification had to be provided, whereas where the experimenter was forbidding, the extrinsic justification was lacking so the subject provided his own justification for engaging in the behavior by increasing his liking of grasshoppers. Those subjects who chose not to eat showed the reverse effect; they were more negative toward grasshoppers in the positive communicator treatment than in the negative one. This presumably reflects a greater tendency to justify *not* complying with the communicator in the positive than in the negative communicator condition.

In an experiment similar to the one just described, Weick (1964) investigated other modes of dissonance reduction. Because the subject in a forced-compliance experiment must actually perform the task he is committed to, we would expect him not only to evaluate the task in a manner that will reduce his dissonance but also to perform the task in a manner consistent with his attitude toward it. Thus the greater the dissonance aroused by the subject's commitment to perform the task, the harder he should work at it and consequently the more successful he should be. To test this hypothesis Weick ran subjects under one of two treatments that varied the justification for commitment. In the high-justification condition the subjects received the course credit they expected for participating in the experiment, whereas in the low-justification condition the experimenter tricked them into participating for no course credit. In the latter condition the experimenter was made to appear dishonest and rather unpleasant in his manner. In the low-justification condition subjects were also given the choice as to whether or not they wanted to go through with the experiment. This factor of choice tends to confound the design, as does the factor of experimental credit, for the two treatments differ in at least three respects: whether the subject is to receive experimental credit, the degree of honesty and pleasantness of the experimenter, and whether the subject has a choice in going through with the experiment. We can expect that this will raise some problems in interpreting any difference in effects between the two treatments. The subject engaged in a concept formation task and a close, running record was kept of various indicators of effort expenditure and task accomplishment.

The results are clear and striking. Under low justification subjects work harder and perform more effectively than under high justification. It is interesting to note that subjects in the low-justification condition not only expended more effort and showed greater achievement but also found the task more pleasant. This latter effect coincides with the results in the other work we have been discussing, but it is not clear which aspect of the justification manipulation was responsible for the results. Also, we cannot tell from the data the order in which the effects occurred. In the low-justification condition, did the task become more attractive because the subject had worked harder at it or did the lack of justification produce an initially favorable attitude that then caused the subject to work harder? Perhaps both effects occurred simultaneously. Further research is obviously needed to answer these questions.

In an ingenious experiment that offers some further clarification of the issues just raised, Zimbardo (1965) varied effort expenditure in advocating a discrepant stand on the subject's subsequent attitude toward the issue involved. The subject either read or improvised a speech advocating the admission of Red China to the United Nations. All of the subjects were initially opposed, at least mildly, to Red China's admission. The delivery of the speech was interfered with by delayed auditory feedback; that is, there was a delay between the subject's verbalization and his hearing what he had said. In one condition the delay was minimal, 0.01 second, whereas in the other condition there was a considerable delay of 0.25 second. The latter condition is quite distressing for anyone and forced the subject to work hard at delivering the speech. The results are what we would expect from dissonance theory. Subjects in the long-delay treatment showed more attitude change in favor of admitting Red China to the United Nations than subjects in the short-delay condition, this being true both of subjects who improvised a speech and of those who merely read the speech. These results are reminiscent of the Aronson (1961) fishing experiment described in Chapter Three in which the subject liked the color of the container to the extent that he had worked hard to get it.

Coercion as an Incentive

So far we have been considering the relationship between attitude change and the size of a positive incentive to engage in discrepant behavior. Clearly, if an action-sequence–dissonance analysis of role-playing is tenable, we would expect threats of punishment to act in much the same way as positive incentives. To the extent that a subject engages in some discrepant behavior to avoid punishment, he requires no additional justification to support his having engaged in the behavior. This implies that the smaller the threat for not engaging in the discrepant behavior, the greater will be the subject's attempt to support his behavior by other means, including attitude change.

An experiment by Brehm (in Brehm and Cohen, 1962) used two levels of threat by a fraternity member to get the subjects, who were pledges in that fraternity, to copy random numbers for three hours. In the low-threat condition the pledge was threatened with a paddling if he refused to cooperate, whereas in the high-threat condition he was threatened with being called before a fraternity tribunal and possibly being expelled from the fraternity. The subject then engaged in the task and his attitude toward the task was measured after it was completed. The subject in the high-threat condition showed a less favorable attitude toward the task than the subject in the low-threat condition. There are other interpretations to this finding, such as the obvious one that anything connected with the dire threat of possibly being expelled from the fraternity would be evaluated negatively, but the finding is also consistent with a dissonance interpretation.

Reactance

It is possible for coercion to boomerang. Brehm and Cole (1966) postulate that when a subject's freedom to act is restricted, he will *react* by attempting to regain his freedom. This "psychological reactance" is a motivational state that will be aroused to the extent that the person's freedom is restricted and to the extent that the behavior involved is important to him; that is, to the extent that it is important for him to be free to make a choice. Reactance can manifest itself in a variety of ways. The person may attempt physically to remove the barrier to behavior; he may derogate the restricting agent; or he may actually enhance the outcome value of the act he is unable to engage in relative to those that are still open to him.

In order to test these ideas Brehm and Cole designed an experiment in which there was a subtle restriction of the subject's freedom to act under conditions of either high or low importance. The experiment called for two subjects to appear together, but one was actually an accomplice of the experimenter. After the two had arrived, they were asked to sit in the hall while the experimenter prepared the necessary materials in the experimental room. The accomplice asked for permission to leave for a few minutes. In the "favor" conditions he returned shortly with a single Coke which he gave to the subject, refusing to accept any money. In the "no-favor" conditions the accomplice simply came back and seated himself by the subject.

When the subjects were admitted to the experimental room, they were asked to engage in a first-impression study—each subject was to be evaluated by the other after each responded orally to three special questions. The importance of this task was varied by telling some of the subjects (high-importance condition) that the impression ratings were being collected for Professor Terrell who had just received a large grant from the National Science Foundation. The first-impression "test" was described as very important to Dr. Terrell, and the experimenter expressed the hope that each subject would take great pains to be as accurate as possible in her assessment ratings of the other. It was also made clear that the ratings were to be based solely on the other subject's answers to the three special questions. Subjects in the low-importance condition were informed that the impression ratings would be examined by an undergraduate sociology student for a class project; importance of accuracy was not stressed.

After the ratings were made and collected, the experimenter picked up a stack of typing paper, placed it in front of the accomplice and looking at him said, "Will one of you stack these papers into 10 piles of five for me please?" The accomplice started stacking the papers and the experimenter noted when the subject started to help, if he helped at all. This served as the main dependent measure in the experiment and was an index of the subject's tendency to return the favor.

From reactance theory Brehm and Cole predicted that subjects in the high-importance–favor condition would be suffering the most from feelings that their freedom had been restricted. It was assumed that these subjects would be inclined to react against the favor which threatened to interfere with their rating objectivity. The specific prediction, therefore, was that fewer subjects in the high-importance–favor condition would return the favor than in the low-importance–favor condition. Subjects in the no-favor conditions should be intermediate on this measure, having received no favor to return. The results on this measure, simply in terms of the number of subjects who helped the accomplice stack papers, are presented

Table 12.12. Number of Subjects Who Helped the Accomplice Stack Papers (From Brehm and Cole, 1966)

	Low Importance	High Importance
No favor		
Helped	9	7
Did not	6	8
Favor		
Helped	14	2
Did not	1	13

in Table 12.12. It is quite clear that they strongly confirm the reactance theory prediction. The subjects' ratings of the accomplice after the first-impression procedure did not show any systematic effects of favor or importance. Brehm and Cole attribute this to the subjects' concern with following instructions to be objective and to ignore information other than that revealed in answer to the three questions. By comparison, "the stacking of papers apparently had nothing to do with the rating task (or any formal aspect of research) and therefore more clearly revealed the subjects' true motivational state in regard to the confederate" (Brehm and Cole, 1966, 425–426).

A number of additional studies have been conducted by Brehm and his students to explore the reactions of persons when their freedom is in some way restricted. In the main, these studies show that restricted alternatives become more attractive to the extent that the process of restriction is seen as genuinely lowering the subject's freedom. These studies are described in Brehm (1966). They tell us much about the conditions under which attempts to control behavior can result in a boomerang effect.

SUMMARY

In this chapter we have attempted to review the literature on attitude change and to cast relevant findings into the attitude framework presented in Chapter Five. The data reviewed were organized into three main sections: the characteristics of the communicator, the nature of the message, and the condition of the audience. In analyzing the characteristics of the communicator we examined a number of factors that affect the credibility the audience attaches to the communicator's message. Credibility is a function of both expertise and co-orientation. While most previous studies have confounded these factors by emphasizing both in one condition and removing both in another, expertise has received more research attention to this point and is clearly an important determinant of accepting persuasive communications when matters of belief are involved. The co-orientation of the communicator is more important when the problem is to bring about a change in values.

Various characteristics of the message itself have been studied. We examined the evidence regarding the effects of the organization of the message on its impact, such as whether presenting one or both sides of the issue is more effective and whether, if the communicator presents both sides, he should present *his* side first or second. Evidence for primacy and recency effects was discussed. We also considered the evidence relating to whether the communicator should state his conclusion explicitly or frame his message in such a manner that the conclusion is apparent but the members of the audience are left to frame it for themselves. Here, as in a number of areas, there are conflicting results, but generally it is more effective to draw the conclusion.

We next considered the work done on the manipulation of values as a technique for changing attitudes. We reviewed some of the work carried out within the classical conditioning framework and saw that attitudes could indeed be changed by transferring value from one stimulus to another. We also saw that there was apparently no direct relationship between the intensity of an appeal to values and the effectiveness of a message. This was true at least for fear appeals which can easily lead to avoidance of the recommendation designed to reduce fear.

We next considered aspects of the audience's reaction before and during the message. The first set of studies dealt with the effect of forewarning the audience as to the nature of the message to which it would be exposed. The research here stumbled onto some interesting distinctions that must be made between forewarning and distraction. Forewarning may, at times, diminish the effect of the message, whereas distraction increases its effect.

We next considered the effect of the audience's point of view on how the speaker's message is perceived. Obviously, if the message is to have its effect it must be perceived correctly. In reviewing this literature we discovered a tendency for a person to assimilate a message that is close to his point of view so that he perceives it as closer than it actually is, and for him to contrast a message that departs from his point of view so that it seems more discrepant to him than it actually is. We discussed the transformation of these terms borrowed from the psychophysical laboratory into the concepts of latitude of acceptance and latitude of rejection and reviewed a study based on these concepts.

We then considered the problem of inoculation against messages countering firmly held beliefs. Here we viewed the measures that might be taken to immunize a person effectively against arguments threatening his attitudes. We examined a number of studies in which supportive and refutational defense inoculations were tried and found that in general refutational defenses were more effective. Active versus passive combinations of defenses were also evaluated in some of the experiments described.

A consideration of active participation led us into the literature that began with an attempt to answer questions about the efficacy of role-playing as an attitude change technique. Studies were reviewed in which such factors as voluntariness in taking the role and incentives for taking it were found to be related to attitude change. Here we discovered the dissonance analysis of the role-playing situation to be especially helpful in understanding the nature of the underlying process, though a full understanding of the processes of reacting to persuasive communications obviously will require the insights generated by a variety of theoretical perspectives.

CHAPTER THIRTEEN

Dyadic Interaction: a Conceptual Framework

The purpose of this chapter is to consider some useful ways of talking about influence processes as they occur in the give-and-take of live social interactions. The studies of attitude change and of responses to the conformity conflict are among the most dramatic instances of social influence; but what of the more casual social encounter in which influence is continuous and subtle in its operation? Take, for example, a conversation between two persons. This is a complex sequential event that cannot be adequately analyzed in terms of the concepts introduced thus far. A conceptual framework that deals with *contingencies* among responses is called for.

A conversation is many things. It is an exchange of information. It is a stimulant of laughter, anger, or affection. It is a context in which we test our ideas and learn about our impact on others. We convey and perceive normative expectations in conversations. And so on. We normally think of a conversation in terms of what was said, in terms of its meaning. There is no reason in principle why we could not classify conversations in terms of their content: what kinds of things were said and what might have been their implications for the participants. But it is also possible to put aside questions about content and start our analysis by framing a different question: in a given social interchange, *how much* was the behavior of one person affected by the other and vice versa? Speaking loosely, this is akin to asking how social the social interchange was. Speaking more technically and precisely, we may ask what proportion of a given social response (or a collection of them) was contingent on preceding responses of the other person.

AN ABSTRACT VIEW OF INTERACTION CONTINGENCIES

Dyadic interaction commences when two persons begin to behave in each other's presence. Each comes into the situation with certain goals in mind, certain cognitions about how these goals may be achieved, and a pattern of attitudes about the situation and the other person. Thus the person approaches the interaction with a set of motivationally relevant *plans* that serve to launch his end of the conversation. These plans may themselves try to take into account the probable responses of the other, or they may be less elaborate in specifying alternative contingencies. Although normally these plans are vague and implicit, and often incidental to the actual interchange that follows, a plan tends to become quite prominent in awareness when important goals are at stake—a raise or promotion, use of the family car, membership in a fraternity.

Once the conversation begins, social contingency is immediately present. To some extent, thereafter, the next response of person A will be contingent on the last response of person B. B's next response will in turn be determined by the preceding A response, and so it goes. The plans of each actor continue, however, to exert some influence on the unfolding responses, so that person A in effect responds to his own last response as well as to the last response of B. The response is thus jointly determined by self-produced and socially produced stimulation. Even if we assume that no other events are occurring while the two persons converse—that no "alien" events enter the system—our contingency model seems sufficiently burdened with great complexity. Matters are further complicated when we concede that plans often change as the conversational sequence unfolds. In addition, we have no effective ways of analyzing or measuring plans or separating self-produced from social stimulation in determining the magnitude and patterning of social contingency.

But this way of looking at social versus internal determinants is helpful in classifying types of interaction. Continuing our concern with the degree to which social interactions involve true social influence, and ignoring the content and mechanisms of influence, we can in principle identify four rather interesting classes of interactions that vary in the pattern of weights to be attached to self-produced versus social stimulation. Schematic representations of these four classes may be seen in Figure 13.1. Persons A and B are partners to the interaction, which flows through a series of responses over time from the top to the bottom of the diagram. The solid arrows reflect the predominant source of influence or response determination, the dotted arrows reflect the less important or more minor source. Both the diagram and the discussion assume that other events stay constant during the interaction.

Pseudocontingency

This might be described as the limiting case of social interaction; it appears that a contingency exists between A and B, but in fact social stimuli are only minimally involved. Each individual's responses are thus largely determined by his pre-established plan, but a semblance of interaction is

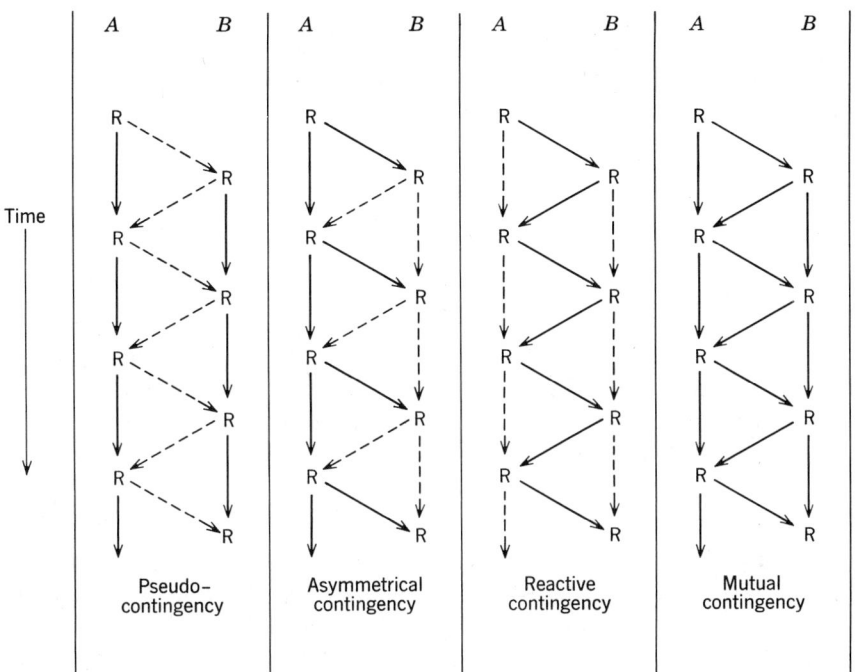

Figure 13.1. *Classes of social interaction in terms of contingency.*

maintained in that responses are alternated and the timing of the alternation requires that each read certain signs emitted by the other. A further distinction within this class may ultimately prove useful. The plan of each may encompass the plan of the other. In this case the person may know the other person's behavioral plan and be able to predict with some precision the exact content and sequence of his responses. Alternatively, pseudo-contingency may arise out of total ignorance of the other's plan and A attends to B's responses merely to time his own next entrance into the conversation.

Perhaps the prototype of the first kind of pseudocontingency is two actors running through a well-rehearsed episode in a play. At least to the extent that the other's part has been memorized along with his own, each actor's plan comprehends the other and the course of interaction is preordained. Certain ritual performances similarly involve a relative lack of social contingency; coronations, weddings, and inaugurals, for example, are socially significant playlets in which each person's part is supposedly known before the "interaction" begins. Although we might argue that well-rehearsed plays and rituals are rather incidental and unimportant examples of social behavior, we have only to stretch the notion of ritual into that of social role to make the pseudocontingency class much more interesting and significant. Role-determined behavior differs from ritual behavior in the degree to which minute details of behavior are specified. Yet there are many role-based interchanges in which the general plan involved in each role meshes with the general plan involved in the other role, with the result that self-produced stimulation (i.e., plans based on things learned during socialization) clearly encompasses or predominates over social stimulation. The waitress and the customer, the guest thanking his host, the doctor and the patient, the young man and his date's father interact in ways that partake of some of the features of pseudocontingency.

The second kind of pseudocontingency may exist when one person's plan does not encompass or allow for the other's, but merely ignores it. We are all too often exposed to debates or arguments in which the antagonists make little effort to answer each other's claims. Thus one debater merely waits anxiously for the other to finish a point before jumping in to make the point *he* was planning to make anyway. The disjunction is often smoothed over with a veneer of courtesy but a listener doubts whether, in such cases, either could reproduce later much of what the other had said. Pseudocontingent conversations may sometimes be observed between psychotic patients, and between children who are more concerned with the amenities of conversation than its substance. In both cases an observer may note that the form and style of conversation (the give-and-take, the encouraging nods, the attentive look) are preserved but the words of one seem to bear little relation to the following words of the other.

Another interesting case of pseudocontingency shows that this class of interaction requires the capacity to learn, perhaps, but not necessarily the capacity to develop cultural roles. In the early 1950s, B. F. Skinner and his students trained pairs of pigeons to play a form of ping-pong by first training each pigeon individually to peck at a ping-pong ball to obtain food. In the actual game each pigeon was placed at the base of an inclined plane. The planes were joined at the top so that the birds could look up to the joint but could not see each other. Each "point" was begun when a ball was released where the planes were joined and allowed to roll toward one or the other pigeon. True to his training, the pigeon would peck at the ball and thus send it over the top onto the comparable plane facing the other pigeon. The other pigeon—true to *his* training—would send it back and the game would be on. These responses could be maintained by reinforcing the ball-pecking response by delivering occasional food pellets to a cup near each pigeon. An observer watching such a performance is amused because, although neither pigeon is really responding to the other, the two are executing individually learned "plans" having social implications and the illusion of social interaction is maintained.

Asymmetrical Contingency

In this class of interaction the responses of one person are largely determined by self-produced stimuli or plans, whereas the responses of the other are largely determined by social stimuli produced by the first. At first glance it might appear that this class of interactions has clear implications for the differential social power of the actors, because only one of them is "influenced" by the other. But this is not necessarily the case. The standard responder, the actor whose responses are largely plan-determined, might be an autocratic master whose responses unfold from a plan he himself concocted. Insofar as the variable responder is affected by the autocrat's responses, he clearly enjoys less power than the standard responder. But the standard responder might be acting on a plan imposed upon him by another agency or person. Here the balance of power is not so clearly determined. The standard responder might be an interviewer trained to ask certain questions in a certain sequence. The person being interviewed is affected by these questions in that he tries to answer them, and thus his behavior is more contingent on the interviewer's than vice versa. Or the standard responder might be an encyclopedia salesman who follows the salesman's manual to the letter in dealing with a prospect who tries to wriggle from his grasp while very much affected by his behavior.

An example from the animal realm points up the possible relationship between asymmetrical contingency and imitation. As Skinner (1953) reports, two pigeons may be trained to engage in rather complex behavior in which one leads and the other follows. Separated only by a glass partition, each pigeon confronts a panel containing three buttons in a vertical column. The apparatus is so designed that both pigeons must peck corresponding buttons simultaneously for either to obtain a food reward, and the pair of corresponding buttons that will produce food changes randomly from trial to trial. Gradually one pigeon, the "follower," begins to adapt his pecking to that of the other pigeon, the "leader." Thus "the behavior of the follower is controlled almost exclusively by the behavior of the leader, whose behavior in turn is controlled by the apparatus which randomizes the reinforcements among the three pairs of buttons" (p. 306). The function of leading may shift from one bird to another over a period of time, but tends to remain stable for identifiable periods. In this example an asymmetry of contingency arises out of the nature of the situation. The follower cannot affect the leader—even though his cooperation is essential to the leader's receipt of food—without in effect changing roles with him.

Most of the examples of asymmetrical contingency that come to mind, however, involve cases in which one person is in a better position to work out a plan of his own devising and the other must adapt his behavior in part to the first. Thus the standard responder has greater freedom to maintain his own prepared behavior than the variable responder, who is enmeshed willy nilly in the other's plan. This is often the road to victory in competitive sports, of course, in which such comments as "He forced him to play his kind of game" are often heard. It is also the "secret" weapon, apparently, of those occasional persons whose own rigidities force others to adapt to *them*.

Reactive Contingency

It is at least logically possible that interaction could occur in a sequence in which each actor's response is almost entirely contingent on the preceding response of the other. This would imply the absence of internal plans or at least their abandonment once the interaction begins. Paradoxically, each actor does exert some influence over his own next response through the response he evokes in the other. Thus, if A's response a largely determines the nature of B's response b, b largely determines $a + 1$, and $a + 1$ largely determines $b + 1$, there is a sense in which each actor exerts a secondary influence on his own subsequent responses through his previous responses.

In the normal course of human, adult interactions it is difficult to develop anything like pure examples of this logical extreme. We begin to see what reactive contingency might involve when we think of two novices playing a game of chess. In the early stages of learning the game a player whose knowledge is limited to the ground rules and the values of the pieces typically plays in a reactive, impulsive manner. Two such players without plans or strategies can respond only to the immediate debacle into which each has been forced by the other's preceding move.

Because reactive contingency places no demands on either memory or foresight, and because it seems to involve little more than a series of reflex reactions strung together over time, we might expect this class of interactions to be more common in animals and children than in socialized adults. Nevertheless, there seem to be conditions that push adults in the direction of reactive contingency and tend to disrupt their best-laid plans of interaction. An intriguing example of such a condition is perhaps a theater fire or other disasters that can lead to panic. Mintz (1951) conducted a series of demonstration experiments designed to reveal some of the major determinants of "nonadaptive group behavior." The subjects participated in the experiment in pairs; each was to remove a separate cone from the same bottle by pulling a string attached to the cone's apex. A situation analogous to that involved in a theater fire was created in view of the fact that only one of the two cones in the bottle could squeeze through its neck at one time. Near the bottom of the bottle was an opening through which water could flow into the bottle. When subject pairs were instructed to get their cones out of the bottle before they were touched by water, or merely told that they would be financially rewarded if the cones were pulled out before certain designated time limits, traffic jams characteristically developed so that each pair member interfered with the other's chances to avoid the water or to be rewarded for success. If one subject had permitted the other to remove his cone without a contest for priority, both could easily have escaped without a traffic jam developing. Here would seem to be a case, then, where reactive contingency—impulsive and essentially planless socially determined behavior—characterizes the interaction taking place. Indeed, when subjects were given a chance to discuss the problem before the experiment, the frequency and severity of traffic jams were reduced (though not entirely eliminated). Such discussions presumably let the subjects develop plans that would inhibit reactive contingency.

A similar conclusion may be drawn from a more recent series of experiments by Kelley, Condry, Dahlke, and Hill (1965). These investigators used an electronic switching device as a sophisticated replacement for cones in a bottle. If two subjects pushed their switches "on" at the same time, neither could "escape." An escape was only possible if the subject was the sole occupant of the escape route (the only one with his "on" switch pushed) for a three-second interval. Subjects were led to believe that if they did not achieve an escape within a certain unspecified time, they would receive a powerful electric shock.

Mintz had argued that fear was not a crucial variable and that the incoordination and jamming up was the result of reasonable reactions to the reward structure of the situation. When a few subjects conflict in trying to escape, others will perceive that their best interests lie in trying to escape as soon as possible. Kelley's results, showing more traffic jams under high-fear conditions, speak against Mintz's conclusion. What is more relevant in the present context is that traffic jams are reduced by any circumstance that permits the coordination of individual plans. In a condition when subjects were given a signal switch to indicate their willingness to wait for the others to escape, the percentage of escapees was high.

Mutual Contingency

The major class of remaining interactions is that in which each response is partially determined by the preceding responses of the other and partly by the individual's own planned or internal stimulation. Interactions in this mutual contingency class thus require that a plan govern the responses of each actor, but the plan becomes continually recast in the light of the other's responses. As far as we can judge, it is this class that is most commonly referred to under the general term interaction in the social psychology literature. It has often been stressed that interaction involves a mutual responsiveness, in which each person's responses become stimuli for the other; the fact that interaction also involves a persistence of self-regulated ongoing responses has been less clearly emphasized. For this reason we believe it is helpful to view the case of true mutual contingency in comparison with the other forms that interaction can take, and thus recognize explicitly the jointly determined nature of any response in a conversational sequence. As Allport (1924) noted many years ago, conversation "involves the opposed efforts of two persons for expansion and control through language, each being only partly successful" (p. 288).

Examples of mutual contingency are numerous and varied. Political antagonists reaching a compromise, bridge experts bidding toward a grand slam, two articulate friends discussing a common experience, lovers moving toward a passionate disagreement that neither initially anticipated or desired, all seem to qualify as examples of the class. An essential attribute of mutually contingent interactions seems to be that each actor both contributes to and takes something from the exchange. The interaction might be a triumph of social creativity in which each is enriched by the other, or it might be a spiraling debacle of increasingly mutual hostility from which neither benefits. Whatever the content of the interaction's course, there is implied a mixture of dual resistance and mutual change that distinguishes mutual contingency from other classes of interaction.

Implications of Variations in Contingency

It is important at this point to review the preceding remarks on contingency and clarify their implications. First let us make clear what the preceding classification scheme was *not* designed to, and therefore did not, accomplish. Armed with our four classes of interaction, we are in no better position than before to predict the course of any given interaction, or even to determine precisely, after the fact, how much contingency was involved. We have made no statements about the settings in which we are more likely to find conversations taking the form of, say, mutual rather than asymmetrical contingency. We have deliberately ignored *what* is said and have tried to avoid considering the psychological mechanisms whereby contingencies develop and operate. Although it is easy to slip into the view that mutual contingency is somehow more beneficial than asymmetrical contingency, that it is more "democratic" and jointly enriching, we have refrained from this kind of value judgment. It is difficult if not impossible to evaluate the personal consequences of an interaction solely on the basis of the amount and distribution of interpersonal influence.

On the other hand we *have*, it is hoped, provoked some reflection on the range of phenomena that are often lumped under the heading of social interaction. It is important to recognize that some interactions involve little more than the running off of complementary roles or individual plans. At the other extreme there are interactions that reflect a kind of primitive, planless, reactivity. The intersection and joint modification of individual communicative plans are featured in mutual contingency, and it is here that we can begin to appreciate the complexity of partial give-and-take in the dyad when behavior is neither exclusively governed by roles nor totally "captured" by incoming social stimulation. The class of asymmetrical interaction represents a special case wherein one actor is able to execute his communicative plan while the other reacts primarily to the acts of the first. In sum, by thus crudely mapping the terrain of social interaction in contingency terms, we have brought to the forefront the interweaving roles of self-stimulation and social stimulation in dyadic interaction.

The classification might thus be viewed as reflecting different patterns or blends of individual autonomy and social dependence. Is there a relationship between this classification scheme and the functional processes discussed in previous chapters? For example, can we derive any implications for the relative frequency of interaction classes from our unequivocal behavior principle (UBO)? Is it possible that the class of reactive contingency is less stable, for example, than mutual contingency, and that those interactions that begin as merely reactive tend to move in the mutual direction? Do mutually contingent interactions become reactive under stress? In general, what might be the conditions in a given relationship that affect movement from one class of interaction to another? Can we extract anything of interest from looking at contingency variations from the standpoint of the antinomy between self-persistence and openness to change?

Although a few answers to such questions can be tentatively suggested on intuitive grounds, we are not as yet in a strong position to provide them. The contingency analysis has perhaps taken us to the threshold of certain psychological insights, but we can go no further without considering the underlying processes of social influence in the dyadic interchange. In effect, our diagram contains arrows that represent stimulation or response-determining input. We need to take a closer look at what these arrows stand for, at the psychological processes they represent.

MODES OF SOCIAL INFLUENCE IN THE DYAD: OUTCOME CONTROL AND CUE CONTROL

The diagram in Figure 13.1 highlights two features of social interaction between two persons: (1) the responses of one person become part of the stimulus environment of the other, and (2) the impact of this environment on the other person's responses has important variations. Having seen some of the variations in amount and patterning of contingency, we now examine the major ways in which one person's responses become stimuli for another.

We shall see that the basic distinction between informational influence and effect influence continues to have applications here.

Our primary problem is to explain why a person would modify his on-going actions to take account of the acts of another. A most general, but not very helpful, explanation might be that he changes his behavior to fit an altered outcome expectancy. Something about the other's act redefines the routes to goal attainment, or substitutes new goals that must be satisfied. Such a conclusion makes sense only if we recognize that the induced change in outcome expectancy may be subtle, trivial, or temporary. If A is about to make a conversational point, and B says, "Excuse me, but what time is it?", A's behavior will normally be altered to complete this intruding sequence by looking at his watch and answering B's question. He may then continue with his remarks, though it is conceivable that he will start off on a new tack. But has this trivial question changed A's outcome expectancy? It would seem so, because the request for the time ties into norms of courtesy and *not* to answer immediately would affront B, possibly leading him to "punish" A with a pained frown or to leave the room in search of a clock.

It might be argued that A's response to B's request was purely reflexive, having nothing to do with outcomes—at least in A's mind. By his request, in other words, B merely touched off a highly overlearned response sequence that went into operation without affecting the outcome expectancies of A. Undoubtedly, these alternative explanations shade into each other at some point and it is extremely difficult to maintain a clear separation between episodes in which behavior changes because the path to goal attainment is affected and episodes in which behavior is elicited by some adequate stimulus. The problem of distinguishing between these alternatives may be seen more clearly, perhaps, in animal learning. Let us imagine that for some reason, someone wants to train a pigeon to shakes its head four times when a yellow light goes on. We know that this may be accomplished by reinforcing the bird (providing a food pellet) when he turns his head, and gradually shifting the process to reinforce only two, then three, and finally four head turns. It is clear that the successful trainer has modified the pigeon's outcome expectancies so that food has become contingent on four head turns. Loosely speaking, the pigeon shakes his head *in order to* get fed; the trainer has acquired some control over the pigeon's behavior by manipulating outcome contingencies. He may then complicate life for the pigeon by feeding him after four head shakes only when a yellow light is on. If the sequence light–head-shaking–food is maintained long enough, the pigeon's head-shaking response will easily be triggered by the onset of a yellow light.

Now assume that this response to the light stimulus becomes highly overlearned, and the pigeon never hesitates to shake his head four times when a yellow light goes on. The original trainer, or anyone else, can now elicit fourfold head-shaking by turning on the yellow light, regardless of the provision of the reinforcing food pellet. This may continue for a great number of trials before the bird gradually extinguishes. Until the extinction does take place, anyone with information about the light–head-shake contingency, and with access to the switch illuminating the yellow light, presumably has a kind of control over the pigeon.

In human interaction it is also possible to identify, at least in principle, these two kinds of control. Let us call them *outcome control* and *cue control* to distinguish between the direct manipulation of rewards and punishments and the provision of information that gears into pre-established environment-behavior contingencies. Outcome control seems to be the necessary precursor to cue control, except for those cases in which innate reflexive behavior is elicited by appropriate stimulation. Presumably, however, such innate contingencies between stimuli and reactions do not play an important role in human social behavior. Although outcome control seems to underlie cue control in most cases, the former requires some command over reinforcement resources, whereas the latter requires appropriate information and the ability to put it to use. Let us now turn to a more detailed examination of each form of interpersonal control.

Outcome Control in Social Interaction

Most behavior theories or learning theories make heavy use of the concept of reinforcement. Although considerable controversy exists about how reinforcement operates, there is substantial agreement on how the term should be defined. The basic feature of most definitions (e.g., Kimble, 1961) is that a reinforcing event is one that increases the likelihood that the response immediately preceding it will recur when the same setting presents itself again. This complicated phrasing breaks down into simpler components when we think of the typical conditioning experiment. An organism makes a response to a stimulus, which is then immediately followed by another stimulus. If the tendency to respond to the first stimulus is strengthened by this sequence (i.e., if the organism is more likely to make the same response the next time the stimulus occurs than it was initially), we conclude that the second stimulus must have had some reinforcing properties. We do not have to insist that all learning requires reinforcement—to do so would enter us on one side of a continuing debate in the learning field—but it seems undeniable that reinforcement (reward or punishment) is an important condition for learning and performance in many life settings. Our problem is to put the reinforcement concept to work in so complex a setting as human social interaction.

Thibaut and Kelley (1959) have developed a useful framework for doing precisely this. In essence, their approach is to assume that each member of a dyad comes to the interaction setting with a repertoire of responses that he might conceivably make. These repertoires intersect in such a way that each member attains different outcomes depending both on what he does and what the other person does. Thus to be effective in the interaction—to maximize, or optimize his outcomes—the individual must take into account not only the various costs involved in making the different responses in his repertoire, but also the likely consequences of his responses for the other person. Each person, in effect, plays a game with the other. He tries to produce the response that will cost him the least or yield him the greatest pleasure, while trying to get the best outcomes available from the other.

In order to express the game-like features of social interaction, Thibaut and Kelley make extensive use of the kinds of matrices used by economists to explicate the theory of games, though it is not necessary to understand the mathematics of game theory in following the main lines of Thibaut and Kelley's reasoning. An elementary account of game theory is presented in Chapter Fourteen. As an introduction to "matrix" reasoning, consider the two-person response matrix in Figure 13.2. The letters at the head of each column refer to the various responses in person A's repertoire. These are acts of which A is capable and which he might conceivably perform in one situation or another. The letters at the left of each row represent the similar but never identical acts that B has in his repertoire of responses.

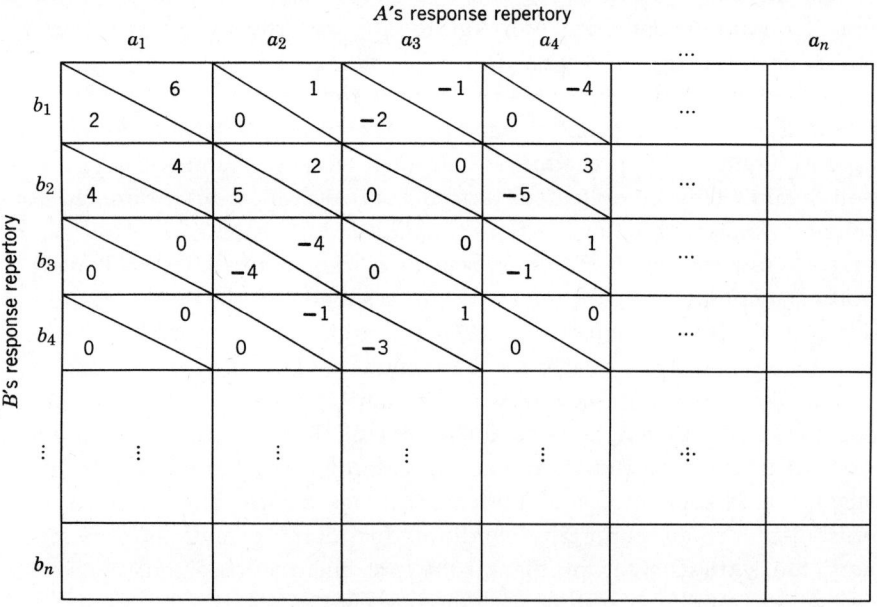

Figure 13.2. Matrix of act combinations, indicating goodness of outcome values for selected pairs (adapted from Thibaut and Kelley, 1959, Table 2-2, p. 15).

By definition, any interaction between persons A and B must involve an exchange of a column act and a row act; that is, an act of A and an act of B occur close to each other in time, and a sequence of these "close occurrences" constitutes the interaction. When two acts occur in close proximity there are presumably consequences for each actor. First of all, each actor must bear the costs of his own act—an act requires some expenditure of energy, some anticipated risks, some anxiety over its effects, some giving up of the possible fruits of other acts at the time, and so on. Second, one person's act has positive, neutral, or negative consequences for the other person. In various ways the act helps or hinders the other person in attaining his goals in the situation. Finally, A is at least indirectly affected by the consequences his own acts have for B: if A hurts B with a glance or a remark, B is usually free to respond in kind.

The consequences of paired or contingent acts are represented in the matrix by sets of plus or minus numbers. Each cell stands for an intersection between an act of A and an act of B. The consequences of this pairing of acts for A are summarized in a number above the diagonal in that cell; the consequences for B are summarized in a number below the diagonal. Where do these consequences come from and how may numbers be assigned? Let us assume that when two people exchange responses both costs and rewards are involved. Every response incurs some degree of cost for the person who makes it. This is easy to see in examples in which the response involves giving money or physical help, but there are also the more psychological costs associated with intellectual effort or emotional arousal. Theoretically, even a transient smile involves some cost even though it may be so minimal as to be a trivial consideration. Once the response is produced, it typically creates certain effects on the other person and on the actor himself. The interaction matrix selects for attention the relative goodness or badness of these effects. Thus, when two persons make responses in close temporal proximity, each response incurs some cost to the actor and provides some value of reward or punishment to the other. If, in the actor's mind, the rewards received match in value (justify) the costs incurred, we may assign a zero to the cell representing the response intersection. If the rewards are greater than normally expected, given the costs incurred, a plus value may be assigned; if less, a minus value. The numbers themselves are arbitrary and may be taken to reflect the relative extent to which the reward-cost balance is positive or negative for a given response combination.

We may call the resulting number the *goodness of outcome* value, remembering that it summarizes both the costs incurred and the rewards and punishments received. The goodness of outcome value in a given cell may be the value of an actually experienced outcome, or may represent the actor's estimate or prediction of the most likely outcome. It will usually be clear from the context of the discussion whether actual or estimated outcomes are involved. As we shall see, the actor may try to predict or take account of the other's various outcomes in order to estimate more accurately the cell in which his own responses will land him. There are obvious cases, such as that of an employer deciding on a change in the piece rate, when one actor has a fairly clear idea of the relative outcome value that the other will receive from his actions. The actor's most direct and ultimate concern, however, is with his own actual or expected outcomes. The model is ruthlessly self-centered, then, though it is possible to represent self-administered rewards that accrue to one person for helping another.

Returning to our own basic assumption that the individual acts to maximize the goodness of his outcomes, or makes the response that is associated with the best outcome expectancy, we would expect both A and B to attempt to move into those cells having the highest positive value. Given the abstract matrix in Figure 13.2, A would like to end up in cell a_1b_1 and B would like to end up in cell a_2b_2. Because both A and B cannot maximize their outcomes in this way at the same time (a relationship cannot be in two cells at once) the relationship either has to move toward some kind of alternation between response pairs or perhaps to a stable compromise (such as cell a_1b_2 in the diagram). But this excursion into the implications of various matrix patterns moves us ahead of the story. Suffice it to say that it is possible to predict an individual's responses by studying the matrix as he probably perceives it and following the assumption that the individual will try to obtain his best outcomes. In cases when each actor knows something about the distribution of outcomes available to the other actor in the relationship, predictions of behavior should be based on the more complex assumption that an individual will attempt to obtain the best outcomes *under the circumstances created by the other's most likely behavior.*

Figure 13.2 may be viewed as an abstract model of two interacting response repertories. The model brings out the fact that any response in one person's repertory can theoretically be made in conjunction with any response in the other person's repertory. However, we are rescued from the horrors of having to work with total repertories by the fact that in any given behavior setting only a limited number of responses have any likelihood of occurring. Thus the interaction context delimits the number of potential acts that need to be considered by the members of the dyad. At any given time only a portion of each actor's repertory is, in effect, "available" to him.

Examples of Mutual Outcome Control

It may be useful to consider three simplified, concrete examples of how the interaction matrix might characterize social interactions. In the first example (Figure 13.3a) we consider two children involved in a bartering

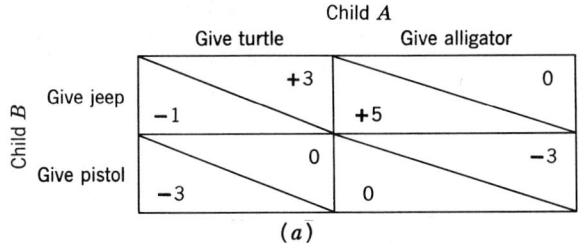

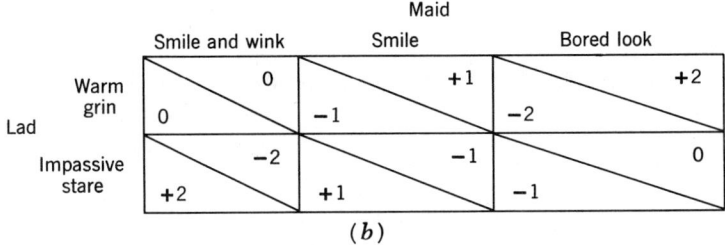

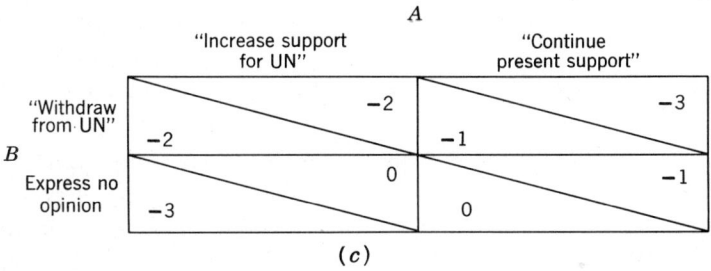

Figure 13.3. Three simplified examples of social interaction. (a) Setting: "exchange" between two children; (b) Setting: a handsome lad and a pretty maid have just been introduced; (c) Setting: two acquaintances exchange opinions on United Nations (A favors UN, B opposes it).

relationship. One child (A) has a small turtle and a baby alligator; the other (B) has a toy plastic jeep and a cap pistol. The children enter the interaction situation motivated to carry out some form of exchange. A likes the alligator better than the turtle and views the former as more valuable; so does B. B would rather keep the cap pistol than the jeep, whereas A would rather have the jeep than the cap pistol. The matrix tries to represent the situation by assigning values to each cell that are arbitrary but in general keeping with the hypothetical preferences described. As these values show, it is obvious that the pistol will not change hands because Child A does not particularly want it and Child B wants to keep it. The only question is whether A views the jeep as sufficiently attractive to be willing to part with his alligator to get it. The top row of Figure 13.3a presents values from which we would predict a final exchange of jeep and alligator. The matrix has been used here to predict where an interchange will eventually end up and not to predict a particular single response. A and B may haggle and threaten withdrawal from the relationship at many points, but the outcome values show that A considers the jeep a fair exchange for the alligator (indicated by the 0 in his half of the cell) and B is likely to be persistent in trying to secure the alligator instead of the turtle: the cost of B's giving up the jeep is not quite compensated by the reward of the turtle (-1), whereas the alligator is clearly more desirable in his eyes than the jeep.

In the second example (Figure 13.3b) the matrix tries to capture a fleeting moment during the first meeting of a "handsome lad" and a "pretty maid." First of all, we note that the boy's available responses are slightly different from the girl's though the setting makes similar responses relevant to each. The fact that two zeroes appear in the upper left-hand cell indicates that both members of this particular dyad would consider this to be a fair exchange. From the lad's point of view, the maid's smile and wink are adequate repayment for the costs incurred in grinning warmly. These costs are probably less a matter of physical energy expended in the grinning process than of the anxiety involved in sticking one's neck out. The warm grin presumably commits the lad to the relationship more than the impassive stare, and this would explain why it is especially devastating for the lad to receive a bored look after grinning (-2). Correspondingly, a smile and a wink is more highly valued in conjunction with an impassive stare than with a warm grin. We might say intuitively that the smile and the wink "mean more" when not solicited by a warm grin, or we may derive the different outcomes from the greater cost involved in the warm grin versus the impassive stare, or this particular lad may simply enjoy being "one-up" in a relationship.

What would be the most sensible prediction of a response combination during this fleeting moment? Unlike the "exchange" described in the previous example, there is no time for negotiation and clarification in the present case. What each person does depends on what he expects the other person to do. There is no time for deliberation and the responses must be simultaneously displayed. If the lad and the maid accurately perceive the matrix, it would seem that the best predictive hunch would call for a bored look met by an impassive stare. This prediction may be derived by looking at each person's position in turn. It seems clear that the maid, since we assume she is governed by self-interest, will express a bored look. At best she will be richly rewarded by a warm grin, at worst by an impassive stare that would fit her expectations under the circumstances. Any other choice would make it possible for her to receive less than her just deserts. The lad's position may be similarly analyzed. Clearly he has less to lose by an impassive stare, especially if he correctly intuits the matrix values and predicts that the maid will look bored.

The final example (Figure 13.3c) considers a setting in which two acquaintances are in the process of exchanging opinions on the future of the United Nations. Person A clearly favors the existence of the UN and can under no circumstances imagine endorsing anything less than continuation of the present support given by the government to the UN. For simplicity's sake, the matrix assumes that he either has to make this response or (as he would prefer) the stronger endorsement of increasing support for the UN. Person B, on the other hand, is opposed to the UN in the extreme. The closest he can come to compromise on this issue is to express no opinion or to change the subject. Once again, the values in the matrix represent the relative goodness of outcome when a particular response in one repertory is placed in conjunction with a response from the other repertory. The matrix shows, first of all, that this particular exchange of opinions is not likely to be an especially pleasant one. If each person expresses his most "extreme" response (increased support vs. withdrawal), the emotional cost of producing these responses is presumably low for both—this represents the way they really feel—but the punishments involved in extreme disagreement make the upper left-hand cell moderately unpleasant for both. All things considered, however, this exchange might very well end up in this unpleasant cell. Since A is likely to come out in favor of increased support for the UN (his outcomes are on the average less negative in the left column), B can spare himself the most extreme discomfort only by shifting to an adamant position on the other side of the issue.

This last example shows how behavior that is rational in one sense can be quite irrational, or self-defeating in another. Clearly, both members of the dyad would be better off in the lower right-hand cell, but it is not at all certain or even likely that they would end up there given the present matrix. It is interesting to speculate on the background factors that might affect whether the dyad ends up in the upper-left or lower-right cell—the degree to which they like each other, whether or not they have been instructed to cooperate, whether or not exploratory communications are allowed, and so on. Such considerations will concern us in Chapter Fourteen.

The preceding examples point up the range of interaction content that can be squeezed into the artificial confines of the dyadic matrix. The examples were deliberately chosen to show how "responses" of different complexity or duration might be similarly characterized in goodness of outcome terms. The examples have also brought out the fact that outcomes in a social interaction can be viewed as jointly determined by the responses of each actor. This seems to bring us back to a clearer understanding of what is meant by outcome control.

In the sense conveyed by the three examples, one actor may exert outcome control over the other when his responses at least partly determine the goodness of outcomes the other can attain. The lad has outcome control over the maid at the instant of their meeting because it makes a difference to the maid whether he grins warmly or stares impassively; she is effect dependent on him. By the same logic, the maid has outcome control over the lad. This fleeting episode may thus be characterized as involving *mutual* outcome control. As the interaction unfolds in a series of responses through time, we can envision a series of matrices flipping into place like frames in a motion picture projector. As the topic changes, or as the mode of dealing with it shifts as a consequence of prior responses, different portions of the two total response repertoires become available to the actors. Viewed in this way, the relative balance of outcome control—which actor can exert the greater control at a given moment in time—may vacillate from conversational episode to episode. Recalling our basic assumption that each actor strives to attain the best available outcomes in the relationship, outcome control clearly implies control over behavior. The individual should choose those responses in his repertoire that reflect his interpretation of the matrix, and thus his behavior will adjust to the actual or expected behavior of the other.

Comparison Level (CL) and Comparison Level for Alternatives (CL_{alt})

We may talk about outcome control with reference to a particular setting (as in the preceding discussion), or we may broaden our framework of analysis to consider what happens to a relationship over time. As the relationship develops and the two actors become increasingly familiar with the values of the matrix in different settings, how may we characterize the general balance of outcome control between them? In order to deal effectively with this kind of question, Thibaut and Kelley make the strong assumption that the reward-punishment value of an outcome must always be calculated with reference to the actor's expectations. They in fact propose two alternative bases for deriving outcome values. The first of these is the actor's *comparison level* (CL), which they define as the average value of all the outcomes known to the person, each outcome weighted by its salience. The actor comes to the relationship with a backlog of experiences in other relationships and knowledge concerning still other relationships he has observed or read about. All of these presumably form a standard against which he may judge the present relationship. All such experiences are not weighted equally, however; some will be more salient than others. The CL may be assigned the value of zero in the matrix and outcomes exceeding this value are subjectively rewarding or gratifying, those at the value are subjectively neutral, and those below CL are unpleasant or punishing.

The second basis for deriving values to put in the matrix is the actor's *comparison level for alternatives* (CL_{alt}). This is defined as the best currently available alternative to the present relationship. The less the average probable outcome in the present relationship exceeds the average available in the best alternative relationship (the smaller it is relative to CL_{alt}), the more the person will be tempted to disrupt or leave the present relationship.

Thibaut and Kelley suggest that the level of outcomes received relative to CL defines the actor's degree of *attraction* to the relationship, whereas the level of outcomes received relative to CL_{alt} defines his *dependence* on the relationship. Attraction and dependence are often closely related. A person who is attracted to a relationship is usually, therefore, dependent on it. The CL–CL_{alt} distinction makes clear, however, that an individual may stay in a relationship that is not satisfying to him simply because no better alternative is currently available. Such a person would presumably receive average outcomes below his CL and above his CL_{alt}.

As we shift from moment-to-moment outcome control to questions concerning the general pattern of outcome control in a more enduring relationship, we become concerned with the conditions defining one person's power over another. Since, as we shall see presently, power is the obverse of dependence, it is the CL_{alt} that is specifically relevant in the present discussion. In all subsequent matrix diagrams, therefore, the numbers reflect goodness of outcomes as compared with those available in the best alternative relationship.

Varieties of Power and Dependence

If the matrix numbers are scaled in terms of the CL_{alt}, each person's dependence on the other may be read from the distribution of outcome values in the matrix. Figure 13.4 shows that there are three kinds of dependence that may be distinguished. In order to simplify the present argument, we consider only the outcomes B derives, and then only in a two-response repertory. Figure 13.4a describes a relationship in which B's outcomes are much affected by his own response but not by any response available to A. Because the numbers are scaled in terms of CL_{alt}, however, it is clear that B is dependent for his highly positive (+4) outcomes on the presence of A. Thus A has the power to keep B in the relationship, but no power to affect the particular response B is likely to select from his own repertory. We might say, then, that A has *contact control* over B. There is some reason why B enjoys responding with b_1 when A is around considerably more than he enjoys responding with b_1 when in the next best available relationship. How might this state of affairs come about? One possibility is that B enjoys A's presence when he himself is acting in, say, a

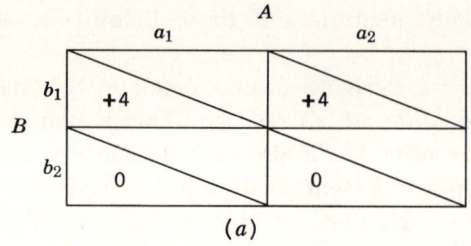

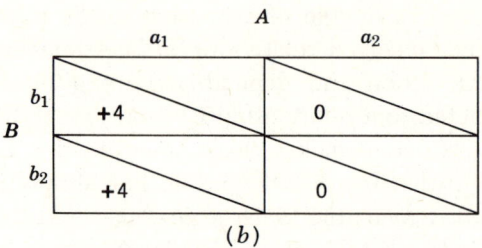

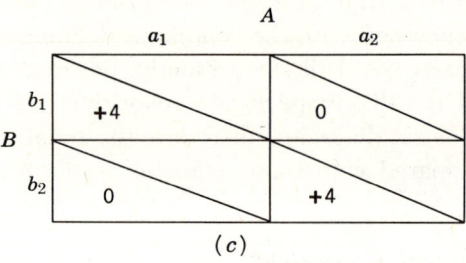

Figure 13.4. Three cases of B's dependence on A. (a) Person B is dependent on the relationship; A has contact control; *(b) Person B is totally dependent on A's responses in the relationship; A has* fate control; *(c) Person B is contingently dependent on A's responses in the relationship; A has* behavior control.

depressed way (b_1) but not otherwise (b_2); furthermore, it does not seem to make any difference how A responds to B's behavior (a_1 versus a_2). Another possibility is that A for some reason reduces the costs to B of response b_1 relative to other people, and it is a response that must be made in someone else's presence. A may create some special atmosphere that makes it easy for B to complain about his job, make love, or laugh.

In the natural world of social relationships, this pure form of contact control is probably rare and fleeting because the matrix form depicted in Figure 13.4a tends to gravitate toward other forms. It is highly unlikely that B will continue to enjoy his own response b_1 regardless of contingent responses from A. From some hidden corner in A's repertory will come a response that *does* affect B's outcomes, or perhaps the cost of making response b_1 will increase precisely because it elicits no predictable reaction from A. Nevertheless, Figure 13.4a points up the possibility that there may be relationships that one actor will try to maintain because his own responses are more gratifying there than in alternative relationships.

In Figure 13.4b and 13.4c the responses of A *do* make a difference in B's outcomes. In the first case (4b), we say that A has *fate control* over B because his choice of response determines B's outcome fate—regardless of B's response. As long as B stays in the relationship, in other words, he remains the passive victim of A's decision to produce response a_1 versus a_2. In Figure 13.4c, B can have a say in the outcomes he receives as long as A responds first or B can correctly anticipate A's behavior. Thibaut and Kelley refer to A's position in this kind of a matrix as that of *behavior control* over B. A is not in a position to control B's outcomes in the direct way that he could in fate control, but he can implicitly control B's behavior. If he wants to elicit b_1 from B he can himself emit, or threaten to emit, a_1. If we conceive of A as the trainer and B as the learner, it is clear that A can "teach" B to make a particular response by selectively emitting behaviors that reward B when he makes that response.

In order to appreciate the differences between fate control and behavior control it is necessary to consider possible variations in A's outcomes. This means filling in some values above the diagonals in the matrices of Figure 13.4. If we begin by entering nothing but zeroes above the diagonals, we imply that A is indifferent both with respect to his own responses and to variations in B's responses. In this case of indifference it is clear that B has more to gain when he is under behavior control than when he is under fate control. If he is under behavior control, he can guarantee decent outcomes for himself by correct anticipation of A's behavior and adaptive modification of his own. If he is under fate control, still assuming that A is indifferent, B is simply at the mercy of momentary variations in A's behavior. If B is unable to predict A's behavior—if A's acts follow his in some totally random fashion—then it will make no difference to B whether he is under behavior control or fate control. The distinction has clear implications only if B, by predicting A's behavior, can get himself into a cell yielding a good outcome.

To continue discussion of the examples in Figure 13.4, because A has potential control over B, he would presumably *not* be indifferent to B's responses. A more likely situation would be that diagrammed in Figure 13.5. This matrix assumes that A has some interest in getting B to make the correct response. He can respond to B with either reward or punishment and, like trainers everywhere, he assumes that B is more likely to make the correct response if that response is rewarded than if it is punished. If he

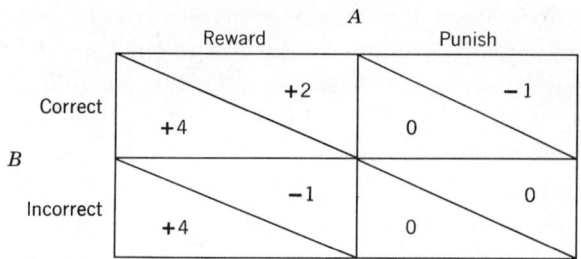

Figure 13.5. Conversion of fate control: A has fate control over B; B has countercontrol over A.

were to punish B for making the correct response or reward him for an error, this would defeat his training objectives and therefore result in negative consequences for him (-1). If B's response were incorrect and A's response were "punish," this would be consistent with A's training objectives ($+$), but the fact that B is incorrect is not a satisfying state of affairs for A ($-$), result: 0. In the event that B is correct and A responds with reward, the state of affairs is satisfying to both of them. It seems obvious that the exchange of responses will gravitate toward the upper left-hand cell in the matrix. At that point we might say that B has learned the correct response.

This example indicates how fate control may be converted in such a way as to have the same training potential as behavior control. If the person who has fate control over another wishes to get that other to perform a certain response, he may get him to do so by controlling his fate positively after the response he favors and negatively after the response(s) he disfavors. This assumes, of course, that B has the desired response somewhere in his repertory. We emphasize again that the *conversion of fate control* will not occur so long as A is indifferent to B's behavior. As Figure 13.5 shows, one person's fate control over another will be converted only when the other exercises some *counterpower* over the one. We are reminded at this point of the cartoon that pictures an albino rat in his home cage talking to a fellow rat: "Boy, have I got that psychologist trained. Every time I press the bar, he gives me food." In the example schematized in Figure 13.5, B counters A's fate control with behavior control. In Chapter Fourteen we shall see that counterpower may either involve fate control or behavior control. Counterpower is not then a special *kind* of control, it is merely any kind of control viewed from the perspective of power that one actor may utilize to blunt, resist, or divert the power of another.

Having introduced the notion of counterpower, we come face to face with the distinction between the outcome control that could be exerted and the control actually exerted. The nature and amount of *potential* control actor A has over actor B may be read from the values on B's side of the matrix diagonals. To the extent that these values are positive on the average, A has contact control: B is generally dependent on the relationship. To the extent that these values differ among each other and there is a wide range between the least attractive and the most attractive outcome, A has either fate or behavior control. As Thibaut and Kelley (1959) put it, a person's power over another (whether over his fate or his behavior) is determined by the range of outcomes through which he can move the other. The distinction between fate and behavior control, finally, derives from the patterning of outcomes in the matrix rather than their average value or their range.

As we take into consideration matrix values above as well as below the diagonal, power and counterpower are both involved and it is only from the "full" matrix that we can predict whether A (or B) will actually use the power he has over B (or A). Once again, the best way to clarify the possibilities seems to be by way of example. In Figure 13.6a, inspection of the values below the diagonal shows that A has fate control over B or C: if A chooses to make response a_1, B's (C's) outcomes just barely exceed his CL_{alt}; if A chooses to make response a_2, B's (C's) outcomes exceed his CL_{alt} considerably. Assuming that A understands the matrix and its implications, it is unlikely that he would actually end up choosing a_1 in interaction with either B or with C. B and C both have sufficient counterpower

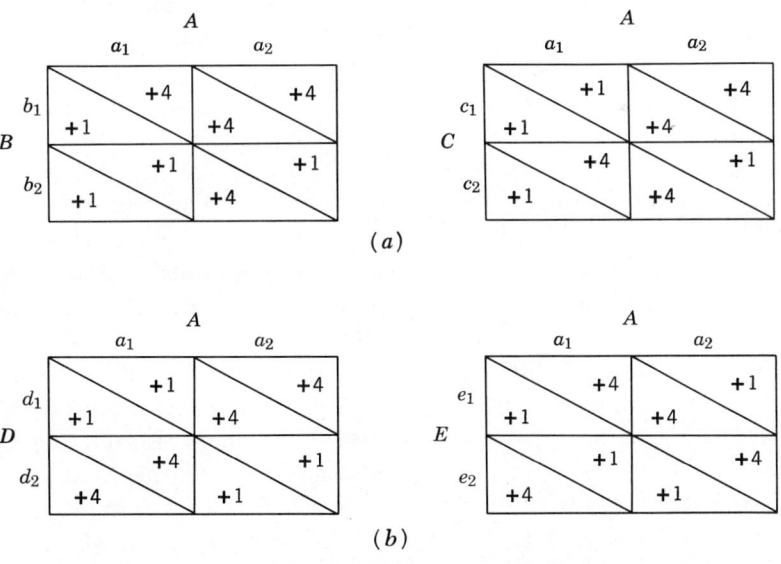

Figure 13.6. Potential and usable power (adapted from Thibaut and Kelley, 1959, pp. 107–109). (a) B and C have power counter to A's fate control over them; (b) D and E both have power counter to A's behavior control. But D's outcomes are correspondent with A's; E's are not.

to get A to make response a_2; otherwise B or C can insure that A's outcomes stay at the minimum level of $+1$.

Figure 13.6b portrays two matrices that differ strikingly with respect to the correspondence of each actor's outcomes. A and D would seem to have strong potential for a harmonious relationship. Whenever one actor responds in a way designed to benefit himself, he benefits the other as well. If, for example, the matrix referred to a ballroom dancing interaction of A and D, responses a_1 and d_1 might be moving forward, a_2 and d_2 moving backward. It should be obvious why the outcomes of both dancers should be more positive when one is moving forward and the other backward. The matrix underlying the A–E interaction, on the other hand, strongly suggests that A and E will have problems. Every time either one responds to the other in a way that maximizes his own satisfaction, he thereby minimizes the other's satisfaction. This is a prominent feature of most competitive situations. A and E could thus be antagonists in a boxing match or a tennis game, in which the success of a punch or a stroke depends very much on the current position or reaction of the other.

It now seems appropriate to take stock of the ingredients of outcome control and to review the major implications of locating outcomes in a reward-cost matrix that interrelates the acts of two persons. Many of the important outcomes toward which people strive rest in the hands of other people. Because this is so, it is apparent that we will try to behave in ways that will influence others to reward us (provide these outcomes) rather than punish us (deny them). Reciprocally, they will naturally be trying to influence us to reward rather than punish them. It is this basic potential for influencing and being influenced that the matrix approach tries to capture.

The kind of interpersonal power represented by a matrix of outcomes can best be understood in terms of a subtle exchange of goods and services. In coordinating his actions to the pattern of rewards available in the matrix, a person is exerting and responding to power, but we also may say that he is exchanging actions that please the other for actions by the other that please him. He thus uses the power resources available in his repertory to exact a fair exchange from the other. The other, of course, is similarly engaged. Homans (1961) has emphasized the exchange character of social interaction in terms bearing considerable similarity to the treatment by Thibaut and Kelley. In Chapter Fourteen we shall deal with the conditions and the consequences of differential power. What do we mean when we say that one person's power exceeds another? How does this come about and what are the implications for action in such an asymmetrical relationship? Our primary concern here has been to show how power and control are implicit in the distribution of available outcomes, and how the potential one person has to exert power over another is tempered by the other's power over him.

We have introduced a number of new terms in developing a "language" of outcome control, and shown how these terms can be represented as variations in the dyadic matrix. If a matrix makes clear that one person has outcome control over another, it must also show that the other is dependent on the one. Thus it is important to recognize that power is the inverse of dependence, for the crucial implication is that the person who has other relationships to which he can turn is least susceptible to influence in the present one. Perhaps the must crucial ingredient of outcome control is for one person to have responses in his repertory that make a difference to the other. If one actor can only make the other happy and never make him sad, he may keep the other in the relationship but he has no clear way to control or influence the other's behavior. It is the *range* of outcomes controlled, then, that is crucial to the capacity for outcome control. The permissive father who rewards all of his son's actions may have contact control over his son, but he has little power to affect his behavior. At the other extreme, the father who does nothing but punish his son will quite likely drive the latter from the relationship at the earliest possible moment. In neither case are the son's outcomes contingent on variations in the father's behavior. It is, then, reward in the context of possible punishment, and punishment in the context of reward which shapes behavior in particular directions.

Cue Control: a Neglected Source of Interpersonal Power

Earlier in the chapter the distinction between outcome control and cue control was introduced to emphasize two rather different sources of contingency in social interaction. Although it was acknowledged that these two forms of control shade into each other and may be difficult to isolate in a given example, the distinction turned upon the directness of reward-punishment manipulation in the dyad. Outcome control, it was argued, involves the direct provision or withholding of reinforcements to guide or shape the course of behavior. Cue control, on the other hand, involves one actor's provision of stimuli that elicit pre-established habit patterns in another. Although these habit patterns ultimately derive from past variations in outcome, an actor may exercise cue control by eliciting learned environment-behavior sequences even when he has no direct control over the other's outcomes. Thus it is sufficient for the pigeon trainer to know about the bird's well-established habit of responding to a yellow light with four head turns if he wants to elicit head-turning behavior—he does not need to have or provide food pellets in order to control the pigeon's behavior.

The distinction between outcome control and cue control has been introduced in various guises by previous writers, but never emphasized. Analysts of the interaction process have apparently been so impressed by the role of reinforcement in human affairs that their accounts of social behavior have been dominated by the reward-punishment theme. This is not to say that other response determinants are never mentioned. Skinner (1938, 1953), for example, distinguished between the following stimulus functions: elicitation, discrimination, emotional, and reinforcing. In his view, a stimulus can affect behavior for a number of reasons and its significance in the sphere of reinforcement is only one of these. However, in spite of acknowledging the variety of ways stimuli affect behavior, his discussion is heavily weighted toward the importance of reinforcement in establishing new stimulus-response connections. Thibaut and Kelley (1959) begin their analysis of social behavior by assuming that "the probability of any one of A's behaviors being elicited is a function of two factors: (1) the strength of instigation to it (from either external or internal stimuli) and (2) previously experienced reinforcement resulting from it" (p. 26). Under the term instigation they include stimuli that elicit innate reflexive behaviors such as "startle," but also "overlearned habits or routines that occur dependably whenever appropriate cues set them off." Although they acknowledge the importance of social instigations to innate and overlearned responses, Thibaut and Kelley nevertheless build their analysis exclusively around the reward-cost matrix (outcome control). Their deliberate decision to restrict their attention to outcome variations is defended on the grounds that, as the interaction proceeds and the relationship stabilizes, instigation and outcome tend to coincide. Thus, as pointed out earlier in the chapter, yesterday's outcome variations set the stage for today's instigations—that is, past reinforcements lead to learning, and learned sequences of behavior may be triggered by appropriate instigations.

Thibaut and Kelley's decision to concentrate on the role of reinforcement (reward-cost) in social interaction reflects their strategic concern with trends of change in a relationship over substantial periods of time. Without wishing to question their emphasis on the long-range significance of reinforcement, we do feel that there are some distinct advantages of separating outcome and cue control and paying some attention to the latter. For one thing, the separation makes good sense in terms of our previous analysis of the determinants of social behavior. Chapter Five emphasized the pervasive effects of the socialization process in the learning of cultural norms. We argued there that one important consequence of socialization is that an increasing number of behavior decisions become automated so that larger and larger patterns of action run their course without conscious planning and deliberation. These automated patterns originally develop out of the individual's attempts to accommodate his behavior to the expectations of others and remain sensitive to these expectations. Insofar as one actor provides the key to unlock the automated sequences of another, he would in our present terms be exercising cue control. By comparison, the individual in novel situations—those not covered by his learning of the cultural map—is likely to be more self-consciously concerned with his outcomes and more sensitively attuned to outcome variations. The implication of these remarks is that the previously drawn distinction between the application of well-established habits on the one hand and behavioral improvisation on the other has a parallel in the distinction between sensitivity to cue control and to outcome control.

Of more apparent relevance is the distinction between informational and effect influence that so dominated the last four chapters. In the context of ongoing social interaction, cue control seems clearly to imply that one person influences another by the information he makes available, whereas outcome control seems closely related to the direct mediation of goal attainment involved in effect influence. The parallel between effect dependence and outcome control is more straightforward than that between information dependence and cue control. A major assumption of the Thibaut and Kelley matrix approach is that each actor is effect dependent and strives to maximize his outcomes under available conditions. But it is much less clear that an actor *strives* to obtain the kind of information, cues, or stimuli, that will have a controlling influence over his actions. Information is transmitted in any episode of cue control, and it affects the recipient's behavior through its relevance to his pre-established dispositions. But the recipient may or may not desire the guidance of the cue controller, just as the latter may be either deliberately exploitative or quite unwitting in the control he exercises.

In a recent review of the group problem solving literature, Kelley and Thibaut (in press) try to find a place for information dependence within the framework of their model of social interaction. They argue as we have in earlier chapters, that each individual is eager to gain a clear picture of those sectors of the environment relevant to action, and they treat information as a kind of outcome sought by the actor in a relationship. Just as the actor will compare prospective interaction partners with respect to the direct outcomes each can provide, so will he compare them with respect to their ability to provide useful information about the environment. When A is under the (outcome) behavior control of B, he will be especially interested in B's predictability and the extent to which he telegraphs his responses, allowing A to adjust to them.

Kelley and Thibaut (in press) handle the interplay between information and effect dependence in an interesting way. They propose that as long as the person is above his comparison level he will act simply and directly to enjoy his outcomes. Below his CL the person adopts an information-seeking and processing set in which the goal is to maximize information;

he becomes temporarily unresponsive to variations in outcome and very concerned with developing a clearer picture of the situation. In short, the more dissatisfied the person becomes with the current state of affairs, the more effect dependence gives way to information dependence.

The notion of information dependence implies an explicit desire for facts that will give the environment more meaning or greater structure. Information is sought primarily for its instrumental value, its potential for improving outcomes. Cue control involves informational influence, but there is no prior awareness by the person that he lacks information and intends to seek it. Opportunities to exercise cue control arise out of the recipient's past history of commerce with outcomes in the presence of cues that the controller is now able to provide. Its effectiveness does not depend on the recipient's present comparison level, but rather on the state of his total response repertoire and the relative availability of various response sequences. In a way, the cue controller helps to specify the responses relevant to the interaction—the $a, b, \ldots,$ of the matrix; and he typically does this by providing the conditioned stimuli previously associated with reinforcement. Cue control differs from outcome control to the extent that those outcome values the actor expects to find in the matrix are actually unavailable.

One implication of this line of reasoning is that the cue controller's capacity to exploit is limited by the possibility of extinction. In the long run, A cannot repeatedly cue B to the same response sequence unless that sequence is periodically reinforced. However, the more A knows about B's past learning history, the more *different* stimulus-habit contingencies he may be able to take advantage of. Just as the effective propagandist should know something about the dispositions of those in his audience, so the cue controller should have insight into the dispositions of the one he wishes to control. Whether we refer to motives, cognitions, or attitudes, each of these dispositional terms contains some reference to those events appropriate to their arousal. Cue control involves some capacity to shape these events, to move the other into a psychological position in which the stimuli for well established stimulus-response connections become available or salient. Cue control is synonymous with dispositional arousal or inhibition. At least in the short run, knowledge is power for the cue controller.

Chapters Ten through Twelve reviewed in some detail the experimental literature bearing on informational influence when specific, persuasive communications are involved. Comparable studies concerned with cue control are exceedingly rare. This seems to reflect the exaggerated emphasis on reinforcement, but also doubtless reflects the primitive level of concept and theory for dealing with cue control phenomena. And perhaps there *are* special difficulties involved in conceptualizing the entry of one actor's behavior into the well-established response systems of another. Whatever the underlying reasons are for the relative neglect of these phenomena, our discussion will be necessarily brief and anecdotal.

Can we specify more clearly the range of phenomena falling under cue control? One way of proceeding would be to attempt an answer to another question: what kinds of factors might interfere with the relationship between available outcomes and behavior? Assuming that we could identify the reward-cost (goodness of outcome) values in a particular two-person matrix, under what conditions would we do a poor job in attempting to predict behavior from these values alone? As Thibaut and Kelley suggest, one person might be able to provide instigations to the other that trade on past contingencies conflicting with the current state of affairs. As an example they use the game "Simon says." In this game the "leader" establishes in the "follower" a strong disposition to behave imitatively. Under the requirement of acting quickly, thereafter, the follower is induced to imitate the action of the leader even when it constitutes an error (presumably a negative outcome for the follower). But the error makes sense in terms of the prior history of the follower. This kind of cue control is extensively used in competitive sports when, as in football especially, each team tries to capitalize on (and thus confound) the expectations of the other by faking and deception.

More dramatic examples of the importance of cue control occur in the field of medicine. The physician is obviously in a position to exert direct outcome control in relating to his patient. Many of his activities provide striking examples of fate control: prescribing a bitter medicine, relieving an excruciating pain by sedation, and so on. But the physician's activities often involve decisions about cue control as well. The doctor may discover that his patient has cancer but withhold this information from him, on the grounds that such information would engage dispositions calling out behavior interfering with the treatment process.

Psychological analyses of the conditions for brainwashing also reveal the importance of cue control. In Korea, for example, Chinese Communist guards effectively played on the dispositions of many American prisoners to bring them to the brink of defection. Schein (1958) reports that the Chinese went to great lengths to obtain a complete personal history from each prisoner. "The purpose was apparently to determine which prisoners' histories might predispose them toward the Communist philosophy and thus make them apt subjects for special indoctrination" (p. 320). This exploitation of individual history seems quite in line with the notion of cue control, for the subsequent indoctrination attempt typically involved trying to make the individual prisoner's personal grievances about America salient and to attach the blame to the capitalist system. The Chinese also tried to remove cues that would normally operate to sustain the prisoners' beliefs. This was done by cutting off all reliable information from the external world and substituting heavily biased Communist magazines and papers. The delivery of mail was systematically manipulated to prevent the prisoner from getting information about the progress of the war, and there were often systematic attempts to break down the stabilizing role of the prisoner group itself by attempting to foster suspicion among the men and by segregating the prisoners by rank.

To bring the discussion closer to home, many students knowingly or unwittingly practice the arts of cue control in constructing examination answers. An interesting strategy available to the bright student who is not properly prepared is that of constructing an answer that triggers a chain of relevant associations in the grader. By placing a few incontrovertible facts in the midst of otherwise ambiguous verbiage, the student may succeed in cuing the grader to substitute his own structure for the student's.

Parents are continually involved in cue control insofar as they structure a child's environment to foster desirable behavior. At bedtime many parents carry the child through a number of elaborate rituals to ease the way to sleep. Eventually, as the child grows older, a few minimal cues will be sufficient to launch the child into his own version of these rituals. It is a rare parent who has not at some time tried to distract his child in order to stop him from crying or to check a temper tantrum. A dramatic instance of cue control may be seen when a two-year-old, in the midst of what portends to be a long cry, is asked a simple and matter-of-fact question having nothing to do with the tears or the incident that provoked them. It is surprising how often the child will, in these circumstances, stop crying and answer the question.

Implicit in the distinction between outcome control and cue control is an underlying distinction between exchange and arousal. As we have seen, in order for one person to vary the outcomes of another, he must typically adjust to applications of the other's counterpower. This implies that action in the dyad tends to gravitate toward the cell representing the fairest exchange of outcomes. Cue control, in our view, is likely to involve more subtle exploitation and there is no necessary exchange involved. By his contributions to the definition of the situation one person may make certain of the other's response options more available, more salient, than others. If one actor wants to avoid engaging in a political discussion with another, for example, he may attempt to exercise cue control by keeping other topics salient, by carefully avoiding remarks that might lead to political associations in the other's mind.

Viewed this way, cue control becomes a way for *A* to affect his own outcomes by eliciting a class of responses in *B* that are, on balance, gratifying to *A*. There is no necessary exchange involved—*A* does not necessarily have to "pay" for the outcomes he receives in the course of eliciting *B*'s behavior. A's success in this elicitation process depends, as noted above, on his understanding of the other's repertory and of the connective links between repertory responses and triggering cues. By capitalizing on the learning history of the other person, then, a person attempts to provide stimulation calling forth actions that he prefers.

SUMMARY

This chapter was concerned with the various meanings of social influence in the setting of ongoing social interaction. Consideration was restricted to the dyad. Even with this restriction it is clear that interaction is extremely complex, and may be approached by the would-be analyst from many perspectives. Our own approach began with an attempt to classify dyadic relations in terms of the degree to which one person's responses are determined by the previous responses of the other. This contingency model suggested four interesting types of interaction: pseudo-contingency, asymmetrical contingency, reactive contingency, and mutual contingency. Only in mutual contingency is the full complexity of human interaction revealed. Our discussion emphasized that this (probably most rewarding and sophisticated) kind of interaction involves a delicate interplay between autonomy in carrying out a person's own conversational plan and reactive dependence on the other's responses.

Going beyond this preliminary analysis of variations in the general patterning of social influence, we considered the psychological foundations of this influence. We proposed that the events of interpersonal contingency could be classified under the headings of outcome control and cue control. The former heading refers to the mutual adjustments of each actor to the outcomes provided by the other. The latter refers to the arousal of certain dispositions by provision of appropriate cues. For the discussion of outcome control we borrow the matrix model of Thibaut and Kelley (1959) and attempted to show how variations in the distribution of outcomes had implications for the flow of influence during an interaction. One person's power was coordinated to the other's dependence, but it was pointed out that power almost inevitably confronts counterpower and that therefore the application of power usually involves compromise through a kind of fair-exchange principle. In general, one person has to present something the other person values in order to receive something of value in return.

Cue control is not directly hemmed in by any such exchange principle. Here the notion is that one person may elicit or make salient certain portions of the other's response repertory by providing appropriate cues. Effective presentation of appropriate cues depends in turn on some knowledge of the other's past history and therefore his dispositions. It is this feature that most clearly establishes the parallel between cue control and informational influence in the area of persuasive communication. Informative persuasion and cue control both require a certain kind of expertise or knowledge, though the subtlety with which this knowledge is used is likely to be much greater in the ongoing interaction situation.

CHAPTER FOURTEEN

Power and Influence in Dyadic Interaction: Experimental Findings

The research to be reported in this chapter includes studies with widely differing theoretical antecedents, but each has the same basic procedure or paradigm: two persons exchange behavior in a setting in which the responses of each are experimentally linked to outcomes for the other; that is, there is mutual outcome control.

The general plan is to proceed from the more simple, contrived, and artificial cases of interaction to the more complex and realistic cases.

Certainly one of the simplest situations in which one person influences another's responses is that of teacher and learner or trainer and trainee. It is customary to think of the teacher-trainer as an expert who provides the trainee with information concerning the most effective routes to attainment of a goal. The trainee is willingly "influenced" by this information to adopt certain beliefs or courses of action because they appear to bring him closer to his objectives. In our parlance the trainer is exercising informational influence or cue control.

But there is another aspect to the training process that is easily overlooked. Instead of, or in addition to, pointing the way for effective goal-directed action, the trainer may himself control access to a desired goal. He may dispense grades, certify readiness for promotion or advancement, pay wages. This places him in a position to reward the trainee for actions that please him (are, perhaps, "correct"), and punish him (withhold the goal) for actions that displease him. The trainee may thus be effect dependent on the trainer or the trainer may be said to exercise outcome control over the trainee. In most training situations effect and information dependence—outcome and cue control—are simultaneously involved. Eventually the trainee performs the "correct" responses because he thinks they are right and also because his outcomes from interacting with the trainer are higher if he does. Many of the previous chapters have dealt at length with the role of expertise, information dependence, and cue control. Our emphasis in the present discussion is on the role of effect dependence or outcome control in dyadic interaction. Nevertheless, the cue– outcome–control distinction is an important one, and we shall remain alert to its psychological implications in evaluating the experimental results to be reviewed.

DYADIC INTERACTION AND OPERANT VERBAL CONDITIONING

One kind of training situation that has recently received considerable attention is operant conditioning in human subjects. The word "operant" refers to behavior that is emitted by an organism in a situation when it is difficult to identify a particular eliciting stimulus (Skinner, 1938). In the typical operant conditioning experiment, a subject is placed in a situation in which in the normal course of events he will emit a variety of operants. At a certain point in the procedure the experimenter selectively rewards or reinforces a particular operant or all operants in a certain class. The reinforcement may be the word "right," "good," or some other signal indicating the experimenter's approval of the operant emitted by the subject. If the operant, or members of the operant class, are emitted with increasing relative frequency, we may say that the experimenter has conditioned the subject's behavior or that he has trained the subject.

Let us imagine an experiment in which the experimenter instructs the subject to emit verbal operants (or words) as rapidly as they come to mind. In order to reduce response variety, he tells the subject to restrict himself to words having to do with food. He informs the subject that he, the experimenter, is thinking of a particular class of foods and the subject's task is to learn what this class is. As the subject complies with this general instruction, he notices that the experimenter says "correct" following the words "orange," "peach," and "lime." The subject might quickly conclude that the experimenter is thinking of the category "fruit" and proceed to name all the other fruits he can think of. Most people would agree that this is not an impressive accomplishment and that the example is trivial and not theoretically interesting. The subject has solved the simple problem which, in common-sense language, merely required him to abstract a common feature of the words the experimenter reinforced—they were all fruits.

But it is easy to imagine how we could make the situation more interesting. We could, of course, make the category to be learned more subtle or complicated. Learning would then take longer and would be subject to influence by a greater number of variables. Or we could try to trick the subject into thinking that he was not in a learning task and that the experimenter was interested in something else—say, the number of words the subject emits in a particular time, or his autonomic reactivity in the process of speaking. If, having tricked the subject in this way, the experimenter were to reinforce fruits (saying "good" or "mmhmm" rather than "correct" to contribute to the deception), would the subject show an increasing tendency to name fruit? And if he did, would he be aware that he had done so because of the contingency between his fruit naming and the experimenter's saying "good"?

It is this latter situation to which we first turn, for it is our conviction that much of the interpersonal influence that occurs in casual social interactions happens rapidly and without awareness. Although the individual may later reconstruct some of the reasons why he did or said certain things rather than others, we assume on intuitive grounds that he is often influenced by outcome control (and by cue control as well) without responding to this interpersonal influence in a deliberate, self-conscious way.

A large number of experiments have been performed in recent years in the area of operant verbal conditioning. Many of these have involved attempts to trick the subject in some way so that he would have difficulty in recognizing the response-reinforcement contingency. This has typically been done by diverting the subject's attention toward a manifest task that is incidental to the hidden learning task. Two early studies in this tradition set the pattern for many of those which followed.

The first, by Greenspoon (1955), involved the verbal reinforcement ("mmhmm") of plural nouns emitted by the subject in response to the simple instructions to say words. In the second, by Taffel (1955), subjects were reinforced in a task of constructing sentences using one of several pronouns. The experimenter said "good" in a flat, unemotional tone whenever the subject formed a sentence with the pronoun "I" or "we."

In both studies there was an increase in the use of the reinforced response, an increase that did not occur in a control (no reinforcement) condition. Both authors reported that the subjects were "unaware"—they could not verbalize the contingencies between response and reinforcement. However, rather strong evidence has since accumulated (Spielberger, 1962), to show that when subjects are classified as aware or unaware on the basis of more exhaustive questioning, the only subjects who show a performance increment are those who later report awareness of the contingency between their response and the experimenter's "good" or "mmhmm." If this is generally true, the findings of Greenspoon, Taffel, and many others certainly become less interesting and more trivial in their implications. The experimenter is playing a game with the subjects and those who figure out the rules do better at the game. It may be, however, that the Greenspoon and Taffel procedures are not particularly suited for studying "learning without awareness." This seems to be Verplanck's (1962) contention, and it does seem likely that many subjects in the foregoing experiments would develop hypotheses about why the experimenter was saying "mmhmm" or "good" and be generally sensitized to the contingencies between their own and the experimenter's responses.

Perhaps it is necessary to bring the interaction closer to the status of a naturally occurring event, thus reducing the subject's tendency to reflect on an experimenter's purpose. Consider, for example, Hildum and Brown's (1956) study, which took the form of an attitude survey conducted by telephone. By reinforcing the expression of opinions on one side of an issue, they were able to influence the opinions subsequently expressed. However, this was true only when "good" was the reinforcement; "mmhmm" had no discernible effect on their response. All subjects rejected the notion that their answers had been influenced by the interviewer's reactions and none expressed any awareness of the contingency between the interviewer's "good" and their own pro- or anti-opinions.

Previously, Verplanck (1955) had apparently demonstrated that casual conversations could be shaped by various kinds of reinforcements in a nonexperimental setting. Using the students in an undergraduate course as experimenters, Verplanck turned them loose on unsuspecting friends in such casual settings as a dormitory room, a restaurant, a public lounge, over the telephone, and in a hospital ward room. The experimenter's task was to start a conversation, provide no reinforcement for 10 minutes, reinforce every opinion statement (those beginning with "I believe that," "I think that," and so on) for the next 10 minutes, and not reinforce again for the final 10 minutes. The reinforcement provided was either agreement with or paraphrase of the opinion expressed. Opinions were surreptitiously tabulated by the reinforcer. The results showed that each of the 24 subjects approached in this way expressed more opinion statements during the middle 10 minutes (the conditioning period) than the first 10 minutes (the base-line period or operant level), and 21 out of 24 subjects expressed more opinions during the conditioning than the extinction period. Paraphrasing was slightly more effective than agreement in increasing the opinion rate but not significantly so. Verplanck reports that none of these subjects ever gave any evidence that he was in an experiment or that there was anything peculiar about the conversation.

Azrin, Holz, Ulrich, and Goldiamond (1961) tried to replicate Verplanck's findings and found that their student-experimenters had great difficulty conducting the experiment in a reliable way. The experimenters initially came up with results confirming Verplanck's data but it was discovered later that many had fabricated their recording to complete the "assignment" and others were strongly influenced at some point in the process of eliciting and recording data by their preconceptions of what the effect of reinforcement should be.

In an attempt to pursue the "conversation procedure" in a laboratory setting, with more rigorous control over possibilities of bias, Centers (1963) developed an ingenious procedure. In a first attempt to explore its possibilities, Centers recruited 49 undergraduate subjects for a laboratory experiment of undefined purpose. When the individual subject showed up at the laboratory room, he was met by another "subject" (carefully trained in his role by the experimenter) who explained that he had come early for the experiment and that Dr. Centers had told him "the machine had broken down and that he had to go downstairs to get someone to fix it. He said he ought to be right back but if he isn't we are to wait a half hour before we can leave."

As the two students waited, the experimental accomplice adopted a standard role in the ensuing 30-minute conversation. In a fashion similar to the student-experimenters of Verplanck, he listened to the naive subject talk for the first 10 minutes with a general show of interest and attention. He tried to keep his participation at a minimum, though he occasionally had to ask "pump-priming" questions to keep the conversation going. During the second 10-minute period the accomplice agreed with or paraphrased all of the subject's opinion statements, was attentive and understanding when the subject made an information statement ("I flunked chemistry"), and answered all questions asking for information. Each of these reactions of the accomplice was designed to reinforce opinion, information, or question operants respectively. During the last 10 minutes, the extinction phase, the accomplice either disagreed with or ignored the subject's conversational comments. The interaction was secretly tape-recorded and monitored by observers stationed behind a one-way mirror.

The results showed that total verbalization by the naive subject was significantly greater during the reinforcement period (the second 10 minutes) than in the base-line operant period or the extinction period. When total verbalization was divided into opinion statements, information statements, and questions, each of these subcategories also showed the predicted increase during the reinforcement period. Centers reported that in no case did a subject express his awareness that the accomplice was trying to influence his behavior.

Although Centers' method may prove useful in studying the impact of reinforcement on conversation, the results of this first study are difficult to interpret. The main problem is that Centers chose to reinforce every kind of statement in the conditioning period and it is not clear whether the results show a specific reinforcing effect or whether the general interest shown by the accomplice during the reinforcement period merely created an atmosphere that induced the subject to become more expansive and talkative. As Centers points out, this is not an inherent limitation of the procedure, but the specific role of reinforcement in shaping the internal structure of a conversation remains unclear.

There are, however, other sources of evidence indicating that the content of conversation can be manipulated by appropriate reinforcement. Some of the more interesting examples are nonexperimental findings from content analyses of psychotherapy sessions. Murray (1956) looked at those categories of patient speech of which the therapist expressed disapproval in psychotherapy and found a decrease in their usage. Bandura, Lipsher, and Miller (1960) found that the patient's hostile statements increased when the psychotherapist "approached" such statements and that they decreased when the therapist "avoided" such statements. Approach in this case involved largely probing, interpretation, and paraphrase, but also approval. Avoidance involved largely ignoring or changing the subject. Winder, Ahmad, Bandura, and Rau (1962) replicated this finding with hostile statements and demonstrated that the same results occurred with dependency statements in the psychotherapy interview.

There is thus fairly impressive empirical evidence that a wide variety of responses emitted by one person (operants) can be conditioned by a wide variety of responses emitted by another (reinforcements). Whether such learning can take place without any awareness of the contingency has not yet been, and may never be unequivocally, established. The problems involved in determining awareness after-the-fact are extremely complicated and difficult to deal with (cf. Eriksen, 1962). We have suggested that learning without awareness is more likely to occur if the setting is natural and the subject is not alerted to the problem-solving possibilities in the situation. It is also true, however, that rigorous control is difficult to maintain in such natural settings and that the response to be reinforced must be carefully defined and objectively recorded.

What Kind of Control?

Are both outcome and cue control involved in the kind of operant conditioning situations reviewed above? Let us start the inquiry by considering the various reasons why the subject might increase his production of responses in the reinforced class. The subject may treat the word "good" or the utterance "mmhmm" as a desirable outcome in and of itself. Perhaps "good" is taken to mean "I approve of you" or "your performance pleases me" or "you are doing what I like, keep it up." If the subject is primarily interested in obtaining "good" responses and goes after them by saying or doing the things that elicit "good" from the reinforcer we would describe the situation as primarily involving outcome control. There is, in effect, an exchange of commodities or outcomes. The person doing the reinforcing seems to like plural nouns (I-we sentences) and the subject likes to hear "good." Each gives the other what he wants. The subject may, however, place the "good" in a somewhat different context. He may see himself in a problem-solving situation in which "good" simply means "the response you just gave is one of the class of responses considered correct in this experiment; see if you can produce other correct responses that show you have discovered the rule under which I am operating." In this case "good" serves as a cue, a bit of information that helps the subject in his efforts to solve the experimental problem. The reinforcer has cue control over the subject in that he—as if in the role of expert—points out (little by little, as it happens) the proper paths toward goal attainment. Perhaps the critical factor in determining the predominance of cue versus outcome control in the situation is the subject's motive state and how this state is linked to the reinforcement. The subject who is primarily interested in winning the experimenter's favor is under his outcome control; the subject who is primarily interested in discovering a solution to the problem posed by the experimenter is under his cue control.

Most studies of conformity, attitude change, and other instances of social influence, as we have seen, are theoretically ambiguous because it is not clear whether the target of influence is effect dependent, information dependent, or both. There is no clear way to sort out the proportion of influence attributable to each source. Similarly, in the case of the operant conditioning studies, there remains an ambiguity concerning how a given subject perceives the situation and what significance he attaches to the reinforcement. Presumably some of the subjects who do not "learn"—more precisely, who do not show an increase in the use of responses in the reinforced class—do not do so because (a) they do not particularly like to hear the word "good" from the other person, or (b) they have no interest in solving what they perceive to be a circumscribed and not very challenging experimental problem. Spielberger, Levin, and Shepherd (1962) found that 19 out of 30 of their subjects in a sentence-construction task were aware of the contingency between "I-we" sentences and "good." All aware subjects were asked by the reinforcer, "Would you say you wanted me to say good?" Nine of the aware subjects said that they did not care one way or the other. In contrast to those who said they cared very much, these "don't care" subjects showed no change in performance.

Although the studies reviewed have simply assumed that "good" or "mmhmm" is reinforcing to the average subject, an interesting approach to the outcome– cue–control distinction involves manipulating the reinforcement value of the supposedly reinforcing response. Whereas the reward or outcome value of the word "good" may be systematically varied from low to high, the cue value of the word would presumably be held constant by an appropriate experimental design.

One approach to the separation of outcome control from cue control is illustrated by Gewirtz and Baer (1958a). These investigators reasoned by analogy to learning experiments involving primary drive variations that the value of the reinforcing stimulus is a function of the state of deprivation of the organism. That is, a rat that has just been fully fed will not be as likely to condition for a food reward as a hungry, food-deprived rat. Similarly, perhaps, a subject who has in the immediate past been deprived of approval or social contact may be more likely to condition in response to the reward "good" than a subject who has not been so deprived.

In their experiment 32 nursery-school children were asked to play a game that consisted of dropping marbles one at a time into a boxlike structure containing two holes. Each child played the game twice: once on arrival at the experimental room and once after 20 minutes of social deprivation. The sequence of the two experimental sessions was reversed for some of the subjects, and it was determined that session order did not make any difference. The condition of social deprivation was arranged by telling the child when he arrived that the toy was broken and asking him to wait (by himself) until it was repaired. In both deprivation and nondeprivation conditions, once the game started the experimenter reinforced dropping a marble into a particular hole by saying "good," "fine," "good one," and so on. These reinforcing comments did not follow every successful marble drop, but were administered according to a predetermined schedule of partial reinforcement. The results showed that on the average subjects made more correct drops in response to approving reinforcement after deprivation than in the nondeprivation condition. This was especially true for those subjects rated high by their teachers in the degree to which they typically sought approval.

It would appear then that the experimenter is in a better position to exert outcome control when the subject has been recently cut off from approval sources than when he has not been so deprived. This is especially true if this subject is a child who has a high general need for approval from adults. We may reasonably assume that, whereas the outcome value represented by approval varies from one condition to the other, the informational or cue value of the reinforcer remains constant. As Gewirtz and Baer conclude, "the effectiveness of a social reinforcer may be increased by its own deprivation" (1958a, p. 54).

Essentially the same conclusion may be applied to the results of a second, similar study by Gewirtz and Baer (1958b). Here the same game along with the same reinforcement schedule was used, but each of 102 children participated in only one of three conditions: a deprivation condition, a nondeprivation condition, or a satiation condition in which playing the game was preceded by a session of drawing and cutting out designs during which the experimenter dispensed continuous approval and friendly conversation. As predicted, subjects in the satiation condition showed the least subsequent responsiveness to reinforcement in the game, those in the nondeprivation condition were intermediate, and deprived subjects were most responsive. It is also interesting to note that children in the deprived condition spontaneously initiated more interaction with the experimenter during the baseline or operant stage of the game (before the reinforcing period) than those in the nondeprivation condition. This may be taken as providing some independent evidence of the deprived children's hunger for approval and contact.

An alternative theoretical explanation of this result is offered by Walters and Parke (1964). They suggest, on the basis of additional experimental evidence, that social deprivation produces general emotional arousal and therefore heightened attentiveness to the experimenter's responses. These responses then serve as cues to previously established habits of continuing to perform in a way that is labeled correct.

Sapolsky (1960) conducted two related experiments with adult female subjects addressed to the same general set of issues as those raised by Gewirtz and Baer. Instead of manipulating the level of deprivation of the subjects, however, he manipulated the attractiveness of the person doing the reinforcing. The subject's task was, in the Taffel tradition, to construct sentences using one of several pronouns; "I" or "we" sentences were again reinforced.

In the first experiment attractiveness was directly manipulated by attempting to convince the subject that she would either be very attracted to the experimenter, indicated by scores on a certain questionnaire both had taken, or not attracted. In the second experiment attraction was indirectly manipulated by selecting subjects and experimenters according to their measured compatibility on a personality questionnaire (FIRO-B, developed by Schutz, 1958). In both experiments subjects in the high-attraction condition showed a significant rise in the construction of "I" or "we" sentences. Those in the low-attraction condition showed no such change.

It is of further interest that in both experiments a curious thing happened during an extinction period when the experimenter was called out of the room to answer a phone call and the subject was told to continue constructing sentences into a tape recorder. In the low-attraction conditions, there was a significant rise in the number of "I" or "we" sentences *after* the experimenter left the room. Although this might be explained in a number of ways, it seems quite possible that the subjects did learn from the experimenters in the low-attraction–incompatibility conditions, but their performances were inhibited by the experimenter's presence. We have here, then, evidence akin to that of the sleeper effect in opinion change (see Chapter Twelve).

The third study in which there was an attempt to manipulate the outcome value of the reinforcer was that of Cohen, Greenbaum, and Mansson (1963). This study is particularly interesting because, in addition to showing the direct effects of social deprivation on responses to social reinforcement, the investigators introduced a variation in commitment to further deprivation. The experiment involved extremely complicated procedures, and we shall present only a brief summary of the experimental design. Adult subjects were put through the Taffel sentence-construction procedure either after they had received considerable social reinforcement on a prior task (low-deprivation) or after they had received a pattern of initial reinforcement followed by silence (high-deprivation). This was a variation of the procedures followed by Gewirtz and Baer. Out of 60 subjects in the high-deprivation condition, 40 were induced to commit themselves to an additional experiment (described as a projected interview) in which it was made clear that they would be exposed to a considerable amount of disapproval from the interviewer-experimenter. Half of these subjects were assured that they would receive $5.00 for participating in this additional experiment; the remaining subjects were told that they would receive $1.00. The $1.00 condition may be viewed as a high-dissonance condition because the subjects were, in effect, asked to commit themselves to further social deprivation without the kind of recompense that would justify submitting themselves to disapproval. The $5.00 condition may be considered a low-dissonance condition because the money itself would seem to provide adequate justification for participation.

The experimental design thus created four conditions to which 80 subjects were randomly assigned: low-deprivation–no-committment, high-deprivation–no-committment, high-deprivation–high-dissonance, and high-deprivation–low-dissonance. Let us first examine the direct effects of deprivation in the two conditions in which no question of further deprivation was involved. In keeping with the Gewirtz and Baer findings, high-deprivation subjects showed a significant increase in the construction of "I" or "we" sentences; low-deprivation subjects did not. Subjects who were aware of the contingency showed more of a performance increment than unaware subjects, but even among the unaware, high-deprivation subjects conditioned significantly more than low-deprivation subjects.

What about the effects of dissonance, defined as commitment to further deprivation of approval? As predicted by the investigators, subjects in the high-deprivation–high-dissonance ($1.00) condition showed no conditioning; subjects in the high-deprivation–low-dissonance ($5.00) condition did show conditioning. In common-sense terms, subjects who have commited themselves to a subsequent session, in which disapproval is expected, seem to reduce their motivation for approval. If they can convince themselves that approval is not important, commitment to further disapproval will be less dissonance-producing. Subjects in the $5.00 group have adequate justification for participating in the later experiment without having to reduce their own needs for approval.

The dramatic and interesting finding is that in those conditions in which the need for approval is predicted to be low—either because the subject has received ample approval in the recent past or because he has convinced himself that approval is unimportant—social reinforcement has no discernible effects on the choice of pronouns in the sentence construction task.

Again we see that through appropriate experimental manipulation outcome control may be distinguished from cue control in the setting of human operant conditioning.

Outcome Exchange and the Distribution of Power

Although those working in the operant-conditioning field sometimes write as though the experimenter were nothing but a programmed "machine" dispensing pellets of reinforcement following selected responses, the studies described deal, of course, with a social interaction between two persons. In terms of the matrix model presented in Chapter Thirteen we may envision a response matrix in which both experimenter and subject have two response classes that "matter" in the relationship. The experimenter has two basic options: he may say "good," "mmhmm," "right," paraphrase, (depending on the particular experiment); or he may remain silent, disagree, scowl, or change the topic. For the time being let us assume, along with the investigators, that the first class of responses is reinforcing, the second class is non- or negatively reinforcing. The subject, on the other hand, has only two response classes that matter to the reinforcer: the reinforced versus all others; for example, plural nouns versus all other words, sentences beginning with "I" or "we" versus all other sentences, hostile comments versus all others, opinion statements versus all others. Of course the subject is not likely at first to realize the importance of the distinction between these two classes. In terms of the matrix values, in other words, the subject has no information about the matrix values above the diagonal—he is unaware of which behaviors the experimenter wants—that is, are reinforcing to *him*. Eventually, however, whether the subject is aware of the fact that a game is being played, and whether he is aware of its rules, he should gravitate toward more frequent responses in the reinforced class.

Figure 14.1 diagrams the simple contingency involved in all of the experiments described. In some of them there were various classes of

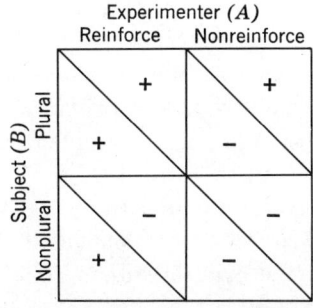

Figure 14.1 Operant verbal conditioning matrix.

reinforcers, various kinds of responses reinforced in the same experiment, or both, but in general the basic situation is given in the figure. Eventually, we would expect most or all of the contingent responses to occur in the upper left-hand cell. An interesting feature of this matrix in that the experimenter has fate control over the subject (see Chapter Thirteen), but the subject also has fate control over the experimenter. As we have pointed out, just as the subject presumably wants to hear the experimenter say, "good," or "mmhmm," so the experimenter wants to hear the subject say plural nouns.

How do the subject and the experimenter differ, then, in the typical operant conditioning paradigm, and what is the best way to characterize this difference? At the outset, the experimenter and the subject are involved in an asymmetrical contingency. In keeping with our characterization, in Chapter Thirteen, of this class of dyadic interactions, one actor (the experimenter) is a standard responder, the other (the subject) is variable. The experimenter enters the relationship with a plan, of which the subject is unaware. The subject enters the relationship with a disposition to be reactive, an orientation to fulfill the experimental task as defined by the experimenter. The case is complicated by the fact that the experimenter's plan has a certain built-in social reference—the plan itself specifies a social contingency. Nevertheless, in essential respects the contingency is initially asymmetrical.

In the course of time, if we ignore those subjects who show no change in performance and no dawning awareness of the contingency, the relationship moves in the direction of increasing mutuality. The subject changes, in other words, from an orientation of simple reactivity to a more complex orientation in which he expresses a behavior plan that is more or less self-consciously pursued. This plan develops as he adjusts to the increasing evidence he receives concerning the contingency of the experimenter's outcomes on his own choice of, say, plural versus singular nouns. In the resulting mutual contingency situation it is apparent that each has power over and each is dependent on the other. The question of who is *more* powerful in the situation boils down to the importance to the subject of receiving "good" versus the importance to the experimenter of receiving plural nouns. If the subject was not involved in the experimental task, that is, not particularly attracted to the experimenter, not especially interested in helping him out, or both, his dependence on the experimenter would not be particularly great. However, the same experimenter might be relatively dependent on him to the extent that the subject's contribution to positive versus negative results was crucial. This would depend, of course, on the strength of the experimenter's belief in the efficacy of verbal reinforcement and the strength of his desire to demonstrate this efficacy. Although this may violate the image of the experimenter as a dispassionate seeker of the truth, we believe that most experimenters would rather see results come out one way than another. This does not mean that experimenters who favor certain hypotheses will do anything not specified in the procedure to influence the results, though Rosenthal (1963, 1966) intimates that such influence is common, if unwitting.

This reasoning about the differential power of subject and experimenter is supported by the findings that subjects learn only when the experimenter's behavior makes a difference to them; when, in effect, the difference in outcome value of "good" versus "silence" is great, and the word "good" has high reward value relative to its absence. The less dependent is the subject on the experimenter, the less likely will his behavior show the effects of learning. The other side of the picture is brought into focus by the suggestive evidence of Azrin et al. (1961) that experimenters who believe more strongly in the effects of reinforcement are, for reasons not as yet clearly understood, more influential in shaping responses than those who are more skeptical of the value of rewards in shaping behavior. In this case, the fact that the subject is showing the effects of reinforcement is in itself a reinforcing event for the experimenter.

An interesting aspect of the operant conditioning procedure is that the process must work through an interpersonal relationship in which power and influence are being exerted. A special feature of the experiments thus far reviewed is that one party of the interchange knows something initially that the other does not know. The experimenter is "one up" on the subject —he is aware of a specific relationship between the subject's verbalizations and his own; the subject is not. It is possible, however, to establish a different kind of situation in which neither partner is initially aware of a particular contingency that is in fact built into their relationship. We turn now to a discussion of such a situation.

INFLUENCE IN A "MINIMAL" SOCIAL SITUATION

In 1956 Sidowski, Wycoff, and Tabory attempted to "re-evaluate the essential features of a social situation as viewed entirely within the framework of conditioning theory, and to investigate the simplest situations that could be considered truly social within this framework" (p. 115). Toward this end, they designed an experiment in which two subjects served simultaneously, but each was unaware that his rewards and punishments were entirely controlled by the responses of the other. Each subject arrived at the appointed room, was met by the experimenter, and was led to a cubicle equipped with a control panel that provided two push buttons. Each subject was led to believe that he was the only one in the experiment. He was hooked into electrodes that could transmit a shock to his left hand and then given the following instructions: "You can press either of these buttons in any manner that you wish and as frequently as you wish. . . . The object of the experiment is to make as many points as you can. Your point score will appear on this counter. The red light will blink and the counter will turn each time that you score a point" (p. 116).

Whether the subject received a score or shock was entirely determined by the button presses of the other subject. If subject A pressed the left button, for example, subject B received a point on his counter regardless of what he was doing at the time. If A pressed the button on the right, B received a shock. B's button presses had similar consequences for A. Both subjects could press either button as often or as seldom as they wished, so that there was no guarantee that shocks or scores received would immediately follow a button press response made by the receiver.

Twenty pairs of subjects were exposed to this experimental procedure. Ten pairs received a strong and painful shock when the other's shock button was pressed; 10 pairs received a rather weak and just barely painful shock. All subjects received a score when they did not receive a shock. The main questions of interest are whether the average subject pair learned through trial and error to reward rather than punish each other, and whether this tendency to learn was greater in the strong-shock than in the weak-shock pairs.

The results showed that the average subjects in the strong-shock pairs learned rapidly (within the first five minutes) to press the button that positively reinforced the other, and continued to press this button throughout the 25-minute duration of the experiment. No evidence of learning was found in the weak-shock group. No subject later expressed any awareness of the "social" nature of the experiment—the fact that another subject was involved. Most of them apparently assumed they were on some complicated learning schedule that was controlled by an automatic device.

In a later study Sidowski (1957) replicated the above experiment with a number of variations. In addition to the strong-shock–score condition that had given rise to learning in the previous experiment, a condition in which only a strong shock was administered and a condition involving only a score were added. In an effort to test the importance of awareness, half of the subjects in each condition were not informed about the presence of another subject, whereas half of them were told that another subject was in an adjacent cubicle and that their scores and shocks were controlled by him as his were controlled by them.

The results of this second experiment strongly supported those of the first: the shock-score subjects showed a significant increase in their use of the score button. Such an increase was also observed in the score-only group. The shock-only subjects did not show a significant increase in their use of the score (nonshock) button. The importance of receiving a positive reward (score) is thus emphasized by these results, though we are left with the problem of explaining why subjects in the weak-shock–score group did not learn in the first experiment, whereas those in the score-only condition did learn in the second experiment.

A further finding in the second experiment was that learning was unaffected by informing the subject that his own rewards and punishments were controlled by another and vice versa. This finding obviously pleased Sidowski because he was eager to show that behavior in a social situation could be affected by reward-punishment variations without necessarily being accompanied by insight or a clear cognitive conception of any social interdependence.

Kelley, Thibaut, Radloff, and Mundy (1962) found the Sidowski experiments quite relevant to the Thibaut-Kelley conception of dyadic interaction. The minimal social situation can be nicely represented as an instance of mutual fate control, which, in the case of successful learning, becomes *converted* to mutual behavior control. The conversion is implicit, however, because the players remain unaware of the structure of rewards in the relationship or even that they are in a relationship at all. It is now appropriate to ask *why* learning takes place or *why* there is a conversion of fate control. A partial answer may be found if we contemplate the various possible response sequences that may occur in Sidowski's minimal social situation. Let us assume, as Sidowski et al. (1956) did, that a given subject will repeat his last response if he was rewarded with a score for it and that he will change his response if he was punished. These may be called the win-stick, lose-shift rules. If this assumption in fact characterizes the subject's implicit or explicit response decision, it follows logically that the subject pair should gravitate toward a state of mutual reward no matter where they start. This is demonstrated in Figure 14.2. If the responses of the two subjects appear simultaneously or in close proximity there are only three possible distributions of reward and punishment (plus-plus, minus-minus, and minus-plus). As Figure 14.2 shows, in any of these cases faithful application of the win-stay, lose-shift rules leads to a solution in which each subject delivers reward to the other. Through time, Case III changes into Case II, which in turn becomes identical to Case I.

Although there was a significant increase in "score" button presses throughout the Sidowski experiments, detailed sequence analysis was difficult because the subjects were allowed to respond as often or as seldom as they wished. This means that instead of learning a particular contingency, subjects could merely learn to decrease their rate of responding. Not surprisingly, this is what happened in the shock-only treatment of the second experiment. Here the total frequency of responding was low at the outset and remained low throughout the experiment.

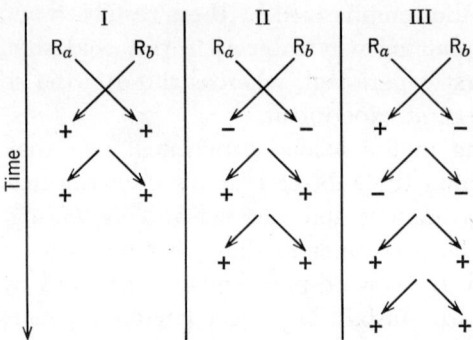

Figure 14.2. Routes leading to mutual reward in a minimal social situation (mutual fate control).

Kelley et al. (1962) attempted to avoid this problem by conducting two experiments in which both subjects were cued to respond simultaneously. Because shock had been demonstrated to be unnecessary for the learning effect to occur, the reinforcements were simply points added or points taken away. Under these conditions an over-all learning (or fate-control conversion) effect was obtained in both replications of the experiment. Their findings thus generally confirmed those obtained by Sidowski, but were now obtained under restrictions of response pacing so that a person was always reinforced (positively or negatively) immediately after making his response.

More careful inspection of the data under conditions of simultaneity revealed that score responses showed no discernible increase in 46 percent of the dyads. Furthermore, solution and no-solution dyads did not initially differ in their tendency to follow the win-stay rule: both were at the outset just as likely to shift their response after a reward as to stay with it.

Kelley et al. inferred from this that the win-stay rule was *learned during the experiment* and was not necessarily imported as a prior learned principle. (There was no systematic shift in the frequency with which the lose-shift rule was followed; its role remains obscure in these experiments.) By means of a partly logical and partly empirical analysis too complicated to report here, the authors developed the hypothesis that out of initially random responding certain accidental response combinations get reinforced and lead to learning of the win-stay rule whereas other, equally accidental combinations do not get reinforced and therefore the rule is not learned. To give one example of contrasting cases, if A rewards B immediately after B has repeated the same response, B is more likely to repeat the response again than if A (inadvertently) punishes B for repeating himself. The point is that subjects must not only learn which button to press; somewhere along the way they must also learn the rule of staying with a response when rewarded. The resulting picture is very different from that supposed by Sidowski and his colleagues, since in both of the Sidowski studies it was assumed that adherence to the win-stay rule is a built-in property of the organism.

It might be pointed out that such considerations strengthen the supposition that these experiments largely involve outcome control and not cue control. If cue control were primarily involved we would have a situation in which an incoming score would serve merely as a signal, triggering a previously learned win-stay rule. The score would indicate that the time for applying the rule was at hand. However, the evidence suggests that the rule develops out of the subject's attempts to increase his score-outcomes and that, initially at least, this pursuit is merely a matter of trial-and-error.

An additional contribution of the Kelley et al. study is the further light shed on the consequences of informing the subject about the social nature of the problem. In the Sidowski (1957) experiment, half of the subjects were informed that another subject controlled their fate, just as they controlled the fate of the other. This information had little or no effect on their rate of learning. In one condition of the Kelley et al. experiments the subjects were also informed of the existence of a social contingency. Greater pains were taken, however, to insure that each subject understood the nature of his complete dependence on the other and of the other's complete dependence on him. Essentially the same information was conveyed as in the Sidowski "informed" conditions, but it was conveyed more carefully and explicitly. As a result, those dyads that were informed about the social contingency showed more rapid and complete learning on the average than the uninformed dyads. Furthermore, this superiority had its basis in the subject's knowledge of the social nature of the contingency and not just in his superior insight into the *mechanics* of the game. One or both subjects in the great majority of solution dyads later reported their assumption that the partner's behavior would be stable if he were receiving positive scores and variable if he were receiving negative scores. This reasonable assumption would seem sufficient to account for the informed subjects' superiority of performance.

Kelley et al. addressed themselves also to the importance of response coordination in the mutual-fate control situation. Solutions are much more likely to occur when responses are simultaneous than when subjects are signaled to respond in alternation. In the alternation case, when A responds, then B, then A, . . . , the dyad cannot move to a mutually reinforcing (plus-plus) state by following the win-stick, lose-shift rules. Assume, for example, that A begins by helping B and is punished in return. A changes his response, thus punishing B. B changes his response, thus rewarding A, who therefore continues to punish B. This constitutes a cycle, then, which starts and ends with B being punished for helping A.

In a pair of subsequent experiments by Rabinowitz, Kelley, and Rosenblatt (1966) comparisons were made between learning in an outcome matrix with a mutual-fate control pattern and in a matrix where A has fate control over B and B has behavior control over A. Under conditions in which subjects were signaled to respond simultaneously, movement toward the mutually reinforcing solution was greater in the mutual-fate-control dyads than in the mixed-fate–behavior-control case. However, in a second experiment in which subjects were permitted to respond as frequently or as seldom as they wished, the fate–behavior-control combination produced more movement toward the correct solution than did the mutual-fate-control condition.

Both of these differences were predicted, and though the reasoning is too complicated to present here it is reminiscent of that which underlies the development of recurrent cycles in the alternation case. Rabinowitz et al. show by a logical analysis how subjects are likely to be reinforced for hurting or punished for helping in the cases in which progress toward a solution is negligible: simultaneous responding in the mixed-fate–behavior-control matrix and free responding in the mutual-fate-control matrix.

What are the implications of these experiments in a minimal social situation, and wherein lies their theoretical contribution? The experiments have a certain value in dramatizing the fact that mutual fate control can be *implicitly* converted—that a majority of subjects will gravitate toward the cell of mutual reward in a mutual-fate-control matrix though they have no direct knowledge of the consequences of their responses on the other, or even if they are unaware that another person controls their outcomes. The logic of the contingency is such that learning can take place in this implicit way, though it seems clear that information about the social source of their outcomes does facilitate learning. The last experiment indicates that outcome patterns other than mutual fate control can yield solutions also, but coordination may require departures from simultaneous responding.

Although there is a *tour de force* quality about the apparent demonstration that a kind of social influence can take place without the target being aware that the influence is social, perhaps the more important implications of these studies lie in the light they shed on the origins of cooperative behavior. The minimal social situation employed in the experiments reviewed happens to be one in which each person can best serve himself, in the long run, by helping the other. Cooperative responses, in other words, will be reinforced whatever their origin and no matter why they are performed. From the Kelley et al. study we begin to see that in such a situation cooperative successes may emerge out of initial trial-and-error fumbling. The fact that the win-stay rule is no doubt easy to learn is probably responsible for this. But it is as important to recognize that the situation does not inherently or inevitably lead to cooperation. A sizable proportion of dyads neither learned the win-stay rule nor consequently solved the problem. The results demonstrate both that cooperative solutions will emerge in a setting where cooperation leads to mutual reward and that there is a certain amount of accident involved in their emergence. Some dyads, composed of subjects who were presumably eager to solve the problem and were potentially capable of solving it, seemed to fall by the wayside through no fault of their own. There is no way for a given subject to guarantee a high level of outcomes by judicious planning or clever strategy. Each person is ultimately at the mercy of the other.

In seeking real-life examples that seem to parallel the laboratory case of minimal social behavior, Kelley et al. suggest that often in casual conversation there is a drift toward topics of mutual interest and that in the long run certain combinations of topics may come to dominate others in the interchange. Especially in the realm of conversational style, or tempo, the conversion of fate control is likely to be implicit. A person's level of vocabulary, his accent (insofar as this is variable), his seriousness of tone all may be affected by the processes of mutual adjustment indicated in these experiments. The important thing is not that minimal social situations abound in the natural environment, but that "underneath the more explicitly attained social arrangements the mechanism illustrated by (the) experiments provides a primitive and pervasive set of interpersonal adjustments of which the participants are hardly aware" (1962, p. 17).

INTERACTION STRATEGY AND SOCIAL PREDICTION

The dyadic situation arranged by Sidowski and Wyckoff and copied subsequently by Kelley and his associates has been called "minimally" social because the interpersonal nature of the situation is, in a way, accidental. One person is exposed to a series of rewarding and punishing events that are, in some complicated way, contingent on his own behavior. The fact that these events have a social origin is more or less incidental to their controlling effect. Eventually, because the situation is so arranged that a simple win-stay rule is reinforced and therefore learned, the successful subject pairs attain a mutually rewarding cooperative state—with no awareness that they have controlled their own rewards by first gaining control over the rewards of another subject.

In the cases we shall now proceed to examine each subject is not only aware of his dependence on another subject (and vice versa); he also has a complete picture of the structure of this interdependence. In other words, the outcome values in the dyadic matrix are fully revealed to him, and his problem is that of maximizing his own outcomes by taking account of the other person's probable actions to maximize *his* outcomes.

Although it is clear from both Sidowski studies, and from those of Kelley et al. and Rabinowitz et al., that subjects can and do learn to cooperate without being aware of the social nature of the situation, the Kelley et al. study shows that information about the social structure accelerates and refines the learning process. Furthermore, 21 of the 26 dyads achieving the solution in the informed condition of the Kelley et al. study reported making the assumption that their partner's behavior would be stable if he were receiving a positive score and variable if he were receiving a negative one. The successful subjects were able, therefore, to infer the social meaning of their own responses from the apparent effect of these responses on the other's behavior. They were thus capable of some strategic thinking about the details of the contingency in which they found themselves. Having decided that response invariance goes with being rewarded, the informed subject was able to develop a strategy to stabilize his own outcomes.

The notion of a behavior strategy is important in the analysis of social interactions. For present purposes a strategic decision is one that takes into account the social contingency into which a given response enters and that considers the influence of this and alternative responses on subsequent social outcomes. (It may help the reader to think of a military strategy that must inevitably take into account the position and most likely reaction of the enemy.) The word "strategy" has a precise technical meaning in the theory of games. It refers to a fully developed plan or program that specifies what a player will do under every conceivable situation in which he may find himself during the course of the game. If, for example, A and B were to reveal their complete strategies (say, to a referee) before playing a chess game, the referee could in theory state the outcome of the game. If the strategies were complete, every conceivable contingency would be covered from the first to the last move.

We shall speak more loosely of strategic thinking or strategic decisions when it is clear that A takes into account what B is most likely to do when A responds with a given alternative. The strategy might be either long-run or short-run, but it would involve a consideration of the various social contingencies potentially involved. In order to gain a clear understanding of the meaning of strategy we shall make a brief digression into the nature of the theory of games.

Although the mathematician von Neumann had written earlier papers on the mathematics of conflicting interests, it is customary to trace game theory to the publication by von Neumann and the economist Morgenstern, in 1944, of *Theory of Games and Economic Behavior*. In effect, game theory deals with the choices (or moves) a completely rational person should make when he is playing a game involving himself and one or more other people. It is basically a theory of decision-making under conditions of uncertainty. It has been extended to cover a variety of different kinds of game situations, but we will be concerned only with the two-person game in which each player is informed about his available choices, those of the other player, and the outcomes contingent on various response combinations. In Chapter Thirteen we introduced the device of representing dyadic interaction possibilities in the form of an outcome matrix. Exposition of the theory of games relies heavily on such matrices, for they define the nature of a game and indicate the pattern of outcomes corresponding to the behavior choices of the two players.

Let us first consider the two-person zero-sum game, a form of game that is subject to rather simple mathematical solution by completely rational players. The distinctive feature of the zero-sum game is that one player always gains precisely what the other player loses, and vice versa. In other words, the game is purely competitive. Such parlor games as checkers, chess, or tick-tack-toe are zero-sum games for this reason, but these games are so complex in structure that they provide a poor context for illuminating the theory. As Rapoport (1960) points out, even the simple game of tick-tack-toe may be played in thousands of different ways. The first player has nine choices of where to put his X; the second has eight choices for his O; the first then has seven for his X, and so on. Assuming that the game lasts five moves, the number of ways the game can be played is $9 \times 8 \times 7 \times 6 \times 5 = 15{,}120$. In actual play, of course, the game of tick-tack-toe is so simple that it is not customarily played by adults. This is because so many of the conceivable plays are equivalent to each other, and because the number of moves that actually make a difference is extremely limited.

To move to a case for which the theory is more appropriate, consider the game described by the matrix in Figure 14.3a. Both players, A and B, are restricted to two responses. It is clear from the arrangement of scores that each can win only at the expense of the other (and, incidentally, that B is likely to get more out of the game than A). If two players were confronted with such a matrix and induced to play the game by making simultaneous response choices over a series of trials with, say, each point worth a penny, we can well imagine that each would engage in something like the following reasoning: "If I (A) do this and B does that, this will happen; but if I do this (the same 'this') and B does that (a different 'that') then that will happen" (Adapted from Rapoport, 1960).

B would presumably be involved in following out the possible contingencies in the same way. A moment's reflection will make it clear that, either immediately or in the long run, the response combination two rational players should make is $b_1 a_2$. By making response b_1, B guarantees himself at least two and possibly four cents. By making response a_2, A might win three cents, and at worst can only lose two cents rather than four or five. But this is only the first step in the reasoning that would probably lead B to choose b_2. B should realize that A is hardly going to be indifferent between a_1 and a_2—he will surely choose a_2. The choice of a_2 *dominates* a_1; every value in the a_2 column is more favorable than the corresponding value

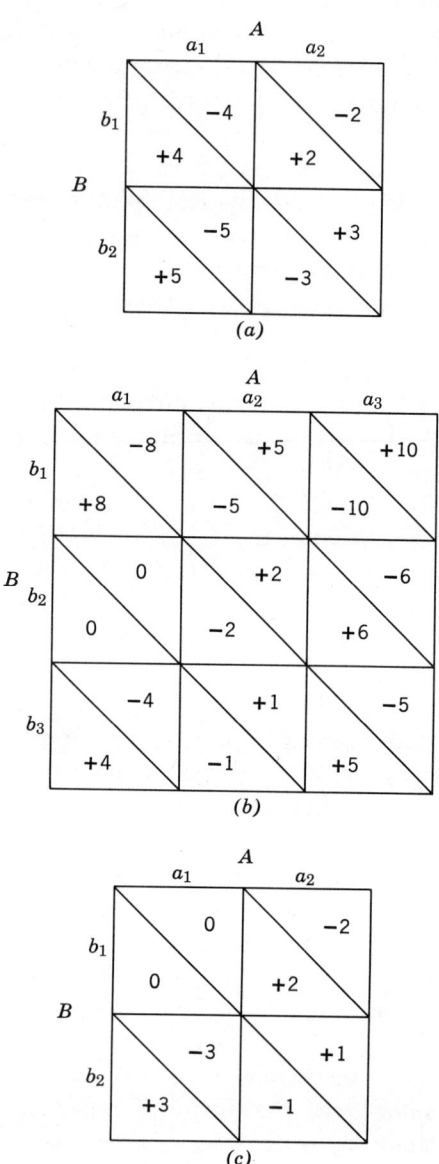

Figure 14.3. *Illustrative two-person zero-sum game matrices.*

in the a_1 column. Therefore there is little point in B trying to win five cents on a given trial at the likely risk of losing three cents. A, for his part, should be able to predict B's reasoning, though his choice would be preordained in any event.

Other matrices can easily be devised in which *both* players are driven, by considering the other's most likely response, to choose an alternative that protects them from disaster but does not yield great riches. Such a matrix is shown in Figure 14.3b. Here, whereas A would certainly like to end up in the b_1a_3 cell, and B would like to end up in the b_1a_1 cell, it would not be rational for either to yield to the temptation of trying to get into their cells of maximum reward. If each takes into account the other's most likely reasoning, they will land in the a_2b_3 cell. Rapoport (1960, adapted, p. 135) spells out how this reasoning might develop.

To focus only on what may be going through B's mind: "Suppose A knows of my policy of minimizing risk. Then he will suppose that I will choose b_3. What is *his* best choice in that situation? Clearly his best is a_2, because there he gains one, whereas he loses four and five in a_1 and a_3 respectively. Now suppose he does come to that decision on the basis of what he supposes I will do. What is *my* best choice in the light of *that* knowledge? Clearly, my best choice is still b_3, because that is where I stand to lose least if A chooses a_2. But b_3 was already my tentative choice on the basis of minimizing risk. I see, therefore, that assuming my decision and assuming that A acts on the assumption that I have acted on that decision, the decision is still the best I can do. Hence my choice is b_3."

The cell represented by the combination of a_2b_3 is called the "saddle point" in game-theory terminology. In any such zero-sum matrix as Figure 14.3a and b a saddle point is the entry or entries that represent at the same time the lowest value in a row and the highest value in a column, looking only at the scores below the diagonal. The saddle point is the response combination that represents the *minimax* (sometimes called *maximin*) solution. This is, roughly, the best solution that either can hope to get under the worst conditions that the other could create. Because the other is in competitive opposition, it may be assumed that the worst conditions are likely to obtain.

Not all matrices have a saddle point, and those that do not have one raise more difficult logical problems for the ideally rational player. Whereas the rational player can solve the saddle-point game by applying the same, rather simple, rule on each trial, the game without a saddle point requires a more complicated strategy. Examine, for instance, the matrix in Figure 14.3c. Here there is no cell in which the lowest score in a row is also the highest score in a column—there is no saddle point. Rapoport imagines a typical sequence of common-sense reasoning:

How shall such a game be played? Let us take B's viewpoint. He would like three, so b_2 is tempting. But minus one threatens there. For security's sake, b_1 is more attractive; it guarantees at least zero. The maximum principle would indicate b_1, because zero is the better of the two worse outcomes. It seems, then, that b_1 should be B's choice.

Now consider A's view. He would like to win 1, and he would play a_2 if he could count on B's playing b_2. But he suspects that B will probably play b_1, because that is where B's minimax lies. If he were sure of B's playing b_1, he would play a_1. But then another suspicion enters A's mind. Suppose B is aware of his (A's) reasoning as far as it has gone. That is, suppose B has guessed that A will play a_1. Might he not on that assumption play b_2 and win 3? If A could only be sure of that, *then* he would play a_2 and win the most he can in this game. But wait. Suppose B has followed *so* far. Will he not play b_1 (to save himself), so as to win two? But if he does, A should play a_1. . . .

We are going around in circles. Ordinary logic will not suffice to establish a rational strategy for either player (adapted from Rapoport, 1960, p. 155).

Here is where game theory—and in particular the minimax theorem of von Neumann—steps in to suggest the most rational strategy. Each subject must behave in such a way that his response on a particular trial cannot be reliably predicted, and this is especially true when the difference between outcomes within a row is high. If there are large differences between the outcomes available to A when he makes response a_1, then he must be especially careful that his a_1 responses are difficult for B to forecast. The only safe way for a player to avoid revealing his plans is for him to randomize his response choices. But complete randomization on the part of both players would not take advantage of any of the information actually contained in the matrix. Therefore the minimax theorem enters to suggest a *mixture* of random strategies. In the particular example B can minimize his losses in the face of a completely rational opposition strategy by playing b_1 33⅓ percent of the time and b_2 66⅔ percent of the time. The rational opposition strategy mixture is for A to play a_1 50 percent of the time and a_2 50 percent of the time. The mathematical formula for deriving these probabilities is quite complicated in the general case, but in the simple case presented (a zero-sum game with two response choices to each player) the procedure is as follows. In order to obtain the minimax strategy mixture for B:

1. Compute the absolute difference between the corresponding entries in the two columns. For B the differences are 2 and 4.
2. Note the ratio of the differences, in this case 2:1.
3. Reverse this ratio to determine the percentage play. Thus the row in which the difference between columns is twice as large should be played half as often—b_2 should be chosen 33⅓ percent of the time.

The minimax strategy for A may be similarly computed. The difference across rows is three points for each column, so column choices should be equally distributed. If both players follow the minimax theorem in this way each will avoid being taken advantage of by the other. However, it must be stressed that, whatever the percentage of choice allocation dictated by the theorem, the choices that go to make up this percentage must be random and therefore, on a given trial, unpredictable. To the extent that one person's choices may be predicted beforehand, the other person can increase his winnings by departing from his minimax strategy to take advantage of his prediction.

Do flesh-and-blood competitors in such a game actually approximate perfect rationality in their play—given full information about the nature of the matrix? A number of experiments have been performed to investigate the behavior of intelligent subjects in zero-sum game situations, and the results of these experiments lead to a rather strong set of conclusions: average college-student subjects tend to move toward the minimax cell when the game is fairly simple and there is a saddle point; their play does not seem to move toward the minimax strategy when there is no saddle point. Thus the findings of experiments on zero-sum games seem to reflect a rather obvious effect of complexity in a problem-solving task. There is a point beyond which subjects "do not have the necessary memory, logical facility, or computational ability to determine mixed minimax strategies . . ." (Rapoport and Orwant, 1962; see this article for more evidence concerning the results of experimental games).

This not very startling conclusion suggests that game theory may be more a plaything for mathematicians than a guide for predicting social behavior. There seems to be no evidence suggesting that subjects unwittingly (as in the minimal social situation) move toward a minimax strategy, unless the strategy called for is simple and unmixed. We might well imagine that in trying to be rational about the game, in attempting to plan with foresight and sensitivity to the other's predicted behavior, the individual player adopts a pattern of responding that recurs and is not by any means random as the minimax theorem requires. Although the results of experiments on zero-sum games are not in themselves of great psychological interest, our digression into the conditions for solving this simple form of game has set the stage for considering games of greater interest to a social psychologist. These are the nonzero-sum games, or those in which one person's gain is not necessarily the other person's loss.

Nonzero-Sum Games, the Prisoner's Dilemma, and Trust

The nonzero-sum game has an appealing relevance to the social psychologist because the play may be a result of competitive motivation, cooperative motivation, or both kinds of motivation in various combinations.

A certain class of nonzero-sum games have been called mixed-motive games (Schelling, 1960) because the player has to choose between increasing his own immediate gain or increasing the total gain of both players. The latter possibility is of course precluded in the zero-sum game. The most widely studied example of the nonzero-sum mixed-motive game is one called the prisoner's dilemma game. The important features of this game are brought out in the following description by Luce and Raiffa (1957):

> Two suspects are taken into custody and separated. The District Attorney is certain that they are guilty of a specific crime, but he does not have adequate evidence to convict them at a trial. He points out to each prisoner that he has two alternatives: to confess to the crime the police are sure they have done, or not to confess. If they both do not confess, then the District Attorney states he will book them on some very minor trumped-up charge such as petty larceny and illegal possession of a weapon, and they would both receive minor punishments; if they both confess they will be prosecuted, but he will recommend less than the most severe sentence; but if one confesses and the other does not, then the confessor will receive lenient treatment for turning state's evidence, whereas the latter will get "the book" slapped at him (p. 95).

Let us consider the important properties of this dilemma, which is diagrammed in Figure 14.4. It is obviously critical that neither prisoner is aware of the other's decision, or the dilemma may be unequivocally resolved. By implication, it is clear that one prisoner's decision will be very much affected by his prediction of what the other will do. Specifically, it will be very much affected by the extent to which he *trusts* the other player not to confess. It seems that, all things considered, both prisoners would be better off refusing to confess. For B, row b_1 is dominated by row b_2; for A, column a_1 is dominated by column a_2. And yet if one prisoner is convinced that the other will not confess, why should he not take advantage of this prediction to reduce his own sentence from a year to three months? It is clear, then, that in studying behavior in a prisoner's dilemma game, we are learning something about how one person's perceptions of another determine his own strategies of responding, though, as we shall see, other factors are also involved.

It should also be noted that the prisoner's dilemma game is a prototype or analogue of many social relationships that involve combinations of competition and cooperation. Other mixed-motive situations have already been described in some detail, such as the Deutsch and Krauss trucking game in Chapter One and the escape-under-pressure dilemma in Chapter Thirteen. Team sports like basketball or ice-hockey involve both cooperation and competition among team members; economic competitors are also cooperatively oriented toward stimulating total sales of the product that each

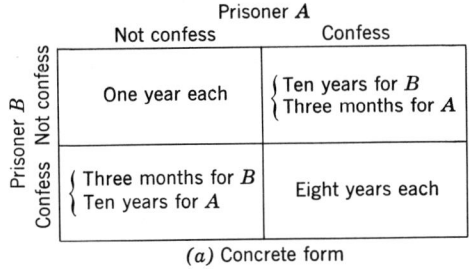

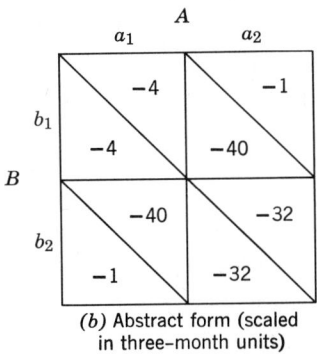

Figure 14.4. *Two representations of the prisoner's dilemma.*

markets—especially in the condition of bilateral monopoly; finally, the current cold war between the United States and the U.S.S.R. is another example of how cooperative and competitive elements can be mixed: "Our foreign policies are very hotly competitive; yet we both seem to cooperate in a precarious abstention from mutual annihilation" (Wilson and Bixenstine, 1962, p. 92).

The true prisoner's dilemma game is a one-play game without repetition. Deutsch appears to have been the first social psychologist to recognize the implications of this game for studying cooperative behavior and attributions of trust in a social situation. Figure 14.5 presents a typical matrix exemplifying the prisoner's dilemma. This matrix constituted the game played by the subjects in an experiment by Deutsch (1960) which explored the effects of different motivational orientations on the frequency of cooperative choice. The features of this game are by now familiar: if neither subject trusts the other, if both subjects choose the second response, each stands to lose an imaginary $9.00. If one subject makes a trusting (a_1 or b_1) response he stands the risk of losing $10.00 while the other wins $10.00. If both subjects are trusting each will gain $9.00. (For obvious economic reasons, the subjects were to *imagine* that these sums of money were in-

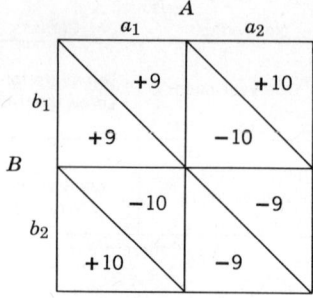

Figure 14.5. Deutsch's (1960) version of the prisoner's dilemma game.

volved in the game.) In this case mutual trust would lead to the same rewarding outcomes for each player.

In a first experiment, each subject participated in the game under one of three different types of motivating instructions: (a) *cooperative*—in which each subject was told to be interested in his partner's welfare and was told that his partner was interested in his; (b) *competitive*—in which each subject was told that the purpose of the game was to win as much money for himself as possible, and also to do better than the other person; (c) *individualistic*—in which each subject was told that the *only* purpose of the game was to win as much money as possible, disregarding the winnings of the other person. Some of these subjects were allowed to communicate to each other before making their choices by exchanging notes. The remainder were allowed no communication. Each pair of subjects played only one trial of the game, and thus each received no information concerning the response chosen by the other subject.

The results are presented in Table 14.1. As would be expected, there are striking differences as a function of motivating instructions. Those given

Table 14.1. Percent of Individuals Making Cooperative (a_1 or b_1) Choice as a Function of Motivational Orientation and Communication Opportunities (From Deutsch, 1960)

	N	% Cooperative Choices
No communication		
Cooperative	46	89.1
Individualistic	78	35.0
Competitive	32	12.5
Communication		
Cooperative	32	96.9
Individualistic	34	70.6
Competitive	48	29.2

the cooperative instructions show greater cooperation than those given individualistic instructions, who in turn are more cooperative than subjects given competitive instructions. What is especially interesting is the extent to which communication increased the level of cooperative choices in the individualistic treatment. Similar findings were obtained by Loomis (1959), making it clear that explicit communication favors cooperation when the subjects are operating under instructions to maximize the amount of imaginary money won, regardless of the other's losses or winnings. As Table 14.1 shows, there was a slight increase in cooperation as a function of communication for the competitive groups too, but this does not approach significance. Many of the competitive pairs did not communicate at all, and a number of those who did communicate tried to mislead the opponents.

Additional treatments were also included, in which the choices were nonsimultaneous (one subject always made his choice first and the choice was announced to the other), or both subjects were free to reverse their choices as often as they wanted to until they were satisfied. In the nonsimultaneous choice condition, the individual subjects behaved quite competitively (only 21 percent of them made a cooperative response). In the reversibility condition they behaved like the subjects in the cooperative condition (77 percent made a cooperative choice). It seems that one person's perception that the other has the capacity to retaliate is one of the factors that promotes cooperative choices in the prisoner's dilemma game.

Implicit Communication through Repeated Plays

When the two players, in the strict version of the prisoner's dilemma game, are allowed to interact for only one trial, there is obviously no opportunity to gain information about the strategy of the other player. As in the experiment just described, conditions of communication before the single trial may be arranged so that useful information about the other player's intentions is conveyed. It is not surprising that communication of intentions has a special effect among the subjects in the individualistic treatment— an effect, derived from the role of the instructions, in reducing uncertainty when either cooperation or competition might be justified as fulfilling the instructions.

As the game changes to one that involves repeated plays with the same matrix, each player has the further opportunity to communicate with the other by means of his choices. We may call this communication implicit to distinguish it from the working out of an agreement through conversation or the sending of notes. Two kinds of information may be discriminated. The first kind may be described as *coordination information;* directly through his choices of alternative plays each player can inform the other concerning his understanding of relevant game properties, thus establishing what his most probable choices will be in the future. Schelling (1960) has written informatively on the subject of tacit coordination between two persons in circumstances where direct communication is impossible. He discusses a number of problem situations in which two persons must converge on a common alternative among several available. To take an everyday example, consider a husband and wife who become separated while Christmas shopping in a large department store. The chances are good that each will hit on the same, preferably unique, place to meet and that they will soon find each other. Where that place is would depend on the particular characteristics of the store and the experiences the pair have shared in similar circumstances, but they would probably converge not because the husband asks himself, "What would I do if I were she?" but because he asks himself, "What would I do if I were she wondering what she would do if she were I wondering what I would do if I were she . . ." As Schelling points out,

> . . . finding the key, or rather finding *a* key—any key that is mutually recognized as the key becomes *the* key—may depend upon the imagination more than on logic; it may depend on analogy, precedent, accidental arrangements, symmetry, aesthetic or geometric configuration, casuistic reasoning, and who the parties are and what they know about each other. Whimsy may send a man and his wife to the "lost and found"; or logic may lead each to reflect and to expect the other to reflect on where they would have agreed to meet if they had had a prior arrangement to cover the contingency (p. 57).

The problem confronted by the husband and wife in this homely example is similar to the problem of players in a prisoner's dilemma game without communication. If the game involves repeated plays, however, certain information may be conveyed by the plays of one that makes it easier for the other to predict the one's future plays. Obviously the man and his wife would be more likely to find each other if they had been separated in department stores before.

In addition to the coordination information that repeated plays make available, the dilemma players develop impressions of each other that become important determinants of their own tendency to cooperate or compete. This *motivational information* derives from more complex inferences than does coordination information and grows out of each player's attempt to discern *why* the other player chose the alternative he did. The primary motivational information conveyed by repeated plays in a prisoner's dilemma game is whether the player is a cooperative and helpful person or whether he is inclined to be deceptive and exploitative.

Resolution of the prisoner's dilemma is conditioned by each player's trust in the other. Part of this trust may grow naturally out of the structure of the game. Although dyads in the individualistic orientation may be afraid to risk a trusting or cooperative response on a one-trial basis, they may become more cooperative over a series of trials. The prospect of repeated trials itself may even make each more trusting of the other at the outset. After all, if trust is met with exploitative malevolence, the person can switch to a counter-exploitative standoff on subsequent trials. As the trials are actually played, however, each player is likely to be more and more influenced by his impressions of the other player and the kind of motivational orientation he attributes to him.

In an attempt to explore these possibilities Deutsch ran a number of pairs through a ten-trial game. None of the subjects was allowed to communicate, except implicitly through his responses, and each of the three motivational orientations was represented in the design. In general, neither the anticipation of the ten-trial game nor the information gained from preceding plays affected the relative preference for cooperative versus noncooperative choices. Subjects given the cooperative instructions started out more cooperative and remained more cooperative than subjects in the other two groups. Subjects in the individualistic conditions started out slightly more cooperative than those given the competitive instruction, but the percentage of cooperative choices actually declined from trial to trial. Deutsch was led to conclude that it was extremely difficult, without explicit communication, for two subjects to get together once the two players' choices were out of phase (one being cooperative and the other being competitive). Without communication the game provides no mechanism for breaking the vicious cycle that begins when one noncooperative choice leads to retaliation by the other. The subjects in the individualistic condition seem to be more determined to protect themselves against possible exploitation than to reap the advantages of banking on mutual trust.

The results are quite similar to those obtained by Scodel, Minas, Ratoosh, and Lipetz (1959), and by Minas, Scodel, Marlowe, and Rawson (1960). Both of these experiments involved repeated play nonzero-sum games played under individualistic instructions. Using a series of different matrices, varying in the extent to which collaboration would be more lucrative than noncollaboration, these investigators found that noncooperative choices predominated and became increasingly prominent as the game wore on. This was even true given the matrix presented in Figure 14.6 where mutual trust seems eminently rational. Here cooperative choices were slightly predominant at first, but noncooperative choices became significantly predominant as the game wore on. Unfortunately, it is not clear to what extent the failure to achieve stable cooperation is determined by changes in the players' impressions of each other. We may only infer that at first the accumulation of points (and in some experiments small amounts of money)

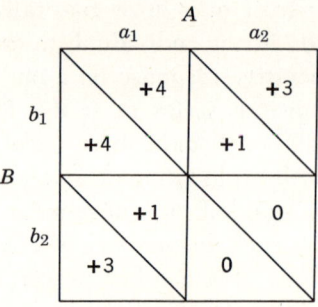

Figure 14.6. A non-zero sum game in which mutual cooperation leads to the highest outcomes for both players (after Minas et al., 1960).

is regarded as important, but that the importance of competitive success—of outscoring the other player—becomes more important as the game goes on.

This explanation for a decrease in cooperative choices is supported by Komorita's (1965) analysis of interviews after repeated play of the prisoner's dilemma game. Most of his subjects reported that they wanted to "beat" the other person rather than maximize their gain. Messé and Sawyer (in press) argue strongly that the use of either imaginary or negligible monetary incentives, typical of most prisoner's dilemma research, encourages the subject to convert what is supposed to be an individualistic game into a competitive one. They present confirming data from an experiment in which more valuable incentives were at stake. Subjects played an elegant electronic version of the prisoner's dilemma game in which gradations of cooperative versus competitive behavior could be measured. There were 10 trials and on each of these a subject could win up to 75 cents. Under this circumstance of high potential payoff there was little initial conflict and rapid movement toward mutual cooperation. Even when subjects were taught in a preliminary training session that the other player could not be trusted, there was a distinct trend toward cooperation under the payoff conditions described. Payoff arrangements that enhance the value of an individualistic orientation are therefore able to counteract tendencies toward pure competition that would otherwise be dominant.

Patterns of Choices Received

We have not dealt specifically with the effect on a player's choices of receiving cooperative versus noncooperative choices from the other player. In the studies reviewed it would have been possible to reconstruct the sequence of incoming and outgoing responses to provide tentative answers to questions about such effects. However, a more powerful and precise experimental procedure was that chosen by Bixenstine, Potash, and Wilson (1963), Bixenstine and Wilson (1963), Solomon (1960), Lave (1965), and Shure, Meeker, and Hansford (1965). In each of these studies the responses of one player were controlled at a predetermined level of cooperative choice. This was accomplished by transmitting responses preprogrammed by the experimenter under the deception that they were coming from another player-subject.

In the Bixenstine experiments each subject was seated in a soundproof booth. He faced a panel containing a matrix of four lights forming a square of two columns and two rows. The subject was instructed that he could respond by pressing the button beneath either column. The other (simulated) subject would be choosing between two rows. After each had responded on a particular trial, the light representing the intersection between the chosen row and the chosen column would light up. The payoff values for each person were listed over each light, forming a familiar prisoner's dilemma matrix (see Figure 14.7).

In the first experiment (Bixenstine, Potash, and Wilson, 1963) 48 college-student subjects were recruited to play the game. After being instructed completely about the mechanics of the game and the nature of the outcome matrix, the subjects were exposed to 30 trials in which the simulated subject chose cooperatively either 83 percent of the time or 17 percent of the time. In both conditions these choices were randomly distributed throughout the 30 trials. For 60 additional trials the subject received responses that matched his own 83 percent of the time. These matches were also random to avoid the appearance of a systematic schedule or deliberate pattern.

The results, rather surprisingly, showed that the number of cooperative choices made by the subjects was not affected by the dramatic variation in the amount of cooperation received. The average subject gave a cooperative choice a little less than a third of the time, whether the incoming

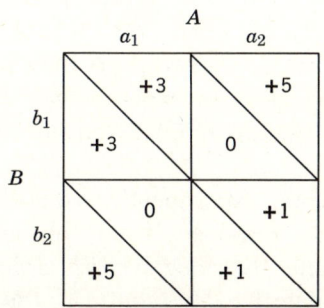

Figure 14.7. *Matrix of prisoner's dilemma game used in the Bixenstine et al. (1963) and Bixenstine and Wilson (1963) experiments.*

responses were 83 percent or only 17 percent cooperative, thus suggesting that despite the individualistic instructions the subjects played the game competitively and were relatively unaffected by the information conveyed through the programmed responses of the simulated other.

It should be noted that if a subject is mainly concerned with doing better than the other player his chances are increased if the other makes largely cooperative choices. If the subject can begin to count on the likelihood that the other player will make a cooperative choice he can enhance both his absolute and relative winnings by choosing competitively. Thus, whereas the receipt of 83 percent cooperative choices would invite reciprocal cooperation for one reason (returning trust with trust), it would invite a noncooperative rejoinder for another reason (maximization of competitive advantage). The question of which reaction would predominate would presumably depend on the subject's definition of the situation, his personal feelings about the other player, and the norms he considered relevant to the playing of the game.

Reasoning that perhaps the 83 percent cooperative choice might not be perceived as reflecting true commitment to a cooperative orientation by the other player, Bixenstine and Wilson (1963) conducted a second experiment in which programmed cooperative or noncooperative choices were made as much as 95 percent of the time. This second experiment actually involved quite complicated sequences of cooperative versus noncooperative responses. Each subject was exposed to one of two sequences of programmed responses. In the first sequence, hereafter called the *initial 95 percent sequence*, 48 subjects received 40 trials of 95 percent cooperative choices, then 20 trials of 50 percent cooperation, 80 trials of 5 percent cooperation, 20 trials of 50 percent cooperation, and 40 trials of 95 percent cooperation. In the second, the *initial 5 percent sequence* treatment, 32 subjects received a complementary pattern of 40 trials of 5 percent cooperative choices, 20 trials of 50 percent cooperation, 80 trials of 95 percent cooperation, 20 trials of 50 percent cooperation, and 40 trials of 5 percent cooperative choices. In effect, one group of subjects was exposed to a build-up and decline, the other to a decline and a build-up of received cooperation. In all other respects the experimental arrangements were the same as in the previous experiments: the matrix outcomes had the same value, the instructions emphasized an individualistic orientation, and so on.

The results of this second experiment were striking. The condition that most favored cooperative responses from the subject was the initial 5 percent sequence—the one that began with a low level of cooperation and became more cooperative. In contrast, the subjects became least cooperative when the other player started with 95 percent cooperation and shifted first to medium and then to low levels of cooperation. The authors offer the reasonable interpretation that a high initial level of cooperation from the other is likely to evoke a suspicion concerning his motives or logic that is justified by decreasing cooperation, whereas advancing from a low to a high level of cooperative choice serves more as an overture to follow suit after an initial period of cautious exploration governed by understandable self-interest. We may conclude that, at least under conditions of low or artificial incentives, sheer repetition of the prisoner's dilemma game does not lead to cooperation, but that systematic increases of cooperative choice from a simulated other do evoke reciprocation and trust. Apparently the choices that one person makes influence the impression the other forms of him and therefore condition the other's tendency toward benevolence or malevolence in the interaction.

A further study dealing with the development of trust in a nonzero-sum game is that of Solomon (1960). He was interested both in the effects of various strategies, as revealed to each player through incoming choices, and the effects of variations in the relative power of the two players. Toward this end, Solomon constructed a number of matrices whose outcome entries defined the power relations between players. As in several of the experiments described, each subject was actually paired with a simulated other who responded with choices programmed by the experimenter. The game was repeated for six trials for each subject. In the Solomon experiments, however, the subject always made his own choices before the simulated other did so that he was deprived of much of his potential control over the other's outcomes. Two of the matrices used in the experiment are presented in Figure 14.8. The numbers refer to earnings and losses that the subjects are to imagine are involved. In matrix 14.8a, in line with the distinctions drawn in Chapter Thirteen, the simulated other has high power over the subject because his outcomes are unaffected by the subject's responses but his responses clearly affect the subject's. This matrix does not technically qualify as a prisoner's

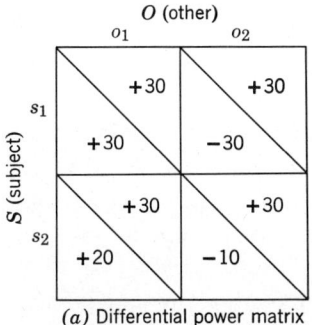
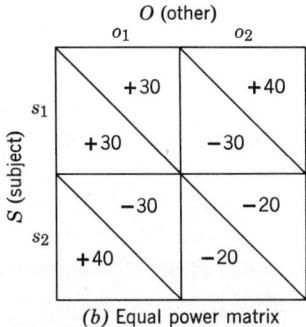

Figure 14.8. Two of the matrices used in Solomon's (1960) experiment.

dilemma game, though it preserves the feature that the subject's choice of response depends on his trust in the benevolence of the other. In matrix 14.8b, on the other hand, the subject and the simulated other have equal power in that the responses of each are crucial to the outcomes of the other. The equal power matrix is a prisoner's dilemma game similar to that used by Deutsch (1958).

Within the framework of each of these matrices (and two others that are ignored for the purposes of this discussion) each subject was exposed to one of three types of strategy from the simulated other: (1) an *unconditionally cooperative strategy*—O makes a cooperative choice (o_1) on every trial regardless of what S chooses; (2) a *conditionally cooperative strategy*—on the first trial O makes a cooperative choice, and for each trial thereafter O's choice is adjusted to that of the subject so that O makes a cooperative choice only when he receives one from S; (3) a *noncooperative strategy*—O makes a noncooperative choice (o_2) for every trial, regardless of what S chooses.

Given these conditions, let us summarize the results in the realms of both perception and action, specifically comparing those subjects playing the game within the differential power matrix with those playing within the equal power matrix. First, it is clear that differential power creates different expectations with regard to the receipt of cooperative behavior. On the very first trial (before any responses from O) subjects in the differential power treatment made significantly more trusting choices than those in the equal power treatments. Apparently, subjects confronting a high-power other assume that because the other has nothing to gain or lose he will make a benevolent choice (that is, choose o_2). However, as we have seen in previous experiments in the prisoner's dilemma game, when power is equated the subject is more likely to expect a noncooperative choice (o_2) and therefore to act in a noncooperative way in order to protect himself.

From the second to the sixth trial, any effects of the different strategies received should be discernible. As predicted, subjects in the equal power condition made more cooperative choices when the others' choices were *conditionally* cooperative than when they were unconditionally cooperative. The number of cooperative choices was consistently lowest when a noncooperative strategy was received. The high amount of cooperation induced by the conditionally cooperative strategy is precisely what would be expected, because the conditionally cooperative O is enforcing his behavior control over S—the subject presumably learns that his own cooperation is necessary in order to elicit O's cooperation.

Interestingly enough, the equal-power subjects expressed greater liking for the conditionally cooperative other than for the unconditionally cooperative other. Precisely the reverse was true in the case of the differential power subjects: they expressed more positive sentiments toward the *un*-conditionally cooperative other. A glance at the two matrices involved (Figure 14.8a and b) suggests why this might be so. In the differential power condition an unconditionally cooperative choice is a gratefully received expression of benevolent motivation. O is a nice guy because he does not exercise the potential fate control he has over S or exploit his position of superior power (cf. Thibaut and Riecken's 1955b experiment, discussed fully in Chapter Seven). In the equal condition, however, the unconditionally cooperative choice becomes naive and irrational if the subject himself chooses the second, exploitative, role. After all, under such circumstances, the other must see that he has defeated himself and, in effect, has gone against instructions by making the choice that helps the subject at his own expense. Solomon presents evidence to support the hypothesis that such an unconditionally cooperative other is viewed as stupid and unwilling or incapable of understanding the game.

Two recent studies provide further evidence that subjects are quite willing to exploit a partner programmed as cooperative. Lave (1965) confronted subjects in a prisoner's dilemma game with behavior patterns to which he later assigned the colorful labels Stalin, Khrushchev, Coolidge, and Gandhi. The Stalin pattern involved consistently noncooperative choices. The Khrushchev pattern was similar except for an occasional sally over to the cooperative strategy. The Coolidge pattern was one of cautious, conditional cooperation: this type of partner was to make the cooperative choice after the subject had been cooperative five times in a row. The Gandhi pattern was unconditionally cooperative.

Not surprisingly, the Stalin pattern was typically met by reciprocal refusal to cooperate. Khrushchev's occasional switches to cooperation seemed to stir the subject's hopes, leading him to make cooperative moves for several trials. These, of course, were then exploited by programmed noncooperative rejoinders. By the fourth such switch the subject no longer was enticed into hopeful cooperation and the Khrushchev and Stalin patterns became identical. Data on the Coolidge pattern were not separately analyzed. The Gandhi pattern tended to elicit cooperation when the matrix values were such that the subject earned little more by exploiting than by reciprocating cooperation. However, when the rewards for a successful double-cross were increased, the subjects responded to unconditional cooperation with exploitation.

Exploitation of cooperative overtures was also common in a study by Shure et al. (1965). These investigators attempted to contrive a laboratory analogue of pacifism in the face of potential violence, in the form of electric-shock administration. A game of transmitting message units was devised with mixed-motive features very similar to the Kelley et al. (1965) escape paradigm described in Chapter Thirteen. Only one subject could transmit at a time, and yet the more immediate the transmission, the greater the reward. Under certain conditions one player could gain control over the other and could push him out of the common transmission path, an action that simultaneously delivered shock. Naive subjects played against a programmed rival who was completely pacifistic. The rival in effect abdicated control to the subject by his moves in the early trials, and put himself at the subject's mercy. The common reaction of most subjects was to take complete advantage of the bogus other, even when the subject was led to believe that his preemptive actions resulted in a painful shock to the other player, and when he knew that the other player could shock him but did not. Personal communications from the pacifist, urging fair play, improved the level of cooperation to some extent, but not markedly. Shure et al. concluded that, within the special confines of their situation, pacifism is an ineffective strategy. This adds some emphasis to the findings already reported on reactions to unconditional cooperation.

Varying the Other Player's Characteristics

Although it seems highly probable that personal impressions of the other player do develop and do influence the subject's own plays, the evidence presented so far is unclear about the relative weight that should be assigned to motivational versus coordination information in the repeated play of prisoner's dilemma games. It is possible, of course, to obtain subjects' impressions of the other player after the game is played, but there are many reasons not to take the reports of these impressions entirely at face value. One such reason is the person's need to justify his own plays after the fact—to explain his own competitiveness, perhaps, by emphasizing the exploitative character of the other player.

A study by Marlowe, Gergen, and Doob (1966) makes an important contribution to this problem by examining the effects of experimentally varying the personal characteristics of the other player. Before a 30-trial prisoner's dilemma game subjects were provided with self-descriptive questionnaires allegedly filled out by the other player, but in fact pre-designed and standardized. Half of the subjects received questionnaires so answered that the other player seemed extremely egotistical; to the remaining subjects he appeared to be extremely modest and humble. These differences were clearly perceived by the subjects, as revealed in their impression ratings of the other player immediately after the questionnaires were received.

Crosscutting this contrived variation in the personality of the other player, half of the subjects were led to expect a subsequent confrontation with their partner "to discuss why they behaved as they did." The remaining subjects were given no such expectation of a postgame discussion. The investigators predicted that subjects expecting a subsequent confrontation would exploit the egotistical partner more than the humble partner; when no further interaction was anticipated, the reverse would be true. This prediction was based on the needs of subjects with egotistical partners to protect their power in the relationship, especially when the relationship was to be more than fleeting, as in the confrontation condition. The optimum strategy for protecting one's power when dealing with an egotist would seem to be successful competition. When dealing with a humble, modest partner, however, exploitation arouses guilt feelings, especially when a subsequent confrontation is anticipated.

In the game itself the partner's responses were programmed to be predominantly cooperative. The hypothesis, that the subjects' choices would vary as a joint function of the partner's personal characteristics and the anticipation of further interaction, was confirmed. When a confrontation was anticipated subjects were more exploitative toward an egotistical than a self-effacing partner. When there was to be no confrontation they were more exploitative toward the self-effacing partner.

GAMES, STRATEGY, AND EVERYDAY "SOCIAL INTERACTION": SUMMARY AND COMMENT

We have to this point explored the experimental data from three distinct but related paradigms: operant verbal conditioning; the "minimal social situation" of mutually contingent responses; and, finally, the two-person game. In each of these research domains we have concentrated on the development of outcome control in dyadic interaction. We have moved generally from the simpler and more primitive outcome control arrangements to those in which a wide range of cognitive and motivational factors become relevant. At some point on this continuum of relative complexity the subject's own definition of situational goals, as well as his attribution of motives and intentions, had to be considered in order to interpret the apparently self-defeating or "irrational" behavior of the subjects. It should thus be clear that the analysis of social interaction cannot go very far without a consideration of the social perceptions and judgmental inferences of the actors involved.

In spite of the aforementioned variations in complexity, we have been dealing with highly contrived artificial laboratory interactions. It is appropriate to ask whether the advantage of experimental control is sufficient, in this case, to compensate for the lack of immediate application of findings to everyday social interactions. What are the implications of the research reviewed for a science of social interaction?

At a minimum the research cited is instructive in showing how individuals are affected in their responding by socially mediated outcomes.

Whether we set this outcome mediation in the context of teaching and instruction, evolving cooperation, or winning a game, there is an underlying structure of outcome control that can be viewed in the same terms. In the examples reviewed, each person's power over the other becomes manifest in an outcome exchange, and the course of the interaction is typically predictable from a knowledge of the outcome matrix that governs the relationship.

A crucial complication that must be stressed is that the outcomes, which are in effect assigned by the experimenter to the cells of the matrix, may not have the intended value for the subjects. At best, the values located in the many experimental matrices presented in this chapter are a crude index of the importance attached by the typical subject to being in a particular cell. It was pointed out, for example, that subjects constructed "I" or "we" sentences in the Taffel task only if they acknowledged being pleased when the experimenter said "good." For those subjects who did not particularly care for the reinforcement, the experimenter was unable to influence (control) their sentence construction. Similarly, in the experimental games a persistent finding was that a majority of subjects instructed to think only of their own welfare ended up more concerned with their competitive advantage over the other player. It has been suggested that the conversion of the game from an individualistic to a competitive one occurred because the subjects could not get excited about accumulating imaginary points or pennies; hence, out of something resembling boredom, they imposed their own reward structure on the game. In effect, they redefined the values of a matrix so that the winning of nine points was practically the equivalent of losing nine points as long as the other player was dealt the same fate (see Figure 14.5).

When genuine incentives *are* offered for individualistic play, there is a noticeable decline in self-defeating competitiveness. This is clearly a major implication of Messé and Sawyer's (in press) finding that cooperation increases over trials in which substantial monetary sums are at stake in a prisoner's dilemma game.

The point is even more dramatically made by Gallo's (1966) direct comparison of the effects of real and imaginary incentives in a mixed-motive game. In a study by Deutsch and Krauss (1960), described in Chapter One, subjects were to imagine themselves as the owners of trucking companies interested in sending their trucks to a destination for profit. The amount of profit was greater the less time it took the truck to reach its destination on a particular trial. If both owners sent their trucks along the most direct route they would meet head-on in a one-lane section. The players had to learn, without communicating, a strategy of alternating the priority of crossing the one-lane section from trial to trial. If they did not adopt this alternating strategy, they would use up time in stalemates or on the longer alternate route (see Figure 1.1).

In some conditions of the Deutsch and Krauss experiment one or both players could operate a gate to prevent the other from using the one-lane path. The amount of joint profit was lowest in the bilateral threat condition, where both players had a gate. Gallo (1966) suspected that this self-defeating behavior was not a function of the psychological effects of threat per se, as argued by Deutsch and Krauss, but arose because: (a) the subjects had virtually no motivation to cooperate because the profits and losses were imaginary, and (b) the availability of gates provided more opportunities to express the competitiveness inherent in the game. To support his argument Gallo designed a study featuring a similar trucking game and compared a condition of imaginary money with one in which substantial sums of real money could be won.

The main results of this study were that the real-money dyads were decidedly more cooperative, used their gates less, and earned more money than the imaginary-money dyads (if the latter had been playing for real money). Real-money dyads engaged in five times as much cooperative alternation behavior as did the imaginary-money dyads. The mean joint payoff for the imaginary-money dyads was −$8.62; for the real-money dyads it was +$2.20.

We may conclude that it is extremely important not to jump too quickly from hypothetical laboratory situations to the arena of more significant life events. This is especially true when the laboratory situation calls for imaginary role playing. It is important that motives relevant to the theoretical concepts being compared be aroused by the experimental procedures.

The concept of strategy has an obvious relevance to the task of matching wits in a game situation, but is the concept of much value in the analysis of more casual everyday interactions? This is an intriguing question to which we shall next attempt to give some preliminary answers.

STRATEGIES FOR AUGMENTING OUTCOMES IN SOCIAL INTERACTION

When two persons are bound together in such a way that each affects the other's outcomes, each can maximize the possible outcomes available in the relationship by doing what the other wants him to do—he can learn, comply, or submit to the other's expectations and desires. If the distribution of power in the relationship is fairly equal, this compliance or learning is typically mutual and we are dealing with something like a fair exchange of economic commodities. Each actor is able to make his own outcomes secure by doing what the other wants him to do, and each is therefore likely to be satisfied with this kind of compliance exchange.

There are, of course, many dyads in which one actor is relatively more powerful than the other. This means that the low-power person's outcomes are more affected by the high-power person's actions than vice versa. Such differences in power place the low-power person in a position of greater uncertainty about his moment-to-moment fate than is true for the high-power person. From the unequivocal behavior orientation (UBO) principle, we would expect the low-power person to act to reduce his uncertainty, to reduce the power differential. His actions may be viewed as part of a social strategy to exert maximum control over his environment.

The first and most obvious strategy available to the low-power person in realizing this end is that of behavioral compliance. By doing what the high-power person would prefer to have him do, the low-power person exerts the only influence available to him within the structure of the matrix defining the relative power of the two persons. The fact that the high-power person prefers the low-power person to do X rather than Y suggests that the low-power person has some counterpower over the high-power person. In exercising this counterpower he makes his own outcomes more predictable and more pleasurable. But the low-power person's leverage is by definition weak and his environment is likely not to be as predictable as in an equal-power relationship, where each actor gives as much as he gets and each has an equivalent investment in the relationship. As long as he complies and the high-power person is aware of this compliance, the low-power person can be fairly confident of maintaining good outcomes. But his position is precarious because he has no way to retaliate if the high-power person erroneously or capriciously punishes him. In addition, compliance in and of itself tends to reinforce and perpetuate the power differential. The more reliable the worker becomes in meeting the supervisor's demands, the more confident the supervisor is that these demands are reasonable and that the worker is happy with the bargain symbolized by their differential power.

Owing to the precariousness of his security and the self-perpetuating side effects of compliance, we would expect to find the low-power person often engaging in strategies designed to increase his relative power in the dyad. Before turning to the ways in which this might be accomplished, let us first note some of the conditions under which power augmentation is *not* likely to be a dominant strategy.

Differential power relations usually occur in a social context in which there are often norms supporting the power difference. In our society there are a number of norms that restrict mobility and serve to inhibit changes in the power structure of particular relationships. In most organizations there are norms that support the placing of college graduates in positions superordinate to individuals with less education. Seniority often gives normative legitimacy to a power position, as does being a male rather than a female or white rather than Negro. The organization itself may be so rigidly structured that there are few opportunities for promotion across certain critical ranks. The armed forces serve as an excellent example if we consider the difficulties of changing from enlisted man to officer status.

Another kind of consideration that may deter or inhibit attempts to augment power is the low-power person's calculation of the risks involved. Although it is usually clear to the more dependent member of a dyad that the more powerful member is *capable* of causing wide variations in the former's outcomes, he may in fact avoid responses that are painful or negative to the dependent person. To the extent that the more powerful member does not actually use his power to punish, the less powerful member will not be motivated to risk stimulating such responses by efforts to improve his status. This would seem to be the psychological basis for permissive, paternalistic leadership, or benevolent autocratic rule. The strategy of the paternalistic leader is, presumably, to keep the followers' outcomes at a sufficiently high level that the risks of rebellion, status competition, or other status-augmenting reactions will not appeal to them.

In the absence of clear social norms that support and give legitimacy to a power differential, and in the absence of strategic benevolence of the high-power person, we propose that the low-power person will attempt to augment his power in the relationship. If such an attempt succeeds the individual will be better able to control his own fate and guarantee himself a higher level of outcome than he could previously count on. In terms of the model presented in Chapter Thirteen, the augmentation of a person's relative power involves either reducing the range of outcomes affected by the other's responses, increasing the effect of his own responses on the other's level of outcomes, or both.

In considering the strategies by which power augmentation may be achieved, we first concentrate on those strategies addressed to the reduction of a range of outcomes affected by the other. A primary means for accomplishing this objective is to *raise the attractiveness of alternative relationships*. The reader will recall that the outcome values composing the matrix reflect the CL_{alt}. The values are considered with reference to a zero point, which in turn is the level of outcomes attainable in the next-most-attractive relationship. The more attractive the person's alternative relationships are, the narrower the range of outcomes through which he may be moved in the present relationship without breaking off from it. The other's responses signifying reward are no longer so attractive to the person, relatively speaking, and the other may risk fewer of those that bring punishment for fear that the recipient will leave the relationship. In effect, then, one person can increase his control over another by cultivating attractive alternative relationships *and* by making their attractiveness known to the other. The essence of this strategy is captured by Stephen Potter's humorous version of "Basic Club Play":

> Basic Club Play as we teach it is the Two-Club approach. In other words it is essential to belong to two clubs if you belong to one club. It doesn't matter if your second club is a 5/- a year sub. affair in Greek Street; the double membership enables you, when at your main or proper club, to speak often in terms of regretful discrimination about the advantages of your other one (1951, p. 141; as quoted in Thibaut and Kelley, 1959, p. 20).

A second strategy for reducing the range of outcomes by which a person may be affected involves attempts by the low-power person to conceal the extent to which the other person's responses are rewarding or punishing. When the other delivers positive outcomes, the one can renounce or devalue them, or both. By acting as though the rewards are modest and by accepting them as a matter of course the individual may succeed in conveying that he needs a higher level of positive outcomes to stay in the relationship, that he feels that he deserves more. This should have the effect of increasing his control in the relationship. Such maneuvers are often seen in the area of labor-management negotiations and form a part of the power strategy of desegregation proponents. Both unions and desegregation petitioners sometimes augment their relative power by renouncing modest concessions or by devaluing the "rewards" offered. Both the buyer and seller of used cars often engage in this tactic in combination with the preceding one—each may exaggerate the value of exchanges that can be effected in alternative relationships and (until the final moment) remain unimpressed by the offer being made in the present relationship. Presumably these tactics of *outcome devaluation* weave in more subtle ways through more casual social encounters so that we often consume with relish another's gratifying remarks or actions without letting on that they have impressed us.

On the punishment sides of the outcome range, matters become more complicated. Two conflicting tactics are available: minimizing the hurt and exaggerating it. Minimizing the hurt or pain may induce the other to desist or shift to responses inducing less pain. This seems to be the strategy employed by many fictional (and perhaps real) prisoner-heroes who are exposed to torture by the enemy. If the hero can feign a stoic indifference to his captor's torture, perhaps the captor will give up or shift to punishing tactics the prisoner privately prefers. This is not far from the tactic of Brer Rabbit, who pleaded not to be thrown into the briar patch. The risks of stoic indifference are obvious, however. The high-power person may be driven to more and more extreme punishments in order to achieve his controlling effects. In the punishment realm the choice of strategy seems to depend critically on the extent to which the relationship is voluntary and other relationships are available. The more alternative relationships are available, and the more attractive they are, the more the low-power person can risk a tactic of indifference. By masking his feelings of pain and not modifying his behavior in response to punishment he may convince the high-power person to shift to more positive inducements. The shift to even more negative responses will be inhibited by the desire not to force the low-power person out of the relationship.

A strategy that marks the transition from reducing the effects of the other's responses to enhancing the effects of one's own responses is *resource development*. The low-power person may suffer low outcomes in the short run in order to acquire greater resources for controlling others in the long run. This is clearly implied by Kelley and Thibaut's (in press) suggestion that persons who fall below CL in a relationship will tend to become information dependent to discover new routes to satisfaction. In this context a resource is anything that contributes to the value that one person's responses can have for another. A worker, for example, who has special talents to offer his employer has greater resources for controlling the employer—has greater relative power—than one who has no such talents. Thus, through education, apprenticeship training, identification, psychotherapy, and other forms of resource development, the low-power person may eventually increase his power by increasing the value of his responses for the other. Such resource development may go hand in hand with renunciation of possible short run gains—as in the case of the worker who goes to night school rather than work for overtime pay—or it may involve converting the outcomes received, through a kind of capital investment, into exploitable subsequent resources. The student who takes information from his teacher, for example, can develop this information into a resource that will change the student-teacher relationship from one of power asymmetry to one of more equal power.

As Thibaut and Kelley pointed out (1959, p. 121) the low-power person may build up the value of his behavior product in the eyes of the high-power person by careful propaganda about its worth. This is amply demonstrated in the marketing field, where the power of a producer to control a consumer is often enhanced by successful advertisement of a product requiring modest resources to produce. A related tactic involves the attempt to create a need for behavior products. We have already discussed the phenomenon of increasing the value of a potential reinforcer by experimental operations that first deprive the subject and therefore motivate him to value that reinforcer (cf. Gewirtz and Baer, 1958a; Cohen, Greenbaum, and Mansson, 1963).

Finally we turn to a cluster of strategies that fall under the heading of *ingratiation.* The word ingratiation is a general term that refers to tactics engaged in by one person to make himself attractive to another. Jones (1964) has written at some length on the problems of defining ingratiation and exploring experimentally the antecedents and tactical forms of attraction-seeking overtures. The studies he reports follow a typical procedure of varying A's (the subject's) effect dependence on B (the "target person"), after which A is allowed to communicate to B about himself and his opinions. Under conditions of high effect dependence A is presumably more oriented toward making an attractive impression on B than under conditions of low effect dependence. By comparing the self-presentation behavior of subjects in positions of high versus low effect dependence, various tactics of ingratiation can be identified and analyzed. For example, Jones was able to demonstrate that subjects who are induced to attach importance to a high personal evaluation by a target person tend to avoid disagreements and to engage in flattering compliments more than those to whom a high evaluation is not important. In general, conformity, compliments, and publicizing of strengths and virtues seem to be the major behavioral routes followed by the ingratiator. One of the main messages of Jones' book is that, under the proper conditions, all of us engage in various tactics of ingratiation—in making ourselves as attractive as we can—and that ingratiation is not just a matter of individual differences in the tendency to flatter or conform.

The full implications of ingratiation need not concern us here, but we shall stress the use of ingratiation tactics as part of a more general strategy of augmenting power. In particular, we shall attempt to distinguish between compliance and ingratiating conformity. Given a dyad in which one member (say, B) has more power than the other (A), we have already indicated that A can be reasonably assured of maintaining a higher rate of outcomes by responding the way B wants him to. Thus B, who is relatively high in power, may directly influence A's performance through his ability to reward and punish A. A can avoid punishment and gain rewards by behavioral compliance with B's wishes.

But A is not only interested in locating himself in the best cell of the existing matrix; he also has a long-range interest in changing the outcome values in the matrix so that his responses have more effect on B, B's responses will have less effect on him, or both. One means of accomplishing this is by successfully exploiting various tactics of ingratiation. If A can make himself more attractive to B he can change the outcome values in the matrix in two ways. First of all, B will suffer more (incur greater costs) when he punishes an A whom he likes than an A about whom he feels neutral or actually dislikes. He will also be happy (incur less costs) when his responses reward A. Because attraction carries with it this implication of increased identification with the fate of the attractive person, B tends to bias his responses toward reward whenever the situation permits.

A second development that should occur in the wake of a successful ingratiation attempt involves a change in the outcome value of A's reactions to B. As A becomes more attractive in B's eyes, his capacity to reward and punish B increases. Thus not only is B led by his own cost calculations to reward A whenever possible; in addition, A is in a stronger position to insure that B does so. Both factors point in the same direction: by making himself personally attractive to B, low-power A increases his relative power in the dyad.

In order to put some flesh on these theoretical bones, let us briefly consider two experiments concerning ingratiation in a power hierarchy. The subjects in the first study (Jones, Gergen, and Jones, 1963) were recruited from a natural hierarchy on a college campus: the student Naval ROTC group. Freshmen and upperclassmen were invited to participate in an experiment on leadership. On arrival at the experimental laboratory the subjects were given general instructions and then escorted to separate booths where they remained throughout the experiment. Once in the booths each pair, a freshman and an upperclassman, was instructed to exchange written communications using standard forms provided for the purpose. In actual fact, standardized messages were secretly substituted for the real ones so that each subject actually received the same series of messages from the "other."

The first group of messages, the only ones that concern us here, involved opinions on a variety of issues ranging from leadership in the Navy to the problems of commercial television programming. During the first phase of the exchange, each subject received 12 opinions allegedly coming from the other and taking rather unpopular stands. His task was to record the degree of agreement with the opinions received and to return the answer to the other person. By comparing the opinion expressed by the subject with those endorsed by classmates who did not participate as subjects it was possible to derive a measure of conformity. Approximately half (specifically, 20) of the high-low status pairs "exchanged" opinions after instructions stressing the accuracy of self-expression and the importance of not misleading the other person (*control condition*). The rest of the subjects (22 pairs) were instructed that the experimenter was looking for compatible commander-subordinate pairs and it was strongly implied that each subject should make every effort to make himself attractive to his partner in the opinion exchange (*ingratiation condition*).

The results showed that low-status subjects (freshmen) conformed more than high-status subjects (upperclassmen) in both conditions, and that all subjects conformed more in the ingratiation than in the control condition. In addition, the content of the message turned out to be imporant in a different way to the two status groups. The nine critical opinion items could be reliably classified in terms of their relevance to the basis of the status hierarchy: three items were highly relevant, dealing with opinions about Navy policy and practice; three items were of intermediate relevance as they dealt with college life and academic affairs; the remaining three items were irrelevant to the NROTC hierarchy and were miscellaneous in content. As might be expected, the low-status freshmen conformed more on the relevant than on the irrelevant items; the high-status upperclassmen, on the other hand, conformed more on the irrelevant items than on the relevant ones. The authors interpret this result as largely a reflection of the greater information dependence of the low-status subjects in the area of Naval affairs. Although there is no informational reason why the high-status subjects should bow to the inferior wisdom of the low-status subjects, the reverse is obviously not true for persons confronted with the opinions of one more expert and knowledgeable than they.

For the present purposes the most relevant of the results reported is that, under instructional pressures to be compatible (i.e., attractive), the low-status subjects showed much more agreement with the incoming opinions from the upperclassmen than in a control condition. They seemed to be using conformity as an overture to win favor. But the results of the ROTC study did not really clarify the distinction between the kind of compliance that confirms existing outcome values in the matrix and conformity as a tactic designed to modify these values in the direction of more equal power. A second study by Jones, Gergen, Gumpert, and Thibaut (1965) moved considerably further in this direction.

In this study college-student subjects were assigned an experimental task presented as a business game. The game was to consist of a large number of separate multiple-choice items involving rather difficult and ambiguous choices. On each item the subject was to rank a series of advertising slogans in terms of their predicted effectiveness in raising sales. The correctness of their orderings would be judged by a business-school graduate student and he would determine their score on each trial. It was carefully explained to the subjects that they would have several practice trials to familiarize themselves with the game, that they would then have a chance to exchange get-acquainted information with their graduate-student supervisor, and finally, that they would play the game of ranking slogans "for real." The subjects were informed that substantial sums of money could be won by doing well in the real game. However, in going through the practice trials, it became clear to each subject that he was not likely to do well on the final game and that he might even lose some money. During the middle period of the experiment, which was ostensibly designed to let the subject and the supervisor get to know each other, an opinion exchange modeled after that of the ROTC study occurred. As in the previous study, the subject expressed his opinions after learning how the supervisor felt, but this time a measure of conformity was derived from the extent to which the subject moved toward the supervisor's opinions and away from the position the subject had endorsed weeks before in a questionnaire including the same opinion items. The investigators were primarily interested in how the subjects, all low in status relative to the supervisor, used their opportunity to conform in preparation for the final game. The final game was actually never played—the subjects were dismissed and the purpose of the experiment explained to them.

This part of the procedure was common to all subjects, but there were two major variations crosscutting each other in the experimental design. For approximately half of the subjects it was made clear that the supervisor had recorded his ranking of the advertising slogans before his contact with the subject and that he would automatically score the subject's answers in terms of his own answer sheet. Because the supervisor could not entertain afterthoughts or make on-the-spot decisions during the game, this was called (in the published report of the study) the closed judgment or *closed* condition. The remaining subjects were led to believe that the supervisor was generally familiar with the materials but would actually judge whether the subject was right or wrong from trial to trial. This was called the *open* condition, as the supervisor was potentially open to influence during the experiments.

The variation that crosscut the open-closed manipulation concerned the set of values and beliefs expressed by the supervisor in an interview overheard by the subjects immediately after the practice game. Approximately half of the subjects in both the open and closed conditions heard the supervisor describe himself as convinced that getting along with others was the most important contributor to successful group action; to the remaining subjects the supervisor emphasized getting the job done and belittled the importance of such things as morale and cooperative spirit. Because of his emphasis on group solidarity the supervisor in the former role was called Sol in the experimental report. In the latter role he was called Prod because of his emphasis on productivity. The design was thus a 2×2 design with four conditions: Open-Sol, Open-Prod, Closed-Sol, and Closed-Prod. The investigators predicted that subjects in the Open-Sol condition would show the greatest amount of conformity to the supervisor, whereas those in the Open-Prod condition would show the least amount of conformity. Subjects in the two closed conditions might be slightly influenced by the information contained in the supervisor's incoming opinion ratings, but the extent of their conformity should be negligible by comparison with the Open-Sol subjects. Those in the latter condition, it was expected, would be as information-dependent as those in the closed conditions and in addition, motivated to curry favor with the influenceable supervisor. Low conformity was predicted in the Open-Prod condition because, it was assumed, the way to win Prod's favor was to manifest independence and autonomy.

The results gave statistically significant support to these predictions: subjects in the Open-Sol condition showed the greatest movement toward the supervisor's opinions; those in the Open-Prod condition showed the least; and subjects in the two closed conditions were intermediate. It may be concluded that the supervisor's openness to influence was an important factor in the inducement to use conformity or manifest independence as an ingratiation tactic. The supervisor's personal values, as revealed by the contrived interview, determined whether conformity or independence would be the preferred overture for creating an attractive personal impression.

These and other studies reported by Jones (1964) indicate that social conditions may easily be arranged to bring forth strategic considerations in an interaction. From the last example we can see that an individual who is unable to insure adequate incomes through compliance (by doing well in the business game) may attempt to improve his power position by increasing his attractiveness to the person who controls his fate. Through such ingratiation he tries to earn favor not by doing well within the confines of the immediate task but by introducing extraneous, illicit considerations in an effort to enhance his attractiveness and thus revise the outcome values of the matrix.

The distinction between compliance and ingratiating conformity depends on one final but crucial factor. This is the extent to which the effectiveness of strategic ingratiation depends on clever concealment of the ingratiator's ulterior motive. One of the prime objectives of the ingratiator is to go beyond compliance and provide evidence that the compliance is spontaneous. Compliance, as used here, involves straightforward acquiescence to the realities of power symbolized by the distribution of outcomes in the matrix. Conformity in the service of ingratiation, however, must appear to be a happy coincidence in order to be successful. Or, if not a coincidence, the ingratiator must at least convey that he is influenced only by the impressive logic of the target person's argument and not by his power to affect the ingratiator's outcomes.

The evidence on this latter point is indirect but fairly persuasive. We have noted, in Chapter Seven, that the compliance of a low-power person typically conveys no information to a supervising high-power person regarding the former's spontaneous loyalty or affection (cf. Thibaut and Riecken, 1955b). Conformity as an ingratiation tactic involves an attempt to create the illusion of spontaneity, the illusion that the person's overt statements validly reflect his covert attitudes. An experiment by Jones and Jones (1964) may be viewed as a partially successful attempt to demonstrate the ingratiator's worries about making his conforming overtures seem obvious to A, the target person and B, himself. In that experiment subjects who were motivated to create a favorable impression adopted a complicated and subtle strategy involving the combined use of moderate conformity and public expressions of confidence in opinions that were in agreement with the target person's. Thus, when they did not agree with the target person they reduced the sting of their disagreement by expressing little public confidence in their opinions. This did not happen with subjects who were not so dependent on the target person—whose relative power was not so low.

Finally, an experiment by Davis and Florquist (1965) added further evidence concerning the subtlety of ingratiation tactics and showed that persons can be induced to be ingratiating to protect themselves from an irascible person with power over them. The experiment was set in the context of a training experience. Each subject (all were female undergraduates) appeared for the experiment and saw that another subject was also there. Each was informed that she would be given extra credit in her psychology course for assisting in the preparation and analysis of data from a large experiment. As part of her assistantship duties she was to learn how to operate certain IBM equipment under the tutelage of the experimenter. When the supervisor-experimenter took the two subjects into a room containing an IBM key punch, one of the subjects was selected to undergo training first, while the other was given an elementary boardwiring task. Actually, the subject selected for key-punch training was an accomplice of the supervisor, and both had been carefully trained to play standardized roles during the training session. Because the subject's task required little concentration she could readily observe the training across the room. As the training of the accomplice proceeded, the supervisor played one of two roles: either he was irascible, supercilious, and contemptuous of the accomplice, criticizing her errors in an emotional manner (the *emotional* condition), or he was relatively helpful and matter-of-fact (the *stable* condition).

As in the experiments previously discussed, this comparison was crosscut by another variation in the degree to which the subject was effect dependent on the supervisor. In the *high-dependence* condition it was stressed that the subject would be expected to return for two additional training and data-analysis sessions, and the supervisor made it clear that he himself was going to rate the quality of her performance, a rating that would constitute 15 percent of her course grade. In the *no-dependence* condition the original supervisor was called away after training the accomplice and stating his opinions, and it was made clear that the subject would be working with another supervisor.

After the accomplice had received her training (under the emotional or the stable supervisor) it was clearly pointed out to the subject that she would be trained in the use of the key punch during the next session. The supervisor then gave each girl a copy of a 20-item opinion questionnaire that was supposedly in use on the project for which she was being trained. He suggested that she fill out the questionnaire in order to become familiar with it. Before she began, however, he commented, "As you can see, there is only one sensible answer for some questions; for others, there is more room for disagreement." He then read the first five items and gave his alleged opinion, backed up with brief arguments. On three of these items he clearly deviated from college norms. On each of the three items, furthermore, he presented certain arguments supporting his opinions. Three of the remaining 15 items were clearly related to the arguments expressed by the supervisor. Thus it was possible to derive two different measures of conformity: one, a direct measure of agreement on opinions explicitly endorsed by the supervisor; the other, a more indirect measure of agreement with certain arguments or premises that had formed a part of his supporting statements.

In planning the experiment Davis and Florquist had reasoned that the threatening or emotional manner of the supervisor would have radically different implications for conformity, as a function of the degree to which the subject was dependent on him. Specifically, they predicted that highly dependent subjects would agree more with the emotional than with the stable supervisor, and that independent subjects would agree more with the stable than with the emotional supervisor. The highly dependent subject would agree with the emotional person in the interest of self-protection, to decrease the likelihood that she would later be ridiculed and embarrassed by the supervisor. In the no-dependence condition, the investigators reasoned, agreement would be prompted by belief in the credibility of the information source and would not be professed as a protective maneuver. The stable supervisor was in fact seen as more able and intelligent and as less dogmatic and opinionated than the emotional supervisor.

Direct measures of agreement with the supervisor on the five items he had read aloud showed no important variations that could be attributed to the experimental conditions. On the other hand, the predictions were rather well supported when the second, more indirect measure of conformity was used. When dependence was high there was more agreement with the implied views of the emotional supervisor than with those of the stable supervisor. When dependence was low the converse was true.

Apparently, tactical conformity shows itself only in the indirect measure because agreeing with someone's premises while disagreeing moderately with his conclusions is a more subtle form of ingratiation than slavishly endorsing the conclusions he directly advocates. In addition, the subject's own picture of himself should be considered. Presumably, if he resists the inclination to agree on issues on which he is openly invited to conform he may continue to see himself as autonomous and able to resist the self-protective urge to curry favor by agreeing with a threatening target person.

Although considerably more research needs to be done in this area to clarify the distinction between compliance and ingratiation, the research thus far suggests that the more obvious the dependence of one person is on another, the more subtle his ingratiation tactics must be in order to be effective.

SUMMARY

In the present chapter we have surveyed a number of experiments primarily concerned with the vicissitudes of outcome control in dyadic interaction. Even when each actor has little or no information about the nature of the contingency between his and the other's responses, various primitive mechanisms may play a role in modifying their behavior. When the outcomes of one person are affected by the responses of another, his own behavior should drift toward a greater frequency of the responses associated with reward. The "win-stay" rule implied by this drift was demonstrated, in a number of experiments, to play a potent role in the development of mutual cooperation. A cooperative exchange of rewards can readily develop out of initially random responding, though it was shown that this does not happen under certain conditions of response timing or when the matrix combines fate control and behavior control.

When the parties to the interaction have full information about the response-outcome contingencies governing the dyadic relationship, interaction may be construed as a game in which strategic considerations become important. In order to respond effectively each actor must calculate the most likely act or sequence of acts to be chosen by the other. When the contingencies are such that one person's losses are not necessarily the other person's gains, the development of cooperative action may require that each player impute trust to the other. The experimental evidence thus far accumulated in the playing of games in which both players can win or lose (nonzero-sum games) emphasizes the difficulties of arranging the conditions that favor mutual trust. The evidence also points up the readiness with which persons convert ambiguous social situations into competitive ones. Cooperation may be imposed on the players by experimental instructions; it may emerge out of free communication between the subjects; or it may be furthered by evidence, in the early plays of the game, that the other intends to play cooperatively if he is met halfway. At best, cooperation rests on a shaky base whenever the trust of one person may be competitively exploited by actions of another. There is evidence, however, that cooperation is much more likely to occur when there are high incentives to optimize absolute individual outcomes. In the typical mixed-motive game outcomes can only be optimized if each individual foreswears competition.

In the discussion just completed, we have tried to extend the notion of strategy to the broader arena of everyday interactions by considering the ways in which a person may either insure that he obtain the best outcomes available in the dyadic matrix or change the distribution of outcomes in his favor. The latter course involves strategies designed to augment his relative power and therefore his control over the other's behavior. This may be done through resource development or through tactics of ingratiation—that is, through the development of skills that increase his contribution to the relationship or through the management of an attractive impression. In exploring the modes of attraction-seeking we have concentrated on the tactic of conformity and compared this with compliance. Although the two kinds of social agreement have a superficial resemblance, compliance supports and verifies the matrix values, whereas ingratiation introduces extraneous considerations in order to produce a redistribution of these values. It may be seen, then, that the conformity of a dependent person can be viewed as a resultant of social influence or as an instrument of social influence. In the former case an individual acquiesces to the workings of the dyadic power structure; in the latter he attempts to convey a congruence of private attitudes in order to influence the other to regard him as attractive and worthy of favorable treatments.

CHAPTER FIFTEEN

The Impact of Group Membership on Individual Behavior

We have traveled a long and winding road in order to record the major points at which the life of the individual is touched by the behavior of other individuals. These other individuals have been characterized variously in preceding chapters as socialization agents, stimulus persons, comparison models, communicators, and actors linked to the individual through contingencies of outcome. Now we shall attempt to cope more directly with the phenomena of group life and no longer restrict ourselves to the dyad.

Two or more persons become a group when the individual members feel that their purposes are served by continued affiliation. In some groups the members share the same purpose; in others the group holds together because it fulfills a variety of individual purposes. Although the collective purpose or various individual purposes may not, in the end, be obtained by group action, the crucial condition is that such expectations are held by the individuals concerned. In short, we take the position that a collection of persons becomes a group when all see their actions as interrelated and their fates as to some extent interdependent.

The importance of group memberships to the average individual can hardly be exaggerated. We are formally educated in groups; many of us work in continued collaboration with others; we typically worship in groups; we are well aware that crimes are often carried out in gangs; we make plans as a family (often viewed as the prototype of a small group); some of us strive to improve our working conditions through joint action within a union; and so on.

We may begin to understand why we so often join with others to accomplish our objectives by returning to consider the possibilities of effect dependence in the action sequence. To say that A is dependent on B or C, or the combination of B and C, implies that A requires the assistance of these others to achieve certain goals important to him. We have already dealt at some length with the informational contribution of other persons to a particular *A*'s definition of reality and his assessment of his capacities to cope with reality. Thus, from time to time, people will seek out others—groups will form—because people are mutually dependent on each other for information. Now, in addition to the role of information dependence in the formation of groups, we wish to consider the ways in which *A* may augment his capacities to achieve important personal goals by joint action with others.

That such effect dependence can lead to group formation is hardly a matter for debate. Previous chapters have highlighted the approach of Thibaut and Kelley to the analysis of social interaction. Underlying their approach is the basic assumption that persons will begin and continue interacting as long as their rewards exceed those expected from individual action or from alternative social relationships. The concept of CL_{alt} was introduced to carry precisely this implication. In Chapter Fourteen we reviewed a number of experiments in which subjects attempted to maximize their outcomes (or effects received) by adapting their responses to those of another person. Because each subject's outcome depended both on his response and the response of the other member of the dyad, we might say that the subject was helped by the other person to attain outcomes otherwise beyond his reach.

In everyday life, similarly, there are numerous objectives which can only be achieved through joint action. It is highly unlikely that Mt. Everest will ever be climbed by a single person; an attack on such a formidable objective requires large and expert teams of collaborators and extensive planning and coordination of effort. Many other examples of objectives for which group effort is essential could be cited: moving a piano, submerging a submarine, playing a Mozart quartet. At a more complicated level of organization, the pooling of resources in business and industry, or through taxation, makes possible for each contributor advantages he could never have gained through individual action.

But this is certainly not always the case. Sometimes "too many cooks spoil the broth"; sometimes the presence and the actions of others can have a distracting or inhibiting effect. Just as there are tasks that by their very nature seem to require coordinated group efforts, so there are tasks which more or less defy such group efforts. Certain cognitive tasks like composing a poem or planning and executing a piece of sculpture seem to require the consecutive, highly coordinated thinking of one person. It seems unlikely that the delicate balance of feedback, foresight, and sustained personal imagery involved in such projects could ever be broken down into component tasks for effective group performance. With respect to certain physical performance tasks the point may be made with even less equivocation. Two persons at the same typewriter can hardly type a better or faster report than one, much less a report that would be *twice* as good or fast.

Thus we see at the outset that the nature of the particular task involved is a critical determinant of the relative advantages of group versus individual effort. Students of group versus individual problem-solving have not yet been really successful in classifying tasks in a way that would make it easy to specify the conditions favoring group over individual action. In spite of the difficulties involved, let us briefly consider the reasons why coordinated effort may be superior to the pooling of individual efforts under certain conditions and inferior under others.

RESOURCE POOLING AND GROUP PROBLEM SOLVING

The comparison of individual versus group problem-solving efficiency is one of the few areas in social psychology in which there has been sustained empirical interest. In his review of the field in Murchison's 1935 *Handbook of Social Psychology*, Dashiell was able to cite an extensive literature dating back to 1895 of experiments concerned with the advantages and disadvantages of solving problems in groups. When Lindzey's *Handbook of Social Psychology* was published in 1954, Kelley and Thibaut could build on Dashiell's review in considering the more recent "experimental studies in group problem solving and process." In no other case did a 1954 *Handbook* chapter represent continuation of coverage reported in 1935, bearing testimony to the persistence of interest in the factors affecting the performance of individuals in groups. However, this persistence of interest has not resulted in cumulative research and the progressive development of theory in this area. Hoffman (1965) laments the fact that "the literature on group problem solving [is] a large conglomeration of unrelated experiments, with only the faintest suggestion of commonality" (p. 127). Nevertheless it is possible to extract some relevant and provocative information from the many experiments that have been done.

As Kelley and Thibaut (1954) point out, a persistent methodological problem has been to find an appropriate comparative base line for gauging the effectiveness of group solutions. Let us assume that the task is one on which votes are taken on a correct answer and groups of five are being compared with matched collections of five individuals voting in isolation. If, after a discussion, the majority vote is taken as the solution offered by the group, the correctness of this solution may be compared with the correctness of that proposed by the computed majority of subjects each working in isolation. If the group solution turns out to be superior we can begin to talk about group effects that are *not* due to the simple effects of averaging or pooling individual solutions. It stands to reason that the majority judgment of a number of individuals confronting the same problematic event will be more likely to be accurate than the judgment of any given individual—assuming that there is some basis for making the judgment in the first place, as in the task of judging the number of beans in a jar or guessing the weights of objects. The superiority of group judgments in such cases follows from the arithmetic of adding independent judgments, a plurality of which are likely to converge on the correct answer. A more important practical and theoretical question is whether the interaction of group members is responsible for better solutions than that obtainable from the *same number* of individuals operating independently, with their solutions ultimately pooled in some reasonable way in the absence of social interaction. A still more stringent comparison is whether the group solution is better than that of the most capable individual in the group. In other words, to what extent is a group's effectiveness merely a matter of the members' ability to identify and accept influence from their most capable colleague? (Cf. Lorge and Solomon, 1955.)

A number of studies have shown that group solutions to certain problems are superior to the pooled solutions of comparable individuals. Kelley and Thibaut (1954, pp. 739–741) present and discuss eight separate experiments that showed a superiority of group solutions over pooled individual scores. However, there are also findings that suggest that groups may be quite inferior to individuals on certain kinds of tasks. In order to illustrate some of the issues involved, let us examine a few recent experiments whose conclusions appear to contradict each other.

The first experiment, by Barnlund (1959), clearly supports the superiority of a group solution versus pooled individual solutions in choosing among several possible conclusions to a series of logical syllogisms. Each syllogism was so constructed that either the premises or the alternative conclusions involved attitudinally charged content (e.g., one correct syllogistic conclusion was ". . . then some communists are conservative Republicans"). Parallel forms of a 30-item syllogism test were constructed so that each individual could serve as his own control. Working independently in a classroom setting, each individual first worked out his own solutions to all of the syllogisms on the initial form of the test. Then, eight or nine weeks later, on the basis of the number of correct answers he had given on this first form, he was put together with others who had achieved similar scores and the resultant group was given the task of solving, through group discussion, a second series of syllogisms. In this way the investigator made sure that each group was composed of individuals with similar ability. The group decisions were compared both with average individual scores of the members on the initial form, and with a computed majority score— how the subsequently composed groups would have scored in the first session if their private decisions had been treated as secret ballots in reaching a majority vote.

For both comparisons the group decisions were clearly superior. A control group of subjects who merely took the two forms of the test as individuals at two different times showed no significant change, thus indicating that the superiority of the discussion group was not a simple function of additional practice or familiarity with syllogisms. The Barnlund experiment seems to agree with the older research discussed by Kelley and Thibaut in emphasizing the contribution of group interactions to the solution of cognitive problems.

On the other hand, a study by Taylor, Berry, and Block (1958) makes it clear that group interaction is hardly a panacea for the fallibility of individuals. Taylor et al. attempted to devise a test of the effectiveness of "brainstorming" as defined and championed by Alex Osborn. Osborn, a prominent advertising executive, introduced the concept of brainstorming in 1938 (see Osborn, 1953) and it has since gained wide acceptance as a way of facilitating creative thinking in groups. Brainstorming involves a free and untrammeled interaction of group members under rules of procedure that prohibit criticism, solicit wild ideas, and emphasize quantity rather than quality of suggestions. The notion is that criticism and the selection of ideas can be applied later.

Taylor et al. compared brainstorming groups of four members with "nominal groups" of the same number of individuals working independently. The task of the subjects was to suggest as many answers as possible to three general questions, devoting 12 minutes to each question. One of the questions, for example, concerned the practical benefits or difficulties that would arise if everyone born after a certain date had a second thumb on each hand, opposite to the present one. The groups and nominal groups were composed by random assignment of students in sections of an undergraduate course.

The results clearly argue *against* the effectiveness of brainstorming for all the problems selected. As anyone might expect, the brainstorming groups produced more and better solutions than the *average* individual working in isolation. There were, after all, four times as many sources for such solutions in the group. However, the nominal groups (noninteracting individuals) produced more solutions than the brainstorming groups. Furthermore, the nominal groups produced a greater number of unique solutions and solutions of higher quality as rated by independent judges.

The results of the Taylor et al. study were essentially confirmed by Dunnette, Campbell, and Jaastad (1963). Using research and advertising personnel in separate replications of the basic design, these investigators found that nominal groups of individuals told to generate solutions under brainstorming instructions produced more ideas than the same individuals (working on similar problems) in brainstorming groups of four persons. The quality of ideas was at least as high in the noninteracting, nominal groups. Dunnette et al. did find, however, that subjects were especially productive when working as individuals *after* participation in a brainstorming group.

It is difficult to reconcile these latter findings with those of Barnlund, though the experiments differed in many respects. It is likely that the superiority–inferiority of brainstorming is contingent on such additional factors as whether the participants are close friends, whether they have had prior brainstorming experience, the nature of the problem, and so on (cf. Cohen, Whitmyre, and Funk, 1960). Keeping the conflicting results in mind, let us consider those facets of the problem-solving process that might determine the relative superiority of group versus individual effort.

The Summation and Coordination of Individual Strengths

There is no question that the members of a group can pool their physical strengths (as in moving a piano) to accomplish physical feats that are beyond the capacity of individual members. Comparable truths in the realm of cognition and intellectual work are harder to come by. Here, apparently, it is not the addition of brainpower in some quantitative sense that is important, but rather the blending of intellectual talents so that the strengths of one complement and fortify the strengths of another. If all of the subjects in the Taylor et al. (1958) experiment had the same suggestions to make, there would obviously have been no quantitative superiority of the interacting groups over the average individual. The fact that such a superiority existed indicates that different individuals produce different solutions. The experimental problems used by Taylor et al. did not require coordination of the talents of individual group members. The intellectual work that went into the construction of the first atomic bomb, as a contrary example, was the product of complementary skills brought into harmony and orchestrated, as it were, by J. Robert Oppenheimer. Thus complementary talents must be properly coordinated through discussion or administrative decision; otherwise there is no reason to expect groups to outperform individuals. The more accurately individual talents are judged, and the more the talented are deferred to in their areas of expertise, the more likely it is that a problem will yield to group effort.

Anticipatory Refinement and Objectification of Thinking

If the problems to be solved in a group are intellectual problems and involve discussion and debate, there are a number of reasons why the discussion may result in a group solution that differs from the pooled individual solution. Bos (1937) has suggested that the very act of formulating an opinion or idea for communication to the group may lead to a sharpening and refining of the idea. Barnlund (1959) concluded in his experiment that the prospect of a group discussion made the members more cautious and deliberate in their thinking. This conclusion was based on postexperimental interviews with the subjects and an analysis of the problem-solving discussions. "The necessity of explaining a conclusion (on the syllogism test) forced many students to be more self-critical. Errors that might have been committed privately were checked before they were communicated to others" (p. 58). Barnlund also suggests that the subjects took a more objective view of the problem as group members and were not so ready to act on their individual prejudices. This, of course, would have facilitated a solution of the syllogism problems as these involved attitudinally relevant content that would otherwise be distracting and lead to errors.

Associative Stimulation

In addition, the ideas expressed by one person can stimulate associations in another that, when expressed, may move the group closer to the goal or solution. This is undoubtedly a subtle and complicated phenomenon, and one that would appear to defy precise empirical study; furthermore, relevant evidence from controlled studies is primarily negative. Nevertheless, the notion that new ideas *can* emerge out of the interaction and synthesis of old ones seems to be one plausible factor that may explain those cases in which brainstorming has been apparently successful. In order for associative stimulation to qualify as a genuine interactional phenomenon, however, it is important that the "stimulator" would not have stimulated his own thoughts in the same direction and that the person stimulated needed the push provided by the outside communication.

Error Correction and Social Influence

Sometimes the problem being dealt with provides feedback to the person or persons trying to solve it. That is, it may be obvious that a solution attempt is correct because of certain built-in checks (like multiplying the resulting number by itself in a square-root extraction problem) or because of certain automatic consequences that certify accuracy (the key or the shoe fits, the motor runs, the airplane flies). In other tasks, however, the feedback may be imperfect or delayed. In problems that lack such self-correcting properties, the group may serve the important screening function of distinguishing promising leads from less promising ones. In an early experiment by Shaw (1932), for example, groups proved more accurate than individuals in solving a variety of intellectual problems. "Perhaps . . . the greatest point of group supremacy," she reports, "is the rejection (by others) of incorrect ideas that escape the notice of the individual when working alone" (p. 502). If every individual did not present the same solutions, and if good solutions tended to drive out bad ones, it is not surprising that groups were more accurate than the average individual in Shaw's experiment. It is not clear from Shaw's analysis how much of the superiority of the groups may be attributable to the pooling of individual solutions, though there appear to be some problems that are not solved by any individuals but are solved by several of the groups.

Returning to the rejection of incorrect suggestions, we might ask why such suggestions should be more often rejected than correct ones. If the person who makes the suggestion cannot reject it himself, why does he go along with the efforts of others to reject it? In most of the problems used by Shaw, those who wished to reject an incorrect suggestion were probably able to point to obvious chinks in the maker's reasoning or to certain clearly undesirable consequences of taking the suggestion seriously. It might also have been true that the superior members of the group contributed more than their equal weight to the final solution. Marquart (1955) replicated Shaw's study and concluded that in neither study did group performance exceed that of the most proficient individual. These individuals may have expressed their suggestions with greater confidence and authority—perhaps because of past experiences of doing well on similar problems—and in this way exerted disproportionate influence.

If there is voting by acclamation those less sure of their answers might not even express themselves. This seems to be the reason for superiority of groups in Gurnee's (1937) investigation. Barnlund (1959) felt that this possibility was minimized in his experiment because his groups were composed of subjects with very similar abilities on the syllogism task. Closely related is the fact that, if erroneous solution attempts are randomly distributed around the true solution, the chances are that a plurality of persons will choose the correct solution rather than the incorrect one. This plurality would then be able to insure, in a democratic vote, that the correct solution was adopted as the group solution, or would be able to exert informational influence on the individuals who are alone in their erroneous opinions and therefore uncertain about them.

In summary, there are four major reasons why a problem solution obtained through group interaction may be more accurate than one extracted from an averaging or other means of pooling individual solutions: the summation or coordination of individual strengths beyond the level necessary to solve the problem; refinements in thinking that precede communication; the social stimulation of associations; and the rejection or suppression of errors through the operation of social influence processes. We have emphasized mainly the positive contributions that may emerge from group interaction, but the study of Taylor et al. reminds us that the mere fact of interaction is hardly a guarantee of solutions superior to pooled individual solutions. The advantages or disadvantages of group interaction undoubtedly are a function of the type of task involved or the type of goal sought as well as the nature of the interaction. The summation of strengths is not important if the task can be easily subdivided and the resultant subproducts easily combined. In the Taylor et al. study, for example, the task involved coming up with independent creative suggestions, and the only real function that the group discussion might have served would have been to motivate the subjects to try harder and to stimulate associations they would otherwise not have entertained. Perhaps analysis of the protocols of the Taylor et al. experiments would show that the social stimulation of associations led to inefficient digressions and detours and that group discussion therefore made it more difficult to achieve creative solutions in the time allotted.

There are group tasks in which the degree of interdependence among the workers is so extreme that an error by one member—the breaking of one link in the chain of performance—means total group failure. Imagine an automobile assembly line, for example, on which the man in charge of installing distributors systematically errs in attaching this vital part of the motor. Obviously every product will be defective, whereas if a number of individual mechanics were each working alone on the construction of a different car at least some functioning automobiles would be completed. McCurdy and Lambert (1952) simulated a comparable situation in the laboratory by comparing groups with individuals in the solution of a problem requiring high member interdependence. They found that individuals were significantly more effective than groups, and attributed the result to the relatively high probability that the group would contain at least one member who was inattentive to experimental instructions or committed an error for other reasons. Groups were able to solve the problem faster when they solved it, but few of them did.

Davis and Restle (1963) compared individuals and groups in the solution of multiple-stage problems—those not susceptible to division of labor but requiring a series of discrete steps to solve. Their groups solved more problems than the same number of individuals working alone, but they were much less efficient than individuals. Individuals in separate rooms solved the multiple-stage problem sooner on the average than the same number of individuals in a face-to-face group. This may be a function of the fact that face-to-face confrontations interfere with the complex intellectual reasoning of individual members, or the fact that multiple-stage problems create special difficulties for identifying the most talented member.

Although the objectification of associations is helpful when emotionally charged materials are to be placed under logical scrutiny, it is also true that group interaction may stifle creativity and give rise to products representing the lowest common denominator. It is certainly possible for the more talented or accurate members to be outvoted by the less talented ones. If the problem is such that solution feedback is extremely vague or long delayed, there is no guarantee that wrong suggestions will be more frequently rejected than correct ones. It also is probable that objectification can limit or constrain the creative process in formulating ideas. As we shall see in the next section, the presence of others is known to promote more conventional associations and avoidance of the unique and idiosyncratic. Judgments tend toward moderation and away from the extremes (Kelley and Thibaut, 1954, p. 750). We can readily imagine many complex problems requiring the kind of originality that would tend to be suppressed by the actual and anticipated presence of others. Whereas it may be possible to establish a group culture supporting the creativity required by brainstorming, the average person's fears of appearing ridiculous in the eyes of others may be difficult to overcome.

Thus we cannot argue the superior merits of group discussion irrespective of the tasks involved, and the advantages that have been listed may shade into disadvantages when task requirements change. In the course of looking at what is gained and lost through group interaction, however, we have raised a number of issues about group process and indicated that there are certain emergent products of group discussion, supporting the claim made by many that the group is a whole that is different from the sum of its parts. We have moved from the general notion that people are sometimes dependent on others for achieving certain goals to a consideration of the specific ways in which individuals may be effect-dependent in solving intellectual problems. We are now prepared to push the concern with accuracy and effectiveness into the background while we deal more directly with the psychological features of group process. What are the major effects of the group on individual thought and behavior? What changes does the individual undergo when he commits himself to group membership?

EFFECTS OF GROUP PARTICIPATION ON COGNITION AND MOTIVATION

In the early attempts to assess the conditions under which groups perform more effectively than individuals, a recurring variable of interest was the effect on individual performance of the mere presence of others. Much of the very early work (from 1898 to 1914) was done by educators who were interested in finding out if school work could be better performed by a student working alone or in the presence of others. A large number of studies followed in the nineteen twenties, essentially addressed to the same "applied" question, though some studies were concerned with applications to industrial rather than educational settings.

Audience and Co-Action Effects

One of the first psychologists to look at the effects of social stimulation as a basic scientific issue was F. H. Allport (1924). In the years 1916 to 1919 he conducted a series of experiments comparing groups of four or five graduate students with the same number working independently but simultaneously in separate rooms—that is, in a *co-action setting*. Whether in a group or in isolation, each subject worked by himself on a series of problems such as vowel cancellation, multiplication, reasoning, and verbal association. Subjects were told that their results would not be compared and that they should avoid thoughts of competition so that, it was hoped, the "pure effects" of social facilitation could be measured. On the basis of his results, Allport proposed that the presence of others increases the quantity and vigor of responses at the expense of their intellectual quality, a generalization that has stood the test of time remarkably well.

Dashiell (1930), a student of Allport's, conducted additional studies on the same problem. He recognized that the problem of audience effects is one of considerable complexity. There are many different types of audience, and it would be unreasonable to think that each type would have the same effect. He identified: (a) the audience of quiet spectators; (b) the audience of vocal supporters or hecklers; (c) the audience of co-working noncompetitors; and (d) the audience of rivalrous competitors. To get at the differential impact of such different audiences on performance, Dashiell conducted a series of experiments in which subjects worked on multiplication problems, analogies items ("rain is to summer as snow is to ----"), and a serial association test to see how quickly the subject could produce a chain of associated words. Each subject worked on each type of problem, in different counterbalanced orders, in each of the following situations:

Alone (A). The subjects met simultaneously in separate rooms and worked on the problems during periods of time signalled to them by a buzzer.
Together (T). Subjects worked in face-to-face groups of 15; they were told not to compete as their results would never be compared with each other.
Rivalry (R). This was the same as the T treatment except that the subjects were urged to compete as their scores would later be compared.
Observation (O). The students were seated three to a small table, and one worked while the other two watched him closely and attentively, gazing at his face, hands, pencil, and so on. (Unfortunately, it is not clear from the experimental report that rivalry was excluded here in the minds of the subjects. Because they took turns as problem solvers and observers it may be assumed that some rivalrous feelings were definitely aroused.)

The results of Dashiell's experiment showed that subjects worked faster and produced more in a situation in which they were under observation

(O) than in the other situations, but the accuracy of their performance suffered somewhat in comparison with the other conditions. There were no large differences among A, T, and R treatments as far as performance was concerned, though subjects were generally faster when in the R condition than when in the A or T conditions in solving multiplication problems and analogies. Dashiell concluded,

> ... the facilitation of speed when work is done merely in the presence of a co-working group over that done in isolation, as observed by some investigators, is not clearly indicated here. What would seem, from our results, to be important phases of a social situation as increasing an individual's speed are the presence of some of the competitive attitude or else some of the being-observed attitude (1930, p. 196).

Especially because many prior studies had shown that working in a group setting generally increases speed of performance, Dashiell wondered why speed was not greater in the T than in the A situation. This caused him to re-examine the A situation in his experiment. Although the A subjects worked privately, they nevertheless worked simultaneously in response to control by buzzers from a common center (a procedure introduced by Allport, 1920), and each was aware that others were working at the same time. Perhaps—although they were not in face-to-face contact—the subjects in the A condition had in fact adopted a "social attitude." To shed further light on the various meanings of being alone, Dashiell conducted an additional study (using the same three types of problem) in which the subjects served in the coworking T situation, in the A situation of simultaneous but separate performance, or in a variation of the A situation (A-different) in which each subject reported individually to the experimenter and was taken to a private room. Unlike the first experiment, each subject participated in only one condition of the experiment.

The results of Dashiell's second study were quite clear. Speed of performance tended to be greatest in the T situation, almost as great in the A-simultaneous condition, and quite a bit less in the A-different condition. Accuracy tended to be highest in the latter condition. If we combine Dashiell's results with those of Allport (1920) and others, it may generally be concluded that the presence of others has an energizing effect on the subject, causing him to work with greater intensity or higher motivation. At the same time, the presence of others may often depress accuracy, either because of the interfering or distracting stimulation other persons provide or simply because an overconcern with speed itself affects accuracy. From Dashiell's results, in addition, we learn that rivalry or competitiveness adds to the audience effect, and that this is especially true of being under intensive observation—when we can only assume that rivalry is involved as well. Also, the increased accuracy and decreased speed of working in isolation do not obtain if the subject is aware that others are working simultaneously in adjacent rooms. The psychological rather than the physical presence of others is what is crucial.

The study of co-action and audience effects has received little attention since the late 1930's. However, two recent reviews by Zajonc (1965, 1966) may help to revive interest in such matters. After a careful re-examination of experimental results on both human and animal subjects, Zajonc (1965) proposes that the presence of others—either in a co-action setting or in one in which the individual performs in front of a passive audience—*impairs the learning of new responses but facilitates the performance of those that have already been learned.* This is presumably because of the generally motivating or arousing effects that people have on other people, animals on other animals. There is considerable evidence from both animal and human learning studies that drive increases the probability of occurrence of those responses dominant in the subject's repertory. If the subject has already learned or almost learned a solution, the correct response will be dominant and the presence of others will facilitate performance. If the task is complex and the correct response is not yet dominant in the hierarchy of possible responses, then the presence of others is more likely to promote incorrect responses. It is to be emphasized that the mere presence of others is being considered. In a co-action setting, if the others are performing at a more advanced level than the subject, he naturally can profit by imitating their responses. Thus the Zajonc proposition can be expected to hold only when imitation and vicarious learning are ruled out.

Zajonc (1965, 1966) marshalls an impressive amount of evidence for his proposition, though he readily admits that it is circumstantial. Going back to Allport's (1920) work, Zajonc notes that the only kind of problem in which interference effects were observed was that involving complex reasoning—precisely where we would expect incorrect answers to be dominant. Pessin (1933) found that subjects made more errors when learning a list of nonsense syllables in the presence of several spectators than when alone. However, recall of the syllables, once learned, was better under social conditions. Ader and Tatum (1963) found that subjects learned a shock-avoidance task more quickly in isolation than when paired with other subjects. Zajonc (1965) concludes with some tongue-in-cheek advice:

If one were to draw one practical suggestion from [this] review . . . he would advise the student to study all alone, preferably in an isolated cubicle, and to arrange to take his examinations in the company of many other students, on stage, and in the presence of a large audience. The results of his examination would be beyond his wildest expectations, provided, of course, he had learned his material quite thoroughly (p. 274).

Zajonc's theoretical proposition is plausible and certainly worthy of additional and more directly relevant research. We agree that the presence of others is probably arousing in the sense that the individual becomes more intense and energetic. But we suspect that the presence of others is distracting as well as motivating, and that the impairment of learning and complex problem-solving may be as much a direct effect of distraction as the increased prominence attached to nondominant solutions. One of the interesting things about Pessin's (1933) experiment, for example, is that learning was equally disrupted by the presence of a spectator and the distracting periodic occurrence of a light and buzzer. Social facilitation of dominant responses may reflect motive arousal, but only secondarily as the organism attempts to overcome the effects of distraction.

What is it about the presence of others that energizes, distracts, and undoubtedly produces other effects on behavior? How may the concepts developed to this point be applied to this problem of analysis? Apparently it is extremely difficult to bring people together for any reason without introducing what psychologists of an earlier generation called "rivalrous motives." We have noted in Chapter Fourteen the relatively irrepressible competitiveness that tends to characterize play in the nonzero-sum game. It is probably true that no matter what subjects are told about how their performances are to be evaluated, as long as the subjects are working together on the same problem they are likely to interpret the situation as vaguely competitive and therefore may be concerned with performing better or at least more rapidly than the other subjects, each of whom, they may assume, is also out to show them up.

Such explicit rivalry or competition cannot account for the effects of a passive audience of spectators on individual performance. It has long been suspected that there are wide individual differences in response to the presence of spectators (Hare, 1962), though the quantity of research addressed to this point is sparse. Paivio (1963; Paivio and Lambert, 1959) has attempted with limited success to develop a measure of sensitivity to "stage fright." Without considering the extreme of stage fright, however, it is reasonable to expect spectators to arouse in a performing subject many of the feelings and anxieties experienced in previous contexts of reflected appraisal. It is in the nature of the performer-spectator role relationship that the former exposes himself to the latter for evaluation. All performers are in the position of being critically observed, of putting themselves under scrutiny. We may thus make some headway in our analysis of audience effects if we consider some of the things that happen to a person when he presents himself for evaluation by another in the reflected appraisal process.

Evaluation Apprehension and Reflected Appraisal

We may start by briefly reporting some evidence on the arousal of affiliation motivation. Shipley and Veroff (1952) were interested in developing a valid measure of the strength of an individual's need for affiliating with others. As one step in the validation process, they attempted to arouse in their subjects a self-conscious interest in being positively appraised by a group of peers. A group of 37 fraternity brothers met to help the investigators in their study of "friendship patterns." Each member was given a booklet whose pages listed 15 adjectives sometimes applied to persons. The subjects first rated these characteristics in terms of their contributions to personal attractiveness. Then each member of the fraternity present stood up, one by one, and while he was standing the others were to check the two adjectives that most clearly applied to him. The procedure was designed to make the issue of attractiveness a salient one and to involve the subjects in thoughts about their standing in the fraternity. Members of a comparable fraternity merely met to take a "food preference test." Both the "adjective rating" and the "food preference" subjects were then asked to write stories to five Thematic Apperception Test cards as a task apparently unrelated to the previous one. As predicted by the investigators, there was significantly more affiliation imagery in the adjective rating group. That is, their stories revealed a greater concern with rejection, loneliness, being jilted, and so on. If we may extrapolate to the more conventional spectator-audience situation, the Shipley and Veroff results suggest that imagery and associative content are very much affected by going through an experience of being observed. Whereas the typical audience situation may be less obviously tied to an appraisal and public evaluation of the performer, presumably there is an increment in this kind of affiliation imagery even in the kinds of audience situation we have been discussing.

In Chapters Ten and Eleven we found abundant evidence for the conclusion that individuals show greater conformity when their responses are monitored by others than when they are permitted to respond privately or anonymously. Because the individual is typically motivated to discover his "reflection" in the reactions of others, and because he is concerned that these reactions be positive, he will try to respond in a manner that will please others. Whether he is or is not in any obvious way effect dependent on the members of his audience, the person will be inclined to modify his responses to bring them closer to what he judges to be the other's expectations.

The problem with introducing conclusions about reflected appraisal and conformity into the present discussion is that the expectations of a particular audience may be either unknown or quite heterogeneous. We have noted in discussing conformity research that the individual often tries to anticipate and to guess the opinions of others, being influenced in subtle ways by these guesses without being aware of a conformity conflict. Insofar as the audience gives out any cues about admired attributes of a performer, this could be one way in which the audience could have an effect on behavior. Whether we can or cannot correctly anticipate or intuit the preferences, opinions, or tastes of others, it is usually possible to identify and to avoid behavior that is bizarre, extreme, or unconventional. The performer may try to ingratiate himself with his audience—even without knowing their specific tastes—by striving at least to avoid offending them.

This reasoning helps us to understand Allport's (1924) finding that individuals tend to produce more common, less personal associations in a group than in an individual context. Subjects were given a piece of paper and were asked to write down words in a chain of associations as rapidly as they came to mind. Each subject met once in a group to do this task and at another time wrote down his associations in the privacy of the laboratory cubicle. After the task was completed (three minutes were allowed) each subject was to go back over his list to underline those associations he felt "derived from some definite personal experience." Almost without exception, subjects wrote more associations in the "together" than in the "alone" condition. However, there were fewer personal associations in the together condition. It is not clear whether subjects merely used different criteria for deciding which associations to underline as personal in the two conditions, or whether they in fact produced more personal associations in the individual treatment. If we assume the latter we have evidence that the presence of others does affect what Allport called the "intellectual or implicit responses of thought" (p. 274). The decline in personal associations can be understood in terms of the subject's tendency to anticipate and adjust to the expectations of others.

If the nature of the audience is unknown and expectations are therefore not communicated to the subject in any way, the distracting and interfering effects of being observed may be even more debilitating. In an experiment by Wapner and Alper (1952) each subject performed a task of choosing between alternative associations to phrases. He did this (a) in front of a one-way mirror and under instructions that he was being observed by an unseen audience, (b) in front of the same mirror with illumination equated in the two rooms so that the subject could actually see the audience, or (c) with the curtain drawn so that only the experimenter was present to monitor the subject's word choices.

A major result that confirmed the investigators' prediction was that decision time was slowest when the subject performed before an unseen audience, intermediate when the audience was seen, and fastest when there was no audience. The difference between the seen and the unseen audience condition tended to be greater than the difference between the seen audience and the alone (except for the experimenter) condition. The word choices were often rather difficult to make, and some were explicitly designed to elicit personal associations. Here is a case, then, in which the desire to avoid unconventional or personally revealing associations was apparently strong enough to induce caution and therefore to counter the normal tendency toward rapid performance in front of audiences. The uncertainty created by the unseen audience added to this tendency toward caution.

An important qualification of the finding was that the differences reported were observed only during the first 10 minutes of the 20-minute experimental session. Subjects apparently adapt to the potentially interfering effects of being observed, and 72 percent of them showed a decrease in decision time from the first to the second half of the experimental session. The decrease was especially marked in the unseen audience condition; there were no differences during the second half of the session.

Perhaps with time the subject loses his initial self-consciousness and learns to cope with the task with greater ease and efficiency. As his performance becomes more routinized it becomes less susceptible to disruption and more facilitated by contributions of motive strength (being more energized in the presence of others). There is good evidence from a study by Schachter, Willerman, Festinger, and Hyman (1963) that the consequences of being placed under the stress of observation and criticism are negligible as long as the performance is routine or has been overlearned. This is consistent, of course, with Zajonc's (1965) argument.

In conclusion, it seems clear that in many respects individuals function differently when they are alone than when they are in the presence of others. We assume that the effects of an audience are mediated primarily through self-consciousness on the part of the subject, a concern with how he appears in the eyes of others. Ultimately, of course, this is a concern with what kind of person he really is. This concern with the appraisals of others has two major effects. On the one hand, the subject's desires to perform well, to acquit himself with distinction or at least to avoid ignominious failure, are strengthened by the presence of others. An audience sits in judgment, and through its reactions the performer judges his own worth and capacities. The increased desire to do well energizes the individual's performance so that speed of movement or reaction and, therefore, the quantity of work per unit of time are typically increased. At the same time, the presence of an audience introduces cognitive considerations that are not germane to task performance and are in fact detrimental to its prosecution. To the extent that the individual is self-conscious—is focused on how well he is performing and is sensitized to others' reactions to that performance—his attention is distracted from the task itself. The tennis player who wonders how he looks to his spectators as he strokes a forehand is likely to be beaten by an opponent who has his eye on the ball.

It must be emphasized, finally, that a theoretical understanding of audience effects will ultimately require detailed analysis of the many varieties of tasks, performers, audiences, and observation settings that may be involved. This is undoubtedly an area in which generalization is quite hazardous. Much depends on the personal significance of the audience for the performer, and this depends in turn on the performer's personality, the nature of the audience, and the type of task involved. Concepts that point to underlying psychological processes are sorely needed in this area. The integrative contributions of Kelley and Thibaut (in press) and Zajonc (1965, 1966) are important steps in this direction.

Individual Motives and Group Goals

One of the most intriguing phenomena characterizing group membership and participation is the relative balance achieved between the satisfaction of individual motives and the attainment of group goals. In Chapter Three the socialization process was viewed as involving the adoption and internalization of the values and beliefs comprising the culture patterns of the larger group. As our focus shifts to the small, face-to-face group, we confront certain aspects of this same process whereby individuals are induced by others to desire to reach objectives that are highly valued by these others and that serve their collective interests. What determines when an individual will identify with group goals and adopt motives consistent with achieving them?

It has often been observed that some of the most noble triumphs and most ignoble defeats of the human spirit are achieved through group action. On the one hand we may point to the heroic self-abnegation of the martyr, who may sacrifice even his life to further the attainment of group goals; on the other hand we may point to the sadistic savagery of the lynch-mob member who seems to be swept along by a group decision that temporarily but radically alters his customary values and his motives as an individual. The dramatic instances in which a person submerges his identity and lends his strength to a group-defined cause have been a source of fascination to students of human behavior for centuries. Such instances assure us that identification with group goals does occur, but the more dramatic examples of motive conversion and group allegiance often involve a tangle of considerations difficult to unravel. The premise of the ensuing discussion is that the processes involved in the conversion of individual motives to group goals may be more readily understood in the less dramatic but more easily controlled context of the problem-solving group.

Cooperation Versus Competition

Let us begin with the simplest case. Many groups are formed because a number of acquaintances have similar individual motives and are aware of this similarity. Insofar as each person seeks the same objective, it may be quite reasonable for all to pool their resources or talents to increase the likelihood that this shared objective will be achieved. In the language of Thibaut and Kelley (1959), we might say that the individuals in this example have a high "correspondence of outcomes" within the matrix of potential interaction: when one person behaves in a way that makes *his* outcomes highly rewarding, the others will be highly rewarded too. Because of this high correspondence of outcomes—this similarity of individual motives—the acquaintances are highly likely to agree readily on a group goal and to help each other in moving toward it. The main problems remaining are those of information distribution and response coordination (cf. Kelley and Thibaut, in press).

We have described in the preceding paragraph the ideal foundations for cooperative action. Because of the congruence of individual motives and the absorption of these motives by the group goal, there is, in effect, no serious problem for the individual of coming to terms with group membership. He will presumably end up doing what he wanted to do before entering the group, with all the added advantages that mutual support and resource pooling can provide. This ideal was roughly approximated in a well-known experiment by Deutsch (1949), who organized the sections of a college psychology course into five-member cooperative or competitive groups. The students in these groups were invited to participate during a three-hour period each week for six weeks as a substitute for part of their regular instruction in introductory psychology. Both cooperative and competitive groups worked on a series of puzzles and a series of human-relations problems. The cooperative groups were told that they were to function as a team in competition with four other teams, and that each person's course grade would depend on the merits of the group solution. The competitive groups were given the same tasks but told that each of the five members would receive a different grade depending on his relative contribution to the group's solutions of the various problems.

In the cooperative group a common goal was thus imposed on the group and the motives of individual members were made to coincide with the group goal by linking performance to a common course grade that each would be given. One member could not detract from the group performance without defeating his own individual purposes. Deutsch described the cooperative groups as *promotively interdependent* for this reason. The competitive groups were, on the other hand, *contriently interdependent*—that is, one person could only achieve his individual purpose of attaining a high grade at the expense of someone else's goal achievement.

As compared with the competitively organized groups, the cooperative groups were generally more productive: they solved the puzzles more rapidly than the competitive groups and produced longer and better recommendations on the human-relations problems. There was a greater volume of communication in the cooperative groups and the members rated themselves as having fewer difficulties communicating to and understanding others. This presumably stemmed from the desire to share insights in the cooperative groups in contrast to the desire for independent, autonomous contributions in the competitive groups. In line with this interpretation, cooperative group members rated themselves as being more affected by the ideas of others and were rated by observers as more friendly during the discussions than competitive group members. Perhaps the most theoretically interesting finding is that the cooperative group members showed greater substitutability in their efforts. These promotively interdependent subjects were aware of withholding contributions on the grounds that "someone else said the same thing." As Kelley and Thibaut (1954) have put it, "A given contribution to the solution by one member is just as valuable to all, at least potentially, as if it were made by another; furthermore, if it is recognized as a step forward, the other members are relieved of the necessity of duplicating it" (p. 754). This tendency toward substitutability is closely related to the tendency to divide up the work in a cooperative group. As an example, the cooperative groups were much more likely than the competitive groups to divide the labor of writing up recommendations among the various members. In addition, participation was more evenly distributed among competitive than among cooperative group members, indicating a greater pressure on each of the competing individuals to make his personal recommendations and suggestions known.

The competitive group in Deutsch's experiment may be seen as a rather peculiar anomaly, as groups go, because the instructions must have appeared somewhat contradictory and confusing to the subjects. They were to be evaluated competitively on their individual contributions to the group solution, and yet the fate and function of this group solution was never spelled out. If the competitive subjects took the grading instructions seriously, there was no need to do anything but go through the motions of the group solution and therefore no need to organize and perform as a group. Nevertheless, as a point of contrast with the cooperative subjects, the competitive groups serve an important experimental function. It is quite clear that the congruence of member goals—the degree of the members' promotive interdependence or correspondence of outcomes—

has important consequences for many phases of group performance and satisfaction.

The more complex the group's objectives, and the more prolonged the interaction necessary to achieve them, the more difficult it is to maintain the cooperative ideal of completely correspondent outcomes. In the pursuit of long-range goals, different members are quite likely to disagree on means or develop competing subgoals and rivalries. Deutsch was able to impose a goal on his subjects that presumably captured the individual motives of the members: everyone was probably interested in obtaining a good grade, and to a roughly equal extent. In many groups, however, the goal is set by the group itself or, if initially imposed from without, it may later be changed by the group itself. Thus, in the give and take of reaching a majority decision, inevitably discrepancies arise between the goal or goals favored by the majority and the motives of particular members in the minority. At some point in the life of the group individuals are carried along decision pathways they did not initially prefer. What happens in these circumstances?

Acquiescence to Group Decisions

The typical group, regardless of its purpose, must from time to time reach decisions that have consequences for the behavior of all members. In order to effect these decisions in an unequivocal way the group must develop or borrow some mechanism for resolving disagreement, some way of legitimizing a particular method of reaching and sustaining decisions. In our society a ubiquitous mechanism is majority vote, but in many industrial and in most military settings the mechanism involves the acquiescence of members to the decisions made by legitimate authority figures. If we concentrate on those groups that operate democratically and reach decisions by majority vote, the problem is to determine the conditions that secure minority acquiescence.

The individual who finds himself in the minority when a group decision is reached has the basic alternative of going along with that decision or leaving the group. (Going along with the decision in this case means that the individual does not obstruct the carrying out of a group decision to the point of being rejected by the majority behind that decision.) Whether the individual publicly accepts the decision depends, of course, on the degree of discrepancy between the majority decision and the individual's minority point of view. It should also depend on the importance of the matter being decided. If the matter is important to the individual he may insist that his viewpoint be adopted and may threaten to leave the group if it is not. If others have more at stake in the decision than he, he will be more likely to acquiesce. Another important variable is the extent to which the individual has internalized certain central values concerning the democratic process, such as the rule that the loser should pledge his support to the winner after an election, or close ranks on an issue that had been hotly contested.

But at the base of all other factors lies the state of the individual's comparison level for alternatives—his CL_{alt}. If the individual is able to enter alternative relationships—join other groups—that are more likely to further his individual motives, minority acquiescence will compete in his mind with the prospects of changing memberships. The Republican candidate who loses his party's nomination is likely to advocate closing ranks behind the nominee because no other party serves his interests any more than the one that just rebuffed him. In many other cases of voluntary group association, however, the loser is in a position to pick up his marbles and enter another game. The individual with a high CL_{alt} may use the power implicit in his prospects for changing membership to exert greater influence on decisions than his single vote would symbolize.

As we consider further the relationship between the CL_{alt} concept and the individual's adoption of group goals, the concept of group cohesiveness again becomes relevant. In Chapter Ten cohesiveness was defined as the resultant sum of pressures on each individual to remain a group member. Pressures from various sources combine to determine cohesiveness, but it is sufficient for our present purposes to equate the extent of cohesiveness with the extent to which each member lies above his CL_{alt}. The CL_{alt}, after all, is a measure of the individual's dependence on the group for positive outcomes. The more dependent each member is on the others (the lower his CL_{alt}), the more cohesive the group will be. It is but a short step to propose that the greater the cohesiveness of a group, the greater will be the tendency for individuals to accept goals imposed by other group members. In other words, the more the individual generally anticipates outcomes in a relationship that exceed his CL_{alt}, the greater is the likelihood that he will adjust his actions to those preferred by other group members.

This general proposition is a variant of those derived from social comparison theory (see Chapter Ten). It was examined in an experiment by Schachter, Ellertson, McBride, and Gregory (1951). Groups of three undergraduate females were brought together and told (rather vaguely) that the experiment concerned "group psychology" and that they were to work as a group on the cooperative production of cardboard checkerboards. There were three jobs or roles involved in the checkerboard construction: cutting the cardboard, mounting it on heavy stock, and painting the boards through a stencil. After the task and the division of labor were described, the subjects were individually taken to private workrooms where they remained until the end of the experiment. The members of the group were thenceforth allowed to communicate with each other only by written messages. Each subject was in fact assigned the job of cutting and given the impression that the other two members were painting or pasting. The messages each subject sent were intercepted by an experimental assistant who, in his role as messenger, substituted standard notes from a prepared set at four-minute intervals throughout the 32-minute work period.

Cohesiveness or the likelihood of mutual attraction was varied by a procedure similar to that used in a number of the experiments in Chapter Ten. Approximately half of the groups were convincingly told that they were preselected because of their congeniality and the "scientific" prediction that they would like each other. This prediction was allegedly drawn from personality data provided earlier by the subjects. The remaining groups were told that it was impossible to arrange a congenial group and that, on the basis of the prior test results, "there is no particular reason to think that you will like them or that they will care for you." The former groups were designated *high cohesiveness* groups, the latter *low cohesiveness* groups.

Within each cohesiveness treatment, subjects in approximately half of the groups were given a *positive induction* and the remainder were given a *negative induction* as they worked on the cutting task. In the positive treatment the subject received notes—apparently from the co-worker but actually from the experimenter—that generally exhorted him to work harder and to produce more boards to maintain the productivity of the "assembly line." In the negative treatment the messages urged a slowdown. On one message, for example, the "painter" had presumably written: "Please work a little slower. I'm flooded in cardboard and drowning in paste." The cutter received notes from the "paster" that supported the direction of the "painter's" exhortations.

The investigators predicted that the direction of the induction would have stronger effects on the high-cohesive subjects than the low-cohesive ones. In other words, being exhorted to speed up or urged to slow down should produce greater influence on the subject's productivity the more attractive he finds his co-workers. The hypothesis is interesting primarily because it qualified the rather naive "common-sense" supposition that groups with members who like each other will produce more than groups with members who are indifferent to each other.

When productivity is measured in terms of the number of cardboards cut during specified intervals of time, the Schachter et al. hypothesis receives partial support. In the positive induction treatments, both high- and low-cohesive subjects increased their production of cardboards about equally as a function of the messages urging faster work. In the negative induction treatments, however, the high-cohesive subjects showed a significantly greater decline in productivity than the low-cohesive subjects. Thus only in the case of the negative induction messages did cohesiveness or mutual attraction have the predicted effects.

Berkowitz (1954) replicated the Schachter et al. study with minor variations in order to explore further the one-sided cohesiveness effect. The task involved cutting small circles that had been predrawn on a blotter, as one step in the construction of ash-trays. The hypothesis that Schachter et al. had originally proposed was strongly supported by Berkowitz's findings. Productivity was greater in the high-cohesive–positive induction condition and less in the high-cohesive–negative induction condition than in the corresponding low-cohesive conditions. Berkowitz suggests that the cutting task in the Schachter et al. experiment may have been enough harder than the cutting task in his experiment to set a ceiling on the productivity of the high-cohesive–positive induction subjects. Even though they were more highly motivated to produce than the low-cohesive–positive induction subjects, they were incapable of working any faster at the job of cutting large rectangles from heavy cardboard.

If we accept the Berkowitz results, at least on a tentative basis, there is evidence that individuals will adopt a goal set by other group members to the extent that they are attracted to these members and value their association with them. When mutual attraction is high, goals established by the majority will tend to be quickly accepted by the minority. In terms of reaching goals imposed from without, however, cohesiveness is a two-edged sword. A high-cohesive group is better able to resist outside influence than a low-cohesive one, and also better able to mobilize effort in the service of what an outsider desires. This suggests that, in an industrial work group for example, the more cohesive the group is, the more important it is for the supervisor to find an acceptable production goal or to find ways to convince the workers that a goal desired by management is one that should be desired by them. If the supervisor succeeds, *then* it will appear that cohesiveness is associated with greater productivity. This conclusion is clearly supported by Seashore (1954) who found in studying a company manufacturing heavy machinery that high-cohesive groups performed better than the average if they accepted company goals but below the average when they rejected company goals. Differences among low-cohesive groups who accepted or rejected company goals were negligible.

We have touched here on a problem of great practical importance to industrial managers: what are the conditions that facilitate the individual worker's acceptance of goals established by management? It becomes especially important for the manager to be able to answer this question when a change in work procedures is required. There is now considerable evidence suggesting that the degree to which an individual *participates* in the decision to establish a certain group goal is of crucial importance in his private acceptance of that goal. Perhaps this conclusion will strike the reader as rather self-evident, but it is nevertheless interesting to find the importance of participation nicely illustrated in a field experiment on different methods of introducing job changes.

Coch and French (1948) began their study well aware that the workers in a particular pajama factory had previously resisted necessary changes in methods and jobs. This resistance took the form of very inefficient production, restriction of output, and high turnover on the job. They were faced, then, with the same kind of general problem that faced Lewin (1947b) in attempting to overcome resistance to changing certain dietary practices. The Coch and French experiment revolved around a minor change in work routines and time allowances that were to be made in the pajama factory. Using groups of workers doing roughly comparable amounts of work at the beginning of the study, Coch and French studied three different methods of introducing job changes: (1) the total participation method in which small working groups were led to discuss the need for the change, learn the new methods, and participate directly in the designing of the new jobs; (2) the representative participation method in which several workers, chosen by the group, went through the same procedures as the total participation groups; (3) a control method in which the change was announced to the workers at a meeting.

The effects of these variations in the degree of participation in the job change were striking. Workers in the control treatment showed an immediate decline in productivity after the change and remained at the same low level for 32 days thereafter, at which point experimental observations ceased. Workers in the total participation treatment, on the other hand, quickly rebounded to their previous performance level and moved steadily beyond it. Workers in the participation-through-representation treatment were adversely affected by the change but gradually improved so that after about 18 days their performance was indistinguishable from that of the total participation workers.

The importance of participation when new goals are being imposed on the members of working groups has also been demonstrated by Bavelas (reported in Maier, 1946), who was able to increase the output of a group of sewing-machine operators by inducing them to decide as a group on new and higher production goals. Schemes have been devised and implemented in selected industrial concerns to insure continued participation of the workers in decisions about production procedures. The boldest of these is the Scanlon plan which involves profit sharing as well as participative decision-making. Katz and Kahn (1966) point out how delicate a matter the institution of such a plan is, and discuss several cases in which the innovation was misinterpreted by the workers. Participation is not an automatic panacea for organizational ills, then, but under proper conditions it certainly may facilitate the internalization of group goals by the individual.

Unfortunately for ease of understanding, there are a number of reasons why participation in a group decision might be effective in facilitating a shift in group goals. Kelley and Thibaut (1954) have summarized several of the possibilities.

(1) Participation increases the likelihood that individual motives will be represented in the group goal. This is not the whole story, however, since initial preferences are sometimes set aside in favor of the group goal. In the Coch and French study, the new goal was defined by management and, we may assume, was not initially favored by any of the workers.

(2) Having discussed the goal and considered the reasons for adopting it, members may have a better appreciation of the value of the goal for themselves and the group. This is not always a potent consideration, however, because Bennett (1955) found that the effects of group decision were not a result of the preceding discussion itself (see Chapter Ten).

(3) A positive evaluation of the goal is derived from hearing that other group members value it. As Kelley and Thibaut pursue this point, it is clear that they have effect dependence primarily in mind—the individual wishes to avoid going against the preferences of friends for fear that he will lose their friendship. But information dependence on co-oriented peers would also operate in the same direction. Both factors help to explain resistance to a goal imposed from without, when this goal is not seen to be favored by the majority of group members. In the Bennett (1955) study, it may be recalled, volunteering (the goal imposed by the experimenter) was highest when the individuals perceived near unanimity within the class in favor of volunteering.

Kelley and Thibaut are quick to point out that the list is not intended to be exhaustive and that finding the specific mechanisms underlying the effectiveness of participation in establishing group goals is an important research problem for the future. At least one additional mechanism deserves to be mentioned that has special significance for the private acceptance or internalization of an imposed group goal. This is the mechanism of postdecision dissonance reduction. Participation, especially if it is followed by a group decision, may be seen as a method for increasing perceived choice and therefore psychological commitment to the decision which is made. Commitment should have strong effects in this case because it is public (cf. Gerard, 1965; Cohen, Brehm, and Latané, 1959). The individual has presumably contributed to the group's decision, so he would suffer dissonance from a number of sources if he remained committed to private motives that were discrepant from the group goal. In keeping with the procedures for inducing the illusion of choice in many dissonance experiments, Coch and French actually imposed a goal on the workers in the total participation treatment, but probably left the workers feeling that they had something to do with choosing the new work procedures. Under these circumstances, dissonance would have resulted from *not* accepting the group goal.

The discussion assumes that the rapid resumption of productivity in the participation conditions follows from the private acceptance of the group goal by the individual worker. This assumption is probably justified, but it would be illuminating to have a more precise and direct measure of the extent to which an individual privately accepts the group decision and gears his motives into attainment of the group goal.

Measuring the Internalization of Group Goals

Bluma Zeigarnik, one of Lewin's early students in Germany, conducted a series of experiments between 1924 and 1926 on the relationship between motivation and memory (Zeigarnik, 1927; summarized by Lewin, 1951). She began with the assumption that the intention to reach a particular goal corresponded to a psychological tension within the individual. This tension would remain active until the goal was reached and would be reflected in thinking about the goal and in activities directed toward its attainment. On the basis of this reasoning, Zeigarnik proposed that if an individual were motivated to complete a task and were interrupted before completing it, there would be residual tension. Therefore he would recall characteristics of the task longer and more vividly than if the task were completed and the tension consequently reduced. In order to test this proposition she conducted a basic experiment in which subjects worked on a series of problems and puzzles, being allowed to complete some and not others. Subjects were later able to recall the incompleted tasks better than the completed ones, thus offering support for Zeigarnik's theory of psychological tension.

Some years later, Lewis (1944; Lewis and Franklin, 1944) attempted to build on the reasoning of the Zeigarnik effect by studying the role of social interdependence in task completion. Specifically, if a task started by the subject were completed by a partner, would such a task be better recalled than one that was completed by the subject himself? She found that recall of the partner-completed and self-completed tasks were equally frequent. This suggests that, under some conditions at least, the activities of a partner can substitute for the person's own activities, implying that the individual goal is converted to a group goal.

An ingenious experiment by Horwitz (1954) carried this line of reasoning several steps further. Horwitz felt that the Lewis studies were difficult to interpret because the subjects may have divided the work with their partners in a way that changed the single task to two subtasks. He was generally interested in whether the motivational concepts developed for individuals who are acting to achieve their own goals can be applied to individuals who are acting so that the group will achieve its goals. Like Lewis, he adopted the incompleted task procedure and attempted to pursue the implications of the Zeigarnik effect for recall of group performance. He needed to create a situation in which the individual would sometimes agree and sometimes disagree with the group about the goal to be followed, and then group action in pursuit of the chosen goal would have to be interrupted in some cases and allowed to be completed in others. To this end he developed rather elaborate procedures.

Female sorority sisters were recruited in groups of five to participate in a "test of group cooperativeness" in which each group would be judged by the quality of its performance in putting together a number of jigsaw puzzles. Upon arrival at the experimental room, the subjects were engaged in a discussion designed to make them quite aware of their group membership and the importance of loyalty and team spirit. The procedure in completing the jigsaw puzzles was as follows: the subjects attempted to direct the experimenter in completing 15 five-piece jigsaw puzzles. At some point in the work on each puzzle, the group members were asked to decide by a majority vote whether they wanted to continue working on that puzzle or move on to the next one. If the group's decision was to continue working, work resumed, but was soon interrupted by the experimenter on half of the tasks. At the end of the series of tasks, the subjects were requested individually to recall the names of the jigsaw puzzles.

Each subject was actually kept in the dark regarding the true votes and communications between each other subject and the experimenter. Therefore it was possible for the experimenter, by communicating bogus information to the subjects, to determine which puzzles would be chosen as the group goal and which would not be, as well as which puzzles would be completed and which would be interrupted. Subjects were seated around a table, but their places were separated by partitions so that they could see the experimenter but not one another. As each trial began the experimenter held up a large outline of the puzzle to be completed, sectioned into five parts to indicate the way to solve the puzzle. At each subject's station there were envelopes containing cardboard pieces corresponding to the sections of the jigsaw "target" figures. Each envelope contained four of the five pieces for a particular puzzle. As work on a particular puzzle began, the subjects were to hold up different pieces to signal which section of the puzzle should be filled in by the experimenter at that time. The subjects were told that if a given (but unspecified) number of subjects and *no more* held up the same piece, the corresponding section would be filled in by the experimenter. The effect of this rule was that a subject could contribute to group progress either by holding or not holding up the piece that was eventually filled in, and thus it was difficult for the subject to feel that she had contributed more than anyone else to the successful placement of a piece. The trials and the successful placements continued until the entire figure was completed. Then the same procedure was followed for the second puzzle, and the third, and so on.

The method of scoring entailed having the group take a vote after two of the five pieces had been placed on the figure to determine whether the group wished to complete the puzzle or move on to the next one. The subjects were to be given a "basic score" for reaching the first stage of placing two pieces. Then if they completed the puzzle rapidly they could receive a bonus added to the basic score. However, inefficient and slow performance from that point on could lead to the subtraction of points from the basic score. The subjects were thus led to believe that their ultimate score would depend on their wisdom in choosing to work first on those puzzles that appeared easiest to complete. It was implied that they might be able to return to work on those that they voted not to complete. The votes to continue or to stop were conducted by the experimenter after the basic score was reached, and each subject was to raise her right hand if she wished to continue and her left hand if she wished to stop. The experimenter then announced what the majority had allegedly decided and the group either continued on the third piece or turned to another puzzle, in line with the *announced* decision.

As indicated, the experimenter controlled the group's "vote" to continue and followed standard sequences in filling in the jigsaw puzzle that bore no relation to the pieces actually held up by the subjects or to the subjects' vote to continue or not. On five puzzles, selected in advance, the group was told that a majority had voted "no," *not* to go on with the work. On 10 selected puzzles the group was told that the majority had voted "yes," to continue. Of these latter 10 the experimenter permitted completion of five puzzles and interrupted work on the third piece of the other five saying that the interruption was temporary and that they would return to the particular puzzle later.

The basic data of the experiment may be reported in terms of the number of tasks recalled in a particular treatment, divided by the total number of tasks in the treatment. The most straightforward and simple test of the "group Zeigarnik effect" would be to see if, among the tasks the group "decided" to work on and thus "accepted" as the group goal, the interrupted tasks were recalled better than the completed ones. The results show that this was indeed the case: whereas the average subject recalled 56 percent of the interrupted tasks, she only recalled 44 percent of the completed ones. This difference was highly significant. By inference, the average subject went along with the group decision and became motivated as an individual to achieve the group goal. The inference that superior recall of interrupted tasks reflected the residual tension associated with unfulfilled motivation is all the more reasonable in view of the percentage of tasks remembered in the *No* treatment. These were the tasks on which, the subject was led to believe, the group decided not to continue working. The average subject remembered only 46 percent of the *No* tasks, roughly the same percentage as the *Yes-completed* tasks. The average individual is not particularly motivated to complete tasks that have not become a group goal.

Horwitz was also able to make a more refined analysis by using two additional sources of data. The actual yes-no vote of each subject was recorded for each puzzle, making it possible to compare those cases in which the individual initially agreed with the group decision with those cases in which the individual and the group were in initial disagreement. In addition, data from a postexperimental questionnaire were used to classify the subjects as *generally* accepting the group's decision when there was disagreement or as generally rejecting it. For convenience the alleged group decision is represented as Y (for continue) or N (for stop), the subject's actual vote on that puzzle is represented as y (yes) or n (no), and C or I designates whether the task was completed or the group's efforts were interrupted by the experimenter.

Table 15.1. Mean Percentage of Tasks Recalled in Cases of Initial Agreement and of Disagreement
(Adapted from Horwitz, 1954)

(a)	Initial agreement		Initial disagreement	
	y Y-I	56%	n Y-I	55%
	y Y-C	41%	n Y-C	52%
	n N	43%	y N	43%
(b)	Further breakdown of disagreement cases			
		Accept	Reject	
	n Y-I	47%	67%	
	n Y-C	17%	66%	
	y N	29%	57%	

Interestingly enough, whether the initial vote was in agreement or disagreement with the group vote does not seem to make a great deal of difference in the subsequent recall percentage—except, perhaps, in the case of the Y-C treatment. When subjects initially vote *not* to work on a task that is later completed by the group they show a better recall for the task puzzle than if they vote to continue and the puzzle is completed. Horwitz suggests that the heightened recall of the nY-C group is caused by the residual tension of being carried into a goal region the subject would prefer to avoid. Regardless of the merits of this explanation, it is clear from the accept-reject figures in Table 15.1b that the rejectors show much better recall than the acceptors in the Y-C treatment. This is certainly what we would expect in line with the Zeigarnik effect for individuals: when the group goal accidentally coincides with the individual's goal (yY-C) or when the individual accepts the group goal after being informed of it (nY-C, $Accept$), there is little residual tension and therefore the names of the puzzles tend to be forgotten (note the respective indices of 41 percent and 17 percent).

Results in the Y-I treatment are a little more difficult to interpret, but still fall into the pattern predicted by Horwitz. Subjects in the position of having accidentally voted for a puzzle that is later interrupted (yY-I subjects) do show high recall, as the individual Zeigarnik effect would predict (56 percent). However, those who do *not* vote for a puzzle that is later interrupted show approximately the same level of recall (55 percent). Looking at the final breakdown in Table 15.1b we see, in fact, that those who tend to maintain their initial disagreement show greater recall than those who change in line with the group decision (67 percent versus 47 percent). Horwitz argues that subjects in the nY-I treatment are somewhat in the position of being damned if they do and damned if they don't. If the subject changes her vote in line with the group decision, there will be residual tension because the group is not allowed to complete the task with which she is now identified. If the subject rejects the group decision and privately adheres to her "no" vote, there still remains the tension of sooner or later being carried into the undesirable goal region, because the experimenter makes clear that the group may be asked to return to the interrupted tasks later.

The present account does not do justice to the subtlety and precision of Horwitz's theoretical argument. Nor does it adequately convey the unusual fit between patterns of empirical data and theoretical predictions stated before conducting the experiment. What we have tried to establish is that group goals can readily be adopted as individual goals and, to the extent that they are, at least some of the consequences are similar to those obtaining when individual motives are aroused. In particular, the average subject recalls better those tasks that the *group* never completes than those completed. The more detailed analysis is generally in accord with this gross conclusion, though it does make some difference whether the subjects initially agree with the group goal, later accept it, or both.

Unfortunately, though the Horwitz study is an encouraging beginning that explores what causes an individual to accept as his own the goal determined by group decision, it is only a beginning. The study confirms that group goals can function for the individual in much the same way as individual motives do, but it does not tell us much about the conditions of group goal internalization. Having established the reasonable presumption that task recall is an index of goal internalization, we now need to determine the social conditions of which this internalization is a function.

We have already mentioned a number of considerations that may be exploited as independent variables in studying how group goals become accepted as individual goals. To speculate further on these considerations, there is the obvious point that the group goal is more likely to be accepted by the individual if it coincides with his original motive for joining the group or reflects his individual vote once he has become a member. If, on the other hand, the individual is in the minority because his vote differs from the group decision, he will tend to go along with the majority if his prospects for joining another group or groups are poor—if he has a low CL_{alt}—or if he is especially attracted to the members of the present group. However, it may be important to distinguish between "going along" publicly with the group and privately internalizing its goals. As a derivation from dissonance theory, it might be predicted that the lower the individual's CL_{alt}, the greater the likelihood of a discrepancy between public avowal and private acceptance. The individual may, as it were, merely go along with the group decision to make the best of a situation in which his bargaining power is low and therefore there is both low choice and low personal commitment. If the individual's low CL_{alt} is combined with high attraction for the members, internalization of the group goal would be more likely to occur on grounds other than those considered by dissonance theory: the desire to be similar to those whom he likes. Finally, if circumstances contribute to the individual's feeling that he has participated in the group decision, even though this decision is at variance with his initial preference, we would expect acceptance to be high on both public and private levels. It should be possible to explore these suggestions by means of the "group Zeigarnik" procedure for identifying goals the individual has privately accepted as his own.

RESPONSIBILITY DIFFUSION

If the goal of the group effectively expresses the motives of each individual, it matters little who contributes to goal attainment as long as somebody does. This assumption underlies the principle of substitutability in cooperative groups (Deutsch, 1949). Of course, groups are seldom ideally cooperative, in the sense that individual motives are completely absorbed in the group goal, but the notion of substitutability is undoubtedly important in most groups in which individuals are concerned with the solution of a common problem. Depending to an important extent on the nature of the task, the group is more likely to attain its goals if steps are taken to avoid duplication of effort and if some attempt is made to allocate duties in line with individual talents and interests.

How these steps are taken, who presides over the allocation of duties, are matters of group organization that we shall examine in Chapter Sixteen. If a formal organization emerges and duties are carefully assigned, then failures to attain the group goal may be traced back to the inadequate efforts of particular individuals. The allocation of personal responsibility is thus made possible by the development of a formal organization in which individual duties are assigned and expectations for individuals are established. As the obverse of this conclusion, it is difficult to locate responsibility for group failure when the allocation of duties—the division of labor—has been haphazard and informal, and when a definite group organization does not exist. It is this latter case with which we are primarily concerned here. In particular, we wish to explore the cognitive and behavioral consequences for the individual of being a member of a group in which individual assignment of responsibility is minimized. We assume that this happens to some extent in any group, but that it is an especially prominent feature of informal, "leaderless" groups, or groups that lack formal organization.

As a dramatic if dimly understood example of responsibility diffusion, let us first consider the lynch mob and similar crowd phenomena. Social scientists who have commented on the lynch mob have been uniformly impressed with the effects of mob membership in eroding the moral constraints that are typically responsible for civilized behavior. Lynch mobs are composed of individuals who, under other circumstances, would be genuinely repelled by the very acts in which they excitedly indulge as members of the mob. Miller and Dollard (1941), in their depiction of a particular 1933 case in which a Negro suspected of murdering a white girl was lynched, go into considerable detail to portray the depths that "group sadism" can reach in lynching. They also make clear that the mob reaction is more than a violent, impulsive outburst of "people who know better." The aggression characterizing the mob is sometimes sustained for hours or even days. The victim in the case they describe was systematically tortured for some 10 hours: castrated, compelled to eat his own genitals, burned by hot irons plunged into his body at various points, hung several times almost to the point of death and then revived, sliced with knives, and finally killed. There is every reason to doubt that any single member of the mob could have engaged in such sustained sadism as an isolated individual. Whereas the victim was actually tortured and killed by those who were most directly involved in vengeance, the body was later delivered to a large crowd of bystanders who drove knives into the corpse, kicked it, and drove automobiles over it. Children came and drove sharpened sticks into the body. Clearly such a frenzy is not the product of some accidental collection of sadists trying to outdo each other. Many of the most prominent citizens of the community were actually involved in the planning and execution of the lynching.

Undoubtedly, the factors involved in the behavior of individuals who are part of a lynch mob are complex and difficult to unravel. But there seems little question that the altered state of the individuals involved is to some extent a function of the responsibility diffusion that characterizes a mob. Several closely related considerations are involved here. In the first place, the individual actually has a certain guarantee of anonymity in the lynch mob in the sense that no one is likely to keep track of who did what to the victim. Even if the individual entertained some doubts about the ultimate morality of his actions, his fears of being identified would be minimized by the nature of the enterprise. Second, there is considerable question whether the average lynch mob member in fact recognizes—at least at the time—the immorality of his actions. After all, a tried and tested way of defining what is right is to do what everybody else seems to be doing. Undoubtedly mob conformity is strengthened by the individual's perception that the acts perpetrated have the quality of group acts—done by and on behalf of the community. The lynch mob member very probably feels that his participation symbolizes his allegiance to community values. Because it was common for lynchings in the 1920's and 1930's to take place with tacit police consent, there is all the more reason to conclude that the lynch mob perceived that it had the powerful sanction of an implicit group decision.

De-individuation

Most accounts of lynchings, riots, and other cases of mob violence emphasize the individual's abdication of personal responsibility for his deeds. He acts as an arm of the larger group, and by submerging himself in the flow of group activity he loses his feeling of accountability for the consequences of his own actions. But the fact that a group exists does not guarantee that its members are genuinely "submerged" in it. Festinger, Pepitone, and Newcomb (1952) have introduced the term *individuation* to suggest a dimension along which groups may fall; some groups may be more individuated than others. In those that are relatively de-individuated, according to their proposed definition, the individual members do not respond to each other as individuals or single each other out for attention during the course of interaction. We have suggested that organized groups in which arrangements have been made for the assignment of specific roles or duties have, through such organizational assignments, counteracted the tendency toward personal-responsibility diffusion in groups. The features associated with organization and role assignment are presumably accompanied by individuation. Role assignment generally requires a leadership structure and, as Festinger et al. point out, prestige and status in a group require singling out an individual and behaving toward him in a special manner. Even if the group is not formally organized, and there are no assigned duties to increase feelings of personal responsibility, we would expect variations from group to group in the amount of de-individuation that prevails. Festinger et al. assumed that this would be the case if rather vague and permissive instructions were given to a group concerning its mandate for functioning. They were interested in examining the correlates of de-individuation when it occurred, and proposed the hypothesis that inner restraints become reduced in groups in which de-individuation occurs and that such groups are therefore more attractive to their members.

The notion of inner restraints was, for Festinger et al., linked ultimately to the freedom to behave impulsively that has been observed in large anonymous crowds like the lynch mob, but is also present in smaller groups of delinquents, partygoers, conventioneers, and so on. It was their position that if de-individuation occurred in a group it would permit greater freedom from the constraints normally holding impulsive behavior in check. The investigators recruited undergraduate male subjects to form 23 groups ranging in size from four to seven members. After seating the subjects around a conference table and placing before each a placard identifying him, the experimenter read a statement that argued convincingly that 87 percent of the population harbored deep-seated hatred of one or both parents. Furthermore, the statement continued, "those individuals who at first vehemently denied having such hostile impulses . . . were subsequently diagnosed as possessing the most violent forms of hostility." The subjects were urged to discuss their own personal feelings toward their parents "in the light of these results." It was expected that individual subjects would have inner restraints against expressing hatred of their parents and that de-individuation—if it occurred—would reduce these restraints.

The conversation of each group of subjects was observed, and each statement expressing positive and negative attitudes toward parents was recorded along with the name of the person who said it. At the end of the 40-minute discussion the experimenter read off a list of 15 statements and asked each subject to indicate whether he remembered the statement's having been made in the discussion and, if so, to indicate by whom. Ten of these statements were actually taken from the observer's records of the discussion, and five had not occurred in the discussion. Two separate error scores were derived from this identification test: errors in recalling who said what ("Identification" or I errors) and errors in remembering the content of the discussion ("Memory" or M errors). The measure of de-individuation for each group was the average number of *I* errors minus the average number of *M* errors for that group. *M* errors were subtracted to correct for the general recall level of the group. The measure of reduction in inner restraint was the number of negative statements made about parents revealed in the discussion of a particular group minus the number of positive statements.

The results showed that those groups that had high de-individuation scores also had high restraint-reduction scores: when the members of the group talked in negative terms about their parents, they showed a tendency to forget who said what. The investigators had initially proposed this as a hypothesis on the grounds that restraint reduction would follow from de-individuation. Is there any evidence that this direction of causal inference is more tenable than the opposite? Is it possible that saying negative things about one's parents leads to de-individuation? The revelation of negative attitudes may have led to repression or selective forgetting, because such attitudes are considered shameful or taboo. However, it so happened that although *I* errors were positively correlated with reduction of restraints (expression of negative attitudes) *M* errors were negatively correlated. Members actually recalled more statements in those groups that expressed more negative attitudes, so it seems hard to account for the identification results in terms of repression.

A second hypothesis was that de-individuation would lead to greater group attraction. The theoretical rationale behind this hypothesis was left somewhat obscure, but the investigators assumed that the greater an individual's freedom to express his deeper impulses in an unrestrained way, the more satisfied he would be with the setting. This hypothesis received tentative support: the larger the *I-M* error index of individuation, the more pleased the members were with the group, though this correlation was not significant.

In spite of the correlational nature of the findings and their borderline statistical significance, the study by Festinger et al. does suggest that the concept of de-individuation may be useful in studying group effects. Furthermore, the linkage between de-individuation and unrestrained behavior calls attention to the general fact that the members of small and rather innocent discussion groups can be affected by being submerged in the group just as the members of a lynch mob can. Though the unrestrained behavior of the lynch mob member is much more dramatic and morally revolting than voicing negative comments about one's parents, the difference between them may be one of degree and it seems that de-individuation may play an important role in breaking down individual restraints in both cases.

In an attempt to establish at least one of the conditions that produces de-individuation, Singer, Brush, and Lublin (1965) investigated the role of identifiable dress. College coed subjects were recruited for a "concept formation experiment" in groups of four. Those in the high-identification condition were told to dress up for the experiment—to "wear a dress or suit and heels and hose." Low-identification subjects were told to wear old clothes and, when they arrived, were asked to put on oversized white lab coats, ostensibly for some later phase of the experiment.

In the experiment proper each four-woman group was either assigned to a taboo topic or a nontaboo topic condition. In the former the subjects were to discuss the "concept" of pornographic literature by considering whether certain possibly salacious literary passages fit into the definition of pornography offered by the Supreme Court. In the latter condition the concept was "a liberal education" and the task was to discuss specific examples of courses to decide which did and which did not belong in a liberal arts curriculum. The ensuing conversations were carefully monitored and measures of obscene word usage, interruptions, silences, and so forth, were taken.

Singer et al. (1965) reasoned that if the members of a group are wearing highly identifiable clothing, they should remain conscious of their identity as persons and de-individuation should be inhibited. In the bulky lab coat, low-identifiability condition, on the other hand, de-individuation should be facilitated. This should show itself in an absence of pauses in the discussion, a tendency toward interruptions (reflecting greater member involvement) and especially in the willingness to use obscene language when appropriate to the topic. The results showed that in the taboo topic condition high-identification subjects made significantly fewer statements containing obscene words than low-identification subjects. Also, if we consider only the taboo topic subjects, the high-identification subjects found participation less enjoyable, had many more seconds of silent time, and showed a tendency toward fewer interruptions. None of these measures showed such differences in the nontaboo topic condition.

It is difficult to evaluate the theoretical significance of these results because there may be a direct connection between formality of dress and the willingness to use obscene language—a connection having nothing to do with the concept of de-individuation, but rather with associations to other occasions on which formal versus informal dress is appropriate. Nevertheless, the fact that the low-identification taboo discussions were generally less restrained and more enjoyable, and featured more obscenity, is certainly consistent with the de-individuation hypothesis. The Singer et al. study makes a contribution by tentatively linking this hypothesis to the presence or absence of self-consciousness through experimental manipulations involving formality of dress.

Is de-individuation the same thing as responsibility diffusion? We would argue that the two concepts are certainly closely related, especially when the individual has some awareness that de-individuation has occurred. If the individual member realizes that his behavior is not likely to be indelibly associated with his name in the eyes of other group members, he will tend to feel anonymous, invisible, and therefore less accountable for the consequences of that behavior. If in the eyes of his fellow members he is not personally responsible for his remarks or actions, the next step is to believe that he shares the responsibility for his actions with them. The process may often work in the reverse direction as well. If a task or group procedure is so defined that the responsibility for a group action is naturally spread among the members, then de-individuation is likely to arise out of this task-derived diffusion of responsibility. In fact, it may be reasonable to use the kind of measure of de-individuation developed by Festinger et al. to compare such groups in the extent to which such responsibility-sharing has in fact occurred.

Risk-Taking in Groups

One of the most intriguing dimensions of behavior that may be affected by the sharing of responsibility for decision-making with others is risk-taking or the tendency to prefer long shots with higher payoffs over sure things with lower payoffs. In spite of the long tradition of research comparing the productivity of individuals in isolation and in groups, a direct attack on the determinants of group risk-taking was not launched until the 1960's. Before an investigation by Stoner (1961) it was generally believed that groups would tend to be more conservative or less risky than individuals responding in isolation. We have already presented Allport's (1924) finding that individuals tend to produce more common or popular associations in a group than in an individual context. This seems to suggest a kind of conservatism, a reluctance to stick one's neck out by producing a unique, and therefore possibly embarrassing, association. Whyte (1956) and various other critics of bureaucracy and the committee system have contended that the process of group discussion leads inexorably to an inhibition of boldness and that the creative innovator is likely to be dragged down to the common denominator of the group. Stoner's results showed, on the other hand, that a group consensus on the degree of risk to be taken in resolving a "life dilemma" situation actually favored alternatives of greater risk than the prediscussion average of individual decisions. This unexpected finding provoked Wallach, Kogan, and their students to design a series of carefully controlled studies on group risk-taking. They were interested, first of all, in establishing the generality of Stoner's results; but beyond this they wished to establish the particular features of a group situation that tend to produce greater boldness in its members.

In the first study Wallach, Kogan, and Bem (1962) recruited over 200 subjects from a large state university. Stoner's subjects had been male graduate students in an industrial management program, and there was a possibility that their greater risk-taking in groups was a function of business-school norms in favor of risk-taking (which would presumably be more salient in the group context). Each subject in the Wallach et al. experiment first took an "opinion questionnaire" privately, but at the same time as five other subjects. The questionnaire asked the subject to respond to 12 hypothetical situations. Although the situations were designed to cover a wide range of content, they all had the same feature: the central person in each situation had to choose between two courses of action, one of which was riskier than the other but also more rewarding if successful. The subject's actual task on each item was to indicate the lowest probability of success he would accept before recommending the choice of the potentially more rewarding alternative. Two examples (p. 77) of the hypothetical situations were:

A. A man of moderate means may invest some money he recently inherited in secure "blue chip" low return securities or in more risky securities that offer the possibility of large gains.

B. An American prisoner-of-war in World War II must choose between possible escape with the risk of execution if caught, or remaining in the camp where privations are severe.

Immediately after filling out the questionnaire in private the subjects were collected around a conference table and unexpectedly told to reach a unanimous decision on each item. The results showed a clear shift in the direction of riskiness for practically every item, with males and females showing approximately the same amount of shift. In addition, a subsequent private retest showed that the "risky shift" maintained itself for both sexes. Although all subjects took the questionnaire immediately after the group discussion under permissive instructions ("some of you may not have agreed with the group's decision. . ."), a smaller group also took the questionnaire for a third time, two to six weeks later, under urging to reconsider each situation. The risky shift was maintained in this smaller group too. It is worth noting that a control group of subjects—who merely took the questionnaire as individuals twice with a week intervening—showed no systematic change in either a risky or conservative direction.

Thus the first study by Wallach, Kogan, and Bem (1962) established convincingly that Stoner's results were not an accident, and that something occurs in the process of interpersonal confrontation and discussion that generates a decision to favor more risky alternatives. Having demonstrated that this shift occurs in both sexes, in very different populations, across items of different content, and that it carries over to private attitudes toward the choices to be made, the investigators turned their attention to a further aspect of generality and to the underlying mechanisms that might be involved in the shift. Is it possible that the group shift toward risk-taking occurs with hypothetical items only and that the introduction of real stakes would inhibit whatever process was operating? To answer this question, it became important to present the subjects with choices having real consequences for them. In attempting to determine the mechanisms at work behind the risky shift, the investigators were left with a number of possibilities after the initial demonstration studies. Perhaps the actual course of group discussion was not important for generating the risky shift, and the greater risk-taking came from the prospect of confronting others and having a kind of pluralistic ignorance concerning their initial attitudes. Conceivably, each individual could have been inclined to assume that he was more conservative than the others were likely to be, and thus he became more prone to take risks out of an attempt to anticipate the opinions of others. Given the fact that a discussion does occur, is the factor of responsibility diffusion really the critical factor behind the risky shift? Although in one sense the individual shares responsibility with the group for the ultimate decision, he also implicates others in the effects of the decision —his actions affect the well-being of others as well as his own well-being. Should this not induce greater caution into the deliberations of the group?

A second experiment by Wallach, Kogan, and Bem (1964) was designed to answer these questions. The experiment again involved a comparison of individual and group risk-taking, but this time there were actual monetary stakes involved in the choices and there were several variations in the condition of group risk-taking designed to reach a clearer understanding of the factors involved in the risky shift.

All subjects met in groups of three. They were told that their main task would be to answer 10 multiple-choice questions taken from old College Board examinations. They would be paid for correct answers but not for incorrect ones. However, each subject was to determine beforehand the difficulty level for each of the 10 questions he would answer. He was told that there were nine different difficulty levels and was given an elaborate schedule indicating the amount of money he would earn for a given level if he answered a problem correctly. The schedule was carefully worked out so that the more difficult the question, the more a correct answer would earn. In the part of the experiment with which we shall be concerned, the subjects never actually saw the problems—they saw merely a booklet containing pages on which they were to indicate the difficulty level they wished to attempt for problem 1, then for problem 2, and so on. Although the problem itself was not presented, there was an indication of its general character (analogies, sentence completions, mathematics) on the top of the booklet page. The actual working of the problems was deferred, so the subject's choices could not be affected by prior successes or failures, though each subject did work on some practice problems that gave him an idea of the range of difficulties involved. After the chosen level of difficulty had been indicated for problems 1 through 5, experimental variations were introduced for the remaining five questions. The effect of these variations was to create four different experimental conditions to compare with a control condition:

1. Group Decision Condition. As in the previous experiment, the difficulty levels chosen for the last five problems were to be determined by unanimous group consensus. Although the consensus was to be binding on each member, he was eventually to solve the problems by himself.

2. Responsibility for Group Condition. Here it was pointed out that each of the last five questions would actually be attempted by a randomly determined member of the group, with the winnings of the other two entirely dependent on his success. The problem-solver would be chosen by a different spin of a spinner for each problem, but each subject had to decide on the difficulty level of all problems before the solver for each (starting with problem six) was randomly designated. Later on, the spinner-designated member would be given a problem at the level *he* had selected for that problem number. There was no group decision.

3. Group Responsibility–Group Decision Condition. This was exactly the same as condition 2 except that the members were to discuss and reach a unanimous decision concerning the difficulty level of the problems to be assigned later by a spin of the spinner.

4. Group Designation Condition. This was exactly like condition 3 except that the group not only was to determine the difficulty level for each problem by discussion to consensus, but was also to designate a representative who would attempt to solve each problem.

5. Retest Control Condition. This condition merely represented a continuation, for problems 6 to 10, of procedures that prevailed during problems 1 to 5. The three subjects, in other words, continued to work individually.

The results of the second Wallach et al. experiment are summarized in Table 15.2. The mean over-all shift index represents the difference between the level of difficulty chosen for problems 6 to 10 by group consensus or individual vote and that chosen for problems 1 to 5 by the individual. Thus positive values indicate a shift in the risky direction.

It is obvious from these results that the experimental treatments had pronounced and divergent effects on the degree of risk-taking. The index for the control group differs significantly from the index for each of the four experimental conditions. As in the previous experiment, the group

Table 15.2. Degree of Shift in Risk-Taking Under Different Conditions of Decision Making (From Wallach, Kogan, & Bem, 1964)

Condition	Shift index mean [a]
1. Group decision (15 groups)	5.6
2. Responsibility for group (15 individuals)	−1.6
3. Group responsibility-group decision (15 groups)	9.4
4. Group designation (15 groups)	12.5
5. Retest control (18 individuals)	2.4

[a] The general nature of this index is described in the text, and more completely in the original article. Positive values indicate a risky shift. All values differ significantly from each other except those for conditions 1 and 3, 3 and 4.

decision condition showed a significant risky shift. The degree of riskiness was further increased when, on top of group discussion to attain consensus, the problem-solver was to be designated by chance or chosen by the group (these conditions were not significantly different from each other). When the group has an opportunity to reach a consensus, but *only* then, the additional factor of having the group represented by one of its members increases risk-taking.

Wallach et al. seemed quite surprised by the high levels of risk-taking in conditions 3 and 4, as they apparently had expected individuals to become more conservative if they envisioned that they might have to stand or fall themselves on behalf of the group. Apparently the designation of an individual performer has a different significance when it occurs in connection with a group consensus about the problem to be solved than when there is no such consensus, as in condition 2. In the absence of consensus the individual has no way of knowing at what level of difficulty the other two individuals would prefer to work. It is therefore not surprising that the subject shifts slightly in the conservative direction in order to avoid the possibility of letting the others down and consequently exposing himself to their ridicule. There is probably built-in cultural resistance to taking risks with other people's money. As evidence of this tendency toward caution, subjects in condition 2 have a significantly smaller shift index than subjects in the retest control condition 5. However, when the group decides on a particular level of difficulty and *then* a member is to be chosen by lot to solve the problem on behalf of the group, there is maximal diffusion of responsibility. Not only is the individual not personally responsible for choosing the particular difficulty level, he is also not even responsible for deciding whether to work on the problem. Thus there is diffusion of responsibility in two senses: the individual shares responsibility with his fellow group members for deciding on the appropriate level of difficulty, and he shares responsibility with "chance" for actually having to work on the problem. If the problem-solver were required to volunteer instead of being chosen by lot, we might expect greater conservatism of choice. The fact that the risky shift is, if anything, slightly greater when the group nominates the member who will actually attempt the problem-solving may reflect the subject's awareness that he can actively avoid personal responsibility for failure by voting for one of the other two group members. Also, if both vote for him it is their fault, in a sense, if he fails.

This study made it clear that a risky shift occurs when the choices involve actual monetary consequences as well as in the case of hypothetical dilemmas. Each subject was informed that he could win anywhere from $1.25 to $15.00, depending on his performance on the 10 problems weighted by their difficulty level. Every attempt was made to assure the subjects that they would actually be confronted with the problems during the last 20 minutes of the experiment and that the payoffs would be delivered. (In point of fact, everything the experimenter told the subjects was correct— a rare case of a nondeceptive experiment in social psychology!)

The results of this second study lend further weight to the interpretation that the mechanism that underlies the risky shift is the diffusion or spreading of responsibility. The critical variation seems to be whether the level of risk is actually decided through the give-and-take of a group discussion in which a unanimous consensus is attained. And yet there are a number of loose ends remaining that make this conclusion premature. Perhaps the decision itself is not critical: it is still possible that risk-taking is seen to be more socially desirable than conservatism and caution, and that the mere anticipation of disclosing his choice is sufficient to make the individual willing to advocate a higher level of risk; or it may be that the presence of others serves as a potential source of solace or comfort in the event that risk-taking incurs negative consequences. To evaluate these explanations for the risky shift—alternatives to the responsibility diffusion hypothesis— a third experiment was designed (Bem, Wallach, and Kogan, 1965). Once again a different kind of risk-taking task was devised in an attempt to extend the generality of conclusions about group risk-taking. This time the consequences of failure were quite unpleasant and involved more than the absence of positive consequences (like monetary gain).

The experiment was presented to the subjects (126 male summer-school students) as a study of various "physiological effects of problem-solving." Subjects signed up for two experimental sessions, the first of which actually constituted the entire experiment. During this "preliminary" session, subjects were dealt with in groups of three but their work space was separated by partitions. Six experiments were described to them, concerned with the effects of various physiological stimulations on the ability to solve simple verbal and mathematical problems. The six were identified as involving "olfactory stimulation," "chromatic stimulation," "movement," "taste," "audition," and sensitivity to "odorless gases." It was explained that subjects would be selected by a random procedure to appear in one of these experiments during their second session, but that within the range of, say, olfactory stimulations to which they might be exposed if assigned by lot to the olfactory experiment, each subject had a degree of choice. The available choices constituted the risk-taking test and concerned the extent to which the subject was willing to undergo painful side-effects if he were more handsomely reimbursed.

In each type of experiment, it was explained, some of the odors, gases, noises, and so on, were known to produce side effects that were temporary but quite unpleasant. Although it was impossible, the experimenter continued, to identify the particular individuals who would suffer these effects, it was possible to determine the probability that any given individual would suffer them. The subject was given a table for each of the six types of experiment, from which he could choose an unidentified odor (or taste, or noise) that had a 10 percent, 20 percent, up to 90 percent chance of producing side effects. The pay ranged from $2.80 if the subject chose the odor with a 10 percent probability of producing side effects to $25.00 if the subject chose the odor with a 90 percent probability. It was emphasized that the money would be paid as the wage attached to the chosen probability only if the individual did *not* actually suffer the side effect and therefore would be available as an experimental subject to work on the verbal and mathematical problems. Otherwise he would be excused from the experiment and paid a flat fee of $1.00. As indicated, the subjects never actually were exposed to "physiological stimulation" or worked on any problems; the entire account of the second session was fictitious and merely served to set the stage for administering the risk-taking measure.

Whereas this much of the procedure was common to all subjects, the following experimental conditions were created by different instructions after the initial private filling out of the risk-taking questionnaire.

1. Discussion to Reach Consensus. The partitions between subjects were removed and plausible instructions urged the group to discuss each of the six possible experiments and reach a unanimous decision about the type of stimulation to be employed if, as the experimenter indicated was possible, the group were chosen to participate in the subsequent experiment *as a group*.

2. Anticipated Public Disclosure. The subjects in this condition were dismissed after they had filled out the questionnaire in private, and were told to return the following week. At that time they were asked to fill out the questionnaire again under instructions that were very permissive about change, and were further told that each person's decisions would be made public and discussed after he filled out the questionnaire because ". . . a number of people have expressed an interest in knowing what the other people have been deciding." Subjects still anticipated that the experimental session itself would be private.

3. *Anticipated Presence of Others.* As in the first condition, the possibility was raised that the experiment might actually be run on a group basis. The subjects were requested to go through the questionnaire again and "mark the stimulation in each experiment you would prefer to undergo for this group problem solving." Unlike the first discussion to reach consensus condition, there was no discussion, and the subjects were not led to anticipate any. They were told that if they were selected for the group version of the experiment they would participate with two other individuals who selected the same stimulation.

4. *Anticipated Discussion to Reach Consensus.* This condition contained all the features of the first condition except for the discussion itself. Subjects were told to select the stimulation they would want to suggest to the group as the stimulation to be used *if* they were selected for a group rather than an individual experiment.

5. *Retest Control Condition.* As in the anticipated public disclosure condition, these subjects returned the following week and the questionnaire was administered for the second time. However, the conditions were the same for the two administrations and there was no anticipation of public disclosure.

The results of the experiment are presented in Table 15.3. The index values here have roughly the same meaning as in the previous table—positive values meaning a shift in the risky direction. Once again the basic comparisons of individual decision versus group-discussion-to-consensus reveals the greater degree of risk-taking in the latter condition. The finding of greater risk-taking in groups withstands the test of generalization to a new type of situation, this time one in which aversive consequences are potentially involved. But the results of the other conditions are also extremely important from a theoretical point of view. It is clear that the mere anticipation that others will learn of his choices does not lead an individual to take significantly more risks. Neither does the prospect that he may end up in a group of like-minded peers who have chosen the same as himself. Thus the risky shift is apparently not a function of anticipating social support in the event of failure. Perhaps the most dramatic finding is that the anticipation of a group discussion actually produces a shift in the *conservative* direction. The investigators suggest that this is comparable to the conservative shift noted in the second experiment, when the individual was forced to make a decision that might be binding on the group. In the present case the individual is asked to record a decision he presumably intends to urge on the group, a decision whose consequences will therefore be experienced by all.

Table 15.3. Degree of Shift in Risk-Taking When Consequences Are Aversive Under Different Conditions of Decision-Making
(From Bem, Wallach, and Kogan, 1965)

Condition	Shift index mean [a]
1. Discussion to consensus (18 groups)	5.43 [b]
2. Anticipated public disclosure (18 individuals)	1.85
3. Anticipated presence of others (18 individuals)	−1.30 [b]
4. Anticipated discussion to consensus (18 individuals)	−4.91 [b]
5. Retest control	1.11

[a] The construction of this index is described in detail in the original article. Positive values indicate a risky shift.
[b] $P < .05$.

The various treatments producing the risky shift in the previous studies feature a combination of face-to-face discussion and group decision or the reaching of consensus. Are both of these essential for the risky shift effect? If not, which is the more critical of the two, discussion or consensus? In order to answer this question Wallach and Kogan (1965) conducted still another experiment in which subjects first made private responses to 12 hypothetical risk-taking situations and then were exposed to one of three subsequent treatments:

1. Discussion and Consensus Condition. Subjects discussed each situation and reached a unanimous consensus about the answer.

2. Consensus without Discussion Condition. Subjects were not allowed to talk, but exchanged messages indicating their recommendations until a unanimous consensus was obtained.

3. Discussion without Consensus Condition. There was no explicit pressure toward agreement but the groups were urged to discuss each situation for five minutes.

In this experiment the risky shift from an initial baseline score to a post-treatment individual score was substantial for both first and third conditions, but there was no tendency toward greater riskiness in the consensus without discussion condition. These findings were essentially replicated in a study by Kogan and Wallach (1967b) under conditions in which the subjects conducted their discussions over an intercom system and could not see each other.

Discussion, then, appears to be the crucial ingredient and Wallach and

Kogan (1965) conclude by suggesting how the give-and-take of discussion may contribute to responsibility diffusion: "It is the affective bonds formed in discussion that may enable the individual to feel less than proportionally to blame when he entertains the possible failure of a risky decision" (p. 18).

By a process of eliminating most of the reasonable alternatives, Wallach and his colleagues have built a strong case for the importance of responsibility diffusion in explaining that groups are more prone than individuals to take risks. It appears that, in some manner facilitated by discussion, group members are led to feel that the responsibility for failure in a high-risk situation will not be attributed to any single member. It is not at all clear, as yet, how the notion of blame-sharing is crystallized or made salient in a discussion of risk-taking problems.

At least one additional factor still lurks in the wings as a plausible explanation for the risky shift. Perhaps those who are initially more inclined to take risks also tend to be dominant and influential in a group interaction. There is some evidence (Wallach, Kogan, and Bem, 1962) that those with high initial levels of risk-taking are perceived as more influential in the discussion. This judgment, however, may simply reflect the fact that the group ends up at a riskier position and therefore, in retrospect, the members assign greater influence to those initially favoring higher risk-taking— whether or not they were actually more influential.

It is not necessary that the group attain consensus in order for the relationship between initial level of risk and imputed influence to obtain. Wallach, Kogan, and Burt (1965) have shown that even when a risky shift is produced by discussion without consensus, group members judge the higher risk-takers to be more forceful in the group discussion. Even here, however, we cannot rule out the effects of coincidence: the members may reason that because most of the group seemed to change toward riskiness, those initially favoring a risky position *must* have been more influential.

Kogan and Wallach (1967a) discuss an unpublished study by Wallach, Kogan, and Burt that attempted to relate the risk-taking proclivity of subjects to influence in group discussions in which risk was not an issue. Groups were systematically composed of individuals varying in their tendency to favor risky choices. These groups were then asked to discuss issues that either had nothing to do with risk or for which the various alternative solutions were balanced for riskiness. After the discussions, members were asked to rank one another for degree of influence in the group discussion. The results were that high-risk-takers were considered more influential among female subjects, but not among males.

Even if there is no general relationship between risk-taking tendency and influence in a discussion group, there may be special reasons why high-risk-takers may be more influential when the discussions involve risk-conservatism dilemmas. Brown (1965) has suggested that the high-risk-taker may have a rhetorical advantage over members in the group favoring a more conservative tack. Kelley and Thibaut (in press) give added weight to this possibility in their discussion of risk-taking phenomena. The contention is that the language available to the proponent of risk is likely to be richer and have more of a dramatic quality than the rhetoric of caution in our culture. The person who, for whatever reason, espouses a risky alternative can trade on powerful Western myths that romanticize risk-taking. The person who stresses caution has only the drab rhetoric of a banker or a Babbitt to fall back on.

The rhetorical interpretation would be exceedingly difficult to test in any direct way, but it might be fruitful to record and analyze the content and style of the discussion in group risk-taking experiments. This would seem to be the appropriate next step in this interesting sequence of research explorations, because whatever is happening to produce the risky shift is obviously mediated by the discussion and the group decision process it serves.

Perhaps the most reasonable conclusion to draw at the present time is that some combination of responsibility diffusion and rhetorical advantage is probably responsible for the shift toward riskiness that occurs in group discussion. At least for female subjects, furthermore, a third factor may be the greater persuasiveness of persons likely to favor risky alternatives.

The practical implications of the reported findings are intriguing, and perhaps a little harrowing, to contemplate. In the area of decisions about military strategy, especially group decisions involving the evaluation of information about the imminence of a potential enemy attack, it is normally assumed that a staff of experts, "communicating about the meaning of incoming information, will . . . have a conservative, check-and-balance type of influence on one another." Yet, as the foregoing experiments have demonstrated, "conditions may be present which generate diffusion of responsibility and thereby increased risk-taking" (Wallach et al., 1964). In other areas where group decision-making may have crucial consequences for community or national planning, or for the fate and prosperity of a particular corporation or institution, the risky shift may also play a role.

Wallach and his colleagues are well aware of the complexity of the risk-taking issue, however, and note the difficulties of generalizing too glibly from the laboratory to the national scene. As they point out, the consequences of military strategy decisions are certainly of greater magnitude than those involved in their experiments and this in itself may change the picture radically. What may be more important, however, is that the decision-making group has a responsibility for the larger society it represents. Although responsibility *within* the group may be shared, the group itself is clearly charged with a definite responsibility for others. In terms of the second experiment, then, the strategic decision group may be more like the responsibility-for-group condition than like the true group decision condition. There are certainly forces operating in the conservative direction at least that would serve to inhibit or modify the risky shift.

Finally, it should be emphasized again that the consequences of responsibility diffusion in a group, including risk-taking, are likely to be vitiated or minimized to the extent that the group is organized and has a leadership structure. In all of the Wallach experiments pains were taken to assure that the groups would be homogeneous, that there would be no grounds for leadership formation, not enough time to develop an organization, and so on. One of the major functions of leadership, and of other organizational developments such as clearly allocated duties and a division of labor, must surely be to counteract the effects of responsibility diffusion and keep them in harness. If the discussion groups in any of the Wallach experiments had been allowed or encouraged to nominate a leader who moderated the deliberations, the risky shift might have been much reduced. It is clear that responsibility diffusion is one of the important consequences of group membership, and that such diffusion mediates important personal feelings (such as satisfaction with a discussion) and actions (such as risk-taking). It is also more than likely that many features of normal group interaction inhibit this diffusion. The conditions that promote versus minimize diffusion have yet to be systematically investigated.

SUMMARY

In this chapter we have concentrated on the ways in which being a member of a group modifies the cognitions, motives, and actions of the individual. In attempting to explore the impact of group membership we started with the practical problem of evaluating the effectiveness of performance by individuals and by groups, recognizing the difficulties of generalizing across different kinds of tasks. A preliminary overview brought out the fact that certain performance possibilities are strengthened by the active and cooperative presence of others. There are tasks in which the summation and coordination of individual strengths makes possible an attack on objectives beyond the reach of an unorganized collection of workers. There are others in which associations are triggered by the discussion itself that would not otherwise have become available in the solution process. The task may require a kind of objectification of thought that is facilitated by the knowledge that others are present and do not necessarily share a person's own private biases and perspectives. Finally, the correction of errors can be the product of social influence processes that occur during problem-solving attempts.

On the other hand, it was pointed out, there is no guarantee that group performance will be superior to the performance of the same number of individuals working in isolation. At least in some group contexts creativity may be stifled by certain fears of derision for deviance, and the group solution may reflect the lowest common denominator of talent. There are also tasks in which the component jobs are so interrelated that the failure of one person disrupts the performance of everyone else.

It may ultimately be possible to develop a detailed classification system that would prescribe the best social arrangement for accomplishing specified tasks. Such a system would surely have to rest on a firm understanding of the basic factors involved in social interaction within the small group. In the second section of the chapter an effort was made to select a few of the issues that have concerned investigators of these basic factors. A considerable amount of early research was addressed to the effects on the individual of performing in the presence of others, and it is now generally recognized that an audience may have an energizing effect on productive effort, and therefore production quantity, but a distracting or disruptive effect on production quality. This distinction may with some justice be rephrased as that between performance (facilitated) and learning (inhibited).

A second basic issue concerns the conditions under which group goals and individual motives reach convergence. Here we discussed in some detail a number of studies examining the conditions of cooperative striving, the role of mutual attraction or cohesiveness in such striving, and the importance of participation in the acceptance of goals imposed on a group from without. Particular attention was paid to an experiment by Horwitz that showed that those who accepted a group goal reacted toward it as they would toward individual goals.

Finally, the role of responsibility diffusion was discussed. The individual apparently entertains different behavioral alternatives when he is a member of a co-acting group than when he is acting as an individual because the group shares in the consequences of his own actions just as he shares in the consequences of theirs. In particular, this diffusion of responsibility appears to affect the extent to which action decisions shift in a risky direction, a fact that may have implications for a variety of important group decision situations.

This chapter is entitled "The Impact of Group Membership on Individual Behavior." In attempting to cover this topic we have ignored or made only passing reference to such central features of group impact as pressures toward uniformity, conformity, and other aspects of social influence in groups. The only reason for this is that such matters have already been discussed at length in other chapters; a full treatment of the issues of membership impact would naturally include an extensive discussion of social-influence processes. It should also be stressed that we have dealt almost exclusively to this point with informally recruited homogeneous peer groups. The groups in most of the experiments discussed can be said to lack even the beginnings of formal structure and are notable in being sufficiently temporary that leaders do not develop. In the next, final chapter, however, we consider the emergence of group structure and the implications of this structure for individual functioning.

CHAPTER SIXTEEN

Psychological Bases of Group Structure

The concept of structure generally expresses the idea of an organization of parts underlying and giving rise to the surface characteristics of an object. When the anatomist speaks of the structure of the human organism, he means more than a disembodied collection of bones, tissues, and fluids. For him, structure is less a matter of the components of the body than of the character of their complex interdependence. The personality theorist refers to structure, too, when he points to the underlying relations and integrating processes that lend stability and consistency to a particular individual's functioning. Similarly, the notion of *group* structure is a convenient abstraction designed to capture the organized quality of group interaction and the persistence or recurrence of the same forms of interaction over a period of time. A group structure may be formally elaborated, as in an established corporation, a university, or an army, each with its clearly specified tables of organization; or the group structure may be informal, as in a streetcorner gang, a car pool, or a family. In either case we may conveniently use the term structure to identify those characteristics of the group that seem to lend stability and order to the behavior of its members.

The structures we wish to define or to single out will depend on the particular problem of group functioning we wish to investigate. Some obvious structural characteristics are the group's leadership hierarchy, interrelated task roles, established networks of communication, and norms governing the making of group decisions. Such characteristics emerge when the group members are more than a mere collection of interchangeable persons.

A detailed discussion of the structural characteristics of groups would take us well beyond the limits of a book on "the foundations of social psychology." Our primary concern has been with individual behavior and the social pressures influencing that behavior, not with the varied forms and patterns of collective life. And yet important psychological factors are involved in the emergence of group structures, and the structures in turn are undeniably important influences on individual behavior. In this final chapter we propose to review briefly and generally some of the psychological conditions that give rise to group structure and some of the consequences for individual members of various structural arrangements.

NORMS AS SUBSTITUTES FOR INFORMAL SOCIAL INFLUENCE

The concept of cultural norm was introduced in Chapter Five to refer to a pattern of commonly held behavior expectations—tacitly agreed-upon rules of responding—that constrain the group member and shape his activities. In order for this shaping to occur it is, of course, important that the individual recognize these shared expectations and be concerned about living up to them. Such concern typically arises because the group rewards normative behavior and punishes deviance. In our earlier discussion the norm was treated essentially as the mediating component of culture. That is, the shared expectations serve as the vehicle through which broader culture patterns affect individual behavior. It was noted that cultural norms develop in order to provide specifications or rules of thumb for behavior in recurring situations and thus to aid the individual in adjusting to his complex and changing environment. The larger the proportion of actions that can follow the lines of the cultural map, the greater is the freedom of the individual to deal with unexpected developments and decisions not covered by the map. The action alternatives confronting a person, as we emphasized in Chapter Seven, can be viewed in terms of the antinomy between holding on to established normative routines and an openness to change and novelty.

Nothing that we say here is intended to conflict with the earlier treatment or to undermine its implications. In Chapters Five and Six we assumed that cultural norms exist as part of the individual's social heritage and went on to discuss problems of decision in areas not covered by the cultural map (including decisions about which of various norms is applicable). Our present interest is to show how norms emerge in the small group and to take a closer look at some of the functions they serve. The norms of the broader culture are developed in similar ways, though the time span is generally more protracted and the individual typically belongs to different groups whose norms are to some extent conflicting and compete for his loyalty.

Most of the experiments dealing with group interaction involve rather homogeneous collections of subjects assembled for a brief experimental period. By studying interaction in such temporary, relatively unstructured, and informal groups, it is possible to gain insight into the workings of social comparison processes and consequent social influence. But it is important to realize that most of the groups investigated in the laboratory lack both a specific history and a projected future existence as a group. We now suggest that the experience of working together and the prospect of continued interaction have effects that modify the nature of the influence processes at work in the group. In particular, members of a continuing group typically move toward the substitution of *normative control* for informal social influence or the direct applications of cue and outcome control. Let us examine the dynamics that underlie this trend toward normative control, starting for the sake of simplicity with the dyad.

It is clear that only trivial questions of social influence arise when the outcomes of each member of a dyad are completely correspondent. As indicated earlier, when outcomes are correspondent in any group ultimate cooperation is guaranteed, in theory, by the coincidence of individual motives and group goals. As each individual tries to maximize his personal outcomes he maximizes the outcomes of others. Problems concerned with coordination of effort, timing of responses, and so on, should be temporary and easily resolved. When the outcomes of two persons are noncorrespondent, more serious difficulties of coordination are involved if each person is to obtain outcomes that are sufficiently positive to keep him above his CL_{alt} and therefore oriented toward continuing membership in the dyad. Collaboration under noncorrespondence—that is, when there is a conflict of interest—usually involves trading, bargaining, and other complex modes of reaching mutually acceptable agreements. This may be clarified by an example drawn from Thibaut and Kelley (1959). Imagine a husband and wife whose outcomes are noncorrespondent in an important sector of recreational preferences. They very much want to be together on their nights out, but the husband enjoys movies and dislikes dancing whereas the wife enjoys dancing and dislikes movies. The situation is reflected in Figure 16.1. It is obvious that the husband and wife will have to trade preferred activities in order to obtain good outcomes even occasionally. The trading might be initiated by either party through the attempt to apply his available personal power. For example, the husband might promise to go dancing next time if the wife goes with him to the movies this time, or threaten to go to the movies if she insists on going dancing.

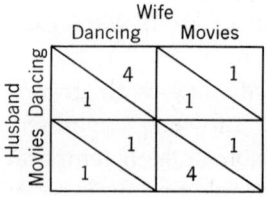

Figure 16.1. Illustration of a relationship requiring trading (from Thibaut and Kelley, 1959, p. 127).

But as Thibaut and Kelley point out, there are many difficulties in the application and threatened application of personal power. In Chapter Ten the point was made that in highly cohesive dyads—those in which each member is dependent on and yet has power over the other—there exists both greater potential for effective social influence and greater potential for resistance. As long as power is exerted on a personal basis, there are dangers of conflict and stand-offs in which neither member can achieve the trade he would like.

The kind of bargain involved in many trading relationships involves the trader's trust that the goods promised in the exchange will actually be forthcoming, that the husband actually will go dancing with the wife next week. Added to uncertainty about whether to be trusting is the problem that each must implicitly acknowledge his dependence on the other in order to negotiate the exchange. Certainly in some relationships this is a difficult thing for the parties to do, because by acknowledging dependence in one area they may invite the application of power in other areas as well. Such considerations are often important in negotiations between management and union, especially if there is a background of mutual distrust. In such situations of noncorrespondent outcomes and roughly equal power, norms may naturally develop as a social device to bypass the uncertainties and frustrations of interpersonal bargaining.

When one person has more power than the other attempts to apply personal power may also have side effects and long-range consequences that are unpleasant to both the high- and the low-power person. By attempting to apply what power he has, the low-power person may invite devastating retaliation from the high-power person. From the point of view of the high-power person, there is always the problem posed by the other's CL_{alt}. If the person low in power is constantly exposed to promises and threats, he may be driven out of the relationship or into a position where he can threaten to leave and therefore exert counterpower to protect his interests. In this way the application of power has a tendency to dissipate the amount of power that might subsequently be applied.

Thus it appears that a major function served by norms is to clarify the stakes involved in a relationship and to coordinate the action of group members to insure that each receives an equitable share of available outcomes. Norms protect the interests of individuals in a social relationship by protecting the integrity and stability of the relationship. In the absence of norms, influence is personalized and likely to involve all the costs incurred in argument, conflict, and the use of threats and bribes. The existence of norms generally insures that friction will be reduced in the relationship and, as appeals to impersonal norms replace personal influence attempts, the dyad can function without a continual re-examination of who is capable of doing what to whom.

Norms and Patterns of Stress in the Dyad

It is perhaps easier to list the various functions served by norms than to specify the conditions under which norms are likely to develop. Thibaut and Faucheux (1965) have recently turned their attention to the latter problem under circumstances of power inequality in the dyad. They propose an intriguing hypothesis, that norms develop naturally under certain conditions of group stress associated with noncorrespondence of outcomes. In developing the background for this hypothesis they distinguish between two kinds of stress, internal and external. *Internal stress* refers to any condition in which the members of a dyad have differential power and their outcomes are negatively correlated. In such a case one person can only achieve good outcomes at the expense of the other, and the low-power member of the dyad—who is in a position to be badly exploited—may be expected to appeal to norms of equity and of fair sharing. *External stress* may be said to exist whenever outcomes available outside the dyad become attractive enough to compete with those available inside. Under these circumstances the low-power member may be especially tempted to be disloyal, thus posing a threat to the high-power member who has more to gain by keeping the dyad going. In order to preserve the integrity of the group in which he holds a natural advantage, the high-power member will be expected to appeal to norms of loyalty and team spirit.

The mere fact that one member is tempted to appeal to the other, either in terms of equity or loyalty, hardly guarantees that the appeal will be successful. The member receiving the appeal must have some reason to conform to the norm being invoked or he will simply resist its application. The next step is to realize that if there is *both* internal and external stress, the high-power member can trade acceptance of the equity appeal or norm in return for the low-power member's acceptance of the loyalty norm. Each member is threatened by behaviors that the other is tempted to perform, so each can reduce the threat to the other by an exchange of adherence to the other's normative appeal. Such an exchange is less meaningful when there is only one kind of stress: the co-occurrence of internal and external stress should be a condition especially favorable for the formation of norms.

The general hypothesis predicting greater norm formation when both internal and external stress are present was tested in an experiment (Thibaut and Faucheux, 1965) in which 100 14-year-old Parisian school boys were the subjects. They appeared in pairs and were introduced to a game of bargaining with each other for points. At the beginning of each experimental session one member of each dyad was randomly assigned to the high-power position (designated as P) and the other to the low-power position (designated as X). The subjects were handed copies of the matrix reproduced in Figure 16.2a and instructed to begin playing the game ac-

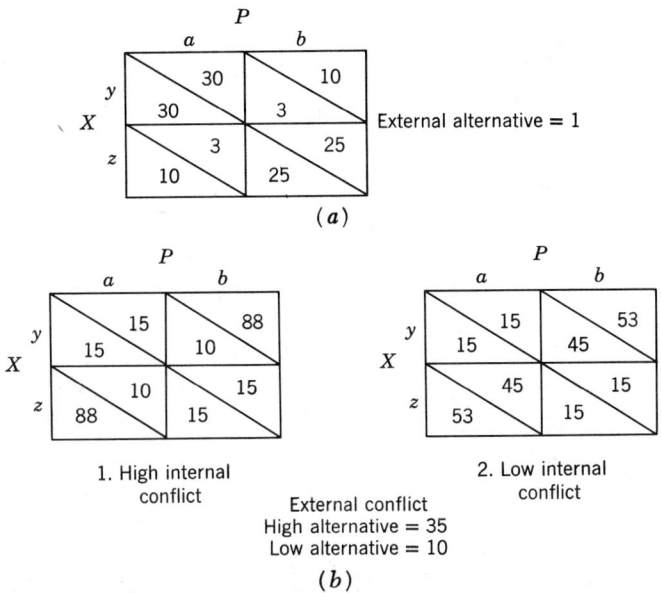

Figure 16.2. Matrices used in the experimental bargaining games of Thibaut and Faucheux (1965). (a) Preliminary practice game matrix. Power implications: in case of either a z or b y, P may take any number of points from 3 to 10. (b) Matrices varying internal and external conflict. Power implications: in case of either a z or b y, P may take any number of points from 10 to 88 (high conflict) or from 45 to 53 (low conflict).

cording to the following procedures (closely paraphrased from Thibaut and Faucheux, 1965, p. 62): By open discussion, the two subjects were to reach a tentative agreement about their joint behavior. Each subject then recorded his private decision about his actual intentions, which did not have to coincide with that implied by the tentative agreement, and then the decisions were made public and the points allocated for that trial. Duplicity was thus possible. In playing the game each subject had three options. He could play either of the two columns (or rows) of the matrix, or he could go outside the matrix to secure a guaranteed alternative. If both subjects actually decided to play this external alternative each received one point. If only one subject chose the external alternative he received one point and the other subject received none. The alternative was thus a dependable (though in this case, a paltry) outcome that each subject could obtain independently of the other's behavior, and it provided a method for threatening the other subject.

If neither subject chose the external alternative, then their outcomes would be determined by the particular cell in which their joint responses located them. The matrix may be interpreted in the usual way (see Chapters Thirteen and Fourteen), with an important exception creating differences in the power of P and X. This exception was embodied in the rule that when there was a difference between the values contained within a particular cell, P was allowed to take any number of points up to the value of the larger cell number. X had to settle for the remainder. Also, it made no practical difference which value was above and which was below the diagonal—another departure from the usual manner of representing the potential outcomes of each player. In matrix A, therefore, if the players' responses landed them in either $b\,y$ or in $a\,z$, then P could take up to 10 points, leaving X with 3. If P took 8, X would receive 5, and so on. Clearly, insofar as there are differences in the numbers above and below the diagonal of a cell, this rule endows P with more power than X.

The matrix in Figure 16.2a was a preliminary matrix designed to acquaint the subjects with the basic properties of the game. Note that $a\,y$ is an obviously harmonious solution and the conflictful solutions ($b\,y$ and $a\,z$) are relatively unattractive to either subject. After three trials with the preliminary matrix, the experiment proper began and the experimental variations were introduced by providing each pair of subjects with a new matrix that had different properties depending on the treatment condition to which the dyad was assigned. The alternatives are presented in Figure 16.2b. Subjects in the high internal conflict conditions were presented with matrix $b\,1$. The main property of this matrix is that P can gain up to 88 points (leaving X with 10) if their mutual choices land them in cells $b\,y$ or $a\,z$. This is consistent, of course, with the previous definition of high internal conflict. Subjects in the low internal conflict matrix ($b\,2$) were more evenly matched in that P, at best, could only gain 53 points whereas X was guaranteed at least 45. Each of these matrices was paired with either a high external alternative (35) or a low external alternative (10). The crucial feature to note is that the high alternative is more than the worst possibilities for X in the high internal conflict matrix. He would thus be very tempted to choose the external alternative if he thought he would be exploited by P.

In playing the crucial series of games with their particular assigned matrix, subjects were given the orientation of competing with all other (past and future) subjects in their position. Thus X was not to compete with the particular P with whom he was paired, but with all other Xs in the experiment. The purpose was to promote an individualistic rather than a narrowly competitive orientation to the game.

After playing the matrix game for six trials, the procedures for forming contracts (that is, explicit norms) were introduced. The experimenter emphasized that contracts were entirely voluntary. On each of the following three trials each subject recorded privately: (1) whether he wanted a contract to be formed, and (2) if so, the single *rule* (among three presented to him) that he would most prefer to have incorporated in the contract. The three rules among which each subject wanting a contract had to choose were as follows (p. 94):

EA-rule. It is prohibited to play the *external alternative* on this trial if a tentative agreement has been reached to play within the matrix.
D-rule. If on this trial a tentative agreement has been reached concerning the *division and distribution* of points between the partners, it is prohibited in the actual play to change the distribution agreed upon.
RC-rule. If on this trial a tentative agreement has been reached such that each partner is to play a specific *row or column* of the matrix, it is prohibited to shift in the actual play to the other row or column.

Recalling our remarks in introducing this experiment, the first two rules should appeal differentially to P and to X, reflecting as they do reactions to external and internal stress respectively. The third rule was introduced primarily as a plausible third option, the choice of which was not predicted by the theoretical formulation. This rule was included to permit a more precise test of the hypothesis because choice of the predicted rule would involve rejection of two that were not predicted.

Finally, each subject was to indicate the type and amount of sanction that he would like to have applied to the violator of any contract rule. He could ask to have an indemnity incorporated in the contract. Indemnities referred in the experiment to payments (in points) the violator of the rule must make to the injured party. In his private recording of his preference for aspects of a contract, the subject could indicate any number of points from 0 to 100 to be applied as an indemnity.

After recording their individual preferences, the partners discussed the matter and decided whether to form a contract, and if a contract were to be formed, the rules and sanctions to be incorporated. They were permitted to include in their contracts as many of the three rules as they liked and to specify the amount of indemnity they wanted incorporated. This procedure was repeated for three trials. Adherence to the various provisions of contracts was enforced by the experimenter.

The *results* of primary interest are those reflecting the frequency and intensity of "contractual activity," but the indications of preference made before contract negotiations are also of interest. In their statements of private preference regarding which rule should be upheld, it was expected that P would prefer prohibiting the external alternative more than X would, whereas X's preference should exceed that of P for a rule prohibiting the violation of any agreement reached about the distribution of points within the matrix. This expectation was strongly confirmed, though neither the degree of conflict nor the size of the alternative made a reliable difference in these comparisons. The major hypothesis of the study was that these variables of internal and external stress would affect the actual contract formation process. Specifically, Thibaut and Faucheux predicted that more contracts would be formed when both forms of stress were present—that is, in the high internal conflict–high external alternative condition—than when there was no stress or only stress of one kind.

As may be seen in Table 16.1, the results provide excellent support for this main hypothesis. In the high-high condition, relative to the other three conditions, there are more contracts formed by the average dyad (as many as 3.00 being possible), more dyads forming contracts, more dyads incorporating both EA and D rules in the contracts formed, and a greater point-indemnity involved. As an over-all measure of the extent of contractual activity, an index was constructed for each dyad by multiplying the number of rules adopted times the magnitude of indemnity to be paid for violations. Again, as the table shows, the condition in which internal and external stress is high stands alone, being significantly larger on this index than the mean of the other conditions combined.

Table 16.1. Frequency and Intensity of Contractual Activity in the Various Treatments

Conflict of Interest	Level of External Alternative	
	High	Low
High		
Mean number of contracts	2.75	1.33
Number of dyads forming one or more contracts	12.00	6.00
Number of dyads adopting both EA- and D-rules [a]	9.00	2.00
Mean indemnity	65.56	26.39
Index of quantity and intensity	315.83	175.00
Low		
Mean number of contracts	1.67	1.92
Number of dyads forming one or more contracts	9.00	8.00
Number of dyads adopting both EA- and D-rules [a]	2.00	3.00
Mean indemnity	35.83	42.22
Index of quantity and intensity	194.17	184.17

[a] EA-rules are prohibitions against playing the alternative; D-rules protect agreements about the division of points (from Thibaut and Faucheux, 1965, p. 99).

Thibaut and his students have done several additional studies (as yet unpublished) extending this reasoning. In general, the results of these studies (all using American college students) offer strong additional support for the proposition that norms (contracts) will be formed when each member of the dyad has a means of threatening the other.

The game matrix developed by Thibaut and Faucheux was designed to provide an experimental analogy for natural group conditions in which members can exploit each other in various ways. Consider a small firm in which the employer divides company earnings between himself and his employees. Naturally he will be more concerned about potential defection of his employees if they can readily sell their services elsewhere. For their part, the employees are likely to be very concerned with their boss's sense of fair play when the firm's earnings are high and he is free to divide them in any way he wishes. From the Thibaut and Faucheux results we would expect contracts protecting both the employer and his employees to develop under the combined circumstances of attractive outside offers and high company earnings. Each should be willing to accede to a contract that prevents him from being exploited by the other. In this way potential stress from different sources can generate the climate for norm formation.

Norm Formation in Larger Groups

As we turn to groups of three or more members, the inevitability and importance of norms increase. As the number of group members grows, the number of possible interpersonal relationships rises at a much more rapid rate. In a triad three simple two-person relationships (A with B, B with C, A with C) are possible; in a quartet there are six; in a quintet ten; and so on. In addition to the simple relationships that may be counted, the number of *mediated* relationships also increases with member size. In terms of influence, for example, the possibility arises that A can influence C by influencing B who in turn influences C. Because of the sheer complexity of relationships in larger groups, the efficient distribution of necessary information and the coordination of individual actions become serious problems that can be at least partially solved by the development of norms and regulations to which everyone adheres.

An even more important factor that facilitates the emergence of norms in larger groups may be the tendency to endow the group with powers and properties that exist independently of the individual members. This is a point emphasized by Georg Simmel (1908) who perceived an abrupt difference between the dyad and larger groups. Each member of the dyad, he reasoned, feels himself to be confronted only by the other, not by a superindividual unit. The secession or death of one member immediately terminates the group; this "is bound to influence the inner attitude of the individual toward the dyad" (p. 124). One aspect of this inner attitude is that any norms that are formed by the dyad tend to remain little more than implicit agreements backed up by each member's bargaining power.

When there are three or more members, on the other hand, the group acquires a kind of durable identity in the minds of these members, at least partly because the loss of one member does not automatically dissolve the group. This perceived identity may be important for normative development. Norms that are seen to operate on behalf of or in the service of the "group" have an important impersonal quality that distinguishes them from informal personal influence. Conformity in a small group may be considered expedient; in a larger group conformity is more likely to seem morally right. The individual acquiesces not to other persons but to the group as an impersonal entity.

This conversion of a practical into a moral arrangement probably has complex origins in the socialization histories of the parties involved. Blau (1964) discusses how the development of conscience can support adherence to group norms by changing the value of rewards available in a social exchange. The members typically import into newly formed groups norms that they have internalized in growing up. These internalized norms affect the matrix values for group-centered versus self-centered behavior. Guilt feelings that would arise from violating group norms must be included as an important cost of actions that are purely self-seeking. "Men who forego the advantages made possible by cheating do not act contrary to their self-interest *if* the peace of mind . . . they obtain for their honesty is more rewarding to them than the gains they could make by cheating" (Blau, 1964, p. 258).

In addition, through the implications of effect dependence and reflected appraisal, "social norms substitute indirect exchange for direct transactions between individuals" (p. 259). A group member may not receive approval in direct exchange for cooperation or conformity to norms, but he may through such actions set the stage for later social rewards by enhancing his reputation. He thus may increase the likelihood that support from others will be forthcoming when he needs it. Especially as the group increases in size, exchange becomes indirect in another sense. A may help B on one occasion; B may help C on another; at still another time, C may help A. As Blau points out, "the same principle applies to formal organizations. Staff officials do not assist line officials in their work in exchange for rewards received from them, but furnishing this assistance is the official obligation of staff members, and in return for discharging these obligations they receive financial rewards from the company" (p. 260).

Once formed, norms seem to have an existence apart from the relationship itself, a quality of "exteriority" as Durkheim observed years ago. Even in the dyad, "it appears to the pair almost as if a third agent had entered the relationship, a feeling that undoubtedly is reinforced by the fact that in earlier relationships the enforcers of rules often actually were third persons (e.g., the mother in the case of two squabbling brothers, the referee in athletic contests, etc.)" (Thibaut and Kelley, 1959, p. 129).

We realize that we are flirting here with ideas that have an ancient and honored history, going back at least to the social contract theories of Hobbes and Rousseau. There are many variants of the notion that men escape the danger and the chaos of living in a social jungle by relinquishing some of their personal power to governing and regulating agencies. Coherent social organizations have been thought to emerge, in other words, out of individuals negotiating a contract with each other concerning rules and principles by which they all agree to abide. We believe that the advantages of such agreements may be just as real in smaller groups as in large societies, and that norms and other forms of group structure serve a function similar to that served by laws in the larger society. However, it has perhaps not been sufficiently stressed that the course of normative growth and development in a group is often implicit. It *may* happen that the members of a group actually sit down together and make out a set of explicit ground rules they propose to follow, conduct a vote, codify the rules as by-laws, and so on. But at least as often norms develop through the kind of trial-and-error process described in Chapter Fourteen, where we referred to several experiments involving the development of implicit cooperation in a minimal social situation. Perhaps by chance, perhaps because of appropriate transfer from other relationships, perhaps through the give-and-take of rather subtle exchanges of social reinforcement, silent understandings may develop that govern the judgments of each group member concerning the right and the wrong ways to behave.

SOURCES OF ROLE DIFFERENTIATION IN GROUPS

In attempting to discover how a group develops an internal structure and selectively accepts certain norms rather than others, we must again confront the fact that groups develop in a variety of ways and ultimately become stabilized in a variety of forms. As an opening wedge into the sources of this variety, we may make the obvious point that group structure is in an important way determined by group function. In other words, groups formed for different purposes and confronting different kinds of environments tend to develop different internal structures (recurrent patterns of interaction that become stabilized and supported by explicit and implicit group norms).

We may refer to the component patterns of interaction that compose group structure by the term *social role*. We take the position that groups normally develop different functional positions—different roles—the content and interrelations of which define the particular structure of the group. These roles evolve in response to the nature of the tasks confronting the group, the particular needs and styles of the members, and the relevance or salience of roles common to experiences in other groups. The members might conveniently reapply the latter in the present instance.

Roles imply differential expectations. As Thibaut and Kelley (1959) put it, "Whereas some of the norms within a group apply to all members, others apply only to specific individuals or sub-classes of individuals. The sub-classes provide a basis for identifying different *roles* within the group . . . By a role . . . we mean the class of one or more norms that applies to a person's behavior with regard to some specific external problem or in relation to a special class of other persons" (p. 142–143).

Usually the same person performs more than one role. This is especially true if both formal (explicit) and informal roles are considered. The group's secretary may have the role of recorder, taker of the roll, and substitute chairman in the absence of the group leader. Each of these roles may be formally specified as duties that go along with his position as secretary. He may also have the role of subtle disciplinarian, dispensing frowns and smiles in response to members who act in ways that thwart or fulfill the group norms, and of conversation summarizer—roles that are not formally designated duties associated with his position. It is customary in sociological analyses of group structure to treat the different group roles as the building blocks of an analysis. These roles may be inferred from observed regularities in behavior, from questionnaire data concerning expectations and perceptions, or both, though roles are of course constructs and like all such convenient fictions they may be described differently by analysts with different interests or perspectives.

The External System and the Internal System

We have said that the particular roles that develop are largely determined by the kinds of problems that the group confronts in the external environment. This is undoubtedly true, but it is only part of the truth. Homans (1950), following the early lead of Barnard (1938), proposed that each group has a social system that may be further analyzed into an external system and into an internal system. According to Homans, the *external system* includes those roles and role relationships that develop directly out of the requirements of group survival and goal achievement— in short, out of the group's attempts to adapt to the external environment confronting it. In the operation of a submarine there are obviously certain tasks that must be performed, such as operating the engines, opening and closing the ballast tanks during submersion and surfacing, looking through the periscope to maintain visual contact when necessary, operating the underwater sound equipment, feeding the crew, and so on. These task requirements naturally create specific roles that must be performed in certain ways. It would be rather silly and inefficient, for example, for each submariner to take an equal responsibility for monitoring underwater sounds.

Equally important, the separate roles must be coordinated both by general regulations and by specific communications from the captain or other designated representatives of the submarine's leadership hierarchy. The differentiation of functional roles (which we may more loosely describe as the division of labor) combines with the allocation of decision-making authority within the leadership hierarchy to constitute the external system of the submarine's social system.

Whereas the external system of role relationships emerges directly out of task requirements, the group's environment is more indirectly reflected in a second system. This has been labeled the *internal system* by Homans, to indicate that it is a set of roles that develop in response to internal group problems rather than to externally imposed tasks. The internal system emerges out of the external system and reacts upon it. Thus, in the submarine example, the roles of Assistant Engineering Officer and Chief of the Boat may require a considerable amount of social interaction and contact between a 45-year-old noncommissioned officer and a 22-year-old naval Ensign. Although the Ensign has formal authority over the noncommissioned Chief Petty Officer, the Chief may develop a personal role of tutor and model in his relations with the Ensign. The Chief may use his superior age and experience to take over spheres of authority and control that threaten the authority structure of the boat. The Ensign's accommodation to this threat will then be an important determinant of how well the boat functions.

In developing further examples of internal system phenomena, Homans argues that a high degree of interaction between two workers—brought about, let us say, by the fact that they are assigned adjacent work benches or must exchange work products in an assembly line—will lead to changes in interpersonal attitudes or, to use his term, sentiments; chances are that the workers will like each other more after intensive contact. This increase in liking, in turn, may lead to increased interaction. The increased interaction may well interfere with production activities and thus bring about changes in the external system. Homans stresses this mutual interdependence of the two systems: relationships and interaction patterns that develop out of necessary job contacts often change in ways that can only be understood if the existence of something like an internal system is recognized.

The distinction between the external and the internal system nicely fits many of the observations made by Roethlisberger and Dickson (1939) in the now classical "Hawthorne Studies" conducted between 1927 and 1932 at the Western Electric Company's Hawthorne Works in Chicago.

Based on a reanalysis of the early observations of this work group, Homans (1950) recounts how personal attractions and animosities—the internal system—interfered with the efficient operation of the external system. As a consequence of various patterns of mutual help, job trading, game playing, engaging in controversies, and so on, the men were producing *and* earning less than they easily could have.

Many of the activities constituting the internal system arise as a way of coping with the boredom that is often inherent in industrial jobs. Roy (1959–1960) spent two months as a participant observer in a small work group of factory machine operators. The work was exceedingly monotonous but Roy began to take note of elaborate and almost ritualized byplay among the workers. It became increasingly clear to him that the men had gradually evolved an intricate series of interaction patterns to help them get through each day. These patterns were easy to identify. Indeed, their occurrence could be predicted from day to day, and Roy's perceptive account of recurrent horseplay and repeated conversational themes provides an excellent illustration of an internal system whose function was to tame "the 'beast of boredom' . . . to the harmlessness of a kitten."

The distinction between external and internal systems might help to classify major clusters of roles in a group. Unfortunately, it is difficult in an actual group to distinguish between roles that compose the external system and internal system roles. This discrimination task seems to be more readily solved by substituting for the distinction between external and internal systems, the closely related distinction between *task roles* and *group maintenance roles*.

Roles Arising Out of Task and Group Maintenance Functions

Thibaut and Kelley (1959) begin their functional analysis of group roles from much the same perspective as Homans, and Barnard before him. Groups typically face two kinds of problem: external problems of dealing with tasks in the environment and internal problems of the relations among members. Both kinds of problem must be solved in such a way as to keep the outcomes of each group member above his comparison level for alternatives (CL_{alt})—otherwise the group will lose members to other relationships and ultimately fail to survive.

Thibaut and Kelley refer to the activities required to maintain externally derived outcomes as *task functions*. Just as an individual may have high power to extract good outcomes from nature or from another individual, so a group may have this same kind of power to secure rewards for its members. It is easy to maintain morale on a winning team. However, efforts to solve the external problems of dealing with tasks in the environment usually involve costs that are not equally distributed among the members. On occasions, furthermore, the group may fail to solve the tasks it has set for itself and therefore fail to gain the rewards associated with task solution. Or, if the task is ultimately solved, there may be long and frustrating delays during which costs are incurred but no rewards are forthcoming.

For the group to survive under these less-than-ideal circumstances, ways must be found of keeping the members above their CL_{alt} and thus of maintaining the group intact. Thibaut and Kelley propose that maintaining the positions of all members above their CL_{alt} is equivalent to maintaining a stable interdependence among the group members. This proposal follows from their analysis of the relations between CL_{alt} and dependence. Activities by which the interdependence of members is maintained are the *maintenance functions* of the group.

Different roles are often associated with these two kinds of function. Many complex organizations employ persons in roles that satisfy primarily group maintenance functions: cooks, messengers, guidance counselors, nurses, repairmen, legal advisors, receptionists, and so on. These roles are ancillary to the external system roles involved in production, but they may be vital for keeping the group in proper working trim.

A Task and a Maintenance Leader?

As far as leadership roles are concerned, maintaining morale and satisfying the followers' needs are among the most important responsibilities of leadership. If the task is complex enough to require role differentiation in the external system (that is, a division of labor among task roles) then one of the functions that must be met by some person or combination of persons is that of coordinating the different contributions to task completion. There may be involved in this both the development of elaborate networks of communication and complicated plans for distributing personnel and insuring that their incomes are coordinate with their talents and the costs they incur on the job. These functions are, of course, maintenance functions and they require the kind of regulatory power that inheres in the leader's position. Most leaders are also centrally involved in performing such task roles as perceiving and diagnosing the nature of the problem presented by the task, training new members, working out new techniques for cutting costs or augmenting total group power, fending off interference from the outside, making friendly alliances in the environment, and so on. An interesting and important question concerns the extent to which the same persons in the group—whether they are leaders or followers—perform both task roles and group maintenance roles.

In the judgment of Bales and Slater (1955),

> The appearance of a differentiation between a person who symbolizes the demands of task accomplishment and a person who symbolizes the demands of social and emotional needs is implicit in the very existence of a social system responsive to an environment. Any such system has both an "inside" and an "outside" aspect and a need to build a common culture which deals with both (p. 303).

They suggest that in the typical small group there is a difference between the one who contributes the most in directly solving task problems, and the one who is liked the most of all the group members.

Thibaut and Kelley (1959) paraphrase Bales and Slater's account of the basic events that lead to a differentiation between the task specialist and the maintenance specialist:

> When any newly formed group is confronted with a task or problem, the members of the group begin to incur costs as they set about working at the task. These task-related or problem-solving behaviors are instigated by one of the members who is at least temporarily the task specialist (or task leader) and who is identified simply by virtue of his initiating the largest number of task-relevant interactions. (We are not concerned at the moment with whether he is a "good" or competent leader.) The task leader's role thus induces increased costs in the other members. Unless the task quickly yields compensating rewards, the result is that the other members tend to drop below CL. The annoyance and aggression that the group members develop from this below-CL experience may be in part directed toward the task specialist who instigated the cost-incurring behavior. If this process continues so that the members' outcomes begin to fall toward CL_{alt}, the group may begin to disrupt if special action is not taken, and it is here that, for groups that survive, the maintenance (or social-emotional) specialist enters. His contribution is to increase the rewards to members by warm supportive behavior toward them, and/or to reduce their costs, by such behavior as making jokes that relieve tension and, in general, by reducing their anxieties (pp. 279–280).

This picture is undoubtedly oversimplified. It assumes that the task is indeed *imposed* on the group members and that they have no initial interest in achieving task goals. It also assumes that leaders have to goad and frustrate their followers, whereas one of their common duties is to facilitate the attainment of goals the followers have chosen by providing materials, facilities, expert advice, and so on. Nevertheless, there is probably enough truth in Thibaut and Kelley's account to propose some reasonable and testable hypotheses.

Thibaut and Kelley suggest further that these roles are likely to be performed by different persons partly because different talents may be involved, talents that tend not to exist in the same person, and partly because one role is in a sense incompatible with the other. The task specialist must exhort, move, and disturb his followers; the maintenance specialist must soothe, quiet, and comfort them.

What evidence is there that this differentiation of task and maintenance roles in fact occurs? Is there any support for the hypothesis that these two kinds of role tend not to be performed by the same individual? Much of the relevant evidence bearing on these questions comes from observations of discussion groups made by Bales and his colleagues. In the late 1940's Bales developed a system of categories for recording the process of social interaction in a discussion group. The final set of categories, described fully in *Interaction Process Analysis* (Bales, 1950), emerged from trying many different classification schemes in the process of observing hundreds of different groups in action. The IPA system instructs the observer to place individual statements or idea units in one of 12 general categories, noting who made the remark and to whom it was directed. One comment might be recorded, for example, under the category "gives suggestion"; another might be put in the category "shows antagonism." The full list of categories is shown in Figure 16.3. As an illustration of how the remarks in a typical interchange would be scored, Bales (1958, p. 439) presents the following excerpt from the beginning of an actual discussion:

Member 1. I wonder if we have the same facts about the problem? [asks for opinion] Perhaps we should take some time in the beginning to find out. [gives suggestion]
Member 2. Yes, [agrees] we may be able to fill in some gaps in our information. [gives opinion] Let's go around the table and each tell what the report said in his case. [gives suggestion]
Member 3. Oh, let's get going. [shows antagonism] We've all got the same facts. [gives opinion]
Member 2. (Blushes) [shows tension]

For the present discussion, perhaps the most important aspect of the IPA system is the division of categories into task-related and social-emotional acts. Categories 1 to 3 and 10 to 12 involve social-emotional or expressive actions. Categories 4 to 9, on the other hand, encompass actions that are more instrumental in nature, more directly concerned with decision making, task-accomplishment, and other requirements imposed by the external environment.

Bales and Slater (1955; Slater, 1955; Bales, 1958) have examined the interaction data of a number of discussion groups and have attempted to relate these data to various attitudes and perceptions of the group members toward each other. The results are quite consistent and provide strong evidence for the natural emergence of role differentiation in face-

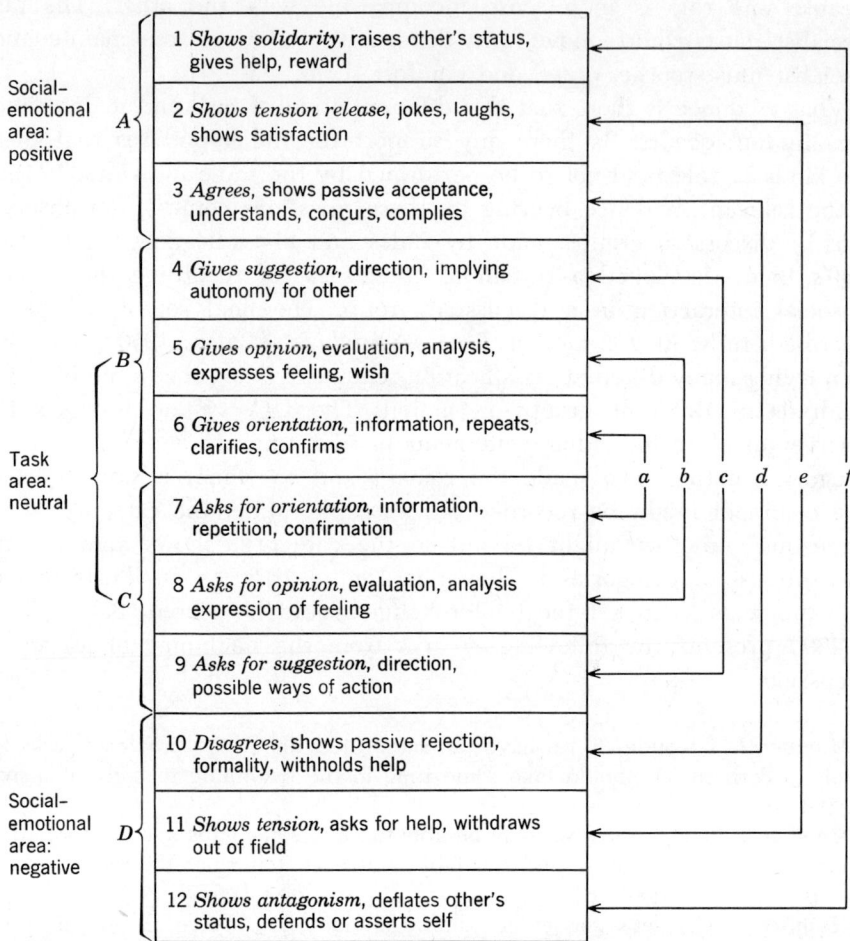

Figure 16.3. The system of categories used in observation and their major relations (from Bales, 1950, p. 59). Key:

a. Problems of communication
b. Problems of evaluation
c. Problems of control
d. Problems of decision
e. Problems of tension reduction
f. Problems of reintegration

A. Positive reactions
B. Attempted answers
C. Questions
D. Negative reactions

to-face groups. As the three articles cited refer to the data on many of the same groups, we shall concentrate on the most fully reported of them, Slater's 1955 report.

Twenty groups, each containing three to seven members, met for four different sessions to discuss typical human-relations problems. A standard procedure was followed in each group: the members were initially unacquainted with each other and were given no clues or suggestions as to how they might organize as a group. When they arrived at the laboratory conference room, the experimenter presented a five-page set of facts about a problem facing an administrator in his organization. Each member was given a copy of the case to read ahead of time and, although they were assured that all information provided was accurate, doubts were raised concerning the presumption that each member was given exactly the same information. In point of fact, the information given to each member was identical but it was thought important to leave this an open issue so that there would be more incentive for the members to communicate with each other. The task defined for each group was to assemble the information, to discuss why the people involved were behaving as they did, and to decide what should be recommended as action for the solution to the problem presented. The groups were asked to time themselves for 40 minutes and to dictate the group solution into a tape recorder in the final one or two minutes of the meeting.

At the end of each meeting, the members were asked to fill out questionnaires that included the following questions:

(a) Who contributed the best ideas for solving the problem? Please rank the members in order. *Include yourself*.

(b) Who did the most to guide the discussion and keep it moving effectively? Please rank the members in order. *Include yourself*.

(c) How well did you personally like each of the other members? Rate each member on a scale from 0 to 7, where zero means "I feel perfectly neutral toward him," and 7 means "I like him very much."

The questionnaire data show that the best-liked member was seldom the member judged to have the best ideas, or to have done the most to guide the discussion. Of special interest is the fact that the tendency for the same person to be best-liked and most highly respected for his ideas is fairly strong after the first session but drops sharply in subsequent sessions. Thus, by the fourth session, the chances that the same person will be judged to be most popular and also rated highest on task ability are slim.

This impression of increasing differentiation of a task specialist and a specialist at being liked is further substantiated by an analysis of the subject's actual interactive behavior—as recorded in the IPA categories. Ignoring the occasional sessions in which the same person was judged both to be most popular and to have the best ideas, there is a distinct difference between the categories featured by the popular man versus the idea man. The member who is nominated as the best idea man tends to concentrate his communications in categories 4, 5, and 6, the problem-solving categories of giving suggestions, opinions, and orientation. Nearly

60 percent of his actions fall in these categories, whereas the corresponding percentage is only 52 percent for the best-liked man. On the other hand, the best-liked man is more active in categories 1, 2, and 3—positive and agreeable reactions. The best-liked man contributes 28 percent of his actions to showing solidarity, releasing tension, and showing agreement; the idea man contributes only 23 percent of his actions to this set of categories.

The emerging pattern is quite consistent with the notion that roles directly concerned with instrumental or task functions tend to attach themselves to some group members, whereas social-emotional or maintenance roles tend to attach themselves to others. It appears that a dual leadership structure often develops in discussion groups, with both a task leader and maintenance leader clearly evident. Some persons, of course, are equally competent at providing leads for solving the task and at soothing and gratifying other members of the group, but this "single leadership" structure is uncommon, presumably because such individuals are rare.

In the more typical dual leadership case, what is the relationship between the "leaders" and how does it develop? There is fairly good evidence that the two leaders fall into a complementary relationship of mutual support. The best-liked man tends to like the idea man more than the rest of the group members do and he likes him more than he does the other members. The idea man, correspondingly, likes the best-liked man more than the others do, and more than he likes the others. Not only are the two leaders involved in something like a mutual admiration society, but they tend to interact with each other more than either does with other members.

In an article summarizing the results of 30 five-man discussion groups, Bales (1958) argues strongly for the hypothesis of two complementary leaders. After presenting data that generally confirm the earlier data presented by Slater, Bales contends:

> The husband and wife in many families seem to play complementary roles of the sort described. Many administrators find cases in their experience where organizations in fact have two leaders, one who specializes on the task side, one on the social-emotional side. It is a kind of political maxim that it is almost impossible to elect the person who is technically best suited for an office—he is generally not popular enough. Surely there must be many persons in leadership positions who welcome any theory that explains to them that their lack of popularity is no fault of their own but is the result of a specialization that is in the nature of things (p. 443).

These results and speculations are provocative and point up the relevance of the task role–group maintenance role distinction, but they should be qualified in at least one major respect. A dual or complementary leadership structure is more common in groups where a fairly high degree of consensus exists among the members as to which member had the best ideas and the best capacity for guidance. In the low-consensus groups the same general relationships tend to hold, but not to the same degree. It is not clear whether the dual leadership structure is made possible by this consensus, or whether the consensus emerges as a consequence of having a viable structure of dual leadership. Bales and Slater (1955) suggest that variations in consensus may reflect accidental variations in the personalities or values of members. Whatever underlies the consensus variations, Bales and Slater feel that the development of a differentiated leadership structure is predicated on some minimal amount of consensus among the members. There must be a sharing of expectations about the criteria of good and bad performances, for example, before role differentiation is likely to arise and become stabilized. In their view, consensus on an idea man is an index of the "latent basis" for role differentiation. The fact remains that a certain amount of differentiation probably must exist before consensus can develop.

Some Reflections on Group Structure, UBO, and the Basic Antinomy

We argued in Chapters Five and Six that the individual is often placed in the position of choosing between alternative courses of action, and that his ability to achieve an unequivocal behavior orientation is important in the process of adapting to environmental demands. This achievement of UBO, however, commits the individual to a stance that often has implications for perception, exposure to information, and attitude change, as well as repercussions for the developing phenomenal self. Much of the present book has concerned the adjustive cognitive processes that occur in these different spheres because of the irrevocability of many actions and the individual's need to take an unequivocal stance toward the environment.

We may now briefly note that many of the internal adjustments that occur in the process of group organization and role differentiation are analogous to the cognitive adjustments of the individual as he works toward a set of cognitions that are consistent with his actions and with each other. Individual group members take action on behalf of the group in the process of task solution. These actions often produce strains, momentary imbalances between individual motives and group goals, that must be dealt with in some way by the other members of the group. Just as cognitions and attitudes tend to change in ways that make them more consistent with personal actions and commitments to action, the roles in the group develop in accommodation to the actions of individuals in confronting the external environment.

The distinction between task roles and group maintenance roles is relevant in this context. Task roles arise in response to the need for action in the environment external to the group. Group maintenance roles represent the ensuing and anticipated accommodation to actions in the task sphere, the internal readjustments that are necessary to support action decisions.

We are reluctant to make too much of the parallel between individual cognitive accommodation and group role accommodation, but there is one further aspect that deserves comment. In discussing the impact of values on perception in Chapter Seven, we suggested that there is a fundamental antinomy in life between stability and self-maintenance on the one hand and openness to change and stimulation on the other. If either side of this antinomy should become completely dominant, it is hard to see how the individual could survive as an intact, effective organism. In the small group it may be that the roles that develop actually represent, in rough terms, the two sides of the same antinomy. In order for the group to survive it must meet its obligations in the larger world; it must show a sensitivity to changing task requirements and a flexibility of response to such changes. At the same time, however, there must be some concern within the group for the preservation of useful traditions, time-tested ways of doing things and of organizing member effort.

Such considerations bring us close again to the distinction between task roles and group maintenance roles, between the task specialist and the social-emotional specialist. In support of this view we may cite Bales and Slater (1955), who suggest that the differentiation into task and maintenance roles represents a difference

> . . . of responsibility for, or vested interest in, maintaining the internal state of affairs of the system in *steady state,* (including existing emotional attachments to persons, objects, modes of gratification, and modes of symbolic control over behavior), vs. responsibility for, or vested interests in *change,* usually for the sake of some improved adjustment vis-a-vis the environment (p. 304).

It should finally be pointed out that the proponents of change and the proponents of the status quo may generate considerable friction in group life. To recognize that a dual leadership structure is characteristic in many groups and organizations is not to suggest that task achievement and group maintenance forces necessarily thrive in harmony. The fact that the task and maintenance leader tend to admire and support each other may be a critical condition for group survival. Without this solidarity at the top the conflict between change and maintenance forces might prove too divisive. When there is little or no consensus concerning the best idea man, perhaps this potentially divisive conflict between maintenance and change pressures is replaced by smaller and less damaging disagreements about proper objectives. Without agreement about the best course to follow, there is little danger of movement and change and therefore little threat to those members favoring the status quo.

Personality Factors and Role Differentiation

For the sake of simplifying the presentation we have to this point ignored the role of personality factors—of individual differences—in determining the kind of group structure most likely to develop. It is important not to overemphasize the external environment as a determinant of group structure, and to recognize the potential importance of differences in member personalities. Situational demands, including the specific requirements of a group task, do not completely override the influence of personality factors and individual talents without the latter leaving some imprint on the formation of group structure. First of all, the range of abilities and personality types sets limits on the possibilities of role differentiation. Some knowledge of member values, areas of competence, and working styles might be vitally important in choosing between organizational forms for accomplishing a particular group objective. For example, a decisive division of labor makes more sense in a group that is characterized by persons with widely differing talents. Second, given the fact that there are pressures toward role differentiation, personality factors are critical determinants of which person will fulfill which role.

The basic problem of organizational planning is to find a suitable and effective compromise between task demands and personal needs and capabilities. In an important sense the task role—group maintenance role division arises out of the attempt to manage this compromise. We have pointed out that if there were complete correspondence of outcomes among group members, the purposes of group organization would be reduced largely to coordination of actions and decisions about timing. In a group in which there is role differentiation, correspondence of outcomes will presumably be greatest when there is appropriate matching of personality with role. Such matching makes it more probable that the individual members will enjoy themselves in carrying out their respective duties. The better the fit of role and personality, the less need for elaborate organizational structures to insure that everyone does his share.

THE EMERGENCE OF LEADERS

A discussion of leadership is traditionally included in any comprehensive treatment of social psychological phenomena. The topic is an obvious point at which psychological research might inform administrative action, and serves as a major testing ground for the application of psychological principles. However, we intend to deal with the problem in a most cursory way in spite of the huge volume of research devoted to the processes of leader functioning and the selection of effective leaders. The major reason we shall follow this course of action is our belief that the leadership topic does not call for or contain any new theoretical principles. We agree with Thibaut and Kelley's (1959) diagnosis that although leadership is a phenomenon of great complexity, there are not any properties unique to it. Leadership seems to be analyzable in terms of other, simpler, concepts, such as outcome and cue control, norms, and expertise.

Nevertheless, our attention is drawn to the problem of leader emergence as a crucial part of the development of group structure, and we shall try to suggest in these concluding pages the major factors that determine the course of this development. The first problem confronting the student of leadership is to find a definition of the leader's role that helps to identify him in groups without a formal leadership structure. A large number of leadership studies evaluate the effectiveness of various ways of performing the functions of leadership once the incumbent of a leadership position is identified. However, as a number of observational studies have shown, the nominal leader of a group is often not the real or effective leader. Thus the definitional problem is not entirely solved by considering only those organizations in which the leader is formally designated.

In any event, because we are more interested in the psychological bases than the sociological origins of group structure, our focus continues to be on the more informal, and typically more temporary, face-to-face group. With reference to such groups we wish to gain insight into the development in which one or more persons rise to the top and begin to exert a disproportionate amount of influence over group decisions. The leaders of such informal groups may be identified through sociometric questionnaires —as in the Bales line of research in which members are asked to identify in retrospect the most influential figures in their group—or through observation by neutral observers. Many studies of leadership emergence attempt to define the leader (or leaders) in terms of the frequency of suggestions made and accepted, or in terms of similar observational measures.

It is of considerable interest when the leader identified by sociometric questionnaires is not the same person identified by observer judgments, and the matching of these two defining criteria is often much less than perfect. For present purposes we shall assume that a general hierarchy of influence does tend to emerge in a flourishing group and that the leaders can be identified with reasonable reliability, either by asking the members or observing the actual course of interaction. We shall attempt to consider the conditions that give rise to such a hierarchy as a general phenomenon and to discuss which individuals gravitate to positions of leadership.

General Conditions Favoring the Development of Leadership Structures

In analyzing the factors that give rise to the separation of leader and follower roles, a first consideration is the fact that an uneven distribution of influence among group members is in a sense inevitable. Given the necessity of making a decision, any decision, initial disagreement must give way to ultimate agreement. (In this case "agreement" implies nothing about private attitude change or even public enthusiasm about the decision —only, at a minimum, a resigned acceptance of it.) That agreement exists where there was once disagreement clearly implies that some group members have exerted and others have accepted influence. Especially if open discussion precedes a vote or decision, an instance of unequal influence has occurred. It may be difficult to locate the source of greatest influence in developing a consensus on a particular topic, but the detection of leaders becomes easier when a series of votes or decisions is observed. This is especially true when the initial majority does not always carry the decision. A person who is always on the winning side in group debates or discussions may be a leader or a follower. If this recurrent winner has sometimes started from a minority position his leadership status is easier to detect. The extreme case, of course, is that in which the "leader" imposes his will in opposition to every other member.

The transition from a single case in which a person may accidentally find himself in the majority to a condition of stabilized, recurrent, disproportionate influence is undoubtedly facilitated by a number of factors. Small groups can, and sometimes do, operate with all decisions determined by majority vote. It would appear, however, that voting procedures easily become cumbersome vehicles for decision-making—especially when decisions are numerous and often trivial. In such cases an elementary concern with efficiency dictates the investment of decision-making power in the hands of one or more executives. The choice of a particular executive may not be a matter of great importance to the group, but it *is* important that someone be vested with the responsibility for making routine decisions, if not those of great importance. Thus it is easy to see why some form of leadership structure emerges out of the need to avoid chaos and contention in the decision-making process. (It may in some cases make sense to distinguish between the procedural leader and the substantive leader—the former being primarily concerned with administrative arrangements, the latter being of greatest influence in the actual decision-making process. However, in the typical small group these positions are difficult to distinguish.)

An implication of this analysis is that the greater the complexity of the task confronting the group, the greater the need for decision-making power to rest in the hands of one or a few designated persons. That is, the more numerous the decisions that must be made by someone, and the greater the interdependence of these decisions, the greater is the likelihood that a strong leadership structure will emerge. Such a proposition fits the earlier comment that leadership is a natural consequence of functional role differentiation—that is, of division of labor. Labor that is "divided" must at some stage be "integrated." This is a major problem of leadership, to coordinate the divided and differentiated roles and to harmonize their contributions to task solution.

Two further variables have been shown to condition the emergence of leadership and to affect the range of decision-making power assigned or conceded to the leader. One of these, group size, is clearly related to task complexity. In a large-scale questionnaire study Hemphill (1950) found that more demands are placed on the leader in groups with more than 30 members than in smaller groups, but also that there is more tolerance of behavior that is highly directive and leader-centered. Not surprisingly, leaders judged to be superior by the members in larger groups were less likely to consult follower opinion and more likely to act on their own initiative than superior leaders in small groups. To this often cited finding of Hemphill's, we may add Bales' (1953) finding that observed equality of participation (and presumably influence) decreases as group size increases—that is, the difference in volume of talking between the one who participates the most and the one who participates the second most, third most, and so on, grows as a function of group size.

A second variable is more closely related to the involvement of the members in group achievement than to complexity per se. This is the variable of *urgency* or the importance of taking decisive and effective action. Many commentators on the political scene have noted that authoritative powers are more willingly granted to national leaders in times of emergency than in normal times. Certainly it would appear that the powers of Churchill and of Roosevelt were magnified as the executive authority in their respective countries became centralized during World War II. From such observations it is natural to suggest that crisis conditions generally promote a willingness of followers in a group to submit to more direction from above.

Although it is a long way from leadership in a national bureaucracy to leadership in small face-to-face groups, it is a reasonable working hypothesis that crisis increases the normal inequality of power distribution whatever the size or organizational complexity of a group. This hypothesis was tested by Hamblin (1958) in an ingenious experiment in which three-person groups were observed under stressful versus nonstressful conditions. Each group was given the task of discovering and applying the proper rules in a modified shuffleboard game. The instructions were designed to arouse a high degree of motivation because the subjects (all adults beyond the age of 25) were to be compared with high-school students who had worked on the game earlier. That these instructions were effective was indicated by informal observation that "the average group behaved as though they were in a tournament. They rushed, ran, and not infrequently shouted" (p. 326).

The rules of the game were to be learned by a process of trial and error. A green light flashed every time a score was made, and a red light flashed every time a rule was violated. For half of the subjects the rules remained the same throughout each of the six five-minute periods. Subjects in these groups constituted the control condition. The remaining groups were in the crisis condition. From the beginning of the fourth task period to the end of the experiment rules were constantly changed for them so that as soon as the group earned a green light, a repetition would bring only a red light.

Experimental observations were made of each attempt of any member to influence the other two, and it was also recorded whether the influence attempt was accepted. From these observations it was possible to derive an index for each individual of the proportion of accepted influence attempts initiated by him, divided by the proportion attributed to the other group members. This *influence ratio* was a measure of the individual's tendency to initiate successful influence attempts relative to his two partners.

If a condition of urgency or crisis in fact increases leadership centralization, we should expect to find that the most influential person is more influential under crisis conditions than control conditions. The results of Hamblin's experiment show this to be true, if allowances are made for the fact that there is often a change in leadership under crisis. Thus whoever is leader at a given point in time is more directive in a crisis than in a controlled condition, a finding that provides good support for the general hypothesis of an increasing centralization of authority under stress.

There may appear to be a contradiction between this conclusion and the earlier statement that members are willing to turn over decision-making powers to a leader when the decisions are trivial and involve arrangements that are largely a matter of convenience and efficiency. Possibly both conclusions are right: it may very well be that group members are least willing to concede influence and power to a leader when matters of *intermediate* importance are involved. Perhaps there is some threshold of importance beyond which the dynamics of crisis enter the picture. Or it may be crucial that threats to group survival are directly involved. Perhaps when things get bad most followers are content to bury their heads in the sand and leave the responsibility for decision-making to others. To assume leadership in a time of crisis involves risks that not all persons are willing to assume. It must be pointed out, however, that the crisis leaders in Hamblin's experiment were more often deposed than the corresponding leaders in the control condition. Thus it appears that ineffective leaders are not tolerated when the stakes are high.

The conclusion that followers are more sensitive to the effectiveness of leader performance when the stakes are high is given further support in a recent study by Marak (1964). He showed that a person who proves to be especially competent in the eyes of other group members exerts disproportionate influence only if the group task involves high rewards. If the members are relatively unconcerned with group success they are almost as likely to be influenced by incompetent as by competent fellow members. If this is combined with the Hamblin findings, we may conclude that poor leaders are quickly rejected and good leaders quickly obeyed when the stakes are raised and high rewards or severe punishments are involved. An important feature of both experiments was that there was immediate feedback as to the correctness of a particular leader's decision.

Conditions Favoring Specific Persons as Leaders

Having dealt briefly with the conditions that generally favor the development of inequalities in the distribution of influence, let us turn finally to examine why particular individuals become leaders and others become followers. Here again it is important to recognize the potential role of chance in the emergence of particular leaders. In the early stages of group formation it may happen that a particular person quite accidentally makes a correct suggestion or two and as a consequence finds himself thenceforth in the leadership role. The possibilities of chance take on a special importance if the initial luck of being correct lands the person in a position that protects him from subsequent error. This presumably can happen in large organizations, where promotions are often to positions in which the decisions to be made are very complex and the feedback as to their correctness is vague and unreliable.

If we disregard the possibilities of random or chance determination of leader emergence, it would appear that the leader does or is something that gains him his high status. It is reasonable to assume that the leader in an informal, voluntary group, is thought by the followers to be capable of making contributions that are valuable enough to warrant their deference to him. Blau (1964) treats the emergence of status differences as a special outgrowth of the exchange of outcomes. Insofar as the leader supplies services, advice, or other benefits for the followers that are not reciprocated in kind, they must pay for these services by deference to the leader and obedience to his orders or requests. Blau draws a picture of leader emergence that begins—taking again the informal face-to-face discussion group as an example—when members start to compete with each other for "participation time." Out of this initial competition it becomes apparent that some are more successful at taking and monopolizing participation time than others. More speaking time is allocated to those who, as a matter of first impression, appear most likely to advance the solution of the group's problems.

Those members who find that they cannot compete in task-relevant participation may search for other ways to be of value to the group. These other ways may include tension-reducing reactions or other group maintenance behavior. After the initial stage of competing merely for participation time, Blau continues, the object of competition shifts toward the winning of approval and positive evaluation of each other's remarks. The emphasis on quantity of contribution gives way, then, to an emphasis on quality. The next stage in the emergence of a leadership hierarchy is a shift from a concern with approval to a concern with commanding respect. The final stage involves a working out of the obligations incurred in the exchange of services for deference and obedience:

> Initially, the high respect of the rest of the group may be sufficient reward for the contributions a group member makes, and short-term discussion groups in laboratories may never advance beyond this stage, but in the long run it is likely to prove insufficient. Since the value of a person's approval and respect is a function of his own social standing, the process of recurrently paying respect to others depreciates its value. Hence, respect often does not remain an adequate compensation for contributions that entail costs in time and effort to the one who makes them, such as assistance with complex problems. Those who benefit from such instrumental help, therefore, become obligated to reciprocate in some other way, and deferring to the wishes of the group member who supplies the help is typically the one thing the others can do to repay him. As a result of these processes in which the contributions of some come to command the compliance of others, a differentiated power structure develops (Blau, 1964, p. 127).

Participation Rate and Leader Emergence

One of the most important implications of Blau's theory of leader emergence is that later stages in the competition for status are outgrowths of earlier stages. Thus it is unlikely that a low initial participator will ever become the task leader, simply because the eventual leader must participate enough to have his abilities validated, his suggestions accepted. In our discussion of the separation of task and maintenance roles, a separation that is minimized by Blau's analysis, we presented Bales' (1953) finding that the high participator was usually identified by the members as their leader—especially during the early stages of group formation. Bass (1949) and Norfleet (1948) provided earlier evidence supporting this same conclusion.

The question might be raised whether the high participator in fact contributes the most to the solution of group tasks or whether the group members are simply too lazy to distinguish between quantity and quality during the early stages of group formation. Riecken (1958) conducted an experiment in which two standard human-relations problems were discussed in four-man groups. On the basis of these discussions the lowest and the highest participators were identified. Then a third problem was posed to the group; it had a solution that was correct but sufficiently elegant that it was not likely to appear in free discussion. In half of the groups a hint containing this elegant solution was slipped to the highest participant; in the remaining half the same hint was slipped to the lowest participant. Riecken was interested primarily in whether the "groups in which great talkers have the best solutions are more likely to agree upon that solution than are groups in which infrequent interactors have it" (p. 309).

The results showed that the top participators were almost uniformly perceived by the other members as contributing more and that placing the hint in the hands of a low interactor did little to change these perceptions. The correct solution was much more likely to be accepted if it were offered by the high participator (11 out of 16 acceptances) than if offered by the low participator (5 out of 16 acceptances). The practical implications are obvious: if we want a group to make the right decisions, we should give relevant information or hints to those in the group with high interaction rates. The theoretical implications of the Riecken findings are a little less clear, because many important personal attributes may be correlated with participation rate. The study does show that the high participator is given considerable credit for the same substantive contributions that are rebuffed when made by low participators.

Bavelas and Hastorf have developed a technique for experimentally changing the participation rates of subjects in a discussion group (for example, see Bavelas, Hastorf, Gross, and Kite, 1965). In their basic procedure four subjects were seated around a conference table that was unobstructed except for a microphone and four small boxes containing signal lights, all grouped at the center of the table. Each subject could see only one box and thus different signals could be delivered independently to each. In a typical instance the subjects were given a standard human-relations problem to discuss and allowed 10 minutes to reach a solution on the problem. On a second human-relations problem the members were told that each subject would be given feedback concerning his contribution to the discussion: "Whenever you make a contribution to the discussion which is helpful or functional in facilitating the group process your green light will go on. . . . Whenever you behave in a way which will eventually hamper or hinder the group process your red light will go on . . ." (p. 58). On a third problem the light signals were not used and all subjects were so instructed.

By differential use of the green and red signal lights, it proved possible to change a low participator into a high participator, and vice versa. This was most effective if the initial high participator was discouraged with the red lights while the initial low participator was being encouraged with green lights. When subjects were asked to nominate the person making the greatest contribution and to answer other questions concerning leadership qualities, the high participator was quite uniformly chosen—in spite of the fact that his participation had been artificially induced. The high participator was probably seen as being encouraged by approval from the experts—he must have been receiving green lights and talked so much as a result. Therefore the subjects may merely have been conceding the validity of the expert's opinion in their own appraisals of the high participator as leader. However, the artificially induced high participator continued to talk more in the third session, in the absence of signals, and continued to be highly evaluated by the other members. Although much more needs to be learned about the bases of these member-evaluations, the findings are at least consistent with the notion that rate of participation, regardless of its quality or mode of induction, is a prime index of leadership qualities in the eyes of other members.

This is not to suggest, of course, that participation is the only thing that matters, even in the early stages of group formation. Participation is an easy variable to measure and this probably accounts for its early appearance and continued prominence in research into how leaders are identified. There are undoubtedly many factors involved in the tendency to participate. Participation indices may merely reflect the operation of other variables as determinants of leader identification. To take one example, there are many easily identifiable physical and social characteristics that may serve as cues in the early assignment of leadership roles. Age, physical size, looks, and grooming may certainly correlate with both participation rate and subsequent leadership nomination. Older people, to take one example, may feel justified in talking more because of their greater experience and maturity and younger members of their group may feel that an older person should be the leader because of his age and therefore his superior wisdom. This would give rise to an observed relationship between participation rate and leadership nomination but the relationship would actually be mediated by age. This same case could be made for any aspect of appearance that is likely to have the effect on the leader himself of increasing his confidence (and therefore his participation) and to have the effect on the followers of increasing their respect for him.

There is also the likelihood that cues emitted early in discussion establish, at least tentatively, the differential expertise of the members. After some preliminary jousting, an expert is likely to feel like an expert, thereby talking more, and is likely to be so judged unless he has completely miscalculated his relative knowledge.

Communication Networks

There may be certain features in the setting and structure of the group that influence leadership emergence quite independently of personality factors or signs of expertise. If the group being studied is not conveniently situated around a conference table but instead the members are located in physically separated positions, as in a factory or governmental agency, it is likely that some people will be more strategically located than others in the network of communication. It is also likely that the satisfaction and productivity of the members will be affected by the degree to which communication possibilities are appropriate to the distribution of functions in the group.

Because of the potential practical and theoretical importance of this problem some interesting work has been done with artificially imposed communication networks. These may be constructed in a variety of ways, ranging from elaborate intercom systems to restrictions on message sending, but the basic idea in all the communication-net studies is to vary the direction of permissible communication and the openness of the various channels between group members.

Some four- and five-person networks that have received experimental attention are portrayed in Figure 16.4. In each case the circles refer to positions in the communication structure and the lines refer to channels that can be used in either direction. Asymmetrical or one-way channels have also been investigated, but we shall restrict ourselves to the symmetrical channel network.

A first distinction among the networks is between those that are centralized and those that are not. The wheel, chain, and Y are centralized in the

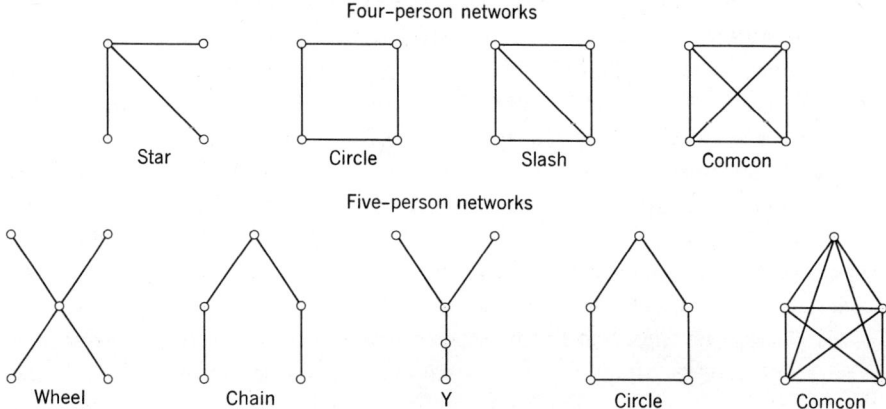

Figure 16.4. Selected communication networks in a four- and five-person group. Circles represent positions, lines represent communication channels.

sense that one position naturally has access to more information than any of the others. The positions in the circle and comcon, on the other hand, are all equivalent, none being more central than any other. It would be expected that a person in the most central position of the wheel, chain, or Y would assume the functions of a leader in assembling information and distributing attempted solutions.

Bavelas (1948) and his student Leavitt (1951) were the first to investigate systematically the social psychological consequences of network variations. Leavitt presented to each of 20 five-man groups a problem of discovering the single symbol that each member held in common on a card containing several symbols such as square, triangle, asterisk. Each subject was supplied with blank message cards whose colors matched that of his working space, which was a section of a large circular table divided by partitions. Subjects could send messages to certain other members of the group, as designated by the network condition to which they were assigned, in this case the circle, chain, Y, or wheel. When a subject thought that he had discovered the common symbol, he was to throw a switch that recorded his answer on a master board of lights in an observer's room. When all five members had thrown the correct switch, that trial was over. Each group of subjects was given 15 consecutive trials in the same network, with variations in the common symbol.

The main result of this experiment was that stable organizations developed by the fourth or fifth trial in the more centralized networks but not in the circle. In the wheel, Y, and chain the subject in the most central position characteristically received information during the early stages of problem solution and transmitted the answer when it became clear to him. As a consequence the central subject transmitted more messages than any other subject in the centralized groups, he enjoyed his job more than the more peripheral members, and he was typically designated the leader on a postexperimental questionnaire. The circle was typically the most inefficient, sending many more messages than the other groups and making significantly more final errors in attempting to identify the common symbol. However, subjects in the circle network typically enjoyed their jobs more than peripheral members in the centralized groups, and became increasingly satisfied as the trials progressed.

Subsequent research has tended to confirm Leavitt's findings that, when the problems posed are simple ones, centralized networks are more efficient but personal satisfaction is often greater in the decentralized circle or comcon. However, subsequent research also suggests that some of the differences between centralized and decentralized networks are *reversed* when the problem is a complex one such as arithmetic, sentence completion, or discussion to a consensus. Typical of results with more complex problems are those of Shaw (1954), who compared a three-person circle network with a three-person wheel in solving simple and complex problems. The simple problems were similar to the symbol identification problems used by Leavitt (1951). The complex problems required arithmetical computations of the sort involved in determining how many trucks of various load capacities would be required to move a certain number of chairs, desks, and so on, from one office building to another. Shaw's (1954) results showed that the circle networks, relative to the wheel, took less time to solve the complex problems and more to solve the simple problems—especially on the early trials.

Shaw and Rothschild (1956) later compared four-person groups in star, slash, and comcon networks (see Figure 16.3) on problems requiring arithmetical computation. Although more messages were transmitted in the slash and comcon networks than in the star, time to solution was lower in the decentralized comcon than in the more centralized slash and star. Shaw, Rothschild, and Strickland (1957) also found that the comcon network was significantly more rapid in reaching a unanimous decision on human-relations discussion problems.

In a recent review of his own and others' work Shaw (1964) firmly endorses the proposition that centralized networks are more effective in solving simple problems of information exchange but decentralized networks are more effective when a group is faced with problems of greater complexity and ambiguity. Shaw surveyed 18 experiments producing data relevant to this proposition and found that they strongly support it. The decentralized groups always send more total messages, regardless of the complexity of the problem, but their solution time is slower with simple problems and faster with complex problems than the solution times of centralized groups.

Shaw believes that two concepts—*independence* and *saturation*—nicely account for many of the phenomena discovered through communication network research. Leavitt (1951) introduced the concept of independence to account for differences in satisfaction among network positions. If features of a network position restrict the incumbent's freedom of action and decision, his culturally supported needs for autonomy are frustrated. Centrality of position permits these needs for autonomy and independence to be fulfilled. Participation in a decentralized network is not quite so satisfying as being in a central position, but it is more satisfying than being a dependent peripheral member of a centralized network.

If independence is primarily reflected in satisfaction and morale, saturation is more intimately involved in performance on a task. A position tends to become saturated when it is threatened by an overload of incoming messages or the necessity to communicate too rapidly to too many others. Shaw (1964) argues that saturation is a function both of the communication demands on a position and the task demands—how much inference, interpretation, or data manipulation are required to solve the problem posed. The possibilities of saturation and the members' needs for independence should both be especially high when subjects in a centralized network attempt to solve a complex problem. Saturation is high because a great deal of solution data must come to one position and these data must be transformed in appropriate ways to solve the problem. Independence needs also enter the picture, however, because the more complex the problem to be solved the more individual solution attempts will be linked to needs for achievement and recognition. Because individuals will gain recognition and prestige by contributing more than their share to the correct solution, subjects in centralized networks with complex problems should be less willing to accept the solutions reported by the central person. The central person, in turn, is less likely to transmit the correct solution because his position is saturated. This could explain, then, why the superiority of the centralized network breaks down when the difficulty level of the problem increases beyond a certain critical point.

When the problem is difficult, the less centralized network may be more effective for several reasons. Everyone is presumed equal in the decentralized network, so there should be a greater tendency for all members to contribute their suggestions to all other members, thus increasing the total information available to the group. Perhaps more important, because the organization in decentralized groups tends to take the form of each-to-all, and each suggestion eventually becomes known by each member, there is a greater likelihood that erroneous solutions will be detected and corrected. In support of this conclusion Mulder (1960) found that more errors were in fact corrected in his circle than in his wheel groups.

Shaw's hypotheses pertaining to saturation are plausible and have some empirical support; they have not, however, gone unchallenged. Mulder (1960) contends that the communication network merely limits the possibilities but does not determine what happens. What happens is determined by the *decision structure* that actually develops as the group gains experience in working together toward the solution of problems. The decision structure of a group may be more or less centralized depending on the extent to which the contributions of individual members are integrated by one member—the leader or the central person. Centralization of decision structure should facilitate problem solution, regardless of whether it occurs in a centralized or a decentralized network.

Mulder (1960) conducted an experiment on Dutch subjects, comparing the performance of four-man circle and wheel networks in solving the same complex problems Shaw (1954) had used. His results showed that the initial advantage of the circle over the wheel gave way to an actual advantage for the wheel. Circle groups were faster than the wheel groups on the first two problems, but the wheel groups were superior thereafter.

These are similar to Shaw's (1954) findings on the same problems, though he found merely a decline in the superiority of the circle over time and no tendency toward a reversal toward superiority of the wheel.

Mulder feels that his results support the importance of decision-structure centralization—his wheel groups did better as the actual decision-making became more centralized. So did the circle groups, but the centralization of decision structure *and* performance effectiveness increased more slowly in the more decentralized network. Mulder's main point is that a centralized decision structure is best for complex as well as simple problems; it simply takes longer for the structure to develop when the problems are complex.

Thus the major problems of network research are far from resolved; Shaw and Mulder are arguing contrary conclusions from very similar data. We suspect that substantial further progress will not be made until there is a more precise delineation of the simple-complex task dimension so that this may be viewed in relation to the subjects' own capacities. At the present time this cluster of research studies is especially of interest in showing that leadership emergence is strikingly affected by communication arrangements among group members and that, starting from rather mechanical variations in whether certain communication links are open or closed, the researcher soon finds himself concerned with intriguing problems of individual motivation, morale, and decisions about how best to make his contribution to group performance.

Other Factors Involved in Leadership Assumption and Assignment

We have only scratched the surface in our analysis of the factors involved in the emergence of particular persons as leaders. Participation rate, age, or appearance may not ultimately be important factors in groups that meet over a long period of time. This is especially so if the group confronts many different problems and receives precise feedback concerning the effectiveness of the leaders' decisions. If there is feedback, and if correct solution of the group's problems is important to the members, presumably true competence will come increasingly to the fore as a leadership criterion. The ineffective pretenders to power will fall by the wayside.

This idealized view of leadership evolution must be qualified by all the factors that contribute to the perpetuation of particular leadership structures once they have emerged. There are, of course, many institutional arrangements, such as specified term of office, that protect the leader from power loss—at least for a brief period of time. But there is also the more subtle protection that comes from something akin to social inertia. Once a person has functioned in the role of leader—even if he has moved into that role without the explicit consent of the other members—it may be difficult to depose him without a disrupting confrontation that may shatter the cohesiveness of the group. For his part, the leader may hold tenaciously to his prerogatives and augment his power by various strategies. These may include gaining allies through favoritism, disarming potential antagonists by appeals to the sympathy of other group members, exaggerating the difficulty of the decisions he has been forced to make, or threatening to leave the group if thwarted. As Deutsch (1962) has suggested, individuals tend to develop vested interests in their social roles, especially those connected with leadership functions. The leader's goal may consequently diverge from the goals underlying leader-follower cooperation and what Deutsch calls the *pathology of self-perpetuating leadership* may result.

There are many cases of effective leadership, too, in which the leader is not the most competent or expert member of the group. We may recall Bales' lament on the difficulty of electing the most competent man to public office. When one person is officially elected or chosen to be the group leader it may be because of his superior competence in meeting the demands of the tasks confronting the group, but it may also be because of his ability to organize the talents of others, to conciliate warring factions, to symbolize and articulate group values, to recognize and support the talents of other members, to represent the group in its dealings with outsiders, and so on. When we consider that a leader may be chosen primarily for his contributions to group maintenance rather than task accomplishment it becomes obvious that the traits of elected leaders may often bear an intimate relation to the traits of the followers who support them. It is for this reason, as much as any other, that psychologists have become less and less interested in the search for personality characteristics of *the* leader. The emergence of particular leaders must be seen as a complicated resultant that is conditioned by the values or needs of the followers, the nature of the task or group goal, the state of the immediate situation, and a number of miscellaneous additional factors that are, as far as our analytic tools can presently reveal, accidental or chance events.

SUMMARY

In the present chapter we have tried to complete a circular, chicken-and-egg, argument begun much earlier in the book. To recapitulate this argument briefly, in Chapter Five we examined the products of socialization against the backdrop of stable cultural realities. We spoke of the cultural map and argued that a sizable proportion of individual actions are reflexive responses to norms carefully charted on the map. Having acknowledged the importance of this cultural backdrop, we proceeded in subsequent chapters to consider the social determinants of thought and action in settings where the cultural guidelines are anything but clear. In this chapter we have tried to show how social structures develop (in a sense, how cultures are made) in the microcosm of the small group. Whereas from a purely descriptive point of view such structural developments often seem haphazard and accidental in their evolution, from a functional point of view the formation of norms, roles, and other structural arrangements is a rational response of actors in settings where each does not always benefit the other by benefiting himself—that is, when outcomes are noncorrespondent.

Our first concern in this chapter was with the reasons norms develop when two or more persons are bound in the mutual dependence that signifies group formation. Norms, we argued, may be viewed as substitutes for informal social influence. Without the development of normative understandings about the trading of outcomes, the sharing of costs, and the timing of responses, a group is vulnerable to whimsical applications of power by various members, and it is soon likely to realize the costs of overlapping or poorly coordinated actions. Norms represent common understandings that, when initially upheld, serve to bind the group into a superordinate unit. Norms may start as practical agreements, but for various dimly understood reasons soon take on moral overtones.

For norm formation to occur, members have to relinquish various temporary claims in order to achieve reasonable long-range objectives. A rational appraisal by each member of his interests, seen in competition with the interests of others, may lead to such normative agreements. Recent studies have shown that norms are much more likely to develop, however, when each member of the group is in a position to threaten the other with a clear loss of outcomes. If, for example, one member controls the distribution of outcomes within the relationship but the other member has attractive alternatives in other relationships, they will readily move toward a contract that offers mutual protection. Norms are especially valuable in larger groups because of the greater complexity of relationships potentially involved. Here they are also especially likely to take on a moral reality that is independent of their enforcement by particular group members.

An extremely important feature of most social structures is role differentiation. It is very useful to distinguish between those roles that directly concern task accomplishment and those roles primarily concerned with group maintenance. In fact, many have argued that the byplay between task and group maintenance functions and the roles generated by these functions is a critical feature of all social systems. In relatively small groups that are groping toward a viable organization we can usually distinguish between two kinds of leaders: a task specialist and a maintenance specialist. The former tends to exhort, arouse, and disturb; the latter tends to mollify, sympathize, and soothe. The one who participates most and who therefore is often judged to have contributed most, tends not to be the most popular member of the group. However, it is common for the high participator to be supported and liked by the maintenance specialist, who in turn is very popular with group members.

Such considerations lead to a concern with the question of how leaders emerge and are detected. We have made little progress toward answering this question, though a number of studies have emphasized the importance of participation rate as an index of leadership assumption. At least in the early stages of group formation, the one who initiates the greatest volume of communication is seen as the leader by the other members. This is true even if this participation rate is artificially induced by experimental reinforcement of the potential leader. Undoubtedly, sheer participation rate recedes in importance as an index of leadership as the group has more experience with a greater variety of tasks and develops standards for evaluating the quality of suggestions made by individual members.

The phenomena of leadership are extremely complex. It is almost impossible to draw conclusions in this area without immediately adding many qualifications about the size of the group and its longevity, the nature of the task, and the broader social and physical contexts within which group interaction takes place. Our intent has not been to draw a comprehensive picture of norm formation, role differentiation, or leader emergence, but rather to illustrate how the principles developed in previous chapters have a bearing on these aspects of social structure.

References

Abelson, R. P. and Rosenberg, M. J. 1958. Symbolic psycho-logic: a model of attitudinal cognition. *Behav. Sci.*, **3**, 1–13.
Adams, J. S. 1961. Reduction of cognitive dissonance by seeking consonant information. *J. abnorm. soc. Psychol.*, **62**, 74–78.
Ader, R. and Tatum, R. 1963. Free-operant avoidance conditioning in individual and paired human subjects. *J. exp. anal. Behav.*, **6**, 357–359.
Adorno, T. W., Frenkel-Brunswik, Else, Levinson, D. J. and Sanford, R. N. 1950. *The authoritarian personality*. New York: Harper and Row.
Allen, V. L. 1964. Uncertainty of outcome and post-decision dissonance reduction. In L. Festinger (Ed.), *Conflict, decision, and dissonance*. Stanford: Stanford Univer., pp. 34–42.
Allen, V. L. and Crutchfield, R. S. 1963. Generalization of experimentally reinforced conformity. *J. abnorm. soc. Psychol.*, **67**, 326–333.
Allport, F. H. 1920. The influence of the group upon association and thought. *J. exp. Psychol.*, **3**, 159–182.
Allport, F. H. 1924. *Social psychology*. Cambridge, Mass.: Riverside Press.
Allport, F. H. 1955. *Theories of perception and the concept of structure*. New York: Wiley.
Allport, G. W. 1935. Attitudes. In C. Murchison (Ed.), *A handbook of social psychology*. Worcester, Mass.: Clark Univer., pp. 798–844.
Allport, G. W. 1937. *Personality: a psychological interpretation*. New York: Holt.
Allport, G. W. 1954. The historical background of modern social psychology. In G. Lindzey (Ed.) *Handbook of Social Psychology*. Vol. I. Cambridge, Mass.: Addison-Wesley, pp. 3–56.
Allport, G. W. and Postman, L. 1947. *The psychology of rumor*. New York: Holt.
Allyn, Jane and Festinger, L. 1961. The effectiveness of unanticipated persuasive communications. *J. abnorm. soc. Psychol.*, **62**, 35–40.
Alper, Thelma G. and Korchin, S. S. 1952. Memory for socially relevant material. *J. abnorm. soc. Psychol.*, **47**, 25–38.
Anderson, L. R. 1962. Effects of peer disagreement on the efficacy of prior belief defense in immunization against persuasion. M. A. Thesis, Univer. of Illinois.
Anderson, N. H. 1965. Primacy effects in personality impression formation using a generalized order effect paradigm. *J. Pers. soc. Psychol.*, **2**, 1–9.
Anderson, N. H. and Barrios, A. A. 1961. Primacy effects in personality impression formation. *J. abnorm. soc. Psychol.*, **63**, 346–350.
Anderson, N. H. and Hubert, S. 1963. Effects of concomitant verbal recall on order effects in personality impression formation. *J. verbal Learn. verbal Behav.*, **2**, 379–391.
Argyle, M. 1957. Social pressures in public and private situations. *J. abnorm. soc. Psychol.*, **54**, 172–175.

Aristotle. 1941 (original date unknown). *The basic works of Aristotle,* R. McKeon, Ed. New York: Random House.
Aronfreed, J. 1964. The origin of self-criticism. *Psychol. Rev.,* **71,** 193–219.
Aronfreed, J. and Reber, A. 1965. Internalized behavioral suppression and the timing of social punishment. *J. Pers. soc. Psychol.,* **1,** 3–17.
Aronson, E. 1961. The effect of effort on the attractiveness of rewarded and unrewarded stimuli. *J. abnorm. soc. Psychol.,* **63,** 375–380.
Aronson, E. and Carlsmith, J. M. 1962. Performance expectancy as a determinant of actual performance. *J. abnorm. soc. Psychol.,* **65,** 178–183.
Aronson, E. and Carlsmith, J. M. 1963. Effect of the severity of threat on the devaluation of forbidden behavior. *J. abnorm. soc. Psychol.,* **66,** 584–588.
Aronson, E. and Carlsmith, J. M. In press. The social psychology experiment. In G. Lindzey and E. Aronson (Eds.), *Handbook of social psychology* (Second Edition). Cambridge, Mass.: Addison-Wesley.
Aronson, E. and Golden, B. W. 1962. The effect of relevant and irrelevant aspects of communicator credibility on opinion change. *J. Pers.,* **30,** 135–146.
Aronson, E. and Linder, D. 1965. Gain and loss of esteem as determinants of interpersonal attractiveness. *J. exp. soc. Psychol.,* **1,** 156–172.
Aronson, E. and Mills, J. 1959. The effect of severity of initiation on liking for a group. *J. abnorm. soc. Psychol.,* **59,** 177–181.
Aronson, E., Turner, J. A. and Carlsmith, J. M. 1963. Communicator credibility and communication discrepancy as determinants of opinion change. *J. abnorm. soc. Psychol.,* **67,** 31–36.
Asch, S. E. 1946. Forming impressions of personality. *J. abnorm. soc. Psychol.,* **41,** 258–290.
Asch, S. E. 1948. The doctrine of suggestion, prestige, and imitation in social psychology. *Psychol. Rev.,* **55,** 250–277.
Asch, S. E. 1951. Effects of group pressure on the modification and distortion of judgments. In H. Geutzkow (Ed.), *Groups, leadership, and men.* Pittsburgh: Carnegie.
Asch, S. E. 1956. Studies of independence and conformity: a minority of one against a unanimous majority. *Psychol. Monogr.,* **70,** No. 9 (Whole No. 416).
Azrin, W. M., Holz, W., Ulrich, R. and Goldiamond, I. 1961. The control of the content of conversation through reinforcement. *J. exp. anal. Behav.,* **4,** 25–30.

Bach, G. R. 1946. Father-fantasies and father-typing in father-separated children. *Child Develpm.,* **17,** 63–80.
Back, K. W. 1951. Influence through social communication. *J. abnorm. soc. Psychol.,* **46,** 9–23.
Back, K. W., Festinger, L., Hymovitch, B., Kelley, H. H., Schachter, S. and Thibaut, J. W. 1950. The methodology of studying rumor transmission. *Hum. Relat.,* **3,** 307–317.
Bales, R. F. 1950. *Interaction process analysis.* Cambridge, Mass.: Addison-Wesley.
Bales, R. F. 1953. The equilibrium problem in small groups. In T. Parsons, R. F. Bales, and A. Shils, *Working papers in the theory of action.* Glencoe, Ill.: Free Press. pp. 111–161.
Bales, R. F. 1958. Task roles and social roles in problem-solving groups. In Eleanor Maccoby, T. M. Newcomb and E. L. Hartley (Eds.), *Readings in social psychology* (Third Edition). New York: Holt. pp. 437–447.
Bales, R. F. and Slater, P. 1955. Role differentiation in small decision-making groups. In T. Parson and R. F. Bales, *Family, socialization, and interaction process.* Glencoe, Ill.: Free Press. pp. 259–306.
Bandura, A. 1965. Influence of model's reinforcement contingencies on the acquisition of imitative responses. *J. Pers. soc. Psychol.,* **1,** 589–595.

Bandura, A. and Huston, A. C. 1961. Identification as a process of incidental learning. *J. abnorm. soc. Psychol.*, **63**, 311–318.

Bandura, A., Lipsher, D. and Miller, P. 1960. Psychotherapists' approach-avoidance reactions to patients' expressions of hostility. *J. consult. Psychol.*, **24**, 1–8.

Bandura, A., Ross, D. and Ross, S. A. 1961. Transmission of aggression through imitation of aggressive models. *J. abnorm. soc. Psychol.*, **63**, 575–582.

Bandura, A., Ross, D. and Ross, S. A. 1963a. Imitation of film-mediated aggressive models. *J. abnorm. soc. Psychol.*, **66**, 3–11.

Bandura, A., Ross, D. and Ross, S. A. 1963b. A comparative test of status envy, social power, and secondary reinforcement theories of identificatory learning. *J. abnorm. soc. Psychol.*, **67**, 527–534.

Bandura, A., Ross, D. and Ross, S. A. 1963c. Vicarious reinforcement and imitative learning. *J. abnorm. soc. Psychol.*, **67**, 601–607.

Bandura, A. and Walters, R. H. 1959. *Adolescent aggression.* New York: Ronald.

Bandura, A. and Walters, R. H. 1963. *Social learning and personality development.* New York: Holt, Rinehart, and Winston.

Barnard, C. I. 1938. *The functions of the executive.* Cambridge, Mass.: Harvard Univer.

Barnlund, D. C. 1959. A comparative study of individual, majority, and group judgment. *J. abnorm. soc. Psychol.*, **58**, 55–60.

Bartlett, F. C. 1932. *Remembering.* Cambridge, England: Cambridge Univer.

Bass, B. M. 1949. An analysis of the leaderless group discussion. *J. appl. Psychol.*, **33**, 527–533.

Bates, F. L. 1956. Position, role, and status: A reformulation of concepts. *Soc. Forces*, **34**, 313–321.

Bavelas, A. 1948. A mathematical model for group structures. *Appl. Anthrop.*, **7**, 16–30.

Bavelas, A., Hastorf, A. H., Gross, A. E. and Kite, W. R. 1965. Experiments on the alteration of group structure. *J. exp. soc. Psychol.*, **1**, 55–71.

Bem, D. J., Wallach, M. A. and Kogan, N. 1965. Group decision making under risk of aversive consequences. *J. Pers. soc. Psychol.*, **1**, 453–460.

Bennett, Edith B. 1955. Discussion, decision commitment, and consensus in "group decision." *Hum. Relat.*, **8**, 251–274.

Bergin, A. E. 1962. The effect of dissonant persuasive communications upon changes in self-referring attitudes. *J. Pers.*, **30**, 423–438.

Berkowitz, L. 1954. Group standards, cohesiveness, and productivity. *Hum. Relat.*, **7**, 509–519.

Berkowitz, L. 1957. Liking for the group and the perceived merit of the group's behavior. *J. abnorm. soc. Psychol.*, **54**, 353–357.

Berkowitz, L. 1958. The expression and reduction of hostility. *Psychol. Bull.*, **55**, 257–283.

Berkowitz, L. 1962. *Aggression: A social psychological analysis.* New York: Mc-Graw-Hill.

Berkowitz, L. and Cottingham, D. R. 1960. The interest value and relevance of fear arousing communications. *J. abnorm. soc. Psychol.*, **60**, 37–43.

Berlyne, D. E. 1960. *Conflict, arousal and curiosity.* New York: McGraw-Hill.

Berlyne, D. E. 1965. *Structure and direction in thinking.* New York: Wiley.

Bettleheim, B. 1943. Individual and mass behavior in extreme situations. *J. abnorm. soc. Psychol.*, **38**, 417–452.

Bixenstine, V. E., Potash, H. M. and Wilson, K. V. 1963. Effects of levels of cooperative choice by the other player on choices in a prisoner's dilemma game. Part I. *J. abnorm. soc. Psychol.*, **66**, 308–313.

Bixenstine, V. E. and Wilson, K. V. 1963. Effects of level of cooperative choice by the other player on choices in a prisoner's dilemma game. Part II. *J. abnorm. soc. Psychol.*, **67**, 139–148.

Blau, P. M. 1964. *Exchange and power in social life.* New York: Wiley.
Bos, Maria C. 1937. Experimental study of productive collaboration. *Acta psychologica,* **3,** 315–426.
Bowerman, C. and Day, B. 1956. A test of the theory of complementary needs as applied to couples during courtship. *Amer. Sociol. Rev.,* **21,** 602–605.
Braine, M. D. S. 1963. On learning the grammatical order of words. *Psychol. Rev.,* **70,** 323–349.
Braithwaite, R. B. 1953. *Scientific explanation; a study of the function of theory, probability, and law in science* (based on the Tanner lectures, 1946). Cambridge, England: Cambridge Univer.
Brehm, J. W. 1956. Postdecision changes in the desirability of alternatives. *J. abnorm. soc. Psychol.* **52,** 384–389.
Brehm, J. W. 1962. An experiment in coercion and attitude change. In J. W. Brehm and A. R. Cohen, *Explorations in cognitive dissonance.* New York: Wiley. pp. 84–88.
Brehm, J. W. 1966. *A theory of psychological reactance.* New York: Academic.
Brehm, J. W. and Cohen, A. R. 1959. Reevaluation of choice alternatives as a function of their number and qualitative similarity. *J. abnorm. soc. Psychol.,* **58,** 373–378.
Brehm, J. W. and Cohen, A. R. 1962. *Explorations in cognitive dissonance.* New York: Wiley.
Brehm, J. W. and Cole, Ann H. 1966. Effect of a favor which reduces freedom. *J. Pers. soc. Psychol.,* **3,** 420–426.
Brock, T. C. 1965. Commitment to exposure as a determinant of information receptivity. *J. Pers. soc. Psychol.,* **2,** 10–19.
Brock, T. C. and Becker, L. A. 1965. Ineffectiveness of "overheard" counterpropaganda. *J. Pers. soc. Psychol.,* **2,** 654–660.
Brodbeck, May. 1956. The role of small groups in mediating the effects of propaganda. *J. abnorm. soc. Psychol.,* **52,** 166–170.
Bronfenbrenner, U. 1960. Freudian theories of identification and their derivatives. *Child Develpm.* **31,** 15–40.
Brown, J. S. 1953. Problems presented by the concept of acquired drives. *Nebraska Symposium,* Lincoln: Univer. of Nebraska. pp. 1–22.
Brown, R. 1958. *Words and things.* Glencoe, Ill.: Free Press.
Brown, R. 1965. *Social psychology.* New York: Free Press.
Brown, R. and Bellugi, Ursula. 1964. Three processes in the child's acquisition of syntax. In E. H. Lenneberg (Ed.), *New directions in the study of language.* Cambridge, Mass.: M.I.T. pp. 131–161.
Brown, R. and Lenneberg, E. 1954. A study in language and cognition. *J. abnorm. soc. Psychol.,* **49,** 454–462.
Bruner, J. S. 1957a. On perceptual readiness. *Psychol. Rev.,* **64,** 123–152.
Bruner, J. S. 1957b. Going beyond the information given. In *Contemporary approaches to cognition.* Cambridge, Mass.: Harvard Univer.
Bruner, J. S. 1964. The course of cognitive growth. *Amer. Psychologist,* **19,** 1–16.
Bruner, J. S., Busiek, R. D. and Minturn, A. Leigh. 1952. Assimilation in the immediate reproduction of visually perceived figures. *J. exp. Psychol.,* **44,** 151–155.
Bruner, J. S. and Goodman, Cecile C. 1947. Value and need as organizing factors in perception. *J. abnorm. soc. Psychol.,* **42,** 33–44.
Bruner, J. S. and Postman, L. 1949. On the perception of incongruity: a paradigm. *J. Pers.,* **18,** 206–223.
Bruner, J. S., Postman, L. and Rodrigues, J. 1951. Expectation and the perception of color. *Amer. J. Psychol.,* **64,** 216–227.
Bruner, J. S., Shapiro, D. and Tagiuri, R. 1958. The meaning of traits in isolation and

in combination. In R. Tagiuri and L. Petrullo (Eds.), *Person perception and interpersonal behavior.* Stanford: Stanford Univer. pp. 277–288.

Burnstein, E. and Worchel, P. 1962. Arbitrariness of frustration and its consequences for aggression in a social situation. *J. Pers.,* 30, 528–541.

Campbell, D. T. 1950. The indirect assessment of social attitudes. *Psychol. Bull.,* 47, 15–38.

Campbell, D. T. 1957. Factors relevant to the validity of experiments in social settings. *Psychol. Bull.,* 54, 297–312.

Canon, L. K. 1964. Self-confidence and selective exposure to information. In L. Festinger, *Conflict, decision and dissonance.* Stanford: Stanford Univer. pp. 83–95.

Cantril, H. 1940. *The invasion from Mars.* Princeton: Princeton Univer.

Carlsmith, J. M., Collins, B. E., and Helmreich, R. K. 1966. Studies in forced compliance: I. The effect of pressure for compliance on attitude change produced by face-to-face role playing and anonymous essay writing. *J. Pers. soc. Psychol.,* 4, 1–13.

Carlson, E. R. 1956. Attitude change through modification of attitude structure. *J. abnorm. soc. Psychol.,* 52, 256–261.

Carmichael, L., Hogan, H. P. and Walter, A. A. 1932. An experimental study of the effect of language on the reproduction of visually perceived form. *J. exp. Psychol.,* 15, 73–86.

Carroll, J. B. and Casagrande, J. B. The function of language classification in behavior. In Eleanor E. Maccoby, T. M. Newcomb and E. L. Hartley (Eds.), *Readings in Social Psychology.* New York: Holt, Rinehart, and Winston, 1958.

Cartwright, D. and Harary, F. 1956. Structural balance: a generalization of Heider's theory. *Psychol. Rev.,* 63, 277–293.

Centers, R. 1963. A laboratory adaptation of the conversational procedure for the conditioning of verbal operants. *J. abnorm. soc. Psychol.,* 67, 334–339.

Chapman, I. W. and Volkmann, J. 1939. A social determinant of the level of aspiration. *J. abnorm. soc. Psychol.,* 34, 225–238.

Cherry, C. 1957. *On human communication.* New York: M.I.T. and Wiley.

Child, I. L. 1954. Socialization. In G. Lindzey (Ed.), *Handbook of social psychology.* Vol. II. Cambridge, Mass.: Addison-Wesley. pp. 655–692.

Cline, M. G. 1956. The influence of social context on the perception of faces. *J. Pers.,* 25, 142–158.

Coch, L. and French, J. R. P., Jr. 1948. Overcoming resistance to change. *Hum. Relat.,* 1, 512–532.

Cohen, A. R. 1955. Social norms, arbitrariness of frustration, and status of agent of frustration in the frustration-aggression hypothesis. *J. abnorm. soc. Psychol.,* 51, 222–226.

Cohen, A. R. 1957. Need for cognition and order of communication as determinants of opinion change. In C. I. Hovland (Ed.), *The order of presentation in persuasion.* New Haven: Yale Univer. pp. 79–97.

Cohen, A. R. 1959. Some implications of self-esteem for social influence. In C. I. Hovland and I. L. Janis (Eds.), *Personality and persuasibility.* New Haven: Yale Univer. pp. 102–120.

Cohen, A. R. 1961. Cognitive tuning as a factor affecting impression formation. *J. Pers.,* 29, 235–245.

Cohen, A. R. 1962. A "forced compliance" experiment on repeated dissonances. In J. W. Brehm and A. R. Cohen, *Explorations in cognitive dissonance.* New York: Wiley. pp. 97–104.

Cohen, A. R. and Brehm, J. W. 1962. An experiment on illegitimate coercion, volition, and attitude change. In J. W. Brehm and A. R. Cohen, *Explorations in cognitive dissonance.* New York: Wiley. pp. 206–210.

Cohen, A. R., Brehm, J. W. and Fleming, W. H. 1958. Attitude change and justification for compliance. *J. abnorm. soc. Psychol.,* 56, 276–278.

Cohen, A. R., Brehm, J. W. and Latané, B. 1959. Choice of strategy and voluntary exposure to information under public and private conditions. *J. Pers.*, **27**, 63–73.
Cohen, A. R., Greenbaum, C. W. and Mansson, H. H. 1963. Commitment to social deprivation and verbal conditioning. *J. abnorm. soc. Psychol.*, **67**, 410–422.
Cohen, D., Whitmyre, J. W. and Funk, W. H. 1960. Effect of group cohesiveness and training upon creative thinking. *J. appl. Psychol.*, **44**, 319–322.
Cohen, M. R. and Nagel, E. 1934. *An introduction to logic and scientific method.* New York: Harcourt.
Cooley, C. H. 1902. *Human nature and the social order.* New York: Scribner.
Cooper, E. and Dinerman, H. 1951. Analysis of the film "Don't be a sucker": a study in communication. *Publ. Opin. quart.*, **15**, 243–264.
Cooper, E. and Jahoda, Marie. 1947. The evasion of propaganda: how prejudiced people respond to anti-prejudice propaganda. *J. Psychol.*, **23**, 15–25.
Cromwell, H. 1950. The relative effect on audience attitude of the first versus the second argumentative speech of a series. *Speech Monogr.* **17**, 105–122.
Crutchfield, R. S. 1955. Conformity and character. *Amer. Psychologist*, **10**, 191–198.

Dailey, C. A. 1952. The effects of premature conclusion upon the acquisition of understanding of a person. *J. Psychol.*, **33**, 133–152.
Darley, J. M. and Aronson, E. 1966. Self-evaluation vs. direct anxiety reduction as determinants of the fear-affiliation relationship. In B. Latané (Ed.), *Studies in social comparison.* New York: Academic.
Darley, J. M. and Berscheid, Ellen. 1967. Increased liking caused by the anticipation of personal contact. *Hum. Relat.*, in press.
Dashiell, J. F. 1930. An experimental analysis of some group effects. *J. abnorm. soc. Psychol.*, **25**, 190–199.
Dashiell, J. F. 1935. Experimental studies of the influence of social situations on the behavior of individual human adults. In C. Murchison (Ed.), *Handbook of social psychology.* Worcester: Clark Univer. pp. 1097–1158.
Davidson, J. R. and Kiesler, Sara B. 1964. Cognitive behavior before and after decisions. In L. Festinger (Ed.), *Conflict, decision, and dissonance.* Stanford: Stanford Univer. pp. 10–19.
Davis, J. H. and Restle, F. A. 1963. The analysis of problems and prediction of group problem solving. *J. abnorm. soc. Psychol.*, **66**, 103–116.
Davis, K. E. 1962. Impressions of others and interaction context as determinants of social interaction and perception in two-person discussion groups. Unpublished doctoral dissertation, Duke Univer.
Davis, K. E. and Florquist, Carolie C. 1965. Perceived threat and dependence as determinants of the tactical usage of opinion conformity. *J. exp. soc. Psychol.*, **1**, 219–236.
Davis, K. E. and Jones, E. E. 1960. Changes in interpersonal perception as a means of reducing cognitive dissonance. *J. abnorm. soc. Psychol.*, **61**, 402–410.
Deutsch, M. 1949. An experimental study of the effects of cooperation and competition upon group process. *Hum. Relat.*, **2**, 199–231.
Deutsch, M. 1958. Trust and suspicion. *Conflict resolution.* II, 4, pp. 265–279.
Deutsch, M. 1960. The effect of motivational orientation upon trust and suspicion. *Hum. Relat.*, **13**, 122–139.
Deutsch, M. 1962. Cooperation and trust: some theoretical notes. In M. R. Jones (Ed.), *Nebraska symposium on motivation.* Lincoln: Univer. of Nebraska. pp. 275–319.
Deutsch, M. and Gerard, H. G. 1955. A study of normative and informational social influence upon individual judgment. *J. abnorm. soc. Psychol.*, **51**, 629–636.

Deutsch, M. and Krauss, R. M. 1960. The effect of threat on interpersonal bargaining. *J. abnorm. soc. Psychol.*, **61,** 181–189.

Deutsch, M., Krauss, R. M. and Rosenau, N. 1962. Dissonance or defensiveness. *J. Pers.*, **30,** 16–28.

Deutsch, M. and Solomon, L. 1959. Reactions to evaluations by others as influenced by self evaluations. *Sociometry,* **22,** 93–112.

Dickoff, Hilda. 1961. Reactions to evaluations by another person as a function of self evaluation and the interaction context. Unpublished doctoral dissertation, Duke Univer.

Dittes, J. E. and Kelley, H. H. 1956. Effects of different conditions of acceptance upon conformity to group norms. *J. abnorm. soc. Psychol.,* **53,** 100–107.

DiVesta, F. J. and Merwin, J. C. 1960. The effects of need-oriented communications on attitude change. *J. abnorm. soc. Psychol.,* **60,** 80–85.

Dollard, J., Doob, L., Miller, N., Mowrer, O. and Sears, R. 1939. *Frustration and aggression.* New Haven: Yale Univer.

Dollard, J. and Miller, N. 1950. *Personality and psychotherapy.* New York: McGraw-Hill.

Doob, L. 1947. The behavior of attitudes. *Psychol. Rev.,* **54,** 135–156.

Dorfman, D. D. 1961. Some effects of drive on the affective intensity of a stimulus. *Psychol. Reports,* **9,** 87–98.

Dreyer, A. 1954. Aspiration behavior as influenced by expectation and group comparison. *Hum. Relat.,* **7,** 175–190.

Dulany, D. E., Jr. 1957. Avoidance learning of perceptual defense and vigilance. *J. abnorm. soc. Psychol.,* **55,** 333–338.

Dunnette, M. D., Campbell, J. and Jaastad, Kay. 1963. The effect of group participation on brainstorming effectiveness for two industrial samples. *J. appl. Psychol.,* **47,** 30–37.

Durkheim, E. 1897. *Suicide.* Paris: F. Alcan. Translation, Glencoe, Ill.: Free Press, 1951.

Ebbinghaus, H. 1913. *Memory.* (Trans. H. A. Ruger and C. E. Bussenius) New York: Teachers College. p. viii. Originally *Über das Gedachtnis.* Leipzig, Germany: Duncker, 1885.

Edwards, A. L. 1941. Political frames of reference as a factor influencing recognition. *J. abnorm. soc. Psychol.,* **36,** 34–50.

Ehrlich, Danuta, Guttman, J., Schonbach, P. and Mills, J. 1957. Postdecision exposure to relevant information. *J. abnorm. soc. Psychol.,* **54,** 98–102.

Emerson, R. M. 1954. Deviation and rejection: an experimental replication. *Amer. soc. Rev.,* **19,** 688–694.

Eriksen, C. W. (Ed.) 1962. *Behavior and awareness: a symposium of research and interpretation.* Durham, N.C.: Duke Univer.

Ewing, T. 1942. A study of certain factors involved in the study of changes of opinion. *J. soc. Psychol.,* **16,** 63–88.

Faigin, Helen. 1953. Child rearing in the Rimrock community with special reference to the development of guilt. Unpublished doctoral dissertation, Radcliffe College.

Fauconnet, P. 1928. *La responsibilité* (Second Edition). Paris: Alcan.

Feather, N. T. 1962. Cigarette smoking and lung cancer: a study of cognitive dissonance. *Australian J. Psychol.,* **14,** 55–64.

Feather, N. T. 1963. Cognitive dissonance, sensitivity, and evaluation. *J. abnorm. soc. Psychol.,* **66,** 157–163.

Feather, N. T. 1964. Acceptance and rejection of arguments in relation to attitude strength, critical ability, and intolerance of inconsistency. *J. abnorm. soc. Psychol.,* **69,** 127–137.
Feshbach, S. 1955. The drive-reducing function of fantasy behavior. *J. abnorm. soc. Psychol.,* **50,** 3–12.
Festinger, L. 1942. Wish, expectation, and group standards as factors influencing level of aspiration. *J. abnorm. soc. Psychol.,* **37,** 184–200.
Festinger, L. 1950. Informal social communication. *Psychol. Rev.,* **57,** 271–282.
Festinger, L. 1954. A theory of social comparison processes. *Hum. Relat.,* **7,** 117–140.
Festinger, L. 1957. *A theory of cognitive dissonance.* Evanston, Ill.: Row, Peterson.
Festinger, L. 1961. The psychological effects of insufficient reward. *Amer. Psychol.,* **16,** 1–12.
Festinger, L. 1964. *Conflict, decision, and dissonance.* Stanford: Stanford Univer.
Festinger, L. and Carlsmith, J. M. 1959. Cognitive consequences of forced compliance. *J. abnorm. soc. Psychol.,* **58,** 203–211.
Festinger, L. and Freedman, J. L. 1964. Dissonance reduction and moral values. In P. Worchel and D. Byrne (Eds.), *Personality change.* New York: Wiley. pp. 220–243.
Festinger, L., Gerard, H. B., Hymovitch, B., Kelley, H. H. and Raven, B. H. 1952. The influence process in the presence of extreme deviates. *Hum. Relat.,* **5,** 327–346.
Festinger, L. and Maccoby, N. 1964. On resistance to persuasive communications. *J. abnorm. soc. Psychol.,* **68,** 359–366.
Festinger, L., Pepitone, A. and Newcomb, T. 1952. Some consequences of de-individuation in a group. *J. abnorm. soc. Psychol.,* **47,** 382–389.
Festinger, L., Riecken, H. W. and Schachter, S. 1956. *When prophecy fails.* Minneapolis: Univer. of Minnesota.
Festinger, L., Schachter, S. and Back, K. 1950. *Social pressures in informal groups: a study of human factors in housing.* New York: Harper.
Festinger, L. and Thibaut, J. 1951. Interpersonal communication in small groups. *J. abnorm. soc. Psychol.,* **46,** 92–99.
Festinger, L., Torrey, J. and Willerman, B. 1954. Self-evaluation as a function of attraction to the group. *Hum. Relat.,* **7,** 161–174.
Festinger, L. and Walster, Elaine. 1964. Post-decision regret and decision reversal. In L. Festinger, *Conflict, decision, and dissonance.* Stanford: Stanford Univer. pp. 100–110.
Fishbein, M. 1965. A consideration of beliefs, attitudes, and their relationships. In I. D. Steiner and M. Fishbein (Eds.), *Current studies in social psychology.* New York: Holt. pp. 107–120.
Fisher, S. and Lubin, A. 1958. Distance as a determinant of influence in a two-person serial interaction situation. *J. abnorm. soc. Psychol.,* **56,** 230–238.
Fisher, S., Rubinstein, I. and Freeman, R. W. 1956. Intertrial effects of immediate self-commital in a continuous social influence situation. *J. abnorm. soc. Psychol.,* **52,** 200–207.
Flavell, John H. 1963. *The developmental psychology of Jean Piaget.* Princeton, N.J.: Van Nostrand.
Freedman, J. L. 1965. Confidence, utility, and selective exposure: a partial replication. *J. Pers. soc. Psychol.,* **2,** 778–780.
Freedman, J. L. 1965. Long-term behavioral effects of cognitive dissonance. *J. exp. soc. Psychol.,* **1,** 145–155.
Freedman, J. L. and Sears, D. O. 1965. Warning, distraction, and resistance to influence. *J. Pers. soc. Psychol.,* **1,** 262–266.

Freud, Anna. 1946. *The ego and the mechanisms of defense.* New York: International Univer. (First German Edition, 1936.)

Freud, S. 1933. *New introductory lectures on psychoanalysis.* New York: Norton. (Translated from *Neue Folge der Varlesungen zur Einfuhrung in die Psychoanalyse,* Vienna, 1933.)

Freud, S. 1940. *An outline of psychoanalysis.* New York: Norton. (Translated from Abriss der Psycho-analyse, *Internationale Zeitschrift für Psychoanalyse und Imago,* XXV, 1940.)

Gallo, P. S. 1966. Effects of increased incentives upon the use of threat in bargaining. *J. Pers. soc. Psychol.,* **4,** 14–20.

Gerard, H. B. 1953. The effect of different dimensions of disagreement on the communication process in small groups. *Hum. Relat.,* **6,** 249–271.

Gerard, H. B. 1954. The anchorage of opinions in face-to-face groups. *Hum. Relat.,* **7,** 313–326.

Gerard, H. B. 1961a. Some determinants of self-evaluation. *J. abnorm. soc. Psychol.,* **62,** 288–293.

Gerard, H. B. 1961b. Disagreement with others, their credibility, and experienced stress. *J. abnorm. soc. Psychol.,* **62,** 559–564.

Gerard, H. B. 1963. Emotional uncertainty and social comparison. *J. abnorm. soc. Psychol.,* **66,** 568–573.

Gerard, H. B. 1964. Physiological measurement in social psychological research. In P. H. Leiderman and D. Shapiro (Eds.), *Psychobiological approaches to social behavior.* Stanford: Stanford Univer.

Gerard, H. B. 1965. Deviation, conformity, and commitment. In I. D. Steiner and M. Fishbein (Eds.), *Current studies in social psychology.* New York: Holt, Rinehart and Winston. pp. 263–277.

Gerard, H. B. 1966. Conflict and the decision sequence. Unpublished manuscript. To be submitted for publication.

Gerard, H. B., Blevans, S. A. and Malcolm, T. 1964. Self-evaluation and the evaluation of choice alternatives. *J. Pers.,* **32,** 395–410.

Gerard, H. B. and Greenbaum, C. W. 1962. Attitudes toward an agent of uncertainty reduction. *J. Pers.,* **30,** 485–495.

Gerard, H. B. and Mathewson, G. C. 1966. The effects of severity of initiation on liking for a group: a replication. *J. exp. soc. Psychol.,* **2,** 278–287.

Gerard, H. B. and Rabbie, J. M. 1961. Fear and social comparison. *J. abnorm. soc. Psychol.,* **62,** 586–592.

Gerard, H. B. and Rotter, G. S. 1961. Time perspective, consistency of attitude, and social influence. *J. abnorm. soc. Psychol.,* **62,** 565–572.

Gewirtz, J. L. and Baer, D. M. 1958a. The effect of brief social deprivation on behavior for a social reinforcer. *J. abnorm. soc. Psychol.,* **56,** 49–56.

Gewirtz, J. L. and Baer, D. M. 1958b. Deprivation and satiation of social reinforcers as drive conditions. *J. abnorm. soc. Psychol.,* **57,** 165–172.

Gilchrist, J. C. and Nesberg, L. S. 1952. Need and perceptual change in need-related objects. *J. exp. Psychol.,* **44,** 369–376.

Glass, D. C. 1964. Changes in liking as a means of reducing cognitive discrepancies between self-esteem and aggression. *J. Pers.,* **32,** 531–550.

Glueck, S. and Glueck, Eleanor. 1950. *Unraveling juvenile delinquency.* New York: Commonwealth Fund.

Goldberg, S. C. 1954. Three situational determinants of conformity to social norms. *J. abnorm. soc. Psychol.,* **49,** 325–329.

Goldberg, S. C. and Lubin, A. 1958. Influence as a function of perceived judgment error. *Hum. Relat.,* **11,** 275–280.

Goldstein, M. J. 1959. The relationship between coping and avoiding behavior and response to fear arousing propaganda. *J. abnorm. soc. Psychol.*, **58**, 247–252.
Gollin, E. S. 1954. Forming impressions of personality. *J. Pers.*, **23**, 65–76.
Graham, F., Charwat, W., Honig, A. and Weltz, P. 1951. Aggression as a function of the attack and the attacker. *J. abnorm. soc. Psychol.*, **46**, 512–520.
Greenbaum, C. W. 1966. Effect of situational and personality variables on improvisation and attitude change. *J. Pers. soc. Psychol.*, **4**, 260–269.
Greenspoon, J. 1955. The reinforcing effect of two spoken sounds on the frequency of two responses. *Amer. J. Psychol.*, **68**, 409–416.
Gurnee, H. A. 1937. A comparison of collective and individual judgments of fact. *J. exp. Psychol.*, **21**, 106–112.

Haire, M. and Grunes, W. F. 1950. Perceptual defenses: processes protecting an organized perception of another personality. *Hum. Relat.*, **3**, 403–412.
Hamblin, R. L. 1958. Leadership and crisis. *Sociometry*, **21**, 322–335.
Hardyck, Jane A. and Braden, Marcia. 1962. Prophecy fails again. *J. abnorm. soc. Psychol.*, **65**, 136–141.
Hare, A. P. 1962. *Handbook of small group research.* New York: Free Press of Glencoe.
Harvey, O. J. and Consalvi, C. 1960. Status and conformity to pressure in informal groups. *J. abnorm. soc. Psychol.*, **60**, 182–187.
Harvey, O. J., Kelley, H. H. and Shapiro, M. M. 1957. Reactions to unfavorable evaluations of self made by other persons. *J. Pers.*, **25**, 393–411.
Hatfield, R. O. 1959. The influence of an affective set on disyllable recognition thresholds. *J. abnorm. soc. Psychol.*, **59**, 439–441.
Heider, F. 1944. Social perception and phenomenal causality. *Psychol. Rev.*, **51**, 358–374.
Heider, F. 1946. Attitudes and cognitive organization. *J. Psychol.*, **21**, 107–112.
Heider, F. 1958. *The psychology of interpersonal relations.* New York: Wiley.
Hemphill, J. K. 1950. Relations between the size of the group and the behavior of "superior" leaders. *J. soc. Psychol.*, **32**, 11–22.
Heron, W. 1961. Cognitive and physiological effects of perceptual isolation. In P. Solomon, P. E. Kubzansky, P. H. Leiderman, et al. (Eds.), *Sensory deprivation.* Cambridge, Mass.: Harvard Univer.
Hess, E. H. 1965. The pupil responds to changes in attitude as well as to changes in illumination. *Scientific Amer.*, **212**, 46–54.
Hildum, D. C. and Brown, R. W. 1956. Verbal reinforcement and interviewer bias. *J. abnorm. soc. Psychol.*, **53**, 108–111.
Hochbaum, G. M. 1954. The relation between group members' self-confidence and their reaction to group pressures to uniformity. *Amer. soc. Rev.*, **19**, 678–688.
Hochberg, J. and Brooks, Virginia. 1958. Effects of previously associated annoying stimuli (auditory) on visual recognition thresholds. *J. exp. Psychol.*, **55**, 490–491.
Hoffman, L. R. 1965. Group problem solving. In L. Berkowitz (Ed.), *Advances in experimental social psychology.* Vol. II. New York: Academic. pp. 99–132.
Hoffman, P. J., Festinger, L. and Lawrence, D. H. 1954. Tendencies toward group comparability in competitive bargaining. *Hum. Relat.*, **7**, 141–159.
Hollander, E. P. 1958. Conformity, status, and idiosyncracy credit. *Psychol. Rev.*, **65**, 117–127.
Hollenberg, Eleanor. 1953. Child training among the Zeepi with special reference to the internalization of moral values. Unpublished doctoral dissertation, Radcliffe College.
Homans, G. C. 1950. *The human group.* New York: Harcourt.

Homans, G. C. 1961. *Social behavior: its elementary forms.* New York: Harcourt, Brace, and World.

Horwitz, M. 1954. The recall of interrupted group tasks: an experimental study of individual motivation in relation to group goals. *Hum. Relat.,* 7, 3–39.

Hovland, C. I. (Ed.) 1957. *The order of presentation in persuasion.* New Haven: Yale Univer. pp. 13–22.

Hovland, C. I. 1959. Reconciling conflicting results derived from experimental and survey studies of attitude change. *Amer. Psychologist,* 14, 8–17.

Hovland, C. I., Campbell, Enid H. and Brock, T. 1957. The effects of "commitment" on opinion change following communication. In C. I. Hovland (Ed.), *The order of presentation in persuasion.* New Haven: Yale Univer. pp. 23–32.

Hovland, C. I., Harvey, O. J., and Sherif, M. 1957. Assimilation and contrast effects in reaction to communication and attitude change. *J. abnorm. soc. Psychol.,* 55, 244–252.

Hovland, C. I., Janis, I. L. and Kelley, H. H. 1953. *Communication and persuasion.* New Haven: Yale Univer.

Hovland, C. I., Lumsdaine, A. A. and Sheffield, F. D. 1949. Experiments on mass communication. Vol. 3 of *Studies in social psychology in World War II.* Princeton: Princeton Univer.

Hovland, C. I. and Mandell, W. 1952. An experimental comparison of conclusion drawing by the communicator and by the audience. *J. abnorm. soc. Psychol.,* 47, 581–588.

Hovland, C. I. and Weiss, W. 1951. The influence of source credibility on communication effectiveness. *Publ. Opin. quart.,* 15, 635–650.

Howes, D. H. and Solomon, R. L. 1951. Visual duration threshold as a function of word probability. *J. exp. Psychol.,* 41, 401–410.

Hull, C. L. 1933. *Hypnosis and suggestibility.* New York: Appleton.

Hunt, W. A. 1941. Anchoring effects in judgment. *Amer. J. Psychol.,* 54, 395–403.

Hyman, H. H. 1942. The psychology of status. *Arch. Psychol., Columbia University,* No. 269.

Insko, C. A. 1964. Primacy and recency in persuasion as a function of the timing of arguments and measures. *J. abnorm. soc. Psychol.,* 69, 381–391.

Itard, J.-M.-G. 1962. *The wild boy of Aveyron.* New York: Appleton-Century-Crofts. (Translated from *Rapports et memoires sur le sauvage de l'Aveyron,* Paris, 1894.)

Ittelson, W. H. 1952. *The Ames demonstrations in perception.* Princeton: Princeton Univer.

James, W. 1892. *Psychology.* New York: Holt.

Janis, I. L. and Feshbach, S. 1953. Effects of fear-arousing communications. *J. abnorm. soc. Psychol.,* 48, 78–92.

Janis, I. L. and Gilmore, J. B. 1965. The influence of incentive conditions on the success of role playing in modifying attitudes. *J. Pers. soc. Psychol.,* 1, 17–27.

Janis, I. L. and King, B. T. 1954. The influence of role-playing on opinion change. *J. abnorm. soc. Psychol.,* 49, 211–218.

Janis, I. L., Lumsdaine, A. A. and Gladstone, A. I. 1951. Effects of preparatory communication on reactions to a subsequent news event. *Publ. Opin. quart.,* 15, 488–518.

Janis, I. L. and Milholland, H. C. 1954. The influence of threat appeals on selective learning of the content of a persuasive communication. *J. Psychol.,* 37, 75–80.

Jecker, J. D. 1964. The cognitive effects of conflict and dissonance. In L. Festinger, *Conflict, decision, and dissonance.* Stanford: Stanford Univer. pp. 21–32.

Jecker, J. D. 1964. Selective exposure to new information. In L. Festinger, *Conflict, decision, and dissonance.* Stanford: Stanford Univer. pp. 65–81.

Jones, E. E. 1964. *Ingratiation: a social psychological analysis.* New York: Appleton-Century-Crofts.

Jones, E. E. and Aneshansel, Jane. 1956. The learning and utilization of contravaluant material. *J. abnorm. soc. Psychol.,* **53,** 27–34.

Jones, E. E. and Daugherty, B. N. 1959. Political orientation and the perceptual effects of an anticipated interaction. *J. abnorm. soc. Psychol.,* **59,** 340–349.

Jones, E. E. and Davis, K. E. 1965. From acts to dispositions: the attribution process in person perception. In L. Berkowitz (Ed.), *Advances in experimental social psychology.* Vol. II. New York: Academic. pp. 219–266.

Jones, E. E., Davis, K. E. and Gergen, K. J. 1961. Role playing variations and their informational value for person perception. *J. abnorm. soc. Psychol.,* **63,** 302–310.

Jones, E. E. and deCharms, R. 1957. Changes in social perception as a function of the personal relevance of behavior. *Sociometry,* **20,** 75–85.

Jones, E. E., Gergen, K. J. and Davis, K. E. 1962. Some determinants of reactions to being approved or disapproved as a person. *Psychol. Monogr.,* **76,** No. 521.

Jones, E. E., Gergen, K. J., Gumpert, P. and Thibaut, J. W. 1965. Some conditions affecting the use of ingratiation to influence performance evaluation. *J. Pers. soc. Psychol.,* **1,** 613–626.

Jones, E. E., Gergen, K. J. and Jones, R. G. 1963. Tactics of ingratiation among leaders and subordinates in a status hierarchy. *Psychol. Monogr.,* **77,** No. 566.

Jones, E. E. and Harris, V. A. 1967. The attribution of attitudes. *J. exp. soc. Psychol.,* in press.

Jones, E. E., Hester, S. L., Farina, A. and Davis, K. E. 1959. Reactions to unfavorable personal evaluations as a function of the evaluator's perceived adjustment. *J. abnorm. soc. Psychol.,* **59,** 363–370.

Jones, E. E. and Jones, R. G. 1964. Optimum conformity as an ingratiation tactic. *J. Pers.,* **32,** 436–458.

Jones, E. E. and Kohler, R. 1958. The effects of plausibility on the learning of controversial statements. *J. abnorm. soc. Psychol.,* **58,** 315–320.

Jones, E. E., Wells, H. H. and Torrey, R. 1958. Some effects of feedback from the experimenter on conformity behavior. *J. abnorm. soc. Psychol.,* **58,** 207–213.

Jordan, N. 1953. Behavioral forces that are a function of attitudes and of cognitive organization. *Hum. Relat.,* **6,** 273–288.

Kaplan, A. 1964. *The conduct of inquiry.* San Francisco: Chandler.

Kastenbaum, A. 1951. An experimental study of the formation of impressions of personality. Unpublished M.A. thesis, Graduate Faculty of Political and Social Science, New School for Social Research.

Katz, D. and Kahn, R. L. 1966. *The social psychology of organizations.* New York: Wiley.

Katz, D. and Stotland, E. 1959. A preliminary statement to a theory of attitude structure and change. In S. Koch (Ed.), *Psychology: A study of a science.* Vol. 3: *Formulations of the person and the social context.* New York: McGraw-Hill. pp. 423–475.

Kelley, H. H. 1950. The warm-cold variable in first impressions of persons. *J. Pers.,* **18,** 431–439.

Kelley, H. H. 1952. The two functions of reference groups. In G. E. Swanson, T. M. Newcomb, and E. L. Hartley (Eds.), *Readings in social psychology.* (Second edition) New York: Holt. pp. 410–414.

Kelley, H. H. 1955. Salience of membership and resistance to change of group-anchored attitudes. *Hum. Relat.,* **8,** 275–289.

Kelley, H. H. 1966. Effects of incentive magnitude on interpersonal negotiations. Paper presented at International Congress of Psychology. Moscow, U.S.S.R. (August).

Kelley, H. H., Condry, J. C. Dahlke, A. E. and Hill, A. H. 1965. Collective behavior in a simulated panic situation. *J. exp. soc. Psychol.*, 1, 20–54.

Kelley, H. H. and Lamb, T. W. 1957. Certainty of judgment and resistance to social influence. *J. abnorm. soc. Psychol.*, 55, 137–139.

Kelley, H. H. and Shapiro, M. M. 1954. An experiment on conformity to group norms where conformity is detrimental to group achievement. *Amer. soc. Rev.*, 19, 667–677.

Kelley, H. H. and Thibaut, J. W. 1954. Experimental studies of group problem solving and process. In G. Lindzey (Ed.), *Handbook of social psychology*. Vol. II. Cambridge, Mass.: Addison-Wesley. pp. 735–785.

Kelley, H. H. and Thibaut, J. W. In press. Group problem solving. In G. Lindzey and E. Aronson (Eds.), *Handbook of social psychology*. (Rev.) Reading, Mass.: Addison-Wesley.

Kelley, H. H., Thibaut, J. W., Radloff, R. and Mundy, D. 1962. The development of cooperation in the "minimal social situation." *Psychol. Monogr.*, 76, No. 19 (Whole No. 538).

Kelley, H. H. and Volkhart, E. H. 1952. The resistance to change of group-anchored attitudes. *Amer. soc. Rev.*, 17, 453–465.

Kelley, H. H. and Woodruff, C. L. 1956. Members' reaction to apparent group approval of a counternorm communication. *J. abnorm. soc. Psychol.*, 52, 67–74.

Kelman, H. C. 1953. Attitude change as a function of response restriction. *Hum. Relat.*, 6, 185–214.

Kelman, H. C. 1961. Processes of opinion change. *Publ. Opin. quart.*, 25, 57–78.

Kelman, H. C. and Hovland, C. I. 1953. "Reinstatement" of the communicator in delayed measurement of opinion change. *J. abnorm. soc. Psychol.*, 48, 327–335.

Kerckhoff, A. and Davis, K. A. 1962. Value consensus and need complementarity in mate selection. *Amer. sociol. Rev.*, 27, 295–303.

Kimble, G. A. 1961. *Hilgard and Marquis' conditioning and learning*. New York: Appleton-Century-Crofts.

King, B. T. and Janis, I. L. 1956. Comparison of the effectiveness of improvised versus non-improvised role-playing in producing opinion changes. *Hum. Relat.*, 9, 177–186.

Kluckhohn, C. 1954. Culture and behavior. In G. Lindzey (Ed.), *Handbook of social psychology*. Vol. II. Cambridge, Mass.: Addison-Wesley. pp. 921–976.

Koch, S. 1956. Behavior as "intrinsically" regulated: work notes toward a pretheory of phenomena called "motivational." In M. Jones (Ed.), *Nebraska symposium on motivation*. Lincoln: Univer. of Nebraska. pp. 42–86.

Kogan, N. and Tagiuri, R. 1958. Interpersonal preference and cognitive organization. *J. abnorm. soc. Psychol.*, 56, 113–116.

Kogan, N. and Wallach, M. A. 1967a. Risk taking as a function of the situation, the person, and the group. In *New directions in psychology III*. New York: Holt, Rinehart and Winston.

Kogan, N. and Wallach, M. A. 1967b. Effects of physical separation of group members upon group risk taking. *Hum. Relat.*, in press.

Komorita, S. S. 1965. Cooperative choice in a prisoner's dilemma game. *J. Pers. soc. Psychol.*, 2, 741–745.

Krech, D. and Crutchfield, R. S. 1948. *Theory and problems of social psychology*. New York: McGraw-Hill.

Kuhn, T. S. 1962. *The structure of scientific revolutions*. Chicago: Univer. of Chicago.

Lair, W. S. 1949. Psychoanalytic theory of identification. Unpublished doctoral dissertation, Harvard Univer.
Lambert, W. W., Solomon, R. L. and Watson, P. D. 1949. Reinforcement and extinction as factors in size estimation. *J. exp. Psychol.*, 39, 637–641.
Latané, B. (Ed.) 1966. *Studies in social comparison.* New York: Academic.
Lave, L. B. 1965. Factors affecting cooperation in the prisoner's dilemma, *Behav. Sci.*, 10, 26–38.
Lawrence, D. H. and Festinger, L. 1962. *Deterrents and reinforcement: the psychology of insufficient reward.* Stanford: Stanford Univer.
Lazarsfeld, P. F. 1949. The American soldier—an expository review. *Publ. Opin. quart.*, 13, 377–404.
Lazarsfeld, P. F., Berelson, B. and Gaudet, H. 1948. *The people's choice.* New York: Columbia Univer.
Leavitt, H. J. 1951. Some effects of certain communication patterns on group performance. *J. abnorm. soc. Psychol.*, 46, 38–50.
Le Bon, G. 1896. *The crowd.* London: Unwin. (Translated from *Psychologies des foules.* Paris: Oleon, 1895.)
Leventhal, H. and Niles, P. 1964. A field experiment on fear-arousal with data on the validity of questionnaire measures. *J. Pers.*, 32, 459–479.
Leventhal, H. and Singer, R. P. 1966. Affect arousal and positioning of recommendations in persuasive communication. *J. Pers. soc. Psychol.*, 4, 137–146.
Leventhal, H., Singer, R. P. and Jones, S. 1963. Effects of fear and specificity of recommendations upon attitudes and behavior. *J. Pers. soc. Psychol.*, 2, 20–29.
Levin, H. 1952. Permissive child-rearing and adult role behavior in children. Paper presented at East. Psychol. Assn., Atlantic City, N.J.
Levine, J. M. and Murphy, G. 1943. The learning and forgetting of controversial material. *J. abnorm. soc. Psychol.*, 38, 507–517.
Levine, R., Chein, I. and Murphy, G. 1942. The relation of the intensity of a need to the amount of perceptual distortion: a preliminary report. *J. Psychol.*, 13, 283–293.
Lewin, K. 1935. *Dynamic theory of personality.* New York: McGraw-Hill.
Lewin, K. 1936. *Principles of topological psychology.* New York: McGraw-Hill.
Lewin, K. 1947a. Frontiers in group dynamics. *Hum. Relat.*, 1, 5–41.
Lewin, K. 1947b. Group decision and social change. In T. M. Newcomb and E. L. Hartley (Eds.), *Readings in social psychology.* New York: Holt. pp. 330–344.
Lewin, K. 1951. *Field theory in social science.* New York: Harper.
Lewin, K., Dembo, Tamara, Festinger, L. and Sears, Pauline. 1944. Level of aspiration. In J. McV. Hunt (Ed.), *Personality and the behavior disorders.* New York: Ronald. pp. 333–378.
Lewin, K., Lippitt, R. and White, R. K. 1939. Patterns of aggressive behavior in experimentally created "social climates." *J. soc. Psychol.*, 10, 271–299.
Lewis, Helen B. 1944. An experimental study of the role of the ego in work. I. The role of the ego in cooperative work. *J. exp. Psychol.*, 34, 113–127.
Lewis, Helen B. and Franklin, Muriel. 1944. An experimental study of the role of the ego in work. II. The significance of task orientation in work. *J. exp. Psychol.*, 34, 194–215.
Libo, L. M. 1953. *Measuring group cohesiveness.* Ann Arbor: Research Center for Group Dynamics.
Leiderman, P. H. and Shapiro, D. (Eds.) 1964. *Psychobiological approaches to social behavior.* Stanford: Stanford Univer.
Lifton, R. J. 1961. *Thought reform and the psychology of totalism: a study of "brainwashing" in China.* New York: W. W. Norton.

Lindzey, G. (Ed.) 1954. *Handbook of social psychology.* Vols. I and II. Cambridge, Mass.: Addison-Wesley.

Lindzey, G. and Borgatta, E. F. 1954. Sociometric measurements. In G. Lindzey (Ed.), *Handbook of social psychology.* Vol. I. Cambridge, Mass.: Addison-Wesley.

Loomis, J. L. 1959. Communication, the development of trust, and cooperative behavior. *Hum. Relat.,* 12, 305–315.

Lorge, I. 1936. Prestige, suggestion, and attitudes. *J. soc. Psychol.,* 7, 386–402.

Lorge, I. and Solomon, H. 1955. Two models of group behavior in the solution of eureka-type problems. *Psychometrika,* 20, 139–148.

Lowenfeld, J. 1961. Negative affect as a causal factor in the occurrence of repression, subception, and perceptual defense. *J. Pers.,* 29, 54–63.

Luce, R. D. and Raiffa, H. 1957. *Games and decisions: introduction and critical survey.* New York: Wiley.

Luchins, A. S. 1948. Forming impressions of personality: a critique. *J. abnorm. soc. Psychol.,* 43, 318–325.

Luchins, A. S. 1957. Experimental attempts to minimize the impact of first impressions. In C. Hovland (Ed.), *The order of presentation in persuasion.* New Haven: Yale Univ. Press. pp. 63–75.

Lumsdaine, A. A. and Janis, I. L. 1953. Resistance to "counterpropaganda" produced by one-sided and two-sided "propaganda" presentations. *Publ. Opin. quart.,* 17, 311–318.

Lund, F. H. 1925. The psychology of belief: IV. The law of primacy in persuasion. *J. abnorm. soc. Psychol.,* 20, 183–191.

Lynn, D. B. and Sawrey, W. L. 1959. The effects of father-absence on Norwegian boys and girls. *J. abnorm. soc. Psychol.,* 59, 258–262.

Maccoby, Eleanor E. 1959. Role-taking in childhood and its consequences for social learning. *Child Develpm.,* 30, 239–252.

Maccoby, Eleanor E., Maccoby, N., Romney, A. K. and Adams, J. S. 1961. Social reinforcement in attitude change. *J. abnorm. soc. Psychol.,* 63, 109–115.

Maccoby, Eleanor, Newcomb, T. M. and Hartley, E. L. (Eds.) 1958. *Readings in social psychology* (Third Edition). New York: Holt.

MacKinnon, D. W. 1938. Violations of prohibition. In H. A. Murray et al., *Explorations in personality.* New York: Oxford Univer. pp. 491–501.

Maier, N. R. F. 1946. *Psychology in industry.* Boston: Houghton-Mifflin.

Malewski, A. 1962. The influence of positive and negative self-evaluation on post-decisional dissonance. *Polish sociol. Bull.,* 3–4, 39–49.

Mangan, G. L. 1959. The role of punishment in figure-ground reorganization. *J. exp. Psychol.,* 58, 369–375.

Marak, G. E. 1964. The evolution of leadership structure. *Sociometry,* 27, 174–182.

Marlowe, D., Gergen, K. J. and Doob, A. N. 1966. Opponent's personality, expectation of social interaction, and interpersonal bargaining. *J. Pers. soc. Psychol.,* 3, 206–213.

Marquart, Dorothy I. 1955. Group problem solving. *J. soc. Psychol.,* 41, 103–113.

Mausner, B. 1954a. The effect of prior reinforcement on the interaction of observer pairs. *J. abnorm. soc. Psychol.,* 49, 65–68.

Mausner, B. 1954b. Prestige and social interaction. The effect of one partner's success in a relevant task on the interaction of observer pairs. *J. abnorm. soc. Psychol.,* 49, 557–560.

McClelland, D. C. 1951. *Personality.* New York: William Sloane.

McClelland, D. C. and Atkinson, J. W. 1948. The projective expression of needs: I.

The effects of different intensities of the hunger drive on perception. *J. Psychol.*, **25**, 205–222.

McClelland, D. C., Atkinson, J. W., Clark, R. A. and Lowell, E. L. 1953. *The achievement motive.* New York: Appleton-Century-Crofts.

McCurdy, H. G. and Lambert, W. E. 1952. The efficiency of small human groups in the solution of problems requiring genuine cooperation. *J. Pers.*, **20**, 478–494.

McDougall, W. 1908. *An introduction to social psychology.* London: Methuen.

McGinnies, E. 1949. Emotionality and perceptual defense. *Psychol. Rev.*, **56**, 244–251.

McGinnies, E. and Sherman, H. 1952. Generalization of perceptual defense. *J. abnorm. soc. Psychol.*, **47**, 81–85.

McGuire, W. J. 1960. A syllogistic analysis of cognitive relationships. In C. I. Hovland and I. L. Janis (Eds.), *Attitude organization and change.* New Haven: Yale Univer. pp. 65–111.

McGuire, W. J. 1961a. The effectiveness of supportive and refutational defenses in immunizing and restoring beliefs against persuasion. *Sociometry*, **24**, 184–197.

McGuire, W. J. 1961b. Resistance to persuasion conferred by active and passive prior refutation of the same and alternative counterarguments. *J. abnorm. soc. Psychol.*, **63**, 326–332.

McGuire, W. J. 1962. Persistence of the resistance to persuasion induced by various types of prior belief defenses. *J. abnorm. soc. Psychol.*, **64**, 241–248.

McGuire, W. J. and Papageorgis, D. 1961. The relative efficacy of various types of prior belief-defense in producing immunity against persuasion. *J. abnorm. soc. Psychol.*, **62**, 327–337.

McGuire, W. J. and Papageorgis, D. 1962. Effectiveness of forewarning in developing resistance to persuasion. *Publ. Opin. quart.*, **26**, 24–34.

McNamara, H. J., Solley, C. M. and Long, J. 1958. The effects of punishment (electric shock) on perceptual learning. *J. abnorm. soc. Psychol.*, **57**, 91–98.

Melikian, L. 1959. Preference for delayed reinforcement: an experimental study among Palestinian Arab refugee children. *J. soc. Psychol.*, **50**, 81–86.

Mensch, I. N. and Wishner, J. 1947. Asch on "Forming impressions of personality": further evidence. *J. Pers.*, **16**, 188–191.

Menzel, H. 1957. Public and private conformity under different conditions of acceptance in the group. *J. abnorm. soc. Psychol.*, **55**, 398–401.

Merton, R. K. and Kitt, A. 1950. Contributions to the theory of reference group behavior. In R. K. Merton and P. F. Lazarsfeld (Eds.), *Continuities in social research: studies in the scope and method of "The American soldier."* New York: Free Press of Glencoe. pp. 40–105.

Messé, L. A. and Sawyer, J. Submitted for publication. Unexpected cooperation: the prisoner's dilemma resolved?

Miller, G. A., Bruner, J. S. and Postman, L. 1954. Familiarity of letter sequences and tachistoscopic identification. *J. gen. Psychol.*, **50**, 129–139.

Miller, G. A., Heise, G. A. and Lichten, W. 1951. The intelligibility of speech as a function of the context of the test materials. *J. exp. Psychol.*, **41**, 329–335.

Miller, N. and Campbell, D. T. 1959. Recency and primacy in persuasion as a function of the timing of speeches and measurements. *J. abnorm. soc. Psychol.*, **59**, 1–9.

Miller, N. E. 1941. The frustration-aggression hypothesis. *Psychol. Rev.*, **48**, 337–342.

Miller, N. E. 1944. Experimental studies in conflict. In J. McV. Hunt (Ed.), *Personality and the behavior disorders.* New York: Ronald. pp. 431–465.

Miller, N. E. and Dollard, J. 1941. *Social learning and imitation.* New Haven: Yale Univer.

Mills, J. 1958. Changes in moral attitudes following temptation. *J. Pers.*, **26**, 517–531.

Mills, J. 1965a. Avoidance of dissonant information. *J. Pers. soc. Psychol.*, **2**, 589–592.

Mills, J. 1965b. Effect of certainty about a decision upon postdecision exposure to consonant and dissonant information. *J. Pers. soc. Psychol.*, **2**, 749–752.

Mills, J. In press. Interest in supporting and discrepant information. In R. Abelson, E. Aronson, W. McGuire, T. Newcomb, M. Rosenberg, and P. Tannenbaum (Eds.), *Cognitive Consistency Theories.* New York: Rand McNally.

Mills, J., Aronson, E. and Robinson, H. 1959. Selectivity in exposure to information. *J. abnorm. soc. Psychol.*, **59**, 250–253.

Minas, J. S., Scodel, A., Marlowe, D. and Rawson, H. 1960. Some descriptive aspects of two-person non-zero-sum games. II. *J. Conflict Resol.*, **4**, 193–197.

Mintz, A. 1951. Non-adaptive group behavior. *J. abnorm. soc. Psychol.*, **46**, 150–159.

Mirels, H. and Mills, J. 1964. Perception of the pleasantness and competence of a partner. *J. abnorm. soc. Psychol.*, **68**, 456–460.

Mischel, W. 1958a. The effect of the commitment situation on the generalization of expectancies. *J. Pers.*, **26**, 508–516.

Mischel, W. 1958b. Preference for delayed reinforcement: an experimental study of a cultural observation. *J. abnorm. soc. Psychol.*, **56**, 57–61.

Mischel, W. 1961a. Preference for delayed reinforcement and social responsibility. *J. abnorm. soc. Psychol.*, **62**, 1–7.

Mischel, W. 1961b. Delay of gratification, need for achievement, and acquiescence in another culture. *J. abnorm. soc. Psychol.*, **62**, 543–552.

Mischel, W. and Gilligan, Carol. 1964. Delay of gratification, motivation for the prohibited gratification, and responses to temptation. *J. abnorm. soc. Psychol.*, **69**, 411–417.

Mischel, W. and Metzner, R. 1962. Preference for delayed reward as a function of age, intelligence, and length of delay interval. *J. abnorm. soc. Psychol.*, **64**, 425–431.

Mittman, L. R. and Terrell, G. 1964. An experimental study of curiosity in children. *Child Develpm.*, **35**, 851–857.

Moore, H. T. 1921. The comparative influence of majority and expert opinion. *Amer. J. Psychol.*, **32**, 16–20.

Morrissette, J. O. 1958. An experimental study of the theory of structural balance. *Hum. Relat.*, **11**, 239–254.

Mouton, Jane S., Blake, R. R. and Olmstead, J. A. 1956. The relationship between frequency of yielding and the disclosure of personal identity. *J. Pers.*, **24**, 339–347.

Mowrer, O. H. 1950. *Learning theory and personality dynamics.* New York: Ronald.

Mowrer, O. H. and Ullman, A. D. 1945. Time as a determinant in integrative learning. *Psychol. Rev.*, **52**, 61–90.

Mulder, M. 1960. Communication structure, decision structure and group performance. *Sociometry*, **23**, 1–14.

Murchison, C. (Ed.) 1935. *Handbook of social psychology.* Worcester, Mass.: Clark Univer.

Murray, E. J. 1956. A content-analysis method for studying psychotherapy. *Psychol. Monogr.*, **70**, No. 13 (Whole No. 420).

Murray, H. A. 1938. *Explorations in personality.* New York: Oxford Univer.

Mussen, P. H. and Distler, L. 1959. Masculinity, identification, and father-son relationship. *J. abnorm. soc. Psychol.*, **59**, 350–356.

Nash, M. 1958. Machine age Maya: the industrialization of a Guatemalan community. *Amer. Anthropologist*, **60**, No. 2, Part 2 (Memoir 87).

Newcomb, T. M. 1943. *Personality and social change.* New York: Dryden.

Newcomb, T. M. 1947. Autistic hostility and social reality. *Hum. Relat.*, **1**, 69–86.

Newcomb, T. M. 1953. An approach to the study of communicative acts. *Psychol. Rev.*, **60**, 393–404.

Newcomb, T. M. 1956. The prediction of interpersonal attraction. *Amer. Psychologist,* **11,** 575–586.
Newcomb, T. M. 1961. *The acquaintance process.* New York: Holt, Rinehart, and Winston.
Newcomb, T. M. 1963. Persistence and regression of changed attitudes: long range studies. *J. soc. Issues,* **19,** 3–14.
Norfleet, Barbara. 1948. Interpersonal relations and group productivity. *J. soc. Issues,* **4,** 66–69.

Orne, M. T. 1959. The nature of hypnosis: artifact and essence. *J. abnorm. soc. Psychol.,* **58,** 277–299.
Osborn, A. F. 1953. *Applied imagination.* New York: Chas. Scribner.
Osgood, C. E. 1952. The nature and measurement of meaning. *Psychol. Bull.,* **49,** 197–237.
Osgood, C. E. 1953. *Method and theory in experimental psychology.* New York: Oxford Univer.
Osgood, C. E., Suci, G. J., and Tannenbaum, P. H. 1957. *The measurement of meaning.* Urbana, Ill.: Univer. of Illinois.
Osgood, C. E. and Tannenbaum, P. H. 1955. The principle of congruity in the prediction of attitude change. *Psychol. Rev.,* **62,** 42–55.

Paivio, A. 1963. Audience influence, social isolation, and speech. *J. abnorm. soc. Psychol.,* **67,** 247–253.
Paivio, A. and Lambert, W. E. 1959. Measures and correlates of audience anxiety ("stage fright"). *J. Pers.,* **27,** 1–18.
Pastore, N. 1952. The role of arbitrariness in the frustration-aggression hypothesis. *J. abnorm. soc. Psychol.,* **47,** 728–731.
Pavlov, I. P. 1927. *Conditioned reflexes: an investigation of the physiological activity of the cerebral cortex.* London: Oxford Univer.
Pepitone, A. and Hayden, R. 1955. Some evidence for conflict resolution in impression formation. *J. abnorm. soc. Psychol.,* **51,** 302–307.
Pepitone, A. and Reichling, G. 1955. Group cohesiveness and the expression of hostility. *Hum. Relat.,* **8,** 327–339.
Pessin, J. 1933. The comparative effects of social and mechanical stimulation on memorizing. *Amer. J. Psychol.,* **45,** 263–270.
Piaget, J. 1936. *The origins of intelligence in children.* New York: International Univer. (Translated from *La naissance de l'intelligence chez l'enfant.* Neuchâtel and Paris: Delachaux and Niestlé, 1936.)
Postman, L. and Brown, D. R. 1952. The perceptual consequences of success and failure. *J. abnorm. soc. Psychol.,* **47,** 213–221.
Postman, L., Bruner, J. S. and McGinnies, E. 1948. Personal values as selective factors in perception. *J. abnorm. soc. Psychol.,* **43,** 142–154.
Postman, L. and Schneider, B. 1951. Personal value, visual recognition and recall. *Psychol. Rev.,* **58,** 271–284.
Postman, L. and Solomon, R. L. 1950. Perceptual sensitivity to completed and incompleted tasks. *J. Pers.,* **18,** 347–357.
Potter, S. 1951. *One-upmanship.* New York: Holt.
Precker, J. A. 1952. Similarity of valuings as a factor in selection of peers and near-authority figures. *J. abnorm. soc. Psychol.,* **47,** 406–414.
Proshansky, H. and Murphy, G. 1942. The effects of reward and punishment on perception. *J. Psychol.,* **13,** 295–305.

Pustell, T. E. 1957. The experimental induction of perceptual vigilance and defense. *J. Pers.*, **25**, 425–438.

Rabbie, J. M. 1964. Differential preference for companionship under threat. *J. abnorm. soc. Psychol.*, **67**, 643–648.

Rabbie, J. M., Brehm, J. W. and Cohen, A. R. 1959. Verbalization and reactions to cognitive dissonance. *J. Pers.*, **27**, 407–417.

Rabinowitz, L., Kelley, H. H. and Rosenblatt, R. M. 1966. Effects of different types of interdependence and response conditions in the minimal social situation. *J. exp. soc. Psychol.*, **2**, 169–197.

Radloff, R. 1962. Opinion evaluation and affiliation. *J. abnorm. soc. Psychol.*, **62**, 578–585.

Radloff, R. 1966. Social comparison and ability evaluation. In B. Latané (Ed.), *Studies in social comparison*. New York: Academic.

Rapoport, A. 1960. *Fights, games and debates*. Ann Arbor: Univer. of Michigan.

Rapoport, A. and Orwant, Carol. 1962. Experimental games: a review. *Behav. Sci.*, **7**, 1–38.

Raven, B. H. 1959. Social influence on opinions and the communication of related content. *J. abnorm. soc. Psychol.*, **58**, 119–128.

Razran, G. H. S. 1938. Conditioning away social bias by the luncheon technique. *Psychol. Bull.*, **35**, 693.

Razran, G. H. S. 1940. Conditioned response changes in rating and appraising sociopolitical slogans. *Psychol. Bull.*, **37**, 481.

Reece, M. M. 1954. The effect of shock on recognition thresholds. *J. abnorm. soc. Psychol.*, **49**, 165–172.

Riecken, H. W. 1958. The effect of talkativeness on ability to influence group solutions of problems. *Sociometry*, **21**, 309–321.

Roethlisberger, F. J. and Dickson, W. J. 1939. *Management and the worker*. Cambridge, Mass.: Harvard Univer.

Rokeach, M. and Rothman, G. 1965. The principle of belief congruence and the congruity principle as models of cognitive interaction. *Psychol. Rev.*, **72**, 128–143.

Rosen, A. C. 1954. Change in perceptual threshold as a protective function of the organism. *J. Pers.*, **23**, 182–195.

Rosen, S. 1961. Postdecision affinity for incompatible information. *J. abnorm. soc. Psychol.*, **63**, 188–190.

Rosenberg, M. J. 1956. Cognitive structure and attitudinal affect. *J. abnorm. soc. Psychol.*, **53**, 367–373.

Rosenberg, M. J. 1960. Cognitive reorganization in response to the hypnotic reversal of attitudinal affect. *J. Pers.*, **28**, 39–63.

Rosenberg, M. J. 1965. When dissonance fails: on eliminating evaluation apprehension from attitude measurement. *J. Pers. soc. Psychol.*, **1**, 28–43.

Rosenberg, M. J. and Abelson, R. P. 1960. An analysis of cognitive balancing. In C. I. Hovland and I. L. Janis (Eds.), *Attitude organization and change*. New Haven: Yale Univer. pp. 112–163.

Rosenthal, R. 1963. On the social psychology of the psychological experiment: the experimenter's hypothesis as unintended determinant of experimental results. *Amer. Scientist*, **51**, 268–283.

Rosenthal, R. 1966. *Experimenter effects in behavioral research*. New York: Appleton-Century-Crofts.

Ross, E. A. 1908. *Social psychology: an outline and a source book*. New York: Macmillan.

Roy, D. F. 1959–60. Banana time. *Hum. Organization*, **18**, 158–168.

Saltzman, I. J. 1949. Maze learning in the absence of primary reinforcement: a study of secondary reinforcement. *J. comp. physiol. Psychol.*, **42**, 161–173.
Samelson, F. 1957. Conforming behavior under two conditions of conflict in the cognitive field. *J. abnorm. soc. Psychol.*, **55**, 181–187.
Sanford, R. N. 1936. The effects of abstinence from food upon imaginal processes: a preliminary experiment. *J. Psychol.*, **2**, 129–136.
Sapolsky, A. 1960. Effect of interpersonal relationships upon verbal conditioning. *J. abnorm. soc. Psychol.*, **60**, 241–246.
Sarnoff, I. and Zimbardo, P. G. 1961. Anxiety, fear, and social affiliation. *J. abnorm. soc. Psychol.*, **62**, 356–363.
Schachter, S. 1951. Deviation, rejection, and communication. *J. abnorm. soc. Psychol.*, **46**, 190–207.
Schachter, S. 1959. *The psychology of affiliation.* Stanford: Stanford Univer.
Schachter, S. and Burdick, H. 1955. A field experiment on rumor transmission and distortion. *J. abnorm. soc. Psychol.*, **50**, 363–372.
Schachter, S., Ellertson, N., McBride, Dorothy and Gregory, D. 1951. An experimental study of cohesiveness and productivity. *Hum. Relat.*, **4**, 229–238.
Schachter, S. and Singer, J. E. 1962. Cognitive, social, and physiological determinants of emotional state. *Psychol. Rev.*, **69**, 379–399.
Schachter, S., Willerman, B., Festinger, L. and Hyman, R. 1963. Emotional disruption and industrial productivity. General Electric Corporation, *Behavioral Research Service Report.*
Schafer, E. and Murphy, G. 1943. The role of autism in a visual figure-ground relationship. *J. exp. Psychol.*, **32**, 335–343.
Schein, E. H. 1958. The Chinese indoctrination program for prisoners of war: a study of attempted "brainwashing." In Eleanor Maccoby, T. M. Newcomb, and E. L. Hartley (Eds.), *Readings in social psychology* (Third Edition). New York: Henry Holt. pp. 311–334.
Schelling, T. C. 1960. *The strategy of conflict.* Cambridge, Mass.: Harvard Univer.
Schopler, J. and Bateson, N. 1962. A dependence interpretation of the effects of a severe initiation. *J. Pers.*, **30**, 633–649.
Schramm, W. and Carter, R. F. 1959. The effectiveness of a political telethon. *Publ. Opin. quart.*, **23**, 121–127.
Schutz, W. C. 1958. *FIRO: a three-dimensional theory of interpersonal behavior.* New York: Rinehart.
Scodel, A., Minas, J. S., Ratoosh, P. and Lipetz, M. 1959. Some descriptive aspects of two-person non-zero-sum games. I. *J. Conflict Resolut.*, **3**, 114–119.
Sears, D. O. and Freedman, J. L. 1963. Commitment, information utility, and selective exposure. *USN tech. Rep. (ONR),* NONR. 233 (54) NR 171–350, No. 12, August.
Sears, R. R. 1957. Identification as a form of behavioral development. In D. B. Harris (Ed.), *The concept of development.* Minneapolis: Univer. of Minnesota. pp. 147–161.
Sears, R. R., Pintler, Margaret H. and Sears, Pauline S. 1946. Effect of father separation on preschool children's doll play aggression. *Child Develpm.*, **17**, 219–243.
Seashore, S. E. 1954. *Group cohesiveness in the industrial work group.* Ann Arbor: Institute for Social Research.
Secord, P. F. and Backman, C. W. 1964. *Social psychology.* New York: McGraw-Hill.
Secord, P. F., Bevan, W. and Katz, B. 1956. The Negro stereotype and perceptual accentuation. *J. abnorm. soc. Psychol.*, **53**, 78–83.
Secord, P. F., Stritch, T. M. and Johnson, L. 1960. The role of metaphorical generalization and congruency in the perception of facial characteristics. *J. soc. Psychol.*, **52**, 329–337.

Shannon, C. E. and Weaver, W. 1949. *Mathematical theory of communication.* Urbana, Ill.: Univer. of Illinois.

Shaw, Marjorie E. 1932. A comparison of individuals and small groups in the rational solution of complex problems. *Amer. J. Psychol.,* **44,** 491–504.

Shaw, M. E. 1954. Some effects of problem complexity upon problem solution efficiency in different communication nets. *J. exp. Psychol.,* **48,** 211–217.

Shaw, M. E. 1964. Communication networks. In L. Berkowitz (Ed.), *Advances in experimental social psychology.* Vol. I. New York: Academic. pp. 111–147.

Shaw, M. E. and Rothschild, G. H. 1956. Some effects of prolonged experience in communication nets. *J. appl. Psychol.,* **40,** 281–286.

Shaw, M. E., Rothschild, G. H. and Strickland, J. F. 1957. Decision processes in communication nets. *J. abnorm. soc. Psychol.,* **54,** 323–330.

Sherif, M. 1935. A study of some social factors in perception. *Arch. Psychol.,* No. 187.

Sherif, M. and Hovland, C. I. 1961. *Social judgment: assimilation and contrast effects in communication and attitude change.* New Haven: Yale Univer.

Shipley, T. E. and Veroff, J. A. 1952. A projective measure of need for affiliation. *J. exp. Psychol.,* **43,** 349–356.

Shure, G. H., Meeker, R. J. and Hansford, E. A. 1965. The effectiveness of pacifist strategies in bargaining games. *J. Conflict Resolut.,* **9,** 106–117.

Sidowski, J. B. 1957. Reward and punishment in a minimal social situation. *J. exp. Psychol.,* **54,** 318–326.

Sidowski, J. B., Wycoff, L. B. and Tabory, L. 1956. The influence of reinforcement and punishment in a minimal social situation. *J. abnorm. soc. Psychol.,* **52,** 115–119.

Simmel, G. 1950. In K. H. Wolff (Ed. and Translator), *The sociology of Georg Simmel.* Glencoe, Ill.: Free Press. (Translated from *Soziologie, Untersuchungen über die Formen der Vergesellschaftung.* Leipzig: Duncker und Humblot, 1908.)

Singer, J. E., Brush, Claudia A. and Lublin, Shirley C. Some aspects of deindividuation: identification and conformity. *J. exp. soc. Psychol.,* **1,** 356–378.

Singer, J. E. and Shockley, V. L. 1965. Ability and affiliation. *J. Pers. soc. Psychol.,* **1,** 95–99.

Skinner, B. F. 1938. *The behavior of organisms.* New York: Appleton.

Skinner, B. F. 1953. *Science and human behavior.* New York: Macmillan.

Slater, P. E. 1955. Role differentiation in small groups. *Amer. Sociol. Rev.,* **20,** 300–310.

Smith, C. E. 1936. A study of the autonomic excitation resulting from the interaction of individual opinions and group opinion. *J. abnorm. soc. Psychol.,* **30,** 138–164.

Smith, E. E. 1961. The power of dissonance techniques to change attitudes. *Publ. Opin. quart.,* **25,** 626–639.

Snyder, A., Mischel, W. and Lott, Bernice E. 1960. Value, information, and conformity behavior. *J. Pers.,* **28,** 333–341.

Solley, C. M. and Murphy, G. 1960. *Development of the perceptual world.* New York: Basic.

Solomon, L. 1960. The influence of some types of power relationships and game strategies upon the development of interpersonal trust. *J. abnorm. soc. Psychol.,* **61,** 223–230.

Solomon, R. L. and Postman, L. 1952. Frequency of usage as a determinant of recognition thresholds for words. *J. exp. Psychol.,* **43,** 195–201.

Sommer, R. 1957. The effects of rewards and punishments during perceptual organization. *J. Pers.,* **25,** 550–559.

Spielberger, C. D. 1962. The role of awareness in verbal conditioning. In C. W. Eriksen (Ed.), *Behavior and awareness: a symposium of research and interpretation.* Durham, N.C.: Duke Univer. pp. 73–101.

Spielberger, C. D., Levin, S. M. and Shepherd, Mary. 1962. The effects of awareness and attitude toward the reinforcement on the operant conditioning of verbal behavior. *J. Pers.*, **30**, 106–121.
Staats, A. W. and Staats, C. K. 1958. Attitudes established by classical conditioning. *J. abnorm. soc. Psychol.*, **57**, 37–40.
Steiner, I. D. and Field, W. L. 1960. Role assignment and interpersonal influence. *J. abnorm. soc. Psychol.*, **61**, 239–245.
Steiner, I. D. and Fishbein, M. (Eds.) 1965. *Current studies in social psychology.* New York: Holt.
Stewart, R. H. 1965. Effect of continuous responding on the order effect in personality impression formation. *J. Pers. soc. Psychol.*, **1**, 161–165.
Stoner, J. A. F. 1961. A comparison of individual and group decisions involving risk. Unpublished M.A. thesis, M.I.T.
Stouffer, S. A., Suchman, E. A., De Vinney, L. C., Star, S. A. and Williams, R. M., Jr. 1949. *The American soldier: adjustments during army life.* Vol. 1 of *Studies in social psychology in World War II.* Princeton: Princeton Univer.
Stouffer, S. A., Lumsdaine, A. A., Lumsdaine, M. H., Williams, R. M., Jr., Smith, M. B., Janis, I. L., Star, S. A. and Cottrell, L. S., Jr. 1949. *The American soldier: combat and its aftermath.* Vol. 2 of *Studies in social psychology in World War II.* Princeton: Princeton Univer.
Strickland, L. H., Jones, E. E. and Smith, W. P. 1960. Effects of group support on the evaluation of an antagonist. *J. abnorm. soc. Psychol.*, **61**, 73–81.
Swanson, G. E., Newcomb, T. M. and Hartley, E. L. (Eds.) 1952. *Readings in social psychology.* (Second edition) New York: Holt.

Taffel, C. 1955. Anxiety and the conditioning of verbal behavior. *J. abnorm. soc. Psychol.*, **51**, 496–501.
Taft, R. 1954. Selective recall and memory distortion of favorable and unfavorable material. *J. abnorm. soc. Psychol.*, **49**, 23–29.
Tagiuri, R. 1958. Social preference and its perception. In R. Tagiuri and L. Petrullo (Eds.), *Person perception and interpersonal behavior.* Stanford: Stanford Univer. pp. 316–336.
Tagiuri, R., Blake, R. R. and Bruner, J. S. 1953. Some determinants of the perception of positive and negative feelings in others. *J. abnorm. soc. Psychol.*, **48**, 585–592.
Tannenbaum, P. H. 1966. Mediated generalization of attitude change via the principle of congruity. *J. Pers. soc. Psychol.*, **3**, 439–499.
Tarde, G. 1903. *The laws of imitation.* Translated, New York: Holt.
Taylor, D. W., Berry, P. C. and Block, C. H. 1958. Does group participation when using brainstorming facilitate or inhibit creative thinking? *Admin. Sci. quart.*, **3**, 23–47.
Taylor, F. K. 1956. Awareness of one's social appeal. *Hum. Relat.*, **9**, 47–56.
Thibaut, J. W. and Coules, J. 1952. The role of communication in the reduction of interpersonal hostility. *J. abnorm. soc. Psychol.*, **47**, 770–777.
Thibaut, J. W. and Faucheux, C. 1965. The development of contractual norms in a bargaining situation under two types of stress. *J. exp. soc. Psychol.*, **1**, 89–102.
Thibaut, J. W. and Kelley, H. H. 1959. *The social psychology of groups.* New York: Wiley.
Thibaut, J. W. and Riecken, H. W. 1955a. Authoritarianism, status, and the communication of aggression. *Hum. Relat.*, **8**, 95–120.
Thibaut, J. W. and Riecken, H. W. 1955b. Some determinants and consequences of the perception of social causality. *J. Pers.*, **24**, 113–133.

Thibaut, J. W. and Strickland, L. H. 1956. Psychological set and social conformity. *J. Pers.*, 25, 115–129.

Thistlethwaite, D. L. and Kamenetzky, J. 1955. Attitude change through refutation and elaboration of audience counter-arguments. *J. abnorm. soc. Psychol.*, 51, 3–12.

Thomas, E. J., Webb, S. and Tweedie, J. 1961. Effects of familiarity with a controversial issue on acceptance of successive persuasive communications. *J. abnorm. soc. Psychol.*, 63, 656–659.

Thorndike, E. L. 1920. A constant error in psychological ratings. *J. appl. Psychol.*, 4, 25–29.

Triplett, N. 1898. The dynamogenic factors in pacemaking and competition. *Amer. J. Psychol.*, 2, 507–533.

Tuddenham, R. D. and McBride, P. D. 1959. The yielding experiment from the subject's point of view. *J. Pers.*, 27, 259–271.

Verplanck, W. S. 1955. The control of the content of conversation: reinforcement of statements of opinion. *J. abnorm. soc. Psychol.*, 51, 668–676.

Verplanck, W. S. 1962. Unaware of where's awareness: some verbal operants—notates, monents, and notants. In C. W. Eriksen (Ed.), *Behavior and awareness: a symposium of research and interpretation*. Durham, N.C.: Duke Univer. pp. 130–158.

von Neumann, J. and Morgenstern, O. 1944. *Theory of games and economic behavior*. Princeton: Princeton Univer.

Vygotsky, L. S. 1962. *Thought and language*. (Ed. and translated by Eugenia Hanfmann and Gertrude Vakar.) New York: Wiley.

Wallach, M. A. and Kogan, N. 1965. The roles of information, discussion, and consensus in group risk taking. *J. exp. soc. Psychol.*, 1, 1–19.

Wallach, M. A., Kogan, N. and Bem, D. J. 1962. Group influence on individual risk taking. *J. abnorm. soc. Psychol.*, 65, 75–87.

Wallach, M. A., Kogan, N. and Bem, D. J. 1964. Diffusion of responsibility and level of risk taking in groups. *J. abnorm. soc. Psychol.*, 68, 263–274.

Wallach, M. A., Kogan, N. and Burt, R. B. 1965. Can group members recognize the effects of group discussion upon risk taking? *J. exp. soc. Psychol.*, 1, 379–395.

Walster, Elaine. 1964. The temporal sequence of post-decision processes. In L. Festinger, *Conflict, decision, and dissonance*. Stanford: Stanford Univer. pp. 112–127.

Walster, E. and Festinger, L. 1962. The effectiveness of "overheard" persuasive communications. *J. abnorm. soc. Psychol.*, 65, 395–402.

Walters, R. H., Banks, R. K. and Ryder, R. R. 1959. A test of the perceptual defense hypothesis. *J. Pers.*, 27, 47–55.

Walters, R. H. and Demkow, L. 1963. Timing of punishment as a determinant of response inhibition. *Child Develpm.*, 34, 207–214.

Walters, R. H. and Parke, R. D. 1964. Social motivation, dependency and susceptibility to social influence. In L. Berkowitz (Ed.), *Advances in experimental social psychology*. Vol. 1. New York: Academic. pp. 231–276.

Wapner, G. and Alper, Thelma G. 1952. The effect of an audience on behavior in a choice situation. *J. abnorm. soc. Psychol.*, 47, 222–229.

Warren, R. P. 1956. *Segregation, the inner conflict in the south*. New York: Random House.

Watson, J. B. 1925. *Behaviorism*. New York: Norton.

Watson, N. S. and Hartmann, G. W. 1939. The rigidity of a basic attitudinal frame. *J. abnorm. soc. Psychol.*, 34, 314–335.

Weik, K. E. 1964. Reduction of cognitive dissonance through task enhancement and effort expenditure. *J. abnorm. soc. Psychol.*, **68**, 533–539.
Weiss, W. 1957. Opinion congruence with a negative source on one issue as a factor influencing agreement on another issue. *J. abnorm. soc. Psychol.*, **54**, 180–186.
Wells, F. L. 1907. A statistical study of literary merit. *Arch. Psychol.*, **16**, No. 7.
White, R. W. 1959. Motivation reconsidered: the concept of competence. *Psychol. Rev.*, **66**, 297–334.
Whiting, J. W. M. 1959. Sorcery, sin and the superego: a cross-cultural study of some mechanisms of social control. In M. R. Jones (Ed.), *Nebraska symposium on motivation*. Lincoln: Univer. of Nebraska. pp. 174–195.
Whiting, J. W. M. 1960. Resource mediation and learning by identification. In I. Iscoe and H. W. Stevenson (Eds.), *Personality development in children*. Austin, Tex.: Univer. of Texas. pp. 112–126.
Whiting, J. W. M. and Child, I. L. 1953. *Child training and personality: a cross-cultural study*. New Haven: Yale Univer.
Whorf, B. L. 1956. *Language, thought, and reality*. Cambridge: Technology.
Whyte, W. H., Jr. 1956. *The organization man*. New York: Simon and Schuster.
Wilson, K. V. and Bixenstine, V. E. 1962. Forms of social control in two-person, two-choice games. *Behav. Sci.*, **7**, 92–102.
Winch, R. F. 1958. *Mate selection: a study of complementary needs*. New York: Harper and Row.
Winder, C. L., Ahmad, F. Z., Bandura, A. and Rau, L. 1962. Dependency of patients, psychotherapists' responses and aspects of psychotherapy. *J. consult. Psychol.*, **26**, 129–134.
Wishner, J. 1960. Reanalysis of "impressions of personality." *Psychol. Rev.*, **67**, 96–112.
Wispe, L. G. and Drambarean, N. C. 1953. Physiological need, word frequency and visual duration thresholds. *J. exp. Psychol.*, **46**, 25–31.
Wolfe, J. B. 1936. Effectiveness of token-rewards for chimpanzees. *Comp. Psychol. Monogr.*, **12**, No. 60.
Wrightsman, L. S., Jr. 1960. Effects of waiting with others on changes in level of felt anxiety. *J. abnorm. soc. Psychol.*, **61**, 216–222.

Yaryan, R. B. and Festinger, L. 1961. Preparatory action and belief in the probable occurrence of future events. *J. abnorm. soc. Psychol.*, **63**, 603–606.

Zajonc, R. B. 1960. The process of cognitive tuning in communication. *J. abnorm. soc. Psychol.*, **61**, 159–167.
Zajonc, R. B. 1965. Social facilitation. *Science*, **149**, 269–274.
Zajonc, R. B. 1966. *Social psychology: an experimental approach*. Belmont, Cal.: Wadsworth.
Zajonc, R. B. and Dorfman, D. D. 1964. Perception, drive, and behavior theory. *Psychol. Rev.*, **71**, 273–290.
Zander, A. 1944. A study of experimental frustration. *Psychol. Monogr.*, **56**, No. 256.
Zeigarnik, Bluma. 1927. Über das leehalten von erledigten und unerleigten Handbengen. *Psychol. Forsch.*, **9**, 1–85.
Zimbardo, P. G. 1960. Involvement and communication discrepancy as determinants of opinion conformity. *J. abnorm. soc. Psychol.*, **60**, 86–93.
Zimbardo, P. G. 1965. The effect of effort and improvisation on self-persuasion produced by role-playing. *J. exp. soc. Psychol.*, **1**, 103–120.
Zimbardo, P. G. and Formica, R. 1963. Emotional comparison and self-esteem as determinants of affiliation. *J. Pers.*, **31**, 141–162.

Zimbardo, P. G., Weisenberg, M., Firestone, I. and Levy, B. 1965. Communicator effectiveness in producing public conformity and private attitude change. *J. Pers.*, **33**, 233–256.

Zimmerman, Claire and Bauer, R. A. 1956. The effect of an audience upon what is remembered. *Publ. Opin. quart.*, **20**, 238–248.

Glossary

Action sequence The course of events traced from a confrontation of behavioral alternatives, through instrumental responses, to the attainment of outcomes.

Affect A general term for emotion or feeling.

Aggression Action taken by an organism, the main purpose of which is to cause injury (in a very broad sense) to another organism.

Anaclitic identification Identification arising out of the loss or threatened withdrawal of a love object. Closely related to *developmental identification*.

Assimilation In perception or judgment, a process by which a presented stimulus is experienced as more similar to a standard (or anchoring) stimulus than objective measurement would indicate. (See *contrast*.)

Asymmetrical contingency A type of dyadic interaction in which the responses of one person are mostly determined by his own plan for the interaction, while the responses of the second person are mostly determined by the responses of the first. The second person reacts, without a plan, to the planned responses of the first person.

Attribution process In person perception, the process of assigning stable, enduring characteristics to a person; of inferring dispositions from actions.

Attitude In the model presented in the book, an attitude is the result of combining a belief premise with a relevant value premise in a syllogism. Attitudes are essentially values derived from other values that are more basic or were internalized at an earlier point in development. (See *belief, value, cognitive category*.)

Authoritarian personality syndrome A set of attitudes and personality characteristics that have been found to occur together in prejudiced individuals. That is, a person who exhibits one of these characteristics (ethnic prejudice) is likely also to possess the others (latent hostility, deference to authority figures, etc.).

Bargaining The process by which persons or groups with partly conflicting and partly harmonious interests try to agree on a procedure for dividing available resources. Bargaining is likely to occur when each person controls resources desired by the other and a range of agreements can be made that will benefit both persons more than no agreement.

Behavior control In Thibaut and Kelley's analysis one person has behavior control over another when the level of outcome that the first can deliver is contingent on the other's response. The person cannot unilaterally control the level of outcome of the other as in *fate control*, but he can influence the other's behavior because if he chooses a particular response some responses available to the other will be rewarding whereas others will not.

Belief An assertion about the nature of objects in a *cognitive category* that is more than definitional. Since both objects and attributes fall in cognitive categories, a belief may be said to express the relations between two cognitive categories when neither defines the other.

Category accessibility A category is said to be highly accessible when apparent instances of the category are recognized and assigned on the basis of minimal information.

Catharsis In relation to the *frustration-aggression hypothesis*, catharsis refers to any hypothesized reduction in the instigation to aggression following the occurrence of any overt aggressive act. Sometimes used more generally to refer to the release of *emotion*.

Central trait A trait or disposition that plays a critical role in organizing an impression of a *stimulus person*, determining the way that other more peripheral traits are interpreted.

Centralized communication network A communication network in which one member has access to more channels of communication and thus is likely to process more information than other members who are in peripheral positions. (See *decentralized communication network*.)

Circular reactions A term introduced by Piaget that refers to a particular sequence of events noted in very young children. The infant emits a response, often quite accidentally, that produces some change in the environment; he will then repeat the response.

Classical conditioning A procedure in which a previously neutral event (the conditioned stimulus) is paired with an event (the unconditioned stimulus) that has the power to elicit a particular response (the unconditioned response). After a number of pairings the conditioned stimulus acquires the power to elicit a conditioned response (very like the unconditioned response) in the absence of the unconditioned stimulus. This procedure is to be distinguished from *instrumental learning*.

Clique A subgroup of members within a larger group, all of whom are more positively attracted to one another than they are to other members of the larger group. Cliques may be detected within a group by the use of a *sociometric questionnaire*.

Codability The accessibility of *cognitive categories* to which verbal labels are applied.

Cognitions Knowledge, interpretations, understandings, thoughts that an individual has about himself and the environment. A cognition is a discrete bit of knowledge, an element of understanding.

Cognitive balance Equivalent to *cognitive consistency* in Heider's model. Various combinations of unit and sentiment relations may be in or out of balance. A balanced relation is one in which, for example, things or persons perceived as belonging together are evaluated similarly.

Cognitive category A set of rules for classifying objects that are similar to one another. When a particular object is recognized as belonging to a certain category then its probable attributes can be ascribed on the basis of previous experience with objects in that same category.

Cognitive consistency The notion that a person's *cognitions* (*beliefs, values, attitudes*, etc.) will tend to be logically or psychologically consistent with one another. When this condition does not obtain, the person will experience discomfort or strain. The general consistency notion is basic to many models of attitude structure and change. (See *cognitive balance, cognitive dissonance, congruity*.)

Cognitive dissonance A term introduced by Festinger and used in the book to refer to the state of tension generated when a person holds two *cognitions* that are inconsistent with one another. Inconsistency, within the framework of dissonance theory, refers to cognitions that carry contradictory implications for behavior.

Cognitive process The process by which concepts, interpretations, and understandings are achieved.
Cohesiveness A property of a *group* that refers to its capacity to resist dissolution. Formally defined as the resultant of forces acting on members to remain in the group. A group is usually cohesive if the group members are attracted to one another.
Commitment Commitment exists to the extent that an action, decision, or *attitude* cannot be revoked, rescinded, or changed.
Comparative appraisal Evaluation of one's own relative standing with respect to an *attitude, belief,* ability, or *emotion* by observing the behavior of appropriate reference persons. These observations may be "at a distance," not requiring interaction between the reference persons and the evaluation seeker.
Comparison function A function of *reference groups,* in which the individual compares himself with a reference group in order to evaluate his own behavior and outcomes. (See *normative function.*)
Comparison level (CL) The level of reward, or positive outcomes, that a person expects based on his experience in previous relationships and interactions. Outcomes more positive than the comparison level are gratifying; those below comparison level are disappointing or frustrating. A concept used systematically by Thibaut and Kelley.
Comparison level for alternatives (CL_{alt}) The level of reward, or positive outcomes, that a person could realize in the best currently available alternative relationship. If a person's outcomes in a relationship fall below his comparison level for alternatives he will tend to leave the current relationship in favor of the more attractive alternative. This concept is used systematically by Thibaut and Kelley.
Compliance Overt *conformity* or the act of openly acceding to another's wishes. Usually contrasted with internalization, though overt compliance may or may not reflect private attitude change.
Conceptual conflict *Conflict* between *beliefs, attitudes,* thoughts, and ideas. A term used by Berlyne to denote a state of uncertainty or ambiguity that leads to *epistemic behavior.*
Concrete operations A stage of development posited by Piaget, including the period from about 18 months to 12 years. During this time the child develops language and cognitive ability, but operations are performed in concrete terms; abstract and symbolic manipulation are absent.
Conditioned avoidance response The result of a particular kind of *instrumental learning* in which the organism must emit a specific response in order to avoid a negative or painful event.
Conditioned stimulus See *classical conditioning.*
Conflict A state that obtains for an individual when he is motivated to make two or more mutually incompatible responses, as when we are attacked and experience both anger and fear, the first impelling us to return the attack and the second impelling us to flee.
Conformity A general term referring to adherence to a group *norm* concerning *beliefs, values, attitudes,* or behavior. Such adherence may reflect a variety of underlying psychological processes.
Congruity The key concept in Osgood and Tannenbaum's model of *cognitive consistency.* Congruity exists when two objects that are positively related in an assertion have the same evaluative meaning for the person, or when two negatively related objects have evaluative meanings of the same intensity but of opposite sign. When these conditions do not exist there will be in-

congruity and the evaluation of both objects involved will be changed in specifiable ways to attain a state of congruity.

Contact control Contact control exists in a relationship when one person's outcomes are determined more by his own selected responses than by the other person's, but these responses must be made within the relationship in order to be rewarding.

Contentives A class of words (nouns, verbs, adjectives) that are most crucial for conveying the semantic content of a statement. Words that convey the basic meaning of a communication as distinct from those conveying grammatical form. (See *functors*.)

Contrast In perception or judgment, a process by which a presented stimulus is experienced as less similar to a standard (or anchoring) stimulus than objective measurement would indicate. (See *assimilation*.)

Contrient interdependence A condition of group interdependence in which the actions necessary for the attainment of one individual's goals will have a negative effect on goal attainment by other group members. A condition that gives rise to competition.

Conversion of fate control The use of *fate control* to shape the behavior of another person (Thibaut and Kelley). This is done by responding positively when he emits a desired response and negatively when he emits an undesired response.

Co-action setting A performance setting in which two or more persons work simultaneously on the same problems in each other's presence or work in separate rooms but know that others are also working. The setting and instructions are so arranged that competition and opportunities for imitation are reduced to a minimum, making it possible to study the "pure" effects on performance of the presence of others.

Co-oriented peer Two persons are co-oriented peers when they face the same life situation, share similar *values*, or have the same basic interests and perspective.

Correspondence of outcomes In Thibaut and Kelley's analysis, the extent to which the outcomes obtained by group members vary together. When the outcomes of group members are correspondent cooperation will usually ensue. When outcomes do not correspond competition will develop, unless headed off by *normative control*.

Counter power In a dyad one person's power is the counter power confronting the other.

Credibility A characteristic of a communicator that, in part, determines his effectiveness in eliciting attitude change. A communicator's credibility is determined by the extent to which he is perceived by the audience as having expert knowledge (expertise) and *attitudes* and *values* similar to their own (*co-orientation* or trustworthiness).

Cue control The use of information about previously learned contingencies to trigger certain responses in another. Unlike the case of *outcome control*, the controlling person need not possess resources desired by the other; he need only provide a cue that elicits a habitual response sequence.

Culture A system of shared *beliefs*, *values*, symbols, artifacts, and performance styles that characterizes a *group*, community, or society.

Decentralized communication network A communication network in which all members have access to an equal number of communication channels, and thus all have an equal opportunity to acquire information from each other. (See *centralized communication network*.)

Decision structure The structure for group decision-making emerging over time in a problem-solving communication network. The extent to which the emergent decision structure is centralized is determined primarily by the structure of the communication network.

Defensive identification Similar to the concept of *identification with the aggressor*. The child internalizes attributes of more powerful and potentially threatening persons, partly to reduce his own powerlessness and partly to produce behavior that will gain him acceptance and protection. Both these ends are achieved by becoming like the more powerful person.

Deindividuation See *individuation*.

Dependence A term widely used in psychology to indicate one person's reliance on another for need satisfaction. In Thibaut and Kelley's analysis the extent to which one person's outcomes vary with another's responses. Dependence is thus the inverse of power. (See *effect dependence, information dependence, power.*)

Dependent variable Responses of subjects, or dimensions of such responses selected for study, that are expected to exhibit systematic change as a consequence of changes in the *independent variable*.

Developmental identification Identification arising out of the problem-solving and *reinforcement* experiences of childhood. The attributes of the *nurturant* parent are *internalized* because these attributes have acquired *secondary reinforcing power*. Closely related to *anaclitic identification*.

Deviate (noun) An individual who behaves in a manner other than that specified by the *group* or *culture* in which he is functioning. In research on communication and consensus in discussion groups, refers to anyone whose views are distinctly different from the mode or majority.

Displacement A phenomenon in which a response, such as *aggression*, is directed at an object other than its appropriate target.

Dispositions The more or less enduring characteristics of a person that, in combination with favorable circumstances, determine his actions.

Dynamism factor A cluster of attributes, applied to a person, that results from the combination of the potency and activity factors. (See *semantic space.*) Activity and potency are generally independent factors of meaning but tend to co-vary when social objects are being rated.

Effect dependence A subcategory of social *dependence* in which one person relies on another for the direct satisfaction of needs. The other person is, then, in a position to provide gratifying effects.

Effectance motivation A term used by White to describe the motivation behind responses that have as their only apparent purpose finding what effect such a response has on the environment.

Effort justification hypothesis Derived from Festinger's theory of *cognitive dissonance:* if an organism expends effort in order to obtain rewards and then finds that the rewards obtained are not sufficient for the effort expended, the organism will attempt to justify the effort by attaching *value* to some aspect of the environment in which the effort was expended.

Emotion A state or feeling, such as anger, fear, joy, or love, experienced by individuals for relatively brief periods of time. An emotion is, during its arousal, equivalent to a very strong *attitude*.

Empathic cognizance The process of understanding and being able to predict the particular actions of others so as to prepare our own responses to them.

Empathy The state of feeling-with-others; sharing the emotions or internal states of another person.

Empirical A descriptive term that indicates an appeal to reliable observations. Thus an empirical investigation is one in which observations of actual events are recorded and examined; an empirical fact is one obtained as the result of an empirical investigation.

Enactive mode A stage in cognitive and linguistic development in which the child identifies objects by describing the actions that can be performed with them (from Bruner).

Encode To transform information into a form that may then be transmitted.

Epistemic behavior Behavior of a sort (exploratory, investigative, or information seeking) that augments knowledge or reduces *conceptual conflict* (from Berlyne).

Error variance The unavoidable variation in responses of subjects who have experienced the same experimental *treatment*. Even though *stimulus* conditions have been objectively identical for all subjects receiving the same treatment, their responses will show some nonsystematic ("error") variation around an average value.

Expansive imitation The tendency of parents, in imitating their child's speech, to add *functors* (prepositions, adverbs, articles, and other grammatical parts of speech) omitted by the child.

Experiment A form of *empirical* research in which antecedent *stimulus* conditions are brought under the manipulative control of the investigator. This is in contrast to other kinds of empirical investigations in which the researcher does not control the relevant aspects of the environment but merely observes the events as they occur.

Experimental design Refers to the plan of an *experiment*. Specifies the way in which conditions will be varied and the comparisons that will be made. A good experimental design permits an unequivocal test of the hypothesis under consideration.

Expert (see page 720)

External stress A condition in a *group* when outcomes available in other relationships become attractive enough to some members to compete with those available within the group. When such a condition exists the high-power member or members may appeal to *norms* of loyalty in order to keep the low-power persons within the group.

External system An interrelated set of roles that develop in response to task and broader environmental requirements faced by the group.

Extinction The process that occurs when *reinforcement* is no longer given in a learning situation. In *instrumental learning* extinction begins when the organism no longer receives a reward after emitting the response that was previously reinforced; the probability of occurrence of the response then decreases. In *classical conditioning* the conditioned stimulus gradually loses its power to evoke the conditioned response when the unconditioned stimulus is no longer presented.

Fate control In Thibaut and Kelley's analysis one person has fate control over another when the responses selected by that person completely determine the level of outcome the other will receive. (See *behavior control*.)

Field experiment An *empirical* investigation that involves the manipulation of antecedent events in a natural setting, often by gaining the cooperation of administrators in a school or industry.

Formal operations The final stage of cognitive development according to Piaget. This stage begins at about 12 years and is characterized by the ability to use abstract and symbolic concepts. In this stage the form of an argument can be followed and divorced from the content.

Frustration Refers to the state of an organism prevented from obtaining some desired goal object or end-state. Usually produces instigation to *aggression* toward the frustrating agent, although aggression may not always occur.

Frustration-aggression hypothesis The hypothesis that *frustration* always produces a tendency toward (often called an instigation to) *aggression,* although, for a variety of reasons, overt aggression may be inhibited.

Functors A class of word forms (verb endings, auxiliary verbs, articles, prepositions) that serve a chiefly grammatical function in language. (See *contentives.*)

Genotype (see page 720)

Gradient of elicitation The relationship (in Miller's conflict model) between the strength of the aggressive response and the degree of similarity to the originally frustrating agent. As objects become less similar to the original frustrator the degree of instigation to *aggression* toward those objects decreases.

Gradient of inhibition The relationship (in Miller's conflict model) between the degree of similarity of objects to the original frustrator and the tendency to inhibit or refrain from *aggression* against that object. As objects become less similar to the original frustrator the tendency to inhibit aggression becomes less and aggression is more likely to occur. The gradient of inhibition falls off more steeply than the gradient of elicitation, thus permitting *displacement.*

Gradient of reinforcement Refers to the decreasing effectiveness of a reinforcer as the time between the response and the presentation of the *reinforcement* is increased.

Group An aggregation of persons becomes a group when all see their actions as interrelated and their fates to some extent interdependent. The members of a group usually expect that their continued affiliation will provide a means of obtaining desired goals.

Group locomotion The movement of a *group* toward whatever objective has been specified as the group goal. This movement may be accomplished by group discussion, group action, or other means appropriate to the particular group goal.

Group maintenance roles *Roles* within a group that develop primarily to insure that the group will have good morale and resist dissolution. In Thibaut and Kelley's analysis these are roles leading to behavior that keeps the group members above CL_{alt} in spite of periods when the costs incurred by performance of task functions are not immediately covered by rewards from task accomplishment.

Halo effect The tendency for trait ratings to show a higher intercorrelation than would be revealed by more objective measurement. Typically this tendency reveals itself in the attribution of favorable characteristics to a person who is already favorably evaluated and unfavorable characteristics to a person who is already unfavorably evaluated.

Horizontal structure (of an attitude) The horizontal structure of an *attitude* (in this book) results from the convergence of distinct syllogistic chains (*vertical structures*) in support of a single attitudinal conclusion. Such an attitude will be more resistant to change than an attitude that is the result of only one chain.

Iconic mode A stage in cognitive and linguistic development in which the child is able to recognize and reproduce objects on the basis of perceptual imagery, but cannot create new forms by applying abstract rules of language (from Bruner).

Identification The general process whereby one person takes on the attributes of another. The term is used in many specific senses that are defined elsewhere. (See *anaclitic, defensive, developmental,* and *incidental* identification; also, *identification with the aggressor.*)

Identification with the aggressor Taking on the attributes of a punitive or harmful person. Such *identification* is said to perform a defensive function by quelling anxieties and allowing the person, in fantasy, to take on the power of the aggressor. (See *defensive identification.*)

Incidental identification Actions or characteristics of a model that are reproduced by the imitator but are incidental to the task being done; that is, mannerisms, gestures, and irrelevant verbalizations.

Independence As applied in research on communication networks, the relative autonomy of a person in a central position. The comparative satisfaction of a central member is believed by some writers to derive from fulfillment of his needs for autonomy and independence.

Independent variable Conditions established or measured by an investigator that are assumed to be causally related to subsequent variations in the behavior of subjects exposed to them. (See *dependent variable.*)

Individual–deindividuation A dimension along which *groups* may vary reflecting the extent to which members respond to each other as individuals and recall who in the group did or said what.

Information dependence A subcategory of social dependence in which one person relies on another for information about the environment, its meaning, and the possibilities for action in it.

Information theory A measurement framework that specifies the amount of information contained in an event in terms of the proportion of uncertainty reduced.

Ingratiation A general term for the tactics engaged in by one person to make himself more attractive to another. Ingratiation may be considered a *strategy* by which a low-power person in a dyadic relationship may reduce the *power* differential.

Inhibition A constraint, usually internal, against emitting a particular response or class of responses. Thus a person may inhibit his aggressive responses, his sexual responses, and so forth.

Inoculation theory A theory that proposes that attitudes can be made resistant to change by "inoculating" the person with a weak form of counter-attitudinal arguments he will encounter later in a much stronger form.

Instrumental learning A procedure in which the organism must perform a certain response in order to receive a reward or *reinforcement.* A contingency is arranged so that immediately after the organism performs the desired response a reinforcement is presented. The probability of occurrence of the response is then increased—the organism becomes more likely to emit the response when placed in the same situation again. This procedure is to be distinguished from *classical conditioning.*

Insufficient deterrence hypothesis Derived from Festinger's theory of *cognitive dissonance:* the severity of a minimally sufficient deterrent is inversely related to degree of *internalization* of the prohibition. That is, the more mild the threatened punishment, assuming the individual refrains from the forbidden behavior, the more likely that the prohibitions will be internalized.

Interaction process analysis (IPA) A procedure developed by Bales for recording and analyzing the process of social interaction in a discussion *group.* An observer places each statement or idea unit into one of 12 formal content categories, noting who makes the remark and to whom it was made. These data may then be analyzed in order to reveal the *role* structure of the group and various interaction trends.

Internal anchor That *stimulus* in a series which is used by the judge as a reference point and to which he compares other stimuli in the series when judging them.

Internal stress A condition in a *group* when there is non*correspondence* of outcomes and in which the members have differential *power*. In such a case the low-power persons can be badly exploited unless there are *norms* of equity and fair sharing.

Internal system An interrelated set of *roles* that develop in response to internal *group* problems rather than to externally imposed task requirements. For example, interactions among group members directed toward task solution may create friendships and frictions. Insofar as these interactions become patterned and recurrent, friendships and frictions become part of the internal system.

Internalization Both a process and product of *socialization* in which *attitudes, beliefs,* and *values* are maintained in the absence of external controls, either rewarding or punishing.

Level of aspiration (LOA) Generally, the standard by which a person evaluates his own performance. This is usually determined partly by what the person would like to achieve and partly by realistic inference from his own past performance or other information.

Love-oriented discipline Techniques of discipline that exploit the child's fear that the parents will withdraw their love, isolate, or ostracize the child if he displeases them.

Manipulation When used with reference to an experiment in social psychology this term indicates the manner in which the experimenter systematically controls and varies *stimulus* conditions.

Minimax solution The response combination in a two-person *zero-sum game* that represents the best solution that either player can hope to obtain under the worst conditions that the other could create.

Mixed-motive game A certain class of *nonzero-sum games* in which the player must choose between increasing his own immediate gain or increasing the total gain of both players. The players' motives are a mixture of the desire to compete and the desire to form a partnership.

Mutual contingency A type of dyadic interaction in which the responses of each person are jointly determined by the responses of the other and by his own motivated plans. That is, the actions of both parties are to an important extent purposeful and self-determined, but each is responsive to the other.

Nonlove-oriented discipline Techniques of discipline that do not exploit the child's fear that the parents will withdraw their love, but that rely on physical rewards and punishments, or on techniques of shaming.

Nonzero-sum games Games in which one person's gain is not necessarily the other person's loss. That is, the sum of the outcomes to the players as a result of a particular response combination may be something other than zero. Includes mixed-motive as well as purely cooperative games.

Normative control The control of interaction by *norms* that establish rules for the division of rewards and costs among the members, thus avoiding recurrent interpersonal *bargaining*, the application of personal *power*, and informal social influence.

Normative function A function of a *reference group* in which the individual is evaluated by the group and rewards or punishments are applied depend-

716 FOUNDATIONS OF SOCIAL PSYCHOLOGY

ing on the degree to which the person conforms to its norms. Assumes that the person values or aspires to membership. (See *comparison function*.)

Norms Expected modes of behavior and *belief* that are established either formally or informally by a *group*. Positive and negative sanctions are usually applied for normative obedience and disobedience respectively. Norms guide behavior and facilitate interaction by specifying the kinds of responses expected and acceptable in a particular situation.

Nurturance A motive, or related behavior, directed toward caring for and providing aid and comfort to another.

Operant A response for which it is difficult to identify a particular eliciting *stimulus*, but which can be reinforced once it has been emitted. This kind of *reinforcement* procedure is called operant conditioning.

Orienting responses A set of responses that prepare the organism to receive and process information. Such responses as repositioning the body, dilating the pupils, flaring the nostrils, are included.

Outcome control One person's ability to determine directly the outcomes (rewards and punishments) of another, and therefore to exert influence over his behavior (differs from *cue control*).

Paradigm A general model for classifying variables and for analyzing and interpreting broad ranges of data in a scientific discipline. In psychology the S-O-R paradigm provides a general orientation that is useful in collecting and interpreting environment-behavior relations.

Partial reinforcement Denotes an arrangement of learning conditions such that *reinforcement* follows some but not all of the occurrences of the response being conditioned.

Participant observers Investigators who participate in the activities of a *group* or community to make detailed observations of ongoing processes of interaction.

Perceptual defense A concept used to account for the finding that a person will fail to perceive, take longer to identify, or incorrectly identify *stimuli* that have negative *value* for him.

Perceptual process A *cognitive process* that attempts to represent the current state of the environment. Usually refers to the process of depicting the physical characteristics of objects and events, and is distinguished from sensation on the one hand and interpretation on the other. (See *sensory process*.)

Perceptual vigilance Enhanced readiness to perceive certain stimuli that have information value for the person, including those that alert him to impending danger—in contrast to *perceptual defense*. (See *category accessibility*.)

Phenomenal self A person's awareness, arising out of his interactions with the environment, of his own *beliefs, values, attitudes,* the links between them, and their implications for his behavior.

Phenotype (see page 720)

Placebo A control *treatment*, especially in drug research, where an agent known to have no intrinsic effects is administered under the same conditions as the experimental drug.

Positivity effect The finding that there is a strong tendency to evaluate favorably others who have favorably evaluated us.

Power A person's power in a relationship is his capacity to influence others in that relationship. In Thibaut and Kelley's analysis this is determined by the range of outcomes through which he can move his partner, or by his *outcome control*. Power may also derive from *cue control*.

Primacy effect If early information is found to have a stronger influence than later information on *cognitions,* impressions, or *attitudes,* such a finding is called a primacy effect. (See *recency effect.*)

Primary reinforcement An event that reinforces a member of a given species without need of prior training. (See *reinforcement, secondary reinforcement.*)

Prior entry effect Refers to the increasing difficulty of changing the nature of *cognitive categories* as the categories grow to reflect more and more experience. Of two experiences of equal intensity, the earlier will do more to shape the category, the later will be more shaped by it.

Prisoner's dilemma game A particular form of *mixed-motive game* whose characteristics derive from the example of a situation in which a prisoner must decide whether to confess to a crime without knowing whether his partner has confessed. The crucial feature of such a game is that one player can gain the most by not confessing if the other player has not confessed but otherwise confession is the better *strategy.* A player's strategy thus reflects his trust in his partner.

Promotive interdependence A condition of group interdependence in which the members' fates are intertwined and they attain or do not attain their goals together. A condition that gives rise to cooperation. (See *correspondence of outcomes.*)

Pseudocontingency A type of dyadic interaction in which the responses of each participant reflect primarily the unfolding of self-determined plans and are not contingent on the other's responses.

Random A set of events is said to be random when the occurrence of any single event or subset of events is determined by chance and has an equal probability of occurring. A random sample, therefore, is a sample taken in such a way as to ensure that each member of the population being sampled has an equal chance of appearing in the sample.

Reactive contingency A type of dyadic interaction in which the responses of each participant are mostly determined by the last response of the other, without reference to any pre-established plan for the interaction.

Recency effect If later information is found to have a stronger influence than early information on *cognitions,* impressions, or *attitudes,* such a finding is called a recency effect. The opposite of a *primacy effect.*

Reductive imitation The tendency of a child to imitate only the *contentives* (nouns, verbs, etc.) in the parent's speech.

Reference groups Groups or classes of individuals that we use as standards to evaluate our *attitudes,* abilities, or current situation. (See *normative* and *comparison function, social comparison, comparative appraisal,* and *reflected appraisal.*)

Reflected appraisal Any evaluation of the self that is inferred from the behavior of other persons during interaction with them. The person inferring the evaluation typically does not directly ask another to evaluate him but judges his own value from subtle cues the other person reveals.

Refutational defense A technique used to develop a person's resistance to persuasive attacks that combines a mild form of the attack and a suitable refutation. The mild attack itself may be sufficient to stimulate effective resistance. (See *supportive defense.*)

Reinforcement An event that follows a response and increases the likelihood that the response will occur again.

Repression A psychoanalytic concept referring to the involuntary exclusion from consciousness of certain cognitions whose admission to consciousness would be painful for the person.

Risky shift The finding that after group discussion the individual members will privately recommend a less conservative course of action than they had privately espoused before.

Role Behavior that is characteristic and expected of a person or persons who occupy a position in the *group*. Such positions and their interrelations define the group structure.

Saddle point In a two-person *zero-sum game* the saddle point is the cell of the game matrix that represents, simultaneously, the lowest value in a row and the highest value in a column, considering only the entries below the diagonal in each cell. Because this value is the best a player can do under the worst and most probable conditions, it represents the *minimax solution* to the matrix. Not all matrices have a saddle point.

Sampling The process of obtaining a subset of subjects or observations from a larger population to serve as a basis for inferring certain characteristics of that population.

Saturation As applied in research on communication networks, the degree to which a position is overloaded with incoming information or the person in that position is faced with the necessity of communicating too rapidly with too many other positions.

Secondary reinforcement A *stimulus* or event that has been paired with a primary reinforcer over a number of trials and has acquired the power to function itself as a reinforcer. (See *reinforcement, primary reinforcement.*)

Semantic space A term used metaphorically to refer to the framework within which different dimensions of connotative meaning may be represented. Within Osgood's system any word or concept may be located on three dimensions: evaluation (good-bad), potency (weak-strong), and activity (activity-passive).

Sensorimotor operations A stage of development, posited by Piaget, including the first 18 months, in which the infant learns the concept of objects—that things exist even when they cannot be currently seen. Coordination of hand and eye movements also develops during this stage.

Sensory process Conversion of physical stimulus energy into neural energy by one of the sense organs. Distinguished in the text from *perceptual process*.

Sentiment relation A term used in Heider's balance model to denote the positive or negative evaluation of an object or person. Synonymous with the concept of *attitude*. (See *cognitive balance*.)

Social comparison The general process of reducing uncertainty about our *beliefs*, abilities, and *emotions* by observing the statements and performances of others. Festinger's theory of social-comparison processes is an attempt to interrelate such concepts as communication, competition, *conformity*, and rejection. (See *comparative appraisal, reflected appraisal*.)

Social reality A general term that refers to the information conveyed by others about the world around them, especially when they agree.

Socialization The *internalization* by individuals of *values, beliefs,* and ways of perceiving the world that are shared by a *group*.

Sociometric questionnaire A questionnaire in which group members are asked to indicate those members with whom they would most like to associate in some specified activity, as well as those they would like to exclude. The pattern of resulting choices can then be used to analyze the structure of the group in terms of mutual attraction between members, subgroup formations, *cliques*, and so on.

Status envy A concept used by Whiting as a determinant of *identification* and imitation. An individual will envy the status of those resource mediators who withhold resources from him, deprive him of resources that were formerly his, and consume or enjoy those resources.

Stereotype A class of objects is said to be steretoyped when identical characteristics are attributed to any object of that class, regardless of the actual degree of variation within the class. Familiar stereotypes are those sets of characteristics attributed to ethnic and racial groups. Stereotypes usually go along with a positive or negative evaluation of the class of objects.

Stimulus Any condition of or change in the physical or social environment to which a person can respond. Stimuli enter into contingencies with responses in the formation of habits and other *dispositions*.

Stimulus person In research on person perception the stimulus person is the target of attribution, perceptual judgment, or evaluation.

Strategy In the theory of games, a fully developed plan that specifies what a player will do under every conceivable situation during the game. More generally, a strategic decision is one that takes into account the current situation and the most probable future contingencies.

Stratification The process of dividing a larger population into distinctive subpopulations according to such criteria as social class, educational level, sex, or race. This is usually in preparation for *sampling* and is done to insure that these subpopulations are all represented in the sample. This procedure is called "stratified random sampling."

Supportive defense A technique used to develop a person's resistance to persuasive attacks in which the subject receives arguments that support his belief prior to the attack. (See *refutational defense*.)

Symbolic mediation The general role of language and other symbols in facilitating association among *cognitions*. Used in this book to explain the ability of organisms to bridge the delay between response and *reinforcement*.

Symbolic mode A stage in cognitive and linguistic development in which the child is able correctly to form concepts or say things he has neither said before nor heard said, by combining words according to rules of usage (from Bruner).

Task roles Roles within a group governing primarily those actions that must be taken so that the group may accomplish its task. Closely related to the concept of *external system*.

Temporal extension In person perception when a characteristic that is momentarily revealed is assumed by the perceiver to be an enduring attribute.

Treatments In social psychological experimentation, the distinctive *stimulus* configurations that the experimenter creates and to which he allows his subjects to respond. Treatments are the result of combining various *independent variables* within a meaningful *experimental design*. For example, an experimenter may combine high or low communicator *credibility* and large or small communication discrepancy (as independent variables) to study the effects on the amount of attitude change shown by subjects who experience these combinations.

Unconditioned stimulus See *classical conditioning*.

Unequivocal behavior orientation (UBO) An orientation of the person toward his decisions and commitments that permits effective and nonconflicted action. As a consequence of this orientation, foregone alternatives tend to be deprecated and the value of the chosen course of action enhanced.

Unit relation A term used in Heider's balance model to denote the cognitive association or dissociation of two objects. If the two objects are seen as associated or belonging together the unit relationship is positive, if they are seen as dissociated the unit relationship is negative.

Value Refers to a broad class of motivational phenomena. Anything that a person approaches, desires, or espouses is a positive value; anything that he avoids, dislikes, or deplores is a negative value. A value exists whenever an *emotion* implying either liking or disliking attaches to a *cognition*.

Value appeals An attempt to change an *attitude* by changing the value premise in the attitude structure.

Value expansion The process of increasing the range of rewarding or punishing *stimuli* that may be effective in controlling behavior. This process derives from *secondary reinforcement*.

Veridicality A property of *perceptions*. Veridical perceptions are those that are confirmed by increased contact with the objects perceived, and especially by precise physical descriptions and measurements.

Vertical structure (of an attitude) The vertical structure of an attitude (in this book) is the chain of syllogisms that leads both logically and developmentally to the final attitude. In such a structure the *beliefs* or *attitudes* resulting from prior syllogisms are used as belief or value premises in subsequent ones. (See *horizontal structure*.)

Zeigarnik Effect A finding, named for its discoverer, that a person has greater recall for tasks that have been interrupted and left uncompleted than for those that have been completed.

Zero-sum game A game in which the outcomes of the players sum to zero, so that on any given play one player gains precisely the amount that has been lost by his opponent. In this sense such games are purely competitive.

Expert Someone who has superior knowledge relative to the person of how to move from one state to another in an action sequence.

Genotype The underlying theoretical factor assumed to be involved in some behavior and to be able, at least in part, to explain that behavior. A theoretical construct which can appear as different *phenotypes*.

Phenotype The surface appearance of some aspect of behavior that the psychologist must relate to some theoretical construct, i.e., a *genotype*.

Author Index

Abelson, R. P., 167, 168, 169, 170, 174, 183, 682, 700
Adams, J. S., 208, 211, 682, 696
Ader, R., 603, 682
Adorno, T. W., 173, 682
Ahmad, F. Z., 542, 705
Allen, V. L., 215, 216, 217, 420, 682
Allport, F. H., 3, 230, 333, 512, 601–603, 606, 628, 682
Allport, G. W., 2, 87, 162, 251, 254, 682
Allyn, Jane, 475–479, 682
Alper, Thelma G., 244, 606, 682, 704
Anderson, L. R., 483, 682
Anderson, N. H., 277, 278, 682
Aneshansel, Jane, 246, 247, 693
Argyle, M., 394, 682
Aristotle, 433–434, 436, 446, 449, 451–452, 456–457, 683
Aronfreed, J., 99, 100, 683
Aronson, E., 30, 32, 40, 48, 50, 51, 53, 60, 67, 69, 72, 89, 90, 91, 101, 102, 103, 104, 198, 223, 224, 246, 285, 286, 378, 442, 443, 463–464, 500, 683, 687, 698
Asch, S. E., 270–274, 277, 278, 387, 388, 390–394, 396, 398, 400, 401, 403, 405, 406, 417, 418, 419, 420–422, 429, 438, 683
Atkinson, J. W., 233, 676, 697
Azrin, W. M., 540, 549, 683

Bach, G. R., 115, 683
Back, K. W., 252, 336, 338, 341–343, 353, 683, 689
Backman, C. W., 260, 701
Baer, D. M., 543–546, 581, 690
Bales, R. F., 658–660, 662–664, 666, 668, 671, 683
Bandura, A., 99, 108, 109, 111, 112, 113, 116, 117, 129, 130, 542, 683, 684, 705
Banks, R. K., 237, 704

Barnard, C. I., 654, 656, 684
Barnlund, D. C., 594–598, 684
Barrios, A. A., 277, 682
Bartlett, F. C., 243, 250, 254, 684
Bass, B. M., 671, 684
Bates, F. L., 177, 684
Bateson, N., 32, 53, 701
Bauer, R. A., 248, 706
Bavelas, A., 615, 672, 675, 684
Becker, L. A., 445, 685
Bellugi, Ursula, 146, 147, 149, 685
Bem, D. J., 628–633, 636–638, 684, 704
Bennett, Edith B., 335, 616, 682
Berelson, B., 196, 695
Bergin, A. E., 439, 441–442, 684
Berkowitz, L., 293, 295, 368, 465–466, 614, 693
Berkowitz, M. I., 291, 684
Berlyne, D. E., 121, 122, 123, 124, 125, 154, 684
Berry, P. C., 595, 703
Berscheid, Ellen, 300, 301, 687
Bettleheim, B., 112, 113, 684
Bevan, W., 140, 701
Bixenstine, V. E., 563, 569–570, 684, 685, 705
Blake, R. R., 64, 284, 395, 698, 703
Blau, P. M., 652, 670–671, 685
Blevans, S. A., 215, 218, 219, 690
Block, C. H., 595, 703
Borgatta, E. F., 287, 696
Bos, Maria C., 596, 685
Bowerman, C., 287, 685
Braden, Marcia, 24, 210, 691
Braine, M. D. S., 147, 150, 151, 156, 685
Braithwaite, R. B., 36, 685
Brehm, J. W., 190, 191, 206, 207, 212, 213, 214, 215, 492, 494, 497–498, 500–502, 616, 685–687, 700
Brock, T. C., 199, 445, 453, 685, 692

Brodbeck, May, 201, 208, 369, 685
Bronfenbrenner, U., 105, 106, 685
Brooks, Virginia, 238, 691
Brown, D. R., 699, 700
Brown, J. S., 88, 685
Brown, R., 153
Brown, R. W., 137, 138, 144, 146–147, 149, 150, 152–154, 156, 235, 540, 638, 685, 691
Bruner, J. S., 132, 134, 137, 138, 139, 144, 145, 149, 230, 231, 234, 236, 240, 272, 273, 284, 685, 699, 703
Brush, Claudia A., 626–627, 702
Burdick, H., 252, 254, 701
Burnstein, E., 296, 297, 686
Burt, R. B., 637, 704
Busiek, R. D., 139, 144, 685
Byrne, D., 689

Campbell, Enid H., 453, 692
Campbell, D. T., 59, 162, 453–456, 686, 697, 698
Campbell, J., 595, 688
Canon, L. K., 201, 202, 203, 246, 686
Cantril, H., 13–16, 686
Carlsmith, J. M., 60, 67, 101, 102, 103, 104, 442, 463–464, 491–494, 496–497, 683, 686, 689
Carlson, E. R., 459, 468, 686
Carmichael, L., 139, 686
Carroll, J. B., 153
Carter, R. F., 197, 701
Cartwright, D., 166, 303, 686
Casagrande, J. B., 153
Centers, R., 540–541, 686
Chapman, I. W., 326, 362, 686
Charwat, W., 291, 691
Chein, I., 232, 233, 695
Cherry, C., 127, 135, 136, 141, 686
Child, I. L., 92, 108, 110, 111, 686, 705
Clark R. A., 697
Cline, M. G., 257, 686
Coch, L., 615–617, 686
Cohen, A. R., 190, 191, 206–207, 214–215, 291, 296, 300, 439, 465, 467, 484, 492–494, 496–498, 500, 545, 581, 616, 685, 686, 687, 700
Cohen, D., 596, 687
Cohen, M. R., 36, 434, 687
Cole, Ann H., 500–502, 685
Collins, B. E., 496–497, 686
Condry, J. C., 511, 694
Consalvi, C., 415, 691

Cooley, C. H., 323, 687
Cooper, E., 457, 469, 494, 495, 687
Cottingham, D. R., 465, 466, 484
Cottrell, L. S., Jr., 703
Coules, J., 292, 293, 294, 703
Cromwell, H., 452, 687
Crutchfield, R. S., 162, 393, 420, 682, 687

Dahlke, A. E., 511, 694
Dailey, C. A., 279, 687
Darley, J. M., 300, 301, 378, 687
Dashiell, J. F., 593, 601–602, 687
Daugherty, B. N., 289, 693
Davidson, J. R., 217, 687
Davis, J. H., 280, 281, 599, 687
Davis, K. E., 264, 265, 269, 284, 288, 297, 304, 305, 587–588, 687, 693, 694
Day, B., 287, 685
deCharms, R., 67, 298, 693
Dembo, Tamara, 363, 695
Demkow, L., 99, 704
Deutsch, M., 27, 28, 29, 30, 73, 215, 284, 285, 309, 314–315, 322, 393, 395, 398, 403, 407–410, 419–421, 452–453, 562–564, 567, 572, 576–577, 609–611, 622, 679, 687, 688
De Vinney, L. C., 703
Dickoff, Hilda, 285, 688
Dickson, W. J., 54, 655, 700
Dinerman, H., 457, 687
Distler, L., 113, 698
Dittes, J. E., 413, 415, 416, 417, 688
DiVesta, F. J., 459, 688
Dollard, J., 88, 129, 130, 290, 292, 623, 688, 697
Doob, L., 162, 290, 292, 574, 688, 696
Dorfman, D. D., 479, 688, 705
Drambarean, N. C., 233, 705
Dreyer, A., 362–363, 688
Dulany, D. E., Jr., 237, 688
Dunnette, M. D., 595, 688
Durkheim, E., 331, 332, 335, 652, 688

Ebbinghaus, H., 242, 453, 688
Edwards, A. L., 244, 688
Ehrlich, D., 197, 688
Ellertson, N., 612–614, 701
Emerson, R. M., 346, 688
Eriksen, C. W., 230, 542, 688, 702–704
Ewing, T., 474, 688

Faigin, Helen, 111, 688
Farina, A., 284, 693

AUTHOR INDEX

Faucheux, C., 646, 647, 650, 651, 703, 704
Fauconnet, P., 262, 685
Feather, N. T., 171, 199, 688, 689
Feshbach, S., 293, 460–466, 689, 692
Festinger, L., 22, 26, 42, 88, 89, 90, 101, 104, 118, 188, 190, 191, 192, 204, 206, 207, 209, 216, 217, 220, 223, 309–312, 313, 315, 318, 326, 336, 338, 339, 340, 341, 347, 349–354, 361, 362, 363, 365, 366, 367, 369, 444–446, 475–479, 491–494, 496, 607, 624–626, 682, 683, 686, 687, 689, 691, 692, 693, 695, 701, 704, 705
Field, W. L., 266, 703
Firestone, I., 66, 498, 706
Fishbein, M., 161, 689, 690, 703
Fisher, S., 398, 399, 420, 441, 689
Flavell, John H., 143
Fleming, W. H., 497–498, 686, 689
Florquist, Carolie C., 587–588, 687
Formica, R., 382, 705, 706
Franklin, Muriel, 617, 695
Freeman, R. W., 420, 689
Freedman, J. L., 101, 102, 103, 104, 203, 211, 246, 478, 689, 701
French, J. R. P., Jr., 615–617, 686
Frenkel-Brunswick, Else, 173, 682
Freud, Anna, 106, 690
Freud, S., 86, 87, 105, 230, 290, 690
Fry, D. B., 136
Funk, W. H., 596, 687

Gallo, P. S., 30, 576–577, 690
Gaudet, H., 196, 695
Gerard, H. B., 50, 53, 72, 195, 200, 215, 218, 219, 223, 225, 309, 314, 315, 351, 352, 355, 357, 359, 363, 369, 374, 376, 377, 380, 382, 393, 395, 398, 402–404, 405–406, 407–410, 419–423, 426, 453, 483, 616, 687, 689, 690
Gergen, K. J., 265, 284, 574, 583, 584, 693, 696
Geutzkow, H., 683
Gewirtz, J. L., 543–546, 581, 690
Gilchrist, J. C., 233, 690
Gilligan, Carol, 96–98, 698
Gilmore, J. B., 492–493, 496, 692, 693
Gladstone, A. I., 470, 480, 692
Glass, D. C., 305, 690
Glueck, Eleanor, 111, 690
Glueck, S., 111, 690
Goldberg, S. C., 401, 439, 690
Goldiamond, I., 540, 683

Goldstein, M. J., 462, 691
Golden, B. W., 443, 683
Gollin, E. S., 278, 691
Goodman, Cecile C., 234, 685
Graham, F., 291, 691
Greenbaum, C. W., 405–406, 488, 545, 581, 687, 690, 691
Greenspoon, J., 539, 691
Gregory, D., 612–614, 701
Gross, A. E., 672, 684
Grunes, W. F., 271, 691
Gumpert, P., 584, 693
Gurnee, H. A., 598, 691
Guttman, J., 197, 688

Haire, M., 271, 691
Hamblin, R. L., 668–670, 691
Hansford, E. A., 569, 702
Harary, F., 166, 303, 686
Hardyck, Jane A., 24, 210, 691
Hare, A. P., 604, 691
Harris, D. B., 701
Harris, V. A., 267, 693
Hartley, E. L., 82, 153, 683, 693, 696, 701, 703
Hartmann, G. W., 244, 704
Harvey, O. J., 301, 322, 415, 441, 471, 472, 474, 691, 692
Hastorf, A. H., 672, 684
Hatfield, R. O., 239, 691
Hayden, R., 278, 699
Hebb, D., 370
Heider, F., 165, 166, 167, 168, 174, 259, 261, 262, 263, 268, 284, 299, 300, 302, 303, 691
Heise, G. A., 136, 697
Helmreich, R. K., 496–497, 686
Hemphill, J. K., 668, 691
Heron, W., 370, 684, 691
Hess, E. H., 218, 691
Hester, S. L., 284, 693
Hildum, D. C., 540, 691
Hill, A. H., 511, 694
Hochbaum, G. M., 356, 357, 691
Hochberg, J., 238, 691
Hoffman, L. R., 593, 691
Hoffman, P. J., 365–366, 691
Hogan, H. P., 139, 686
Hollander, E. P., 412, 415–416, 691
Hollenberg, Eleanor, 111, 691
Holz, W., 540, 683
Homans, G. C., 528, 654–656, 691, 692
Honig, A., 291, 691

Horowitz, A. E., 153
Horwitz, M., 617, 620, 621, 692
Hovland, C. I., 139, 172, 433, 437–440, 441, 447–449, 453, 455–457, 471–472, 474, 480, 686, 692, 694, 696, 700, 702
Howes, D. H., 137, 692
Hubert, S., 278, 682
Hull, C. L., 331, 692
Hunt, J. McV., 695
Hunt, W. A., 140, 692
Huston, A. C., 108, 109, 113, 116, 684
Hyman, H. H., 81, 313, 692
Hyman, R., 607, 701
Hymovitch, B., 228, 352–354, 369, 683, 689

Insko, C. A., 456, 692
Iscoe, I., 705
Itard, J. M. G., 6, 7, 8, 692
Ittelson, W. H., 134, 692

Jaastad, Kay, 595, 688
Jahoda, Marie, 469, 687
James, W., 382, 692
Janis, I. L., 433, 450, 455, 460–466, 470, 480, 485–488, 492–493, 496, 686, 692, 694, 696, 700, 703
Jecker, J. D., 215, 216, 217, 692, 693
Johnson, L., 261, 701
Jones, E. E., 67, 246, 247, 264, 265, 267, 269, 284, 289, 295, 297, 298, 304, 305, 408–410, 464, 494, 582–584, 586, 687, 693, 703
Jones, M. R., 687, 694, 705
Jones, R. G., 583, 586, 693
Jones, S., 695
Jordan, N., 302, 693

Kahn, R. L., 615, 693
Kamenetsky, J., 451, 704
Kaplan, A., 36, 70, 73, 74, 693
Kastenbaum, A., 278, 693
Katz, B., 140, 701
Katz, D., 170, 615, 693
Kelleher, R. T., 122
Kelley, H. H., 73, 82, 271, 272, 301, 302, 309, 312–314, 315, 322, 352–354, 359, 360, 369, 397, 404, 412–415, 416, 417, 433, 456, 511, 515–516, 522–523, 525, 527, 528, 530–531, 533, 535, 551–556, 573, 580–581, 592–595, 600, 608–610, 616, 638, 644–645, 652, 654, 656–658, 666, 683, 688, 689, 691, 692–694, 700, 703
Kelman, H. C., 112, 439–440, 490, 694
Kerckhoff, A., 288, 694
Kiesler, Sara B., 217, 687
Kimble, G. A., 85, 515, 694
King, B. T., 485–488, 692, 694
Kite, W. R., 672, 684
Kitt, A., 82, 313, 320, 697
Klein, G. S., 230
Kluckhohn, C., 178, 694
Koch, Helen L., 228, 695
Koch, H., 12
Koch, S., 228, 694
Kogan, N., 303, 628–633, 636–638, 684, 694, 704
Kohler, R., 247, 693
Komorita, S. S., 568, 694
Korchin, S. S., 244, 682
Krauss, R. M., 27, 28, 29, 30, 73, 215, 562, 576–577, 688
Krech, D., 162, 694
Kubzansky, P. E., 691
Kuhn, T. S., 46, 694

Lair, W. S., 106, 695
Lamb, T. W., 397, 694
Lambert, W. E., 599, 604, 697, 699
Lambert, W. W., 234, 695
Latane, B., 206, 207, 366, 378, 616, 687, 695, 700
Lave, L. B., 569, 573, 695
Lawrence, D. H., 88, 89, 90, 118, 223, 365, 366, 691, 695
Lazarsfeld, P. F., 34, 196, 695, 697
Leavitt, H. J., 675–676, 695
LeBon, G., 331, 332, 695
Lenneberg, E., 137, 138, 144, 685
Leventhal, H., 463–464, 465–467, 695
Levin, H., 111, 695
Levin, S. M., 543, 703
Levine, J. M., 244, 247, 695
Levine, R., 232, 233, 695
Levinson, D. J., 173, 682
Levy, B., 66, 498, 706
Lewin, K., 4, 51, 65, 187, 189, 316–318, 333–335, 336, 340, 341, 363, 385, 615, 617, 695
Lewis, Helen B., 617–618, 695
Libo, L. M., 369, 427, 695
Lichten, W., 136, 697
Leiderman, P. H., 690, 691, 695
Lifton, R. J., 19, 20, 21, 22, 695

Linder, D., 285, 286, 495, 683
Lindzey, G., 287, 593, 682, 683, 686, 694, 696
Lipetz, M., 567, 701
Lippitt, R., 4, 65, 695
Lipsher, D., 542, 684
Long, J., 237, 697
Loomis, J. L., 565, 696
Lorge, I., 438, 594, 696
Lott, Bernice E., 401, 702
Lowell, E. L., 697
Lowenfeld, J., 238, 696
Lubin, A., 398, 399, 401, 441, 689, 690
Lublin, Shirley C., 626–627, 702
Luce, R. D., 562, 696
Luchins, A. S., 271, 277, 696
Lumsdaine, A. A., 447–449, 450, 470, 480, 692, 696, 703
Lumsdaine, M. H., 703
Lund, F. H., 452, 453, 696
Lynn, D. B., 116, 696

Maccoby, Eleanor E., 113, 114, 115, 131, 153, 208, 476–478, 683, 689, 696, 701
Maccoby, N., 208, 696
MacKinnon, D. W., 110, 696
Maier, N. R. F., 615, 696
Malcolm, T., 215, 218, 219, 690
Malewski, A., 219, 696
Mandell, W., 172, 456–457, 692
Mangan, G. L., 239, 696
Mansson, H. H., 545, 581, 687
Marak, G. E., 670, 696
Marlowe, D., 567, 574, 696, 698
Marquart, Dorothy I., 598, 696
Mathewson, G. C., 50, 53, 72, 223, 225, 690
Mausner, B., 401, 696
McBride, P. D., 392, 704
McBride, Dorothy, 612–614, 701
McClelland, D. C., 87, 88, 98, 230, 233, 696, 697
McCurdy, H. G., 599, 697
McDougall, W., 2, 3, 697
McGinnies, E., 230, 236, 237, 697, 699
McGuire, W. J., 172, 478–485, 488, 697, 698
McNamara, H. J., 237, 697
Mead, G. H., 485
Meeker, R. J., 569, 702
Melikian, L., 97, 697
Mensch, I. N., 271, 697
Menzel, H., 417, 697

Merton, R. K., 82, 313, 320, 697
Merwin, J. C., 459, 688
Messé, L. A., 568, 576, 697
Metzner, R., 96, 97, 698
Milholland, H. C., 462, 692
Miller, G. A., 136, 137, 697
Miller, N., 453–456, 697
Miller, N. E., 88, 93, 94, 129–130, 290, 623, 688, 697
Miller, P., 542, 684
Mills, J., 30–32, 40, 48, 50, 51, 53, 72, 89, 103, 197, 198, 200, 201, 202, 204, 223, 224, 246, 300, 301, 683, 688, 697, 698
Minas, J. S., 567, 568, 698, 701
Minturn, A. Leigh, 139, 144, 685
Mintz, A., 510-511, 698
Mirels, H., 300, 301, 698
Mischel, W., 96–98, 364, 401, 698, 702
Mittman, L. R., 123, 698
Morgenstern, O., 556, 704
Moore, H. T., 333, 698
Morrissette, J. O., 303, 698
Mouton, Jane S., 64, 395, 698
Mowrer, O. H., 95, 96, 106, 107, 290, 292, 688, 698
Mulder, M., 677–678, 698
Murchison, C., 162, 376, 593, 682, 687, 698
Mundy, D., 551–556, 694
Murphy, G., 230–233, 235, 244, 247, 695, 699, 701, 702
Murray, E. J., 541, 698, 699
Murray, H. A., 110, 260, 696, 698
Mussen, P. H., 113, 698

Nagel, E., 36, 434, 687
Nash, M., 130, 698
Nesberg, L. S., 233, 690
Newcomb, T. M., 81, 82, 153, 166, 281, 282, 284, 287, 288, 295, 360, 624–626, 683, 689, 693, 696, 698, 699, 701, 703
Niles, P., 463–464, 695
Norfleet, Barbara, 671, 699

Olmstead, J. A., 64, 395, 698
Orne, M. T., 331, 699
Orwant, Carol, 561, 700
Osborn, A. F., 595, 699
Osgood, C. E., 168, 169, 174, 242, 274, 275, 276, 699

Paivio, A., 604, 699
Papageorgis, D., 478–479, 481–484, 697

Parke, R. D., 545, 704
Parsons, T., 683
Pastore, N., 295, 296, 699
Pavlov, I. P., 121, 434, 699
Pepitone, A., 278, 293, 294, 624–626, 689, 699
Pessin, J., 603–604, 699
Petrullo, L., 686, 703
Piaget, J., 122, 143, 243, 699
Pierce, C., 48
Pintler, Margaret H., 115, 701
Postman, L., 137, 138, 139, 230, 235, 236, 237, 251, 254, 682, 685, 698, 699, 702
Potash, H. M., 569, 684, 685
Potter, S., 580, 699
Precker, J. A., 287, 699
Proshansky, H., 235, 699
Pustell, T. E., 239, 700

Rabbie, J. M., 374, 377, 380, 498, 690, 700
Rabinowitz, L., 554, 556, 700
Radloff, R., 366, 370, 376, 551–556, 694, 700
Raiffa, H., 562, 696
Rapoport, A., 557, 559–561, 700
Ratoosh, P., 567, 701
Rau, L., 542, 705
Raven, B. H., 352–354, 369, 395, 689, 700
Rawson, H., 567, 698
Razran, G. H. S., 459, 700
Reber, A., 100, 683
Reece, M. M., 238, 700
Reichling, G., 293, 294, 699
Restle, F. A., 599, 687
Riecken, H. W., 22, 66, 209, 283, 291, 292, 294, 298, 573, 586, 672, 689, 700, 703
Robinson, H., 198, 246, 294, 698
Rodrigues, J., 139, 685
Roethlisberger, F. J., 54, 655, 700
Rokeach, M., 158, 700
Romney, A. K., 208, 696
Rosen, A. C., 237, 238, 700
Rosen, S., 199, 700
Rosenau, N., 215, 688
Rosenberg, M. J., 56, 163, 164, 167–171, 174, 183, 468, 493–495, 682, 698, 700
Rosenblatt, R. M., 554, 556, 700
Rosenthal, R., 55, 549, 700
Ross, D., 113, 116, 117, 684
Ross, E. A., 2, 3, 700
Ross, S. A., 113, 116, 117, 684
Rothman, G., 158, 700
Rothschild, G. H., 676, 702

Rotter, G. S., 422, 690
Roy, D. F., 656, 700
Rubenstein, I., 420, 689
Ryder, R. R., 237, 704

Sait, E. M., 691
Saltzman, I. J., 85, 701
Samelson, F., 401, 701
Sanford, R. N., 173, 232, 682, 701
Sapir, S., 152
Sapolsky, A., 545, 701
Sarnoff, I., 380, 701
Sawrey, W. L., 116, 696
Sawyer, J., 568, 576, 697
Schachter, S., 22, 53, 209, 252, 254, 336, 338, 343, 345, 346, 371–377, 382–385, 607, 612–614, 683, 689, 701
Schafer, E., 235, 701
Schein, E. H., 112, 533, 701
Schelling, T. C., 562, 566, 701
Schneider, B., 137, 699
Schonbach, P., 197, 688
Schopler, J., 32, 53, 701
Schramm, W., 197, 701
Schutz, W. C., 545, 701
Scodel, A., 567, 698, 701
Sears, D. O., 203, 211, 478, 689, 701
Sears, Pauline, 363, 695, 701
Sears, R. R., 107, 109, 115, 290, 292, 688, 701
Seashore, S. E., 614, 701
Secord, P. F., 140, 260, 261, 701
Shannon, C. E., 124, 702
Shapiro, D., 272, 685, 690, 695, 696
Shapiro, M. M., 301, 322, 412, 414, 691, 694
Shaw, M. E., 676, 702
Shaw, Marjorie E., 597–598, 675–678, 702
Sheffield, F. D., 447–449, 692
Shepherd, Mary, 543, 703
Sherman, H., 237, 697
Sherif, M., 139, 333, 441, 471, 472, 474, 692, 702
Shils, A., 683
Shipley, T. E., 605, 702
Shockley, V. L., 370, 702
Shure, G. H., 569, 573, 574, 702
Sidowski, J. B., 549–553, 556, 702
Simmel, G., 651, 702
Singer, J. E., 370, 382–385, 626–627, 701, 702
Singer, R. P., 464–467, 695
Skinner, B. F., 508–509, 530, 538, 702

Slater, P. E., 658–660, 662–664, 683, 702
Smith, C. E., 402, 403, 404, 702
Smith, E. E., 498, 702
Smith, M. B., 703
Smith, W. P., 295, 703
Snyder, A., 401, 702
Solley, C. M., 232, 233, 237, 697, 702
Solomon, H., 594, 696
Solomon, L., 284, 285, 322, 569, 571, 573, 688, 702
Solomon, P., 691
Solomon, R. L., 137, 234, 235, 692, 695, 699, 702
Sommer, R., 235, 702
Spielberger, C. D., 539, 543, 702, 703
Staats, A. W., 458–459, 703
Staats, C. K., 458–459, 703
Star, S. A., 703
Steiner, I. D., 266, 689, 690, 703
Stevenson, H. W., 705
Stewart, R. H., 278, 703
Stoner, J. A. F., 628, 629, 703
Stotland, E., 170, 693
Stouffer, S. A., 33, 703
Strickland, J. C., 676, 702
Strickland, L. H., 295, 309, 315, 410, 676, 703, 704
Stritch, T. M., 261, 701
Suchman, E. A., 703
Suci, G. J., 274, 276, 699
Swanson, G. E., 82, 693, 703

Tabory, L., 549, 702
Taffel, C., 539, 545, 576, 703
Taft, R., 244, 703
Tagiuri, R., 259, 272, 284, 303, 685, 686, 694, 703
Tannenbaum, P. H., 168, 169, 174, 274, 276, 698, 699, 703
Tarde, G., 331, 332, 703
Tatum, R., 603, 682
Taylor, D. W., 595, 596, 598, 599, 703
Taylor, F. K., 233, 703
Terrell, G., 123, 698
Thibaut, J. W., 66, 283, 291–294, 298, 309, 315, 347, 349–351, 410, 515–516, 522–523, 525, 527–528, 530–531, 533, 535, 551–556, 558, 573, 580–581, 584, 586, 592–595, 600, 608–610, 616, 638, 644–652, 654, 656–658, 666, 683, 689, 693, 694, 703
Thistlethwaite, D. L., 451, 704
Thomas, E. J., 456, 704

Thorndike, E. L., 272, 704
Torrey, J., 367, 408–410, 689, 693
Triplett, N., 704
Tuddenham, R. D., 392, 704
Turner, J. A., 442, 683
Tweedie, J., 456, 704

Ullman, A. D., 95, 96, 698
Ulrich, R., 540, 683

Veroff, J. A., 605, 702
Verplanck, W. S., 539–541, 704
Volkhart, E. H., 359, 694
Volkmann, J., 326, 362, 686
von Neumann, J., 556, 560, 704
Vygotsky, L. S., 145, 704

Wallach, M. A., 628–633, 636–639, 684, 694, 704
Walster, Elaine, 220–222, 444–446, 689, 704
Walter, A. A., 139, 686
Walters, R. H., 99, 111, 112, 129, 130, 237, 545, 684, 704
Wapner, G., 606, 704
Warren, R. P., 16–18, 704
Watson, J. B., 162, 704
Watson, N. S., 244, 704
Watson, P. D., 234, 695
Weaver, W., 124, 702
Webb, S., 456, 704
Weick, K. E., 498–499, 705
Weisenberg, M., 66, 498, 706
Weiss, W., 437–439, 443, 692, 705
Wells, F. L., 272, 705
Wells, H. G., 12
Wells, H. H., 408–410, 693
Weltz, P., 291, 691
White, R. K., 4, 65, 695
White, R. W., 121, 122, 123, 705
Whiting, J. W. M., 92, 108, 110, 111, 113, 114, 115, 116, 117, 119, 130, 131, 705
Whitmyre, J. W., 596, 687
Whorf, B. L., 152, 154, 705
Whyte, W. H., Jr., 628, 705
Willerman, B., 367, 607, 689, 701
Williams, R. M., Jr., 703
Wilson, K. V., 563, 569–570, 684, 685, 705
Winch, R. F., 287, 705
Winder, C. L., 542, 705
Wishner, J., 271, 273, 274, 697, 705
Wispe, L. G., 233, 705
Wolfe, J. B., 84, 705

Wolff, K. H., 702
Woodruff, C. L., 404, 694
Worschel, P., 296, 297, 686, 689
Wrightsman, L. S., Jr., 379, 383, 705
Wyckoff, L. B., 549, 555, 702

Yaryan, R. B., 223, 705

Zajonc, R. B., 300, 479, 603–604, 607–608, 705
Zander, A., 295, 705
Zeigarnik, Bluma, 617–619, 621, 622, 705
Zimbardo, P. G., 66, 380, 382, 439, 488, 498–499, 701, 705, 706
Zimmerman, Claire, 248, 706

Subject Index

Ability, and response to discrepancy, 401–405
  considered in action sequence, 316–318
  measured by social comparison, 326–328, 361–367, 401–404
  related to opinion comparison, 365–367, 386
  see also Competition, Level of aspiration, Performance
Acceptance by group, and conformity, 411–415
  see also Cohesiveness, Conformity, Reflected appraisal
Achievement, need for, 96, 98
Action(s), 225, 262
  ability aspect of, 316–318
  as effective compromise, 180
  as target for attitude change, 431
  commitment to (UBO), 185
  conflict and, 179–180
  consequences of, 179–180
  culture as framework for, 176
  dispositions and, 261–269
  distinguished from thought, 180
  coordinated by group norms, 645
  in a decision-framework, 187–195
  informational value of observed, 264–269
  irrevocable, 180
  restrictions on, 179–180
  under conditions of uncertainty, 178–181
  urgency of, variable in leadership structure, 668
  see also Action sequence, Choice, Commitment, Cognitive dissonance, Unequivocal behavior orientation
Action sequence, 187–188, 315–318
  effect dependence in, 591
  pre-decisional phase of, 188–190
  post-decisional phase of, 188–190

Action sequence, referral in, 318–320
  schematic picture of, 317
Activity factor (active-passive), 275, 276
Advice, 128–129
Affect, 707
  see Emotion
Affiliation, imagery as a measure of, 605
  due to comparative appraisal, 370–380
  see also Fear, Uncertainty
Aggression, 707
  attack in social interaction, 308
  attraction and, 290–299
  catharsis of, 292–294
  displacement of, 93–95
  imitation of, 109, 112–113
  in adolescence, 111–112
  inhibition of, 291–297
  see also Frustration, Hostility, Responsibility diffusion
Anchorage of opinions, 357–361
Antinomy, and social contingency, 513
  basic, 227–230, 663–665
  in perception, 229–240
  in learning-retention, 246–248
Anxiety, reduction, through identification with aggressor, 106
  self-criticism developed through reduction of, by adult, 99, 379
  versus fear as cause of affiliation, 380–381
  see also Fear
Approval, social reinforcement in operant conditioning, 543–549
Arbitrariness, related to frustration, 296–297
  related to perceived causality, 297
Argument, in attitude change
  Aristotle on, 446, 449, 451–452

Argument, one-sided versus two-sided communication, 446–451, 503
  order of presenting, 451–456, 503
  with and without conclusions, 456–457
Assimilation, 707
  and prior entry effects, 141–142
  involvement and, 472–474
  to typical instance in perception, 138–142
  see also Contrast
Asymmetric contingency, 509–510, 535, 707
  adaptation in, 509
  in operant verbal conditioning, 548
  see also Contingency
Attitude, 184, 328–329, 707
  action orientation of, 163
  affect-cognition model of, 163–165
  as syllogistic conclusion, 159–162
  cognitive differentiation of, 163
  consistency between, 172–175
  consistency within, 170–172
  dimensions of, 162–163
  direction and extremity of, 162
  functions of, 432
  horizontal structure of, 160–161, 712
  impact on perceiving and remembering, 227–255
  models of internal structure of, 162–170
  related to belief and value, 159–162, 328
  saliency of, 162
  verifiability of, 163
  vertical structure of, 160–161, 720
  see also Attitude change
Attitude change, 431–504
  and conclusion drawing, 456–457
  and initial attitude, 469–474
  and belief and value appeals, 457–468
  communicator, role in, 436–446
  effects of audience distraction on, 474–480
  effects of forewarning on, 474–480
  effects of overhearing on, 444–447
  effects of roleplaying for varying incentives on, 485–497
  learning paradigm of, 434–435
  mass media and, 431
  prestige suggestion in, 437
Attraction, 342
  and being liked, 283–287
  and comparison, 367–368
  and consensus development, 386

Attraction, and expertise, 368
  and reducing imbalance, 299–306
  and similarity, 287–290
  complementarity and, 287–289
  determinants of, 282–306
  frustration or attack and, 290
  in response to flattery, 284–285
  mutual, and acquiescence to group decisions, 613–614
  see also Cohesiveness
Attributes, associated and defining, 158
Attribution process, 262–269, 707
  see also Impressions
Audience, and co-action effects, 601–608
  and evaluation apprehension, 493–497, 605–608
  effect of in perceiving and remembering, 248
  participation in persuasive communication, 485–502
  susceptibility to message, 468–471, 476
Authoritarian personality syndrome, 173–174, 707
Autistic hostility hypothesis, 281, 294–295
Autistic thinking, 230

Balance theory, 165–167
  see also Cognitive balance
Bargaining, 27–30, 561–574
  and norm formation, 644–650
  in interests of social comparison, 365
Behavior control, 525–527, 707
Belief, 157–158, 707
  and comparative appraisal, 325–326
  appeals to, in communication, 457–459
  as minor premise in syllogism, 159–162
  discrepancy between, and action, 25–26
  inoculation and resistance to change of, 480–485
  see also Attitude, Attitude change
Boomerang, 471, 500, 502
Brainstorming, 595, 600
Brainwashing, 18–22
  and cue control, 533–534

Catharsis, 292–294, 708
Causality, perceived (phenomenal), 262–264, 268–269
  and response to frustration, 295–299
  personal versus impersonal, 262
Causation, and correlation research, 40–41
Central trait, 270–274, 708

SUBJECT INDEX 731

Choice, degree of, and person perception (attribution), 267–269
  in the decision-making process, 186–226
  see also Action, Games, Strategy
Circular reactions, 122, 146, 708
Classical conditioning, 84–85, 434–435, 708
  used in manipulation of belief premise of attitude, 458–459
  see also Extinction, Learning, Reinforcement
Co-action, effects on problem solving, 601–608
Coalitions, 365–366
Codability, 137–138, 708
  see also Cognitive category
Cognition, 708
  effects of group participation on, 600–622
  in dissonance theory, 190–191
  see also Cognitive category
Cognitive balance, 184, 708
  attraction and evaluation of persons, 299–306
  in perceiving persons, 284
  in relation to congruity model, 169
  see also Balance theory, Cognitive consistency, Cognitive dissonance
Cognitive category, 132–134, 708
  accessibility of, 136–138, 231, 235, 239–240, 708
  and language, 144–145
  and prior-entry effect, 141–142
  belief expresses relationships between, 157–158
  effect of expectancy on perception of, 136–140
  resistance to change, 227–229
  threshold of, 140
Cognitive consistency, 162–170, 708
  see also Attitudes, Balance theory, Belief, Cognitive balance, Cognitive dissonance
Cognitive development, 142–145
Cognitive dissonance, 190–225, 708
  and certainty of outcome, 215–216
  and commitment, 201–203, 215
  and decision confidence, 201–203
  and effort justification, 88–92, 222–225
  and importance, 191
  and overlapping alternatives, 193
  and reevaluation of choice alternatives, 211–219

Cognitive dissonance, and the decision process, 190–194
  and selective exposure to information, 196–211
  and voluntariness, 214–215
  reduction in "forced-compliance" paradigm, 491–498
  theoretical determinants, 190–191, 494, 546
  see also Cognitive balance, Cognitive consistency
Cognitive process, 709
  and perceptual process, 131–132
Cognitive socialization and information dependence, 120–156
Cognizance, 113–114
Cohesiveness, 339–340, 709
  and attitude change, 341–347, 353–355, 357–360
  and CL_{alt}, 612
  and communication, 346–347, 357–360
  and rejection of group members, 345–347
  and social comparison, 367–368
Commitment, 418–429, 709
  and conformity, 418–419
  and dissonance, 201–203
  and importance of consequences, 214–219
  audience, to initial position, 468–469
  public, 207–208, and self-, 419–420
  reduces desire for evidence, 211
  see also Action, Choice
Communication, 128–136
  and reduction of uncertainty, 127–128
  and social comparison, 331–386
  in game situations, 565–568
  persuasive, 446–504; one-sided versus two-sided, 446–451, 503; order of presenting arguments in, 451–456, 467, 503
  role of, in attitude change, 446–485
  theory of informal social, 309–312, 340–341
  see also Argument, Attitude change, Belief, Co-orientation, Discrepancy, Expertise, Social comparison, Values
Comparative appraisal, 321, 324–329, 396–407, 709
  of abilities, 361–368
  of beliefs and persons, 340–361
  of emotions, 369–385

732 SUBJECT INDEX

Comparative appraisal, methods for distinguishing from reflected appraisal, 392–396
   see also Attitude, Ability, Belief, Communicator, Emotion, Reflected appraisal
Communication networks, 674–678
   centralized, 708
   decentralized, 710
   independence in, 714
Communicator, 436–446
   co-orientation of, 442–446
   credibility of, 439–446, 710
   expertise of, 436–442
Comparison function of group, 312–314, 709
   see also Comparative appraisal, Informational influence, Normative function, Reference group
Comparison level (CL), 522–523, 709
Comparison level for alternatives (CL_{alt}), 522–523, 709
   and acceptance of group goals, 622
   and acquiescence to group decisions, 611–612
   and norm development, 643–651
   and power augmentation, 579
Competition, and audience effect, 602–604
   and performance comparison, 326–328, 361–367
   in prisoner's dilemma game, 562–570
   in problem-solving groups, 609–611
Complementarity, in attraction of person, 287–290
   see also Attraction and being liked
Compliance, behavioral, 577–589, 709
   forced, 485–499
   see also Conformity, Ingratiation
Conceptual conflict, 124, 155, 709
   see also Epistemic behavior
Concrete operations, stage of, 143–144, 709
Conditioned avoidance response, 92–95, 709
Conditioned stimulus (CS), 84, 434, 458, 709
   see also Classical conditioning
Conflict, 187–190, 203–204, 709
Conformity, 387–430, 709
   and a nonunanimous majority, 405–407
   and ability, 401–404
   and acceptance, 411–418
   and majority size, 399–401

Conformity, and the judgmental stimulus, 396–399
   comparative appraisal and, 392–407
   nature of conflict, 390–391
   reflected appraisal and, 392–396, 407–418, 605–606
   see also Acceptance, Comparative appraisal, Reflected appraisal
Congruity principle, 168–170, 709–710
Consensus, and communication in groups, 331–386
   and risk taking, 628–639
   anticipated, 634–635
   recruitment of, 44–45
Conscience, development of, 95–105
Consistency in behavior, 181–182
   see also Cognitive consistency
Consonance, cognitive
   see Cognitive dissonance
Consultation, 128–129
Consummatory behavior, 187
Contact control, 523–524, 710
Contentives, 148, 710
Contingency, 505–536
   asymmetrical, 509–510
   mutual, 511–512
   pseudo, 506–508
   reactive, 510–511
   see also Behavior control, Dependence
Contrast, 140, 471–474, 710
   see also Assimilation
Contrient interdependence, 609–610, 710
Control, in the research process, 37–41
   parental, 78–79, 105–117, 128–129
   power and counterpower, 505–536
   see also Behavior control, Cue control, Outcome control
Conversation, and patterns of social contingency, 505–513
Conversion of fate control, 551–555, 710
Co-action setting, 710
Cooperation, and competition, 556–575, 609–611
   and correspondence of outcomes, 644
   see also Competition
Co-orientation, 319–320, 341, 381–382, 404–405, 436–437, 442–444, 502–503
   see Expertise
Co-oriented peer, 710
Correlational research, 39–41
Correspondence of outcomes, 710
Counterpower, 526, 710

SUBJECT INDEX

Cue control, 513–515, 710
   and interpersonal power, 529–535
   in operant conditioning, 542–543
   see also Outcome control
Cultural map, 176, 179, 227, 530–531, 643
Culture, 176–179, 710
   see also Norms
Curiosity, 121–128, 229

Deception in experiments, 60–62
Decision process, 187–194
   individual versus group, 333–336, 628–639
   see also Action, Antinomy, Choice, Dissonance
Decision structure, 677, 711
Defenses against counterattitudinal arguments, 480–485
   refutational, 717
   supportive, 719
De-individuation, 624–628, 711
Delay of gratification, 95–99
Dependence, 117–118, 711
   and power in dyadic interaction, 523–529
   see also Comparison level for alternatives, Effect dependence, Information dependence, Power
Dependent variable, 711
Deprivation, 370–371, 543–546
   see also Brainwashing
Deterrence, patterning of, 99–105
   see also Insufficient deterrence hypothesis
Deviation
   see Conformity
Disciplinary techniques, 108, 110–112
Discrepancy, and expertise in attitude change, 439–442
   and relative ability, 401–404
   anticipation of, 420–421
   see also Attitude change, Conformity, Cognitive dissonance
Displacement, 94–95, 711
Dispositions, 711
   attribution of, 261–269
   cognitive, and information processing, 131–136
Dissonance
   see Cognitive dissonance
Distraction, and attitude change, 476–480
   effect of, on performance, 602–603

Dual leadership structure, 662–665
Dynamism factor, 275, 711

Effectance motivation, 122–123, 711
Effect dependence, 711
   and group goals, 407–408, 591
   and internalization of values, 83–105
   and outcome control, 515–531, 543
   condition in socialization, 78–83, 117–118, 310
   inducing experimentally, 407–411
   see also Information dependence, Outcome control, Reflected appraisal
Effort justification hypothesis, 88–92, 118, 222–224, 711
Emotion, 329, 711
   comparison of, 369–385
Empathic cognizance, 113–115, 130–131, 711
Empathy, 260, 711
Empirical, 712
Enactive thought mode, 149, 712
Encode, 712
Epistemic behavior, 123–124, 712
   see also Conceptual conflict
Error variance, 712
Ethics of experimentation, 60–62
Evaluation apprehension, 493–496, 605–608
Expansive imitation, 148, 712
Expectancy, effect on attribution process, 265
   and learning, 242–243
   and perception, 136–142
   due to cultural map, 177
   of others and phenomenal self, 183
Experiment, structure of typical, 62–70
   debriefing after, 68
   instructions in, 65
   outcome of, 67–68
   random assignment of subjects in, 51–52, 717
   task in, 67–68
   types of, 70–74
   validating questionnaire in, 68
Experimental design, 712
Experimentation, rationale for, 39–41
Experimenter effects, 55–57
Expertise, 318–319, 357
   and communication, 436–442
   see also Co-oriented peer
Exploitation of game partner, 573–574
   see also Ingratiation

Exploratory behavior, 121–128
External stress, 646–650, 712
External system, 655–656, 712
Extinction, 87, 712
  see also Classical conditioning, Instrumental learning, Reinforcement, Resistance to extinction
Extrinsic investigation, 122

Fate control, 525–527, 712
  conversion of, 526, 710
  mutual, 551–554
  patterning of outcomes in, 527, 554
  see also Behavior control
Fear, affiliation related to, 370–374
  and comparative appraisal, 370–385
  and reflected appraisal, 380–381
  appeals, in communication, 460–467
Field experiment, 712
First impression, 270–281
  see also Impressions, Halo effect
Fixed action pattern, 186
Forewarning, of communicator position, 474–477
Forgetting, 242–244
  and order of presentation, 453–454
  see also Learning, Memory
Formal operations, 143–144, 712
Frustration, 290–299, 713
  and attraction in person perception, 290
  perceived cause of, 295–299
  see also Aggression
Frustration-aggression hypothesis, 290–292, 295–296
Functional autonomy, 87
Functors, 148–149, 713
  see also Contentives

Games
  see Nonzero-sum games, Prisoner's dilemma, Reward-cost matrix, Zero-sum games
Game theory, 556–559
  and minimax solution, 559
  "saddle point" in, 559
  strategy in, 556
Genotype, 51, 71–72
  see also Phenotype
Gradient, of elicitation, 93–94, 713
  of inhibition, 92–94, 713
  of reinforcement, 96–97, 713
Gratification, delay of, 95–99

Group, 713
  acceptance by, and conformity, 411–418
  consensus and communication in, 331–412
  emergence of leaders in, 665–668
  formation of, 592
  initiation severity and liking for, 30–33
  maintenance, 656–663
  normative and comparative functions of, 312–314
  norm formation in, 651–653
  risk taking in, 628–631
  role differentiation in, 653–665
  sociometric position in, 415–418
  see also Reference group
Group decision, acquiescence to, 611–617
  and cohesiveness, 341–343, 353–354
  and consequences for attitude change, 333–336
  responsibility for, 631
  see also Risk taking
Group goals, 310, 407–411, 592–593, 608–611
  and individual motives, 608
  internalization of, 617–622
Group locomotion, 309–312, 713
Group maintenance roles, 656–663, 713
Group problem-solving, and emergence of leaders, 671–673
  effects of co-action on, 601–608
  resource pooling in, 593–600
  versus individual problem-solving, 593–598
  see also Co-action, Cooperation, Group decision, Group goals, Risk taking
Group structure, 642–681
  see also Antinomy, Communication networks, External system, Internal system, Leader, Leadership structure, Unequivocal behavioral orientation
Guilt, and identification, 110–112
  in brainwashing, 19–20

Halo effect, 272, 275, 713
Heterogeneity of group member characteristics, 347–357
Horizontal structure of attitude, 160–162, 170, 713
  see also Vertical structure

Iconic mode, 149–150, 713
Identification, 105–117, 714
  anaclitic, 106–109, 707

Identification, and resource mediation, 112–115
  cognizance, precondition of, 130–131
  defensive, 106, 112–117, 711
  developmental, 106, 112, 711
  Freudian analysis of, 105–106
  guilt, an index of, 110–112, 119
    developmental, 106, 112, 711
  with the aggressor, 112–117, 714
Idiosyncracy credit, 412
Imitation, 108–110, 146–149, 324
  and asymmetrical contingency, 509
  expansive, 148
  Tarde's laws of, 332
  reductive, 148, 717
  see also Identification, Reinforcement
Impressions, 256–282
  and reflected appraisal, 321–324
  organization of, 269–282
  see also First impression, Halo effect, Traits
Independent variable, 714
Information, 124–125, 714
  categorization of, 132–136
  derived from observing action, 264–269
  seeking and avoidance, 194–211
  utility of, 201–203
Information dependence, 79, 120–156, 309–320, 714
  and cue control, 515–532, 543
  and social influence, 340–341
  cognitive processes and, 131–142
  curiosity in, 121–128
  in the action sequence, 316–318
  of child, 78–79, 126–127
  see also Comparative appraisal, Epistemic behavior, Information
Informational influence, 314–315
Information theory, 124–125, 264–296, 714
Ingratiation, 581–589, 714
  and differential power, 583–584
  distinguished from compliance, 582–583
  see also Conformity
Inhibition, 99, 296–297, 714
  and impulse control, 92–95
  see also Aggression, Gradient
Initiation, 30–33, 50–51, 129–130
Inoculation, and resistance to counterarguments, 480–488, 714
Instrumental behavior, 187
Instrumental learning, 84, 714
Insufficient deterrence hypothesis, 100–104, 714

Interaction process analysis, 659–663, 714
Interaction matrix
  see Reward-cost matrix
Internal anchor, 139–140
Internalization, of values, 77, 715
  of group goals, 617–622
  related to extinction, 86–92
  see also Delay of gratification, Effect dependence, Effort justification hypothesis, Guilt, Insufficient deterrence hypothesis
Internal stress on group, 646, 649–650, 715
Internal system, 654–663, 715
Internal validity, 59
Intrinsic investigatory responses, 122
Investigatory responses, 122–124

Judgments, group versus individual, 593–594
  see also Attitudes, Beliefs, Opinions
Justification, 100–104, 487–498

Language, acquisition, 146–152
  and cognition, 137–138, 142–154
  see also Cognitive category, Cognitive development
Latitude of acceptance and rejection, 471–473
  see also Assimilation, Contrast
Law of effect, 235
Law of emphasis, 235
Leader, climate created by, 4
  conditions favoring certain persons as, 670–679
  emergence of, 665–669
  see also Leadership structure
Leadership structure, 642, 665–679
  and group size, 668
  conditions favoring development of, 667–670
  crisis in, 668–669
  distribution of influence in, 667–670
  emergence of, 667
  see also Leader
Learning, avoidance, 87–88
  embedded in language, 269–270
  of mutual fate control in dyad, 549–555
  observational, 129–130
  of values, 84–86
  paradigm for studying attitude change, 434–436
  thematic verbal content, 240–248

see also Classical conditioning, Cognitive category, Extinction, Instrumental learning
"Least-effort" principle, 227
Level of aspiration (LOA), 326–327, 361–363, 385–386, 715
Life space, 187, 189, 316
Locomotor exploration, 122
Love-oriented discipline, 106–108, 715
  and guilt, 110–112

Majority size, effects on social influence, 399–401
Manipulation, 715
Matrix
  see Reward-cost matrix
Maximin solution
  see Minimax solution
Measurement, 52–58
Memory, for thematic material, 243–248
  in testimony and rumor, 249–252
Minimal social person, 157
Minimal social situation, 549–555
Minimax solution, 559–561, 715
Mixed-motive game, 562, 715
Motivation, achievement, 96, 98
  affiliation, 605
  effectance, 122–123
  effect of, on perceptual responses, 229–235
  group participation and, 600–604, 608
  individualistic, 564–570
  perception of, 261–262
  see also Values
Mutual contingency, 511–512, 715
Mutual-fate control, 554–555

Nonlove-oriented discipline, 108, 715
Nonzero-sum games, 561–575, 715
  see also Mixed-motive games, Prisoner's dilemma
Normative control, 715
Normative function of reference group, 312–314, 715–716
  see also Reference group
Norms, 176–178, 643–653, 716
Nurturance, 107–109, 112, 117, 716

Objectification of thinking, 596–597, 599
Oedipus complex, 105–106
  see also Identification

Openness to change, one side of basic antinomy, 227–229, 513
Operant, 538, 716
Operant conditioning, 538–549
Opinions, 432
  anchorage of, 357–360
  comparison of, 341–342, 345–357, 367–368, 370–371
  see also Attitudes
Orienting responses, 121–122, 716
Outcome control, 513–514, 515–529, 716
  cue control, precursor to, 515
  contingencies in, 514
  effect dependence and, 531
  fair-exchange principle in, 535
  in operant conditioning, 542–544
  in training, 537–538
  see also Cue control, Outcomes, Reward-cost matrix
Outcome expectancy, 514, 518
Outcome level (OL), 187, 317–318, 328, 514, 523
  range of, 579–580
  variations in, 522, 532, 554
Outcome potential, 191
Outcomes, certainty of, 215–216
  correspondence of, 609, 644
  exchange of, 534, 547–549
  see also Outcome control, Reinforcement
Out-of-role behavior, 265–267

Partial reinforcement, 88–90, 100, 716
Participant observers, 716
Participation rate and leadership emergence, 671–673
Perception, 131–134
  a decision-making process, 134
  and the basic antinomy, 229–239
  effects of expectancy on, 136–142
  see also Cognition, Person perception
Perceptual defense, 236–239, 716
  see also Perceptual vigilance
Perceptual process, 131–132, 716
  see also Cognitive process
Perceptual vigilance, 231, 239, 240, 245–247, 716
  see also Category accessibility, Perceptual defense
Performance, social factors affecting, 326–327, 363–364
  see also Ability, Co-action, Comparative appraisal, Group problem-solving, Reflected appraisal, Social facilitation

SUBJECT INDEX

Personal integration, 174–184
 see also Unequivocal behavior orientation
Person, as a construct, 157–162
 concepts regarding: attitude, 159–162; belief, 157–158; value, 158–159
Person perception, 256–308
 attraction and hostility and, 282–306
 inferring disposition from acts in, 261–269
 order effects in, 276–282
 personal causality and, 262–264
 see also Impression, Perception, Traits
Persuasion, to change attitudes, 431, 435–436
 to create attitudes, 435
 to modify intensity of attitudes, 435
 see also Attitude change, Communication
Phenomenal self, 182–185, 716
Phenotype, 51, 71–72
 see also Genotype
Pilot study, 70
Placebo, 716
Plan, in dyadic interaction, 506–508, 510, 513
 see also Strategy
Positivity effect, 284, 717
Power, 509, 716
 as exchange, 528
 varieties of, 523–529
 see also Contingency, Control, Cue control, Outcome control
Prestige suggestion, 436–438
Primacy effect, 717
 in persuasion, 451–457
 in impression formation, 277–278
 see also Prior-entry effect
Primary reinforcement, 85, 91, 717
Prior-entry effect, 141–142
 and primacy, 454–455
Prisoner's dilemma game, 562–575, 717
 see also Mixed-motive game, Nonzero-sum game
Problem-solving
 see Group problem-solving
Promotive interdependence, 609, 717
 see also Cooperation
Pseudocontingency, 506–509, 535, 717
Psycho-logic model of attitude structure, 167–168
Punishments, 92–93, 107–108
 and identification, 111

Punishments, and internalization of values, 99–105
 in matrix, 517, 525
 in "minimal" social situation, 550–551
 reinforcement in learning, 515
 timing of, 119
 see also Displacement, Identification, Insufficient deterrence hypothesis

Reactance, 500–502
Reactive contingency, 510–511, 535, 717
Recall
 see Memory
Recency effect, 717
 in impression formation, 227–228
 in persuasion, 451–457
Recipathy, 260
Recruitment of consensus, 44–45
Reference group, 11–12, 362
 anchorage of opinions in, 357–360
 comparison function of, 81–83, 312–314, 719
 normative function of, 82–84, 312–314, 715–716
 see also Group
Reflected appraisal, 321–324, 395, 717
 anticipated, 380–381
 evaluation apprehension and, 605–608
 role in conformity research, 407–418
 see also Ability, Attitude, Emotion, Conformity
Refutational defense, 480–485, 717
 see also Supportive defense
Regret, postdecisional, 193–194, 219–222, 226
Reinforcement, and imitation, 129–130
 approach to socialization, 84–86
 gradient of, 96, 713
 immediate versus delayed, 96
 in attitude change, 494–497
 in operant conditioning, 538–549
 see also Extinction, Learning, Outcomes, Outcome control
Relevance of cognitions to each other, 190
 of issue to group goal, 341, 343–347
Remembering
 see Memory
Repression, 717
Resistance to extinction, 86–89
 based on conditioned avoidance, 83, 93
 discrimination hypothesis, 88
 effort-justification hypothesis, 89–92
 role of partial reinforcement, 88–91

see also Values, Extinction
Resource development, 581
Resource pooling and group problem-solving, 593–600
Response, coordination in mutual fate control, 553
  in conversational sequence, 505, 512
  observation and measurements, 52–57
  see also Actions
Response repertory in dyadic matrix, 515–516
Responsibility diffusion, 622–639
  see also Risk-taking
Retention
  see Memory
Reverse imitation, in language development, 146–149
Rewards
  see Reinforcement
Reward-cost matrix, 516
Rhetoric, Aristotle on, 433–434
Risk-taking, in groups, 628–639
Risky shift, 718
  see also Risk-taking
Role playing, 114–115, 280, 718
  as an attitude change technique, 485–500
  in fantasy, 107
  see also Audience, Participation in persuasive communication
Roles, 177–178
  differentiation in, 653–665
  in pseudocontingency, 508
  person perception and, 265–266
Rumor, 249–254

"Saddle point," 559, 718
Sampling, 64–65, 718
Saturation, 718
Science, goals of, 37–41
  methods of, 42–45
Secondary reinforcement, 718
Segregation, attitudes toward, 16–17
Selective exposure to information, 197–214
  see also Cognitive dissonance, Information
Semantic space, 275–282, 718
Sensorimotor operations, 143, 718
Sensory deprivation, 370–371
Sensory interaction, 479
Sensory process, 120, 718

Sentiment relation, 165, 718
  see Attitude
Sleeper effect, 437–439
Social comparison, 128–131, 309–315, 321–330, 718
  see also Comparative appraisal, Effect dependence, Impressions, Information dependence, Reflected appraisal, Social reality, Socialization
Social facilitation
  see Group problem solving
Social reality, 309–312, 718
Socialization, 76–78, 80, 93, 117, 227, 718
  cognitive, and information dependence, 120–156
  effect dependence in, and value internalization, 83–86
  products of, 157–186
Socialization demands, consistency of, 99, 104–105
  intensity of, 99–100
  timing of, 99–100
Sociometric status, 415–418, 718
S- [O] -R paradigm, 46–58
Stability, of dispositions, 263–264, 431
  of environment, 256–257
  one side of antinomy, 228–229
Standing, 321, 324
Status, 412
  acquired, 416–417
  and conformity, 411–412
  of agent of frustration, 294
  see also Group structure
Status-envy hypothesis, 114–115, 718–719
Stereotype, 140, 719
Stimulus, 1–2, 47–50, 719
  ambiguity, 396–398
  perception of negative, 236–239
  perception of positive, 232–236
  see also Conditioned stimulus, S- [O] -R paradigm, Unconditioned stimulus
Strategy, 555–589, 719
  see also Game theory, Ingratiation, Non-zero-sum games, Prisoner's dilemma game
Stratification, 64, 719
Subgroups, 349–351, 412
Superego, 95, 105–106
Supportive defense, 480–485, 719
  see also Refutational defense
Syllogism, model of attitude structure, 159–162

Syllogism, and classical conditioning, 434–435
Symbolic mediation, 719
Symbolic mode, 150, 719

Task maintenance roles, 656–664, 719
Task set, 315
Temporal extension, 260, 719
Testimony, 249–250
Threat, 29, 484, 500, 577, 645
Time binding, 99
Traits, attribution of, in person perception, 261–262
  central, role of, 270–272
  meaning as additive, 272–273
  see also First impression, Halo effect, Person perception
Trust in the nonzero-sum game, 561–565
  and repeated plays, 566–567
Typical instance, 133
  assimilation, 60, 138–141
  see also Assimilation, Expectancy, Latitude of acceptance

Unconditioned stimulus (UCS), 84–85
  in appeal to beliefs, 458
  in learning paradigm, 434
  see also Classical conditioning, Conditioned stimulus
Uncertainty, action under conditions of, 178–181
  and comparative appraisal, 369–378, 396–398
  and information seeking, 124–125, 318
  in person perception, 264–265
  of outcome, 215–216
  reduction by socialization agents, 126–128
  see also Information, Information theory
Unequivocal behavior orientation (UBO), 179–181, 188, 211, 513, 578, 663–665
Unit relation, 165, 719

Validity, internal and external, 59
  of experimental manipulations, 68
Value expansion, 85–88, 720
Values, 83, 158–159
  acquisition of, 84–92
  appeals to, 435, 457, 459–468
  impact of, on perception and memory, 227–255
  premise in attitude syllogism, 158–159
  see also Attitudes, Motivation, Resistance to extinction
Veridicality, 230–232, 720
Vertical structure of attitude, 160–162, 184, 720
  see Horizontal structure
Vigilance
  see Perceptual vigilance

War of the Worlds, 12–16
When prophecy fails, 22–23
Wild boy of Aveyron, 5–8
Win-stay rule, 552–555, 589

Yielding
  see Conformity

Zeigarnik effect, 617–622, 720
Zero-sum game, 557–561, 720
  see Nonzero-sum game, Competition, Outcomes